Arthur, Origins, Identities and the Legendary History of Britain

Explorations in Medieval Culture

General Editor

Larissa Tracy (*Longwood University*)

Editorial Board

Tina Boyer (*Wake Forest University*)
Emma Campbell (*University of Warwick*)
Kelly DeVries (*Loyola Maryland*)
David F. Johnson (*Florida State University*)
Asa Simon Mittman (*CSU, Chico*)
Thea Tomaini (*USC, Los Angeles*)
Wendy Turner (*Augusta University*)
David Wacks (*University of Oregon*)
Renée Ward (*University of Lincoln*)

VOLUME 25

The titles published in this series are listed at *brill.com/emc*

Arthur, Origins, Identities and the Legendary History of Britain

By

Jean Blacker

BRILL

LEIDEN | BOSTON

Cover illustration: King Arthur (from the Heroes Tapestries), South Netherlandish, ca. 1400–1410. The Metropolitan Museum of Art (Cloisters): Munsey Fund, 1932; Gift of John D. Rockefeller Jr., 1947 (https://www.metmuseum.org/art/collection/search/467528, last accessed 28 September 2023).

Library of Congress Cataloging-in-Publication Data

Names: Blacker, Jean, 1952- author.
Title: Arthur, origins, identities and the legendary history of Britain / by Jean Blacker.
Description: Leiden ; Boston : Brill, [2024]. | Series: Explorations in medieval culture, 2352-0299 ; volume 25 | Includes bibliographical references and index.
Identifiers: LCCN 2023053054 (print) | LCCN 2023053055 (ebook) | ISBN 9789004691032 (hardback) | ISBN 9789004691889 (ebook)
Subjects: LCSH: Arthur, King–In literature. | Arthurian romances–History and criticism. | Geoffrey, of Monmouth, Bishop of St. Asaph, 1100?-1154. Historia regum Britanniae. | Wace, approximately 1100-approximately 1175. Roman de Brut. | Gaimar, Geffrei, active 1136-1137. Estoire des Engleis. | Great Britain–In literature
Classification: LCC PN686.A7 B53 2024 (print) | LCC PN686.A7 (ebook) | DDC 820.9/351–dc23/eng/20231219
LC record available at https://lccn.loc.gov/2023053054
LC ebook record available at https://lccn.loc.gov/2023053055

Typeface for the Latin, Greek, and Cyrillic scripts: "Brill". See and download: brill.com/brill-typeface.

ISSN 2352-0299
ISBN 978-90-04-69103-2 (hardback)
ISBN 978-90-04-69188-9 (e-book)
DOI 10.1163/9789004691889

Copyright 2024 by Koninklijke Brill NV, Leiden, The Netherlands.
Koninklijke Brill NV incorporates the imprints Brill, Brill Nijhoff, Brill Schöningh, Brill Fink, Brill mentis, Brill Wageningen Academic, Vandenhoeck & Ruprecht, Böhlau and V&R unipress.
All rights reserved. No part of this publication may be reproduced, translated, stored in a retrieval system, or transmitted in any form or by any means, electronic, mechanical, photocopying, recording or otherwise, without prior written permission from the publisher. Requests for re-use and/or translations must be addressed to Koninklijke Brill NV via brill.com or copyright.com.

This book is printed on acid-free paper and produced in a sustainable manner.

Contents

Acknowledgements XI

Introduction 1
1   Contextualizing Geoffrey's *Historia*, Arthur, and the Early French *Brut* Tradition   20
2   Structure of *Arthur, Origins, Identities*   23

1   Geoffrey of Monmouth's *Historia Regum Britanniae*: Part 1   28
1   Introduction   28
    1.1   *Galfridian Scholarship*   28
    1.2   *Introductory Overview of Geoffrey's Contemporaries*   33
    1.3   *Geoffrey's Possible Intentions*   38
2   Description of Britain, Arrival of Brutus, Foundation Myth: Geoffrey and His Predecessors   44
    2.1   *Gildas, Bede, and "Nennius"* (*the* Historia Brittonum)   44
    2.2   *Geoffrey and the Foundation Myth of the Britons*   54
3   *Adventus Saxonum* and the Passage of Dominion   62
    3.1   *Geoffrey's Predecessors*   62
      3.1.1   Gildas   64
      3.1.2   Bede   67
      3.1.3   *Historia Brittonum*   72
    3.2   *Geoffrey's Contemporaries: William of Malmesbury and Henry of Huntingdon*   75
      3.2.1   William of Malmesbury: *Gesta Regum*   75
      3.2.2   Henry of Huntingdon: *Historia Anglorum*   79
      3.2.3   Henry of Huntingdon: *Epistola ad Warinum*   83

2   Geoffrey of Monmouth's *Historia Regum Britanniae*: Part 2   91
1   Geoffrey of Monmouth: *Adventus Saxonum* and Preview of Other Landmark Events   91
2   King Arthur   107
    2.1   *King Arthur and His Precedents in Gildas, Bede, and the* Historia Brittonum   107
    2.2   *King Arthur in William of Malmesbury and Henry of Huntingdon*   111
    2.3   *King Arthur: Geoffrey of Monmouth. Overview*   113
      2.3.1   Arthur's Birth   121
      2.3.2   Arthur as Military Commander and Statesman   123

3 Post Arthur: Gormund's Donation, Augustine's Conversion of the English, the Passage of Dominion (Reprise) – Cadwallader and the Final Days 131
4 Postscript: Geoffrey's Ideas on Multiple Ethnicities, Nationalities, Allegiances – including His Prejudices Interwoven with Origin Stories as Part of His Endeavor to Negotiate Identities 137

3 The First Variant Version 154

1 Introduction 154
2 Dating and Authorship of the First Variant Version 157
3 The Description of Britain and the Foundation Myth 167
4 *Adventus Saxonum* 182
5 King Arthur 190
6 Stages of the Passage of Dominion 204
7 Cadwallader and the Final Passage 219
8 Conclusion 232

4 Wace's *Roman de Brut*, Part 1 239
Gaimar's Estoire des Engleis

1 Introduction 239
2 Setting the Stage: Gaimar's *Estoire des Engleis* 241
3 The Prologue to the *Estoire des Engleis* 243
4 The Foundation Myth, the *Adventus Saxonum*, and the Passage of Dominion 253
5 The Epilogue to the *Estoire des Engleis* 258

5 Wace's *Roman de Brut*, Part 2 259

1 Wace's *Roman de Brut*: Organization of the Chapter 259
2 Foundation Myth 259
  2.1 *The Britons Settle the Land* 259
  2.2 *The Giants* 268
  2.3 *The Importance of Language, and the Changing of Names* 272
  2.4 *Shifting Identities: Brittany and the Theme of Ethnic Separatism* 278
3 The *Adventus Saxonum* 281
4 King Arthur 287
  4.1 *Introduction* 287
    4.1.1 Birth and Rise to Power 288
    4.1.2 Arthur's Battles 292
      4.1.2.1 *Arthur and the Scots* 300

CONTENTS VII

		4.1.2.2	*The Beginning of Arthur's Foreign Conquests* 307
	4.1.3	The Founding of the Round Table and More Foreign Conquests 308	
	4.1.4	Organization and Governance; Arthur's Plenary Court 312	
	4.1.5	The Roman Campaign and Its Context 326	
	4.1.6	Arthur's Last Battle: The Battle of Camlann 337	
		4.1.6.1	*The "Breton Hope"* 339

5 Gormund's Donation and the Passage of Dominion; Gormund and Arthur as Leaders 342

6 Augustine's Conversion of the English 359

7 Cadwallader and the "Final Days" 368

8 Conclusion: The Role of Language, Ethnic/Cultural Separatism, and the Characterization of Arthur as Insider/Outsider, Barbarian and Civilizer 374

6 The Anonymous Verse *Brut* Tradition 383

1 General Introduction 383

2 Contextualizing the Anonymous Verse *Brut*s: Wace and Authorial Voice 386

3 Overview: Anonymous Verse *Brut*s 388

4 Common Content of the Anonymous Verse *Brut*s Relative to the *Historia* and Wace 392

5 Anonymous Verse *Brut*s 394

5.1	*Munich* Brut (*Munich, Bayerische Staatsbibliothek C. Gall. 29*) 394	
	5.1.1	Background 394
	5.1.2	Roman Material/Universal History 395
	5.1.3	Description of Britain 397
	5.1.4	More Roman History/War against Pandrasus/ Founding of New Troy 398
	5.1.5	Leir 400
	5.1.6	Conclusion: Comparative Look Back at Membritius; *MB*'s Political Agenda 405
5.2	*The Royal* Brut (*London, British Library Royal 13.A.XXI*) 408	
	5.2.1	Overview 408
	5.2.2	Trojan Foundation Myth 411
	5.2.3	Giants; Group Identities 412
	5.2.4	Coming of Christianity to Britain 416

	5.2.5	The *Adventus Saxonum* 417
	5.2.6	Revival of Christianity among the Britons 418
	5.2.7	Conclusion 422
5.3		*London, College of Arms 12/45A* 423
	5.3.1	Overview of the Narrative(s); Prologues 423
	5.3.2	Comparative Study of Cassibellanus (Geoffrey, Wace, Royal, and CA) 429
	5.3.3	Hengist and Horsa 432
	5.3.4	Vortigern's Search for Merlin, Opening of the Prophecies 435
	5.3.5	Ending of CA's Anonymous Verse *Brut* 437
	5.3.6	Introduction to Incomplete Copy of Wace's *Brut*, and Summary of Remainder of Dorse 438
	5.3.7	Lacunae in CA's Copy of Wace's *Brut* 441
	5.3.8	Continuation of the Anonymous *Brut* and Wace Text; Conclusion 443
5.4		*The Harley* Brut (*London, British Library Harley 1605*) 445
	5.4.1	Overview of the Five Fragments 445
	5.4.2	Fragment 1: the *Adventus Saxonum* 449
	5.4.3	Fragments 3 and 4: Arthur's Reign 451
	5.4.4	Fragment 5: the Last of Arthur's Battles 454
	5.4.5	Fragment 2: Merlin's Prophecies and Merlin's Prediction of Vortigern's Death Up through Uther's Capture of Octo and Eosa 455
	5.4.6	Tentative Conclusions 462
5.5		*The Egerton* Brut (*London, British Library Egerton 3028*) 462
	5.5.1	Overview of the Manuscript, the Poem, Authorial Voice, and Egerton's Goals 462
	5.5.2	Egerton's Cutting of Passages to Achieve Its Goals 471
	5.5.2.1	*Trimming of Maritime and Martial Scenes* 471
	5.5.2.2	*Trimming of Speeches* 472
	5.5.2.3	*Trimming of Naming Passages, and Other Cultural Markers Such as Court Festivities* 473
	5.5.3	Egerton and the Church 475
	5.5.4	The *Adventus Saxonum* 475
	5.5.5	Future of the Britons 476
	5.5.6	Scotland 478
	5.5.7	Continuation of the Egerton *Brut* on English History 479
	5.5.8	Egerton: Conclusions 480

CONTENTS

6 Chapter Conclusion 481

Conclusion 486

Appendix 1: Wace's *Roman de Brut* in Its Manuscript Contexts 497
Appendix 2: Anonymous Verse *Brut*s 507
Appendix 3: Arthur's "Twelve Battles": Comparative Chart 512
Bibliography 515
Index of Persons 558

Acknowledgements

When a book takes as long as this one has to complete (though other projects intervened), one has many, many people to thank. Many thanks are due to Glyn S. Burgess for his help with the translations from the Old French (though any errors remaining are of course my own), to Ian Short for his guidance regarding Wace manuscripts in particular, to Michael Barich for his assistance with some of the Latin translations (especially for those where I have elected to substitute my translations of the First Variant for David Burchmore's edition/translation), to David Burchmore for his willingness to share his manuscript of the First Variant before it was published, and to the anonymous reader for Brill for his invaluable assistance throughout the process.

Many thanks go to Kenyon College for financial and other support (including letters of introduction time and again), to Graham Coursey (Kenyon College Library Access Services Manager) for his never-ending patience with my myriad requests for Interlibrary Loan items and his very prompt and gracious efficiency, to the IRHT in Paris for their generosity during my many visits to consult their archives and manuscripts on microfilm, to the Bibliothèque nationale de France, the Bibliothèque Sainte-Geneviève, and the Bibliothèque de l'Arsenal for their generosity as well, and to the National Endowment for the Humanities for summer assistance early on in this project.

Last but not least, infinite thanks are due to Marcella Mulder, my sponsoring editor at Brill, without whose gracious assistance this book would never have appeared, to Theo Joppe for his patience and excellent work and the entire production staff at Brill, to my daughter Edwina Finefrock who has shared me enthusiastically with King Arthur for what seems like eons, and to my husband, Jack, for whose editorial advice and assiduous never-ending support I will always be grateful.

If there are people and institutions whose names do not appear here, I hope they will realize that this is due to my oversight, and not to any lack of gratitude.

Introduction

In the first years of the twenty-first century, the "Arthur industry," to borrow Richard Barber's term,[1] continues to grow exponentially as demonstrated by the robust number of studies in a broad range of areas, both popular and academic, from those that bring recent archaeological discoveries in the British Isles to bear on questions of Arthur's historicity to those that apply postcolonial theory to Arthurian motifs in fiction (and historiography as well). The recent upsurge in interest in the Arthurian legend in the last century is also suggestive of a contemporary need for Arthurian myth; simply put, without a need, these legends would not speak to so many in so many diverse ways. Beyond the ever-present search for escape and nostalgia, by understanding the formative texts of early Arthurian historical narrative and the foundation stories with which Arthur is inextricably linked as well as the eras which produced them, we may better understand our own struggles to come to terms with our own ethnic and individual identities in an age of increasing anonymity and globalization.

Medieval Arthurian narrative is as rich – and as potentially overwhelming – as the current spectrum of scholarly production, including the major genres of Latin prose historiography, Latin heroic poetry, vernacular chronicles (verse and prose) and romances, first in Anglo-Norman and Continental French and later in Middle English, and Welsh literature. *Arthur, Origins, Identities* takes as its primary material historical texts – that is, texts that we as modern readers might not consider historically accurate but which were nonetheless perceived by their producers and audiences as historical – which focus on what is commonly referred to as the "legendary history" of Britain.[2] Not only were these historical texts the first to have had a widespread, inescapable impact

---

1   *King Arthur: Hero and Legend* (New York: St. Martins, 1961; repr. 1986), 199. For a cogent survey of many perspectives on Arthur, aspects of medieval British/English identity and their modern-day implications, see Nicholas Higham's Introduction in *Britons in Anglo-Saxon England*, ed. N. J. Higham, Publications of the Manchester Centre for Anglo-Saxon Studies 7 (Woodbridge: Boydell, 2007), 1–15.

2   For a discussion of medieval perceptions of historical writing which for us contains many elements which appear fictional, see the new Introduction (pp. 1–50) which accompanies the revised electronic version of my *The Faces of Time: Latin and Old French Historical Narrative of the Anglo-Norman Regnum* (Austin: University of Texas Press, 1994; rev. electronic ed., 2019, https://utpress.utexas.edu/books/blafac). When citing this book, I will use the 1994 pagination (rather than approximations in the revised e-book, since the latter may not have uniformly stable pagination for all individual or library readers, except for the new Introduction, which has conventional, hard-copy pagination).

2   INTRODUCTION

on subsequent Arthurian history – and romance – which followed, they also contain Arthur in his "historical" context, the early history of the British Isles, a context which informs so many later "presentations" of Arthur.

Although King Arthur was originally a British mythical figure, the earliest and most widely disseminated historical – or "pseudo-historical" – texts in which he appears were written in Latin and French. The Latin history most influential in disseminating the Arthurian myth – Geoffrey of Monmouth's *Historia Regum Britanniae* (*c.*1138) (hereafter *HRB*)[3] – received considerable attention when it was written and subsequently through the ages from both the scholarly and popular communities. However, the roughly contemporaneous Variant Versions (particularly the First Variant which was roughly contemporaneous with Geoffrey) of the *HRB* as well as the early French and Anglo-Norman verse translations – Wace's *Roman de Brut* (1155) and anonymous versions including the Royal *Brut*, the Munich, Harley, and Egerton *Brut*s (12th–14th c.) – remain much less well known today, although Wace's *Brut* is gaining ground among scholars.[4] These texts, as well as Laȝamon's middle English *Brut* (*c.*1185–1216) and the Latin verse epic the *Gesta regum Britanniae* (*c.*1230–40), are distinguished from fictional texts – Welsh, French, and English lays and romances – in that, instead of creating a separate kingdom for Arthur

---

3   Although Geoffrey's vulgate history has recently been edited under the title of the *De gestis Britonum*, I am choosing to retain the traditional title (Geoffrey of Monmouth, *The History of the Kings of Britain: An Edition and Translation of the De gestis Britonum* [*Historia Regum Britanniae*], ed. Michael D. Reeve, trans. Neil Wright, Arthurian Studies 69 (Woodbridge: Boydell, 2007). All references will be to this edition unless otherwise noted, as to *The Historia Regum Britannie of Geoffrey of Monmouth, II: The First Variant Version: a critical edition*, ed. Neil Wright (Cambridge: D. S. Brewer, 1988), to sections using the § symbol (but rarely to Book numbers [for the vulgate]).

4   Until recently, the oldest version of the Anglo-Norman prose *Brut* (*c.*1272) – a text which fused Arthurian history to later Saxon and English history and was one of the most popular of medieval books – was almost unknown to either the scholarly or the popular audience; Julia Marvin's outstanding edition has opened this text for detailed study (*The Oldest Anglo-Norman Prose Brut: An Edition and Translation*, ed. and trans. Julia Marvin, Woodbridge: Boydell, 2006). The prose *Brut* chronicle tradition in its many permutations is profoundly complex and can only be touched on tangentially here. For an overview, see J. Blacker, "The Anglo-Norman and Continental French Reception of Geoffrey of Monmouth's Corpus from the 12th to the 15th Centuries," in *A Companion to Geoffrey of Monmouth*, ed. Georgia Henley and Joshua Byron Smith, Brill's Companions to European History 22 (Leiden: Brill, 2020), 454–66, and the work of historians, literary scholars, and editors including Julia Marvin and Heather Pagan (and with Geert de Wilde, Anglo-Norman prose *Brut*s), Lister Matheson (English prose *Brut*s), John Spence (Anglo-Norman prose chronicles), and most recently Trevor Russell Smith ("National Identity, Propaganda, and the Ethics of War in English Historical Literature, 1327–77," unpub. PhD thesis, University of Leeds, 2017); see Bibliography below.

INTRODUCTION 3

out of time and place, they contextualize the Arthurian legend as part of the history of the British peoples and form a parallel foundation story similar in many ways to those created by peoples throughout northern Europe.

By providing close readings of the early French verse texts in relation to their Latin precedents as well as occasionally in comparison with the Anglo-Norman prose *Brut*, Laȝamon's *Brut*, the *Gesta regum Britanniae*, the later French verse Chronicle of Peter of Langtoft (*c.*1296–1307) and Robert Mannyng's English verse Chronicle (*c.*1338) as fruitful counterpoints where appropriate,[5] *Arthur, Origins, Identities* will illuminate many of the processes involved in the formation of the Arthurian myth and ultimately suggest political, cultural, and psychic purposes which those narratives – as historical, not romance, narratives – may have been intended to serve.

Arthurian history and fiction are often characterized by two elements, that of the barbarian or outsider and that of the civilizer or insider; these elements are in continual tension, with the one never completely erasing the other, often existing simultaneously. Broadly speaking, each Arthurian text, whether history or fiction, contains each of these elements to differing degrees, though it can be argued that for example, the theme of civilizer or insider tends to dominate certain genres such as French romance where the society of knights of the Round Table becomes the quintessential symbol of court civilization. The extent to which a text participates in the hierarchy of values evident in these themes in turn suggests the nature of the ethnic or social identities to which the text either appeals or which its author (or authors) seeks to create.[6]

---

5 As with the Old French prose *Brut* tradition(s), Laȝamon's *Brut*, the *GRB*, Langtoft and Mannyng's Chronicles, can only be referred to in this study tangentially as they relate to the presentations of the Arthurian (and pre-Arthurian) worlds in the main texts under consideration here. On the rich Welsh tradition including the *Brutiau*, see Patrick Sims-Williams, "The Welsh Versions of Geoffrey of Monmouth's 'History of the Kings of Britain,'" in *Adapting Texts and Styles in a Celtic Context: Interdisciplinary Perspectives on Processes of Literary Transfer in the Middle Ages: Studies in Honour of Erich Poppe*, ed. A. Harlos and N. Harlos, Studien und Texte zur Keltologie, 13 (Munster: Nodus Publikationen, 2016), 53–76. This article is particularly important for its tracing of the history of the adaptations of the *HRB* in Welsh – including the scholarship on those adaptations – as well as its revelations on the early Welsh interest in the First Variant version.

6 Similarly, Robert Hutton writes "to a post-war Britain caught in the process of resigning its imperial and Great Power status, and jettisoning most of the attitudes and ideologies left over from its Victorian apogee, the Arthur of the *Historia Brittonum* seemed to be a traditional hero better fitted than most to adapt to changing needs. He was a warrior who had defended his nation with the courage and success of traditional patriotic leaders, while cutting a less stuffy and conventional figure than most. He could be said to belong equally to all the different peoples of Britain and – clad imaginatively but plausibly in the furs, leathers, long hair, trailing moustaches and jewellery of a Celtic warlord – function both as a national icon and

Arthur, Origins, Identities and the Legendary History of Britain will suggest answers to the following questions: How did these Arthurian texts containing versions of the British foundation myth respond to prevailing images of individual or collective identity and what role may those texts have played in the creation of those identities? What is the nature of the "imagined communities" constructed by these texts and what is the significance of the variations among them? In what ways did each author respond to his particular audience and which elements of the Arthurian narrative were more essential to his plan? What cultural, political or psychic needs did these Arthurian narratives meet and what might be the origins of those needs? Finally, to what extent and in what ways does each text contribute to a "larger picture" of Arthur and are thus instrumental in the construction of a myth that still remains so compelling today?

In working with Arthurian material, particularly in historical texts, it is impossible to ignore the question of Arthur's historicity, a question that is raised, tentatively or resoundingly "answered," often in new ways by succeeding generations of scholars and popularizers. To echo Rosemary Morris's sentiments in the face of the seemingly innumerable theories attempting to explain Arthur's origins, and the central debate for or against his historicity,[7] I too find the "puzzle of Arthur" fascinating but "unanswerable"; like Morris and others, I wonder "why Arthur, rather than a dozen other legendary figures, should attract attention, as he undeniably does even pre-Geoffrey" and how "the ensuing phenomenon of Arthur's adoption as a prime literary symbol of the Middle Ages" came about.[8]

However, although I occasionally will incorporate elements of archetypal-mythological criticism in discussions of literary symbols,[9] I intend to move principally in a different direction, toward analysis of projected ethnic and social group interrelationships, in order to articulate more broadly the role of Arthur in the social imaginary of the twelfth and thirteenth centuries in the Anglo-Norman sphere. I need to emphasize that this is not a book aimed at

---

a count-cultural one, an establishment figure and a noble savage" ("The Early Arthur: History and Myth," in *The Cambridge Companion to the Arthurian Legend*, ed. Elizabeth Archibald and Ad Putter, Cambridge: Cambridge University Press, 2009, 11–35, cited at 31).

7 See Chapter 2, nn. 41–42, for references to this debate.

8 *The Character of King Arthur in Medieval Literature*, Arthurian Studies 4 (Cambridge: D. S. Brewer, 1982; repr. 1985), 4.

9 Although archetypal criticism as a primary approach is no longer widely practiced, the intersections between folklore analysis, tale-type studies, and archetypal criticism can still be illuminating in the case of "eternal" heroic figures such as King Arthur when seen in relation to specific social or political contexts. See Norris J. Lacy, ed., *A History of Arthurian Scholarship* (Cambridge: D. S. Brewer, 2006).

INTRODUCTION

unearthing new historical evidence or confirming socio-political conditions at the time(s) our authors were writing, but rather to explore and highlight the socio-political frameworks they sought to evoke or create in their texts, regardless of whether or not those frameworks can be shown to be grounded in historical "fact."

The primary focal points of *Arthur, Origins, Identities* will be the connections between 1) foundation myths[10] including the "description of Britain"[11] (which as a sub-narrative reveals fascinating intercultural dynamics); 2) narratives of the *adventus Saxonum* as a process rather than a single event – including the conversion of the English, whose different versions can be very revealing of authorial perspectives toward the Britons and the Saxons – and the eventual passage of dominion from the Britons to the Saxons;[12] and 3) Arthur's world

---

10   The emphasis will be primarily on the early British foundation myth of Brutus, based on Trojan origins with reference, when pertinent, to the later-appearing myth of Albina, which aimed to create a "prehistory" for Britain before the arrival of the Trojans. On the Albina legend, see Lesley Johnson, "Returning to Albion" in *Arthurian Literature XIII*, ed. James P. Carley and Felicity Riddy, Cambridge: D. S. Brewer, 1995, 19–40; Anke Bernau, "Beginning with Albina: Remembering the Nation," *Exemplaria* 21.3 (2009): 247–73; and eadem "Myths of Origin and the Struggle Over Nationhood in Medieval and Early Modern England," in *Reading the Medieval in Early Modern England*, ed. Gordon McMullan and David Matthews, Cambridge: Cambridge University Press, 2007, 106–18, 249–53 (notes). On the foundation myths of the Angles, Saxons, Scots, Picts, and other groups, see especially Susan Reynolds, "Medieval 'Origines Gentium' and the Community of the Realm," *History* 68 (1983): 375–90; J. Turville-Petre, "Hengest and Horsa," *Saga Book of the Viking Society for Northern Research* 14 (1953–57): 273–90; Nicholas Brooks, "The English Origin Myth," in idem *Anglo-Saxon Myths: State and Church, 400–1066* (Rio Grande, OH: Hambledon Press), 79–90; Molly Miller, "Matriliny by Treaty: The Pictish Foundation-Legend," in *Ireland in Early Mediaeval Europe: Studies in Memory of Kathleen Hughes*, ed. Dorothy Whitelock, Rosamond McKitterick, and David Dumville (Cambridge: Cambridge University Press, 1982), 133–61; Marjorie O. Anderson, "Dalraida and the Creation of the Kingdom of the Scots," in *Ireland in Early Mediaeval Europe*, 106–32; and Matthew H. Hammond, "Ethnicity and the Writing of Medieval Scottish History," *The Scottish Historical Review* 85.1 (2006): 1–27.

11   I am using this term as Nicholas Higham does in his study of the description of Britain in Bede, that is, as a type of text or genre, rather than as a reference to a specific text such as the twelfth-century Anglo-Norman *Description of England* (N. J. Higham "Old Light on the Dark Age Landscape: the Description of Britain in the *De Excidio Britanniae* of Gildas," *Journal of Historical Geography* 17.4 (1991): 361–72); Lesley Johnson, "The Anglo-Norman *Description of England*: An Introduction," in *Anglo-Norman Anniversary Essays*, ed. Ian Short, Anglo-Norman Text Society Occasional Publications Series 2 (London: ANTS, 1993), 11–30; Alexander Bell, "The Anglo-Norman *Description of England*: An Edition," *Anglo-Norman Anniversary Essays*, 31–48.

12   Discussions of Arthur's role in history and Geoffrey of Monmouth's radical departure from Bedan chronology have been invariably influenced by R. William Leckie

6   INTRODUCTION

and its variations. The goal will be to demonstrate how each of those elements contributes to the fabric of the social imaginary of the contemporary societies as seen in specific texts, and ways in which that (or those) social imaginary(-ies) still speak to us today – the latter as demonstrated by the fact that Arthurian scholarship has shown no signs of slowing down in recent years.[13]

Arthur, Origins, Identities draws on a number of theoretical approaches – including those commonly associated with postcolonial studies,[14] historical and anthropological work on early European "barbarian" peoples and processes of ethnogenesis or "ethnopoiesis" to borrow Sigbjørn Sønnesyn's term,[15] Indigenous methodologies,[16] and archetypal-mythological criticism – in order

---

     Jr.'s groundbreaking study, *The Passage of Dominion: Geoffrey of Monmouth and the Periodization of Insular History in the Twelfth Century* (Toronto: University of Toronto Press, 1981).

13   Norris Lacy concludes a very useful survey of current Arthurian scholarship with the observation on the "Arthur industry," that "evidence has led [him] to believe that this is one industry that is entirely recession-proof" ("Arthurian Research in a New Century: Prospects and Projects," in *New Directions in Arthurian Studies*, ed. Alan Lupack, Arthurian Studies 51, Cambridge: D. S. Brewer, 2002, 1–20, cited here at 17). While it is not possible to provide here a comprehensive overview of the protean figure of Arthur in the Galfridian or romance traditions, nor more than a sample bibliography, particularly useful with respect to the major works of historical writing that appeared in the century following Geoffrey's *Historia* (in addition to studies already cited here) are Michelle R. Warren, *History on the Edge: Excalibur and the Borders of Britain, 1100–1300* (Minneapolis: University of Minnesota Press, 2000); N. J. Higham, *King Arthur: Myth-making and History* (London: Routledge, 2002); on early medieval historians' "historicization" of Arthur, Thomas Green, *Concepts of Arthur* (Stroud, Glos.: Tempus Publishing, 2007); and John Gillingham, *The English in the Twelfth Century: Imperialism, National Identity and Political Values* (Woodbridge, Suffolk: Boydell Press, 2000), esp. "The Context and Purposes of Geoffrey of Monmouth's *History of the Kings of Britain*', pp. 19–39, reprinted from *Anglo-Norman Studies XIII. Proceedings of the Battle Conference, 1990*, ed. Marjorie Chibnall, Woodbridge, Suffolk: Boydell, 1991, 99–118). Henceforth, I will be citing the articles in John Gillingham's collection, *The English in the Twelfth Century*, at initial reference, with their original publication information, and placement in the book of collected essays, but subsequent references, by book pagination only (unless cited by other scholars, where I will use their methods of citation).

14   For the vast field of postcolonial studies, including references to colonialism in the Roman Empire, see Ania Loomba, *Colonialism/Postcolonialism* (Abingdon, Oxon: Routledge, 3rd ed. 2015), esp. pp. 1–60.

15   "The Rise of the Normans as *Ethnopoiesis*," in *Norman Tradition and Transcultural Heritage: Exchange of Cultures in the "Norman" Peripheries of Medieval Europe*, ed. Stefan Burkhardt and Thomas Foerster (London: Routledge, 2016), 203–18, on the literary creation of the *gens Normannorum*.

16   For a broad range of studies informed by Indigenous perspectives and methodologies by scholars on five continents, see the *Handbook of Critical and Indigenous Methodologies*, ed. Norma K. Denzin, Yvonna S. Lincoln, and Linda Tuhiwai Smith (Los Angeles: Sage

INTRODUCTION

to best illuminate the goals and shape of each particular text. I argue in part that Arthur may have been so central to the literary and political milieu in twelfth-century England, Wales, Scotland, Ireland and France not only because he embodied, on one level, the growing courtly and military ideals of the dominant Anglo-Norman/Anglo-Angevin[17] aristocracy in England, but also because he was an outsider who rose to rival and then surpass other outsiders (including any king the Saxons, Scots and Picts could put forward) but also the emperor of Rome.[18] The nature of Arthur's role as outsider, from royal stock but of "barbarian" (British) origins – in many ways analogous to "subaltern" peoples – may appeal particularly in the modern age where the blurring of national boundaries and globalization have evoked strong nationalistic (and in some instances xenophobic) sentiments throughout the world, rendering the eternal, archetypal struggle between insider and outsider both more threatening and potentially rewarding, though always extremely complex.

Because each of the texts studied in *Arthur, Origins, Identities* originates in a different cultural setting, each conveys different sets of group identities, defining the polarity of self and other – "us" and "them" – differently. Some identify Arthur as a British king (as distinguished from the English/Saxon settlers)[19] – at the same time royal, illegitimate, barbarian, and civilizer, others

---

Publications, 2008); see also Linda Tuhiwai Smith, *Decolonizing Methodologies: Research and Indigenous Peoples*, 2nd ed. (London: Zed Books, 2012). Although not exact of course, numerous parallels exist between the treatment of native peoples by dominant invaders/colonizers in North America (and elsewhere) and the British archipelago, as well as the suppression or minimizing of historical narratives produced by the marginalized communities.

17 See John Gillingham on the complex and problematic nature of characterizing the Angevin Empire with respect to Britain in the twelfth century, *The Angevin Empire* (London: Arnold, 2nd ed. 2001), esp. 2–5.

18 For perspectives on outsiders, and fundamental questions raised concerning human identity, including boundaries between "racial" and cultural difference, see Sylvia Huot, *Outsiders: The Humanity and Inhumanity of Giants in Medieval French Prose Romance* (Notre Dame, IN: University of Notre Dame Press, 2016), esp. her Introduction, 1–25.

19 See Michelle Warren's unusual use of the adjective "Briton" in place of "British," an approach she follows "so as to avoid the imperialist connotation of *British*" (*History on the Edge: Excalibur and the Borders of Britain 1100–1300*, Medieval Cultures 22, Minneapolis: University of Minnesota Press, 1). See also Ben Guy on the "Britons" to whom he does not apply the collective term "British" (but for different reasons than Warren). Guy notes in particular that Geoffrey of Monmouth, "had he not possessed an intricate understanding of the cultural self-awareness of different groups of Britons in his own time, he would not have been so careful to distinguish between the origins of the Cornish, Bretons, and Welsh in his history"; Guy proposes that "Geoffrey attributed to the Cornish an ethnic distinction that arose prior to the foundation of Britain by Brutus ... whereas the Bretons and the Welsh, on the other hand, are, in no uncertain terms, latter-day Britons" ("Geoffrey of

as a new and better Roman emperor analogous to the Norman conquerors, while still others – primarily the later authors such as Egerton and the prose *Brut* writer(s) – a quintessentially English hero, the "same" hero who must be relied upon to save England by throwing off the Norman Yoke as envisaged by later English chroniclers including Robert of Gloucester and Robert Mannyng. Arthur as descendant of Brutus, eponymous leader of the Britons and founder of New Troy, retains that essential identity while establishing Caerleon (later Camelot) outside of New Troy (London) as his seat of government, on the geographical plane thus both insider and outsider; the Round Table simultaneously inclusive and exclusive repeats this dynamic and encompasses the essential tension between these two poles. Even Arthur's relation to death is by analogy one of insider and outsider – with simultaneously one foot in this world and one foot in the next: for some, the king dies, for others he is wounded (though he disappears from the scene), for still others he is taken away to someday return (the so-called "Breton hope"). Each text's portrayal of Arthur's "death" in turn reveals further political preoccupations – or agendas, to use a stronger but rather overused term – beyond those involved in the portrayal of his "life".[20]

Monmouth's Welsh Sources," in *A Companion to Geoffrey of Monmouth*, 32–66, cited at 33). In the present study, I will avoid the term "Celtic" except when referring to language and will use "British" in referring to the identities of the Welsh, Cornish, and Bretons who considered themselves Brittonic-speaking Britons (although not all scholars I will cite do so).

20   For a very useful survey of the thematic and symbolic importance and political implications of Arthur's death from Geoffrey's antecedents through Malory, see Felicity Riddy, "Contextualizing *Le Morte Darthur*: Empire and Civil War," in *A Companion to Malory*, ed. Elizabeth Archibald and A. S. G. Edwards (Woodbridge: D. S. Brewer, 1996), 55–73. On the so-called Breton hope and William of Malmesbury's famous denunciation thereof, see also Siân Echard, "'Hic est Artur': Reading Latin and Rereading Arthur," in *New Directions in Arthurian Studies*, ed. Alan Lupack (Cambridge: D. S. Brewer, 2002), 49–67. Patrick Sims-Williams suggests that "the first positive testimony to such a belief in Arthur's survival, among the Cornish and Bretons is in the account of the journey of the Canons of Laon to Bodmin in 1113" ("The Early Welsh Arthurian Poems," in *The Arthur of the Welsh: The Arthurian Legend in Medieval Welsh Literature*, ed. Rachel Bromwich, A. O. H. Jarman, and Brynley F. Roberts, Cardiff University of Wales Press, 1991, 33–72, cited at 49); cf. Christopher M. Berard who proposes that this account not be read "as a witness to belief in Cornwall in 1113, but rather as a testament to the European vogue for Arthurian tales at the time of the *Miracula*'s composition – which coincided with the dissemination of Geoffrey of Monmouth's *Historia* (ca. 1138)," that it was rather an interpolation by Herman of Tournai twenty-five years after the events, meant to "censure the clergy and nobility of [his] day for their passion for secular Arthurian tales at the expense of religious devotion" ("King Arthur and the Canons of Laon," *Arthuriana* 26.3, 2016: 91–119, cited at 91). J. E. Lloyd has argued that Geoffrey balanced or conflated a Breton and Cornish belief in Arthur's survival with a Welsh belief that he was killed at the battle of Camlann,

INTRODUCTION 9

and that Geoffrey solves the problem of the "flagrant contradiction between the Welsh and the Breton account of the same historical event [by] setting both accounts before the reader and leaving him to make his choice" ("The Death of Arthur," *Bulletin of the Board of Celtic Studies* 11, 1941–4: 158–60, cited at 160). Rachel Bromwich refers to a commentary on the Prophecies from the second half of the twelfth century which claims that "the belief in Arthur's departure was common to the Bretons, the Welsh and the Cornish (*Omnium scilicet haec est supersitito, Britonum, Guallorum et Cornubiencium*)" [she is presuming that by Britones/Britonum are meant Bretons], adding further that Étienne de Rouen's *Draco Normannicus* includes a story that when Henry II was preparing to attack Brittany in 1167, the king "received a letter from Arthur announcing his return!" ("Brittany and the Arthurian Legend," in *The Arthur of the Welsh*, 249–72, cited at 262); J. Hammer, "A Commentary on the *Prophetiae Merlini*," *Speculum* 10 (1935): 3–30 and *Speculum* 15 (1940): 409–31, esp. pp. 414–15. In "'*Exspectare Arturum*': Arthur and the Messianic Hope," Constance Bullock-Davies investigates the evolution of the "Breton hope" from the time of Carausius (d. 293), a Roman military commander who was remembered in British legend, especially in the North and Scotland, as "a great warrior who had kept the enemy at bay," having fought off the Romans (against whom he had revolted) and the Picts, the only emperor who "was styled or styled himself '*Exspectatus*'," (436) to the early thirteenth century including reactions of historians, clerics, and rulers; since the belief "embodied, in the first place, an anti-establishment political ideal and in the second, an anti-Christian concept, it met with strenuous opposition from both State and Church ... [it offered] a totally unacceptable challenge to the sovereignty of the English reigning monarch [and as] far as Churchmen were concerned, belief in the second coming of Arthur was pure heresy"; in order to render him palatable to a wide range of courtly audiences, Arthur "had to undergo literary purgation; he had to be shorn of local political aspirations and divested of every trace of Judaic or Christian Messianism" (439) although he remained for many "not only the national hero of the Welsh but the fairy and Christian counterpart of the political Messiah he once was" (440) (*Bulletin of the Board of Celtic Studies* 29 (1980–81): 432–40, cited at 436, 439, and 440). See also Paul Dalton, "Topical Concerns of Geoffrey of Monmouth's *Historia Regum Britannie*: History, Prophecy, Peacemaking, and English Identity in the Twelfth Century," *Journal of British Studies* 44.4 (2005): 688–712; Victoria Flood, "Arthur's Return from Avalon: Geoffrey of Monmouth and the Development of the Legend," *Arthuriana* 25.2 (2015): 84–110; and Helen Fulton who comments that "Geoffrey's reluctance to engage with the already pervasive idea of Arthur's return is perhaps the strongest evidence we have for his ideological alignment with Norman, rather than Welsh, interests" ("Originating Britain: Welsh Literature and the Arthurian Tradition," in *A Companion to British Literature: Volume 1: Medieval Literature 700–1450*, ed. Robert DeMaria, Jr., Heesok Chang, and Samantha Zacher, Hoboken, NJ: John Wiley & Sons, 2014), 308–22, cited here at 314). Cf. Virginie Greene who systematically surveys both scholarship on this question as well as primary sources (medieval historians primarily), concluding that this "belief" was instead a *topos* repeated often for a variety of purposes, without any documentary or archeological (or other) evidence that people – either the insular or Continental Britons or others – actually believed in Arthur's "non-death" and eventual return ("Qui croit au retour d'Arthur?" *Cahiers de Civilisation Médiévale* 45.180, 2002: 321–40). On the mockery of the Breton hope with parallels to mockery of the Jews awaiting the Messiah, see Christopher M. Berard, *Arthurianism in Early Plantagenet England: From Henry II to Edward I* (Woodbridge: Boydell, 2019), esp. 69–73, and on the

In terms of analytical perspectives not directly related to the Arthurian sphere, one needs to take into account Benedict Anderson, whose seminal work on the origins of nationalism in the modern period and the concept of imagined communities has now become virtually second nature to any study of how communities create themselves and perpetuate their autonomy relative to their neighbors.[21] In writing about religious community and dynastic realm before the modern period, he states that "both of these, in their heydays, were taken-for-granted frames of reference, very much as nationality is today. It is therefore essential to consider what gave these cultural systems their self-evident plausibility, and at the same time to underline certain key elements in their decomposition."[22] Most useful for our purposes is the concept "taken-for-granted frames of reference," that is, presumed ideas that are not always openly articulated, and in fact often go unstated.

The notion of "taken-for-granted frames of reference" also comes into play in Charles Taylor's formulation of the "modern social imaginary" by which is meant the elements that are assumed when people think of modernity and modernism; Taylor uses the term "social imaginary" rather than "social theory" to emphasize the mechanisms apparent in the thinking of the public at large in any society rather than those of only the elites, with the emphasis on the "common understanding that makes possible common practices and a widely shared sense of legitimacy"; this "common understanding" is not expressed as theories but rather conveyed "in images, stories and legends."[23]

---

      connections between those alleged "beliefs" in the return of Arthur and colonialism, see esp. 24–74.

21   *Imagined Communities: Reflections on the Origin and Spread of Nationalism* (London and New York: Verso, 1983; rev. ed. 2006).

22   *Imagined Communities*, 12.

23   *Modern Social Imaginaries* (Durham, NC: Duke University Press, 2004). Taylor defines his terms thus: "There are important differences between social imaginary and social theory. I adopt the term imaginary (i) because my focus is on the way ordinary people 'imagine' their social surroundings, and this is often not expressed in theoretical terms, but is carried in images, stories, and legends. It is also the case that (ii) theory is often the possession of a small minority, whereas what is interesting in the social imaginary is that it is shared by large groups of people if not the whole society. Which leads to a third difference: (iii) the social imaginary is that common understanding that makes possible common practices and a widely shared sense of legitimacy" (23). Though at times criticized for being euro-normative in taking Western modernism as his primary focus, Taylor's work is perhaps most valuable in its promotion of the idea of multiple modernities, with the Western formulation being only one among many. See also Bronislaw Baczko, *Les imaginaires sociaux: Mémoires et espoirs collectifs* (Paris: Payot, 1984) from whom he adapted the term "social imaginary."

INTRODUCTION 11

The concepts of "taken-for-granted frames of reference" and the ways ordinary people "imagine" their social milieu and communicate those imaginings in images, stories, and legends, form very useful constructs through which to approach Arthurian history within the framework of foundation myths of Britain and stories of those who shared (or did not share) power over the island. Although Michael Hechter concentrates on the early modern period to the modern, his central arguments in *Internal Colonialism* provide analyses which are directly applicable to the social dynamics in Britain in the twelfth and thirteenth centuries.[24] Although his rhetoric can often be perceived as polarizing – one need only look at the full title of the book and imagine a wide range of reactions – Hechter's formulation of the concept of internal colonialism itself – how some groups dominate others to the latter's detriment, perpetuating a class system where some are second-class citizens within their "own" country – is universally applicable (without even wishing to "take sides"),[25] and certainly to medieval Britain where, described in broad strokes,

---

24 *Internal Colonialism: The Celtic Fringe in British National Development, 1536–1966* (Berkeley and Los Angeles: University of California Press, 1975; 2nd ed., New Brunswick, NJ: Transaction Publishers, 1999). Although the term "Celtic fringe" is dismissive, it is used almost exclusively by scholars including Hechter to signal the marginalization of "Celtic" populations or institutions – in their support, and not the contrary; see for example also W. R. Jones, "England Against the Celtic Fringe: A Study in Cultural Stereotypes," *Cahiers d'Histoire Mondiale* 13.1 (1971): 155–71 and idem, on what he terms "English political and ecclesiastical imperialism" in "Medieval State-Building and the Churches of the Celtic Fringe," *Journal of Church and State* 16.3 (1974): 407–19. Similar views and sentiments inform this statement that "the 'New British History' has confronted but not yet fully resolved this problem of constructing the Celtic fringe as a *problem* in English history rather than a *contributor* to British history [my emphasis] ... Students might see Ireland, Scotland, and even Wales as culturally different, but those differences are still too often only glimpsed as divergence from a normative Englishness" (David Eastwood, review of *Celtic Identity and the British Image*, by Murray G. H. Pittock, Manchester: Manchester University Press, 1999, *English Historical Review* 116.465 (2001): 249–50, cited at 249).

25 I do not intend to "take sides" between the cultures and groups I will be discussing through the major texts in this book and am well aware that although I am writing about the Middle Ages, feelings of identity in our own time (as well as toward the past) run deep and must be respected. However, on the importance of increasing our awareness of the role of historical writing in creating, fostering, or perpetuating inequality among groups, see nn. **31** and **34** below. On a related matter, I am also aware of the current debate – particularly within universities in the United States – regarding the use of the term "Anglo-Saxon" as both an adjective and a noun. Given the history of the term used referring to "white" people (and regrettably by the far-right with respect to the "superiority" of "white" people), in order to be more inclusive and welcoming to people of all races and ethnicities, scholarly groups such as the International Society for Anglo-Saxonists have begun to change their names to emphasize the "pre-Conquest" aspect of the field disassociated from connotations of ethnoracial superiority through usage of the term

12   INTRODUCTION

the Britons gave way to the Saxons, who then struggled with the Vikings, and finally the Normans:

> A defining characteristic of imperial expansion is that the center must disparage the indigenous culture of peripheral groups. To the extent that the 'impingement of the center [is] much weaker than the permeation of the periphery by the center'[26] the periphery will tend to develop a reactive solidarity.[27] This insistence of cultural superiority on the part of the expanding metropolitan state is a characteristic of more recent imperialism as well. The imperial structure is weak because the center is quickly forced to rely on coercion to establish political order, since its legitimacy is frequently in question.[28]

Each of these statements has vast implications, many of which have been addressed by numerous scholars in a variety of contexts.[29] In a seminal article

---

"Anglo-Saxon." In this book, I will avoid the use of the term "Anglo-Saxon" whenever possible (except for the numerous texts such as the Peterborough Chronicle or Winchester Chronicle and other recensions which are often referred to under the collective title, "the Anglo-Saxon Chronicles"); I will retain "Angles" and "Saxons" as referred to by the authors I am studying. In addition, I will use the term "English" to distinguish those descended from or associated with the Germanic settlers/invaders from the Britons. On these very complex issues of terminology and cultural sensitivity, see David Wilton "What Do We Mean by *Anglo-Saxon*? Pre-Conquest to the Present," *Journal of English and Germanic Philology* 119.4 (2020): 425–56, for his analysis, numerous references, as well as a list of occurrences of "Anglo-Saxon" as used by some medieval writers (though not Geoffrey of Monmouth); see also Mary Rambaran-Olm and Erik Wade, "The Many Myths of the Term 'Anglo-Saxon'," *Smithsonian Magazine* July 14, 2021: https://www.smithsonianmag .com/history/many-myths-term-anglo-saxon-180978169/. For other perspectives, see also n. 10 above and n. 100, Chapter 2 below. On the relationships between the tremendously complex issues of race, hierarchies, and the medieval cultural and social imaginary, see Geraldine Heng, *The Invention of Race in the European Middle Ages* (Cambridge: Cambridge University Press, 2018); Rees Davies, "Race Relations in Post-Conquest Wales: Confrontation and Compromise," The Cecil-Williams Lecture for 1973, *Transactions of the Honourable Society of Cymmrodorion* (1974–75): 32–56; Cord J. Whitaker, *Black Metaphor: How Modern Racism Emerged from Medieval Race-Thinking* (Philadelphia: University of Pennsylvania Press, 2019); and other studies cited below in *Arthur, Origins, Identities*.

26   Shmuel N. Eisenstadt, *The Political Systems of Empires* (New York: The Free Press, 1969), xii.
27   Frank Young, "Reactive Subsystems," *American Sociological Review* 35.2 (1970): 297–307.
28   *Internal Colonialism*, 64.
29   For example, R. R. Davies, *The First English Empire: Power and Identities in the British Isles 1093–1343* (*The Ford Lectures Delivered in the University of Oxford in Hilary Term 1998*) (Oxford: Oxford University Press, 2000), esp. ch. 6, "The Anglicization of the British Isles," 142–71; John Gillingham, "Conquering the Barbarians: War and Chivalry in Twelfth-Century Britain," *Haskins Society Journal* 2 (1992): 67–84 (repr. in idem, *The English in the Twelfth*

INTRODUCTION   13

on the writing of English and British history in the twelfth century and the
attitudes of nineteenth-century English scholars valorizing English history at
the expense of British history – and the ways in which the writing of history
both forms and reflects public opinion – the late R. Rees Davies argues that
Geoffrey's *Historia* "may well have been a retaliatory response to the appearance of an authoritative and monopolistic English version of Britain's past,"
elaborating a "counter-history of British resistance and imperial glories under
Arthur."[30] Davies points out how marginalized the Britons were in the justifiably highly respected historical narratives of Bede, William of Malmesbury,
and Henry of Huntingdon:

> Britain beyond England and the Britons and their descendants hardly
> figure at all in their histories. They are for the most part geographically
> and chronologically off-stage. It was impossible, of course, not to men-
> tion them in recounting the story of English advance and triumph, but

---

     Century: Imperialism, National Identity and Political Values, Woodbridge: Boydell, 2000,
     41–58); and Sarah Foot, "The Making of *Angelcynn*: English Identity Before the Norman
     Conquest," *Transactions of the Royal Historical Society*, ser. 6 (Cambridge: Cambridge
     University Press, 1996), 25–50.

30   *The Matter of Britain and Matter of England: An Inaugural lecture delivered before the
     University of Oxford on 29 February 1996* (Oxford: Clarendon Press, 1996), cited here at
     11 and 10, respectively. I must acknowledge the tremendous debt I owe to the work of
     R. R. Davies (whom I never had the privilege of meeting), and to stress that my essential
     thesis about Geoffrey – that the vulgate *Historia* was written largely in order to counter
     Bede's and other historians' Anglo-centric views of the British past – is of course not new,
     but that I want to use this book to build on that view to see how this thesis plays out in
     other works which followed in Geoffrey's tradition, including the First Variant, Gaimar's
     Estoire des Engleis, Wace's *Roman de Brut*, and several of the early anonymous verse *Bruts*.
     Although many have considered Geoffrey's *Historia* "nonsense," I intend to argue that it
     was, at the very least, "politically necessary" nonsense and inspired many different reac-
     tions, even, and perhaps most notably, very soon after its appearance. Among numer-
     ous articles on the reception of Geoffrey of Monmouth, see Simon Meecham-Jones,
     "Early Reactions to Geoffrey's Work," in *A Companion to Geoffrey of Monmouth*, 181–208
     (https://brill.com/view/title/39588); Jean Blacker, "The Anglo-Norman and Continental
     French Reception of Geoffrey of Monmouth's Corpus from the 12th to the 15th Centuries,"
     in *A Companion to Geoffrey of Monmouth*, 454–66; and the very rich collection of essays
     which hadn't yet appeared when I was writing my survey on the early French reception
     of Geoffrey, *L'Historia regum Britannie et les "Bruts" en Europe, II: Production, circula-
     tion, réception*, ed. Hélène Tétrel and Géraldine Veysseyre, Rencontres 349, Civilisation
     médiévale 32 (Paris: Classiques Garnier, 2018), esp. Jaakko Tahkokallio, "Publishing the
     History of the Kings of Britain," 45–57, Diana Tyson "A Study of Medieval French *Brut*
     Manuscripts in London Collections," 125–45, and Olivier de Laborderie, "L'incorporation
     de l'*Histoire des rois de Bretagne* de Geoffrey de Monmouth dans les généalogies des rois
     d'Angleterre (XIIe–XIVe siècles)," 255–80.

14   INTRODUCTION

they put in an appearance only to be defeated; they have virtually no
other identity.[31]

Applauding recent efforts to work the history of Wales, Scotland, and Ireland
into histories of the United Kingdom, the latter which is so often dominated in
the academy by the history of England, Davies comments that

> It is in part an attempt to make amends for an act of historiographical
> oversight and neglect. The streamlined neatness of English historiogra-
> phy, even of Anglocentric British historiography, was built on privileging
> the history of the nation-state, its political story-line, and its dominant
> elite at the expense of underestimating the plurality of Britain.[32]

---

31   *The Matter of Britain and the Matter of England*, 15. This historiographical side-lining
      can be seen to reflect a cultural component as well. As Bryan Ward-Perkins comments
      "Anglo-Saxon Britain is undoubtedly a particularly extreme case of cultural domina-
      tion"… "the experience of post-Roman Britain confirms the observation, that the amount
      of borrowing between one culture and another is determined, not only by the amount
      of contact between the two, but also by the perceived status that each culture has in
      the eyes of the other. When invaders find a native culture that they feel to be superior to
      their own, they borrow heavily and readily from it, as happened amongst the Franks in
      romanized Gaul; but when, as in Britain, they find a culture that they, rightly or wrongly
      perceive to be inferior, the story is very different" ("Why Did the Anglo-Saxons Not
      Become More British?" *The English Historical Review* 115. 462 (2000): 513–33, cited at 526
      and 530). Similarly, Nicholas Brooks finds that modern historians' "over-reliance" on Bede
      may have led them to overlook or downplay archaeological and place-name evidence –
      primarily though not exclusively of churches – and the fact that many of Bede's sources
      were almost exclusively from the eastern areas, which suggests that British Christians
      and their churches may have played a more significant role in the Christianization of the
      Saxons than previously thought ("From British to English Christianity: Deconstructing
      Bede's Interpretation of the Conversion," in *Conversion and Colonization in Anglo-Saxon
      England*, ed. Catherine E. Karkov and Nicholas Howe, Medieval and Renaissance Texts
      and Studies 318, Essays in Anglo-Saxon Studies 2, Tempe, AZ: Arizona Center for Medieval
      and Renaissance Studies, 2006, 1–30). On Bede's "agenda" to side-line the Britons, see
      also Robert Hutton who writes that, in general, Bede's "purpose was to make out his own
      people the English, to be the chosen people of God and the true heirs of the Romans. To
      justify that view, the native British had to be like the Biblical Canaanites: the low life that
      got swept aside in the proper implementation of God's plan for Britain. Gildas was an
      absolute gift to Bede, because he was a native Briton who called his own people a sinful
      bunch of losers who had deserved all they had suffered at English hands. … Arthur does
      not appear in Bede's history [for to have done] so, as a very successful native British sol-
      dier, would have wrecked the entire argument of the book" ("The Early Arthur," 25). See
      also Chapter 6, nn. 62 and 67.
32   *The Matter of Britain and the Matter of England*, 23. On the one hand, while Davies argues
      for more inclusion of the contributions of the "margins" on the part of English historians –
      arguing in favor of viewing outlying areas' histories as contributions rather than as

problematic – he takes a balanced view as well, questioning the often "proprietorial attitude of historians of Ireland, Scotland, and Wales towards 'their own' history" (23); one of
the strengths of this lecture is Davies's attempt to speak about differing poles of historical
material, and inevitably about those who write about those poles, without engaging in an
"us versus them" binary. While at the same time arguing against what he calls "the stream-
lined neatness of English historiography" which was built on "privileging the history of
the nation-state, its political story-line, and its dominant elite at the expense of underes-
timating the plurality of Britain," Davies is careful to avoid questioning "the achievement,
the validity, or the future of the history of England" or of its people. When he suggests that
"the length of the matter of England needs to be balanced in some degree by the breadth
of the Matter of Britain," he is seeking to encourage a broader base from which history
can be written but also from which history of the past can be perceived and understood,
encouraging plurality and richness while avoiding the sorts of evaluation and specializa-
tion that can lead to exclusion. However, there is a much larger issue beyond the specific
treatment both of the Britons in medieval historical writing and any contemporary tendency on the part of scholars of the English nation to overlook the "Celtic fringe" in assess-
ing the history of Britain, and that is the role of historical writing in both the creation
of popular myths or their perpetuation. There is a surprisingly useful analogy between
Davies's observations on mainstream academic production in Britain – emphasizing his
pointing to the necessity for more inclusion of "border peoples" in writing a more pluralis-
tic and holistic history of the island – and the writing of the history of the First Peoples in
the United States (though the latter is arguably more extreme given the genocide involved
in nearly four hundred years of "resettlement," including the forced removal of the 1830
Indian Removal Act), including the extent of changes to the educational system currently
being advocated by scholars in the US in order to educate students living in mainstream
society about the native peoples who occupied the lands before the European settlers
came. On the influence of historical writing in shaping views of the dominant society
toward those on the margins, on "settler colonialism" particularly in the Americas (with
references to other settler states such as Australia and Canada), and the necessity of dis-
rupting the idea of *terra nullius* – the so-called "Doctrine of Discovery" which holds that
the Europeans "discovered America" which was in their view empty of human civilization before they came – see for example Roxanne Dunbar-Ortiz, *An Indigenous People's
History of the United States*, ReVisioning American History 3 (Boston: Beacon Press, 2014);
Emma Battell Lowman, "*An Indigenous Peoples' History of the United States*: A Review,"
Decolonization: Indigeneity, Education & Society 4.1 (2015): 118–28; Frederick E. Hoxie, "The
Presence of Native American History," in *The Organization of American Historians and
the Writing and Teaching of American History*, ed. Richard S. Kirkendall (Oxford: Oxford
University Press, 2011), 198–206; and Jean M. O'Brien, *Firsting and Lasting: Writing Indians
out of Existence in New England* (Minneapolis: University of Minnesota Press, 2010).
Both Davies and Dunbar-Ortiz (among others) advocate going beyond the articulation
of theories of historical writing as a more purely intellectual pursuit, toward promoting awareness of social inequalities potentially perpetuated by historical scholarship,
and ultimately toward the improvement of peoples' lives through changing of attitudes,
starting with the academy and spreading outward to governments and societies at large.
Similar work is being conducted on African-American history in the US (as well by historians and others on behalf of multiple groups around the world); among the vast resources
on that topic, for an introduction, see Gerald Horne, *The Counter Revolution of 1776: Slave*

16 INTRODUCTION

Michelle Warren writes, paraphrasing R. W. Southern:

> the cultural trauma of Norman colonization focused attention on the near and distant past, as both dominant and dominated groups defended their collective identities and sought therapeutic cures for alienation in history. In this process, King Arthur became the most contested of all Britons.[33]

Recognizing that so many groups fought over Arthur claiming him as "theirs" in order to further their own political ends, Warren highlights the political messages of the Arthurian myth by reintegrating Arthurian history back into the texts and traditions from which it is too often extracted, working against many critical approaches that have tended to view the Arthurian story in isolation, as a sort of literary beast out of time and place. While embracing a number of postcolonial perspectives, Warren specifically engages a subset of those perspectives often applied to "border writing" from border cultures, seeking to break through national, generic or regional perspectives to look at culture in literature more holistically and less divisively[34] – treating Arthurian texts as analogous to aspects of cultures often in conflict with one another, aspects more easily understood when viewed as dynamic parts of a whole.

While I share Warren's desire to consider Arthurian sections of individual texts as part of a larger whole, both textually and culturally, as well as her engagement with postcolonial approaches – in addition to many of the primary texts we study in common including the *HRB*, First Variant, and Wace's *Brut*[35] – my readings of those texts often part ways with hers, without

---

Resistance and the Origins of the United States of America (New York: New York University Press, 2016) and idem, *The Apocalypse of Settler Colonialism: The Roots of Slavery, White Supremacy, and Capitalism in Seventeenth-Century North America and the Caribbean* (New York: Monthly Review Press, 2018).

33 *History on the Edge*, xi.

34 Often considered the groundbreaking book in this field is D. Emily Hicks, *Border Writing: The Multidimensional Text* (Minneapolis: University of Minnesota Press, 1991); see also Bruce W. Holsinger, "Medieval Studies, Postcolonial Studies, and the Genealogies of Critique," *Speculum* 77.4 (2002): 1195–1227. Davies also comments that with reference to Gerald of Wales and Geoffrey of Monmouth: "Both men were, in their different ways, victims, exponents, and beneficiaries of their own cultural ambivalence; they were men of the frontiers; therein undoubtedly lay part of the richness of their characters and the fertility of their imaginations" ("Matter of Britain and Matter of England," 7).

35 In terms of texts, there is a not-surprising overlap between Warren's work and my own since she also works with historical texts, not romance (though she does devote considerable energy to symbols of chivalry and their cultural weight). However, texts which form a major focus in Warren's *History on the Edge* but which do not figure widely in *Arthur,*

INTRODUCTION

necessarily fundamental (or at least troublesome) disagreement but with different meanings attached.[36]

Laurie Finke and Martin Shichtman's work with the "idea" of Arthur and his role in the social imaginary, rather than more traditional – but always vexing – questions of historicity or folkloric origins is informed by the question of why a group of narratives about King Arthur suddenly appears to emerge full-blown in the twelfth century, and why Arthur has continued to be such an enduring cultural and semi-historical figure.[37] Finke and Shichtman argue that "King Arthur has been used by historians – medieval and modern – as a potent, but empty, social signifier to which meaning could be attached that served to legitimate particular forms of political authority and cultural imperialism."[38]

While I agree with Finke and Shichtman's fundamental premise that Arthur has been used to serve a broad spectrum of political – and often imperialist[39] – ends from the Middle Ages to the present, I see Arthur less as an empty signifier or cipher but rather as a tension-filled symbol and tool (but some may see these readings as more similar than I am portraying them here). For my reading, it is Arthur's dual status of insider/outsider in all its complexities – allying him with the most universal of heroes from world literature – that has contributed to making Arthur an ever-malleable, even transcendent, figure, particularly compelling in the articulation of ethnic or national identities and dreams of equality, independence or glory – or dreams of a return to former conditions once enjoyed, of equality, independence or glory.

Lastly, another study on Arthur engages twelfth-century historical narrative with Arthurian connections, but envisages Arthur less as metaphor for the marginalized or as a broader symbol of cultural and political triumph – or other

---

Origins, Identities include Laȝamon's *Brut*, the *Brut y Brenhinedd*, Robert of Gloucester's *Historia rhythmis Anglicanis*, and William of Rennes's *Gesta regum Britanniae*.

36 See for example discussions in Chapters 1, 2, 3 and 5.

37 Laurie A. Finke and Martin B. Shichtman, *King Arthur and the Myth of History* (Gainesville: University Press of Florida, 2004). In this book, they address issues of historical writing and cultural formation in William of Malmesbury's *Gesta Regum Anglorum*, Geoffrey of Monmouth's *HRB*, Wace and Laȝamon, John Hardyng's *Chronicle*, Malory's *Morte Darthur*, and two modern texts that relate the history of Adolf Hitler's "acquisition" of the Holy Grail.

38 *Myth of History*, p. 2. Although with the risk of oversimplification, the term "cultural imperialism" describes a situation where the culture of a dominant group is imposed upon a less dominant group since the latter's culture is considered inferior to that of the dominant group.

39 More recently, Finke and Shichtman have continued their examination of the nefarious uses of, or connections to, Arthur and his court, in texts sympathetic to, or produced by, the Nazi regime or Nazi sympathizers elsewhere. See especially "Exegetical History: Nazis at the Round Table," *Postmedieval: A Journal of Medieval Cultural Studies* 5 (2014): 278–94.

18 INTRODUCTION

possibilities among the broad range of meanings along that continuum – than either Warren or Finke and Shichtman is Kristin Over's *Kingship, Conquest, and Patria*.[40] While Over appreciates and argues cogently for the duality inherent in Geoffrey's Arthur whom she characterizes as simultaneously "warrior-chieftain and cultural trendsetter,"[41] the strength of her study lies less in its promotion of Arthur as a binary and transcendent hero and more in her arguments underscoring Geoffrey's Welsh connections or biases, a theme that has been sounded often but is put forward by Over with renewed vigor and persuasive power.[42] While providing excellent background on early Welsh historical and literary allusions to Arthur and Arthur-like leaders, her book is less focused however on the ancient, mythical foundational precedents of Arthur's connections to the Britons' hegemony than on the contemporary twelfth-century politics of Welsh resistance to Anglo-Norman territorial domination,[43] and the significant mirroring of those pulls and tensions within Anglo-Norman England as seen in French and Welsh romance.

---

40   Kristin Lee Over, *Kingship, Conquest, and Patria: Literary and Cultural Identities in Medieval French and Welsh Arthurian Romance* (New York: Routledge, 2005). My apologies to the many other literary scholars and historians, to whose work I owe an immeasurable debt of gratitude but who are too numerous to mention here; many of their contributions will be engaged in more specific ways at various junctures in *Arthur, Origins, Identities*.

41   *Kingship, Conquest, and Patria*, 65.

42   On both the centrality and marginality of the Welsh and Wales in Geoffrey's historical endeavor, see also Michael A. Faletra, *Wales and the Medieval Colonial Imagination: The Matters of Britain in the Twelfth Century* (New York: Palgrave MacMillan, 2014), and the numerous publications of John Gillingham referenced throughout *Arthur, Origins, Identities*, particularly "The Context and Purposes of Geoffrey of Monmouth's *History of the Kings of Britain*"; it is important to note that Gillingham does not insist that Geoffrey was Welsh. On Geoffrey's identity which is often – but not always – perceived as inseparable from his arguments or goals in the *Historia*, Michelle Warren writes: "Scholars have often identified Geoffrey as a member of one of these groups, either Breton (Tatlock [*Legendary History*] 396–402, 443), Cornish (Padel, 4), Welsh (Gillingham ["Context and Purposes," orig. pagination] 100–03, 106–10), or Norman, usually on the basis of perceived biases toward the group. The identity politics of a colonial culture like twelfth-century Monmouthshire, however, militate against the deduction of ethnicity from politics or blood relationships" ("Making Contact: Postcolonial Perspectives through Geoffrey of Monmouth's *Historia regum Britannie*," *Arthuriana* 8.4 (1998): 115–34, cited at 117); see O. J. Padel, "Geoffrey of Monmouth and Cornwall," *Cambridge Medieval Celtic Studies* 8 (1984): 1–28. See also Chapter 1, n. 45 for more views on Geoffrey's identity, as well as Joshua Byron Smith's Introduction to *A Companion to Geoffrey of Monmouth*, eds. Henley and Smith, 1–30, where Smith leans toward Welsh as Geoffrey's origins.

43   Following Gillingham, referring specifically to Geoffrey's possible reactions to the "great revolt" of 1136–37, where Welsh princes regained many of the lands previously lost to Henry I (*Kingship, Conquest, and Patria*, 48–49 and nn. 40–42).

INTRODUCTION

Over rightly sees Geoffrey's "counter-history" on one level as a message against "foreign control in Britain," yet I would like to broaden this view of counter-history as an argument against "internal foreign" control as well: in addition to a reaction against the Norman conquering half of the Anglo-Norman equation, Geoffrey's work promoted resistance to the English perception of cultural superiority over the Britons as seen in historical texts and elsewhere in society. As Over herself notes, while the early tenth-century *Armes Prydein* for example prophesies "nationalist opposition" to the Saxons as foreigners it hoped to drive out of Wales forever,[44] Geoffrey writing in the early to mid-twelfth century could have been referring both to actual foreigners – the Norman conquerors who were firmly in place[45] – but also to those now native English who were treating the Britons as foreigners in their own land.

---

44 *Armes Prydein: The Prophecy of Britain from the Book of Taliesin*, ed. Ifor Williams, trans. Rachel Bromwich, Mediaeval and Modern Welsh Series 6 (Dublin: School of Celtic Studies Dublin Institute for Advanced Studies, 1972; repr. 1982, 2006; orig. published in Welsh in 1955), xxvi. In his review of Williams's edition with Rachel Bromwich's translation, Bedwyr Jones suggests that the author of the poem, the *Battle of Brunaburh* which is included in the Anglo-Saxon Chronicle for the year 937, must have known of the anti-Saxon propaganda in the *Armes Prydein* because the Anglo-Saxon poem seems to answer it, exulting in the resounding defeat of the Welsh and other Brythonic troops at Brunanburh in 937 (Bedwyr L. Jones, review of *Armes Prydein: The Prophecy of Britain from the Book of Taliesin*," *Medium Ævum* 43 (1974): 181–85, 183; *The Anglo-Saxon Chronicles*, ed. and trans. Michael Swanton, London: J. M. Dent, 1996; rev. ed., London: Phoenix, 2000). Although Williams did not think that the poem could have been written following such a setback (that is, post-937), David Dumville points out that this "makes no allowance for the resilience of the mediaeval warrior-politician, for the rapid shifts in fortune which could and did occur, as in the winter of 939/40 when the anti-English coalition resumed its military activities and undid what Æthelstan seemed to have achieved at Brunanburh" ("Brittany and 'Armes Prydein Vawr'," *Études Celtiques* 20.1 (1983): 145–59, cited at 148–49). For other perspectives, see for example, Elizabeth M. Tyler who argues that "the poem's clear emphasis on the West Saxons' imperial designs on all the peoples of Britain and its delight in violence points to the messy origins of a polity that only later became 'English' in anything like the modern sense … When read alongside Athelstan's charters and 'Armes Prydein Vawr,' 'Brunanburh' brings both the diversity of Britain and the hegemony of England into full view" ("England between Empire and Nation in the 'Battle of Bruanburh'," in *Whose Middle Ages? Teachable Moments for an Ill-Used Past*, ed., Andrew Albin, Mary C. Erler, Thomas O'Donnell, Nicholas L. Paul, Nina Rowe, and David Perry, New York: Fordham University Press, 2019, 166–80, cited at 176).

45 In *Faces of Time*, which was written in many respects from different perspectives than this current book, I argued that Geoffrey's text fulfilled an educative and legitimizing function for the Anglo-Norman elite, teaching them how the Britons descended from the Trojans (as did the Normans), as if to educate them partially regarding the background of many of the inhabitants of the land called England which they now occupied and governed (1994, 163–66). As Olivier de Laborderie notes with respect to the audiences of early thirteenth-century genealogical rolls, "in adopting the Anglo-Saxon – and sometimes

20   INTRODUCTION

1   Contextualizing Geoffrey's *Historia*, Arthur, and the Early French
        Brut Tradition

In terms of the ancient history of the Britons, as Felicity Riddy summarizes
handily in her contextualization of Malory's *Morte DArthur*, by Malory's time,
people looked back nine hundred years

> and did not see an unconquered island; they saw discontinuities, not
> continuity. They saw the Norman invasion of the eleventh century, the
> Danish invasion of the ninth, the Anglo-Saxon invasion of the fifth,
> which was preceded by a failed attempt by the Picts and the Scots, and
> the Roman invasion of the first century BC.[46]

In the few extant medieval texts which even attempt to tackle the history of pre-fifth century Britain, the Britons begin to be mentioned as their
co-existence with the Romans comes to an end – the Romans being the first
conquering people to depart – and they remain behind to fend for themselves
against the Saxons, whose hegemony was ultimately the most enduring.[47]

In brief, in Gildas's sixth-century *De Excidio*, essentially a sermon containing a narrative of the history of the Britons before the coming of the Saxons,
Arthur does not yet appear; instead one finds the Roman Aurelius Ambrosius
who leads the Britons in a victory against the Saxons at Mons Badonicus; in
the ninth-to-tenth century *Historia Brittonum*, Arthur the *dux bellorum* fights
and wins twelve battles, yet does not secure ultimate victory for the Britons; in
the mid-tenth-century Cambro-Latin chronicles, the *Annales Cambriae*, there
is one mention of Arthur: entry 72 (*c.*516 AD) which relates Arthur's victory at
Badon Hill and his having carried the Cross on his shoulders for three days and
three nights before his victory.[48]

> even the British – past as part of their own history, they went one step further in becom-
> ing Englishmen: French-speaking Englishmen, but English nonetheless" ("A New Pattern
> for English History: The First Genealogical Rolls of the Kings of England," in *Broken Lines:
> Genealogical Literature of Medieval England and France*, ed. Raluca L. Radulescu and
> Edward Donald Kennedy, Turnhout: Brepols, 2008, 45–61, cited at 61).

46   "Contextualizing *Le Morte Darthur*: Empire and Civil War," 57.

47   For resources on the current debates among historians, anthropologists, art historians,
       sociologists and others on theories of settlement in early Britain, see Chapter 1, esp.
       nn. 55 and 99.

48   The only surviving early mention of Arthur is found in Aneirin's Welsh *Y Goddodin*
       (*c.*600), though he is not openly eulogized as is his descendant Cynon throughout the
       poems; the brave but not victorious warrior Gwawrddur, is compared with Arthur unfa-
       vorably in stanza 99 "though he was no Arthur"; for the edition and further discussion,

INTRODUCTION   21

As will be discussed in more detail in Chapter One, Arthur does not appear as a king and potential savior of the Britons until Geoffrey of Monmouth's *Historia*, the text that puts Arthur on the literary and historical map; in fact, according to Bedwyr Jones, it would appear that "the evidence of Welsh tradition surely is that the characterization of Arthur as the political deliverer of the Britons is a post-Norman creation."[49] In Geoffrey's *Historia*, Arthur is the 99th of 107 kings whose reigns stretch in unbroken succession from Brutus, the great-grandson of Aeneas to Cadualadrus (Cadwaladr or Cadwallader), the last king of the Britons who allegedly died in 689 – though Geoffrey goes on to imply that the Britons shared rule of the Island with the Saxons until the reign of Athelstan, thus opening up a window of roughly 300 years of shared rule until the late tenth century.[50] Although Arthur is only one of 107 kings, his reign occupies three books of eleven (not including the book of Prophecies) of the *Historia*, significantly more than any other king.[51]

Geoffrey gives Arthur what in later literature becomes his "standard biography,"[52] perhaps most notable for the fact that during Arthur's reign the

---

     see Chapter 2, n. 44 below. As Over observes, "regardless of attractive conjectures of a vast corpus of oral material about Arthur, surviving Welsh poetry by and large omits him from the praise of military resistance to foreign invaders and neighboring enemies" (18). On the status of Badon Hill (vs. Bath) and Arthur's shield in Geoffrey, Wace, and other texts, see esp. Chapter 1, n. 76, Chapter 2, n. 16 and nn. 46–49, Chapter 5, nn. 66, 71, 89–90, and Appendix 3.

49   Bedwyr L. Jones, review of *Armes Prydein*, 183. Although this does not preclude Arthur's having possibly also been an early messianic figure in oral legend, the lack of evidence from the Welsh tradition suggests otherwise, as Dumville concludes "the author of our poem inherited as a legendary convention the messianic joint role of Cynan and Cadwaladr. Their function was to personify or represent the Continental and Insular Britons respectively, indicating that the whole of the British world ('o Vynaw hyt Lydaw', etc. ["from Manaw (an area around the head of the Firth of Forth) to Brittany," l. 172]) would eventually shake off its political fragmentation, uniting to recover its ancient territory" ("Brittany," 156). Cf. however n. 20 above with references to the "Breton hope," some of which suggest that the belief in Arthur as deliverer may have been circulating in Brythonic areas before the Normans came to England. See also the numerous essays in *The Arthur of the Welsh* which argue for the vibrancy of the early Welsh literary and historical traditions.

50   The roughly 300-year gap first proposed by Leckie in *The Passage of Dominion* and articulated most clearly in his work on Wace whom he sees as reconciling the Galfridian gap with the FV's having made the tenth-century Athelstan a contemporary of seventh-century Cadwallader (esp. pp. 110–17). See also Chapter 5 below.

51   See Chapter 1, n. 4 below on the king count.

52   Riddy, "Contextualizing *Le Morte Darthur*: Empire and Civil War," 60. See also Judith Weiss, "Arthur, Emperors, and Antichrists: The Formation of the Arthurian Biography," in *Writers of the Reign of Henry II: Twelve Essays*, ed. Ruth Kennedy and Simon Meecham-Jones, The New Middle Ages (New York: Palgrave Macmillan, 2006), 239–48.

22   INTRODUCTION

conquered become conquerors, the colonized become colonizers, and the man
who is outsider by birth – an illegitimate son of a marginalized population –
becomes the ultimate insider – a king whose realm spreads across most of
northern Europe, and nearly becomes Roman emperor. Arthur's journey can
be broken down into the following stages:

1)   a complex and seemingly contradictory birth story;
2)   accession to the throne at fifteen;
3)   defeat of the Saxons;
4)   marriage to Guinevere;
5)   a world-renowned court;
6)   the conquest of countries in the north of Europe as well as "France";
7)   a challenge from Rome;
8)   fight with a giant and near-defeat of the Roman army;
9)   treachery of his nephew, Mordred, who has taken his wife Guinevere
      and had himself crowned king in Arthur's absence (hence precipitating
      Arthur's departure from the battles with Rome before their conclusion);
10)   Arthur's return to his kingdom, defeat of Mordred whom he kills and by
      whom he is mortally wounded at the battle of Camlann.[53]

In terms of Arthur's family (who figure largely in the romance tradition,
though not in the histories), for Geoffrey, it is only Arthur's parents, Uther
Pendragon and Ygerne, who seem to matter (though they are rarely present
in his youth, his upbringing not being at issue, although for many writers his
having been conceived in sin is), despite the long line of ancestors Geoffrey
so carefully draws.[54]

    Although Geoffrey does devote some energy to Arthur's role in peacetime,
it is the king's battles that draw the greatest attention from the histories in this

---

53   As will be seen in the discussions of our texts in the following chapters, with variations,
      including mention of the "Breton hope," Arthur is mortally wounded but is not always
      said to have died; in the vulgate, Arthur is "taken away to the island of Avallon to have
      his wounds tended and, in the year of Our Lord 542, handed over Britain's crown to his
      relative Constantinus, son of Cador duke of Cornwall" (§178.81–84). No mention is made
      of his death, Geoffrey leaving this open-ended, perhaps in light of rumors (or a belief)
      already circulating of Arthur's "return"; see n. 20 above.

54   Rosemary Morris notes that "Arthur is a classic case of the legendary figure who attracts
      previously unrelated characters into his orbit. Their proliferation gives his family tree a
      complication rivalled only by Perceval's" (The Character of King Arthur, 94). However,
      unlike the multiple relatives alive during his "lifetime," added by the romance tradition,
      in Geoffrey, Arthur's remote ancestry "by contrast, is never traced further back than
      Constans [eldest son of Constantine II, crowned by Vortigern, assassinated by the latter's
      Pictish agents], and there is confusion even there" (94). See also Morris's discussion of
      Arthur's conception and nuclear family (26–29).

INTRODUCTION

study. Rosemary Morris divides the battles into five categories (though not all of these categories suit each of the texts discussed in this book):

1) Saxon wars
2) Defensive wars, including wars against rebels
3) "Altruistic" wars, on behalf of vassal or ally
4) Wars of conquest
5) The Roman war[55]

Regardless of Arthur's successes on the battlefield, he is unable to help his people achieve lasting dominion, though each text treats the king's victories but ultimate demise differently.[56]

2 Structure of *Arthur, Origins, Identities*

While each chapter will focus on a different chronicle (or set of chronicles), the discussion in each chapter will be organized along three primary lines of inquiry which distinguish the presentations of the legendary history of Britain from text to text, thereby highlighting themes of ethnic identity, sense of community, and the mechanics of cultural assimilation, domination, and imperialism (military, political, and cultural):

1) the foundation story;
2) the *adventus Saxonum* and the passage of dominion from the Britons to the Angles (as minor figures), the Saxons as the major group of Germanic invaders/settlers, and their descendants; and
3) Arthur: his origins, rise to power, conquests, peacetime activities, defeat and "death".

It is important to note that the section on Arthur – which I am choosing to place in third position in each chapter – is, in many texts, technically speaking an interruption to the second section because the *adventus Saxonum* is not a single event, but rather a process, which happens over many years as the Saxons arrive, bring reinforcements, depart and return, with Arthur's reign falling toward the end of the Britons' hegemony, before the final Saxon take-over.

---

55   *The Character of King Arthur*, 51.
56   Felicity Riddy observes further that probably even taking into consideration Geoffrey's brief narrative of the 300-year shared rule between the Britons and the Saxons (between Camlann in late seventh century and the reign of Athelstan mid-tenth), ultimately "any story about the British resistance is bound to be about a last stand, just as narratives about native Americans in the history of the American west inevitably have written into them, implicitly or explicitly, the larger tragic outcome of their story" (Riddy, "Contextualizing *Le Morte Darthur*," 58).

However, for ease of discussion, the section on Arthur (3) follows that of at least the initial stages of the *adventus* (2), with the "final passage of dominion" mentioned in the closing section of each chapter following the discussion of Arthur's presentation, where appropriate.

Chapter 1, "Geoffrey of Monmouth's *Historia Regum Britanniae*: Part One," places Geoffrey's text within a larger historiographical framework. First, Geoffrey's text is seen ideologically and structurally in relation to preceding works by authors such as Bede, Gildas, and "Nennius," then to works by Geoffrey's principal twelfth-century contemporaries William of Malmesbury and Henry of Huntingdon, focusing on the description of Britain, the Brutus foundation myth, the *adventus Saxonum*, and the earlier stages of the passage of dominion.[57] Geoffrey of Monmouth's seminal pro-British text is seen in large part to be a reaction to – or necessary response to – the universally accepted pro-English eighth-century history by Bede (*Historia ecclesiastica gentis Anglorum*).[58] Chapter 2, "Geoffrey of Monmouth's *Historia Regum Britanniae*: Part Two," focuses on Geoffrey's text more closely, analyzing his treatment of King Arthur in the context of his predecessors and his principal contemporaries, and his presentation of Gormund's Donation, Augustine's conversion of the English, and the final stage of the passage of dominion including Cadwallader and the "final days."

Chapter 3, "The First Variant Version," is devoted to the so-called First Variant version (or simply Variant Version) of the HRB (post 1138 to the early 1150s),[59] examining the outstanding features of this near-contemporary revision of the HRB assembled by a largely pro-Saxon (or pro-English) redactor (or set of redactors). The FV will also be contextualized within the Galfridian tradition, with references to other versions, including conflate manuscripts of the vulgate version and the FV.

Chapter 4, "Wace's *Roman de Brut*, Part One: Gaimar's *Estoire des Engleis*," sets the stage for Chapter 5, "Wace's *Roman de Brut*, Part Two." While not containing the narrative of the foundation myth and the early history of the Britons on the island, as the *Estoire des Bretuns* Gaimar refers to in his prologue is no longer extant, the *Estoire des Engleis* provides an important window onto

---

57 Primary works of William of Newburgh, Gerald de Barri (Gerald of Wales), and Gervase of Canterbury, among others, will be referred to where pertinent.

58 See nn. 29–31 above.

59 In his translation of the First Variant, the first to appear in English, David Burchmore argues for the reverse order: that is, that the First Variant was written before the vulgate, as first proposed by Robert Caldwell. See Chapter 3, nn. 10–16, 18.

INTRODUCTION   25

early English history as it was presented to an Anglo-Norman family in the
mid-twelfth century.[60]

In Chapter 5, Wace's *Roman de Brut* is viewed less as a precursor to the medieval French romance tradition – a perspective common to much scholarship
on this writer's *Brut*[61] – and more as an historical text, a central conduit of
the Latin tradition to the French and English vernacular historical traditions.
Among the many distinguishing features of this text are: Wace's tendency to
"equalize" the enemies, to "depoliticize" the presentation of factions in favor
of a more universal, fatalistic view;[62] the creation of a continuum of power,
ranging from Gormund's nearly total destruction of the Britons and subsequent lack of desire to assimilate on the part of the Saxon heirs of Gormund's
Donation, to Arthur's more culturally tolerant, albeit nonetheless colonialist
strategies; the coexisting tension between Arthur's role as civilizer and "equalizer," despite his "irregular" barbarian origins, and his hunger for power and
world domination.

Chapter 6, "The Anonymous Verse *Brut* Tradition," examines five early anonymous French verse *Brut*s (all Anglo-Norman but Munich): the Royal *Brut* (BL
Royal 13.A.XXI), the Munich *Brut* (Munich, Bayerische Staatsbibliothek Gall. 29),
the Harley *Brut* (BL, Harley 1605), the version in College of Arms 12/45A (roll),
and the fourteenth-c. Egerton *Brut* (BL, Egerton 3128), providing an analysis
of "alternative" versions of early British history. Although no identifying prologues or epilogues are extant and the texts are fragmentary, their presentations of Arthur – for example, distinct echoes of the First Variant in the Royal
Brut – reveal ideological transformations, including Harley's inclusion of
the book of Merlin's Prophecies, thereby reinstating allusions to the Britons'

---

60   For editions, Gaimar's patrons, and sociopolitical context of his *Estoire des Engleis*, see
      especially Chapter 2, n. 19, Chapter 3, n. 16, and on the *Estoire des Bretuns* Chapter 4, n. 5.
61   For an overview of recent scholarship on Wace's *Brut*, see Jean Blacker, *Wace: A Critical
      Bibliography*, with the collaboration of Glyn S. Burgess (St. Helier: Société Jersiaise, 2008),
      46–118.
62   A number of scholars have misinterpreted my intentions in coining this phrase as applied
      to Wace's *Brut*: I did not mean that Wace eliminated all political content from his text, but
      that for example he tended to praise figures such as Julius Caesar whom Geoffrey viewed
      as enemies of the Britons, as well as neutralizing Geoffrey's animosity toward the Saxons
      and other groups or individuals by focusing on etymology, genealogy, and geographical
      definitions, as if to set the history in a more universalizing context; the addition of nos-
      talgia, a major theme of the Norman poet, intertwined with the theme of the passage
      of time and Fortune's wheel also serves to dilute the political content ("Transformations
      of a Theme: The Depoliticization of the Arthurian World in the *Roman de Brut*," in *The
      Arthurian Tradition: Essays in Convergence*, ed. Mary Flowers Braswell and John Bugge,
      Tuscaloosa: University of Alabama Press, 1988, 54–74, notes pp. 204–9 [published under
      the name Blacker-Knight].

26 INTRODUCTION

future. The later Egerton *Brut* – on one level a form of abridgment of Wace's *Brut*, 88% of which is made up of lines from that poem – emphasizes Arthur's dominance over Rome, downplays Welsh and Britons' future roles, and reveals distinct anti-Scottish sentiment early in the reign of Edward II whose Scottish campaigns met with mixed success.[63]

In conclusion, the tremendous variety in presentation, perspectives, and goals among these five anonymous verse *Bruts* serves not only to underscore Geoffrey's importance – as if the vulgate text needed its importance underscored! – as well as the multiplicity of meanings his narrative held for various writers and audiences of these verse histories. Whether their patrons were either unable to obtain a copy of Wace's text, or they sought a different "spin" – from an amplification of the role of Roman history in the Britons' background to a realignment of the power structure in Arthur's army during the Roman campaign – they illustrate how "counter" Geoffrey's "counter-history" really was, as they often bring the Britons' story back into a more Bedan orbit, emphasizing how the Britons' story was a subset of English history, and how a united Britain under the aegis of England was truly an accomplishment of universal proportions, equal only to that of the Roman empire.

Although he wouldn't touch translating the book of Merlin's Prophecies, Wace's inclusion of the "Breton hope" as a vital concept – and not a foolish one as his colleague William of Malmesbury portrayed it – shows him to have been, if not a promoter of Arthur in particular as a messianic figure, then a believer in the future renewal and triumph of the downtrodden, no matter how far in the distant future. As I argue in this book, for Wace, Arthur was the ultimate symbol of historical promise, and although the Breton taletellers may have "fabled" too much and thus made Arthur unbelievable in their tales, the Norman poet's comments in the *Roman de Rou* belie at least a desire to believe in a basis for Arthur's reality,[64] or if that idea is not palatable, then beyond that, a belief in what he represents for all peoples.

---

63   As will be seen in Chapter 6, although largely made up of Wace lines, in my view, the organizational principles – omissions and restructuring of key passages – reveal sufficient independence of thought and spirit to consider this a separate text in its own right, and not a Wace fragment. See Chapter 6, n. 174. On dating of these texts and their MSS, see Appendix 2, n. 1.

64   For the famous passage from the *Brut* on the "fablers," see Chapter 5, n. 113. In his Norman history, the *Roman de Rou* (1160–c.1174), Wace comments that he considered himself a "fool" for having believed the stories surrounding Arthur and having gone to the *forêt de Brocéliande* in Brittany to see for himself:

Issi soleit jadis ploveir   Thus in days past, it used to rain.
En la forest e environ,   In the forest, and around,

INTRODUCTION 27

That Arthur as metaphor does not need a basis in historical truth to function with its full power and that it continues to do so into our postmodern era – most preferably of course as symbol of triumphant righteousness, not as tool of fascist oppression as at the hands of the Nazis or fascist sympathizers[65] – is one of the many signs of Geoffrey of Monmouth's genius, and that of those who followed him who were less "logical positivists" and more idealists that one day, the distribution of power would let the subaltern be heard (to borrow Gayatry Spivak's term),[66] and the "other" would no longer be other, the "us" would not be oppositional with "them," but us would just be all of us.

mais jo ne sai par quel raison.	But I don't know why.
La seut l'en les fees veeir,	People used to see fairies there,
se li Breton nos dient veir,	If the Bretons are telling the truth,
e altres mer(e)veilles plusors;	And many other marvels;
aires i selt aveir *d'ostors*	There used to be hawks' nests there
e de grant cers mult grant plenté,	And large stags in abundance,
mais vilain ont *tot* deserté.	But peasants have ruined it all.
La alai jo merveilles querre,	I went there looking for marvels,
vi la forest e vi la terre,	I saw the forest and I saw the land,
merveilles quis, mais nes trovai,	I sought marvels, but I didn't find any,
fol m'en revinc, fol i alai;	I came back a fool, and went a fool;
fol i alai, fol m'en revinc,	I went a fool, I came back a fool,
folie quis, por fol me tinc.	I sought folly, I considered myself a fool.
(*Rou*, III, v. 6384–98)	

See Anthony J. Holden, ed., *Le Roman de Rou de Wace*, 3 vols. Société des Anciens Textes Français (Paris: Picard, 1970–73). The edition is reprinted and translated in Wace, *The Roman de Rou*, trans. Glyn S. Burgess (St. Helier: Société Jersiaise, 2002) (the translation above is my own). David Rollo suggests that by stating that the marvels did not exist, Wace is "doing no less than dismissing his past career, his promulgation of fantasies [in the *Brut*] underwritten by precisely the insubstantial fable he here divorces from empirical history" (*Historical Fabrication, Ethnic Fable and French Romance in Twelfth-Century England*, Edward C. Armstrong Monographs on Medieval Literature 9, Lexington, KY: French Forum Publishers, 1998, cited here at 163.)

65 As ably demonstrated by Finke and Shichtman in ""Exegetical History: Nazis at the Round Table."

66 See Gayatri Chakravorty Spivak's seminal essay, "Can the subaltern speak?" in *Marxism and the Interpretation of Culture*, ed. Cary Nelson and Lawrence Grossberg (Urbana and Chicago: University of Illinois Press, 1988), 271–313.

CHAPTER 1

Geoffrey of Monmouth's *Historia Regum Britanniae*: Part 1

1 Introduction

1.1 *Galfridian Scholarship*

At best, Geoffrey of Monmouth has been judged an inventive historian,[1] at worst, a prevaricator, and the *Historia Regum Britanniae* "one of the greatest romantic novels of all time."[2] The *Historia* traces the history of Britain from

---

1   It should be noted that the scholarship on Geoffrey is so vast that documentation here cannot be encyclopedic; references are intended to point readers in fruitful directions, but regrettably cannot be exhaustive. Although I rely on Michael Reeve's edition as primary text of reference (including the use of his chapter divisions, though not the book numbers; see Chapter 2, n. 9 below), I have chosen to retain the traditional title of the *Historia Regum Britanniae* since it still dominates the scholarship (Geoffrey of Monmouth, *The History of the Kings of Britain: An Edition and Translation of the De gestis Britonum* [*Historia Regum Britanniae*], ed. Michael D. Reeve and trans. Neil Wright, Arthurian Studies 69, Woodbridge: Boydell, 2007).

2   David N. Dumville, "Sub-Roman Britain: history and legend," *History N. S.* 62 (1977): 173–92; repr. in idem, *Histories and Pseudo-histories of the Insular Middle Ages* (Aldershot: Variorum, 1990), cited here at p. 175. Acton Griscom presents a collection of opinions on Geoffrey as a romancer (*Historia*, ed., pp. 109–110), but was himself "perhaps the most earnest modern defender of Geoffrey as a sober historian [from the earlier part of the twentieth century]" (Valerie Flint, "The *Historia Regum Britanniae* of Geoffrey of Monmouth: Parody and its Purpose," *Speculum* 54 (1979): 447–68, cited here at p. 448). Among the numerous treatments of Geoffrey as an historian – though without the expectation that what he wrote was necessarily factually accurate – from roughly 1920–1990, see J. S. P. Tatlock, *Legendary History of Britain* (Berkeley and Los Angeles: University of California Press, 1950); Heinrich Pähler, *Strukturuntersuchungen zur Historia Regum Britanniae des Geoffrey of Monmouth* (Bonn, 1958), esp. pp. 58–60, 92–134; Walter F. Schirmer, *Die frühen Darstellungen des Arthurstoffes*, Arbeitsgemeinschaft für Forschung des Landes Nordrhein-Westfallen, Geisteswissenschaften 73 (Cologne and Opladen: Westdeutscher Verlag, 1958); Robert W. Hanning, *The Vision of History in Early Britain: From Gildas to Geoffrey of Monmouth* (New York and London: Columbia University Press, 1966); Antonia Gransden, *Historical Writing in England, c.550–c.1307* (Ithaca, NY: Cornell University Press, 1974), pp. 206–208; R. W. Southern, "Aspects of the European Tradition of Historical Writing: 1. The Classical Tradition from Einhard to Geoffrey of Monmouth," *Transactions of the Royal Historical Society*, 5th ser. 20 (1970): 173–96; Susan M. Schwartz, "The Founding and self-betrayal of Britain: An Augustinian approach to Geoffrey of Monmouth's *Historia Regum Britanniae*," *Medievalia et Humanistica* n. s. 10 (1981), 33–53; *The Historia Regum Britannie of Geoffrey of Monmouth, 1: Bern Burgerbibliothek, MS. 568*, ed. Neil Wright (Cambridge: D. S. Brewer, 1984) and *The Historia Regum Britannie*

© KONINKLIJKE BRILL NV, LEIDEN, 2024 | DOI:10.1163/9789004691889_003

the arrival of the Trojan Brutus and ostensibly ending with the departure and death of Cadwallader in the seventh century – with a postscript of passing reference to a period of shared rule with the Saxons until the tenth century – covering considerable ground not discussed elsewhere.[3] Although King Arthur appears for the first time by this name and with this title, and compiles a glorious record, he is not the sole focus, but rather the illustrious ninety-ninth of 107 kings of the Britons,[4] many of whom have never been heard of before or since. Not only has Geoffrey's purported principle source, the "liber vetustissimus" supposedly in a Brittonic tongue (Welsh?) and brought to him by Walter archdeacon of Oxford and which Geoffrey claims to have translated into Latin (Prologue, 7–9) never been identified but the *Historia* contains much material that has either been impossible to trace or to identify satisfactorily.[5] Despite the

---

of Geoffrey of Monmouth, 11: The First Variant Version: a critical edition, ed. Neil Wright (Cambridge: D. S. Brewer, 1988); and R. W. Leckie, Jr. *The Passage of Dominion: Geoffrey of Monmouth and the Periodization of Insular History in the Twelfth Century* (Toronto, Buffalo, London: University of Toronto Press, 1980). See Bibliography for fuller details of Griscom's edition.

3 Geoffrey consistently uses the term "Saxon" (*Saxones*) rather than "Angles" (*Angli*) or "Anglo-Saxon." See Leckie on Geoffrey's narrative of shared rule between the Britons and the Saxons filling in a 300-year gap not discussed by other historians, esp. *Passage*, 53–72.

4 In Reeve's Index, the named kings and queens are assiduously numbered, but regrettably the positions "41st" through "49th" were accidentally omitted (§52). Thus, although Cadwallader (Cadualadrus/Cadwaladr) is listed in the Index as the "114th and last king" (p. 287), he is the 107th (and last) king, making Arthur (Arturus) the 99th king (not the 106th); Vortegirnus's (Vortigern) second reign should also be counted in the tally (now 94th and 96th) and Vortimer[ius] takes the 95th. I am very grateful to Professor Reeve for having graciously assisted me in this recalculation (thorough private communications); other recalculations of named kings' and queens' numbers are based on this general recalculation (and noted when they occur in the discussion). However, readers should be aware that such tallies, particularly for a work like Geoffrey's where there are also numerous unnamed monarchs, so few dates and remarkably little historical accuracy, is not an exact science, nor does it need to be. On the kinds of names Geoffrey used, their origins and the often-tenuous relationship to known history, see Tatlock, *Legendary History*, esp. ch. IV "Personages and Their Names," 116–70.

5 Ian Short examines numerous possibilities regarding Gaimar's sources concluding however, with regard to Geoffrey, that "what Gaimar's epilogue does not, unfortunately, allow us to do is to come any closer to finding an answer to the question of the status of Geoffrey's *liber vetusissimus* – of whether it is to be seen more as a metaphorical than as a real book, as the disparate gatherings of collective memory rather than the ordered quires of written record. It could, of course, have been both, as Geoffrey himself suggests" ("Gaimar's Epilogue and Geoffrey of Monmouth's *Liber vetustissimus*," *Speculum* 69 (1994): 323–43, cited here at 340). R. W. Southern considered the "very old book" to have existed ("From Einhard to Geoffrey of Monmouth," 194), but Christopher Brooke was convinced that Geoffrey used the *topos* of translation, "like other writers, to hide a fiction" ("Geoffrey of Monmouth as an Historian," in *Church and Government in the Middle Ages: Essays Presented to C. R. Cheney on his Seventieth*

30   CHAPTER 1

mystery surrounding this work – or perhaps because of it – Geoffrey's text has been one of the most popular and influential histories – or pseudo-histories[6] – the West has ever known, in addition to being the earliest broad-ranging source of Arthurian material.

Aside from philologists for whose studies of vocabulary, names, and the origins of the same do not rely on the historicity of Geoffrey's text as a defining concern, modern scholarly assessments of Geoffrey of Monmouth's impact on historiography[7] and romance through the *HRB* fall into at least four groups:[8]

Birthday, ed. C. N. L. Brooke, D. E. Luscombe, G. H. Martin and Dorothy Owen, Cambridge: Cambridge University Press, 1976, rev. 1978, 77–91, cited at 83).

6   John Gillingham credits Rees Davies with the term "counter-history" when referring to the *HRB* ("The Context and Purposes of Geoffrey of Monmouth's *History of the Kings of Britain*," *The English in the Twelfth Century*, 37, n. 104). "Counter-history" is a more useful term than "pseudo-history" since it underscores the purposeful responsiveness of the text to a stance of political and cultural superiority on the part of both predecessors and contemporaries, whereas "pseudo-history" gives no indication of political perspective, and can additionally be construed as dismissive, since it can be used to label the work as fake, and thus undermine its value, even on a metaphorical level. For an analysis which leans toward seeing Geoffrey's *HRB* as "pseudo-history" – the label though used not to dismiss necessarily, but to distinguish the text from a romance tradition, as if occupying an intermediate place on a continuum between "authentic" history and strictly romance – see Peter Damian-Grint and Françoise Le Saux, "The Arthur of the Chronicles," in *The Arthur of the French*, ed. G. S. Burgess and Karen Pratt (Cardiff: University of Wales Press, 2006), 93–111, at 93.

7   As Alan MacColl notes, Geoffey's *Historia* "exercised such a profound influence on English national historiography," but in a sense, Geoffrey's importance goes beyond historiography, regardless of the often emphasized lack of factual veracity in that work, since "the importance of Britain as a geopolitical concept from the twelfth century onward derives mainly from Geoffrey of Monmouth" (MacColl, "The Meaning of 'Britain' in Medieval and Early Modern England," *Journal of British Studies* 45, 2006: 248–69, cited at 249–50). See also Denys Hay who argues that Geoffrey's text "did more than any anything else to make men conscious of the term Britain" ("The Use of the Term 'Great Britain' in the Middle Ages," *Proceedings of the Society of Antiquaries of Scotland* 89 (1955–56): 55–66; repr. in idem *Europe: The Emergence of an Idea*, Edinburgh: Edinburgh University Press, 1957, rev. ed. 1968, 128–44, cited at 131). Geoffrey's famous "ambiguity" may also in part "have made possible that work's appropriation by both the English and the Welsh as part of their respective national histories" ... "for both, the idea of a unique Britishness was also a way of defining themselves against one another. The English used it as a way of advancing their claims to dominion over Wales, the Welsh to give an ideological backbone to their resistance against the English" (MacColl, "The Meaning of 'Britain'," 252–53, 249). On Geoffrey's complexity and ambiguity, which, as we will see in this chapter, opens the work to a panoply of interpretations ranging from archetypal symbolic patterns to pointed political commentary, see John Gillingham, "The Context and Purposes of Geoffrey of Monmouth's *History of the Kings of Britain*."

8   Because Galfridian scholarship is so vast and his impact was so great both in his lifetime and to the present day, these categories are being laid out for the purposes of understanding a pattern in his reception. Individual contributions to scholarship will not be cited here

1) the assessments of historians who have argued that Geoffrey cannot be considered an historian *due to the dubious contents* of his work, and thus tend to discount the value of his text due to its lack of veracity; 2) those of historians who treat Geoffrey as an historian *despite the often dubious nature of his 'historical reporting'* in large part because the majority of contemporaries accepted him as an historian even if they did not find truth in all he wrote; while considering Geoffrey an historian, these modern historians often approach Geoffrey with a healthy dose of skepticism;[9] 3) those of literary scholars whose focus may be narrative strategies and mentalities (rather than primarily a reconstructive understanding of the past) who treat Geoffrey as an historian *despite the often dubious nature of his 'historical reporting'*, again, because of the reception of his contemporaries or near-contemporaries; and 4) those of literary

---

under these categories in an effort to not reduce studies to their belonging to any one or another "camp."

9   On the reception of the *Historia*, Christopher Brooke writes "It purported to be history, and history it was taken to be: with only a few dissentient voices the Latin world immediately accepted it as genuine, and gave it a tremendous reception and this is remarkable, since we now know that hardly a word of it is true, that there has scarcely, if ever, been a historian more mendacious than Geoffrey of Monmouth" ("Geoffrey of Monmouth as an Historian," 77–78). Brooke continues: "There has been much argument as to how much he invented, and this will never be concluded for no one doubts that some of his sources are lost. What the patient researches of Tatlock and others have made abundantly clear is that he liked to create, as it were, a mosaic pattern in which most of the pieces had some existence in his material, some of the pieces were recognisably historical, but most of the pattern was invention" (79). For John Gillingham, it is not usually a question of how much Geoffrey may have or may not have invented (while not denying that there's a great deal of invention in Geoffrey), but rather the goals of his narrative. While he agrees with Flint that "there was a serious purpose behind this entertainment [parody], but given the overwhelmingly political and military content of Geoffrey's history" he thinks it "more likely that it had to do with matters of politics, the politics of cultural nationalism" rather than being designed to "exalt non-monastic virtues and styles of life" ("The Context and Purposes of Geoffrey of Monmouth's *History of the Kings of Britain*," *The English in the Twelfth Century*, 20–21). Cf. Monica Otter who argues that the wide range of perspectives and potential motivations is "surely indicative of a purpose beyond simply taking sides in contemporary political struggles" ("Functions of Fiction in Historical Writing," in *Writing Medieval History*, ed. Nancy Partner, London: Hodder Arnold, 2005, 109–30, cited at 120) and as cited by Rebecca Thomas, that, "while not dismissing the indications that Geoffrey does, on occasion, show sympathy toward the Britons ... [Otter argues that] the text ought to be understood as a parody in that it takes the same form as other medieval histories, but provides new content which conflicts with these previous works" (Rebecca Thomas, "Geoffrey of Monmouth and the Anglo-Saxon Past," in *A Companion to Geoffrey of Monmouth*, 105–28, cited at p. 108 referring to Otter, *Inventiones: Fiction and Referentiality in Twelfth-Century English Historical Writing*, Chapel Hill: University of North Carolina Press, 1996, 78–79.)

32 CHAPTER 1

critics who view Geoffrey in broader terms beyond that of a practitioner of historical or pseudo-historical writing, but rather as the primary source of Arthurian narrative.

Before proceeding to outline predominant perspectives in modern Galfridian criticism, it is important to point out that another unique aspect of Galfridian studies in addition to the voluminous work of modern scholars is the remarkable number of comments by contemporaries or near-contemporaries of Geoffrey's, though their reactions – like those of moderns – are by no means uniform.[10] As R. William Leckie, Jr. notes, Geoffrey's immediate reception stemmed from the fact that "in place of the meager and often unflattering material on the Britons found in other sources, the *Historia* offered a stunning depiction, one which was eagerly received by an age grown conscious of the past."[11] Furthermore, Geoffrey's extension of the period "during which the Britons constituted the dominant force in Insular affairs well into what was normally reckoned as belonging to Anglo-Saxon history" provided an "alternative and decidedly British view of events in the fifth, sixth, and even seventh centuries," wherein "the presence of small bands of Saxons no longer sufficed as a marker and the gradual nature of the take-over left considerable room for uncertainty"; ultimately "the precise location of the dividing line between British and Anglo-Saxon rule became a matter of paramount concern."[12] Nonetheless, as Leckie asserts, despite initial expressions of amazement and also popularity, "blanket acceptance ... did not mark the first fifty or sixty years following the appearance of the *Historia* ... Historians of the twelfth century moved very cautiously, and conferred upon Geoffrey only grudgingly the status of acknowledged authority."[13] However, according to Leckie, by the early thirteenth century, his authority had been largely accepted, and "a considerable period of time would pass before serious controversy once again swirled about Geoffrey's depiction."[14]

---

10 See Simon Meecham-Jones, "Early Reactions to Geoffrey's Work."

11 Leckie, *Passage*, 20.

12 Leckie, *Passage*, 19.

13 Leckie, *Passage*, 20–21. Leckie also proposes that the two sections of the HRB – pre-Arthurian and post-Arthurian – should be differentiated in any discussion of Geoffrey's immediate reception (43): "the mode and incidence of usage vary depending on the presence, strength, and nature of prior views. For the pre-Roman period Geoffrey was the only source of information on Insular affairs, but the situation became more complex in later sections [particularly regarding the passage of dominion from the Britons to the Saxons] where Geoffrey's perspective was adopted, modified, and even rejected" (51).

14 Leckie, *Passage*, 28.

HISTORIA REGUM BRITANNIAE: PART 1   33

1.2   *Introductory Overview of Geoffrey's Contemporaries*

Among the most well known of Geoffrey's contemporaries[15] is Henry of Huntingdon (c.1088–c.1156). A secular cleric, archdeacon of Huntingdon and canon of Lincoln, Henry was commissioned by Alexander, bishop of Lincoln, to write the *History of the English People*, which he completed in the early 1130s;[16] it was as Alexander's representative that Henry set off to Rome in 1139 to secure a papal privilege for Lincoln. En route, he stopped at Bec where the Norman historian Robert of Torigni (c.1110–1186), monk of Bec and later abbot of Mont-Saint-Michel, showed Henry a copy of Geoffrey's *HRB*. Henry, having expressed "amazement" (having been "*stupens*") at his discovery of the *Historia*, transformed the notes he took at Bec into a summary of Geoffrey's *Historia*, in epistolary form, with changes, addressed to a certain "Warin the Breton" the *Epistola ad Warinum* which he later appended to his own *History* (one of three letters that make up Book VIII in the fourth version of the *HA*, c.1146).[17] Robert incorporated much of Henry's *History* into his own which he began c. 1150, based on a copy that Alexander gave Bec in 1147, though it appears that

---

15   The author of the First Variant can also technically be considered one of Geoffrey's contemporaries since he/she was writing around the same time. A separate chapter (Chapter 3) will be devoted to that text.

16   Henry, Archdeacon of Huntingdon, *Historia Anglorum: The History of the English People*, ed. and trans. Diana Greenway, Oxford Medieval Texts (Oxford: Clarendon Press, 1996).

17   On the dating, see Greenway, ed. and trans., *Historia Anglorum*, lxxi–lxxiii, ci. For more background, see also *Henry of Huntingdon: The History of the English People 1000–1154*, trans. Diana Greenway, Oxford World's Classics (Oxford: Oxford University Press, 1996, 2002), xxvii–xxix, and for the text, and additional information, eadem, ed. and trans., *Historia Anglorum*, 556–83 and 559, n. 2, where Greenway explains that the identity of "Warin the Breton" is unknown, speculating that he might have been a fellow canon of Lincoln, or alternatively, offering the possibility that Henry "was addressing a fictitious person, perhaps even a *Briton* rather than a Breton, invented to serve the purpose of justifying the epistolary form of this piece." See also Neil Wright ed. FV, lxxi and idem, "The place of Henry of Huntingdon's *Epistola ad Warinum* in the text-history of Geoffrey of Monmouth's *Historia regum Britannie*: a preliminary investigation," in *France and the British Isles in the Middle Ages and Renaissance: Essays by Members of Girton College, Cambridge, in Memory of Ruth Morgan*, ed. Gillian Jondorf and David N. Dumville, Woodbridge, Suffolk: Boydell and Brewer, 1991, 71–113. Leckie notes that the composition of the pre-Saxon portion of the *Historia Anglorum* predates Henry's first seeing of Geoffrey's text at Bec. However, it was more because of the revolutionary nature of Geoffrey's pre-Saxon material that Henry chose not to integrate it into his history, but rather appended his summary in the Epistle, in response to Warin's having pointed out (according to Henry) the gap, that is, "between Eli's judgeship (c.1100 BC) and Caesar's expeditions (55–54 BC) lay more than a thousand years; yet not a single historical occurrence was assigned to this period" (*Passage*, 39 and n. 39).

34   CHAPTER 1

he didn't use its information on pre-Arthurian British monarchs.[18] In the late
1130s, Walter Espec had a copy of the *HRB* at Helmsley where Gaimar, author of
the *Estoire des Engleis* (*c.*1136–37), the earliest extant Old French chronicle and
the *Estoire des Bretuns* (no longer extant) came to know of it.[19] Soon after, probably around 1143, Alfred, sacrist of Beverley minster in Yorkshire (fl. 1134–54), in
his *Annales* "asserts that the *Historia* was being widely read, enjoyed and talked
about."[20] Alfred followed Geoffrey primarily, almost exclusively for almost half
his work, often quoting him *verbatim*; he also used Bede, Simeon of Durham,
and Henry of Huntingdon, expressing concerns about the lack of corroborating evidence for the deeds of Arthur and other British kings, in Geoffrey
and elsewhere.[21]

18   Greenway, trans., *Henry of Huntingdon*, xxix. Leckie infers that the real problem was the
      sheer volume of new material in the *HRB*: "Robert's comments betray uneasiness over the
      quantitative impact of Geoffrey's account … Geoffrey had succeeded in rectifying the ear-
      lier quantitative imbalance [between Saxon history and British history], but by so doing
      he had created a new problem" (*Passage of Dominion*, 46–48).
19   On this dating of the text, see Ian Short, "Gaimar's Epilogue," and cf. Paul Dalton who
      argues for 1141–50 ("The Date of Geoffrey Gaimar's *Estoire des Engleis*, the Connections of
      his Patrons, and the Politics of Stephen's Reign," *Chaucer Review* 42 (2007): 23–47); Geffrei
      Gaimar, *Estoire des Engleis: History of the English*, ed. and trans., Ian Short, Oxford: Oxford
      University Press, 2009, ix–xvi; John Gillingham, "Kingship, Chivalry and Love. Political
      and Cultural values in the Earliest History Written in French: Geoffrey Gaimar's *Estoire
      des Engleis*," in *Anglo-Norman Political Culture and the Twelfth Century Renaissance*, ed.
      C. Warren Hollister (Woodbridge: Boydell, 1997, 33–58; repr. in *The English in the Twelfth
      Century*, 2000, 233–58); J. Blacker, "'Dame Custance la gentil': Gaimar's Portrait of a
      Lady and her Books," in *The Court and Cultural Diversity: Selected Papers from the Eighth
      Triennial Congress of the International Courtly Literature Society, The Queen's University
      of Belfast 26 July–1 August 1995*, ed. Evelyn Mullally and John Thompson (Cambridge:
      D. S. Brewer, 1997), 109–19; Paul Dalton, "Geoffrei Gaimar's *Estoire des Engleis*, Peacemaking,
      and the 'Twelfth-Century Revival of the English Nation'," *Studies in Philology* 104 (2007):
      427–53; and Peter Damian-Grint, *The New Historians of the Twelfth Century Renaissance:
      Inventing Vernacular Authority* (Woodbridge: Boydell, 1999), esp. pp. 49–53, 218–25. See
      also Chapter 4, n. 5.
20   Gransden, *Historical Writing in England c. 550 to c. 1207*, 212.
21   Gransden, *Historical Writing*, 212 and n. 250. Leckie cites Alfred as the first to comment on
      the absence of supporting evidence in Geoffrey (*Passage*, 45). He also inserted "a substan-
      tial portion of Geoffrey's account into what was essentially an historical vacuum" without
      apparent difficulty. This was more straightforward than the task facing Robert of Torigni,
      according to Leckie: "The problems were rather different when the data had to be inter-
      polated into a pre-existent frame. A case in point is Robert of Torigni, who grappled with
      the problems attendant upon incorporating materials from the *Historia regum Britanniae*
      into the universal chronicle of Sigebert of Gembloux," since he felt he would have been
      forced to insert a huge regnal list into the combined work of Eusebius and Jerome, two
      inviolable authorities whose histories formed the basis of Sigebert's chronicle (*Passage*,
      46–47). Alfred of Beverley, *Annales, sive Historia de gestis regum Britanniae*, ed. Thomas

HISTORIA REGUM BRITANNIAE: PART 1

Perhaps with Geoffrey's narrative in mind, the Benedictine monk and one of the most highly reputed historians of the twelfth century, William of Malmesbury (c.1097–c.1143) – and perhaps on many levels, Geoffrey's fiercest competitor[22] – comments on the tales of Arthur as spurious and separates them from veracious histories; he apparently also considered English history "comprehensible without a detailed discussion of the Britons (*GRA*, 1.1–4, 1:5–8)."[23] In an extraordinary passage in his epilogue, Geoffrey names William of Malmesbury and Henry of Huntingdon along with the Welsh Caradoc of Llancarfan, warning the latter to stick to the Welsh kings and William and Henry to the Saxon kings,

> "forbid[ding] them to write about the kings of the Britons since they do not possess the book in British which Walter, archdeacon of Oxford, brought from Brittany, and whose truthful account of their history I have here been at pains in honour of those British rulers to translate into Latin" (§208.601–7: "Reges autem eorum qui ab illo tempore in Gualiis successerunt Karadoco Lancarbanensi contemporaneo meo in materia scribendi permitto, reges uero Saxonum Willelmo Malmesberiensi et Henrico Huntendonensi, quos de rebigus Britonum tacere iubeo, cum non habeant librum illum Britannici sermonis quem Walterus Oxenefordensis archidiaconus ex Britannia aduexit, quem de historia eorum ueraciter editum in honore praedictorum principum hoc modo in Latinum sermonem transferre curaui").

Antonia Gransden comments that Gervase of Canterbury (fl. c. 1193–1210) "had little critical sense ... accept[ing] the veracity of Geoffrey of Monmouth without hesitation, asserting (in the *Mappa Mundi*) that if the ancient British buildings had survived they would have proved the truth of the *Historia*."[24] Gerald of Wales appears to have had an ambivalent attitude toward Geoffrey,

---

    Hearne (Oxford, 1716); *Chronique de Robert de Torigni*, 2 vols., ed. Léopold Delisle (Rouen: A. Le Brument, 1872–73); and Sigebert of Gembloux, *Chronographia*, ed. L. C. Bethmann, Monumenta Germaniae Historica: Scriptores 6 (1844; repr. Leipzig, 1925), 268–374.

22   William of Malmesbury and his numerous commentaries on material presented by Geoffrey will be referenced throughout this chapter, rather than concentratedly here. The primary text is William of Malmesbury, *Gesta Regum Anglorum*, 2 vols., vol. 1, ed. and trans. R. A. B. Mynors, R. M. Thomson, and M. Winterbottom, Oxford Medieval Texts (Oxford: Clarendon Press, 1998) and vol. 2: *General Introduction and Commentary*, R. M. Thomson in collaboration with M. Winterbottom (Clarendon Press, 1999).

23   Leckie, *Passage*, 18.

24   *Historical Writing in England*, 260. *The Historical Works of Gervase of Canterbury*, ed. W. Stubbs, 2 vols., Rolls Series (London, 1879–80).

36   CHAPTER 1

at times using material, at times questioning his veracity (not unlike Alfred of Beverley); on the range of Gerald's views, Julia Crick comments that "attempting to rationalise and homogenise Gerald's wildly fluctuating allegiances and sympathies would prove a fruitless enterprise" and that new work demonstrating William of Newburgh's pro-English biases calls for a reevaluation of Gerald's reception of Geoffrey.[25]

William of Newburgh, Augustinian canon (*c.*1136–*c.*1201) was Geoffrey's most outspoken twelfth-century critic, a very well respected historian with a longstanding reputation for critical acumen and impartiality; however, once doubts were cast on his impartiality with respect to the Galfridian material, his views of Geoffrey have been seen in a more balanced light.[26] Nancy Partner has observed that the sole purpose of the prologue to William's *Historia* – a work which did not touch on Geoffrey's body of material but rather the history of England from 1066–1198 – appears to have been to discredit Geoffrey; she notes that it is puzzling that William "gave so much space and effort to an attack on an author whose work was mostly irrelevant to his own," as if he were "arguing with some other body of opinion," perhaps debating the "Geoffrey question" which may have been "a lively topic in literary circles."[27] Leckie adds that William's disquisition on the sources of early insular history "was prompted by the current practices of men like Gervase of Canterbury ... what was new around 1200 was not the Galfridian construct, but the weight assigned to his

---

25   *Historical Writing in England*, 246 and nn. 248–49; *Geraldi Cambrensis opera*, ed. J. S. Brewer et al, 8 vols., 6: *Itinerarium Kambriae et Descriptio Kambriae*, ed. James F. Dimock [1868], Rolls Series (London, 1861–91) and Gerald of Wales, *The Journey Through Wales / The Description of Wales*, trans. Lewis Thorpe (Harmondsworth, Middlesex: Penguin Books, 1978). For an analysis of Gerald's hostility toward Geoffrey – which seems to have been aimed more at the historian than at the material in the *HRB*, given Gerald's use of the material – see Julia Crick, "The British Past and the Welsh Future: Gerald of Wales, Geoffrey of Monmouth and Arthur of Britain," *Celtica* 23 (1999): 60–75, cited at 62. According to Crick, Gerald agreed with and used much of what he found in the *HRB*. Where he parted ways with Geoffrey was in regard to the future: Gerald supported Glastonbury's claim to have Arthur's bones in order to support the Plantagenet monarchy's need for Arthur to be dead (never to return). An auxiliary unintended consequence of the claim to the graves, however, was the corroboration of the historical Arthur. On Glastonbury's claim, see *Glastonbury Abbey and the Arthurian Tradition*, ed. James Carley (Cambridge: D. S. Brewer, 2001), and Richard Rouse and Cory Rushton, "Arthurian Geography," in *The Cambridge Companion to the Arthurian Legend*, ed., Elizabeth Archibald and Ad Putter (Cambridge: Cambridge University Press, 2009), 218–34.

26   Gransden, "Bede's reputation as an historian in medieval England," *Journal of Ecclesiastical History* 32 (1981): 397–425 (repr. in eadem, *Legends, Traditions and History in Medieval England*, London and Rio Grande, OH: Hambledon Press, 1992, 1–29).

27   Nancy F. Partner, *Serious Entertainments: The Writing of History in Twelfth-Century England* (Chicago and London: University of Chicago Press, 1977), 62.

HISTORIA REGUM BRITANNIAE: PART 1   37

testimony. And William focuses his attack on this very point."[28] About Geoffrey, William states that "none except those ignorant of ancient histories can possibly doubt the extent of his wanton and shameless lying virtually throughout his book," particularly in his contradictions of Bede whom William admired greatly.[29] William gives some credence to Gildas, perhaps in part because the latter derided the Britons, thus proving his impartiality to William, rather than trying to create a hero for them in the person of Arthur.[30]

According to Partner, for William, Geoffrey's book "obviously struck a chord of vaguely racial antipathy that [he thought] was justified and substantiated by the authority of Gildas and Bede ... William's denunciation came from his contempt for all Britons, ancient and modern. ... They were perfidious, belligerent but unsteady, uncivilized, and suspicious ... [William] considers the ancient British, the Scots, Irish and Welsh outright barbarians and the Continental Bretons not far advanced over them."[31] Partner attributes a good portion of

---

28 *Passage of Dominion*, p. 95. See also Gillingham, "Context and Purposes," 22–23.
29 [*Historia rerum Anglicarum*] *William of Newburgh: The History of English Affairs*, trans. P. G. Walsh and M. J. Kennedy, Aris and Phillips Classical Texts (Oxford: Oxbow Books, 1988), I, preface, p. 31 (paragraph 5) ("quam petulanter et quam impudenter fere per omnia mentiatur nemo nisi veterum historiarum ignarus" I, preface, p. 30, para. 5). Walsh and Kennedy's translation is based on R. Howlett's edition, Rolls Series, London, 1884. Robert Bartlett notes that William "decried it [the *HRB*] as nonsense, blaming Geoffrey for 'making up absurd fictions' and asserting that 'only a person ignorant of ancient history would have any doubt about how shamelessly and impudently he lies in almost everything'" (*England under the Norman and Angevin Kings 1075–1225*, The New Oxford History of England, Oxford: Clarendon Press, 2000, 633 and n. 47). See also Martin Aurell, "Le discrédit de l'incroyable histoire de Geffroi de Monmouth au XIIe siècle," in *La verité et crédibilité: construire la verité dans le système de communication de l'Occident XIIIe–XVIIe siècle*), ed. Jean-Philippe Genêt (Paris-Rome: Publications de la Sorbonne, 2015), 499–520.
30 *Serious Entertainments*, pp. 63–64. On William's views on these peoples, see also Gillingham, "The English Invasion of Ireland," in *Representing Ireland: Literature and the Origins of Conflict, 1534–1660*, ed. B. Bradshaw, A. Hadfield, and W. Maley (Cambridge: Cambridge University Press, 1993, 24–42; repr. in idem, *The English in the Twelfth Century*, 2000, 145–60, esp. 148, 159–60), "Conquering the Barbarians" (*The English in the Twelfth Century*, 48, 55), "The Foundations of a Disunited Kingdom," in *Uniting the Kingdom? The Making of British History*, ed. A. Grant and K. Stringer (London: Routledge, 1995, 48–64; repr. *The English in the Twelfth Century*, 2000, 93–109, esp. 95, 106, 109), and "The Travels of Roger of Howden and his Views of the Irish, Scots and Welsh," in *Anglo-Norman Studies XX* (1998), 151–69 (repr. *The English in the Twelfth Century*, 2000, 69–91, 69). Although William's views were less than salutary toward the British peoples, apparently his expression of attitudes toward the Jews, for example, was more positive and "contrasts sharply with the dogmatic intolerance of most of his contemporaries" (Gransden, *Historical Writing*, 265).
31 Partner, *Serious Entertainments*, 64. See also Gransden who writes that William's critical acumen was best illustrated by the "remarkable passage" on Geoffrey of Monmouth (264

38   CHAPTER 1

this antipathy to William's view that "before the Albigensian incident in 1166, only the Britons had encouraged heresy in England":[32]

> England had always remained immune from this and other heretical plagues even when heresy was swarming through other parts of the world. When this island was called Britain because of its British inhabitants ... it admitted the errors of Pelagius ... But since the English possessed this island, having expelled the Britons, so that it was called England, the poison of the heretical plague never flourished.[33]

It is worth noting that William believed that the Britons had been chased from the island, and that English possession of England was definitive. In addition to the lack of corroborating evidence, these views on the perceived inferiority of the Britons and the desirability or in fact necessity of their demise are more central to William's criticism of Geoffrey than that the latter was a liar – a "fabulator" – and that Arthur never existed: William felt that he had uncovered a fraud, since the Britons as he saw them could never have produced a hero of the caliber of Arthur.[34]

1.3   Geoffrey's Possible Intentions

Although it is no doubt true that as John Gillingham has put it "it is unlikely, to say the least, that there could ever be a single satisfying explanation of a book as extraordinary and influential as Geoffrey of Monmouth's *History of the Kings of Britain*," a number of theories have been put forward to explain Geoffrey's intentions (not all of which can be listed here);[35] depending on

---

and n. 137); among William's arguments that Geoffrey's portrayal of Arthur was a fiction "if King Arthur had really existed, William affirms, Bede would have mentioned him" and that Geoffrey mentions "three archbishops at Arthur's feast" but "this was impossible, as the Britons had no archbishops" (*Historical Writing*, 265).

32   Partner, *Serious Entertainments*, 64.

33   William of Newburgh, *Historia rerum Anglicarum*, ed. Richard Howlett, Rolls Series 82 (1884–85), 132; Partner's translation (with elipses), *Serious Entertainments*, 64.

34   Scholarship on the early Britons, and the peoples most closely associated with them, is of course voluminous. For useful surveys, and further references, see Tim Clarkson, *The Men of the North: The Britons of Southern Scotland* (Edinburgh: John Donald, 2010) and idem, *Strathclyde and the Anglo-Saxons in the Viking Age* (Edinburgh: John Donald, 2016); Barry Cunliffe, *Britain Begins* (Oxford: Oxford University Press, 2012); Pierre-Roland Giot, Philippe Guigon, and Bernard Merdrignac, *Les premiers Bretons d'Armorique* (Rennes: Presses Universitaires de Rennes, UHB Rennes 2, 2003); T. M. Charles-Edwards, *Wales and the Britons, 350–1064* (Oxford: Oxford University Press, 2013); and the essays in N. J. Higham, ed., *Britons in Anglo-Saxon England* (Woodbridge: Boydell, 2007).

35   "Context and Purposes," 19.

HISTORIA REGUM BRITANNIAE: PART 1   39

one's perspective, each theory has at least some applicability (and most are not mutually exclusive):[36] 1) Geoffrey had no "serious political purpose" but instead aimed at literary effect,[37] parody in particular;[38] 2) he was sending a message aimed at the Anglo-Norman ruling elite during the civil war following the death of Henry I, warning them of the damaging effects of political discord;[39] 3) Arthur's kingdom is symbolic of the Anglo-Norman empire, that

36   Gillingham: "covering almost two thousand years and the reigns of ninety-nine kings it is so full of material of different kinds that almost anyone who reads it with a particular interest in mind will be able to pick out passages to support their own interpretation" ("Context and Purposes," cited at 19). See also Martin Aurell, "Geoffrey of Monmouth's *History of the Kings of Britain* and the Twelfth-Century Renaissance," *Haskins Society Journal* 18 (2006): 1–18, and Fiona Tolhurst, "Geoffrey of Monmouth's *Historia regum Britannie* and the Critics," *Arthuriana* 8: 4(1998), 3–11. For work representing a range of both literary and historical interpretations of Geoffrey's *Historia* as a whole (excluding, for example, manuscript studies or scholarship limited to the *Prophetia Merlini* or the *Vita Merlini*) primarily from 1990 on, see Michael Curley, *Geoffrey of Monmouth* (Michael J. Curley, *Geoffrey of Monmouth*, Twayne's English Authors Series 509 (New York: Twayne, 1994); his annotated selected bibliography remains quite useful for scholarship preceding 1990), and also Laurie A. Finke and Martin Shichtman, *King Arthur and the Myth of History*, esp. 37–70; Blacker, *Faces of Time*; Damian-Grint, *The New Historians*; Heng, *Empire of Magic*; Warren, *History on the Edge*, and the Introduction, nn. 13 and 37 above. Many of the perspectives presented are of course not mutually exclusive: for example, the legend of Troy can be seen to serve as an instrument for arguing that the Welsh were indeed not barbarians as they descended from as noble a line as the French.

37   J. E. Lloyd, *A History of Wales*, London 1939, vol. 2, 528; John Clark, "Trinovantum – the evolution of a legend," *Journal of Medieval History* 7.2 (1981): 135–51, 143.

38   Valerie Flint has argued that Geoffrey's overriding purpose was parody, and that he "meant, ultimately, to call into question the position held and hoped for in twelfth-century Anglo-Norman society by literate and celibate canons regular and monks" ("Parody and Purpose," 449), and that he meant to mock not only the three historians he names in the epilogue – William of Malmesbury, Henry of Huntingdon and Caradoc of Llancarfan – but also others (460). See also Christopher Brooke, "Geoffrey of Monmouth as a Historian."

39   Wright, ed., I, xv; Walter F. Schirmer, *Die frühen Darstellungen des Arthurstoffes*, Arbeitsgemeinschaft für Forschung des Landes Nordrhein-Westfalen Geisteswissenschaften, 73 (Cologne and Opladen: Westdeutscher Verlag, 1958), 25–28; J. Blacker, *Faces of Time* (1994, 78–84, 96, 99, 163–66); Paul Dalton, "Topical Concerns," 690–91 and n. 7. As Gillingham points out, though, "warnings against discord could have applied to the Welsh just as much" as to the Anglo-Norman elite ("Context and Purposes," 21). Cf. Helen Fulton who states that "Geoffrey's history can be read in part as a warning about the dangers of a civil war over the succession, a struggle which could only weaken the central Norman state. While some historians have interpreted Geoffrey's prophecies of a Welsh return as an indication of Geoffrey's pro-Welsh sympathies, it is more likely that he was hinting to his Norman patrons (men such as Robert Earl of Gloucester and Bishop Alexander of Lincoln) that Norman power was not as absolute as they liked to think and that an external threat, whether from Wales, Brittany, or elsewhere, was always a possibility" ("Originating Britain: Welsh Literature and the Arthurian Tradition," 312).

40   CHAPTER 1

Arthur was shaped in the image of Charlemagne and Alexander, and thus by
further developing the myth of Trojan ancestry of the Britons (beyond what
was done by Bede and "Nennius"), Geoffrey was providing the Anglo-Norman
ruling house with a genealogy more glorious than that from which the Franks
were descended; some scholars have gone further to read Geoffrey's treatment
of this genealogy as justification for the Norman Conquest;[40] 4) in addition
to creating a Trojan ancestry, Geoffrey aimed to glorify the Britons' civilizing
influence, for the benefit of the Anglo-Norman ruling house principally in
opposition to the kings of France (rather than in opposition to the English);[41]
5) that instead of being largely a secular historian, Geoffrey wrote "very much
as a man steeped in the tradition of Christian historiography" and wove the
history of Britain into a "structure of founding, betrayal, and diaspora based

---

40   Marjorie Chibnall, *Anglo-Norman England 1066–1166* (Oxford: Basil Blackwell, 1986),
        p. 211; Wright, ed., I, xix; Gordon H. Gerould, "King Arthur and Politics," *Speculum* 2 (1927):
        33–51, esp. 45, 49; Tatlock, *Legendary History of Britain*, 305–20; Schirmer, *Die frühen
        Darstellungen des Arthurstoffes*, 28–30. For a more strongly Norman perspective on
        Geoffrey's construction of a Trojan ancestry as primary motive in writing the *Historia*,
        see Francis Ingledew, "The Book of Troy and the Genealogical Construction of History:
        The Case of Geoffrey of Monmouth's *Historia regum Britanniae*," *Speculum* 69.3 (1994):
        665–704; Martin B. Shichtman and Laurie A. Finke, "Profiting from the Past: History
        as Symbolic Capital in the *Historia Regum Britanniae*," in *Arthurian Literature XII*, ed.
        James P. Carley and Felicity Riddy (Cambridge: D. S. Brewer, 1993, 1–35; repr. as ch 2 in
        Finke and Shichtman, *King Arthur and the Myth of History*); Stephen T. Knight, *Arthurian
        Literature and Society* (London and New York: Macmillan, 1983), esp. chap. 2, p. 44;
        Hugh A. MacDougall, *Racial Myth in English History: Trojans, Teutons, and Anglo-Saxons*
        (Montreal: Harvest House, 1982), p. 8. See also Michael Faletra on Geoffrey's wish to bol-
        ster the Norman state in a number of contexts ("Narrating the Matter of Britain: Geoffrey
        of Monmouth and the Norman Colonization of Wales," *The Chaucer Review* 35.1 (2000):
        60–85, and "The Conquest of the Past in the History of the Kings of Britain," *Literature
        Compass* 4.1 (2007): 121–33). Faletra argues that Geoffrey's inclusion of the prophecies as
        possibly offering "the promise of Briton resurgence" which he then proceeds to "stifle"
        ("Narrating the Matter of Britain," 76), implies that Geoffrey would not have done that
        had he wished to shore up Welsh hopes and claims. Faletra also finds that Geoffrey's text,
        along with William of Malmesbury's *Gesta Regum*, "legitimate[s the] Norman coloniza-
        tion of Wales by creating and perpetuating textual myths of the innate defeatedness – and
        the inevitable defeatability – of the British people" ("Narrating," 82). Faletra is ultimately
        arguing that Geoffrey simultaneously glorifies the history of the Britons while also mini-
        mizing their prospects, implying that as Helen Fulton puts it, according to Faletra, "far
        from being ambivalent toward the claims of the Welsh to original sovereignty in Britain,
        Geoffrey supports the Norman imperium and its colonization of Wales" (Helen Fulton,
        "Originating Britain," 320 n. 4). See also n. 45 below.
41   See R. Howard Bloch, *Etymologies and Genealogies: Literary Anthropology of the French
        Middle Ages* (Chicago: University of Chicago Press, 1983), 82 and also Brooke, "Geoffrey of
        Monmouth as an Historian," 88.

HISTORIA REGUM BRITANNIAE: PART 1   41

on Old and New Testament model," specifically relating the kingdom of King Arthur to that of King David;[42] 6) that romance and historiographical elements mingle in Geoffrey's work as "varieties of cultural work negotiating the shock of communal trauma" in European and Norman history in the years proceeding his work, that is, in response to the upheaval of the Crusades;[43] 7) Geoffrey aimed to construct a "récit total," consciously setting out to integrate the three central "matières," that of Rome (le roman antique), that of France (la *chanson de geste*) and "la matière de Bretagne";[44] and 8) that Geoffrey wrote his narrative of sovereignty, colonization, conquest, domination and assimilation primarily from a Welsh perspective, as a "powerful rejoinder" to English writers – and the Anglo-Norman elites – the majority of whom who increasingly viewed the "colonials" as barbarians, as cultural inferiors to those in power who practiced the high civilization of the French and, by association, the English.[45] In

---

42   S. Shwartz, "The Founding and Self-betrayal of Britain: An Augustinian Approach to Geoffrey of Monmouth's *Historia Regum Britanniae*," *Medievalia et Humanistica* n. s. 10 (1981), 33–53, esp. 34–35.

43   Geraldine Heng, *Empire of Magic: Medieval Romance and the Politics of Cultural Fantasy*, 2003, p. 18.

44   Jean-Yves Tilliette, "Invention du récit: La 'Brutiade' de Geoffroy de Monmouth (*Historia regum Britanniae*, § 6–22)," *Cahiers de civilisation médiévale* 39 (1996): 217–233.

45   Gillingham, "Context and Purposes," 39. Gillingham finds Geoffrey's placing of Arthur's court at Caerleon (when Uther had had his court in London) as evidence of a desire to give a "distinguished pedigree to a people that had suddenly begun to play once more – as their prophecies said they would – a major part in the politics of Britain" (37), as Morgan succeeded in regaining lands lost by his father and in all likelihood "resumed the ancestral title [of 'king'] in the euphoria of 1136–37" ("Context and Purposes," 36); see also Robert Bartlett who describes the events surrounding the Welsh revolt of 1136–37 as a "major resurgence of Welsh power" (*England under the Norman and Angevin Kings, 1075–1225*, The New Oxford History of England, Oxford: Clarendon Press, 2000, here at 74). Karen Jankulak's recent study of Geoffrey and the Welsh tradition proposes that Geoffrey "was not simply a copier of Welsh material, but an interpreter within the spirit of the Welsh tradition. Whatever his own 'ethnic' origins, this sensibility makes Geoffrey very much a Welsh writer" (*Geoffrey of Monmouth*, Cardiff: University of Wales Press, 2010, here at 4); Jennifer Farrel comments that despite similarities between Geoffrey's work and many aspects of the Welsh tradition, to call him a "Welsh writer" is "nonetheless something of an over-simplification" ("History, Prophecy and the Arthur of the Normans: The Question of Audience and Motivation behind Geoffrey of Monmouth's *Historia Regum Britanniae*," in *Anglo-Norman Studies 37: Proceedings of the Battle Conference 2014*, ed. Elisabeth van Houts, Woodbridge: Boydell Press, 2015, 99–114, here at 100–101). It is of course not impossible that Geoffrey's loyalties were mixed between pro-Welsh and pro-Norman as suggested by Brynley F. Roberts ("Geoffrey of Monmouth and the Welsh Historical Tradition," *Nottingham Mediaeval Studies* 20, 1976: 29–40, 40) and Stephen Knight (*Arthurian Lit. and Society*, 1983, 64–66). While Farrell argues for more serious consideration of possible Breton connections, she ultimately favors the view that Geoffrey was "first and foremost

addition, feminist critics have provided a number of compelling studies, often grounded in the historical events of Geoffrey's time – specifically the conflict between King Stephen and the Empress Matilda.[46]

On the literal level, the "Celtocentric" (Welsh) perspective is particularly compelling as it forms the core of a cluster of interrelated perspectives, themes, and responses; it is also illuminating on a number of metaphorical levels as well. As John Gillingham notes, in the *Historia*, Geoffrey deals with the three main themes of the Welsh tradition: first, the two main themes, the rivalry between Britain and Rome, and the loss of dominion to the Saxons, and thirdly, the theme of deliverance and renewal.[47] On a historical level, by integrating British history into English history and by integrating Arthur into a long line of English kings, British history becomes more mainstream and Arthur becomes representative of the best rulers of any people. On a historico-metaphorical level, Arthur is the subject of the "Breton hope" who will one day return and bring the Britons to their former glory, rising above the rival Saxons, the English, and the Normans. On a more purely metaphorical level, Arthur's "people" represent – or speak to – all peoples who through series of circumstances not necessarily of their own doing have been made marginal in their own lands; stories of Arthur's glory speak to dreams of all groups who

---

writing for and inspired by contemporary Anglo-Norman society, and that his concerns were chiefly political," given his treatment of the issues of female rule, and his "almost oppressive sermonising on the perils of civil war and the problems of dynastic succession" ("History, Prophecy and the Arthur of the Normans," here at 114). In the context of the *Prophetiae Merlini*, Victoria Flood contends that Geoffrey's ideological agenda is "a question ... often associated with the indeterminacy of his ethnic background ... By turns, Geoffrey has been understood to be a Welshman championing the lost history of his people; a Breton possessed of enormous pride in his countrymen; and a Normanised cleric closing off a dangerously contemporary Welsh interest in restoration in the distant insular past ... he has also been understood – like Gerald of Wales – as an author who is culturally hybrid: at once Norman and Welsh." She ultimately concludes that while these are fascinating lines of inquiry, they cannot determine per se the political nature of Geoffrey's texts (*Prophecy, Politics and Place in Medieval England: From Geoffrey of Monmouth to Thomas of Erceldoune*, Cambridge: Brewer, 2016, 21–22). Where I do agree more fully with Flood is in her recalling what Gillingham has written, while like him, not insisting that Geoffrey was Welsh: "it is probably no coincidence that Geoffrey made use of 'the theme of the British recovery [...] just at that moment when it seemed to be becoming historical reality [during the Welsh revolt of 1136–37]'" (Gillingham, "Context and Purposes," 38, cited by Flood at 23).

46   See in particular Fiona Tolhurst, *Geoffrey of Monmouth and the Feminist Origins of the Arthurian Legend*, Arthurian and Courtly Cultures (New York: Palgrave MacMillan, 2012) and eadem, *Geoffrey of Monmouth and the Translation of Female Kingship*, Arthurian and Courtly Cultures (New York: Palgrave MacMillan, 2013).

47   "Context and Purposes," 38.

seek to return to the "golden days," or to any days more prosperous than the present, particularly Indigenous groups seeking to actualize the restoration of ancestral lands, full rights, and a central place in historical writing, having been displaced by colonial powers.[48]

Setting aside the vexed question of Geoffrey's personal national/ethnic origins, for many historians (and others), as Neil Wright has noted, "perhaps the paramount problem posed by Geoffrey of Monmouth's immensely influential *Historia Regum Britannie* is the question of the sources on which Geoffrey based the narrative of British history presented in his *magnum opus*."[49] Whereas Geoffrey's methods of adaptation with respect to his earliest known source, Gildas's *De Excidio Britanniae*, can be characterized by borrowings verbatim and scattered verbal echoes most often without acknowledgement of Gildas – there are only seven direct citations of Gildas and all but two are fraudulent,[50] his methods with respect to Bede's *Historia Ecclesiastica Gentis Anglorum* were "entirely different"; although there are verbal echoes, Geoffrey "refused to make any concession to Bede's authority by modifying his customary free approach to his source [citing Bede even less often than he cites Gildas]; rather the *Historia* contradicts Bede at almost every turn."[51] Specifics will appear below, but for now, Wright's insightful summation is most useful: "in the case of Gildas he adapted the *De Excidio Britanniae* freely, and used Gildas's reputation to prop up his inventions; in that of Bede, he twisted, reshaped, and

---

48   In the introduction to his *First English Empire* whose major themes are "exploring the relationship between England and the British Isles, and equally exploring why that relationship did not develop, substantively or historiographically, into an integrative one," Davies points out the appropriation of King Arthur by the end of the twelfth century "into what was in effect the authorized version of the history of England and of the English monarchy ... an appropriation of the tales of a world-conquering hero, whose exploits were too wondrous to be reserved for the defeated Britons" (*The First English Empire: Power and Identities in the British Isles 1093–1343*, Oxford: Oxford University Press, 2000, p. 2). It would be surprising if many groups did not "appropriate" Arthur; see Susan Aronstein on Arthurian "ownership" (*Introduction to British Arthurian Narrative*, Gainesville: University Press of Florida, 2012). See also the Introduction, n. **32** on sources for Indigenous claims to ancestral lands, full rights, and being written back into histories created by colonial powers in North America.

49   "Geoffrey of Monmouth and Bede," in *Arthurian Literature VI*, ed. Richard Barber (Cambridge: D. S. Brewer, 1986), 27–59, cited here at p. 27. On the written sources, including Welsh as well as Latin, for the period 400–600, see in particular David Dumville, "Sub-Roman Britain: History and Legend," esp. pp. 175–82.

50   Wright, "Geoffrey of Monmouth and Bede," 28.

51   Wright, "Geoffrey of Monmouth and Bede," 28 and 53. On Geoffrey's debt to Gildas, see N. Wright, "Geoffrey of Monmouth and Gildas," *Arthurian Literature II*, ed. Richard Barber (Cambridge: D. S. Brewer, 1982), 1–40 and "Geoffrey of Monmouth and Gildas Revisited," *Arthurian Literature IV*, ed. Richard Barber (Cambridge: D. S. Brewer, 1984), 155–63.

44   CHAPTER 1

contradicted the previously accepted Bedan version of the British past while taking shelter behind the authority which the *liber vetustissimus* conferred on his *Historia*."[52]

2   Description of Britain, Arrival of Brutus, Foundation Myth: Geoffrey and His Predecessors

2.1   *Gildas, Bede, and "Nennius"* (*the* Historia Brittonum)

Geoffrey's description of the Trojan foundation of Britain was certainly not taken from Gildas who says virtually nothing of the Britons before the arrival of the Romans. During the Roman occupation, Gildas decries the Britons' rebelliousness and treachery (*DEB*, 4–13, pp. 17–21).[53] According to Gildas, the situation had deteriorated to such an extent both due to internal strife and external attacks, that the Britons begged the Romans to return, but soon after sending a number of fruitless expeditions to help the Britons against barbarian invasions, "the Romans therefore informed our country that they could not go on being bothered with such troublesome expeditions; the Roman standards, that great and splendid army could not be worn out by land and sea for the sake of wandering thieves who had no taste for war" (*DEB*, 181, p. 22). Following his few brief passages on the sorry state of the Britons, Gildas passes to the arrival of the Saxons (to which we will return below).[54]

Nor did Geoffrey take his description of Trojan foundations from Bede, although the latter provides more details of early Britain than Gildas. In Chapter 1 of the *Historia ecclesiastica*, Bede relates that at first the only inhabitants of the island were the Britons who had arrived from Amorica – but no other details are provided than this – followed by "some Picts from Scythia"[55]

---

52   Wright, "Geoffrey of Monmouth and Bede," 55.

53   Gildas, *The Ruin of Britain and other works*, ed. and trans. Michael Winterbottom, Arthurian Period Sources, 7 (London: Phillimore, 1978). I will refrain from entering into the debate as to whether Gildas can legitimately be referred to as an "historian," and will use that term for simplicity's sake.

54   Following the arrival of the Saxons, Geoffrey does incorporate four of Gildas's five kings – Constantine, Aurelius Caninus, Vortipor, and Maglocunus (Malgo, Maelgwn), but omitting Cuneglasus; see Leckie, *Passage of Dominion*, 60 and 64.

55   *Historia Ecclesiastica*, I.i. Generally considered one of three Brittonic-speaking peoples inhabiting Scotland in the early medieval period, descendants of Tacitus's "Caledonian Britons" ("Picts," Kathellirine Forsyth, in John T. Koch, ed. *Celtic Culture: An Historical Encyclopedia*, 5 vols. (Santa Barbara, CA: ABC-CLIO, 2006), IV, 1446–48), there is currently no consensus among historians (including of ancient Rome and sub-Roman Britain), art historians, archeologists, anthropologists and others as to who the Picts actually were – or

HISTORIA REGUM BRITANNIAE: PART 1   45

who asked for permission from the Scots (*Scoti*, the current inhabitants of Ireland)[56] to settle in Ireland but were refused since according to the Scots

of what groups they were made up – or their relationships with other peoples of the territories which are now modern Scotland. Isabel Henderson cautions against thinking of the Picts monolithically, writing of the probability that "the peoples lumped together by the Romans under the name 'Picts' had a mixed racial and cultural background ... there is no trace of the *Picti* having arrived at some point in time to settle in North Britain in the way that the Scots arrived in Argyll and the Anglo-Saxon peoples arrived in the south," arguing that the Picts may have been made up of multiple peoples, including native Britons ("The Problem of the Picts," in *Who are the Scots?*, ed. Gordon Menzies (London: BBC, 1971), 51–65, here at 52). On legends of origins of the Picts, see James Fraser, "From Ancient Scythia to *The Problem of the Picts*: Thoughts on the Quest for Pictish Origins," in *Pictish Progress: New Studies in Northern Britain in the Middle Ages*, ed. Stephen T. Driscoll, Jane Geddes, and Mark A. Hall (Leiden: Brill, 2010), 16–43. In a review article on recent scholarship on the Picts, arguing for greater energy to be directed to archeological excavations and that greater credence be given to the pre-historical aspects of the fifth through the eighth centuries, Martin Carver has characterized the Picts – as an historical phenomenon – as a "quintessentially 'lost people of Europe,'" a perception reinforced by the paucity of written documents and the fact that very little record of the Pictish language remains. However, Carver maintains that there "is no archaeological difficulty in knowing who and where the Picts were. Theirs was an unusually expressive episode in the life of the north-east Britons, and it needs explaining in terms of environment, economy, agency, allegiances, mission, exchanges, beliefs. It is ripe for archaeology ..." ("Lost, found, repossessed or argued away – the case of the Picts," *Antiquity* 85.330 [2011]: 1479–83, here at 1479 and 1483). See also idem, "What were they thinking? Intellectual Territories in Anglo-Saxon England," in *The Oxford Handbook of Anglo-Saxon Archaeology*, ed. Helena Hamerow, David A. Hinton, and Sally Crawford (Oxford: Oxford University Press, 2011), 914–47. On the Picts as one of multiple peoples in early Scotland, see James Fraser, *From Caledonia to Pictland: Scotland to 795*, New Edinburgh History of Scotland 1 (Edinburgh: Edinburgh University Press, 2009); Sally M. Foster, *Picts, Gaels and Scots: Early Historic Scotland* (London: Batsford, 1996; 2nd ed. 2004; rev. ed. London: Birlinn, 2014), and Alex Woolf, *From Pictland to Alba 789–1070*, New Edinburgh History of Scotland 11 (Edinburgh: Edinburgh University Press, 2007). On the Pictish language, see especially Katherine Forsyth, *Language in Pictland: The Case Against "Non-Indo-European Pictish,"* Studia Hameliana 2 (Utrecht: Stichting Uitgeverij de Keltische Draak, 1997), and Chapter 2, n. 15 below.

56   I am using the modern term "Scots" here (and elsewhere) anachronistically, with the understanding that it is usually the English translation used for the Latin *Scotti/Scoti*, a term which referred to the Irish in early texts. Modern historians and critics (as well as translators) often use the term "Scots" when referring to the people of the early Middle Ages who inhabited the territories which eventually became the kingdom of Scotland. Dauvit Broun argues that strictly speaking, the "Gaelic-speaking 'Scots' saw themselves unambiguously as an offshoot of the Gaels of Ireland (as it [*sic*] revealed in the tenth-century text *Senchus fer nAlban*, the 'History of the People of Scotland'). In short, the 'Scots' in this period had no idea of having a distinct ethnic identity: they simply saw themselves as Irish. The confusion caused by modern English terminology is largely a result of Gaedil's translation into Latin as *Scoti*: only later ... did Scoti acquire its modern

46   CHAPTER 1

(Irish), "there was not room for them both" (*HE*, I, p. 39). The Scots (Irish) suggested that the Picts make the voyage to the land at the northern end of the longer island; the Picts soon left for the land which was later to become Scotland, taking with them Scottish (Irish) women for wives, on the condition that, should there be regnal disputes in the future, they would select rulers from the female royal line rather than the male.[57] Bede moves on from the initial chapter containing the few details of early Britain, to Chapter 2, in whose opening lines, one reads that "now Britain had never been visited by the Romans and was unknown to them until the time of Gaius Julius Caesar ..."[58]

Of his three main written sources that survive – Gildas, Bede and the *Historia Brittonum* (hereafter *HB*) sometimes attributed to "Nennius" – Geoffrey was by far the most influenced by "Nennius" regarding the Trojan origins of Britain; in fact, neither Gildas nor Bede provide origin stories for the Britons.[59] With

---

sense of the inhabitants of the Scottish kingdom"; in fact "the first generation to articulate fully a sense of ethnic Scottishness – the Scots as a distinct people with their own unique history and ancient origins" belongs to the late thirteenth to early fourteenth centuries (Dauvit Broun, "When did Scotland become Scotland?" *History Today* 46.10 (1996): 16–21, here at 17 and 18). See also idem, "Alba: Pictish Homeland or Irish Offshoot?" in *Exile and Homecoming: Papers from the Fifth Australian Conference of Celtic Studies, University of Sydney, July, 2004*, ed. Pamela O'Neill (Sydney: Sydney Celtic Studies Foundation, University of Sydney, 2005), 234–75.

57   See Molly Miller, "Matriliny by treaty: the Pictish foundation-legend," 133–6. For a more recent reconsideration of matriliny among the Picts, see Nicholas Evans, "Royal Succession and Kingship among the Picts," *The Innes Review* 59.1 (2008): 1–48 [https://doi.org/10.3366/E0020157X000140], and Clare Downham's review of both James Fraser *From Caledonia to Pictland* and Alex Woolf, *From Pictland to Alba 789–1070* (*Journal of Scottish Historical Studies* 29.2 (2009): 141–43); for additional sources, see also Chapter 2, n. 15 below.

58   Bede gives "the year of Rome" which is 61 BCE, having taken the Roman date from Orosius. The editors state though that "the true dates of the expeditions are the year of Rome 699 and 700, that is, 55 and 54 B.C." (Colgrave and Mynors, 20, n. 1).

59   The textual history of the Welsh Latin text the *Historia Brittonum* (probably originally composed in c. 829/30), and the attribution to "Nennius," is extremely complex, given not only the number of recensions from various periods – at least four, the "Vatican," "Harleian," "pseudo-Nennian" (with the prologue that attributes the text to "Nennius") and the "Gildasian" (or alternatively "pseudo-Gildasian" since the text is erroneously attributed to Gildas), the variety of materials and interpolations contained in those recensions, the disputable identity of the author, as well as the nearly forty manuscripts; David Dumville rejects the authenticity of the "Nennian Prologue" (the earliest extant copy of which is found in the twelfth-century MS Cambridge, Corpus Christi College 139), considering it a later forgery and not part of the original text, and proposing that the *Historia Brittonum* is a carefully constructed amalgam of anonymous texts/recensions rather than a single ninth-century text attributable to a Welsh author named Nennius: "the author remains unknown and ... the ascription to 'Nennius' is no older than a Welsh recension

HISTORIA REGUM BRITANNIAE: PART 1   47

the *Historia Brittonum*, on the other hand, one has hit the proverbial "mother lode" of foundation stories (to be discussed briefly below). As Robert Hanning observes, one of the most noteworthy aspects of the *Historia Brittonum* is the unusually large number of origin stories; he counts four for the Britons – two going back to Rome, a third combining a Germanic tradition with a biblical

of the text in the mid-eleventh century" ("'Nennius' and the *Historia Brittonum*," *Studia Celtica* 10/11 (1975/6): 78–95; repr. in *Histories and Pseudo-histories of the Insular Middle Ages*, Variorum, 1990, Ch. x, cited at p. 78). Cf. Peter J. C. Field, who argues that there was a Welsh Nennius who wrote the *HB* in the late eighth century, and that the prologue (as it is in Corpus Christi College 139) is authentic and was expressly omitted from later versions due to its having contained fairly insulting assessments of the Britons' capacity for historical endeavor: "I Ninnius, disciple of Elvodugus, have undertaken to write down some extracts that the stupidity of the British ['hebitudo gentis Brittannie'] cast out; for the scholars of this island of Britain had no skill and set down no records in books. I have therefore made a heap of all that I have found ..." ("Nennius and his History," *Studia Celtica* 30 (1996): 159–65, Field's translation, 160, based on Dumville's transcription, 79–80, with one emendation (Field, 160 n. 4); see also Christopher A. Snyder, "Arthur and Kingship in the *Historia Brittonum*," in *The Fortunes of King Arthur*, ed. Norris J. Lacy (Cambridge: D. S. Brewer, 2005), 1–12). For detailed accounts of, and views on, these and other vexed questions pertaining to this work including the disputed primacy of the Harleian recension named for BL Harley MS. 3859, see David N. Dumville, ed., *The Historia Brittonum, 3: The 'Vatican' Recension* (Cambridge: D. S. Brewer, 1985), and the following studies by the same author: "On the north British section of the *Historia Brittonum*," *Welsh History Review* 8 (1976/7): 345–54 (repr. in *Histories and Pseudo-histories of the Insular Middle Ages*); "Some aspects of the chronology of the *Historia Brittonum*," *Bulletin of the Board of Celtic Studies*, 25 (1972–74): 439–45 (repr. in *Histories and Pseudo-histories of the Insular Middle Ages*); "The Corpus-Christi 'Nennius'," *Bulletin of the Board of Celtic Studies*, 25 (1972–74): 369–80 (repr. in *Histories and Pseudo-histories of the Insular Middle Ages*); "*Historia Brittonum*: An Insular History from the Carolingian Age," in *Historiographie im frühen Mittelalter*, ed. A. Scharer and G. Scheibelreiter, Veröffentlichungen des Instituts für Österreichische Geschichtsforschung 32 (Munich and Vienna: Oldenbourg, 1994), 406–34; "The Historical Value of the *Historia Brittonum*," *Arthurian Literature* VI, ed. Richard Barber (Cambridge: D. S. Brewer, 1986), 1–26; see Julia C. Crick, *The Historia Regum Britannie of Geoffrey of Monmouth, IV. Dissemination and Reception in the Later Middle Ages* (Cambridge: D. S. Brewer, 1991), 29–30. See also Thomas M. Charles-Edwards, "The Arthur of History," in *The Arthur of the Welsh*, 15–32; Wendy Davies, *Wales in the Early Middle Ages* (Leicester: Leicester University Press, 1982), 47–50, 206–6, 244, n. 35; John T. Koch, "The Celtic Lands," in *Medieval Arthurian Literature: A Guide to Recent Research*, ed. Norris J. Lacy, Routledge Library Editions: Arthurian Literature 7 (New York and London: Garland, 1996), 239–322, esp. 246–54; N. J. Higham, *King Arthur: Myth-Making and History*, esp. 119–28, who notes that "what became clear during the course of the 1990s, was the extent to which we should see this as an authored text and not just a collection of pre-existing source materials lumped together crudely by a poorly qualified copyist and editor" (120), and Siân Echard, "*Historia Brittonum*," in *The Encyclopedia of Medieval Literature in Britain* (Chichester, West Sussex and Hoboken, NJ: John Wiley & Sons, 2017), 1019–20.

48   CHAPTER 1

tradition and a fourth combining a Roman version with a biblical version.[60]
Perhaps due to the manuscript of the *HB* to which Geoffrey had access, he was
very selective in what he took from "Nennius," though what he left behind is
perhaps as revealing as what he took, and then amplified.[61]

Two manuscripts of the "Vatican" recension (Paris, BnF lat. 9768 *olim*
Vatican, Biblioteca Apostolica Reg. lat. 1964, Théodore Mommsen's M and
David Dumville's R; Paris, BnF lat. 11108, Mommsen's N and Dumville's J) and the
Chartres MS. (Chartres, Bibliothèque municipale, 98, the oldest manuscript,
Mommsen's Z)[62] contain a genealogy that links the Romans to Dardanus,
father of Trous, the builder of Troy; Brutus, brother of Romulus and Remus – all

---

60   See Robert W. Hanning, *Visions of History in Early Britain from Gildas to Geoffrey of
      Monmouth* (New York: Columbia University Press, 1966), 102–7, and 213–15, nn. 39–65,
      for a detailed account of these versions, as well as two origin stories for the Scots, 107–8.
      In Hanning's four versions for the Britons, he includes the version in M, N, and Z which
      links the Romans to Dardanus, which I do not discuss below under Harley since it was
      not originally in that manuscript (though it is printed by Morris in his edition/translation
      based on Harley; see **n. 66** below).
61   On the question of which recension of the *Historia Brittonum* Geoffrey may have used,
      Michael Reeve comments "whether or not Geoffrey used more than one, he certainly
      used one that included the three *mirabilia* from *Hist. Brit.* 67 and 69–70 described in
      §§ 149–50 ... That he used the Gildasian recension has nevertheless been inferred by his
      ascription to Gildas of material in § 100 taken from the *Historia Britonum* [sic], and to
      judge from the extant manuscripts it was the manuscript that circulated most widely in
      the twelfth century"; in addition, however, when Geoffrey mentions Gildas, Reeve com-
      ments that "he may have both the *De excidio* and the *Historia Britonum* in mind'" though
      "on the other hand, he says that Gildas did not mention Arthur, which is true of Gildas but
      not of the *Historia Britonum*" (ed., lxviii).
62   See Edmond Faral's facing-page edition of the Chartres MS (the manuscript was since
      destroyed during WWII) and the Harley MS in *La Légende arthurienne: études et docu-
      ments*, 3 vols. (Paris: Champion, 1929), vol. 3, 2–62; Faral includes the *Annales Cambriae*
      where they are found in Harley between the main part of ch. 66 and the list of cities
      in ch. 66a (see n. **65** below on the arrangement of Morris's edition and translation).
      On the list of cities, see Keith Fitzpatrick-Williams, "The xxuiii civitates brittanie [with
      reverse cedilla on e] of the *Historia Brittonum*: Antiquarian Speculation in Medieval
      Wales, *Journal of Literary Onomastics* 4.1 (2015) 1–19. Regarding the Chartres recension,
      Fitzpatrick-Williams writes that "David Dumville's promised edition of the variant recen-
      sions – ten in all – stalled after the publication of Volume 3 (the 'Vatican' recension),
      the only volume so far published (Dumville 1985) (cited at p. 2)." Although it has not
      been possible for me to confirm this definitively, Boydell and Brewer have told me that
      it is not in their database, and that they have not been able to track it down, surmis-
      ing that it may never have appeared in finalized form after having been announced (as
      The Historia Brittonum 2: The 'Chartres Recension,' Cambridge: D. S. Brewer, 1988) (private
      communication).

HISTORIA REGUM BRITANNIAE: PART 1   49

three sons of Silvius – engages in wars on behalf of Rome.[63] After subduing
Spain, Brutus takes Britain, which is later inhabited by his descendants (or the
descendants of his father, Silvius, depending on the manuscript).[64]

London, British Library, Harley 3859 (Mommsen's H)[65] – often considered the oldest, most complete manuscript witness of the *Historia Brittonum*
(though not the original text) – contains a number of foundation stories often
interwoven with genealogies: three foundation stories for the Britons (or two,
depending on how one counts them, one being bi-partite in chs. 17 and 18,
and the initial one in ch. 10),[66] the bi-partite alternate version combining a

---

63   Mommsen's sigla were also used by Lot, and others, but not by Dumville; see Theodor
Mommsen, ed., *Chronica Minor Saec. IV. V VI. VII.*, 3 vols. (Berlin, 1891–98); Ferdinand
Lot, *Nennius et l'Historia Brittonum: étude critique suivie d'une edition des diverses ver-
sions de ce texte*, 2 vols., Bibliothèque de l'École des Hautes Études, Sciences historiques
et philologiques 263 (Paris: H. Champion, 1934); and David N. Dumville, ed., *The Historia
Brittonum, 3: The 'Vatican' Recension*.

64   Hanning, *Vision of History*, 104.

65   Since it is the most widely accessible edition, I am using John Morris's based on the Harley
MS: *Nennius: British History and the Welsh Annals*, ed. and trans. John Morris, Arthurian
Period Sources 8 (London: Phillimore, 1980), containing the *Annales Cambriae*, the earliest extant version, inserted in the Harley MS between ch. 66 and ch. 66a (the list of
cities of Britain) of the *Historia Brittonum*, pp. 85–91, with a prefatory note and English
translation on pp. 44–49. The Welsh genealogies also contained in the Harley MS are not
printed with the others in vol. 8, but rather in idem, ed., *Genealogies and Texts*, Arthurian
Period Sources 5 (Chichester: Phillimore, 1995), 13–55; the Welsh genealogies (as well as
the *Annales Cambriae*), edited by Egerton Phillimore in *Y Commrodor* 9 (1888): 141–83, is
reprinted by Morris; see also Morris's very useful introduction to the Irish, British (Welsh),
and English genealogies in vol. 5, 3–10, and on the so-called "Northern History" containing
the English genealogies, see also Kenneth H. Jackson, "On the northern British Section
in Nennius," in *Celt and Saxon: Studies in the Early British Border*, ed. N. K. Chadwick
(Cambridge: Cambridge University Press, 1963), 21–62. I will use the designation "ch."
for the chapters in *HB*, rather than the "§" symbol, used here only for the chapter sections Geoffrey's *Historia* and the First Variant. In his Introductory note to Morris's edition
(Morris passed away in 1977 before the edition was completed), R. B. White reveals that
the "dagger symbols" (†) before and after a passage indicate that the passage in question was taken from Mommsen's edition (*Chronica Minora*, Berlin, 1892) rather than from
Faral's (*La Légende arthurienne*, 3) upon which Morris based the bulk of his edition.

66   Morris includes from another (unidentified) recension an "addendum" (set off with dagger symbols): the Harley redactor says at the beginning of ch. 10, "If anyone wants to
know when this island was inhabited after the Flood, I find two alternative explanations"
(ch. 10, p. 19; "Si quis scire voluerit quo tempore post diluvium habitata est haec insula,
hoc experimentum bifarie inveni," p. 60) – that is, the "alternative explanation" which
involves "Dardanus, son of Jupiter, of the race of Ham," and is probably the version found
in MSS M, N, and Z. While valuable, this addition without definite annotation tends to
confuse the count as to how many foundation stories there are for the Britons in the *HB*
as represented by Harley (see n. 60 above). On the multilayered nature of this text and the

Germanic tradition – including the Britons – with biblical information (ch. 17), and another genealogy which combines Roman with biblical tradition (ch. 18); two for the Irish (ch. 13 and ch. 15); a genealogy of Vortigern's family (ch. 49); genealogies of the kings of the Bernicians (part 1, ch. 57), kings of Kent (ch. 58) the East Angles (ch. 59), the Mercians (ch. 60), the Deirans (ch. 61), the Bernicians (part 2, ch. 61), and Welsh (Britons) genealogies.[67] The first foundation story (ch. 10, pp. 19, 60),[68] which the redactor says he found in the "Annals of the Romans," relates that after the Trojan war, Aeneas came to Italy with his son Ascanius, defeated Turnus and married Lavinia, daughter of Latinus; after Latinus's death, Aeneas inherits the kingdom of the Romans and the Latins. After Lavinia's death, Aeneas remarries; his wife bears a son named Silvius; Silvius's wife dies while giving birth to Britto or Brutus. Before his birth, a prophecy has foretold that he will kill his father and mother. The prophecy comes to pass (he kills his father in a hunting accident), and Brutus the outcast flees Italy. He arrives in the islands of the Tyrrhenian sea, only to be expelled by the Greeks, who remember that his grandfather had slain Turnus. Brutus leaves in disgrace, and then goes to Gaul where he founds the city of Tours, and then to Britain. Brutus establishes there a new fertile nation, emblematic of a new world order, leaving behind the ancient hatreds.

In Harley, the second foundation story, about which the redactor says "I have found another explanation about Brutus in the old books of our elders" (ch. 17, p. 22)("Aliud experimentum inveni de isto Bruto ex veteribus libris veterum nostrorum," p. 63), is more strictly speaking a genealogy since there is little narration save the list of fathers and sons. In the beginning part (ch. 17) containing a Germanic legend, the European barbarian peoples are traced back to Japheth, one of the three sons of Noah, thus combining a Germanic legend with the Bible.[69] In the second part (ch. 18), the Britons as first inhabitants of Britain are shown to have descended from Brutus, tracing the line all the way back to Japheth and Noah, tying in the thread found in MSS M, N, and Z, where Trous son of Dardanus is also brought in, thereby combining the three threads

---

relative position of the Harley MS. in the textual history, see David N. Dumville, "*Historia Brittonum*: An Insular History from the Carolingian Age."

67 On the Welsh genealogies, see Ben Guy, *Medieval Welsh Genealogy: An Introduction and Textual Study*, Studies in Celtic History 42 (Woodbridge: Boydell Press, 2020).

68 Citations from Morris are by chapter number, page number of English translation, and page number of Latin original.

69 The barbarian peoples in question are 1) allegedly descended from the five sons of Armenon: Goths, Walagoths, Gepids, Burgundians, and Langobards; and 2) from the three sons of Negue: Vandals, Saxons, Bavarians, and Thuringians. Also in this picture are the peoples allegedly descended from Hessito, the first son of Alanus, and brother of Armenon and Negue: Franks, Latins, British, and Albans (ch. 17, pp. 22, 63).

of Roman, Trojan, and biblical descent. As Dumville notes, "the author of the *Historia Brittonum* preferred, like the Franks, a Romano-Trojan origin for his people; but a rival view which he acknowledged situated that origin rather in a context of ultimately biblical genealogy, albeit one which closely associated the Britons with the Romans and Franks, both of whom had claimed Trojan origins."[70]

This rival view, which sets British history within a more universal framework, serves both to raise the history of the Britons to a higher level, but also to deemphasize that group. In fact, given how much of the *Historia Brittonum* is devoted to genealogies and foundation stories in which the Britons are not primary players, one might wonder how the text came to be called the *Historia Brittonum*.[71] As Dumville comments, the author, while never straying too long from the Britons "nonetheless was catholic in his Insular historical interests and his admission that the four nations of the British Isles [Britons, Gaels, Picts, and English] all had a stake – a legitimate stake – in the history of Britain." As a result, "we might feel that it is Britain, or the British Isles rather than the Britons themselves, which provide the principal focus of his historiography."[72]

While on the one hand, "Nennius's" inclusion of numerous English genealogies for quite possibly structural help with his history, and what could thus be construed as an admission of the legitimacy of – or support for – various aspects of Saxon/English rule does not necessarily signal "anglophilic" intent on the whole, the pro-British aspect may not be sufficient for some to think that a goal of the *Historia Brittonum* was to answer Bede's anglocentric history. For example, whereas David Dumville finds the work "is hardly a British counterpart to the Englishman's, either in intention or execution,"[73] Patrick Sims-Williams is of the opposite view, arguing that "the *Historia Brittonum* reads almost like a reply to Bede."[74] Thomas Charles-Edwards takes what some

---

70   "*Historia Brittonum*: An Insular History from the Carolingian Age," 427.

71   Dumville: "Can three or more centuries of modern scholarship have mistaken what this is a history of, as well as what kind of a history it is and was intended to be?" ("*Historia Brittonum*: An Insular History from the Carolingian Age," 415) and on the various names by which this text is referred in different manuscript witnesses see 416–17.

72   "*Historia Brittonum*: An Insular History from the Carolingian Age," 414.

73   "*Historia Brittonum*: An Insular History from the Carolingian Age," 414, 434. Similarly, Dumville maintains that "the *Historia Brittonum* is part of, and the most substantial evidence for, the development of English cultural influence in Wales" ("The Historical Value of the *Historia Brittonum*," 24). One need not assume, however, that *HB*'s author was arguing in favor of any perceived superiority of English cultural influence through his portrayal of the Britons and the Saxons.

74   Sims-Williams maintains that this "reply" is supported by the portrayal of the Britons as "among the most illustrious and ancient nations of Europe, especially by comparison

52   CHAPTER 1

may read as a middle ground, arguing that while *HB* "plainly took much material from English as well as Irish sources [and] appears to have favoured a reconciliation, based upon a common faith, between the Britons and the English,"
the redactor's/author's views did not go as far as Bede's English leanings.[75] The
skeletal list of Arthur's twelve battles in ch. 56,[76] and passages on Vortigern's

---

with the Picts, Irish, and Anglo-Saxons" and that "Geoffrey of Monmouth develops this
theme to its limits" ("Some functions of origin stories in early medieval Wales," in *History
and Heroic Tale: A Symposium*, ed. Tore Nyberg, Iørn Piø, Preben Meulengracht Sørensen,
and Aage Trommer, Odense: Odense University Press, 1985, 97–131, cited here at 117–18).

75   Cf. Charles-Edwards's views of Bede's Anglo-Saxon perspectives and "lack of antipathy"
toward the Britons, Chapter 2, n. 120 below. See also W. Trent Foley and Nicholas J. Higham
who argue that, although Bede does allow for the worthiness of some Britons, recom-
mending that certain British Christians be imitated for their saintliness, in general "Bede
shared with his intended audience such disinterest in and general contempt for the
Britons that he felt himself free to introduce them singly or en masse in various guises
according to quite different agendas, the focus of which always lay in some aspect or other
of this self-consciously 'English' history" and that as far as Bede was concerned more often
than not "their 'Britishness' [i.e., the larger group they belonged to] was significant but
their specificity [individual identity] was not" concluding that there was "something very
stereotypical about his treatment of the Britons" ("Bede on the Britons," *Early Medieval
Europe* 17.2 (2009): 154–85, 175, and cited at 172). For Foley and Higham, more revealing of
Bede's favoritism in his portrayal of the Saxons (English) is that "from a biblical perspective, Bede's failure to link the piety of saintly Britons with their Britishness is unremark-
able, but his tendency to link the piety of saintly Anglo-Saxons with their Englishness
is" (181). Nonetheless Foley and Higham conclude that although Bede was writing for a
Northumbrian elite, and often his treatment of the Britons is condemnatory, especially
on the topic of their refusal to help Augustine in his efforts at converting the Saxons, his
portrayals of the Britons are ultimately mixed, and "his own private thoughts on the matter must remain something of an enigma" (185).

76   When scholars use the phrase "Arthur's twelve battles," they commonly refer to the battles
listed in the *Historia Brittonum*, where Arthur fights alongside the "kings of the British" as
their "leader in battle"; the list of battles in other texts can vary considerably – particularly
in the Galfridian tradition – authors taking free reign no doubt with the vagueness of the
list as they found it, either in a version of the *HB* or in their own source(s). It is important
to note that in the *HB*, Arthur is universally victorious and that neither his "death" nor his
eventual return are reported:
"The first battle was at the mouth of the river called Glein. The second, the third, the
fourth and the fifth were on another river, called the Douglas, which is in the country of Lindsey. The sixth battle was on the river called Bassas. The seventh battle was
in Celyddon Forest, that is, the battle of Celyddon Coed. The eighth battle was in
Guinnion fort, and in it Arthur carried the image of the holy Mary, the everlasting
Virgin, on his [shield,] ['super humeros suos'] and the heathen were put to flight on
that day, and there was a great slaughter upon them, through the power of Our Lord
Jesus Christ and the power of the holy Virgin Mary, his mother. The ninth battle was
fought in the city of the Legion. The tenth battle was fought on the bank of the river
called Tryfrwyd. The eleventh battle was on the hill called Agned. The twelfth battle

HISTORIA REGUM BRITANNIAE: PART 1

infamy and his son, Vortimer's triumphs in chs. 43–49, show that through Arthur and Vortimer, the Britons are victorious, yet "in the end, their victories served only to reveal the more clearly that it was God who had determined that Saxons should settle in Britain under their own kings"; Charles-Edwards concludes in this instance that "whether or not the author of the *Historia Brittonum* knew Bede's *Historia Ecclesiastica*, he had an answer to Bede's accusation (I, 22) that 'together with the other unspeakable crimes which their historian Gildas recounted in tearful prose, they were also adding, this, that they never communicated the word of the Faith by preaching to the people of the Saxons or English who inhabited Britain with them'" – the *HB* author's answer introduced through the narratives on the sustained missionary work of both Patrick (ch. 54) and Rhun ab Urien (ch. 63).[77]

In light of not only the proportion of Bede's text devoted to the Britons and British affairs – approximately 27%, not inconsequential but too low for Geoffrey – but also more importantly Bede's anglocentric perspective – and the fact that the *Historia Brittonum* may not have gone far enough in arguing the British cause to make up for any perceived inadequacies in Bede's work, the temptation for Geoffrey of Monmouth to go further would have

---

was on Badon Hill and in it nine hundred and sixty men fell in one day, from a single charge of Arthur's and no one laid them low save he alone; and he was victorious in all his campaigns" (*HB*, 56; Morris, trans., 35; Morris uses "Douglas" rather than "Duglas" as in Reeve/Wright, and Wace in the original; Weiss translates as "Douglas" as does Greenway; I am choosing "Duglas" in Appendix 3 and elsewhere to disambiguate from the River Douglas, in the north-west, and not the same (probably unlocatable) river referred to in *HB*, allegedly in Lindsey; cf. Andrew Breeze who argues for Douglas Water, Scotland ("The Historical Arthur and Sixth-Century Scotland," *Northern History* 52.2, 2015: 158–81, 174; http://dx.doi.org/10.1179/0078172X15Z.00000000085).

Geoffrey apparently retained the grandeur of Arthur's victory at mons Badonis/Badonicus mons from earlier historians ("pagum Badonis," §146.81) but he places it earlier in the series of Arthur's "domestic" or "national" battles. For perspectives on these battles, their possible locations, their fictitious nature or historical plausibility, see especially David N. Dumville, "The Historical Value of the *Historia Brittonum*," idem "'Nennius' and the *Historia Brittonum*"; Peter J. Field, "Nennius and His History," *Studia Celtica* 30 (1996): 159–65, idem, "Arthur's Battles," *Arthuriana* 18.4 (2008): 3–32; Kenneth H. Jackson, "The Site of Mount Badon," *Journal of Celtic Studies* 2 (1953):152–55; Rachel Bromwich, "Concepts of Arthur," *Studia Celtica* 10/11 (1975–76): 163–81; Andrew Breeze, "The Historical Arthur and Sixth-Century Scotland," and the recent review of scholarship on Badon in Breeze, "The Arthurian Battle of Badon and Braydon Forest, Wiltshire," *Journal of Literary Onomastics* 4.1 (2015): 20–30. R. M. Thomson comments that William of Malmesbury apparently "conflated the eighth of Arthur's battles" in *HB*, that of Guinnion fort, "and the twelfth 'in monte Badonis'," but he was not the only one (*GRA*, Vol. 11, 21). See Appendix 3 as a schematic illustration of the variations on the battles among the texts in question.

77   "The Arthur of History," *The Arthur of the Welsh*, 28.

54 CHAPTER 1

been irresistible.[78] By filling in so many of the gaps left by his major sources, Geoffrey can be seen to position himself as the British Bede; the ambitious nature of the *HRB* itself, as well as his threat to his contemporaries William of Malmesbury and Henry of Huntingdon – that they confine themselves to writing about the Saxons and leave the Britons to him – suggest as much, although this cannot be proven.[79]

2.2 *Geoffrey and the Foundation Myth of the Britons*

Although we cannot say for certain which recension of the *Historia Brittonum* Geoffrey used,[80] it is revealing to outline the most important details he did *not* choose from the origin stories in the *Historia Brittonum* (as seen in Harley):

---

78   As Neil Wright notes, "much of the basic framework of the *Historia Regum Britanniae* was provided by the *Historia Britonum*," i.e., the British foundation legend of Brutus, the main points of the history of Roman Britain from Caesar to Maximianus, the raids of the Picts and Scots, the material on Vortigern and the *adventus Saxonum* ("Geoffrey of Monmouth and Gildas," 4). With a well wrought understatement referring to Geoffrey's "free, yet carefully considered, approach to the adaptation of his literary sources" (5), Wright comments that Geoffrey "fleshed out this skeleton from other sources, including Bede," adding "extensive material on the pre-Roman kings, the Arthur cycle, and traditions about Cadwallon and Cadwaladr, [according to Geoffrey] the last kings of Britain" (4).

79   Wright: "Clearly, Geoffrey intends to emulate and outdo William and Henry in the *Historia*"; the passage where he forbids them to discuss the material on the Britons since only he has the "very old British book" "deliberately invites comparison with them" and, by extension, with Bede as their predecessors and Geoffrey's distant rival (ed., I, 1984, xix). Although certain questions may have been on the minds of many intellectuals of the time, it is tempting to see much of what Geoffrey provides as answers – or inventive guesses – to questions such as that articulated by Henry of Huntingdon regarding Stonehenge: "And no one can work out how the stones were so skillfully lifted up to such a height or why they were erected there" (*HA*, i.7, pp. 22–23). See Richard J. C. Atkinson, *Stonehenge* (London: H. Hamilton, 1956), 183; Tatlock, *Legendary History*, 41; and John Clark, "Trinovantum: The Evolution of a Legend," 138.

80   Lewis Thorpe suggests Geoffrey "had at his disposal something closely related to MS. Harl. 3859" (1966, p. 15); see also Thea Summerfield, "Filling the Gap: Brutus in the *Historia Brittonum, Anglo-Saxon Chronicle* MS F, and Geoffrey of Monmouth," in *The Medieval Chronicle VII*, ed. Juliana Dresvina, Nicholas Sparks, Erik Kooper (Amsterdam: Rodopi, 2011), 85–102. Summerfield points out that the F manuscript of the Anglo-Saxon Chronicle which dates from between 1100 and 1107 also contains a version of this foundation myth featuring Brutus, "slightly abbreviated" but still exhibiting "close verbal parallels with the 'Harleian Recension' of the *HB*" (91). MS. F usually referred to as the "Domitian Bilingual" has been dated by its most recent editor to between 1100 and 1107 "possibly later, but in any case not before 1100"; the F-scribe appears to appears to have had "several obvious agendas, all having to do with protecting and promoting the interests of the monastic community of Christ Church [Canterbury]" (Peter Baker, ed., *The Anglo-Saxon Chronicle: A Collaborative Edition. Volume 8, MS F*, Cambridge: D. S. Brewer, 2000, lxxvi). See also Ben Guy who writes that since "both the annals and genealogies were used by Geoffrey, ... [it]

1) the tracing of Brutus's line back to Noah;
2) the placing of Brutus's line in the context of the lines of the various barbarian peoples as descended from the children of Japheth, son of Noah.

Eliminating the genealogy back to Noah serves to foreground the Trojan and Roman aspects of Brutus's lineage, without clouding matters with biblical information, which on the one hand universalizes the story but on the other hand diffuses the focus considerably. Eliminating the stories of the other European peoples also serves to remove yet another narrative distraction. Also, in the context of the European peoples' narrative, the author of the *Historia Brittonum* refers to his source as the "old books of our elders" (ch. 17, pp. 63, 22), which Geoffrey might have construed as competition for his "very old book in the British tongue."

The elements Geoffrey *does* include in his version of the British foundation story contained in Book I of the twelve books of the *Historia* are the following:[81]

1) Brutus's coming of age;
2) Brutus's leadership of the Trojans, defending them against enslavement by the Greek King Pandrasus;
3) The siege of Sparatinum; Brutus's fierceness in battle; his troops show mercy to none;
4) Brutus captures Pandrasus;
5) Pandrasus releases the Trojans, giving them ships, gifts, and the princess Inoge his daughter to Brutus as his wife;
6) The goddess Diana prophesies to Brutus of the land beyond the sea, once inhabited by giants but now empty and waiting for Brutus's people;
7) Brutus joins up with Corineus, leader of four generations of exiled Trojans, in Aquitaine; Cornwall later named after Corineus;
8) Brutus sacks Aquitaine, held by King Goffar the Pict, leader of the Poitevins;
9) The battle of Tours, named after Turnus, nephew of Brutus; the Gauls are defeated; Brutus and his Trojans set sail for "the promised isle" (*promissam insulam*);

---

is likely he had access to a version of the Harleian recension of the *Historia Brittonum*" ("Geoffrey of Monmouth's Welsh Sources," in *A Companion to Geoffrey of Monmouth*, 31–66, esp. pp. 49–58, cited at 51).

81 The titles of these topics are loosely based on Thorpe's subheadings in the first thematic division which he labels "Part One: Brutus Occupies the Island of Albion" (following the description of Britain, I: 1–2) (trans., pp. 53–74). For a full outline of the text, based on Thorpe's thematic divisions, see the opening pages of Chapter 2, and nn. 9–10 on Reeve's divisions.

56   CHAPTER 1

10)   Corineus defeats Gogmagog, one of the giants who was still remaining in
       Albion; Brutus divides his kingdom and founds his capital, Trinovantum,
       much later renamed Kaerlud after Lud, brother of Cassivelaunus who
       fought against Julius Caesar;

11)   Brutus reigned twenty-three years; his immediate descendants.[82]

In Geoffrey's text, a glance reveals that we have left behind the realm of annalistic reporting and straightforward genealogies strictly speaking; the lines
of a larger narrative are filled in to form an engaging, integrated set of passages likely intended to move the listening/reading audience forward. Given
the level of detail just in these opening pages, it is easy to see how Geoffrey
did not arrive at the invasion of Julius Caesar until Book IV, that is, roughly a
third of the way through the narrative, whereas William of Malmesbury began
the *Gesta Regum Anglorum* at that point, and Henry of Huntingdon came to
Caesar early in the first of ten books of the *Historia Anglorum*.[83]

Like Gildas, Bede, and "Nennius," Geoffrey begins his narrative with a
descriptio insulae, a description of Britain; his version differs considerably
from that of his contemporary Henry of Huntingdon, on whose prefatory
description a number of texts in the "description of Britain" tradition including the Anglo-Norman *Description of England* are based.[84] Lesley Johnson
rightly observes that each version of this kind of description reveals not simply information but also each author's perspectives and thematic interests of
their texts:

---

82   Beginning of Book II (§23).

83   G. H. Gerould, "King Arthur and Politics," 37. Even the opening section – from the news
       of the son expected by Silvius's wife to Brutus's arrival in Britain – which is roughly 270
       words in the *HB* is expanded by Geoffrey to roughly 4,000 words (Summerfield, "Filling
       the gap," 93). In my tally of books of the *Historia Anglorum*, I am not counting Books XI
       and XII since they contain epigrams that do not advance the historical narrative per se.

84   Lesley L. Johnson, "The Anglo-Norman *Description of England*: An Introduction," cited at
       18, and Alexander Bell, ed., "The Anglo-Norman *Description of England*: An Edition." This
       early-to-mid twelfth-century Anglo-Norman poem is largely focused on the geographi-
       cal divisions of the Heptarchy and the history of those divisions and ecclesiastical sees,
       but it does bring in events from the British and Norman periods of Insular history, as
       well as from the Saxon. For a discussion of how this text presents a different view of the
       passage of dominion from those of Gaimar and Wace, as well as an overview of Henry
       of Huntingdon's description of the island, see the above article by Johnson. See also
       Hugh M. Thomas who in his investigation into the development of English national iden-
       tity comments on the tendency of twelfth-century descriptions of Britain "to slide into
       descriptions of England," which MacColl sees as "testimony to the power of 'England'
       as a construct" (Thomas, *The English and the Normans: Ethnic Hostility, Assimilation,
       and Identity, 1066–c. 1220*, Oxford: Oxford University Press, 2003, 265, and MacColl, "The
       Meaning of 'Britain,'" 249 n. 4).

Potentially Britain is a blessed land, a *locus amoenus*, which offers all the natural resources necessary for the cultivation of a Christian society. For Gildas, the fact that the Britons do not thrive on this land is a sign of their spiritual corruption ... the geographical setting of British history becomes an index of its history in Gildas's text: his narrative traces the transformation of the 'vineyard' of Britain into a wasteland. Bede's history, in contrast, goes on to trace the fulfillment of the island's physical (and metaphysical) potential.

In the *De Excidio*, following a brief setting out of the goals of the work, Gildas provides in the description proper a dispassionate account of geographical dimensions and architecture; he then proceeds to undermine the peacefulness of the initial narrative in the very next section with the beginning of his diatribe against the Britons (*DEB*, 3, 4, pp. 16–17). Bede's description found as the first chapter of Book I of the *Historia Ecclesiastica* includes physical geography, climate, resources, the languages of its five main inhabitant peoples, and how all inhabitants were originally Britons, the arrival of the Picts, and how some Irish remained in Ireland and others traveled to what later became Scotland (1:1, pp. 14, 16, 18, 20). "Nennius's" description – not in the prologue where it is mentioned that he simply compiled a "heap of all that [he] had found," which Dumville considers a late forgery[85] – attributes the name of the island to Brutus, a Roman consul, mentions the 28 cities, four nations (Irish, Picts, Saxons, British) and the two principal rivers (Thames and Severn); the remainder of the "description" segues into the various versions of the foundation legends, including biblical and those of other barbarian peoples. Henry of Huntingdon took Bede's description as a frame, including the geographical situation, climate, resources and languages, but then expands to include former cities of Britain, the kingdom of the Saxons, the shires and sees of England and Wales, concluding with an account of the marvels of the island (I: 1–11, pp. 10–34 [even pages]). Although a great admirer of Bede, at the end of Book I of the *Gesta Regum*, William of Malmesbury only follows part of Henry's lead by providing a survey of kingdoms and bishoprics (I: 99–105, pp. 147, 149).

Geoffrey's description of Britain appears to be patterned on the early section of Gildas's (which like Geoffrey's is significantly less detailed than Bede's), including the island's situation with respect to France and Ireland, dimensions, vegetation even to the detail of colorful flowers, and twenty-eight cities; where Gildas has two rivers (the Thames and the Severn), Geoffrey lists three (Thames, Severn, and Humber). Where Bede adds the element of the five

---

85   See n. 59 above.

58   CHAPTER 1

languages, Geoffrey does not, though to Bede's list of three peoples – Britons,
Picts and Irish (including the subset of the latter, the Irish Dalrudini who settled Scotland) – he makes two changes, listing the Normans and naming the
Scots: the Normans, the Britons, the Saxons, the Picts and the Scots. Geoffrey
adds only one non-neutral comment at the end of the short *descriptio* passage:
"ex quibus Britones olim ante ceteros a mari usque ad mare insederunt donec
ultione diuina propter ipsorum superbiam superueniente Pictis et Saxonibus
cesserunt" ("of these the Britons once occupied it from shore to shore before
the others, until their pride brought divine retribution down upon them and
they gave way to the Picts and the Saxons," *HRB*, §5.44–46).[86] Since Geoffrey's
book is a history of the Britons, in his *descriptio insulae* he does not include the
divisions of the Saxon kingdoms as do his contemporaries William and Henry,
nor the ecclesiastical sees associated with early England.[87]

In the vulgate *Historia*, Book I proper is devoted to the core of the foundation
legend. It ranges from the voyages and conquests of Brutus – written about by
neither Gildas, Bede nor William of Malmesbury (Gildas moves straight from
the description of Britain and the diatribe about the Britons to their struggles
with the Romans, bypassing a foundation story altogether; Bede begins with

---

86   In a neutral fashion, William mentions the Normans in his prologue, explaining that in
      the three last books of his *GR*, he will write of the three Norman kings (*GR*, i pr 6, p. 16). In
      his *descriptio insulae*, Henry of Huntingdon is less neutral, first flattering then disparaging
      the Normans: "... ubi modo Normanni, gens noua sed ualidissima, degunt" ("where the
      Normans, a new but extremely powerful people, are now settled" (*HA*, i. 2, pp. 12–13). A bit
      later, Henry includes the Normans in his reference to the five peoples who settled Britain
      as "five plagues" ("quinque plagas") visited upon Britain by "divine vengeance" ("divina
      ultio"), sent to punish the "fideles" as well as the "infideles": "Primam per Romanos, qui
      Britanniam expugnauerunt sed postea recesserunt. Secundam per Pictos et Scotos, qui
      grauissime eam bellis uexauerunt, nec tamen optinuerunt. Terciam per Anglicos, qui eam
      debellauerunt et optinent. Quartam per Dacos, qui eam bellis optinuerunt, sed postea
      deperierunt. Quintam per Normannos, qui eam deuicerunt et Anglis inpresentiarum
      dominantur" ("The first was through the Romans, who overcame Britain but later with-
      drew. The second was through the Picts and Scots, who grievously beleaguered the land
      ˙with battles but did not conquer it. The third was through the English, who overcame and
      occupy it. The fourth was through the Danes, who conquered it by warfare, but afterwards
      they perished. The fifth was through the Normans, who conquered it and have dominion
      over the English people at the present time," *HA*, i. 3, pp. 14, 15).
87   Mary Frances Giandrea explains that while the more universalizing writing of William
      of Malmesbury, Henry of Huntingdon, and Orderic Vitalis has understandably garnered
      a great deal of the attention of scholars, "the majority of the [historiographical] output
      was overwhelmingly local in its focus" including of course on ecclesiastical topics, adding
      that "Anglo-Norman historians were able to rescue the Anglo-Saxon past from the dust-
      bin and use it in defense of the present" (*Episcopal Culture in Late Anglo-Saxon England*,
      Woodbridge: Boydell, 2007), 16.

HISTORIA REGUM BRITANNIAE: PART 1   59

Julius Caesar and William with Severus and Constantinius)[88] – and the Trojans to the founding of Britain and its capital, Trinovantum, a topic of contemporary interest (that is, the founding of London in pre-Roman times).[89] As mentioned above, Geoffrey's contribution of the foundation story distinguishes his work from that of Gildas and Bede; he also creates greater focus on Brutus than "Nennius" by eliminating the alternative foundation legends included in the various recensions of the *Historia Brittonum* and by telescoping the narrative into a full chapter of the *HRB*.

As Brutus leads his people out of slavery and into the promised land, we hear both echoes of Moses as a figure of redemption as well as allusions to the slave trade, not only with reference to the Roman occupation but also in times much closer to Geoffrey's. Under the Roman Empire, the slave trade was an accepted part of the social fabric; slavery continued in early England and was practiced by the Vikings as well, among others.[90] By the late 1130s however, part of the developing contemptuous attitude toward the Celtic peoples focused on war as a slave hunt. William of Malmesbury, Orderic Vitalis and others expressed dismay at the taking of slaves as well as the ferocity often associated with Welsh, Scottish and Irish warring armies, which John Gillingham suggests may have reflected English approval of the Norman-introduced "chivalric" code of behavior that preferred capturing prisoners rather than killing them or selling them into slavery; new attitudes toward warfare were taking hold in more economically prosperous England but not yet in the largely agrarian economies

---

88   Henry of Huntingdon provides little on Brutus in the *Historia Anglorum*; the title of Book 1 – "Liber Primus ... De Regno Romanorum in Britannia" – gives away the focus of that opening book of his seven-book history of the English, that is, the Romans and not the Britons (two books of which are devoted to the coming of the Normans and their administration). What little he writes on Brutus can be found in his epitome of the *HRB*, the *Epistola ad Warinum* (*HA*, ed. and trans. Greenway, pp. 558–83). For an edition, translation, and commentary, in addition to Greenway's, see Neil Wright, "The Place of Henry of Huntingdon's *Epistola ad Warinum*." Greenway commends Wright's article particularly for its setting forth of the adaptations Henry made to the details of the *HRB*.

89   Geoffrey may have been trying to "prove" or at least to support Orosius's attribution to the early Britons of the establishment of a number of city-states, among which that of the Trinovantes was "the strongest" (*Historiae* 6.9–10); Bede transcribed Orosius but did not comment on the *Trinovantum firmissima civitas*, so we cannot know exactly how Bede might have read the phrase, i.e., as "the strongest city of the Trinovantes" or "the strongest city, Trinovantum" (*HE*, 1.ii, p. 21; Colgrave and Mynors translate the phrase as "the strongest city of the Trinovantes," p. 23). See Clark, "Trinovantum,"139, and Wright, "Did Gildas read Orosius?" *Cambridge Medieval Celtic Studies* 9 (1985): 31–42.

90   H. R. Loyn, *Anglo-Saxon England and the Norman Conquest* (New York: St. Martin's Press, 1962), 2nd ed. 1991, 90 and n. 39.

60   CHAPTER 1

of Ireland, Wales, and Scotland.[91] By depicting Brutus leading the Trojans out of slavery – especially at the hands of the highly civilized Greeks – Geoffrey raises Brutus's stature, and by extension, that of the Trojans/Britons, by rejecting slavery and the societies that practiced it, exonerating the Celtic peoples and further demonstrating a cultural superiority beyond that of the Greeks and Romans.[92]

En route to Aquitaine, Brutus and his followers come upon four generations of settlers descended from the Trojan exiles who had accompanied Antenor when he had fled Troy. Eventually, they take all these descendants and their leader Corineus to Albion. First however they must defeat the Gauls – the ancestors of the French who serve occasionally in the *HRB* as an allusion to the courtly neighbors of the Normans but more frequently as the traditional enemy of the Britons (and the English) – and set sail for the "promised isle," fulfilling the prophecy of the goddess Diana. The prophecy, which Brutus fails to distinguish as either a dream or the actual voice of the goddess (§17.313–15), functions in part as evidence of the importance of prophecy in the *HRB*, presaging Merlin's book in the center of the text, but it also highlights the importance of both Brutus and the Trojans who are seen as destined to occupy the island, as it is now empty and waiting for them, according to the divine voice.

After chasing the few remaining giants out of Albion and into the surrounding mountains, Corineus defeats Gogmagog, the last and most formidable of the giants. Jeffrey Cohen comments that "the first Trojan encounter with

---

91   Gillingham writes: "In England disputes over succession to high office, or succession to great estates, certainly involved violence, but it was violence which was controlled so as to spare the lives of the royals and aristocrats who engaged in it. Compared with Celtic politics the so-called 'anarchy of Stephen's reign' was a very 'gentlemanly' affair. What all this suggests is that the conventions of chivalry were appropriate to a certain stage of socio-economic development, one which England had reached by the twelfth century, but which Celtic countries had not" ("Conquering the Barbarians," 55).

92   Although Geoffrey disassociates the Britons from slavery, in part to counteract growing prejudices against British peoples but also to show approval of the Norman rulers by participating in the growing acceptance of clemency in warfare thought to have been introduced into England by William the Conqueror, he did not eschew other forms of violence or atrocities perpetrated by the Britons, using descriptions of great carnage to demonstrate their valor (as in e.g., the battle against the Aquitanians, §18. 339–88). Geoffrey associates the taking of slaves with the Gauls, putting a speech into the mouth of Aquitanian King Goffarius Pictus: "Oh cruel destiny! These dishonoured exiles have even made a camp in my kingdom. To arms, men, to arms, close your ranks and advance. We shall soon capture these effeminates as if they were sheep, and make them slaves in our country" (§20.406–9; "Proh fatum triste! Castra etiam sua in regno meo fecerunt ignobiles exules. Armate uos, uiri, armate et per densatas turmas incedite. Nulla mora erit quin semimares istos uelut oues capiemus atque captos per regna nostra mancipabimus").

HISTORIA REGUM BRITANNIAE: PART 1

the aboriginal giants has a clear biblical subtext. The spies sent by Moses to search Canaan discover dwelling there a race called the Anakim, towering giants in whose sight the invading Israelites say they seemed like small insects (Num. 13:33–34) ... Envisioning the anterior culture as monsters justifies its displacement by making the act heroic." Cohen further observes that "the irony, of course, is that the Celtic ('British') peoples whose history Geoffrey is writing stand exactly in this aboriginal position to the Anglo-Saxons who 'settle' the island – that is, in the preconquest account of English history, the Celts occupy the place of the Galfridian giants, the invading Germanic tribes that of the glorified British."[93]

Geoffrey's narrative of the founding of Trinovantum or Troia Nova is rather spare, certainly when compared with Wace's.[94] Geoffrey relates that Brutus founded the city within a few years of his arrival in Albion, that is, well before the arrival of the Romans. He adds a "simultaneous" chronology directly following the narrative of the founding of the city, to the effect that this occurred during the time "the priest Eli was ruling in Judea and the Ark of the Covenant was captured by the Philistines" (§22.505–7). "Nennius" provides a similar chronology, except that the latter does not specify "by the Philistines" but merely gives "by the foreigners" (*ab alienigenis*) (*HB*, ch. 11, pp. 20, 61); more importantly, though, "Nennius" does not mention Trinovantum but provides the chronological reference for the general time frame of the Britons' arrival in Albion. Thus Geoffrey gives the impression of more precision and drives home the point that the city which was to become London dates from a period significantly preceding the era described by Julius Caesar. In addition, as if to bolster the biblical reference, Geoffrey adds, that "the sons of Hector were ruling at Troy after the descendants of Antenor were exiled. In Italy there ruled the third of the Latins, Silvius Aeneas, the son of Aeneas and the uncle of Brutus" (§22.508–9). In this way, Geoffrey interweaves the illustrious beginnings of British history with both biblical history and Roman history, as one of his attempts to place the history of the Britons in a universal, international framework.[95]

---

93 *Of Giants: Sex, Monsters, and the Middle Ages*, Medieval Cultures 17 (Minneapolis: University of Minnesota Press, 1999), 34–35. See the chapter on Wace for that author's variation on the giants' "removal" from Albion.

94 For Wace's version, see below, Chapter 5.

95 For a different reading of the Troy legend in opposition to biblical tradition, an opposition which may have informed Geoffrey's use of Troy's descendants, see Francis Ingledew who comments that "Troy emerges as a concept expressing a new historical consciousness, intimately associated with an aristocratic and lay cultural environment and at odds with the biblically oriented Augustinian-Orosian paradigm, which instead of claiming birth in

62   CHAPTER 1

3   *Adventus Saxonum* and the Passage of Dominion

3.1   *Geoffrey's Predecessors*

As succinctly put by Martin Grimmer: "The nature of the arrival of the
Anglo-Saxons in Britain *c.*450–660, and the survival of the incumbent Romano-
British population, has long been an emotive topic. Traditional views represented the coming of the Anglo-Saxons as an invasion of entire tribes with large
and aggressive warbands, and used vivid imagery of the Anglo-Saxons 'storming
the earthwork camps ... slaughtering and driving away the Romanised Britons,'
and the Romano-Britons being 'as nearly extirpated as a nation can be'."[96] Up
until the last fifty years or so, archaeologists as well as historians had traditionally taken as the unquestioned starting point of their investigations the general
overview provided by four sources: two British sources, Gildas and "Nennius"
and two early English sources, Bede and the Anglo-Saxon Chronicle.[97] Each of
these early sources presents what Donald White has dubbed the "catastrophic
invasion theory," though each (medieval) writer or redactor has a different
approach and perspective (to which we will return shortly).

    Within the last twenty to thirty years or so, there has been movement toward
an evaluation (or reevaluation) of material evidence – both archaeological and
genetic – which has led to the "minimalist" hypothesis that the arrival of the
Saxons and the ensuing cultural change was due to a settlement of a military
and governing elite; that is, that the Germanicization of Britain was due to the
resultant acculturation of the local population to the Germanic elite, as well as
to independent developments among the original populations.[98] The hypothesis of the "migrationists" who have envisaged large-scale migration, and in

---

Troy, confessed birth in the Fall" ("The Book of Troy," 666). See also Nicholas Birns, "The
Trojan Myth: Postmodern Reverberations," *Exemplaria* 5 (1993): 45–78.

96   G. M. Trevelyan, *History of England* (London, 1926), 28–29 and E. Freeman, *Four Oxford
Lectures: Teutonic Conquest in Gaul and Britain* (London, 1888), 74, as quoted by Grimmer
in "Invasion, settlement or political conquest: changing representations of the arrival of
the Anglo-Saxons in Britain," *Journal of the Australian Early Medieval Association* 3 (2007):
169–186, cited at 169.

97   There are two Continental sources, two Gallic chronicles, though the latter are less frequently known or referenced. See Stephen Muhlberger, "The Gallic Chronicle of 452 and
its Authority for British Events," *Britannia*, 14 (1983): 23–33 and Michael E. Jones and
John Casey, "The Gallic Chronicle Restored: A Chronology for the Anglo-Saxon Invasions
and the End of Roman Britain," *Britannia* 19 (1988): 367–98, also Ian Wood, "The End
of Roman Britain: Continental Evidence and Parallels," in *Gildas: New Approaches*, ed.
M. Lapidge and D. Dumville, Studies in Celtic History 5 (Woodbridge, Suffolk: Boydell
Press, 1984), 1–25.

98   On the "elite dominance" view, see particularly C. J. Arnold, *An Archaeology of the
Early Anglo-Saxon Kingdoms* (London: Routledge, 1988), R. Hodges, *The Anglo-Saxon*

HISTORIA REGUM BRITANNIAE: PART 1 63

the extreme, population replacement – a view promoted by the medieval narratives – has lost favor somewhat but as with any vigorous debate, there are adherents to theories that represent a variety of views between the two poles.[99]

It is beyond the scope of this study to even try to do justice to the myriad complexities of this debate, nor can we resolve the problem by reconciling the two opposing paradigms, if that were even possible. It is important to recognize, though, that each reading of the evidence with regard to both dating and manner of settlement or conquest – whether narrative, archaeological, or genetic – may understandably be informed to an extent by the writer's (both medieval and modern) political perspectives and ethnic attachments.[100] Realizing that

---

Achievement (London: Duckworth, 1989) and Nicholas Higham, *Rome, Britain and the Anglo-Saxons* (London: Seaby, 1992).

99 For the contemporary debate among historians, archeologists, anthropologists and biologists seeking to define the actual nature of the *adventus Saxonum* and its effects upon the native populations, in addition to scholars mentioned above, see also Kevin M. Martin, "The 'aduentus Saxonum,'" *Latomus*, 33 (1974): 608–39; John E. Pattison, "Integration versus apartheid in post-Roman Britain: A response to Thomas et al (2008)," *Human Biology*, 83 (2011): 715–33; Bryan Ward-Perkins, "Why did the Anglo-Saxons not become more British?"; and Helena Hamerow, "Migration Theory and the Anglo-Saxon 'Identity Crisis,'" in *Migrations and Invasions in Archaeological Explanation*, ed. John Chapman and H. Hamerow, *British Archaeological Reports* Series 664 (1997), 33–44. In her cogent survey of recent archaeological work in this area, Hamerow rightly states that it would be best to take an interdisciplinary approach: the "documentary and linguistic evidence should ideally be given parity with the archaeological record" (p. 33). See also Alex Woolf's survey of scholarship on the settlement issue; he argues for the possibility of a system which could be seen as parallel to that of apartheid, positing a "long drawn-out process of economic decline" for the Britons wherein "many individual Britons may have found themselves drifting into Anglo-Saxon households, as slaves, hangers-on, brides and so forth" having minimal impact on "the cultural or linguistic identity of the community" but "the biological contribution of this steady trickle of Britons into English households would have been enormous over several generations"; Woolf concludes that "such a model allows us to escape the problems of both the genocide and the elite emulation models and complies with all the constraints left us by the evidence, archaeological, linguistic and textual" ("Apartheid and Economics in Anglo-Saxon England," in *Britons in Anglo-Saxon England*, 115–29, cited at 129 (a system analogous to that of apartheid perhaps first suggested by Higham in *Rome, Britain, and the Anglo-Saxons*, 193). See also Donald A. White who wisely cautions circumspection regarding the effects of national and cultural chauvinism and contemporary socio-political trends on the study of the *adventus Saxonum*, "Changing Views of the *Adventus Saxonum* in Nineteenth and Twentieth Century English Scholarship," *Journal of the History of Ideas*, 32 (1971): 585–94.

100 In addition, as with any group or period, it is necessary to keep in mind that the idea of an "Anglo-Saxon" – i.e., English, pre-Conquest – identity or culture is not monolithic, although it is often referred to as if it were. Catherine Karkov and Nicholas Howe remind us that "one of the remarkable developments in the field [of Anglo-Saxon studies]

64   CHAPTER 1

complete impartiality is impossible, the immediate goal here is not to uncover
the "historical truth" about the *adventus Saxonum* – or the start of the Saxon
period or the Germanicization of Britain, as the coming of the Saxons was not
an event but a process – but to discover where Geoffrey of Monmouth falls on
the continuum of narrative sources, and evaluate his contribution to the narrative "evidence" as well as the contributions of those who used his material,
including the Variant Version redactors, Wace, Laȝamon, and the anonymous
French verse chroniclers, and contemporaries who took different approaches,
most notably William of Malmesbury and Henry of Huntingdon. Although
modern scholars debate the principle that the migrations were a long and
complex process, extending over many years before and after the mid-fifth
century (approximately the time of the arrival of the celebrated Hengist and
Horsa), most medieval writers sought to assign the initial arrival to specific figures within a fairly limited time frame – although as discussed below, Geoffrey
of Monmouth breaks the mold in the area of dating, as in many others.[101]

3.1.1   Gildas

Although largely a diatribe against the rulers and churchmen of his day,
Gildas's *De Excidio et Conquestu Britanniae* (or just the *De Excidio Britanniae*)

---

over the last twenty years or so is the growing awareness that there are many different
Anglo-Saxon Englands to be studied and, correspondingly, that there are no master
narratives or paradigms that can account for all of them with equal success ... Without
denying necessary filiations of history, religion, language and geography, these new
visions of Anglo-Saxon England are notable for their greater alertness to the presence
of differences in local conditions, chronological periods, and cultural circumstances ...
these new approaches have also reinterpreted or reconceptualized some very familiar
aspects of Anglo-Saxon England, such as conversion and colonization" (*Conversion and
Colonization in Anglo-Saxon England*, "Introduction," xi–xx, cited here at xi.) On the question of changing definitions and how they may reflect fluid – or not so fluid – cultural and
political identities, see esp. Susan Reynolds, "What Do We Mean by 'Anglo-Saxon' and
'Anglo-Saxons'?" *Journal of British Studies* 24 (1985): 395–414.

101   For example, even though recent archaeological evidence would appear to suggest that
by 410 AD (the departure of the Romans) there were already communities of Germanic-
speaking settlers established around the Roman towns of East Anglia and Lindsey (Myres,
Anglo-Saxon Pottery and the Settlement of England, Oxford, 1969, esp. pp. 62–83, and Vera
Evison, "Distribution maps and England in the first two phases," in *Angles, Saxons, and
Jutes. Essays presented to J. N. L. Myres*, ed. V. I. Evison, Oxford, 1981, pp. 126–67), even
this early Germanic material has recently been interpreted in a way more consistent
with the traditional mid-fifth century dating (John Hines, "Philology, Archaeology and
the *Adventus Saxonum vel Anglorum*," in *Britain 400–600: Language and History*, ed.
Alfred Bammesberger and Alfred Wollmann, Anglistische Forschungen 205, Carl Winter:
Heidelberg, 1990, 17–36). See John T. Koch, ed. *Celtic Culture: An Historical Encyclopedia*, 1,
58–61.

(*c.*540), is often considered the earliest substantial source for fifth- and early sixth-century Britain written by a near contemporary.[102] This work has had broad influence on both writers of history and legendary history for many reasons, not the least of which that it was the earliest to associate the figure later to become Arthur (that is, Ambrosius Aurelianus) within this time frame. The *DEB* is divided into three parts: first (following the preface), the history of Britain, including the description, Roman Britain, independent Britain (after the Romans refused to come to the aid of the Britons in 410 AD), the coming of the Saxons and the victory at Badon Hill (*DEB*, 1–26); second, the "complaint" against the kings (*DEB*, 27–65) and the third, the "complaint" against the clergy (*DEB*, 67–110). In brief, on the *adventus Saxonum* – as on other topics in other areas – Gildas paints in broad strokes with relatively few details, attributing the annihilation or exiling of the Britons to their own divisiveness, and finding the Saxon takeover deserved punishment.

The "proud tyrant" ("superbus tyrannus"), first identified by Bede as Vortigern,[103] having invited the Saxons to help him against the "foul hordes of

---

102 David Dumville has dated the Saxon wars to the 490s, Badon to *c.*500, and the composition of the *DEB* to *c.*545 ("The Chronology," 83). Michael Herrn suggests a late fifth-century date for the *DEB* ("Gildas and Early British Monasticism" in *Britain 400–600: Language and History*, ed. Bammesberger and Wolmann, 65–78, esp. p. 78); Nicholas Higham's more radical revision of the dating places the Saxons wars and Badon in the 430s and the writing of the *DEB* between 479 and 484 (*The English Conquest: Gildas and Britain in the Fifth Century*, Manchester University Press, 1994, 137). François Kerlouégan proposes on linguistic grounds late fifth century if not somewhat earlier ("Le Latin du *De Excidio Britanniae* de Gildas" in *Christianity in Britain, 300–700, Papers presented to the Conference on Christianity in Roman and Sub-Roman Britain held at the University of Nottingham 17–20 April 1967*, ed. M. W. Barley and R. P. C. Hanson, Leicester University Press, 1968, 151–76, p. 172–73, and *Le De Excidio Britanniae de Gildas. Les destinées de la culture latine dans l'île de Bretagne au VIᵉ siècle* (Paris: Presses de La Sorbonne, 1987). On the issues involved in the dating of the *DEB* itself as well as Gildas's vague chronology of the major events he describes, see also Patrick Sims-Williams, "The Settlement of England in Bede and the *Chronicle*," *Anglo-Saxon England*, 12, ed. Peter Clemoes (Cambridge: Cambridge University Press, 1983), 1–41, esp. pp. 5–15, David Dumville, "Gildas and Maelgwn: problems of dating," in *Gildas: New Approaches*, 51–60 and idem, "The Chronology of *De Excidio Britanniae*, Book I," in *Gildas: New Approaches*, 61–84, and Thomas O'Sullivan, *The De Excidio of Gildas: Its Authenticity and Date*, Columbia Studies in the Classical Tradition, 7 (Leiden: E. J. Brill, 1978), esp. 158–78.

103 *HE*, i:14, p. 48. The name "Vortigern" is apparently a title meaning "chief lord" (ed., p. 48, n. 2), "perhaps a Latininzation" [of the Welsh "Gwrtheyrn"]. See also H. M. Chadwick, "Vortigern," in ed. Nora K. Chadwick et al, *Studies in Early British History* (Cambridge: Cambridge University Press, 1954), 26–27; *Trioedd Ynys Prydein: The Triads of the Island of Britain*, ed. and trans. Rachel Bromwich (Cardiff: University of Wales Press, 1961, 4th ed. 2014), 386–90; and John H. Ward, "Vortigern and the End of Roman Britain," *Britannia* 3 (1972): 277–89, 277 n. 2.

66   CHAPTER 1

Scots and Picts" in the north ("tetri Scottorum Pictorumque greges," 19:1, p. 95)
opened the floodgates. The "ferocious Saxons (name not to be spoken!), hated
by man and God" were "let into the island like wolves into the fold to beat back
the peoples of the north"; writing of the council of the "proud tyrant," Gildas
says "of their own free will they invited under the same roof a people whom
they feared worse than death even in their absence" (DEB, 23: 1–2, p. 26).[104]
After the withdrawal of the "cruel plunderers" ("crudelissimi praedones," 25:
2, p. 98), the Saxons – not mentioned again by name – are now held back by
Ambrosius's victory at Badon Hill (DEB, 26:1, p. 28). However, "external wars
may have stopped, but not civil ones," with the threat remaining of the Saxons'
future regained strength, due to the irresoluteness and sins of the Britons. As
Patrick Sims-Williams notes, "Gildas was all too successful in presenting a
highly generalized account of the history of Britain from the Saxon devasta-
tions down to his own time" portraying the end of Roman Britain "as a process, not an event," though with an "exclusively moral" rather than specifically
political intent.[105] In terms of this process, Gildas leaves off after the victory of
the Britons at Mount Badon. Although Nicholas Higham argues plausibly that
"Gildas's moral invective in this last chapter of the 'historical' introduction – and
thereafter for the remainder of the work – was conditioned not by the expectation of a Saxon revival following comprehensive defeat at *mons Badonicus*, but
by the reality, and currency of Saxon domination," the text does not explicitly

---

104   For a different interpretation of the "invitation," see K. M. Martin: "Gildas merely states
      that the Saxons were allowed to enter unless he means by the word *intromitterentur* 'they
      were caused to enter' or 'they were sent in'" ("The *aduentus Saxonum*," 615) [DEB, 23.1,
      p. 97]; Winterbottom translates as "should be let into [the island]" (DEB, 23, 1, p. 26). In
      addition, the phrase "primum in orientali parte insulae iubente infausto tyranno terri-
      biles infixit ungues" (23.4, p. 97; "on the orders of the ill-fated tyrant they first of all fixed
      their dreadful claws on the east side of the island," 23.4, p. 26, Winterbottom trans.) is
      ambiguous, meaning possibly that Vortigern ordered the Saxons to arrive, or that once
      they had arrived, he ordered them to settle on the eastern side of the island. See also
      Sims-Williams, "Gildas and the Anglo-Saxons," *Cambridge Medieval Celtic Studies* 6 (1983):
      1–30, p. 20.
105   "Gildas and the Anglo-Saxons," cited at 14, 17, 30. Patrick Sims-Williams provides a use-
      ful (albeit somewhat tongue-in-cheek) gauge of the goals of the DEB: "Like most oral
      tradition, Gildas is concerned not so much with absolute chronology as with relative
      chronology because he is interested in cause and effect, in responsibility, in crime and
      punishment. Some of the questions he answers may well have been asked and answered
      in similar terms before. Why were the Britons conquered by the Romans? Because they
      were cowards. Why did Britain fall to foreign enemies? Because the usurper Maximus
      took away her soldiery. Why did the Romans abandon the Britons? Because they got fed
      up with wasting their time on people who would not help themselves. Why were the
      Walls and the Saxon Shore Forts built? As a last, unsuccessful attempt to help the Britons.
      Why did the Saxons take over? Because of the Britons' foolish invitation" (23–24).

HISTORIA REGUM BRITANNIAE: PART 1   67

mention any establishing of dominant Saxon kingdoms, falling short of that. Rather, Gildas expresses the fear that the Britons will lose control of the island, given the pervasiveness of civil wars among them. Gildas sets the stage for the passage of dominion to the Saxons, but the takeover itself does not play out on Gildas's stage as a "historical" narrative, although there is a prophecy that the Saxons would "reside in/occupy" the land for a further 300 years and for half of that time they would "repeatedly lay [the land] waste," though the starting point of that duration is not clear (*DEB*, 23:3, p. 26).[106]

3.1.2   Bede

As one might expect since Bede was writing at least 200 years after Gildas, his narrative moves the Saxons forward to fuller ascendancy over the central part of the island, an ascendancy which he attributes to God's will, but from an English perspective, that is, with the Saxons serving as the agents of fulfillment of a great destiny for the island (i.e., most likely the first expression of the idea of the "Anglo-Saxon achievement");[107] the Anglo-Saxon Chronicle shares much of Bede's pro-English perspective, not surprisingly.

---

106   On the vagueness of the *DEB*, Sims-Williams notes that "the only periods of time [Gildas] ever mentions are the ten years or more that he had considered before writing (*bilustrum*), the forty-four years that had passed since the siege of *Badonicus mons* and his own birth, and the prophesied 300 years of Saxon conquest" ("The settlement of England in Bede and the *Chronicle*," 14–15). Even the extent or force of the "conquest" referred to here is open to interpretation, however (in fact, Sims-Williams himself refers elsewhere to the "prophesied three hundred years of settlement" ("Gildas and the Anglo-Saxons," 28): Winterbottom translates "certo apud eum praesagio, quo ter centum annis patriam, cui proras librabat, insideret, centum vero quiquaginta, hoc est dimidio temporis, saepius vastaret" (23.4, p. 97) by "[favorable too the omens and auguries, which prophesied], according to a sure portent among them, that they would live for three hundred years in the land towards which their prows were directed, and that for half the time, a hundred and fifty years, they would repeatedly lay it waste" (23.3, p. 26). The key term may be "insideret" which can mean "occupy" both in the sense of "inhabit, live in, settle" and "take possession of, hold." Referring in a different study to the "prophesied three hundred years of settlement," Sims-Williams notes: "Unlike Cadwallon in the early seventh century (as reported by Bede) [*EH* II.20], Gildas does not plan the genocide of the entire English race, though the story of the prophesied three hundred years of settlement perhaps suggests that he may have anticipated its eventual removal" ("Gildas and the Anglo-Saxons," 28). We have no way of knowing whether this was wishful thinking on Gildas's part – the possibility of the "removal" of the Saxons – which might have motivated his reporting of the prophecy.

107   On Bede's English perspective, Nicholas Howe writes, "Blessed with a retrospective vision of events, [Bede] faced no conflict of loyalty between his Germanic ancestry and his Christian faith. For him the defeat of the British Christians stood as a vivid cautionary tale which taught that only the just could possess the island" (*Migration and Mythmaking*

68   CHAPTER 1

Although Bede does not devote much of his narrative to military exploits
of secular figures, he is the first to give the names and a bit of background
for Hengist and Horsa, associating with the invasion legend two brothers who
"owed their names to the cult-image venerated by the warriors of early Kent"
(i.e., names associated with a Germanic horse cult).[108] However, rather than
focusing on military operations, in the *HE*, I, 15, Bede appears to explain the
invasion more in terms of its results than in terms of the process involved in
getting there, that is, as J. E. Turville-Petre puts it, "he gives an ethnographic
analysis based on the political alignments of his day." In a description that was
to become canonical due to the respect given Bede as an historian, he traces
the people of England back to three Continental tribes, the Jutes, Saxons and
Angles, defining the areas occupied by their descendants.[109] Although the

---

  in Anglo-Saxon England, New Haven, Yale University Press, 1989; 2nd ed. South Bend, IN,
  University of Notre Dame Press, 2001, 52).

108 On the various mythic associations of the Hengist and Horsa figures and their incorpo-
     ration into narratives including those of Gildas, Bede, the *Historia Brittonum* and the
     Anglo-Saxon Chronicle, see J. E. Turville-Petre, "Hengest and Horsa," 286. Turville-Petre
     concludes that, "the theme of the *adventus Saxonum* is presented in personal terms, by
     investing religious symbols with a foundation-legend. The cult of these equine deities had
     been fostered by the heathen priests of Kent. Religious practices withered, but genealo-
     gists had a use for the invasion-heroes, who were finally ranged among the forbears link-
     ing the Christian kings of Kent with Germanic antiquity" (p. 289).

109 Turville-Petre, "Hengest and Horsa," p. 273. Later in the context of the peoples to whom
     the monk Ecberht sought to preach the gospel, Bede provides what might be construed as
     alternate account of the Germanic peoples from whom the Angles and Saxons descended:
     "Quarum in Germania plurimas nouerat esse nationes, a quibus Angli uel Saxones, qui nunc
     Brittaniam incolunt, genus et originem duxisse noscuntur; unde hactenus a uicina gente
     Brettonum corrupte Garmani nuncupantur. Sunt autem Fresones, Rugini, Danai, Hunni,
     Antiqui Saxones, Boructuari" ("He knew that there were very many peoples in Germany
     from whom the Angles and the Saxons, who now live in Britain, derive their origin; hence
     even to this day they are by a corruption called *Garmani* by their neighbors the Britons.
     Now these people are the Frisians, Rugians, Danes, Huns, Old Saxons, and *Boruhtware*
     (Bructeri)," v. 9, pp. 476, 477). Although this list is not necessarily accurate, Ian Wood notes
     that "its basic tenor is closer to the evidence of the archaeology of the early Anglo-Saxon
     inhumation cemeteries than is that of the simple story of the three boatloads of Angles,
     Saxons and Jutes" ("Before and After the Migration to Britain," in *The Anglo-Saxons from
     the Migration Period to the Eighth Century: An Ethnographic Perspective*, ed. John Hines,
     Studies in Historical Archaeoethnology 2 (Woodbridge: Boydell, 1997), 41–54, cited at 41).
     Bede's more simplistic model may have been more palatable to his contemporary audi-
     ence, and certainly to later generations of historians – to judge by the number of texts
     which repeat Bede's formula (including the highly reputable William of Malmesbury) –
     where the diversity of Continental origins and also the influence of native peoples
     tended to be neglected. On Bede's more simplistic model – and his popularizing of
     the term *gens Anglorum* – referring not to the Angles specifically but to the Germanic
     settlers collectively, having "adopted what Pope Gregory had created on the basis of a

HISTORIA REGUM BRITANNIAE: PART 1 69

Germanic invasion had to be told to a certain extent in order to demonstrate the establishment of the Germanic settlers in England prior to the conversion in 597,[110] which was the main interest in the early narrative of the *HE*,[111]

misunderstanding" – see Michael Richter, "Bede's *Angli*: Angles or English?" (*Peritia* 3, 1984: 99–114, cited at p. 113). See also Margaret Lamont who suggests that in Laȝamon, "the term 'Ænglisc' ... is part of a larger move in English historiography more generally, in which 'English' becomes a broader, more inclusive term than either 'Saxon' or 'Briton' before it. As far back as Bede's *Historia Ecclesiastica gentis Anglorum*, the Angles, Saxons, and Jutes merge to become the English people" ("When are Saxons 'Ænglisc'? Language and Readerly Identity in Laȝamon's *Brut*," in *Reading Laȝamon's Brut: Approaches and Explorations*, ed. Rosamund Allen, Jane Roberts, and Carole Weinberg (Amsterdam – New York: Rodopi, 2013; *DQR Studies in Literature* 52.1), 295–319, cited at p. 315). We remember though that neither Geoffrey nor Wace fail to distinguish between the Saxons and the Britons.

110 In interpreting 597 as the year traditionally given, following Bede, for the arrival of the mission of St. Augustine in Canterbury to convert the "pagan English," Nicholas Brooks asks, "have we too readily accepted Bede's concept of a separate English ethnic identity and his reluctance to recognize the contribution of British Christians to English Christianity?" He argues that the evidence that "the Christian faith had of course already reached Britain at least four centuries before that date and could indeed claim to have been an established religion for more than 280 years by that time" begs for a reevaluation of the influence of Bede's attitudes toward British Christianity upon his narrative of the conversion in the *Historia Ecclesiastica* ("From British to English Christianity: Deconstructing Bede's Interpretation of the Conversion" in *Conversion and Colonization in Anglo-Saxon England*, 1–30, cited here at 1). Brooks writes elsewhere, "In imagining that English church history began with the Roman mission at Canterbury in 597, they were assisting, indeed encouraging, British cultural amnesia. Bede's account involved both the creation of a national English myth and the necessary amnesia concerning the glories of the British (and Romano-British) Christian past. The church of Canterbury, it would seem, effectively colluded with Rome, and later with Bede, to create a new history for a new English people" ("Canterbury, Rome and the Construction of English Identity," in *Early Medieval Rome and the Christian West: Essays in Honor of Donald A. Bullough*, ed. Julia M. H. Smith (Leiden: Brill, 2000), 221–46, cited at p. 246). On the vast subject of Augustine's conversion of the English, see especially S. D. Church, "Paganism in Conversion-Age Anglo-Saxon England: the Evidence of Bede's *Ecclesiastical History* Reconsidered," *History* 93.2 (310) (2008): 162–80; Ian Wood, "The Mission of Augustine of Canterbury to the English," *Speculum* 69.1 (1994): 1–17; and Nicholas J. Higham, "From Tribal Chieftains to Christian Kings," in idem and Martin J. Ryan, *The Anglo-Saxon World* (New Haven, CT and London: Yale University Press, 2013), 126–78, and also below Chapter 2, nn. 33 and 112, Chapter 3, n. 115, and Chapter 5.

111 As Brooks points out with respect to Bede's narrative of the conversion (which itself needed to bolster English claims to land and hegemony), although Bede's primary subject matter was the ecclesiastical history of the English, he devotes seventeen chapters of Book I to Christianity in Roman Britain (*HE* 1.4–21). Brooks expresses the opinion that "most of these chapters, have, I suspect, been seldom read by modern scholars, since Bede was here conflating known written sources and is not himself a primary authority" and that these chapters "have much to tell us of Bede's own purposes. He needed to explain to

70   CHAPTER 1

according to Richard Sowerby "Bede demonstrates either little knowledge of or little interest in the stories of the invasion which the author of *Historia Brittonum* would come to use for the centerpiece of his work."[112]

It is also possible that Bede was skeptical about the Hengist and Horsa material, hence his use of the phrase "are said" ("perhibentur") – "their first leaders *are said* to have been two brothers" – while at the same time including a Kentish origin myth, tracing the leaders of Kent back to Hengist and Horsa, and the latter back to the god, Woden.[113] Whether Bede was skeptical or not, Book I, chapter 15 is quite short; the third and last paragraph which recounts how the island became so crowded with these peoples that they "became a source of terror to the natives who had called them in" (i. 15, p. 53; "Non mora ergo, confluentibus certatim in insulam gentium memoratarum cateruis, grandescere populus coepit aduenarum, ita ut ipsis quoque qui eos aduocauerant indigenis essent terrori," i. 15, p. 52). In this same passage, derived from Gildas, Bede describes how the foreigners ravaged the land such that "the fire kindled by the hands of the heathen executed the just vengeance of God on the nation for its crimes" (i.15, p. 53).

Chapter 16 which is even shorter recounts how the Britons "regained their strength, challenged their victors to battle, and, with God's help, won the day" under the leadership of "Ambrosius Aurelianus ... the sole member of the Roman race who had survived this storm in which his parents, who bore a royal

---

his English readers that the Britons had been Christian before the Anglo-Saxons, and his account was necessarily sensitive"; among other things "it had to avoid lending credence to British claims to rule areas that had since passed to Anglo-Saxon control" and placed the emphasis "on the one hand, on Roman imperial and papal authority as the source of legitimacy, and on the other on British sinfulness and heresy" ("From British to English Christianity," 6).

112   Richard Sowerby, "Hengest and Horsa: the manipulation of history and myth from the *adventus Saxonum* to *Historia Brittonum*," *Nottingham Medieval Studies*, 51 (2007): 1–19, cited at 4. Bede is the first to name Hengist and Horsa and associate them with Kent (F. M. Stenton, *Anglo-Saxon England*, Oxford University Press, 1943, 1947; 3rd ed. 1971, 16–17).

113   Sowerby, "Hengest and Horsa," 13. For a slightly different interpretation of Bede's use of this genealogy, see also Sims-Williams: 'This genealogy back to Woden (the only one Bede actually quotes) looks like an attempt to link the royal lines of Kent and Wight via a fictitious common ancestor, *Uecta*, who is obviously an eponym of the Isle of Wight,' ("The settlement of England," 23). Turville-Petre notes that there are actually two "invasion-formulas" in Bede, the first in *HE*, I, 15 where Hengist arrives with his brother Horsa, and the second in *HE*, II, 5 where Hengist arrives with his son Oisc; the latter version may have been favored in Kent as it is a dynastic legend, connecting King Æthelberht's lineage back to Hengist (who had himself been traced back to Woden, *HE*, I, 15) ("Hengest and Horsa," 287).

HISTORIA REGUM BRITANNIAE: PART 1

and famous name, had perished" (i.16, p. 55). In Bede, Aurelius Ambrosius is a Roman, as he is in Gildas though Gildas writes "perhaps alone of the Romans" ("qui solus forte Romanae gentis") with less surety than Bede (*DEB*, i.25, 3). Nonetheless, the implications are that the Britons needed a leader more closely associated with the Romans than with the native peoples to bring them out of their misery.[114]

Soon following the narrative of the battle of Mount Badon, Bede's emphasis shifts from the Britons to the Pelagian heresy (i. 17–19), including Germanus's visit *c*.429. He does note that the Britons, being Christians, wanted no part of the heresy, but unable to stamp it out themselves, they turned to Gaulish bishops for aid (i. 17, p. 55). By Book I, chapter 22, Bede again echoes Gildas on the brief hiatus of foreign threats: "Britain had rest for a time from foreign though not from civil wars" (i.22, p. 67). In virtually the same breath, though, after acknowledging Gildas, he mentions the worst of the Britons' crimes, from which point he turns from the Britons, never to write of them again as a subject of his narrative: "To other unspeakable crimes, which Gildas their own historian describes in doleful words, was added this crime, that they never preached the faith to the Saxons or Angles who inhabited Britain with them. Nevertheless God in His goodness did not reject the people whom He foreknew [the Angles and the Saxons], but He had appointed much worthier heralds of the truth to bring this people to the faith" (i. 22, p. 69).[115] Leckie proposes that the way Bede handles the period following Mount Badon – moving from the battle backward in time to Germanus's handling of the Pelagian heresy and then shifting the focus forward to the history of insular Christianity – "offers an instructive example of how writers came to discount the Britons as a significant factor in the struggle for control of the island."[116]

---

114 Whether this figure was intended to be Romano-British, that is, an assimilated native Briton as there must have been especially toward the end of the Roman occupation and onward, there is no possibility of knowing.

115 "Qui inter alia inenarrabilium scelerum facta, quae historicus eorum Gildas flebili sermone describit, et hoc addebant, ut numquam genti Saxonum siue Anglorum, secum Brittaniam incolenti, uerbum fidei praedicando committerent. Sed non tamen diuina pietas plebem suam, quam praesciuit, deseruit; qui multo digniores genti memoratae praecones ueritatis, per quos crederet, destinauit" (i.22, p. 68).

116 *Passage of Dominion*, p. 13. Whether one agrees with this more neutral view of Bede's attitudes toward the Britons – rather than "lacking in antipathy" toward the Britons on the one hand or "anglophilic" on the other – it would appear at the very least that Bede was not particularly interested in the Britons' part of the equation in the evolution of Britain.

3.1.3 Historia Brittonum

Whereas Bede had followed Gildas in reporting the original three keels that arrived with Hengist and Horsa, though without the omens, divinations, and prophecy that Gildas associates with the invasion, the *Historia Brittonum* elaborates significantly with respect to these two previous texts, adding many elements. Among the most notable additions or changes are 1) that the brothers came as exiles – that is, uninvited; 2) the slaughter of three hundred of Vortigern's closest associates at the peace banquet ("the night of the long knives"); and 3) the four battles fought between Vortimer's forces and Hengist's.[117]

In broad outline, in the *Historia Brittonum*, the story of Hengist (also Hengest) and Horsa proceeds as follows:

> Ch. 31: Hengist and Horsa arrive as exiles, (uninvited); Vortigern welcomes them, handing over the island called "in their language" Thanet and in "British" Ruoihm;[118] this transpired during Gratian's second rule with Equitius, 347 years following the passion of Christ;
>
> Ch. 36: The Saxons agree to fight on behalf of the Britons against Vortigern's enemies (Picts, Irish, and Romans) in exchange for supplies of food and clothing but when the Britons can no longer provide supplies and invite them to leave, the Saxons rebel and fight their hosts;
>
> Ch. 37: Hengist summons reinforcements from his homeland with Vortigern's consent; sixteen ships arrive, one carrying Hengist's daughter, whom Vortigern begs to marry;
>
> Ch. 38: Hengist advises Vortigern to invite his son and cousin to fight against the Scots and to give them the northern regions next to the Wall; Octha and Ebissa arrive with 40 keels; more and more forces come until they take the city of the men of Kent;
>
> Ch. 43: Vortigern's son, Vortimer, fights with Hengist and Horsa, expelling them back to Thanet, from where they summon further reinforcements;

---

117   Christopher H. Flack argues that *HB*'s stating Hengist and Horsa arrived as exiles, without an invitation from Vortigern, to a certain extent "minimizes the leader's responsibility ... and transforms his motivation for seeking external aid into very human and sensible terms," while at the same time implicating the Britons more deeply in their own demise ("Writing Conquest: Traditions of Anglo-Saxon Invasion and Resistance in the Twelfth Century," unpublished doctoral thesis, University of Minnesota, Sept. 2013, p. 39, http://hdl.handle.net/11299/159710).

118   The isle of Thanet, at the most easterly point of Kent, was once separated from the mainland by the Wantsum Channel, which has since silted over (last recorded passage of a ship through the channel in 1672); today it is no longer an island.

HISTORIA REGUM BRITANNIAE: PART 1

Ch. 44: Vortimer fights four successful battles and the barbarians flee; Horsa dies in the second battle as does another of Vortigern's sons, Cateyrn; Vortimer dies soon after (but not poisoned by his stepmother, Ronwen, as in the *HRB* (§102));

Ch. 45: The barbarians return soon after through the ministrations of Vortigern and his wife, Hengist's daughter; Hengist arranges for the Britons to meet the Saxons unarmed to secure peace;

Ch. 46: Hengist commands his men to draw their daggers, "*saexas*," and slaughter Vortigern's 300 men; to redeem his own life, Vortigern cedes Essex, Sussex and Middlesex to the East Saxons, South Saxons, and Middle Saxons respectively;

Ch. 56: The numbers of Saxons in Britain continue to grow; on Hengist's death, his son Octha comes from the north to Kent, and from him are descended the kings of Kent; Arthur fights twelve successful battles against them; the defeated Saxons seek help from Germany and considerable numbers continue to arrive, bringing their kings from Germany to rule them in Britain.

In this review of contents, several elements stand out: first, that Hengist and Horsa were the first Saxons to arrive, coming uninvited, as exiles, who agreed at first to serve as mercenaries for Vortigern, but then who later rebelled against the leader of *Britannia*;[119] second, that there was a continuous and steady stream of reinforcements from Germanic regions, which supports the dominant medieval view that the Saxons were not few in numbers when they took over Britain; third, that Hengist is a major symbol of Saxon treachery in this pro-Briton text; fourth, the mention of Arthur, who fought alongside the Briton kings as their war leader, here specifically against the Kentish descendants of Hengist and his son, Octha ("Arthur pugnabat contra illos in illis diebus cum regibus Brittonum, sed ipse dux erat bellorum," ch. 56, p. 76); and fifth, Arthur's twelve battles, which is the first time these battles are found in writing.

---

119 In keeping with his belief that there was substantial Germanic settlement in Britain as early as the fourth century, that is, toward the end of the Roman occupation (*c.*360) but certainly before the end (410), J. N. L. Myres argues that the Hengist and Horsa figures with which Gwrethyrn (Vortigern) is associated should be viewed not literally as the first Saxons but more plausibly as the first significant arrivals who led to the establishment of the English dynasties: "In the story of Hengist and his Jutish or Frisian followers, we are dealing, not with the firsts occurrence in Britain of the familiar Roman practice of controlled barbarian settlement, but with the last" (*Anglo-Saxon Pottery and the Settlement of England*, p. 97).

74 CHAPTER 1

It is generally accepted that the myth of Hengist and Horsa was of Germanic origin, which makes the adaptation contained in the *Historia Brittonum* – possibly written for a Welsh audience at the court of Merfyn Frych (826–44), king of Gwynedd, serving to strengthen Welsh national identity[120] – all the more intriguing. Nicholas Brooks proposes that in addition to the characterization of the Saxons as treacherous ("friendly in word, but wolfish in intent and deed," ch. 46) and "barbarians" (chs. 44, 45) (though the latter term can be used generically to refer to non-Christians), the lumping together of the various Germanic peoples under the name *Saxones* which is characteristic of Welsh and Irish sources, elements of a "Welsh overlay" include the fact that the Saxons do not appear to win any of their newly gained British lands by conquest, that is, through valor, but through Vortigern's mistakes and his own treachery against the Britons: lands are handed over in chs. 31 and 38, through agreements to fight Vortigern's enemies; in ch. 37, as result of the marriage settlement with Hengist's daughter; and ch. 46, in order to ransom Vortigern following the slaughter of his high-ranking comrades at the peace banquet.[121] Brooks concludes

> the fact that *c.*46 of the *Historia* ends with Vortigern's cession of Essex and Sussex (and in some versions Middlesex) to Hengist confirms that this is a Saxon tale, whose function is indeed to justify the rule of the Saxon peoples of south-east England by Hengist's descendants. The account of Hengist's entry into Canterbury (*c.*38) and the four Kentish battles that underly both the *Historia*'s account of Vortemir's [Vortimer's] campaign and the Chronicle's account of Hengist and Æsc's victories may likewise have served as 'charter-myths,' justifying the dynasty's control of both the eastern Jutish half and the western Saxon half of Kent.[122]

In the *Historia Brittonum*, that the Saxons take over "by the will of God" and not through their own strength or merits – "quia non de virtute sua Brittanniam occupaverunt, sed de nutu Dei" (ch. 45, p. 72) – can be seen to both condemn the Britons and create sympathy for them, and undercut or support the Saxons

---

120   Nicholas Brooks, "The English Origin Myth" in *Anglo-Saxon Myths: State and Church 400–1066* (London: Hambledon Press, 2000), 79–90 at p. 84. The Harleian recension, thought to be a version "very close" to original, contains a reference to the fourth year of the reign of King Merfyn of Gwynedd (Dumville, "*Historia Brittonum*: an Insular History from the Carolingian Age," 406 and idem "The Historical Value," 5).

121   Described in the *HB* for the first time but labeled elsewhere as either the "treachery of the long knives" or the "night of the long knives"; see n. 125 below. Brooks, "English Origin Myth," 83.

122   Brooks, "English Origin Myth," 87.

HISTORIA REGUM BRITANNIAE: PART 1   75

through faint praise and fatalism: the Britons are condemned for their divisiveness which led to this situation, and yet pitied for being robbed of their homelands and chased away; the Saxons are unworthy but triumphant, at least in this context. In a way, this ambiguous stance leaves the road wide open to both the Welsh historiographic and prophetic traditions hoping for a British revival as well as to the partisans of the Saxons, who could view this "will of God" as a positive judgment upon the Saxon occupiers.

3.2 Geoffrey's Contemporaries: William of Malmesbury and Henry of Huntingdon

3.2.1 William of Malmesbury: Gesta Regum

Although William took Bede as his model, in the case of the opening of the *Gesta Regum Anglorum*, he dispensed with the description of Britain as well as with the foundation story of the Britons, and begins "with a concise first book on the history of the English from their conquest of Britain to the reign of Ecgberht, who, after various strokes of fortune had dismissed the lesser kings, made himself the sole ruler of almost the whole island" (GRA, I, Prologue, p. 15).[123]

A picture of the Saxons, which couldn't be further from Gildas's, is that of William of Malmesbury who writes with reference to Vortigern's initial invitation:

> To cut a long story short, it was unanimously decided to summon from Germany the Angles and Saxons, who were warlike nomads and thus offered a twofold advantage: being invincible in battle they would easily drive out the enemy, and having hitherto no local attachment, they would reckon it a rich reward if they were given as their dwelling-place even rough ground or barren moorland; *in any case, the memory of such kindness would soften their native ferocity of manners, and they would never raise a finger against the fatherland* [our emphasis]. (GRA, i.4.2, p. 21)

> [Itaque, ut ad summam redigam, placuit omnibus Anglos et Saxones e Germania euocandos, armis ualidos, sedibus uagos: geminum futurum commodum, ut armis inuicti facile hostes propulsarent, et hactenus

---

123   "Procedat iaque primus libellus de Anglorum gestis succinctus, ex quo Brittaniam occupauere usque ad regem Egbirhtum, qui uaria sorte profligatis regulis insulae pene totius nactus est monarchiam" (1, Prol., 5–8). William makes isolated comments about the Britons (aside from his comments on Arthurian tales, to be discussed below), such as the following, during the reign of Cenwealh: "The British, brooding over the memories of their former independence and therefore constantly plotting rebellion, he [Cenwealh] twice completely crushed ..." (1.19.2; "Britannos antiquae libertatis conscientiam frementes, et ob hoc crebram rebellionem meditantes, bis omnino protriuit ...").

76   CHAPTER 1

> locorum incerti pro ingenti annumerarent benefitio si uel squalidum
> solum ieiunumque cespitem ad habitandum suscepissent, ceterum num-
> quam eos aliquid contra patriam molituros, quia genuinam feritatem
> morum emolliret memoria benefitiorum.]

The translation "the memory of such kindness" is perhaps overly generous for
"memoria benefitiorum," but it is in keeping with the general tone of generosity
toward the Saxons in this passage, certainly generous relative to Gildas's portrayal. William adopts Bede's most well known formula of the three Germanic
peoples, stating that the Angles, Saxons and Jutes came over from Germany –
"aptly known as Germany because it is the germinating place of such a horde"
(i.6.2, p. 23) – to relieve the motherland of a press of population "lest she suc-
cumb exhausted beneath the effort of feeding such a numerous progeny" (i.6.2,
p. 23). Although they left in principle to avoid the crowding of their homeland, William implies that the Saxons came in small numbers: "It was from this
Germany, then, that there first came to Britain a band of men whose prowess
made up for their scanty numbers" (i.6.3, p. 23), giving the impression that the
conquering force was a military elite. However, the key here is the idea of "at
first" ("primo"), as they may have been followed later by great numbers of settlers, which William does not explicitly state here – in other words, the first
contingent was invited, and those who followed did so to relieve the press of
population. It is important to note that William states that Hengest [Hencgest]
and Horsa were of "distinguished lineage ... great-great-grandsons of the patri-
arch Woden, from whom the royal family in almost all barbarian nations traces
its descent" (i.6.3, p. 23). He adds, though, a note regarding the error the English
made concerning Woden, "whom the English peoples vainly supposed to be a
god" (i.6.3, p. 23).

   From this early point in Book I, William continues to a brief narrative
of Hengest's adventures, how Vortigern gave him Kent in exchange for his
(unnamed) daughter's hand in marriage, how Guorongus and his men sailed
to Northumbria and settled there, the siege of Mount Badon, Arthur's prowess and his protection by the Virgin Mary, and the death of Hengest. Kristen
Fenton notes that William appears to emphasize the role that Vortigern's
unbridled sexuality plays in the conquest, by highlighting the king's desire for
Hengest's daughter but also his lack of control seen in his impregnation of his
own daughter (*GRA*, i.iv, p. 21); the latter detail is also found in the *Historia
Brittonum* (c.39), but not in Gildas, Bede or the Anglo-Saxon Chronicles.[124]

---

124   *Gender, Nation and Conquest in the Works of William of Malmesbury* (Woodbridge, Suffolk:
        Boydell, 2008), 104–6.

HISTORIA REGUM BRITANNIAE: PART 1   77

Two further details found in the *HB*, but not in Gildas or Bede, are important aspects of William's portrayal of the conquest, and can be seen as both unflattering to the Britons – or at least to Vortigern – and to the Saxons as well, but more indirectly: first is the bride-gift of Kent which Vortigern gives to Hengest in order to gain the marriage, and the second is the handing over of three more provinces: during the so-called "night of the long knives," where 300 counselors of Britain were invited to dinner by the Saxons and then slaughtered all except the king, Vortigern who "was taken prisoner, and had to buy himself out of slavery by the surrender of three provinces" (*GRA*, i.8.4, p. 27) (William does not name the provinces);[125] in the *HB*, Vortigern "to save his life ... ceded several districts, namely Essex and Sussex" with a variant reading "together with Middlesex and other districts that they chose and designated" (ch. 46, p. 32). The marriage gift of Kent suggests that the Saxons did not win that very important region – considered the first of the early English kingdoms – through prowess; the remaining regions were won through what was essentially treachery and coercion.

Unlike Gildas and Bede who have Ambrosius Aurelianus as the military commander victorious against the Saxons at Badon Hill[126] or the *Historia*

---

125   Referring to the "treachery of Scone" from a lost Irish tale but outlined by Geraldus Cambrensis to the effect that the "Scots invite Pictish nobles to a feast, trap them in their seats, and kill them," Marjorie O. Anderson suggests that the "night of the long knives" in the *Historia Brittonum* (ch. 46) is actually but one example of a more widespread literary motif: "The theme of an ostensibly unarmed and festive meeting between two ethnic groups at which one treacherously attacks and kills the other is common to the *Historia Brittonum* (English and Britons), the *Res Gestae Saxonicae* of Widukind of Corvey (Saxons and Thuringians), an Irish tale (vassal people and their Irish lords) and farther afield the *Russian Primary Chronicle* (Olga of Kiev and the Derevlians)." Anderson's further comments on the use of this type of story in Scotish/Pictish material are also suggestive as to why some authors may have used the "night of the long knives" episode in their histories of the English/British (e.g., William of Malmesbury and Geoffrey of Monmouth) and why others didn't (e.g., Bede, Henry of Huntingdon and the Anglo-Saxon Chronicles): "We may guess that in the original Scot/Pict story, as in *Historia Brittonum* and Widukind, the meeting was a feast arranged to ratify a pact of friendship already made. The liquidation of an entire nobility at one blow is an economical way of explaining a people's disappearance. It can hardly be doubted that the story of the Treachery was to some extent fictitious. The question is whether an existing fiction served to elaborate something that actually happened, or was adopted as a convenient myth in answer to the question 'what became of the Picts?'" ("Dalraida and the Creation of the Kingdom of the Scots," 116–17).

126   In the *Chronica Maiora*, Bede dates Ambrosius's victory to the reign of the Emperor Zeno (474–91) (Sims-Williams, "The Settlement of England," 18); *Chronica Maiora ad a. DCCXXV*, ed. T. Mommsen, Monumenta Germaniae Historica Auctores Antiquissimi XIII (Berlin: Weidmann, 1898), 223–327, §504; see also Bede, *Chronica Maiora = De Temporum Ratione*

78   CHAPTER 1

Brittonum (which has at least two different Ambrosius figures),[127] William follows Gildas and Bede but then adds Arthur along with Ambrosius at Badon
Hill, the latter as Vortigern's successor and "sole surviving Roman [who] kept
down the barbarian menace with the outstanding aid of warlike Arthur" (i.8.2,
p. 27). William praises Arthur, saying that "he assuredly deserves to be the subject of reliable history rather than of false and dreaming fable; for he was long
the mainstay of his falling country" (i.8.2, p. 27).

About the English (*Angli*), William writes that "although the sport of
Fortune's wheel" they "made good their wavering ranks by reinforcements
of their fellow countrymen ... so, little by little, as the natives retreated, they
spread over the whole island, not without the favouring providence of God, in
whose hand is every change of lordship" (i.8.3, p. 27). In William, the Angles and
Saxons demonstrate both prowess and an ability to listen to reason, i.e., they
are endowed with enough positive qualities that the judgment of "the favouring providence of God" only supports and does not undercut their potential for
future greatness. From there, William passes to the kings of Kent. The Britons
are out of the picture from this point forward.[128]

    Liber cap. LVI–LXXI seu Chronica Maiora, ed. C. W. Jones, Corpus Christianorum, Series
    Latina 123 B (Turhout: Brepols, 1977), 461–544.

127   In the *Historia Brittonum*, in ch. 31, Vortigern rules in "dread of Ambrosius" though no
    further information is provided; in chs. 40–42, Ambrosius is the fatherless boy whose
    blood must be sprinkled on the base of the king's tower for it to stand, and also Emrys,
    the overlord; in ch. 42, Vortigern gives Ambrosius the boy wizard who has just told the
    king that his father "is one of the consuls of the Roman people" "all the kingdoms of the
    western part of Britain" (p. 31); in ch. 48, Ambrosius is "the 'great' king among all the kings
    of the British nation" (p. 33; "rex †magnus† inter omnes reges Brittannicae gentis," p. 74)
    who granted rule over the regions of Buellt and Gwretheyrnion to Vortigern's son Pascent;
    and in ch. 66 there were to have been twelve years between the beginning of Vortigern's
    reign and the battle of Wallop between Vitalinus and Ambrosius. Numerous scholars have
    tried to sort out these discrepancies and identify an historical Ambrosius from among
    the references, including Léon Fleuriot, *Les origines de la Bretagne: l'émigration* (Paris:
    Payot, 1980), 170 and J. N.L. Myres, "Pelagius and the end of Roman Rule in Britain," *JRS*
    50 (1960): 21–36, esp. 35–36, and idem, *English Settlements*, Oxford History of England
    (Oxford: Oxford University Press, 1989), 14–15, 164, and 212–13.

128   Stating "but this happened in the course of time" (i.8.3, p. 27; "sed haec processu anno-
    rum," p. 26), William backtracks to a brief narrative of the night of the swords, then
    moves on to the English kingdoms. Except for isolated definitional references – such
    as "the Britons (whom we call Welsh)" (ii.125.1, p. 197), "the Northwalians, that is the
    Northern Britons" (ii.134.5, p. 215), and "the Western Britons who are called Cornish"
    (ii.134.6, p. 217) – no references to the Britons as a topic of discussion appear in the *GRA*
    beyond Book 1. Cf. Emily Winkler who critiques Gillingham's and Davies's assessments
    of William's general pro-English stance (190–91), arguing that on the contrary, "William
    endeavoured to restore honour to the Britons in Britain's remote past by minimizing

HISTORIA REGUM BRITANNIAE: PART 1   79

3.2.2 Henry of Huntingdon: *Historia Anglorum*

Henry of Huntingdon's *Historia Anglorum* was intended to reach a wide audience, including "the less educated" ("pluribus, id est minus doctis," *HA* viii, pref., p. 584), and in its final form, consisted of ten books of roughly equal length, "each making a unit that might be read – and read aloud – in a single sitting."[129] Although largely derivative, the vast scope of Henry's text, his interests, organizational techniques, and certain original elements make his *Historia Anglorum* an important source, if not for history itself (the "what actually happened"), then for the history of historical writing in the twelfth century.[130] In the early books of the *HA*, one of the most striking elements is Henry's invention of the Heptarchy (1.4–5), an organizing principle for early English history still in use today. Another is his idea of the five plagues in which

---

their subjection to the foreign invaders. He appropriated Roman imperial claims to represent the Britons as a people of strength, pride and authority in their own right, not merely as inhabitants of an oppressed frontier province and victims of invasion. In this respect he shared a renewed interest in the British past with his contemporaries Henry of Huntingdon and Geoffrey of Monmouth" ("William of Malmesbury and the Britons," in *Discovering William of Malmesbury*, ed. Rodney M. Thomson, Emily Dolmans, and Emily A. Winkler, Woodbridge: Boydell, 2017, 189–201, cited here at 190). While it is reasonable to say that William, Henry of Huntingdon, and Geoffrey of Monmouth "shared a renewed interest in the British past," to lump these historians together with respect to their perspectives toward the Britons goes too far, even acknowledging William's positive comment about Vortimer, that he "would have made a good ruler had God permitted" ("egregie regnum moderaretur si Deus siuisset" 1.8.1, p. 26). Davies acknowledges that "William of Malmesbury could refer, rather patronizingly, to 'our Britons' (*GR*, 1, 6); but his views of the Britons and the Welsh are generally unflattering (e.g. *GR*, 1, 57, 237). He seems to have rather more sympathy for the Irish, at least historically, as noble and innocent savages (*GR*, 1, 57)" ("The Matter of Britain," 15 n. 38). See Gillingham, "The Context and Purposes," 27–30.

129   Greenway, ed. and trans., p. lviii. Greenway demonstrates that there were six versions, the first concluded around 1133 and the sixth soon after King Henry 11 came to the throne in 1154 (pp. lxvi–lxxvi).

130   As Greenway notes, Henry was "one of the 'weaver' compilers of whom Bernard Guenée has written ... For about 75% of the History, Henry was entirely dependent on the work of other writers, which he reproduced in quotation, summary and translation. Roughly speaking, about 25% of the History came from Bede, around 40% derived from the Anglo-Saxon Chronicle, and about another 10% came from other written sources'"(ed., p. lxxxv); see also eadem, "Authority, convention and observation in Henry of Huntingdon's *Historia Anglorum*," *Anglo-Norman Studies XVIII, Proceedings of the Battle Conference 1995*, ed. Christopher Harper-Bill (Woodbridge: Boydell, 1996), 105–21; Bernard Guenée, "L'historien et la compilation au xiie siècle," *Journal des savants* (1985), 119–35 and "L'historien par les mots," *Politique et histoire au Moyen Age, Recueil d'articles sur l'histoire politique et l'historiographie médiévale, 1956–1981* (Paris: Publications de la Sorbonne, 1981), 221–37.

80   CHAPTER 1

the successive invasions of Romans, Picts and Scots, English (*Anglis*, 1.4), Danes
and Normans are viewed as punishments visited upon the island of Britain by
a vengeful God. That the initial elaboration of the Heptarchy occurs in virtually "the same breath" as the five plagues cannot be coincidental. When the
Britons aren't absent altogether from the narrative, they are seen as victims
who lose their rightful place to the land. However, not only do they lose the
land, they are not contributors to the history of Britain worthy of being the
subject of narrative.

The placement of Henry's mention of the Heptarchy is revealing of Henry's
perspectives and goals, as is the overall organization of the early books of the
Historia Anglorum.[131] The initial mention of the Heptarchy falls in Book 1,
whose title is also telling (as is the title of the entire work) entitled "on the
kingdom of the Romans in Britain" ("de regno Romanorum in Britannia"). At
this juncture, it is worth noting that no book in the *Historia Anglorum* is named
after the Britons, nor is there a book devoted to any local groups, including
those who may have preceded the Britons (which in these texts are giants).[132]
Henry organizes the opening chapters of Book 1 thus:

---

131   Henry is often praised for his organizational skills or as Nancy Partner puts it his "rather
       insistent orderliness" (*Serious Entertainments*, p. 23); see also Leckie: "This influential
       work was the most systematic survey of its day and the first to give serious consideration
       to the pre-Saxon era" (p. 73). James Campbell writes, "No less significant is the extent to
       which [the *Historia Anglorum*] reads as a text-book or a set of careful lectures. Its author
       is often anxious to sort out, reorder, clarify ... It is characteristic of Huntingdon that it
       was he who introduced the idea of the Heptarchy which so many generations have found
       useful, if in part so misleading, in seeking a thread to follow through the early English cen-
       turies" ("Some Twelfth-Century Views of the Anglo-Saxon Past," *Peritia* 3 (1984): 131–50;
       repr. in *Essays in Anglo-Saxon History*, London: Hambledon Press, 1986, 209–28, cited at
       213). For example, in Book 3, which is devoted to conversions – of peoples and individu-
       als, including royals – ecclesiastical history has been separated from secular; Henry draws
       extensively on Bede but he has rearranged the latter's material so that the conversions are
       divided by kingdoms, following the organizational principle of the Heptarchy (Campbell,
       "Some Twelfth-Century Views," 212–13).
132   In the early books, mention is made of individual Britons with occasional collective ref-
       erences, but there are no sustained narratives, certainly not on the order of the *Historia
       Brittonum*, let alone the *Historia Regum Britanniae*. For example, in Book 1, ch. 37, Henry
       writes of Constantinus who married St. Helena, the daughter of King Coel of Colchester
       and fathered Constantine the Great with her; in fact, Geoffrey appears to have found
       this bit of information in the *HA* (in a "pre-Geoffrey" version), which has led Tatlock to
       consider this a "reliable case where Geoffrey borrowed from Henry and not *vice versa*"
       (*Legendary History*, 34). One might also conclude that Henry's superlative comments on
       Constantine "the flower of Britain ... of British stock and origin, whose equal Britain has
       not produced before or since" (1.38, p. 61) must also have been made before he saw the
       copy of the *HRB* at Bec in 1139, since it is hard to imagine that Constantine would have

HISTORIA REGUM BRITANNIAE: PART 1   81

Ch. 1 the description of Britain;

Ch. 2 Britain's physical situation within Europe;

Ch. 3 the list of the twenty-eight "very noble cities" in the times of the
    Romans and Britons (note the order, Romans first, Britons second); and

Ch. 4 the five plagues and the Heptarchy.

After listing the five plagues,[133] Henry introduces the Heptarchy – the seven
English kingdoms established early on, that is, Northumbria, Mercia, East
Anglia, Essex, Kent, Sussex and Wessex – but he does not provide historical
precision except through parallels with a rough time frame with respect to the
kingdom of Wessex; all we "know" is that "the emergence of this characteristic
means of government is placed in the century and a half following the initial
landings," based largely on the authority of the Anglo-Saxon Chronicle (rather
than Bede).[134]

Perhaps one reason for this lack of precision on Henry's part was his reliance
on the Anglo-Saxon Chronicle, his main source other than Bede for the first
two books of the *HA*. In general, the Chronicle gives information on isolated
battles and little or no analysis or attempt to construct a larger picture in order
to reconcile the distinct traditions the Chronicle was trying to convey (such as
Henry tries to do with the structuring device of the Heptarchy, for example).[135]
Although Henry does try to make links as a way of explaining, as for example

---

  outshone Arthur once Henry had read Geoffrey's details about the latter. In Book 11, short
  narratives appear on the Britons in the context of Saxon victories against them, except
  for 11.18, which contains an abbreviated account of Arthur's twelve battles, and 11.25, 27,
  29 and 35, which contain accounts of battles, only 25 and 35 having references to British
  victories, albeit temporary. It was only when Henry included his abbreviated adaptation
  of the *HRB*, the "Epistola ad Warinum" (one of three letters that make up Book VIII in the
  fourth version of the *HA*, *c.*1146) that he was able to fill in the gaps concerning the rulers
  of Britain before or even following the English invasions. That way, he was not obliged to
  entirely recast – or openly contradict – the early books of his English history (Greenway,
  ed. and trans., *Historia Anglorum*, lxxi–lxxiii, ci); see also Wright, "The Place of Henry of
  Huntingdon's *Epistola ad Warinum*," 74–75.

133 See Chapter 2, n. 86 above, and Chapter 3, n. 44.

134 Leckie, *Passage*, 75.

135 Leckie writes in reference to the Anglo-Saxon Chronicle that "the entries for the second
  half of the fifth century and first half of the sixth tend to define the significance of any
  given occurrence in relation to the history of a single enclave. This feature of the account
  should doubtless be attributed to the fact that the compilers incorporated a substantial
  number of regional traditions." As a result "the gathering together of discrete traditions
  failed to confer historical insight which was in any way commensurate with the scope of
  the depiction. For this reason the *Anglo-Saxon Chronicle* remains a compilation of narrow
  viewpoints and does not provide a coherent view of the Germanic conquest of Britain"
  (*Passage of Dominion*, 8–9).

82   CHAPTER 1

through his tracing of the "inexorable progress of the kingdom of Wessex and his dating of all other kings in relation to the West Saxon kings"[136] one does not find explanations as to how the fragmentation of the early English kingdoms – and the quest for separate identities – arose, and certainly not a discussion or analysis of this fragmentation within the context of a larger picture to include the original Britons, except through the use of the binary "victors" versus "defeated/destroyed/exiled."

Again, the structure of Henry's *HA* may be more revealing than his analysis. His account of Brutus and the arrival of the Britons in Britain is squeezed into Book 1.9; chapters 10 and 11 contain the arrival of the Picts and the *Dalreudini* (Irish under the leader, Reuda) and a description of Ireland respectively, with the comment that the Britons came to the island in the third age of the world and the Irish came in the fourth (1.11, pp. 30–31). Henry then proceeds to Julius Caesar in ch. 11 and the Roman conquest of the Britons. From ch. 12 on, each chapter is centered on a Roman leader – the Britons become Christians in ch. 28 during the rule of Marcus Antoninus Verus [Marcus Aurelius] and his brother Aurelius Lucius Commodus [Lucius Verus]– until ch. 45 when the Scots and Picts attack and the Britons appeal to Rome for aid. Chapter 46 focuses on the letter to the consul, Aetius, and ch. 47, the final chapter of Book I, reveals a victory for the Britons, followed by great prosperity and then corruption, invasions and Vortigern's arrival on the scene.

That Henry opens Book II on the coming of the English with the arrival of Hengest and Horsa renders the narration of that event more pointed and dramatic than Bede's more blended arrangement, where different topics such as corruption, religious turmoil, invasions of the Scots and Picts, and Vortigern's invitation are all interwoven mostly in the middle chapters of Book I (Bede, *HE*, i. 8–18), with the landing of Hengist and Horsa in i. 15. Like Bede, Henry portrays the initial arrival as materializing through Vortigern's invitation, rather than using the *Historia Brittonum*'s portrayal of the Saxons as exiles who came to Britain by chance. Henry however, departs from Bede in the matter of Aurelius Ambrosius whom Bede writes was victorious forty years before Mount Badon, about which he promises to write later, but doesn't, with no mention of Arthur (Bede, *HE*, i.16).

In the *Historia Anglorum*, Henry follows the *Historia Brittonum* by making two separate characters of Aurelius and Arthur; in the *HA*, Book II.2, Aurelius fights against Hengest and Horsa on the side of the two sons of Vortigern. Arthur appears in II.18, along with the list of twelve battles from the *HB*, including that of Mount Badon. In Book II of the *HA*, between the arrival of the Saxons

---

136   Greenway, ed. and trans., *Historia Anglorum*, lxi.

and the battle of Mount Badon, there is a relentless stream of battles between the various Saxon kings, each associated with one of the seven kingdoms in Henry's Heptarchy. An important exception to Henry's usual association of the Saxons with particular regions comes in the narrative of Arthur's twelve battles, including Mount Badon – there are no associations with any particular Saxon kingdom with reference to Arthur's battles, just as the Britons are rarely associated with regions, or smaller geographical units, except when they lose them, such as the cities of Gloucester, Cirencester and Bath (II.25). Upon completion of "Arthur's chapter," Henry returns to the forward march through the founding of the seven kingdoms and battles among the Saxons and the Britons, and eventually among warring Saxons (beginning in chapter 30).

The Britons receive sporadic mention, as in ch. 25 when the Saxons capture the three important cities of Gloucester, Cirencester and Bath, in ch. 27, when the Britons enjoy a victory at "Woden's barrow," the massacre of Britons at *Beandune* (ch. 29) and the defeat of the Britons at *Peonnan* (ch. 35). There were no future goals, no redemption, no turning back for the Britons, as Henry says in the first chapter of Book II: "We shall have true glory, fame and honour if we rely, with cheerfulness and joy, on Him who is the only true one, if we put all our hope and trust in God, not in the sons of men, as did the Britons, who, deserting God and the grandeur of His fear, sought aid from pagans, and gained their just deserts" (ii. 1, p. 79).[137]

3.2.3 Henry of Huntingdon: *Epistola ad Warinum*

Understandably, the *adventus Saxonum* is portrayed differently in the *Epistola ad Warinum*, which Henry appended to the *Historia Anglorum*, as mentioned above.[138] At approximately 2,800 words, in its entirety shorter than the average book of the *Historia Anglorum*, the *Epistola ad Warinum* is a significant condensation of Geoffrey's text. Neil Wright has convincingly demonstrated that Henry's changes – omissions, additions, and different phrasing – were of his own devising, and not due to his having used an inferior text of the *HRB* from which he took notes at Bec in 1139.[139] While it is quite possible that the

---

137 "Veram autem gloriam et famam et honorem habebimus, si ei qui solus uerus est cum iocunditate et leticia innitamur, si spem nostram et fiduciam omnem in Deo ponamus, non in filiis hominum, sicut Britanni, qui Deo abiecto et magnificentia timoris eius auxilium pecierunt a paganis, habueruntque sed quale decebat" (ii. 1, p. 78).

138 On the textual history of the *Epistola*, see n. 17 above. On the parallels between the patterns of Henry's revisions and those of the author of the First Variant, see Wright ed. (11), *The First Variant Version*, lxx–lxxiv.

139 "The Place of Henry of Huntingdon's *Epistola ad Warinum*," 90.

84 CHAPTER 1

emendations could reveal hesitancy or the seeds of disapproval, it would appear that they are largely politically motivated.[140]

The *Epistola* is divided into ten sections of varying lengths, as follows:

Ch. 1) prologue: ostensibly in answer to Warin's question as to why he began the HA with the deeds of Julius Caesar while omitting the reigns from Brutus to Caesar, Henry explains that he had been unable to find adequate sources of British history when he initially wrote, but to his amazement he found a text at Le Bec on his way to Rome (in 1139), and can now provide a supplementary account based on notes taken from that source;[141]

Ch. 2) from Aeneas through Brutus to Trinovantum;

Ch. 3) Leir and his daughters;

Ch. 4) Belinus and Brennius;

Ch. 5) the rulers who came between Belinus and Luid [Lud];

Ch. 6) Luid's restoration of London, and the version of Cassibellanus's defeat by Julius Caesar [in contrast to the version in the HA];

Ch. 7) in one sentence of 30 words, he states that he will now tell of the remaining British kings from the time of Julius Caesar to the arrival of the English or Cadwallon (Geoffrey's Caduallo), "the last powerful king of the Britons" (though in Geoffrey Cadwallader, Caduallo's son, was the last king of the Britons to rule over Britain);

Ch. 8) heirs to Cassibelanus's kingdom; Lucius was the first to convert to Christianity;

Ch. 9) Arthur; and

Ch. 10) the "passage of dominion."

---

140 See Wright who posits that "the *Epistola*, then, is not simply a précis: Henry's modifications, however tentative, deserve to be recognized as a first, faint adumbration of the misgivings with which some mediaeval historians (most notably William of Newburgh) received Geoffrey's *Historia*, and which were in time to lead to its downfall in the sixteenth and seventeenth centuries" ("The Place of Henry of Huntingdon's *Epistola ad Warinum*," 91). On Henry's political motivations for his changes, see also Olivier Szerwiniack who writes that Henry more often than not substituted Bede's views for Geoffrey's in the *Epistola* ("L'*Epistola ad Warinum* d'Henri de Huntingdon, première adaptation latine de l'*Historia regum Britannie*," in *L'Historia regum Britannie et les "Bruts" en Europe, I: Traductions, adaptations, réappropriations*, ed. Hélène Tétrel and Géraldine Veysseyre, Rencontres 106, Civilisation médiévale 12, Paris: Classiques Garnier, 2015, 41–52).

141 Wright concludes that Robert of Torigni probably asked Henry the same question before he showed him Geoffrey's *Historia* at Le Bec. Robert was also instrumental in the survival of the *Epistola* since he included it (having copied it from the 1147 version of Henry's *Historia Anglorum*) in his extended version of the universal chronicle of Sigbert of Gembloux ("The Place of Henry of Huntingdon's *Epistola ad Warinum*," 74–75; *Chronique de Robert de Torigni*, 2 vols., ed. Léopold Delisle, Rouen: A. Le Brument, I, 97–111).

HISTORIA REGUM BRITANNIAE: PART 1   85

In the early sections of the *Epistola*, as in the *Historia Anglorum*, a good deal
of emphasis remains on the Romans, seen in at least three of Henry's narrative stratagems: 1) through the use of ch. 7 whose sole purpose is to mark the
transition from the pre-Roman period to Caesar's invasion; 2) through the
cross-reference to his own account of Caesar's invasions in his much more
extensive text (*HA*, i.12–14, *Epistola* ch. 6); and 3) in ch. 8 the fact that nearly
every sentence contains a reference to the Romans, either collectively or
through the name of an emperor. With respect to the *adventus Saxonum*, as
if not to contradict the *Historia Anglorum*, in the *Epistola*, Henry repeats the
information that Vortigern invited the Saxons, which lays the blame for their
arrival on the British ruler (in *HB*, they arrive as exiles, ch. 31; in *HRB*, they just
arrive, §98). Henry also omits the scene of the "night of the long knives" where
Hengest and the Saxons treacherously massacre the British leaders; with this
omission, Henry further exonerates Hengest and the Saxons.[142]

Since ch. 10 is greatly condensed, as are all the sections, the concerns
it might raise about its version of the "passage of dominion" in the *Epistola*
are less than they might have been had this been a "full-length" text; in other
words, severe cutting alone could have resulted in a "passage" much more similar to that of the First Variant and Wace than the vulgate *Historia*, rather than
political expediency lying at the heart of the presentation. But given the kinds
of changes that were made, and the originality of those changes – i.e., what he
took from Geoffrey and what he left behind – Henry's political views may have
been more compelling criteria for his selection of details than simply saving
narrative space.

In the *Epistola*, Henry gives not only a highly compressed reading but also
a very unique reading of the passage of dominion. In the vulgate, following
Gormund's destruction and handing over of the island to the Saxons – an
act known as "Gormund's Donation" – Geoffrey posits shared dominion over
England between the Britons and the Saxons until the reign of Athelstan in the
tenth century (924–39), thus pushing the full start of Saxon dominion back
nearly 300 years. In the First Variant, the island is renamed and the Saxons
take over directly after the Donation; Wace makes further changes, trying to

---

142   Apparently in order not to contradict the *HA*, Henry has also avoided the lengthy episode
       where Brutus travels to Greece, frees his people from bondage, and gathers followers who
       eventually settle Britain with him, a narrative contained in Geoffrey's vulgate text but not
       in the *Historia Brittonum* (except for two brief sentences, "and later he came to this island,
       which is named Britannia from his name, and filled it with his race, and dwelt there. From
       that day, Britain has been inhabited until the present day" *HB*, ch. 10, p. 19; "Et postea ad
       istam pervenit insulam, quae a nomine suo accepit nomen, id est Brittaniam, et inplevit
       eam cum suo genere, et habitavit ibi. Ab illo autem die habitata est Brittannia usque in
       hodiernum diem" *HB*, ch. 10, p. 60) (Wright, "*Epistola ad Warinum*," 78).

86   CHAPTER 1

reconcile Galfridian chronology with the First Variant and Bede.[143] In the *Epistola*, the English still invite the African Godmund (Gormund), who proceeds to destroy the whole country and its Christianity, but there is no mention of the Donation or of a Saxon takeover yet.

Next, the arrival of Augustine is just that, an arrival, without even a mention of the conversion, let alone any details either positive (Bede, the FV, and Henry's *HA*) or negative (Geoffrey's vulgate, and to a certain extent Wace).[144] In the *Epistola*, one phrase each is devoted to the battles and/or deaths of Edelfridus, Caduanus, Eadwinus, Cadwallon, Penda, Osfridus, Osricus, and Oswald. The narrative proper (preceding a one-line epilogue and epistolary salutation) ends thus:

> The advent of a severe plague caused him [Cadwaladr] to flee to king Alanus, grandson of Solomon in Brittany. The English came from Germany and occupied the island, which had been emptied by the plague. Cadwaladr journeyed to Rome, never to return. From that point the British entirely relinquished their name and kingdom. (*EW*, ch. 10, p. 113)[145]

In this version, the "passage of dominion" is later than in the First Variant, though not as late in the vulgate, and without any reference to either Augustine's conversion of the English or to Athelstan. In addition, not only does the island receive a new name, but according to Henry, the Britons gave up not only their kingdom which had been emptied by the plague but also their name. In the *Epistola*, the Britons do not go into exile either in their own land or abroad: it is as if they ceased to exist altogether as the land takes on a new identity, a variation on the passage of dominion theme which appears to be found in no other text; according to Geoffrey, the Britons were renamed the Welsh

---

143   See Chapter 5, n. 198.

144   See Chapter 2, n. 33.

145   "Tunc ueniente peste grauissima fugit in Armoriam ad regem Alanum Salomonis nepotem. Angli uero uenientes a Germania terras peste uacuatas possederunt. Chedwalladrus autem rex Romam iuit non reuersurus. Exinde Britanni et nomen et regnum penitus amiserunt" (Wright, *EW*, ch. 10, p. 106). Immediately following the end of the narrative, without a break, Henry closes the letter with these statements: 'This is the sum of the notes which I promised you. If you require a fuller version, seek out the large volume by Geoffrey Arthur, which I discovered at Le Bec; in it you will find a careful and detailed account of the above. Farewell' (*EW*, ch. 10, p. 113; "Hec sunt que tibi breuibus promisi; quorum si prolixitatem desideras, librum grandem Galfridi Arturi, quem apud Beccum inueni, queras, ubi predicta diligenter et prolixe tractata uidebis. Uale" ch. 10, p. 106). On Geoffrey's by-name Arturus, see Wright, ed., I, x, and Tatlock, *The Legendary History*, 438–9.

HISTORIA REGUM BRITANNIAE: PART 1   87

(*HRB*, §§207–8), and while he does not appear happy about this, it is a far cry from being nameless or having one's identity subsumed by the occupiers.

In deference to Henry, we might speculate that perhaps the nameless status of the Britons was simply a shortened version of Geoffrey's account:

> Those Saxons who survived when the dreadful plague was over announced, as was their unfailing custom, to their fellow-countrymen in Germany that, if they came as immigrants, they could easily occupy the island, devoid as it was of its inhabitants. On receiving the news, that wicked people ass[e]mbled a vast crowd of men and women, landed in Northumbria and filled the empty tracts of land from Scotland to Cornwall. There were no natives to stop them, save a few remaining Britons living in the remote forests of Wales. This marked the end of British power in the island and the beginning of English rule. (*HRB*, §204. 550–59)[146]

Yet even Geoffrey's depiction does not convey complete absence of the Britons and certainly not the losing of their name – without a new name being substituted for the old one. However, in Henry's *Epistola*, the emptying of the island is complete, as it was when the Trojans themselves rid the island of the giants early on in the *HRB*. Henry accomplishes in a short amount of space for the English what Geoffrey sought to do for the Britons, that is, recreate an aboriginal situation for the English (Germanic) peoples, to contribute to the legitimacy of their takeover. As Rees Davies has put it, "the historical mythology of a people is ultimately concerned to show that the people in question is literally aboriginal and that its unbroken history as a people validates such a claim. A people's place ... depends on it being able to show that it is immemorially a people and can construct the past to show that is so."[147] Creating a more absolute version of an English foundation myth requiring removal of the

---

146   "Quorum residui, cum tam feralis lues cessauisset, continuem morem seuantes nuntiauerunt conciuibus suis in Germania insulam indigena gente carentem facile illus subdendam si in illam habitaturi uenirent. Quod cum ipsis indicatum fuisset, nefandus populus ille, collecta innumerabili multitudine uirorum et mulierum, applicuit in partibus Northamhimbriae et desolates prouincias ab Albania usque ad Cornubiam inhabitauit. Non enim aderat habitator qui prohiberet praeter pauperculas Britonum reliquias quae superfuerant, quae infra abdita nemorum in Gualiis commanebant. Ab illo tempore potestas Britonum in insula cessauit et Angli regnare coeperunt."

147   R. R. Davies, "The Peoples of Britain and Ireland, 1100–1400: IV. Language and Historical Mythology," *TRHS* ser 6, vol. 7 (1997), 1–24, cited at 20.

88   CHAPTER 1

native peoples may not have been Henry's initial intent in his presentation of
his "notes" to Warin, yet that appears to have been the result.[148]

In addition, at the level of language, there is yet another interesting distinction between Geoffrey's version and Henry's. In Geoffrey, the Britons' power in
the island comes to an end – "potestas Britonum in insula cessauit" – whereas
in Henry, the Britons "relinquish" their kingdom (Wright, *EW*, 113) – "regnum
penitus amiserunt"; the former expression emphasizes that British power had
at least at one time existed, while the latter expression only relates to territorial claims. Unless one equates territory with power one for one, "relinquishing
the kingdom" implies less original power than "loss of power in the island."
In the context of the passage of dominion, Henry has once again undermined
the Britons in this letter whose stated aim was to convey the high points of
Geoffrey's *Historia*. Henry appears to have achieved this goal to a limited
extent with respect to content but to an even more limited extent with respect
to the spirit of the original text. Only rare comments such as Henry's unique
assignation to Arthur of the title "the Breton hope" can be seen to convey some
of Geoffrey's pro-Briton spirit.[149]

---

148   Despite the variant in Robert of Torigni's chronicle in Avranches, Bibliothèque municipal
       MS. 159 which reports Henry as having referred to Geoffrey of Monmouth's history as "the
       legend of the kings of the Britons who held *our* island before the English" – which could
       possibly be read to imply a collective sense of belonging on Henry's part, a shared island
       among Britons and English – rather than as Davies does, as revealing a proprietary view
       of England as belonging only to the English (see n. 149 below), the end of the *EW* provides
       yet another reason to be skeptical of Winkler's contention that Henry "rewrote these
       moments of change to improve the honour of the Britons" ("William of Malmesbury
       and the Britons," 192). On the range of English foundation myths (among others), see
       Introduction, n. 10, and Barbara Yorke, "Anglo-Saxon Origin Legends," in *Myth, Rulership,
       Church and Charters: Essays in Honour of Nicholas Brooks*, ed. Julia Barrow and Andrew
       Wareham (Aldershot: Ashgate, 2008), 15–29; eadem, "Political and Ethnic Identity: A Case
       Study of Anglo-Saxon Practice," in *Social Identity in Early Medieval Britain*, ed. Andrew
       Tyrrell and William O. Frazer (London: continuum, 2000), 69–89; in the same volume,
       Alex Woolfe, "Community, Identity and Kingship in Early England," 91–110; and on the leg-
       end of Cunedda, the kingdom of Gwynedd, as well as Cornish legends, and an application
       of Bourdieu's ideas of how group ethos is produced and transmitted, see David C. Harvey
       and Rhys Jones, "Custom and Habit(us): The Meaning of Traditions and Legends in
       Early Medieval Western Britain," *Geografiska Annaler, Series B, Human Geography* 81.4
       (1999): 223–33 .
149   On the minor role the Britons play in the English histories of William of Malmesbury and
       Henry of Huntingdon as the two most outstanding examples, Rees Davies writes that "it
       was impossible, of course, not to mention them [the Britons] in recounting the story of
       English advance and triumph, but they put in an appearance only to be defeated; they
       have virtually no other identity ... Henry of Huntingdon let the cat out of the bag in his
       letter to Warin, referring to Geoffrey of Monmouth's *Historia* as the "book about the kings

HISTORIA REGUM BRITANNIAE: PART 1   89

The *Epistola ad Warinum* is not only "not simply a précis" of the *HRB* as Wright correctly observes, but also an important distinct witness to the traditions of the passage of dominion and to the larger body of Galfridian material.[150]

of the Britons who held *our* island before the English" (Davies, "The Matter of Britain," 15–16). It is intriguing that the passage Davies cites here from the *Epistola* regarding *"our* island" is found only in one of the five *Epistola* manuscripts, that is, Robert de Torigini's version of the *EW* in Avranches MS. Bibliothèque municipale 159 (fols. 174v–178v) following this phrase "... Hoc tamen anno, cum Romam profiscerer, apud Beccensem abbaciam scripta rerum predictarum stupens inueni [Wright, *"Epistola ad Warinum,"* ch. 1, p. 93; "... But this year, on my way to Rome, I discovered, to my amazement, a history of the above reigns at the abbey of Le Bec" [Wright, p. 106].) [The Avranches variant begins here, following the word "inueni"]: *"Siquidem Robertum de Torinneio eiusdem loci monachum, uirum tam diuinorum quam secularium librorum inquisitorem et coaceruatorem studiosissimum, ibidem conueni. Qui cum de ordine hystorie de regibus Anglorum a me edite me interrogaret et id quod a me querebat libens audisset, obtulit michi librum ad legendum de regibus Britonum qui ante Anglos* **nostram insulam** *tenuerunt";* "But in that place I met *Robert of Torigni (a monk of the same place), a very studious man as eager to research books as collect them both divine and secular. Who, when he had questioned me about the order of my history of the kings of the English, offered me a book to read on the kings of the Britons who held* **our island** *before the English"* (Wright, *"Epistola,"* p. 93 n. 7; my translation). See also Greenway's edition of the *EW* for variants from Robert de Torigini's version in the Avranches MS. (ed. and trans., *HA*, p. 558–83).

150   In fact, Robert de Torigini's version gives yet another perspective. An extra line is added in the Avanches MS. to the end of ch. 10 (text and translation in italics below), perhaps to soften the loss of the Britons' name, emphasizing the change of name of the island: "... Exinde Britanni et nomen et regnum penitus amiserunt. *Ex tunc illa Britannia est Anglia nominata"* (Wright, *"Epistola ad Warinum,"* p. 106 and n. 30; "From that point, the British entirely relinquished their name and kingdom," Wright, *"Epistola,"* trans., p. 113; *"From then on, Britain was named 'Anglia,'"* my translation). This phrasing is reminiscent of the First Variant which explains the renaming of the island immediately following Gormund's Donation: "Hinc Angli Saxones uocati sunt qui Loegriam possederunt et ab eis Anglia terra postmodum dicta est" (186/7, p. 177; "Henceforth the Saxons who possessed Loegria were called 'Angles,' and because of them the land was called 'Anglia' [England] ever since," my translation; Burchmore: "Henceforth the Saxons were called English, who possessed Loegria, and from them the land was afterward called England", 186.1, p, 391). I prefer "Angles" to "English" in this particular context to hearken back to one of the first peoples to have come to the island, whom Wace may have considered to have been the Saxons' ancestors (see Chapter 5, n. 198); see also Gaimar, who uses the name "Ange" (l. 853), which Short translates as "the country named Angle" (ed. and trans., 49), not necessarily referring to the early Angles as a separate group, and Chapter 4, nn. 20–21, 24–26, and 43 on Gaimar's views of English descent. Geoffrey does not mention the renaming of the island, for this would not have served his purpose. In fact, Geoffrey appears to have used the terms *Angli, Anglorum* collectively for a variety of purposes, rather than to refer to the narrower group/tribe of early arrivals: 1) for example, as a "modernizing" touch referring to Henry I, king of the English (§3.20 "Henricus illustris rex Anglorum"), the "Molmutine [laws], which are still renowned even today among the English" (§34.328 "quae usque ad hoc tempus inter Anglos celebrantur"), and the very rare occasions he

Perhaps Henry assumed that Warin (if he were not a straw man) would consult the entire *HRB*, and then attempt to piece together its contents and perspectives with what he had presumably read in the *HA*, and the *Epistola*, but that is not very likely. If Warin never read the *HRB* for himself, then the *Epistola* would certainly have stacked the deck as it were since it contains what can best be characterized as an Anglicized rendition of the *HRB* – with the Romans mentioned at least as often as the Britons (and the former in usually reverential terms),[151] and never a disparaging word for the Saxons – as one of a number of English histories "consigning the Britons to an historical oubliette."[152]

---

uses "English" instead of Saxons, at the end as a temporal collective marking "the end of British power in the island and the beginning of English rule" (§204.558–59 "Ab illo tempore potestas Britonum in insula cessauit et Angli regnare coeperunt") and when Ivor and Yni and the Britons "subjected the English (*gentem Anglorum*) to savage incursions for sixty-nine years" (§207.588–89) ; and 2) when referring to the language "the stone circle known in English as Stonehenge" (§180.103–4 "composita Anglorum lingua Stanheng nuncupatur"). Geoffrey's use of the term "Saxons" rather than "English" was apparently typical of British authors, as Michael Richter writes, in use by "Celtic peoples in referring to their Germanic neighbors," who were "for centuries in the mainstream of European developments. They never abandoned this terminology, but on the continent, 'Saxon' was gradually replaced by 'English'" ("Bede's *Angli*: Angles or English?" 114).

151   Henry's views of the Romans were a far cry from Gildas's, whose resistance to embrace the Romans has been seen to make him "the first known Briton to write from such a post-imperialist perspective" (Sims-Williams, "Gildas and the Anglo-Saxons," 29). Henry's views were considerably more pro-Roman, as if the memory of Roman imperial repression has significantly faded and been supplanted by a "proto-classical" view of Roman efficiency and grandeur.

152   R. R. Davies, "The Peoples of Britain and Ireland," 19.

CHAPTER 2

Geoffrey of Monmouth's *Historia Regum Britanniae*: Part 2

1   **Geoffrey of Monmouth:** *Adventus Saxonum* **and Preview of Other Landmark Events**

Except for the area of Arthur, no topic in Geoffrey's *Historia* reveals more of his effort to include seemingly forgotten peoples, to broaden the focus, and to question accepted assumptions than does the *adventus Saxonum*, which in Geoffrey's text is certainly more of a process than any single event. While it is on the one hand impossible to ignore Geoffrey's favoritism for the Britons – regardless of one's perspectives, it is difficult not to see Geoffrey's work as a "counter-history," to borrow Davies's term – at the same time it is important to acknowledge the breadth his portrayal adds to the larger fabric of the history of the island as a whole. Even though little of what Geoffrey writes can be proven – at least not sufficiently by modern standards – the fact that he writes it at all serves as a reminder that the ancient Britons did exist, although many scholars today feel understandably safer examining the work of biologists, archeologists, and anthropologists who rely on material culture for their reconstructions, rather than on imaginative texts spun out of a "lost" past.[1]

As mentioned above, Geoffrey's narrative of the *adventus Saxonum* is much fuller than that of the *Historia Brittonum*. In fact, in Geoffrey's vulgate *Historia*, for all practical purposes, the *adventus* (and related events) expands to fill the remainder of the narrative after the arrival of Hengist and Horsa; the initial arrival *c*.449[2] is but one in a very long series of events for Geoffrey, going through and beyond the reign of Arthur, who is no longer a battle commander but a glorious king and international conqueror. Although Geoffrey does not narrate in any detail the approximately 250 years between Cadwallader's death

---

1   It is as if Geoffrey suspected that without written histories broadly accessible in the more universally known Latin language, the Britons could someday be dismissed, disenfranchised or worse – or at least relegated to the realm of groups for whom there is only oral history – as many Indigenous peoples have been, particularly in the Americas (a situation which many scholars, including from native communities, are currently seeking to remedy); see the Introduction, n. 32.
2   For the year 449, the A recension of the Anglo-Saxon Chronicle notes the arrival of Hengist and Horsa at Vortigern's invitation (Swanton ed. and trans., p. 12).

© KONINKLIJKE BRILL NV, LEIDEN, 2024 | DOI:10.1163/9789004691889_004

92   CHAPTER 2

in *c.*689 to the reign of Athelstan in 923–39 – skipping over many key figures of early English history such as Alfred the Great, Althelstan's grandfather – with one broad stroke he effectively manages the addition of roughly 250 years of joint rule over the island between the Britons and the Saxons; Geoffrey also finesses the time lag between Gormund's Donation (which cannot be dated precisely) and the final Saxon takeover:[3] at the end, "the Saxons acted more wisely, living in peace and harmony, tilling the fields and rebuilding the cities and towns; thus, with British lordship overthrown, they came to rule all Loegria, led by Athelstan, who was the first of them to wear its crown" (§207.594–97).[4] What is critical for Geoffrey to establish is less when the Saxons *came over* than when they *took over* since, according to his view, those were two remarkably distinct things.

Lewis Thorpe's thematic divisions of the *HRB* remain useful for an overview of this highly detailed yet virtually dateless text:[5]

> *Part One: Brutus occupies the island of Albion* ["prehistory"]
>   Book I – from the description of Britain through the combat of Corineus and Gogmagog
> *Part Two: Before the Romans came* [continuation of "prehistory"]
>   Book II – Brutus's descendants, including King Leir and his daughters
>   Book III – Belinus and Brennius fight in Gaul and sack Rome
> *Part Three: The coming of the Romans*
>   Book IV – Arrival of Julius Caesar; Claudius; Vespasian

---

3 Leckie states that "Wace jumps from the first decade of the seventh century down to the second quarter of the tenth" (p. 113), that is, basically skipping roughly three hundred years between Gormund's Donation and Athelstan, as he attempts to reconcile Geoffrey's gap – Geoffrey's stretch of shared rule between the Britons and the Saxons post-Gormund and pre-Athelstan – with the FV's making Cadwallader a contemporary of Athelstan (though Wace knew that the latter situation was not the case). On Wace's handling of these gaps, which involved his emphasizing the growth of Saxon settlements rather than shared power with the Britons, see Chapter 5, esp. section 7.

4 "At Saxones, sapientius agentes, pacem etiam et concordiam inter se habentes, agros colentes, ciuitates et oppida reaedificantes, et sic abiecto dominio Britonum iam toti Loegriae imperauerant duce Adelstano, qui primus inter eos diadema portauit" (§207.594–97).

5 Trans., *The History of the Kings of Britain*, (1966). Geoffrey is notorious for not having cited sources or dates. His major form of dating is through biblical parallels which themselves are very difficult to locate precisely in time. It should be noted that Thorpe's division into twelve books, following Griscom, has not been adopted by all editors or translators; see nn. 9–10 below on Reese's divisions of the text. Cf. Wright's outline of the books (of the vulgate) and their contents which he uses as a point of comparison with the *Gesta Regum Britannie* of William of Rennes (*Historia Regum Britannie of Geoffrey of Monmouth, V. Gesta Regum Britannie*, ed. and trans. Neil Wright, Woodbridge: D. S. Brewer, 1991, xxxviii–xxxix.)

HISTORIA REGUM BRITANNIAE: PART 2

Book V – Britain converts to Christianity; Diocletian persecutions; Maximianus; Britons settle Armorica; Britain ravaged by Picts and Huns

Book VI – Rome helps Britain for the last time; Romans abandon Britain [in 411]

Part Four: The house of Constantine

Book VI (cont'd) – Britons' counsel; Constantine II comes from Brittany; Vortigern becomes king; arrival of Hengist and Horsa, followed by many Saxons; Vortigern marries Ronwen;[6] Vortigern's tower, the pool and the dragons; Merlin

Part Five: The Prophecies of Merlin

Book VII – prophecies

Part Six: The house of Constantine (cont'd)

Book VIII – Vortigern burnt in his tower; Hengist's execution; Aurelius the Briton restores the churches; Merlin and Stonehenge; Utherpendragon and Ygerne

Part Seven: Arthur of Britain

Book IX – Arthur's coronation; battles of Lincoln, Caledon Wood, Badon Hill, Thanet and Loch Lomond; Arthur marries Guinevere; Arthur's foreign campaigns; Arthur's plenary court; Roman senate arraigns Arthur

Book X – Arthur's defiance; Barfleur; monster of Mont-Saint-Michel; battles with the Romans; battle of Saussy [Siesia];[7]

Book XI – Arthur's victory at the battle of Saussy [Siesia]; Mordred's treachery; battle of Camlann; Arthur mortally wounded and taken to Avalon

---

6 Thorpe has "Renwein"; I have regularized the numerous spellings to "Ronwen," following Wace's usage (and "Ygerne" as well, following the dominant spelling of that name in Wace, rather than "Igerne," or "Ygerna/Igerna," the latter forms often found in the Latin).

7 Thorpe writes that he arrived at this name of Saussy after studying the campaign and before reading Tatlock's note, to the effect that "There is an obscure place thirty-five miles southwest of Langres, named Saussy, on the way to Autun" (*Legendary History*, 103 n. 83); Thorpe remarks that "Tatlock is being too difficult" reminding readers (as does Tatlock) that Geoffrey's sense of distance "can be remarkably vague" (Thorpe, trans., 247 n. 1). Tatlock adds that Geoffrey's narrative of Arthur's military campaign in Burgundy demonstrates, among other things, "his combination of accuracy and vagueness, of rather vivid scenes separated by stretches of haze" (*Legendary History*, 102). Rather than "accuracy" however, it should be said that Geoffrey's use of details most often creates an *illusion* of "accuracy" (though occasionally "accuracy" does occur). Reeve and Wright have opted for "Siesia," a valley en route to Autun, "though which Lucius [and his army] would pass" (§168. 241–42). See Weiss for an account of the various localities that have been proposed (trans. *Roman de Brut*, 309, n. 2).

94   CHAPTER 2

Part Eight: The Saxon domination

    Book XI (cont'd) – Constantine battles Mordred's sons; to defeat King
        Keredic,[8] Saxons invite Gormund, African king; Britain is deci-
        mated, Britons flee to Cornwall and Wales; arrival of St. Augustine

    Book XII – kings Caduan (Briton) and Ethelfridus (Saxon) divide
        Loegria between them (the latter held north of the Humber, the
        former the remainder); Caduallo and Edwin; Penda, king of the
        Mercians; angelic prophecy, Cadwallader abandons Britain, dies in
        Rome; the Britons are given the name of Welsh; the Saxons "with
        British lordship overthrown, they came to rule all Loegria, led by
        Athelstan, who was the first of them to wear its crown" (§207)

As noted above, unlike some earlier editors (Giles 1844 and Griscom 1929),
Michael Reeve, Geoffrey's most recent editor, does not number the Prophecies
of Merlin as Book VII, so that in his edition, the last book is Book XI, not
Book XII.[9] Although this was likely not Reeve's rationale for not numbering the
Prophecies as Book VII, for our purposes here, the result is the same: by excluding the Prophecies from the numbering system (and thus setting it to the side
of the narrative proper), the coming of the Saxons falls almost exactly halfway
through the work – midway through Book V – with six books remaining, 6–11.[10]
Physically marginalizing the Prophecies in this way makes a certain amount of
sense in that the text of the Prophecies does not move the narrative forward,
although it was often taken very seriously and read by medieval scholars (and
others) as referring to events transpiring in the later history of the island.[11]

---

8   Reeve uses Kareticus rather than Keredic (ed., §184.134–35). Reeve comments that "for an
      editor of the *De gestis Britonum*, the worst problem concerns names, of which there are
      over 900, many recurrent" (lii). For simplicity's sake, I have chosen to use Reeve's (and
      Wright's) spellings, indicating alternate spellings where appropriate, though I have occa-
      sionally anglicized some of the more common or well known names such as Edwin for
      Edwinus, and Cadwallader for Cadualadr/Cadualadrus.

9   Reeve's extensive manuscript research supports the division of the *De Gestis Britonum*
      into eleven books of 208 chapters, with the *Prophetiae* (the "Prophecies of Merlin,"
      which also circulated separately) falling between books 7 and 8; Reeve's book 11 contin-
      ues from section 190 (where Thorpe's book 12 begins as outlined above) to the end. In
      his 1984 single-manuscript edition, Wright used just chapter (section) numbers but not
      book numbers, as did Faral in his critical edition of 1929. See also Michael D. Reeve, "The
      Transmission of the *Historia Regum Britanniae*," *Journal of Medieval Latin* 1 (1991): 73–117.

10   For a discussion of the manuscript tradition with respect to book and chapter numbers
      and the elements that entered into Reeve's editorial decisions in this regard, see Reeve,
      ed., pp. lix–lxi.

11   On the Latin manuscript tradition of the Prophecies, including its having circulated
      apart from the vulgate text, see Caroline D. Eckhardt, "The *Prophetia Merlini* of Geoffrey
      of Monmouth: Latin Manuscript Copies," *Manuscripta* 26.3 (1982): 167–76. On the

HISTORIA REGUM BRITANNIAE: PART 2

With its emphasis on the deeds of the Britons, alongside the 107 kings of the Britons[12] in the *Historia* one should not be surprised to find only a handful of Saxon kings. This may in part be due to what Michael Curley has observed

> importance of prophecy in the twelfth century, see especially R. W. Southern, who remarks that of the "still more widely disseminated prophecies of Merlin. Here again we have the strange phenomenon of apparently unrelieved gibberish claiming the anxious attention of men of high intelligence and sophistication, and here again we can only explain the phenomenon by the need which men felt to believe in a wide dissemination of divinely inspired truth about historical events throughout all ages and peoples" ("Aspects of the European Tradition of Historical Writing: 3. History as Prophecy," *Transactions of the Royal Historical Society*, 5th ser., 22 (1972): 159–80, cited at 168). For the early traditions of prophecy, and the place of Geoffrey's *Prophetiae Merlini* within those traditions, see *The "Prophetia Merlini" of Geoffrey of Monmouth: A Fifteenth-Century English Commentary*, ed. and trans. Caroline D. Eckhardt, Speculum Anniversary Monographs 8 (Cambridge, MA: Medieval Academy of America, 1982), esp. pp. 1–15; see also Michael J. Curley, *Geoffrey of Monmouth*, Twayne's English Authors Series 509 (New York: Twayne, 1994), chapter 3 "*The History of the Kings of Britain: The Prophecies of Merlin*," 48–74; Julia C. Crick, "Geoffrey of Monmouth, Prophecy and History," *Journal of Medieval History* 18.4 (1992): 357–71; the essays in *Moult obscures paroles: Études sur la prophétie médiévale*, ed. Richard Traschler with Julien Abed and David Expert (Paris: Presses de l'Université Paris-Sorbonne, 2007); and Victoria Flood, *Prophecy, Politics and Place in Medieval England: From Geoffrey of Monmouth to Thomas of Erceldoune* (Cambridge: D. S. Brewer, 2016), 1–109.

12   On the number of the kings of the Britons, see Chapter 1, n. 4 above. As mentioned earlier, my goal is not to determine Geoffrey's sources, if that were indeed possible with certainty. With respect to the myriad of Briton kings both ancient and closer to Geoffrey's time, Dauvit Broun remarks that "although it has been argued that he made clever use of Welsh material that suited his purpose, [he] had nothing to go on comparable in scale with what was available to Irish and English scholars; but this merely allowed his creative genius the freedom to conjure up a vision of a long and ancient line of kings punctuated by vivid portrayals of strong and weak rulers which captured the imagination not only of English and Welsh writers but of Continental audiences, too" (*Scottish Independence and the Idea of Britain: From the Picts to Alexander III*, Edinburgh: Edinburgh University Press, 2007, 46). On Geoffrey's Welsh sources, see Brinley F. Roberts, "Geoffrey of Monmouth and Welsh historical tradition," *Nottingham Mediaeval Studies* 20 (1976): 29–40, and specifically on possible sources of his king list (including the dearth specifically of Welsh king-lists), see Molly Miller, "Geoffrey's Early Royal Synchronisms," *Bulletin of the Board of Celtic Studies* 28 (1978–80): 373–89; in fact, Miller comments that although the Welsh were producing pedigrees, "in providing a king-list [Geoffrey's] publication marks a new departure in Welsh historiography" (373); see also David Dumville, "Kingship, Genealogies and Regnal Lists," in *Early Medieval Kingship*, ed. P. H. Sawyer and I. N. Wood (Leeds: School of History University of Leeds, 1977), 72–104, Appendix: bibliography 1–5; repr. in *Histories and Pseudo-Histories of the Insular Middle Ages*, Variorum, 1990). Peter C. Bartrum suggests a single poetic source with a king-list, genealogy and a few narrative details, perhaps inspired by the Irish *Lebor Gabála Érenn* ("Was There a British 'Book of Conquests'?," *BBCS* 23 (1968–70): 1–6), though David Dumville wonders why Bartrum had not considered the possibility of the *Historia Brittonum* as just such a source ("The Historical Value of the *Historia Brittonum*," 6), suggesting as well that the *Lebor* could have been one of Geoffrey's

96   CHAPTER 2

as a pattern of Geoffrey's, wherein he replaces major early English leaders
with those from the Britons – some of his own invention – as for example he
does with Edwin of Northumbria whose reign was characterized by Bede as
a "golden age" of peace: "Geoffrey's plan was to supplant Edwin and Alfred
as beacons of culture and peace with their British predecessors, Dunvallo
Molmutius, his son Belinus, and Marcia, sage wife of Guithelinus."[13] Notable
Saxon and other early English figures found in Geoffrey's vulgate *Historia* are
Hengest and Horsa; Cherdric, (Cerdric) founder of Wessex; Cheldric (Celric)
late sixth-century king of the West Saxons; Colgrin (Saxon leader appointed
after the death of Octa, Hengest's son and Eosa, his kinsman); Oswald, king
of Northumbria; Penda, king of the Mercians; and Athelstan, the first king of
a united England. Notable absences are all the remaining early English kings
from the late sixth century up to Athelstan in the mid-tenth, most visibly
absent being Edwin, Ethelbert, Edmund, Offa, Ethelred, Alfred the Great, and
Edward the Elder.

The Saxons are most often referred to as a group – most frequently as
Saxones, seldom as *Angli* – in a total of 79 instances, in contrast with the
relative few mentions of the two other primary enemy groups of the Britons
in Geoffrey's vulgate *Historia*, that is, the Scots (16 instances) and the Picts
(28 instances), with even fewer mentions of other regional enemies, such as
the Irish, who are named as a group only 5 times.[14] In fact, Geoffrey demonstrates little understanding of, or interest in, the Scots and the Picts as peoples
in their own right; besides using that pair of peoples periodically as a set piece
and object of animosity, he has little to say other than "But enough of the Picts,
since it is not my intention to write either their history or that of the Scots, who
are descended from them and the Irish" (*HRB*, §70.386–88).[15]

---

     inspirations (7). See also Stuart Piggott, "The Sources of Geoffrey of Monmouth: I. The
     pre-Roman king-list," *Antiquity* 15 (1941): 269–86.

13   *Geoffrey of Monmouth*, 21. Curley notes as well that "Welsh lore concerning Dufnwal
     Moelmud seem to have suggested to Geoffrey the germ of the idea that the early British
     kings long before the advent of the Romans were not simply great founders of nations
     and great warriors, but they were also wise lawgivers and civil engineers who built and
     protected Britain's impressive roads" (21).

14   These counts are approximate and based on index entries in Reeve, ed., 302, 304. The
     Romans as a group (*Romani*), who are more often seen as rivals – that is, occasionally with
     awe or admiration, and worthy of emulation – rather than as enemies, would appear to be
     mentioned 79 times (index, 303). On *Saxones* vs. *Angli* in Geoffrey, see also n. 110 below.

15   For a range of views regarding the highly complex topic of the origins of the early medi-
     eval Scottish kingdom, the descent relationships between the Irish and the Scots, and
     the "disappearance" of the Picts (and the Pictish language), see Marjorie O. Anderson,
     "Dalraida and the creation of the kingdom of the Scots"; Edward J. Cowan, "Myth and

HISTORIA REGUM BRITANNIAE: PART 2   97

In Geoffrey's *Historia*, the coming of the Saxons and their eventual take-over of England extends over the second half of the text interlarded with references to the Saxons as a group, peppered with references to the Scots and Picts, but whose main course is the "revelation" of roughly 250 years of virtually unknown – and unrecorded elsewhere – history of the Britons, not the least of whom was Arthur. The stages of the growth of Saxon hegemony can be roughly outlined as follows:

1) the welcoming of Hengest and Horsa, the arrival of more Saxons, and the "night of the long knives" and its immediate aftermath;

2) Aurelius's battles against the Saxons, death of Hengest, surrender of Octa, campaign of Loth against Octa and Eosa, and the latter's deaths at the battle of St. Albans;

3) a hiatus of dominion-building for the Saxons, following their defeat by Arthur at Colidon Wood and Bath,[16] his defeat of Frollo, and foreign conquests;[17]

4) following Arthur's defeat at Camlann, and departure from the scene, a resumption of dominion-building for the Saxons with the coming of Gormund and the conversion of the English; and

5) the final battles against the Britons, followed by the sweeping declaration of Saxon supremacy 250 years later.

The Saxons are first mentioned in the Description of the island, where Geoffrey lists the five peoples who have inhabited the island: the Normans, the Britons, the Saxons, the Picts, and the Scots. He adds that "of these the Britons once occupied it from shore to shore before the others, until their pride brought

---

Identity in Early Medieval Scotland," *Scottish Historical Review*, 63:176, pt. 2 (1984), 111–32; Molly Miller, "Matriliny by treaty: the Pictish foundation-legend"; Ewan Campbell, "Were the Scots Irish?" *Antiquity* 75 (2001): 285–92; and Patrick Wormald "The Emergence of the *Regnum Scottorum*: A Carolingian Hegemony?"

16   This is the great battle of *Bade* or Bath (in Geoffrey, *pagum Badonis* §146.81, considered by some to equal Mount Badon, Badon Hill), but not as Arthur's twelfth battle as in *HB*, except in Henry's *HA* (ii. 18; in this text, Henry lists *castellum Guinnion* as the eighth battle as in *HB*, Mount Badon as the twelfth); *Bade* is the only named battle in the *EW* (ch. 9); see also Chapter 5, n. 71 and Appendix 3 on Arthur's battles.

17   During this hiatus of Saxon dominion-building, Arthur is apparently not shown to reclaim the lands Vortigern gave away or that the Saxons seized; rather, for Geoffrey, the focus is largely on Arthur's foreign conquests (and Scotland). This may be because Aurelius Ambrosius was supposed to have restored the land and the Britons' former territorial holdings following the debacle of Vortigern's reigns – see n. 28 below – but the exact nature of Aurelius's "reconstitution" is not clear (and likely purposefully so, as is often the case in Geoffrey's ambiguous text). The Saxons' later gain of "all of Loegria" will be discussed below as it is associated with Gormund's "Donation" and not part of Arthur's reign or dominion.

98   CHAPTER 2

divine retribution down upon them and they gave way to the Picts and the Saxons" (§5.42–46).[18]

It is not until Book VI, section 98 that the Saxons are mentioned again, though not by the name of their people. This is the beginning of stage one of the *adventus* where Vortigern is informed by his messengers "of the landing of warships full of unknown men of large stature" (§98.252–53), that is, the arrival itself. Vortigern asks Hengest (in Geoffrey) and Horsa their "country of origin and their reason for coming to his kingdom" (§98.256–57). Hengest speaks for the others, replying that they are from Saxony, one of the provinces of Germany, and they had been chosen by lots to leave in exile due to overpopulation of their homeland. Here Geoffrey has followed the story of both the *Historia Britonnum* – the exile (ch. 31) – and that of William of Malmesbury – the overpopulation and the drawing of lots as the customary solution for alleviating it (*GR*, i.6.2, p. 23). Hengest states that their purpose in coming "is to offer our service to you or some other lord," to which Vortigern replies that although he is disappointed that they are pagans, their arrival is propitious (*HRB*, §98.285–87).

Geoffrey's version of the arrival itself is therefore arranged to remove at least some of the guilt associated with Vortigern in the "invitation" version (found in Gildas, Bede, and Henry of Huntingdon's *Historia Anglorum*).[19] In the *HRB*, the Saxons are more free agents rather than an instrument of Vortigern and the Britons. The earliest mention of the Saxons as a group comes in the context of an early battle when they fought alongside Vortigern's Britons and they receive praise from Geoffrey here: "but the Britons did not have to fight hard, as the Saxons among their ranks fought so bravely that they quickly routed the enemy, accustomed though they were to winning" (§99.296–98).

Gifts of lands to the Saxons carry various meanings and importance in each of the texts in which they occur. In Geoffrey's *Historia*, on this early occasion, in thanks for their efforts, Vortigern "increases his gifts to them and gave their leader Hengest extensive lands in the region of Lindsey to support himself and his fellow-warriors" (§99.299–301);[20] since no specific gifts are mentioned

---

18   The Normans as a group drop from view, no doubt for the sake of political expediency, except for two mentions in the context of the death of Bedevere at the battle of Saussy (§171.359 and §176.468).

19   There is no mention of the initial arrival of the Saxons or of Hengist and Horsa in Henry's *Epistola ad Warinum*.

20   On the use of Lindsey in Geoffrey, see Tatlock, *Legendary History*, 23–24. For evidence supporting the suggestion that the Anglo-Saxon kingdom of Lindsey had originally been a development of an earlier British kingdom, see Thomas Green, "The British Kingdom of Lindsey," *Cambrian Medieval Celtic Studies*, 56 (2008): 1–43. The *Historia Brittonum* gives Lindsey as the site of one of Arthur's twelve battles (ch. 56) but does not associate that area with Vortigern and his gifts. See Appendix 3, and note.

before this point, however, we have no way of measuring or comparing this "increase." When Vortigern marries Hengest's daughter Ronwen, he gives Hengest the province – later kingdom – of Kent as a wedding gift. In Geoffrey, there are no more gifts of land to the Saxons, given freely[21] – from here on out, what the Saxons do gain they do through their own devices or via Gormund's "Donation."

In other texts, however, at least three more of the lands that made up the Saxons' Heptarchy were gained by virtue of Vortigern. In the *Historia Brittonum*, Kent is given as a wedding gift, and at the "night of the long knives," in order to save his life, Vortigern hands over Essex and Sussex, "together with Middlesex and other [unnamed] districts" (ch. 46). In William of Malmesbury's *Gesta Regum*, in addition to the wedding gift of Kent (i.7, 2), at the feast following the slaughter of the Britons, Vortigern has to "buy himself out of slavery with three [unnamed] provinces" (i.8, 3). From a different perspective, the Anglo-Saxon Chronicles record for the years 456/457 that the Britons, having lost 4,000 men (or "four troops"), abandoned Kent, fleeing in great terror to London (ASC, pp. 12–13);[22] other provinces were gained in due course, but not through the auspices of Vortigern. Henry of Huntingdon in the *HA* records Vortigern's wedding, but no marriage gift, with no other gifts of land from Vortigern; in the *EW* there is no narrative of the wedding and no gifts of land.

Granted, Geoffrey may not have used the same version of the *HB* that William apparently did. Nonetheless, Geoffrey may have had other reasons for associating only the gifts of Kent (marriage gift §100.363–65) and lands around Lindsey (prior to the marriage §99.300) with Vortigern: 1) although the Saxons are involved in a major land-grab following the night of the long knives (§§104–5) – a treachery where the Briton nobility is wiped out, the bloodshed of the narrative extreme enough without the added administrative detail of significant territorial expansion – he saves Vortigern's last ignominy for his defeat by Aurelius Ambrosius, whose role Geoffrey significantly amplifies over any of this predecessors or contemporaries; 2) by not mentioning any other gifts of land (except Lindsey), the emphasis is on Kent, which was traditionally considered the first of the Saxon-held regions; and most importantly, 3) references to additional provinces this early in the text would have called attention

---

21   Later, at the conclusion of the "night of the long knives," in order to buy his life, Vortigern is forced to give the Saxons "cities and castles" and they take London, York, Lincoln, and Winchester "and laid waste to all regions" (§105.491–95); in Wace, Vortigern gives them London, Winchester, Lincoln, York, and Chichester, as well as Sussex, Essex and Middlesex in fee (*Brut*, 7289–94).

22   Reading based on the Winchester and Peterborough MSS (A and E) (*The Anglo-Saxon Chronicles*, ed. and trans. Michael Swanton, 12–13).

100   CHAPTER 2

to the multiple administrative elements of the Heptarchy, which Geoffrey
apparently assiduously wanted to avoid. Furthermore, by mentioning no other
gifts of land passing from Vortigern to the Saxons, Geoffrey may have sought
to give the impression that Vortigern, during the first half of his reign (or his
"first reign" depending on how one chooses to count it),[23] had held the largest
extent of English lands of any single ruler between the end of Roman rule and
the reign of Athelstan – since no single Saxon ruler is said to have reigned over
"all of Loegria" after Gormund's "Donation."[24]

Geoffrey's portrayal of the infamous night of Saxon treachery, the "night
of the long knives," also differs from the portrayals in other texts. In the *HRB*,
six details distinguish the scenario: 1) the treachery takes place on May Day;[25]
2) "around four hundred and sixty barons and earls" were killed (as opposed to
the three hundred in *HB* and William's *GRA*); 3) the killing of many Saxons by
the unprepared Britons before they themselves were slaughtered (the Britons
had no knives but they used rocks and clubs they found on the ground to inflict
damage on the Saxons); 4) rather than Vortigern ransoming himself through
the gift of provinces, he agrees to give castles and cities; 5) he flees to London,

---

23   During Vortigern's "first reign" (§§ 95–101), his land holdings are extensive. At the time of
      St. Germanus's preaching to the Britons in the hopes of defeating both the Pelagian heresy
      and the pagan Saxons, Vortigern invites yet more Saxons via "Octa, Ebissa and Cherdich
      [who] arrived with three hundred ships full of armed men, all of whom Vortigern wel-
      comed warmly and rewarded with generous gifts" (§101.385–87), hoping they would help
      him defeat the barbarians in the north; Geoffrey adds "for with their help he continually
      beat his enemies and was victorious in every battle" (§101.387–88; "Missis ilico legatis,
      uenerunt Octa et Ebissa et Cherdich cum trecentis nauibus armata manu repletis, quos
      omnes suscepit Vortegirnus benigne maximisque muneribus donauit; uincebat namque
      inimicos suos per eos et in omni proelio uictor existebat" §101.385–88). Fearing Vortigern's
      further betrayal, the Britons abandon him, making his son Vortimer king, who proceeds to
      lead the Britons in purging their lands of Saxons and other barbarians; perhaps because
      he was so successful, Vortimer's step-mother Ronwen has him poisoned, and Vortigern
      returns to power, having sought out Hengist in Germany who returns with a fleet of
      300,000 armed men (§103). At the start of his "second reign," Vortigern's subsequent over-
      tures at peace with Hengist lead up to the May Day "peace summit" meeting, at which the
      "night of the long knives" takes place, and subsequent territorial expansion of the Saxons
      (§§ 104–5).
24   For a minority – though intriguing – view of Vortigern as Roman *vicarius*, of his relations
      with the Romans and thus a revision of his interactions with the Saxons, see John H. Ward,
      "Vortigern and the End of Roman Britain," *Britannia* 3 (1972): 277–89, esp. 285–89.
      J. N. L. Myres also proposes that based on the *Historia Brittonum*, Vortigern "could be
      described as living in fear not only of the northern barbarians and of the internal opposi-
      tion led by Ambrosius, but also of Roman invasion" (*Anglo-Saxon Pottery*, p. 98).
25   On the festival of Beltane (not in *HB* or William of Malmesbury's *GRA*), see Tatlock,
      Legendary History, 40.

HISTORIA REGUM BRITANNIAE: PART 2

and the Saxons take London, then York, Lincoln and Winchester; and 6) following Vortigern's ransoming and the taking of London, etc., the Saxons are said to lay waste "to all regions" (§105.493–95). Thus, not surprisingly, in Geoffrey's *Historia*, the night of treachery and its immediate aftermath are portrayed on a grander scale, with the emphasis on death and total destruction, as well as territories taken by the Saxons rather than ceded to them.

Stage two of the march toward Saxon hegemony in the vulgate *Historia* begins with Aurelius's battles against the Saxons. In the *Historia Brittonum* which is Geoffrey's fullest source (except for the *liber vetustissimus*, whose existence we are not going to argue here),[26] as noted above, Ambrosius is a bit of a garbled figure, including one story in chapters 40–42 in which Ambrosius plays the role later played by Merlin in Geoffrey's *HRB*. In Geoffrey, this figure is unified as a king, with the combined name of Aurelius Ambrosius (Ambrosius Aurelianus in Gildas and Bede); he is son of King Constantine II, brother of Constans (murdered by Vortigern) and Uther, father of Arthur. With typical sleight of hand, "Geoffrey inserts three illustrious rulers from the house of Constantine [Aurelius, Uther, and Arthur] into the epoch which was formerly thought to have witnessed the emergence of the Anglo-Saxon kingdoms."[27]

As Leckie notes, "Aurelius Ambrosius wrests control of the island from the usurper Vortigern, restoring British rule to its former estate … [Aurelius] inaugurates a glorious era, which culminates in the reign of Arthur. It is not the Saxons who rise in this period, but the Britons."[28] Aurelius fights three major battles against the Saxons at Maisbeli where he defeats Hengest (§121), Kaerconan where he defeats again and this time captures Hengest (§123), and York where he besieges Octa and Eosa (§126), having had Hengest executed (§125). Upon the urging of Bishop Eldadus who appealed to Aurelius's sense of mercy, Aurelius gives Octa and Eosa "the region adjacent to Scotland," one of the "empty places" referred to by Eldadus (§126.179–86); Octa and Eosa negotiate a truce with Aurelius, but after the latter's death, they resume their belligerence.[29] Aurelius orders the churches rebuilt that had been destroyed

---

26   For one of the most cogent and convincing arguments assembled to date in favor of the existence of Geoffrey's *liber vetustissimus*, see Ian Short, "Gaimar's Epilogue" and the Introduction, n. 5. See also the survey in Siân Echard, "Latin Arthurian Literature," in *A History of Arthurian Scholarship*, ed. Norris J. Lacy (Cambridge: D. S. Brewer, 2006), 62–76.

27   Leckie, *Passage*, p. 59.

28   Leckie, *Passage*, p. 59. Leckie rightly finds that Geoffrey paints a glorious picture of Aurelius, yet the issue of whether the exact territories grabbed by the Saxons earlier during Vortigern's reign were ever restored by Aurelius remains unresolved, or at least, vague.

29   Octa was an Anglo-Saxon king of Kent (the dates of his reign are unclear c. 500–540) and according to some sources, he may have been Hengist's son and Ebissa (Eosa) Hengist's

by the Saxons near York, London, and Winchester (§127), cities and surrounding areas seized by the Saxons at the night of the long knives (or in its immediate aftermath).[30] Geoffrey writes that for Aurelius, "his sole concerns were the restitution of his kingdom, the reorganization of the churches, the renewal of peace and law, and the enforcement of justice" (§127.200–2). The building of Stonehenge through Merlin's miraculous engineering is also credited to Aurelius, as a memorial to the slaughtered Britons.

Following Aurelius's death by poison – at the hands of the Saxon Eopa disguised as a Briton monk – Utherpendragon is crowned and leads the battle of Mount Damen after having been defeated by the Saxons at York by Octa and Eosa. Loth wages a campaign against Octa and Eosa, yet it is Uther who is eventually victorious against them; the latter's deaths at the battle of St. Albans mark the closing of stage two. [Since it is so unique and compendious, stage three containing Arthur's battles against the Saxons will be discussed below under the category of Arthur.]

Stage four opens with the power vacuum left by Arthur's removal to Avalon. In 542 – one of the very few dates in the *Historia Regum Britanniae* – the mortally wounded Arthur hands over Britain's crown to his "relative" Constantinus, son of Cador duke of Cornwall. The Saxons and Mordred's two sons rise up against him but without success (§179). Following the nephew of Constantinus, Aurelius Conanus, came Vortiporius who successfully fought against the rebellious Saxons, who continued to send for reinforcements from Germany; Vortiporius became monarch of the entire kingdom and "in the end ruled his people well and in peace" (§182.113–14). Next came Malgo to whom Geoffrey devotes an exemplary description – in physical beauty, military prowess and generosity – save for his "wallowing in the sin of sodomy" (§183.117). Malgo ruled the entire island "as well as its six neighbors, Ireland, Iceland, Gotland, the Orkneys, Norway and Denmark which he conquered in fierce battles" (§183.118–21). In addition, taking note of this extraordinary post-Arthurian figure who appears virtually unknown to the scholarly and popular communities,

---

nephew; see *HB*, ch. 38. The two are first mentioned by Geoffrey in Hengist's speech about sending for his son, Octa, and his cousin, Ebissa; Wright translates "fratuele suo Ebissa" as his "cousin," Thorpe as his "brother" (§101.380; Thorpe based on Griscom, ed., VIII, xiii). See "*fratruelus*, nephew" in R. E. Latham, *Revised Medieval Latin Word-List from British and Irish Sources* (London: Oxford University Press for the British Academy, 1965; orig. *Medieval Latin Word-List*, ed. J. H. Baxter and Charles Johnson, 1934), 201.

30   As typical with Geoffrey, the chronology of these events is unclear; it is hard to imagine that both the killing of the Britons at the May Day peace gathering and the Saxons' taking of London, York, and Winchester all occurred on one night (and that uncertainty cannot be settled at this point).

HISTORIA REGUM BRITANNIAE: PART 2   103

it is important to also note that in nearly all of the references to the Saxons in this latter part of the text, Geoffrey uses the verb *insurrexere*, which serves to reinforce the Saxons' status as secondary to the Britons, a constant threat to the peace but certainly not in charge of anything more than at the local level.

The Saxons revolt again, and seek the aid of the African king Gormund, to disastrous effect for the Britons. With 160,000 troops, Gormund lays waste to the countryside, driving the Britons to Brittany, Cornwall or Wales, as he gives Loegria to the Saxons. The Britons lose the "royal crown and control over the island" (§187.170–1) fighting among themselves and three usurpers, but at the same time the Saxons do not become "masters of the island, as they too were subject to three kings" just as the Britons were (§187.173–§188.175); thus Geoffrey again forestalls passage of dominion, as if this stage in Saxon hegemony is both moving forward and static.

Geoffrey's portrayal of Augustine's conversion of the English also puts the Saxons in a position of inferiority, and thus in a way, illustrates a form of stasis in the Saxons' march forward. In a pointed but very abbreviated version of the conversion (very short in comparison with Bede and Henry of Huntingdon for example), Geoffrey supports the Britons' position in every way.[31] In response to Augustine's request that the British abbots submit to him and his suggestion that they assist him in converting the English, Abbot Dinoot explains that the Britons already have their own archbishop, and that they refuse to preach to the Saxons since the latter perpetually persist in their attempts to wrest the island from the rightful control of the Britons: "gens Saxonum *patriam propriam* eisdem auferre perstarent" (§188.192–93) [our emphasis]. As Michael Curley observes, after showing via Dinoot's speech that the Britons owe the Saxons nothing, the Britons "despising their faith and beliefs and shunning them like dogs" (§189.194–95), Geoffrey "passes over in silence Bede's obsession with the Celtic Church's non-canonical date for celebrating Easter" since he did not exactly embrace Bede's view of Augustine's twofold mission – that is, to both evangelize the English and recall the British Church "back to the lap of Roman orthodoxy" following the Pelagian heresy.[32] The conversion of the English, which functions as a high point in early English hegemony and a rite of passage in Bede in particular, is yet another source of enmity against the

---

31   As noted above, Chapter 1 n. 110, Bede devotes an extended passage to the conversion whereas Henry divides up the information by regions of the Heptarchy. On Geoffrey's diametrically opposed presentation to that of Bede's, see Michael Curley, *Geoffrey of Monmouth*, 102–4.

32   Curley, *Geoffrey of Monmouth*, 104 and 103.

104   CHAPTER 2

Saxons – nearly to the point of ridicule – in Geoffrey.[33] At best, the conversion is a form of stasis in Geoffrey.

The fifth and final stage of the passage of dominion – which Geoffrey forestalls until the very end – has as its high points the struggles between the Briton king, Cadwallo (son of Briton, Caduan), and the Saxon Edwin (son of Edelfridus and the wife he repudiated), king of Northumbria,[34] raised together at the court of Caduan and later in Armorica at the court of king Salomon (according to Geoffrey, §190.225–44.[35] After they have grown and returned to Britain, having ascended their thrones, Edwin proposes to wear the crown of Northumbria, but Cadwallo is persuaded by Brianus, his nephew, to not permit the ceremonial crown-wearing (although Edwin had been his lifelong friend and was already king north of the Humber), having been advised that only one king should wear the crown at a time, Brianus arguing in light of the Saxons' consistent track record of treachery against the Britons (§191.258–77). Cadwallo threatens Edwin to cut off his head if he dares wear the crown (§192.283–85), and the latter subsequently ravages southern Britain but is eventually killed by Cadwallo at the battle of Hedfield (§197.430–32).

As one might expect, Bede devotes considerable time to Edwin (*HE*, ii. 9–20), to whom he attributes the Christianization of Northumbria, in part through his marriage to a Kentish princess, but perhaps more importantly on the political level, Edwin, "like no other English king before him, he held under his sway the whole realm of Britain, not only English kingdoms but those ruled

---

33   On the subject of ridicule with respect to Augustine's conversion of the English, see the discussion of Wace's treatment of the events in Chapter 5 and also Jean Blacker, "Why Such a Fishy Tale? St. Augustine's Conversion of the English in Wace's *Roman de Brut*," *Romance Quarterly* 52.1 (2005): 45–53.

34   Although not all of Geoffrey's "information" is accurate by any means, (St.) Edwin was an actual king of Northumbria (Deira and Bernicia; *c.*586–632/33, reign *c.* 616 until his death). The location of his early exile in childhood is unknown but Geoffrey and Reginald of Durham report the Welsh legend that he was raised by king Cadfan ab Iago in Gwynedd along with Cadfan's son, Cadwallon ab Cadfan (though Geoffrey adds the Armorican court of Salomon as well, §190). In Bede, Edwin is the fifth in the list of Bretwaldas (see n. 113 below). On the Welsh tradition of Edwin's childhood exile, see Colgrave and Mynors (ed. and trans.), 162 n. 1, and 202–3 n. 2. See also T. M. Charles-Edwards, *Wales and the Britons*, 389 n. 52.

35   In a compelling analysis of family history as political history, Geraldine Heng refers to Geoffrey's story of the two princes, Caduallo the one foundling a Briton and the other Edwin a Saxon, as a "romance" where both "are born of royal women at the same time, in the same household, and fostered together in intimacy through their infancy, childhood, and adolescence – a folkloric motif that drives narrative pretexts in romances and lays through the Middle Ages" (*Empire of Magic*, 52–58). See also Tatlock, *Legendary History*, 390.

over by the Britons as well" (*HE*, ii. 9, p. 163). Bede's portrayal of Cadwallo the Briton resembles one of Geoffrey's portrayals of any Saxon:

> Cædwalla, although a Christian by name and profession, was neverthe-less a barbarian in heart and disposition and spared neither women nor innocent children. With bestial cruelty he put all to death by torture and for a long time raged through all their land, meaning to wipe out the whole English nation from the land of Britain. (*HE*, ii. 20, pp. 203, 205)

Bede continues on Cædwalla, in the same breath reiterating his view of the Britons' role in the evangelization of the English:

> Nor did he pay any respect to the Christian religion which had sprung up amongst them. Indeed to this very day it is the habit of the Britons to despise the faith and religion of the English and not to co-operate with them in anything any more than with the heathen. (*HE*, ii. 20, 205)

Geoffrey may have internalized some of Bede's view of Caduallo/Cadwallon (Cædwalla) as singularly uncooperative and belligerent.[36] When the latter is unable to decide how to resolve the conflicts between King Peanda (Penda) of Mercia and King Oswi of Northumbria, one of his advisers suggests that he play the Saxon kings off one against the other, commenting, "My lord, since it has been your intention to drive the entire English race from Britain's shores, why change your mind and permit them to live among us in peace?" (§200.481–3). Cadwallo is persuaded by this and similar arguments, granting Peanda permis-sion to fight Oswi. After Peanda's death, his son succeeds him with Cadwallo's blessing; the son tries to wage war on Oswi but Cadwallo finally arranges a peace between the Mercians and the Northumbrians (according to Geoffrey).

---

36   Geoffrey may in fact have applauded this ambition attributed to Caduallo by Bede (Caduallo/Cadwallo/Cadwallon, that is, Cadwallon ap Cadfan, king of Gwenedd, 625–34/5, and Northumbria, 633–34/5), called Cædualla by Bede, who uses the same name for the later king of Wessex (born *c*. 659, reigned 685–89); on which other early writers may have shared this negative view of Caduallo, see Patrick Sims-Williams ("Gildas and the Anglo-Saxons," 28). Although Bede was scrupulous and had access to some Welsh sources, "Bede's accusation that Cædualla's aim [referring to the later king of Wessex; *HE* iv.15.382] was to exterminate the people of the isle of Wight should be viewed with caution, as the similar charge [of genocidal goals] against Cadwallon" (Geoffrey's Caduallo, Bede's first Cædualla, *HE* ii.20) ("Cædualla," John T. Koch, ed., *Celtic Culture: An Historical Encyclopedia*, I, 317).

106   CHAPTER 2

The peace among the Britons is short-lived, which Geoffrey decries through a speech by King Cadwallader as he heads to Brittany to escape the plague.[37] In true Galfridian fashion, the Saxons who had survived the plague

> announced as was their unfailing custom, to their fellow-countrymen in Germany that, if they came as immigrants, they could easily occupy the island, devoid as it was of its inhabitants. On receiving the news, that wicked people ass[e]mbled a vast crowd of men and women, landed in Northumbria and filled the empty tracts of land from Scotland to Cornwall. There were no natives to stop them, save a few remaining Britons living in the remote forests of Wales. This marked the end of British power in the island and the beginning of English rule. (§204.550–59)[38]

For the first time referred to as the English (*Angli*), the Saxons grow stronger. Cadwallader plans to return from Brittany when an angelic voice stops him, stating that "God did not want the Britons to rule over the island of Britain any longer, until the time which Merlin had foretold to Arthur" (§205.564–66). Following Cadwallader's death in Rome, Ivor and Yni assemble a fleet, land in Britain and subject the English to "savage incursions" for sixty-nine years, but this is in vain, since

> the once proud race had been so weakened by plague, famine and their habitual strife that they could not ward off their foes. As their culture ebbed, they were no longer called Britons, but Welsh, a name which owes its origin to their leader Gualo, or to queen Galaes or to their decline.[39]

---

37 Cadualadrus/Cadwaladr/Cadwallader, that is, king of Gwynedd, *c.* 655–682, grandson of Cadfan ab Iago and son of Cadwallon ab Cadfan (the latter being Geoffrey's Caduallo, Bede's "earlier" Cædualla; Bede's "later" Cædualla was king of Wessex who lived at least 30 years later than Cadwallon/Cædualla, king of Gwynedd and Northumbria). It is thought though that Geoffrey confused the story of Cadwallader's pilgrimage to Rome with Bede's account of Cædualla of Wessex's pilgrimage to Rome (*Trioedd Ynys Prydein: The Triads of the Island of Britain*, ed. and trans. Rachel Bromwich, 4th ed. 2014, 298–99). In the 10th-century prophetic poem, the *Armes Prydein*, Cadwallader (Cadwaladr; king of Gwynedd, d. late 7th c.; son of Cadwallon) appears along with a prince named Cynan, as one of two messianic leaders expected to restore the Britons to the sovereignty of Britain following the expulsion of the Saxons (*Armes Prydein, The Prophecy of Britain From the Book of Taliesin*, ed. Ifor Williams, trans. Rachel Bromwich, Medieval and Modern Welsh Series VI (Dublin: Dublin Institute of Advanced Studies, 1972, 1982, 2006, ll. 81–100, 163–70, 176–94).

38 See Chapter 1, n. 146 for the Latin passage.

39 "Supradicta namque mortalitas et fames atque consuetudinarium discidium in tantum coegerat populum superbum degenerare quod hostes longius arcere nequiuerant.

HISTORIA REGUM BRITANNIAE: PART 2

For perhaps the first time in the text, Geoffrey gives the Saxons credit for wisdom, while also bemoaning the fate of both the Britons and their successors, the Welsh:

> The Saxons acted more wisely, living in peace and harmony, tilling the fields and rebuilding the cities and towns; thus with British lordship overthrown, they came to rule all Loegria, led by Athelstan, who was the first of them to wear its crown. The Welsh, unworthy successors to the noble Britons, never again recovered mastery over the whole island, but, squabbling pettily amongst themselves and sometimes with the Saxons, kept constantly massacring the foreigners or each other.[40]

Although Leckie implies that Geoffrey fleshes out the extra 250 (-300) years of joint rule of Britons and Saxons, extending the passage of dominion with narrative details in the text, in fact Geoffrey accomplishes the extension through a typical deft application of smoke and mirrors. As noted above, there are numerous comments about joint rule – or at least simultaneous rule – but none of those comments fall between the reign of Cadwallader after the plague when Britons are said to lose dominion, and the coming of Athelstan in the tenth century – though Geoffrey does not give a date for Athelstan. Thus, we have 250 years of extended joint rule brushed over with one stroke.

2   King Arthur

2.1   *King Arthur and His Precedents in Gildas, Bede, and the* Historia Brittonum

Perhaps one of Geoffrey's most audacious moves was the presentation of Arthur, a figure who as Geoffrey portrays him, appears nowhere else.[41] Geoffrey's

---

Barbarie etiam irrepente, iam non uocabantur Britones sed Gualenses, uocabulum siue a Gualone duce eorum siue a Galaes regina siue a barbarie trahentes" (§207.590–94). Wright translates "siue a barbarie trahentes" as "their decline".

40   "At Saxones, sapientius agentes, pacem etiam et concordiam inter se habentes, agros colentes, ciuitates et oppida reaedificantes, et sic abiecto dominio Britonum iam toti Logriae imperauerant duce Adelstano, qui primus inter eos diadema portauit. Degenerati autem a Britannica nobilitate Gualenses numquam postea monarchiam insulae recuperauerunt; immo nunc sibi, interdum Saxonibus ingrati consurgentes externas ac domesticas clades incessanter agebant" (§207.594–600).

41   As is so often (if not always) the case with Geoffrey's *Historia*, both the range and quantity of scholarship on Arthur (both literary and historical) is so voluminous as to defy comprehensive citation; references cannot be exhaustive. Standard references to the Latin and

108   CHAPTER 2

Arthur appears almost as if in a vacuum, simultaneously indefensible –
no sources can be cited to corroborate – and not needing of a defense, i.e.,
untouchable – no sources can be cited to contradict. The multiple aspects of
Arthur, his plasticity, are also as excellent a ploy as the *liber vetustissimus* (if
that is indeed a ploy). As often, with Arthur, Geoffrey is again "playing both
ends against the middle." A comparison with Arthur's precedents, albeit sometimes indirect – since Arthur isn't Arthur until Geoffrey – serve best to point up
the many aspects of Arthur in Geoffrey's *Historia*.

In the early works referring to the figure who came to be known as Arthur,
what sparse references there are are usually to battles and other military
aspects surrounding those battles.[42] In Gildas, Arthur is not named as such,

<hr/>

vernacular historico-legendary traditions not already mentioned above include Robert
Fletcher, *Arthurian Material in the Chronicles, Especially Those of Great Britain and France*,
Studies and Notes in Philology and Literature x (Cambridge, MA: Harvard University,
1906; repr. New York: Burt Franklin, 1973) (dated but still useful); the essays in *The Arthur
of the French, The Arthur of the English* and *The Arthur of the Welsh*; Siân Echard, *Arthurian
Narrative in the Latin Tradition* (Cambridge: Cambridge University Press, 1998), and with a
significant component on the pre-Galfridian tradition, Thomas Green, *Concepts of Arthur*
(Stroud, Gloucester: Tempus, 2007).

42   On the military exploits surrounding Arthur, recent arguments in support of Arthur's his-
      toricity, as well as significant bibliography on both sides of that question, see Peter J. Field,
      "Arthur's Battles." Field takes exception to views debunking the historicity of Arthur such
      as those expressed by Thomas Charles-Edwards who writes that "at this stage of the
      enquiry, one can only say that they may well have been an historical Arthur [but ...] the
      historian can as yet say nothing of value about him" ("The Arthur of History," *The Arthur
      of the Welsh*, 29) and particularly of David Dumville, perhaps the most skeptical of histo-
      rians regarding Arthur, "I think we can dispose of him [Arthur] quite briefly. He owes his
      place in our history books to a 'no smoke without fire' school of thought ... The fact of
      the matter is that there is no historical evidence about Arthur; we must reject him from
      our histories, and above all, from the titles of our books" ("Sub-Roman Britain," 187–88).
      Cf. Oliver Padel, "The Nature of Arthur," *Cambrian Medieval Celtic Studies* 27 (1994): 1–32.
      Padel distinguishes between the "historical" Arthur (of the *Historia Brittonum*, ch. 56,
      and the *Annales Cambriae*) and a pan-Brittonic "folklore" Arthur who is the hero of local
      wonder-tales, arguing that the folklore Arthur is "the true one, and the 'historical' Arthur
      [is] the secondary development" (30), and Thomas Green, whose thesis in *Concepts of
      Arthur* (2007) is that Arthur was originally conceived as a folkloric hero, and later his-
      toricized by the author(s) of the *Historia Brittonum*; see also Nicholas Higham, *King
      Arthur: Myth-Making and History*, whose arguments draw heavily on those of Padel and
      Green. Two useful recent surveys (with broadly based bibliographies) on this debate are
      Alan Lane, "The End of Roman Britain and the Coming of the Saxons: An Archaeological
      Context for Arthur?" in *A Companion to Arthurian Literature*, ed. Helen Fulton, Blackwell
      Companions to Literature and Culture 58 (Oxford: Blackwell, 2009; Chichester: John
      Wiley & Sons, 2012), 15–29, and N. J. Higham, "Early Latin Sources: Fragments of a
      Pseudo-Historical Arthur" in *A Companion to Arthurian Literature*, 30–43. For an addi-
      tional perspective – compelling, but given the nature of the ever-continuing scholarship

HISTORIA REGUM BRITANNIAE: PART 2

but instead one finds the leader of the Britons at a very tumultuous time, Aurelius Ambrosius, "a gentleman who, perhaps alone of the Romans, has survived the shock of this notable storm" (*DEB*, 25.3, p. 28). That is the only description – if it can be called that – of "Arthur" in Gildas, though the historian does not miss an opportunity to decry the weakness and divisiveness of the Britons both before and after Badon Hill ("His descendants in our day have become greatly inferior to their grandfather's excellence" 25.3; "external wars may have stopped but not civil ones" 26.2).[43] Gildas cites the battle of Badon Hill as "pretty well the last defeat of the villains, and certainly not the least" (26.1) and dates it to the year of his birth, "one month of the forty-forth year since then has already passed."[44]

---

on Arthur, probably not the "last word" – see Higham's most recent study, *King Arthur: The Making of the Legend* (New Haven, CT: Yale University Press, 2018). Investigating both global and insular mythologies and texts, Higham concludes here that there were multiple potential King Arthurs, but no one figure can claim the title of the "once and future king," that insofar as early insular as well as Galfridian material is concerned, Gildas, "Nennius" and the *Annales Cambriae* should not be treated much differently than Geoffrey, all being/creating imaginative works in which ultimately "the past was pressed into service of the present, and was subject to the immediate, and highly variable, purposes of political ideology" (271).

43 Field notes that Gildas names only one fifth-century Briton – Aurelius – "and that mainly to lament that the man's descendants were not worthy of him" ("Arthur's Battles," 4).

44 On the difficulties of dating Gildas's *De Excidio*, see many of the sources in n. 102 above, as well as Molly Miller, "Relative and Absolute Publication Dates of Gildas's *De Excidio*," *Bulletin of the Board of Celtic Studies* 26 (1974–76): 169–74 and eadem, "Starting to Write History: Gildas, Bede, and Nennius," *Welsh History Review* 8 (1977): 456–65; Michael E. Jones, *The End of Roman Britain* (Ithaca, NY and London: Cornell University Press, 1996), esp. 43–53, 121–30; and E. A. Thompson, "Gildas and the History of Britain," *Britannia* 10 (1979): 203–26. Field writes that the second and third documents to allude to Arthur are two Welsh elegies, the first *Y Gododdin* ("The Gododdin") on the massacre of an expeditionary force from the British kingdom of the Gododdin (around Edinburgh) wiped out in a raid on Northumbria *ca.* 600, and the *Marwnad Cynddylan* ("Lament for Cynddylan") about a "mid-seventh-century King of Powys who fought the English of what was to become Mercia"; each of the two texts implies that Arthur was exemplary among warriors. Field goes on to speculate intriguingly that "since, however, references to persons in early Welsh heroic verse are exclusively to historical figures, the people who composed these poems must have believed Arthur was a real person, not a mythological or fictional one" ("Arthur's Battles," 5), though of course the authors' beliefs in Arthur's historicity do not necessarily prove it. See also Rachel Bromwich's essential investigation of (and survey of scholarship on) Arthur's origins, where she cites lines 1241–42 of the *Gododdin* as "the third of three fundamentally important early references to Arthur": "*gochore brein du ar uur / caer ceni bei ef arthur*" ("he glutted (?) black ravens in the rampart of the stronghold, though he was no Arthur" Bromwich's translation) ("Concepts of Arthur," *Studia Celtica* 10/11 (1975–76): 163–81, cited at 176); Thomas Charles-Edwards, "The Authenticity of the Gododdin: An Historian's View," in *Astudiaethau ar yr Hengerdd:*

110   CHAPTER 2

Neither Bede writing *c.*820 nor the Anglo-Saxon Chronicles mention Arthur by name. Bede writes of a "certain Ambrosius Aurelianus ... under whose leadership the Britons regained their strength" (i. 16–17, 55). Bede writes that the Britons won, and then their enemies, until the year of the siege of Mount Badon "when the Britons slaughtered no small number of their foes about forty-four years after their arrival in Britain" (i. 16–17, 55). No more details are provided either on the significance of that battle, or on Arthur, who is not named specifically in connection with the battle. Skipping ahead, the early tenth-century *Annales Cambriae* date the battle to 516 (in which Arthur carried the cross on his shield, the first mention of this legend)[45] and Arthur's death as well as Mordred's to 537 at Camlann.[46]

In chapter 56 devoted to Arthur's campaigns, the *Historia Brittonum* names Arthur as the leader of the Britons who fought alongside the kings of the Britons, but who was not a king himself. "Nennius" gives locations for twelve battles, the twelfth and last being at Badon Hill where "nine hundred and sixty men fell in one day, from a single charge of Arthur's." The chronicler adds that "no one laid them low save he alone; and he was victorious in all his campaigns."[47] The *HB* also claims that Arthur carried the image of the Virgin Mary on his shield.[48] There is no more description of Arthur than this.

    Studies in Old Welsh Poetry, ed. Rachel Bromwich and R. B. Jones (Cardiff: University of Wales Press, 1978), 44–71; and the substantial introduction to *The Gododdin of Aneirin: Text and Context from Dark-Age North Britain*, ed. and trans. John T. Koch (Cardiff: University of Wales Press, 1997), ix–cxliii.

45   See Chapter 5, for the discussion of Mary on Arthur's shield in Wace, Geoffrey and others, .as well as n. 48 below.

46   "516 an. Bellum Badonis, in quo Arthur portavit crucem Domini nostri Jhesu Christi tribus diebus et tribus noctibus in humeros suos et Brittones victores fuerunt" ("516 The Battle of Badon, in which Arthur carried the Cross of our Lord Jesus Christ for three days and three nights on his shoulders [*i.e. shield*] and the Britons were the victors" (Morris's italics)) and "537 an. Gueith Camlann in qua Arthur et Medraut corrueunt, et mortalitas in Brittannia et in Hibernia fuit" ("537 The battle of Camlann, in which Arthur and Medraut fell: and there was plague in Britain and Ireland") (Morris, ed. and trans, *Annales Cambriae*, pp. 85 (Latin), 45 (English).)

47   "Duodecimum fuit bellum in monte Badonis, in quo corruerunt in uno die nongenti sexaginta viri de uno impetu Arthur; et nemo prostravit eos nisi ipse solus, et in omnibus bellis victor extitit" (ch. 56; p. 76).

48   The first written occurrence of the variant that it was the Virgin Mary, and not the Cross, that appeared. Morris has read the Latin of the *HB* here as referring to Arthur's shield, but it reads literally "shoulders": "in quo Arthur portavit imaginem sanctae Marie perpetuae virginis super humeros suos" (ch. 56; p. 76) (but this was "clearly" *HB*'s misreading of the Welsh "scuit" – shield – for "scuid" – shoulders, according to William of Malmesbury's editor and translator, R. M. Thomson, *GRA*, vol. II, 21). Geoffrey solves this particular dilemma by saying that Arthur had the shield, Pridwen, at his shoulder: "and shouldered his shield

HISTORIA REGUM BRITANNIAE: PART 2   111

2.2   *King Arthur in William of Malmesbury and Henry of Huntingdon*

In the *Gesta Regum*, William of Malmesbury's narrative on Arthur is equally brief, hitting the major points already mentioned, with some differences, including the distinction made between Ambrosius and Arthur, and the addition of the historian's hopes regarding the validity of future narratives on Arthur:

> With [Vortimer's] decease the Britons' strength withered away, and their hopes dwindled and ebbed; at this point, in fact, they would have collapsed completely, had not Vortigern's successor Ambrosius, the sole surviving Roman, kept down the barbarian menace with the outstanding aid of warlike Arthur. This Arthur is the hero of many wild tales among the Britons even in our own day, but assuredly deserves to be the subject of reliable history rather than of false and dreaming fable; for he was long the mainstay of his falling country, rousing to battle the broken spirit of his countrymen, and at length at the siege of Mount Badon, relying on the image of our Lord's Mother which he had fastened upon his arms,[49] he attacked nine hundred of the enemy single-handed, and routed them with incredible slaughter. (i.8.2, p. 27)

Given these meager and thus perhaps even more tantalizing references to Arthur found in the aforementioned sources, in addition to tales which must have been circulating orally, there is little wonder that Henry of Huntingdon marveled at finding Geoffrey's *Historia* at Bec in 1139, over one quarter of which was devoted to that figure.[50]

---

   called Pridwen, on which was depicted Mary, the Holy Mother of God, to keep her memory always before his eyes" (§147.109–10 "humeris quoque suis clipeum vocabulo Pridwen, in quo imago sanctae Mariae Dei genitricis inpicta ipsum in memoriam ipsius saepissime reuocabit"). On Wace's variation – and precision relative to Geoffrey's text – on the exact location of this image on Arthur's shield, see Chapter 5. On this image in its various forms in early Welsh and Latin texts concerning Arthur, see John Koch, "The Celtic Lands," 252–53.

49 William of Malmesbury's approach to the shoulder/shield situation, having apparently read the Welsh correctly (Thomson, *GRA*, vol. II, 21): "fretus imagine Domincae matris quam armis suis insuerat" (i.8.2; "relying on the image of our Lord's Mother which he had fastened upon his arms"). Just how it was "attached" or where it was "sewn" is another matter, not to be solved here. Thomson comments that Geoffrey "perhaps partly depending upon *GR*, has it both ways: Arthur had 'across his shoulders a shield ... on which was painted a likeness of the Blessed Mary'" (*GRA*, vol. II, 21–22).

50 According to Robert of Torigni, Henry was shown at least some version of Geoffrey's *Historia*. On the possibilities of which manuscript Henry might have seen, see Jaakko

112 CHAPTER 2

However, as Diana Greenway notes, it would have been too great an undertaking for Henry to recast Books I and II already written to accommodate the newly discovered material: "the concept of the *regnum* of the Romans in Britain would have had to be abandoned, as the idea of a line of powerful kings in Britain up to the time of the Saxon invasions challenged Henry's underlying interpretation of the first five hundred years of British history."[51] As a consequence, in the third version of the *HA*, Henry made "only minor revisions" in Book I on the basis of the new information,[52] but he did create a separate compilation, the *Epistola ad Warinum*, which makes up one of the components to Book V of the *HA*, and contains more material on Arthur.[53]

Other than in the *EW*, in the *HA* Arthur appears in Book II, chap. 18. The chapter opens with the following praise: "The valiant Arthur who was at that time the commander of the soldiers and kings of Britain, fought against [the invaders] invincibly. Twelve times he led in battle. Twelve times he was victorious in battle"; an enumeration of the twelve battles follows.[54] Henry adds his own comment: "One historian [author of the *HB*][55] tells of these battles, and the places where they were fought, though none of the places can be identified now. I think this has happened by the providence of God, so that popular favour, adulatory praise, and transitory fame might be set at nought."

In the *EW*, chapter 9 of 10 is devoted to Arthur, who here for the first time – other than in Geoffrey and the First Variant – appears as a king. The elements are:
1) Arthur's investment with royal insignia at age 15;
2) Defeat of Colgrinus, *ducem Anglorum*;
3) Siege of Lincoln ends in concord (not in great slaughter as in *HRB* §§ 144–45);
4) The "enemy" destroy the city of Legions, without warning (not in *HRB*);[56]

Tahkokallio, "Early Manuscript Dissemination," in *A Companion to Geoffrey of Monmouth*, 155–80, esp. 159–61.

51 *HA*, ed. and trans. D. Greenway, c.

52 *HA*, ed. and trans. D. Greenway, c and n. 154 to Book I, chapters 3 (Caerleon), 9 (Silvius), and 12 (Luid).

53 For a summary of the major inclusions and omissions in the "Letter to Warinus," see Greenway, ed. and trans., *Historia Anglorum*, c-ci, including her observation that "at some points Henry seems closer to the First Variant than to the Vulgate *HRB*," to be discussed below in Chapter 3 on the First Variant. For the Letter's relevance to the textual history of the *HRB*, see Wright, "*Epistola*."

54 The source of this chapter was *Historia Brittonum* (Vatican C text, ch. 27) (Greenway, ed. and trans., 100, n. 66).

55 Greenway, ed. and trans., 100, n. 67.

56 *HRB* §§156–62 contain and account of the city, and of Arthur's speeches and ceremonies; in §177 it is the place to which Guinevere flees.

HISTORIA REGUM BRITANNIAE: PART 2   113

5)   The great battle of *Bade* (only named battle);[57]
6)   Arthur "made all the English that remained his tributaries";[58]
7)   Arthur annexes Scotland, and "all the lands surrounding Britain";
8)   Crosses the sea and defeats the Roman forces at Paris;
9)   Before crossing the Alps, returns to England to defeat his nephew, Mordred, but is himself mortally wounded;
10) "But the Bretons [*Britones*], your ancestors, refuse to believe that he died. And they traditionally await his return."[59]

Characterization is sparse; there are no speeches, but here elements are gathered that create the picture that became so well known through Geoffrey's *Historia*: Arthur's kingship, the extent of his kingdom over all England including "foreign" annexation (though not to the extent in the *HRB*), his defeat of the Roman legions, and the final battle with Mordred. When looking at the *EW* as a whole, however, this Arthurian section does not completely change the largely pro-English tenor of the text.

2.3   *King Arthur: Geoffrey of Monmouth. Overview*

Although in his prologue, Geoffrey claims that he found "in the fine works of Gildas and Bede ... nothing concerning the kings who lived here [in Britain] before Christ's Incarnation, and nothing about Arthur and the many others who succeeded after it [i.e., him],"[60] while the first claim is largely true, the second is less so, although information on Arthur named thusly is meager. In comparison with the sources discussed above, the scope of Geoffrey's expansion on Arthur in the three books Geoffrey devotes to this figure clearly stands out and it is not surprising how the presentation forms the nucleus of the

---

57   See n. 16 above, and Chapter 5, n. 71.
58   Greenway, ed. and trans., "Exalted Matters: Letter to Warin," *EW*, ch. 9, p. 579.
59   This element is not in the *HRB*. Wright suggests that Henry included this in the *Epistola* "because of its special relevance to his Breton addressee" ("*Epistola*," p. 79). On the Bretons' belief that Arthur was still alive and would return one day, see William of Malmesbury, who commented in the context of the "discovery" of Gawain's grave, that since Arthur's grave had never been found, there were "old wives' tales that he may yet return" (*GRA* iii. 287, p. 521) and Hermann of Tournai, *De miraculis S. Marie Laudensis*, *PL* clvi 983 (Greenway, ed. and trans., 580, n. 167). For a detailed investigation of this motif in legend, historical texts, and fiction, see Virginie Greene, "Qui croit au retour d'Arthur?" and also the Introduction, n. 20 and Chapter 5, n. 175.
60   "de eis Gildas et Beda luculento tractatu fecerunt nichil de regibus qui ante incarnationem Christi inhabitauerant, nichil etiam de Arturo ceterisque compluribus qui post incarnationem Christi successerunt repperissem ..." (Prol., 3–5, pp. 4, 5).

114 CHAPTER 2

majority if not all subsequent Arthurian history[61] and fiction. The most outstanding features of Geoffrey's presentation of Arthur are as follows:

1) Arthur is now a king (the 99th);[62]
2) His conception via deception out of wedlock (§137.511);
3) His coronation at 15; followed by battles against the Saxons (§143.8–9);
4) Arthur's arms described (§147.107–13), including the shield which is now named Pridwen, on which is depicted the Virgin Mary;
5) "Mercilessly cut down and forced to sail home" the Irish under their leader King Gillamurius, then turning "his attention to the Scots and Picts" he "began wiping them out with utter ruthlessness" (§149.160–66); not unlike his enemies, Arthur is pitiless at first – "No one he came upon was spared, until all the bishops and subordinate clergymen of that wretched country came to the king barefoot, carrying holy relics and church treasures, to beg him for mercy" (§149.166–69) – but then he is moved to pity and pardons them;
6) Pardons the Scots and restores churches in York (§151.192–200);
7) Arthur's reputation for generosity and excellence "spread to the farthest corners of the world"; after learning of the anxieties of other rulers, he "exulted at being universally feared and decided to conquer all Europe" (§154. 229–36);
8) Subjects Norway and Denmark to his rule, then sails to Gaul and begins "to ravage the entire country" (§154. 247–51); defeats the Roman consul Frollo in single combat so that Paris will not be destroyed by a prolonged battle;
9) Arthur spends nine years in Gaul "subduing the remaining rebellious provinces" (§155.298–301); he returns to Britain after giving Normandy to Bedevere and Anjou to Kay;
10) Description of the plenary court and enumeration of guests summoned: "Arthur's world-famous openhandedness had made them all love him" (§156.306–55; cited at 355);
11) Court festivities with a "courtly" scene including: "all its doughty knights wore clothes and armour of a single colour. Its elegant ladies, similarly dressed, spurned the love of any man who had not proved himself three times in battle" (§157. 387–90);

---

61 When I say "history" in this context, I am not taking sides in the debate on Arthur's historicity but am rather referring to texts that were conceived *by their authors* to be historical narratives.

62 See Chapter 1, n. 4.

HISTORIA REGUM BRITANNIAE: PART 2

12) Arthur prepares to take a hundred and eighty-three thousand, two hundred knights and "countless infantry" (promised to him by his liegemen) across the channel to answer the challenge of the Roman emperor, to whom he will never pay tribute, but rather he will exact from them what they are trying to exact from him (§162.529–30; 534–37);

13) Arthur fights the hideous Mont-Saint-Michel giant in single combat (§165);

14) Arthur engages the Romans near Autun (§166);

15) Arthur's plans against Lucius Hiberius (§§167–68); inventory of the fighting against Lucius Hiberius (§§171–75); Arthur hears of Mordred's treasonous usurpation, and of Guinevere's betrayal (§176);

16) Return to his kingdom; battle at the river Camblan; carnage against Mordred (§178.46);

17) Inventory of the fallen on both sides, including Mordred and Arthur: "The illustrious king Arthur too was mortally wounded; he was taken away to the island of Avallon to have his wounds tended, and in the year of Our Lord 542, handed over Britain's crown to his relative Constantinus, son of Cador duke of Cornwall" (§178.81–84).

The remaining mentions of Arthur (§191.272; §195.377, 381; and §205.566) allude to his reputation, his descendants, the descendants of Hoel who fought with Arthur, and a reference to the angelic voice which came to Cadwallader (Cadualadrus) as he sought Alanus's help to "restore him to his former power"; as Cadwallader was preparing a fleet, the voice orders him to give up the attempt, saying that "God did not want the Britons to rule over the island of Britain any longer, until the time came which Merlin had foretold to Arthur."[63]

Strictly in mathematical terms, by preceding Arthur with 98 kings and following him with seven, Geoffrey accomplishes a number of goals: 1) Arthur is preceded by a rich and complex contextual fabric including descendants of famous Trojans, the first "settlers" other than the native giants; 2) although the fabric of preceding generations of kings is rich because numerous, Arthur stands out if only by virtue of the amount of narrative devoted to him, but also because of his territorial ambitions, and the quality of his leadership (though there are ironies, such as those seen in the juxtaposition of his bellicose nature

---

63 "... auxilium ab Alano petiuit ut pristinae potestati restitueretur. At cum id a rege impetrauisset, intonuit ei vox angelica dum classem pararet ut coeptis suis desisteret. Nolebat enim Deus Britones in insulam Britanniae diutius regnare antequam tempus illud uenisset quod Merlinus Arturo prophetauerat" (§205.562–66). As with all references to Merlin's Prophecies, the contents are suitably vague.

116   CHAPTER 2

and talent for establishing a lasting peace);[64] 3) although the implications of
the end of the *HRB* are that following Cadwallader, the Britons shared control of the island with the Saxons for some 250–300 years until the reign of
Athelstan, the reigns of very few Briton kings following Arthur are narrated,
again increasing Arthur's stature by contrast, and no names are given for
those Britons who shared rule with the Saxons, further raising Arthur beyond
the others.

As mentioned in the Introduction, there are two essential threads or poles
in medieval Arthurian history and fiction, that of barbarian or outsider, and
that of civilizer or establishment insider; these elements are often in tension
perhaps no place more so than in Geoffrey's *HRB*. Geoffrey's Arthur is full of
contradictions and perhaps that is why he can be so easily molded to suit
nearly any subsequent text: Arthur is not only "other" simultaneously as he
is both an establishment and a non-establishment figure, but he can "meta-
morphose" within the same text because he can always be positioned as the
"other," depending on the perspectives of the writer and the audience (the
latter itself conceivably composed of a range of individuals from numerous
places and socio-political stations): 1) while born of a great line of kings, beginning with Brutus, great-grandson of Aeneas, and coming to fulfillment as the
son of Uther Pendragon, Arthur is conceived out of wedlock and through
deception (deception which can be seen as well as mystery and magic); 2) one
of the greatest of the British kings,[65] as a Briton Arthur is always "other" in the

---

64   On Arthur's tempered administrative dominion in Wace in contrast with Gormund's
      rapacious military techniques with Geoffrey's *Historia* as a frame of reference, see Jean
      Blacker, "Arthur and Gormund: Conquest, Domination and Assimilation in Wace's *Roman
      de Brut*," in *"Si sai encore moult bon estoire, chançon moult bone et anciene": Studies in
      the Text and Context of Old French Narrative in Honour of Joseph J. Duggan*, ed. Sophie
      Marnette, John F. Levy, and Leslie Zarker Morgan, Medium Aevum Monographs (Oxford:
      The Society for the Study of Medieval Languages and Literature, 2015), 261–82.

65   A further wrinkle is argued by Tatlock who devotes a good deal of energy to what he
      considers the vital importance of Arthur's Breton connections, including that Arthur's
      grandfather (Aurelius) was a Breton, and his "most distinguished vassal is his nephew
      king Hoelus of Brittany" (*Legendary History*, 398). In this vein, also noteworthy is King
      Salomon's speech to the Britons where he explains that after the Britons went to Brittany,
      those who remained behind in Britain "never again enjoyed the privilege of maintain-
      ing uninterrupted control of their land" becoming in a way the inferiors of the Bretons
      who often came to their aid, "… thus I am grieved by the weakness of your people, since
      we share the same origins and you are called British, just as we are, we who bravely pro-
      tect this land you see from the attacks of all its neighbours" (§194.342–44). In an article
      which in part expands on Tatlock's suggestions, Edwin Pace proposes that in Geoffrey's
      vulgate "Britain's first post-Roman ruler, Constantine, is not just a Breton, he is also
      younger brother to Aldroenus, king of Brittany" revealing that "Arthur's Breton dynasty is

HISTORIA REGUM BRITANNIAE: PART 2

context of Saxon England, and Norman England for that matter – one finds at least a double layer of "othering" as the English are "other" for the Normans and British peoples are "other" for the English; 3) Arthur is both a symbol of military domination across western Europe and also of the highest civilization attained in peacetime, thus again an "other" as a "civilized Briton," itself, for many, an oxymoron.

Drawing a very useful analogy, Ananya Jahanara Kabir argues that in large part, the Victorian imperialist trope of British colonial rule as a new Roman empire was predicated upon both a forgetting of its sub-Roman British bar-barian past and a glorification of the "Anglo-Saxon" English, freed from the Norman Yoke and poised to fulfill its self-appointed mission of civilizer of less-than-civilized regions of the world.[66] The forgetting of the British past was essential to the imperialist goal of disseminating latter-day *Romanitas* due to the perception that the Britons were barbarians whose crude ways were not consonant with Roman civilization (unmindful that the Britons had converted to Christianity while the ancient Romans had remained largely pagan).[67] In this conceptualization of Englishness, the "Anglo-Saxon" element is dominant, superior to the British underclass, yet at the same time subju-gated by the Norman overlords.[68] Although to invoke seventeenth-century,

---

thus a *cadet* branch of Conan [Meriadoc]'s line" ("Athelstan, 'Twist-Beard,' and Arthur's Tenth-Century Breton Origins for the *Historia Regum Britanniae*," *Arthuriana* 26.4 (2016): 60–88, here 71–72). On the subject of Breton claims to royal descent (from Conan Meriadoc and Arthur), see also Jean-Christophe Cassard, "La Tradition royale en Bretagne armorique," *Revue Historique* 281.1 (569) (1989): 15–45. On Geoffrey's "promotion" of the Bretons, see also Rosemary Morris, "The *Gesta Regum Britanniae* of William of Rennes: An Arthurian Epic?" *Arthurian Literature VI*, ed. Richard Barber (Cambridge: D. S. Brewer, 1986), 60–125, esp. 98–99.

66   "Analogy in Translation: Rome, England, India" in *Postcolonial Approaches to the European Middle Ages: Translating Cultures*, ed. Ananya Jahanara Kabir and Deanne Williams, Cambridge Studies in Medieval Literature (Cambridge: Cambridge University Press, 2006), 183–204.

67   Kabir writes: "the analogy between the Roman and British empires met the analogy between medieval Britain and colonial India at precisely the moment figured in the 'groans of the Britons' [Trevelyan's translation of Gildas's "gemitus Britannorum"]: the gap between the departure of the Romans from Britain in the early fifth century AD and the arrival of the Angles and Saxons in the sixth. With the help of the trope of *translatio studii et imperii*, this gap sutures two trajectories of conquest into the 'beginning of the nation's narrative' even while calling attention to the 'minus in the origins': the erasure of Britain's Celtic past from this developing teleology" (184).

68   The term "the Norman Yoke" which emerged in English nationalist discourse in the seven-teenth century was used to attribute the oppressive aspects of feudalism in England to the impositions of William the Conqueror; as stated in the late-eighteenth-century anony-mous *Historical Essay on the English Constitution*, "whatever is of Saxon establishment

118   CHAPTER 2

eighteenth-century, and Victorian political rhetoric may appear to overstate
the case, or to obfuscate it with anachronistic references, the Britons as an
original or native, dispossessed people, the early English as both conquerors
and conquered (and thus colonizers and colonized) and the Normans as invisible (not named directly in the text) but omnipresent (metaphorically) – and
possibly civilizing – oppressors are central images in the foundation myth of
the Britons, as seen prominently in Geoffrey of Monmouth's text, particularly
in his presentation of Arthur as insider and outsider, always "other."[69]

In his essay, "The Beginnings of English Imperialism," John Gillingham
argues that William of Malmesbury was the first medieval writer to reincorporate the Roman view of barbarism – the principal criterion being the lack
of civilized behavior – into his own, thereby creating a polarity of civilized vs.
uncivilized to parallel that of Christian vs. pagan, "allow[ing] for the possibility of Christian barbarians."[70] Gillingham also advances the idea that "one of
William of Malmesbury's most creative and influential achievements was to
introduce [an] imperialist perception of Celtic peoples into history," a perception which goes beyond the "traditional enmity of neighbors, ... the virtually
universal feeling that 'we' are 'better' than 'them'" to an "imperialist view that
certain people are so inferior as to belong to a distinctly lower order of society."
Gillingham proposes, however, that William's view of the Celtic peoples as barbarians caught on because he simply made explicit widespread ideas that were
already commonplace in the twelfth century since in his observation, earlier,
"within the Anglo-Saxon world during the ninth, tenth and eleventh centuries [what is striking] is the absence of any clearly defined attitude towards
the Welsh, the Scots and the Irish ... as though they were regarded as people
simply like any other" that the "tenth-century English kings may have been

---

is truly constitutional, but whatever is Norman is heterogeneous to it, and partakes of
a tyrannical spirit" (Obadiah Hulme, *An Historical Essay on the English Constitution*,
London: Edward and Charles Dilly, 1771, 9–10, as cited in Kabir, 188 and n. 14).

69   Michelle Warren characterizes the *Historia* as a portrayal of "the forgotten empire of a
      marginalized people in reaction to an urgently present colonial dynamic" ("Making
      Contact: Postcolonial Perspectives through Geoffrey of Monmouth's *Historia regum
      Britannie*," *Arthuriana* 8.4 (1998): 115–34, 116 ff.). Cf. Patrick Sims-Williams who writes that
      "racial stereotypes of the Celts are not solely invented and maintained by non-Celts in
      an imperialist context, important though this context has often been. A shared sense of
      Celtic 'otherness' can be exploited by Celtic individuals and groups working within, or
      against, the non-Celtic establishment, so it is not surprising that some Celts should have
      an interest in maintaining it," particularly the image of "Celts" as seers and visionaries
      ("The Visionary Celt: the Construction of an Ethnic Perception," *Cambridge Medieval
      Celtic Studies*, 1986 (11): 77–96, cited at 77).

70   "The Beginnings of English Imperialism," 10.

HISTORIA REGUM BRITANNIAE: PART 2 119

imperial rulers, in that they ruled, or claimed to rule, over a number of king-doms; but they were not imperialists."[71] Not unrelatedly, as senses of identity

71 "The Beginnings of English Imperialism," 9. Although on the political level William did share the prevalent view among contemporary (and earlier) historians that the Saxon takeover of the island was an "achievement" and he bemoaned the Norman conquest and continuing domination, with respect to his perceptions of levels of cultural refinement, "it was French culture, not Christianity alone, which made the English civilised" ... "the more 'Frenchified' England and the English became, the better" (Gillingham, "Beginnings of English Imperialism," 29 and 6). Gillingham breaks down those views of "Celtic" inferi-ority into three areas: 1) the barbarian at work; 2) the barbarian at war, and 3) the barbar-ian in bed. In brief, the barbarian at work refers to the perception that the "Celtic" regions were largely supported by an agrarian economy; William of Malmesbury comments "What would Ireland be worth without the goods that come in by sea from England? The soil lacks all advantages, and so poor, or rather unskillful, are its cultivators that it can produce only a ragged mob of rustic Irishmen outside the towns; the English and French, with their more civilized way of life, live in the towns, and carry on trade and commerce" (*GR*, v. 409.1). On the barbarian at war, in an account of a Scottish attack on Northumbria in 1183, Richard of Hexham comments on the savagery of a war targeted against non-combatants, where "by the sword's edge or the spear's point they slaughtered the sick on their beds, women who were pregnant or in labor ... worn-out old men, feeble old women, anyone who was disabled ... they carried off their plunder and the women, both widows and maidens, stripped, bound, and roped together ... to be either kept as slaves or sold to other barbarians in exchange for cattle" (cited by Gillingham, 11; *Chronicle of the Reigns of Stephen, Henry II and Richard I*, ed. Howlett, iii. 156–7); Gerald de Barrie wrote later: "The French ransom soldiers; the Irish and Welsh butcher them and decapi-tate them" (cited by Gillingham, 11; *Journey through Wales*, trans. Thorpe, 269). According to John of Salisbury, the Welsh "live like beasts ... despising the law of marriage, they keep concubines as wives; whenever it suits them they get rid of them for a price ... they do not blush to indulge in incest" (cited by Gillingham, 11; *Letters of John of Salisbury, vol. 1: The Early Letters (1153–61)*, ed. and trans. W. J. Millor, H. E. Butler, and C. N. L. Brooke, Oxford Medieval Texts, Oxford, Clarendon Press, 1986, i. 135–36). Gillingham points out that certain circumstances contributed to these perceptions: agrarian practices in "Celtic" lands were less prosperous than those in England; the slave trade was not active in twelfth-century England but it was in Wales, Ireland, and Scotland; and marriage laws in those regions, based on secular rather than church law, permitted divorce, and in the case of kings, polygamy. Nonetheless, as Gillingham notes, the "perception of Celtic soci-eties as barbarous obviously functioned in part as an ideology of conquest" and goes fur-ther to suggest that "the greater significance of the imperialist outlook was the barrier it set up between the conqueror and the conquered – a barrier which inhibited assimila-tion" ("Beginnings of English Imperialism," 17). See also Silke Stroh, "Colonial Beginnings? Celticity, Gaeldom and Scotland until the end of the Middle Ages," *Scottish Cultural Review of Language and Literature, suppl. Uneasy Subjects: Postcolonialism in Scottish Gaelic Poetry* 17 (2011): 43–68; Jeffrey Jerome Cohen, "Green Children from Another World or the Archipelago in England," in *Cultural Diversity in the British Middle Ages*, ed. idem, New Middle Ages Series (New York: Palgrave MacMillan, 2008), 75–94, esp. 89 on William of Newburgh's attitudes toward the Welsh, Irish, and Scots; R. R. Davies, *The First English Empire*, 113–41.

120   CHAPTER 2

evolved, by as early as the 1130s but certainly by the middle of the twelfth century, it appears that the Norman educated elites at least (the broader populace
is another matter)[72] began to think of themselves as English, as evidenced for
example in Henry of Huntingdon's reference to the collective group in celebrating the victory of the English crown over the Scots at the Battle of the Standard,
in his third redaction of the *Historia Anglorum* – as the *gens Normannorum
et Anglorum*.[73]

However, despite one's perspective on the extent to which the descendants
of the Normans in England assimilated by the middle of the twelfth century
and how closely they may have identified with the English population – and
despite how much "ordinary" anti-Saxon, anti-Norman/anti-French sentiment
there may have been as well as anti-British[74] – the fact remains that, with
respect to the two "dominant" cultures and centers of power (English and
Anglo-Norman), the British cultures and peoples remained largely outsiders.[75]

---

72   For a broad-ranging consideration of nations and senses of national identity with spe-
      cific reference to the peoples of medieval Britain (not necessarily the ruling elites), see
      R. R. Davies, "Nations and National Identities in the Medieval World: An Apologia," *Journal
      of Belgian History* 34 (2004): 567–79. Cf. also Patrick Sims-Williams, "The Visionary Celt."
73   At other times, Henry did not refrain from expressing anti-Norman views, writing in the
      context of the chaos surrounding Stephen's taking of the throne upon Henry I's death,
      about the "mad treacheries of the Normans" (*HA*, x, p. 700). On the very intricate subject
      of the sense of identity of the English and descendants of the Normans in the twelfth
      century, including the extent to which the Normans assimilated into English culture, see
      especially John Gillingham, "Henry of Huntingdon and the Twelfth-Century Revival of
      the English Nation," *The English in the Twelfth Century*, 123–44 (orig. publ. in *Concepts of
      National Identity in the Middle Ages*, ed. Simon Forde, Lesley Johnson, and Alan V. Murray,
      Leeds Texts and Monographs, New Series 14, Leeds: Leeds Studies in English, 1995,
      76–101); Ian Short, "*Tam Angli Quam Franci*: Self-Definition in Anglo-Norman England,"
      in *Anglo-Norman Studies 18*: Proceedings of the Battle Conference 1995, ed. Christopher
      Harper-Bill (Woodbridge: Boydell, 1996), 153–75; Rodney Hilton, "Were the English
      English?" in *Patriotism: The Making and Unmaking of British National Identity: Vol. I
      History and Politics*, ed. Raphael Samuel (London and New York: Routledge, 1989), 39–43;
      and Elizabeth Tyler, "Trojans in Anglo-Saxon England: Precedent Without Descent," *The
      Review of English Studies*, New Series, 64.263 (2013): 1–20.
74   Given the range of human behavior, one can regrettably find ethnic slurs against all sides.
      For an account of such slurs against English and Normans, see Short, "*Tam Angli Quam
      Franci*,"153–54. One would hope that in the "real" world – and not just in an ideal one – as
      Short adds, "it would naturally be a mistake to assume any correlation between this sort of
      national stereotyping, which is as much a cultural constant as it is a literary convention,
      and the actual social realities of the time" (154).
75   The work of other scholars including John Gillingham (esp. the arguments advanced in
      "Henry of Huntingdon and the Twelfth- Century Revival of the English Nation") – and
      readings Ailred of Rievaulx, Henry of Huntingdon, Geoffrey of Monmouth, and Gaimar –
      have led Paul Dalton to suggest that the growing closeness of the English and the

HISTORIA REGUM BRITANNIAE: PART 2   121

In light of this increasing anti-British sentiment on the part of Geoffrey's contemporaries, it becomes all the more compelling to his enterprise as one not
only of inclusion but of redemption. He not only sought to write a history of
the native peoples which his colleagues would take seriously as an integrated
part of the history of the island – as so many of them did take it seriously – but
he also sought to redeem those peoples in the face of growing disapproval,
even scorn.

One of the best means of doing that was of course through Arthur, making
the outsider also insider, and glorious, in addition, on both scores. It is important to note that in Geoffrey for the first time, the character of Arthur is sufficiently developed to be said to have a "life" beyond simple mentions in one
battle or a list of battles.[76] In each of the sections of Arthur's life – 1) conception and birth, 2) accession, 3) peacetime activities and 4) war – the dynamic
between insider and outsider is visible, in a wide range of manifestations, and
altered by each of the historians who took up Arthur's story.[77]

2.3.1   Arthur's Birth

The circumstances of Arthur's birth are notable, as are the fact that in Geoffrey,
Arthur has a "life": Arthur is no longer "simply" a military commander serving
alongside the Romans as in Gildas, Bede, and the *Historia Brittonum*, appearing in battles either singly or multiples, but a descendant of Brutus, with a

---

Normans, that is, the merging of identities or assimilation, was not only closely related
"to the simultaneous emergence of a new hostile representation by Anglo-Norman writers of the 'Celtic' peoples as barbarians" but equally to the perceptions of the "political
crisis of the Anglo-Norman state" in the 1130s, primarily but not exclusively the Welsh
rebellion supported by David, king of Scots; in other words, there is evidence to support
the case that "the 'twelfth-century revival of the English nation,' the demonization of the
'Celtic' peoples, and the political and military crises of the early years of Stephen's reign
were interrelated" ("The Topical Concerns of Geoffrey of Monmouth's *Historia Regum
Britannie*," cited here at 692, and 710).

76   As Gordon Gerould noted nearly one hundred years ago, "there is no evidence, despite
the *Britonum nugae* mentioned by William of Malmesbury, that a coherent legendary
sequence about Arthur existed until Geoffrey created it" ("King Arthur and Politics," 38).
The emphasis here is on "coherent," for this is another of Geoffrey's innovations – the
creation of what was from that time forward was a "life" of the king – though the missing
enfances would only be later supplied in any detail in the romance tradition. Although
most historians today are wary of reconstructing a "coherent" life of Arthur, this is apparently what Geoffrey tried to do.

77   For somewhat different divisions of Arthur's "life" and also of his military engagements,
see Rosemary Morris (*The Character of King Arthur in Medieval Literature*), who it must
be remembered, is constructing a "biography" based on both historical and fictional texts
ranging over a much longer period ("earliest times" to 1500, p. 1) than the present book.

"birthtale" as opposed to simply mentions solely within the adult context of war.[78] Arthur's father was royal,[79] making him the quintessential insider, but he was conceived out of wedlock, making him the quintessential outsider with respect to traditional family expectations and church doctrine.[80] The magic involved in Arthur's conception further increases his extraordinary status, linking him with "Celtic" legends almost like a demi-god, bringing him closer to an "inner circle" of "Celtic" lore, but likewise distancing him from the Saxons.[81]

Arthur is further distanced from the Saxons as none of them or their leaders are involved in his accession; Arthur is chosen as king of the Britons by the Britons only.[82] In fact, when Uther dies suddenly, the Britons are in the difficult

---

78   See Morris's discussion of possible antecedents for Arthur's birth tale (24–35), and Tatlock, *Legendary History*, 312–19.
79   Morris sums up Geoffrey's creation of a family for Arthur: "Geoffrey introduces a new figure: Uther, who is made Ambrosius' brother. Arthur is thus connected to Ambrosius by the privileged uncle-nephew link ... the Saxon struggle is nonetheless a family affair [with] something of the flavour of a dynastic struggle, the House of Constantine versus the House of Hengest ...; the family network also gives Arthur a close connection with the enthralling Vortigern story" and "sets Arthur in the huge descent of the British royal house and its collective destiny" (13).
80   For some, the term "outsider" may not seem strong enough since it does not take into account the question of sin. Robert Hanning has argued that Uther's sin is redeemed by the good inherent in Arthur's birth (*Vision of History*, 153–54). Following an examination of a number of texts reflecting English law (prior to 1926, if a child were conceived out of wedlock but born in it, legitimacy was guaranteed) whereas in French law, this was not the case, Morris concludes with the general remark that "the story of Arthur's conception is, then, a rich and complex one whose legal political, moral and narrative implications are fully and intelligently exploited by a variety of authors with contrasting aims and viewpoints" (32). For our purposes, it is the mark of difference – Arthur's *otherness* – that is important, at least for Geoffrey and his contemporaries, including the anonymous author of the First Variant and Wace, not unresolvable illegitimacy or sin.
81   For a survey which remains useful (although not annotated), see Mary Williams's presidential address to the Folklore Society, "King Arthur in History and Legend," *Folklore* 73 (1962) 73–88. See also Nicholas Higham, *King Arthur: The Making of the Legend*, which includes extensive discussions of analogies of Arthur, demi-gods, and other figures related to deities from western as well as non-Western traditions.
82   Referring to early Welsh literature collectively, Morris notes that Arthur "is not invariably called a king, and even where he receives that title – as in the saints' lives – there is no interest in the circumstances of his accession," declaring as well that "Arthur is not a Welsh king, and there is nothing Celtic about his kingship, or about his accession in any text ... [but] in non-Welsh literature, by contrast, Arthur compelled attention by the mere fact of his kingship" (36). On Arthur's status as national hero or king and related issues of regional or national identity in early Welsh history, literature, and saints' lives, see in *Arthur of the Welsh*, specifically Thomas Charles-Edwards, "The Arthur of History" (15–32), Patrick Sims-Williams, "The Early Welsh Arthurian Poems" (33–72), and Brynley F. Roberts, "Culwich ac Olwen, the Triads, Saints' Lives" (73–96); see also

HISTORIA REGUM BRITANNIAE: PART 2

position of selecting a king under duress; the barons are essentially forced to
urge Dubricius archbishop of Carleon to crown Arthur, Uther's son, his successor, since the Saxons "when they learned of Uther's death, had invited in
their countrymen from Germany, and led by Colgrimus, were aiming to expel
the Britons" (§143.1–3). Although Arthur is the only claimant, he has to be
"suggested" by the barons; Geoffrey makes sure that Arthur gains the crown
through assent of his barons, and not through conquest, usurpation, deposi-
tion, or automatic inheritance.[83] In addition, the Church's role and assent is
vital, as Arthur must be seen as a ruler in the good graces of the Church – and
in this way, yet again an insider.[84]

2.3.2 Arthur as Military Commander and Statesman

Since Arthur fights so many battles in the vulgate *Historia* – his image as a
warrior-king here probably exceeded only by the portrayal of the civilized imperialist in Wace's *Brut* – it is important to see them in relation to one another
and to the few peacetime activities thrown in, as if by afterthought.[85] Geoffrey
not only adds a significant number of details found in the list of battles in the
HB (as well as skipping some of the locales), but he also adds the international
arena, aggrandizing rather than overshadowing Arthur's successes at home
(until Camlann). From Gildas to Geoffrey, Arthur has been transformed from
a Roman leader in the provinces to a king with vast territories, second only to

---

J. S. P. Tatlock, "The Dates of the Arthurian Saints' Legends," *Speculum* 14.3 (1939): 345–65;
Huw Pryce, "British or Welsh? National Identity in Twelfth-Century Wales," *English
Historical Review* 116.468 (2001): 775–801; Thomas Green, *Concepts of Arthur*, esp. chap-
ters 1–4; Catherine Piquemal, "Culwch and Olwen: A Structured Portrayal of Arthur?"
Arthuriana 10.3 (2000): 7–26; and Nerys Ann Jones, "Arthurian References in Early Welsh
Poetry," in *Arthur in the Celtic Languages: The Arthurian Legend in Celtic Literatures and
Traditions*, ed. Ceridwen Lloyd-Morgan and Erich Poppe, Arthurian Literature in the
Middle Ages IX (Cardiff: University of Wales Press, 2019, repr. 2020), 15–34.

83   The difficulties of the accessions of William I, Henry I, as well as Stephen, cannot have
been far from Geoffrey's mind. On the nuances of those complex situations, see especially
David Bates, *William the Conqueror* (New Haven, CT: Yale University Press, 2016) and
idem, *The Normans and Empire* (Oxford: Oxford University Press, 2013); Edmund King,
King Stephen (New Haven CT: Yale University Press, 2010), esp. ch. 2 "The Accession,"
41–81; and David Crouch, *The Normans: The History of a Dynasty* (London and New York:
Hambledon Continuum, 2002).

84   We need to keep in mind that Geoffrey is trying to counter Bede's minimizing of the role
of the Church in the affairs of the Britons, and one means of achieving that is to make visible at all crucial moments ecclesiastical power and positive engagement with the Britons.

85   In Wace's poem, Arthur's peacetime role takes on major significance with his founding
of the Round Table and the narrative space Wace devotes to that symbol and political,
organizational tool. See Chapter 5.

124   CHAPTER 2

the Roman emperor (and in the position to defeat him, if fate in the guise of
Mordred's rebellion hadn't intervened).

Geoffrey's vulgate *Historia* appears to not use the locale of the *HB*'s first
battle at the river Glein (probably the River Glen), passing straight to the
"River Duglas" ("flumen Duglas") where he places Arthur's first battle against
the Saxons, Scots, and Picts.[86] In that same vicinity, Arthur raises a siege at
York (nominally, the second battle); the third is the siege of Lincoln "on a hill
between two rivers in the province of Lindsey" (*HRB*, §145.60), vaguely following the setting of *HB*'s fifth battle. The river Bassas in *HB* ("sextum bellum super
flumen quod vocatur Bassas" *HB*, ch. 56; p. 76) may have given Geoffrey as much
trouble as modern researchers for he gives it a skip, passing straight to the location of "Nennius"'s seventh battle, the siege of Colidon Wood (*HRB*, §145.65).[87]
Still counting the battles, the eighth (located at "Guinnion fort" in *HB*)[88] is "in
the region of Somerset" ("Sumersetensem prouintiam," §146.87) in Geoffrey;
the latter supplies Arthur with a shield with Mary depicted upon it, and a name
(Pridwen), as well as the named sword, Caliburnus (Excalibur), and the lance
Ron; it should be noted that none of the other royal figures in the *HRB* have
named arms.

However, from the ninth battle to the twelfth as they appear in the *Historia
Brittonum*, the *HRB* parts ways: in the latter text, there is no battle at the City
of Legions (Vrbs Legionum, Caerlcon),[89] nor on the banks of the Tryfwyd,[90]
nor Mt. Agned,[91] nor oddly enough, *HB*'s twelfth battle, at Badon Hill (in *HRB*,

---

86   My intention here is not to participate in the debates aimed at establishing the locales
      for these battles, but rather to show where Geoffrey's *Historia* intersects with the *HB* and
      where it does not. On the possible locations of these battles, see Chapter 1, n. 76, Chapter 5,
      n. 66, Appendix 3, N. J. Higham, *King Arthur: Myth-Making and History*, 144–50, and idem,
      King Arthur: The Making of the Legend, Appendix 11, "Arthur's Battles as Described in the
      Historia Brittonum and the *Annales Cambriae*," 285–88.
87   On Bassas as a rhyme-word with Duglas from a Welsh battle-listing poem (possibly a
      source of *HB* §56), see P. J. C. Field, "Gildas and the City of the Legions," *Heroic Age* 1
      (1999): http://www.heroicage.org/issues/1/hagcl.htm (accessed 2019); on views regarding
      the possible underlying battle-poem, see also John T. Koch, "The Celtic Lands," 248–49.
88   See also Robin Melrose, *Religion in Britain from the Megaliths to Arthur: An Archeological
      and Mythological Exploration* (Jefferson, NC: McFarland, 2016), 173–74.
89   Though if in this instance, by the City of Legions is meant York, Geoffrey has mentioned
      that locale for Arthur's celebration of Christmas, as well as for one of the sieges fought
      near the river Duglas. See P. J. C. Field, "Gildas and the City of the Legions."
90   The shore of the river Tribruit remains particularly unresolved. See most recently Sims-
      Williams, "The Early Welsh Arthurian Poems," in *Arthur of the Welsh*, 33–72, here 41, and
      Higham, *King Arthur: The Making of the Legend*, 286.
91   Mount Agned (reminiscent of *HB*'s "the hill called Agned") appears in *HRB* long before
      Arthur comes on the scene, as a city built by Ebraucus (sixth king of the Britons) "now
      called Edinburgh" ("Montis Agned, quod nunc Castellum Puellarum dicitur" §27.93).

pagum Badonis appears earlier), the site of Arthur's most famous defeat of the Saxons. Following the eighth battle (*pagum Badonis*) where Arthur wears Mary on his shield and kills 470 men himself in one day, each with one blow from Caliburnus (§147.126–28) – which many scholars have considered synonymous with Badon Hill given the types of details Geoffrey includes here[92] – Arthur fights on numerous fronts simultaneously, delegating his authority and thereby increasing his reach. He goes to Scotland to take on the Scots and Picts who are besieging Hoelus in Dumbarton, while sending Cador duke of Cornwall to pursue the Saxons. Cador attacks the Saxons who flee to Thanet, killing their leader Chelricus and forcing the remainder to surrender and give him hostages (§147.144–47).

His mission completed, Cador sets out for Dumbarton which Arthur had freed "from barbarian attack" ("a barbarica oppressione liberauerat" §149.149), then on to Moray, where Arthur's forces had formed a blockade against the Scots and Picts, who had fled there, having fought three battles against the king and his nephew.[93] Many of the Scots and Picts starved after a fortnight of the blockade; Guillamurius, king of Ireland, comes to their aid with a "great host of barbarians" ("cum maxima barbarorum copia classe superuenit" §149. 161–62). Arthur lifts the blockade, turns his troops on the Irish, whom he "mercilessly cut down and forced to sail home" ("quos sine pietate laceratos coegit domum refretare" §149.164). Having dispatched the Irish, Arthur turns his attention to the Scots and Picts, "wiping them out with utter ruthlessness" ("uacauit iterum delere gentem Scotorum atque Pictorum, incommutabili saeuitiae indulgens" §149. 165–66). No one was spared until the bishops and other clergy appealed to Arthur stating, "if he let them keep a small portion of their country, they would willingly bear the yoke of slavery for ever" ("sineret illos portiunculam habere patriae, perpetuae seruitutis iugum ultro gestaturos" §149.172–73). Arthur is moved to tears and grants the Scots pardon (§151.192) (though nothing is said about slavery, i.e., no deal is struck based on the bishops' rhetoric).

After pardoning the Scots, Arthur returns to York to celebrate Christmas. Saddened to see that the region's churches had been abandoned, Arthur had the churches rebuilt, "and filled them with throngs of religious men and women" restoring "family titles to the nobles who had been dispossessed by

---

92 See Chapter 1, n. 76, and n. 16 above, and Appendix 3 for the order of the battles in the different texts.

93 No name is specified for the nephew, though the nephew most recently mentioned in the narrative is Hoel (who had been in poor health, §148.136); Gualguainus (many variants including other Latin, as well as English "Gawain," French "Gauvain") and Modred (Mordred) are two more nephews named in the *HRB* (sons of Loth, who had married Arthur's sister, §152. 205–7), though it is unlikely that it is one of them being referred to here.

126   CHAPTER 2

the Saxon incursion" ("Ecclesias usque ad solum destructas renouat atque reli-
giosis coetibus uirorum ac mulierum exornat. Proceres autem inquieitatione
Saxonum expulsos patriis honoribus restituit" §151.198–200). Arthur restores
royal power over the Scots to Auguselus (one of the previous kings of the
region before the Saxons came) and makes the latter's brother Urianus king
of Moray. Loth, who had married Arthur's sister and was the father of Gawain
and Mordred, regained his earldom of Lothian and its connected provinces.
After having reestablished "the old institutions of the whole region" ("tocius
patriae statum in pristinam dignitatem reduxisset" §152. 208–9), Arthur marries Gahnhumara (Guinevere), "a woman of noble Roman ancestry brought up
at the court of duke Cador, who was the most beautiful woman in the island"
(§152. 209–11; "ex nobili genere Romanorum editam quae in thalamo Cadoris
ducis educata tocius insulae mulieres pulcritudine superabat").

A number of elements should be noted here. First, as mentioned above, following *HB*'s battle eight, the *HRB* departs: the increase in the number of battles
or sieges is prodigious, as if Geoffrey wished to create a situation beyond mathematical calculation; as a result, the focus tends to leave behind the impulse to
tally and moves to the quality and detail of the encounters. Second, Arthur's
reach and authority have expanded: he delegates battles to others, and once
the battles are done, he restores ancestral rights, conferring kingship over
Scotland since he has the authority to do so. Third, Arthur's ruthlessness is
mentioned more often than his capacity for pity, but at least he does have the
latter (a point to which we will return later). Fourth, he restores churches, supporting the idea that the British church was thriving before the Saxons came –
and further undermining the notion promoted by Bede and the Anglo-Saxon
Chronicle that the British church was neither well established nor organized
by the time Augustine arrived in 597.[94] Fifth, Arthur reestablishes "old institutions of the whole region" implying again a large cultural structure, but also a
king with the means to do such widespread work. Sixth, there are mentions of
Arthur's nephews – a central institution in the Middle Ages being that of the

---

94   On the extent and influence of the British church some two hundred years before
     Augustine's arrival, see Steven Bassett, "How the west was won: the Anglo-Saxon take-
     over of the west midlands," *Anglo-Saxon Studies in Archaeology and History* 11 (2000):
     107–118; Nicholas Brooks, "Canterbury, Rome and the Construction of English Identity";
     and Karen George, *Gildas's "De excidio Britonum" and the Early British Church*, Studies in
     Celtic History 26 (Woodbridge: Boydell and Brewer, 2009). See also Felicity Heal, "What
     Can King Lucius do for You? The Reformation and the Early English Church," *The English
     Historical Review* 120.487 (2005): 593–614, and Chapter 1, n. 110.

uncle-nephew relationship[95] – but also of his marriage to the "most beautiful woman in the land," phrasing and ideology reminiscent of folklore and myth, as well as the hyperbole of the growing vernacular culture seen in *chansons de geste* and romances, as Geoffrey expands Arthur's network.

The summer following his wedding (which remains undescribed), Arthur devotes to conquering Ireland; king Gillamuri's (Guilamurius) "defenceless warriors were horribly butchered and fled wherever they could find refuge" (§153.215–16), the king and other chiefs are captured, forced to surrender, together with the whole country. Arthur immediately proceeds to Iceland, which he conquers; kings Doldauius of Gotland and Gunuasius of the Orkneys come unbidden to pay tribute. The following spring, Arthur returns to Britain, restoring peace that lasts twelve years.

At some point during the peaceful hiatus, Arthur decides to increase his court by inviting "all the best men from far-off kingdoms"; his court becomes so renowned that other leaders fear Arthur will steal their subjects from them, and thus begin preparing themselves with fortifications. Arthur's fame has apparently gone to his head and he "exulted at being universally feared and decided to conquer all Europe" (§154.234–36). His fleet's first stop is Norway, where he seeks to reinstate Loth, the rightful heir to the throne after the death of Sichelmus. The Britons are victorious, adding Norway and Denmark to Arthur's territories. Next, Arthur sails to Gaul where the Roman tribune Frollo proposes single combat to Arthur, to spare Paris. Arthur kills Frollo in a single combat of epic proportions, complete with Arthur splitting Frollo's head in two. Paris surrenders to Arthur; following nine years securing "the surrender of all the Gallic provinces," Arthur returns to Paris, holds court there, giving Normandy to his butler, Bedevere, Anjou to Kay his steward, and many other regions of Gaul to members of his retinue (§155.298–305). Having secured peace, he returns to Britain.

There is a brief respite from the battle narratives[96] focused on the images of Caerleon – including the "college of two hundred scholars" (§156.322–23) – and

---

95   For a survey of this topic, see Robin Fox, "In the Company of Men: Tribal Bonds in Warrior Epics," in idem *The Tribal Imagination: Civilization and the Savage Mind* (Cambridge, MA: Harvard University Press, 2011), 196–225.

96   It is unclear whether the nine years in Gaul should be counted as a long stretch of the twelve years' peace or not, but very little of the nine years of land-grab in France or the twelve years' peace is narrated beyond the skeletal upshot: "After nine years had passed, in which he secured the surrender of all the Gallic provinces, Arthur returned to Paris and held court there, summoning clergy and laymen to confirm the rule of peace and law in the kingdom. He presented Estrusia, now called Normandy, to his butler Bedeverus, the province of Anjou to his steward Kaius, and many other regions to noble men of his retinue. Then, having secured peace for his cities and their people, he returned to

128   CHAPTER 2

the court at Pentecost upon Arthur's return from France. The guest list contains thirty-two named military and ecclesiastical dignitaries and "many others too numerous to name" (§156.344). Foreign leaders include twenty-five named kings and nobles, plus the twelve peers of France (all unnamed but Gerinus of Chartres), and the (unnamed) nobles subject to Hoelus, duke of the Armorican Britons. At this occasion one finds the famous passage of the knights in their colors, and ladies in similar colors, "spurn[ing] the love of any man who had not proved himself three times in battle," creating a model situation wherein "the ladies were chaste and better women, whilst the knights conducted themselves more virtuously for the sake of their love" (§157.387–91). Three days are devoted to field games, the fourth to Arthur's giving gifts of cities or castles to those who served him, and the fifth to the giving of "archbishoprics, bishoprics, abbeys or some other [ecclesiastical] honour" (§157.402–3).

While the latter honors were being distributed, twelve men "of mature age with reverend expressions" arrive with olive branches and a letter from Lucius Hiberius (§158. 411–14). Arthur, who at Geoffrey's pen has conquered most of western Europe, is now faced with the challenge of capitulating to the Roman emperor, which he will not do.[97] He and his troops head to Rome; en route, Arthur defeats the Mont-Saint-Michel giant, though is unable to save Hoel's niece, viciously killed by the monster after his attempts at rape had failed.[98]

In addition to the fact that the narrative of Arthur's battles against the Romans (§§163–76) are significantly more detailed than those against the Saxons – in part because the Saxons are only local villains whereas the Romans are shown to hold sway over a much vaster territory, both physically

---

Britain at the beginning of spring" ("Emensis interim nouem annis, cum totius Galliae partes potestati suae submisisset, uenit iterum Arthus Parisiis tenuitque ibidem curiam, ubi conuocato clero et populo statum regni pace et lege confirmauit. Tunc largitus est Beduero pincernae suo Estrusiam, quae nunc Normannia dicitur, Kaioque dapifero Andegauensium prouinciam, plures quoque alias prouincias nobilibus uiris qui in obsequio eius fuerant. Deinde, pacificatis quibusque ciuitatibus et populis, incipiente uere in Britanniam reuersus est" §155.298–305).

97   As Le Saux notes, an important element of Geoffrey's unconventionality was to present Britain "equal (if not superior) to Rome in its origins and achievements" (*Companion*, 89). See also Gioia Paradisi, *Le passioni della storia: Scrittura e memoria nell'opera di Wace*, Dipartimento di Studi Romanzi Università de Roma "La Sapienza," Testi, Studi e manuali 16 (Rome: Bagatto Libri, 2002), esp. ch. 9, "Polisemia del paradigma troiano e riscrittura del passato romano" (137–82).

98   See Laurie A. Finke and Martin B. Shichtman, "The Mont St. Michel Giant: Sexual Violence and Imperialism in the Chronicles of Wace and La3amon," in *Violence against Women in Medieval Texts*, ed. Anna Roberts (Gainesville: University Press of Florida, 1998), 56–74; Sylvia Huot, *Outsiders*, 27–68, esp. 65–68; and Jeffrey Jerome Cohen, *Of Giants: Sex, Monsters, and the Middle Ages*, 29–61, and 70, 105, and 109–10.

HISTORIA REGUM BRITANNIAE: PART 2

and culturally – the characterization of the king in his speeches is crucial to Geoffrey's design. A key multi-layered speech is that of section 169, where Arthur addresses the legion of 6,666 men he has with him:

> You, my friends, have made Britain the mistress of thirty kingdoms, and I congratulate you on your resolve, which, I see, never falters, but grows ever stronger. Although you have not campaigned for five years and are devoted to the pleasures of rest rather than to military service, you have by no means lost your natural prowess, but have stood firm and put the Romans to flight. In their arrogance they desired to deprive you of your freedom and advanced to attack in superior numbers, yet they could not stand up to your assaults and have retreated in disgrace to this city, from which they will shortly emerge to march to Autun down this valley, where you will be able to take them by surprise and catch them like sheep. Clearly they considered you to be as cowardly as easterners when they planned to exact tribute from your country and make you slaves. Have they not heard of the wars you waged against the Danes, the Norsemen and the leaders of the French, whom you placed in my power and freed from the shameful domination of Rome? Having won that greater victory, we will surely prevail in this lesser affair, as long as we show the same determination to crush these effeminates. What reward each of you will obtain if, like faithful comrades, you obey my wishes and commands! Once the enemy is defeated, we shall march on Rome, capture it and take it over, so that you shall have gold, silver, palaces, towers, castles, cities and all the spoils of victory. (§169.268–89)[99]

---

[99] "Domestici mei, qui Britanniam terdenorum regnorum fecistis dominam, uestrae congratulor probitati, quam nullatenus deficere, immo magis ac magis uigere considero. Quamquam quinque annis inexercitati oblectamentis ocii potius quam usui miliciae dediti sitis, nequaquam tamen ab innata bonitate degenerauistis sed in ipsa perseuerantes Romanos propulistis in fugam. Qui instimulante superbia sua libertatem uobis demere affectauerunt, qui ampliori numero incedentes ingenere proelia coeperunt, qui congressui uestro resistere non ualuerunt, sese turpiter infra ciuitatem istam receperunt, ex qua ad praesens egressuris et per istam uallem Augustudunum petituris obuiam poetritis adesse et nichil tale praemeditatos uelut pecudes occupare. Sane orientalium gentium segnitiam in uobis esse existimabant dum patriam uestram facere tributariam et uosmet ipsos subiugare affectarent. Numquid nouerunt quae bella Dacis atque Norguegensibus Gallorumque ducibus intulistis, quos meae subdidistis potestati et ab eorum pudendo dominio liberauistis? Qui igitur in grauiore decertatione ualuimus in hac leuiori sine dubio praeualebimus si pari affectu sermiuiros illos elaborauerimus opprimere. Quantos honores quisque uestrum possidebit si uoluntati meae atque praeceptis meis ut fideles commilitones adquieueritis! Subiugatis etenim ipsis, continuo Romam petemus, petitam

130   CHAPTER 2

As in the numerous speeches in this part of the text (§§165, 166, 169, 170, and 174), Geoffrey packs a great deal in here. Noteworthy elements of this particular speech are: 1) the declaration that there have been thirty kingdoms conquered by the Britons; 2) the usual braggadocio that the Britons are outnumbered but still stronger; 3) the expression "cowardly as easterners" ("sane orientalium gentium segnitiam in uobis esse existimabant" §169.278–79) may refer to the Saxons, possibly drawing them into a context unrelated to them for additional calumny; 4) slavery is not criticized as such, but rather that Britons would never become slaves of the Romans;[100] 5) *semiuiros*, (translated by Wright as "effeminates" §169.285) is a fairly unusual usage, in this case applied to the Romans, but certainly not confined to them;[101] 6) the Britons have performed the social service of freeing the Danes and others from "the shameful domination of Rome" ("pudendo dominio" §169.282), but this domination referenced by Arthur in this speech, has itself been replaced by Arthurian domination, colonialism viewed from the perspective of the colonizer, that is, from the standpoint of the insider; and 7) Arthur's plan to conquer Rome is spelled out with no uncertainty – demonstrating, among other things, just how far Arthur has come since his questionable birth and accession; for Arthur, at the zenith of his power before the fall, Rome is just another source of the spoils of war.

The account of Arthur's victory against the Romans in Seisia (see note 7 above) is quite detailed, making up sections 169–76, the most extensive account of an Arthurian battle. Tragic as it is, the battle against the usurper Mordred, of whose treachery Arthur learns at the end of section 176, takes less narrative space. The battle of Camlann passes quickly; at the end, Arthur is said to have been mortally wounded, though in the very next sentence, one reads "he was taken away to Avallon to have his wounds tended, and in the year of Our Lord 542, handed over Britain's crown to his relative Constantinus, son of Cador duke of Cornwall" (§179.81–84). Having his wounds tended is ambiguous and leaves the famous opening for other interpretations, including that of the "Breton hope," though the handing off of the crown is ominous.

---

     capeiemus, captam autem possidebimus, et sic aurum, argentum, palatia, turres, oppida, ciuitates, et ceteras uictorum diuicias habebitis" (§169.268–89).

100   On slavery and how it may have affected views of the Britons in the twelfth century, see Chapter 1, n. 92 and n. 71 above.

101   Sarah Allison Miller reports that the term *semivir*, although uncommon in classical Latin, appears several times in Ovid's corpus to denote an unnatural creature, either half-man half-beast or half-man half-woman: "the Ovidian *semivir*, then, is monstrous in a corporeal sense .... not simply an effeminate man or a eunuch, but a 'boundary violation' in hybrid form"; see also the "*semivir* Paris" in *Aeneid* 4.215 (*Medieval Monstrosity and the Female Body*, Routledge Studies in Medieval Religion and Culture 8, New York and Abingdon: Routledge, 2010, cited here at 149).

HISTORIA REGUM BRITANNIAE: PART 2

3 Post Arthur: Gormund's Donation, Augustine's Conversion of the English, the Passage of Dominion (Reprise) – Cadwallader and the Final Days

No sooner has Arthur left the scene, than the Saxons return, fighting against Constantinus and Mordred's two sons. Of those who succeed Constaninus, the most notable is the fourth king, Malgo, "probably the most handsome of all Britain's rulers" who "drove out many tyrants" (though his reputation was plagued by "the sin of sodomy" §183.117). Geoffrey claims that he "ruled the whole island as well as its six neighbours, Ireland, Iceland, Gotland, the Orkneys, Norway and Denmark, which he conquered in fierce battles" (§183. 118–21),[102] though why "fierce battles" were necessary to secure those countries since Arthur had already done so, is not clear. However, regardless of the efforts expended to gain those territories, the emphasis is on the imperial reach of the Britons, and their king, whom it is implied ruled over all the Britons throughout their territory (which is never succinctly defined).

Almost every incident remaining in the *Historia*'s narrative following Malgo's reign (sections 184–208) pertains directly to the passage of dominion, although not expressed by Geoffrey in so many words. In order to defeat King Kareticus (see note 8 above) the Saxons invite the African king Gormund(us) who had been subduing the Irish at the time. With one hundred and sixty thousand Africans, he crosses to Britain, and together with the Saxons (who had already gotten a head start), lays the country waste. Following the making of a pact with Isembard who promises to renounce Christianity if Gormund will help him defeat this uncle, King Lodewicus of France, the slaughter is so bad that survivors tried to flee "to any place of safety they could find."[103]

At this point in the narrative, we have one of the only occasions Geoffrey chooses to rail against the anticipated eventual tragic fate of the Britons,[104] brought on by their penchant for civil war:[105]

---

102 Geoffrey's charge of sodomy leveled against Malgo follows the suggestion in Gildas "a man drunk on wine pressed from the vine of the Sodomites" (Faletra, trans., 201, n. 2). On the possible connections between Geoffrey's Malgo and the Welsh Maelgwyn Gwynedd, see Karen Janulak, *Geoffrey of Monmouth* (Cardiff: University of Wales Press, 2010), 48.

103 On Geoffrey's use of the Gormund and Isembard legend, as well as differences between his portrayal of Gormund's predations and that of Wace, see J. Blacker, "Arthur and Gormund: Conquest, Domination and Assimilation."

104 This moralizing narratorial aside is not found in either the First Variant or Wace (Le Saux, *Companion*, 99).

105 On the theme of civil war in the *Historia* and Geoffrey's veiled – or not so veiled – (see Farrell, Chapter 1, n. 45 above) warnings to the Anglo-Norman aristocracy regarding its perils, see Chapter 1, n. 39.

132   CHAPTER 2

> Your kingdom is divided against itself, lust for civil strife and a cloud of
> envy has blunted your mind, your pride has prevented you from obeying
> a single king, and so your country has been laid waste before your eyes
> by most wicked barbarians, and its houses fall one upon another. Your
> descendants will regret it one day, when they see the cubs of the bar-
> barian lioness take their towns, cities and other possessions, whilst they
> themselves will become miserable exiles who will scarcely if ever regain
> their past glory.[106]

In this rhetorical outpouring, Geoffrey returns to several themes which had
been largely set aside during the sections on Arthur's foreign conquests and his
engagement with the Romans: 1) internecine warfare; 2) the barbarian nature
of the Saxons; 3) prophetic predictions of future travails directly resulting from
the Britons' current behavior; 4) exile; and 5) the possibility – albeit meager, he
fears – of future glory.

Embedded within the reprise of these themes comes the final coup de grace
and setting of the stage for the passage of dominion: Gormund the "infaustus tyrannus" with his "innumerabilibus Affricanorum milibus" ("countless
thousands of Africans") lays waste almost the entire island, and gives "the
largest portion of it, called Loegria" to the Saxons, while the Britons retreat to
Cornwall and Wales, from where they continue to "launch frequent damaging
incursions" (§186.154–60). Geoffrey continues, that "more priests sailed in a
great fleet to Brittany, with the result that the churches of the two provinces
of Loegria and Northumbria lost their entire congregations" and adds about
himself and projected future writings, "but I shall relate their story elsewhere,
when I translate the book about their exile" (§186.168–69).[107]

Unlike in the First Variant and Wace, Geoffrey does not mark the passage
of dominion with Gormund's "donation."[108] With his usual chronological

---

106   "Quia ergo regnum tuum in se diuisum fuit, quia furor ciuilis discordiae et liuoris fumus
      mentem tuam hebetauit, quia superbia tua uni regni oboedientaiam ferre non permisit,
      cernis iccirco patriam tuam ab impiissimis paganis desolatam, domos etiam eiusdem
      supra domos ruentes, quod posteri tui in futurum lugebunt. Videbunt etenim barb-
      arae leaenae catulos oppida, ciuitates atque ceteras eorundem possessiones optinere,
      ex quibus misere explusi prioris dignitatis statum uel numquam uel uix recuperabunt"
      (§185.147–54).
107   "Sed haec alias referam, cum librum de exulatione eorum transtulero" (§186.168–69).
      Scholars have apparently overlooked this claim to translate "*the* book" on the exile of the
      congregations of Loegria and Northumberland, quite possibly due to its ambiguity and its
      inferior status to that of the "Britannici sermonis librum uetustissimum" (Prol., 9).
108   Leckie, *Passage of Dominion*, esp. 101–19 (and notes pp. 136–37), and Chapters 3 and 5 of
      this volume.

HISTORIA REGUM BRITANNIAE: PART 2   133

vagueness, Geoffrey continues, "then for a long time" the Britons lost the crown over the whole island; they did not try to regain it but rather ravaged their own lands that were ruled by three usurpers. The Britons' lack of organization is matched by that of the Saxons, who also did not rule a united kingdom since "they too were subject to three kings" and sometimes fought against each other, and sometimes against the Britons (§187.170–75). It is as if the Britons and the Saxons are tied in a dead heat, locked in struggles among themselves, with no one at this point able to prevail.

At this juncture, Geoffrey introduces Augustine's mission, though he does not provide the year 597 or any other date.[109] Geoffrey's account is the most pro-Briton of any of his contemporaries: he emphasizes that Pope Gregory sent Augustine to "preach God's word to the English" – one of the only instances he uses the term "Angli"[110] – because the latter had destroyed Christianity in the "part of the island they occupied," making it clear to his readers that at this juncture at least, the Saxons did not control the entire island. He comments on how organized the Briton church was: "in their province" there were seven bishoprics with an archbishop; Bangor itself had so many monks that it was itself divided into seven subunits, each with its own prior and 300 monks – it is only to legions and battalions that Geoffrey ordinarily devotes this level of mathematical detail, underscoring again the level of organization which characterized the British church.[111]

Geoffrey readily admits that the Britons did not cooperate with Augustine, but he does so with pride, painting Augustine in the wrong and the Britons in the right, and in addition as victims of the Saxons: "To Augustine's request for the submission of the British bishops and his suggestion that they should share in his efforts to convert the English, Dinoot [their abbot] replied with various objections to the effect that they owed no obedience to him, since they had their own archbishop,[112] nor did they preach to their enemies, since the

---

109   See Chapter 1, nn. 110–111.

110   The vulgate *Historia* contains thirteen instances of the term "Angli," almost all falling toward the end of the text – that is, in the portion leading up to the transition from partial to complete Saxon domination (§§3.20, 34.328, 180.103, 188.176, 189, 194, 194.331, 197.428, 198.435, 200.469, 481, 204.559, 207.589); there appear to be seventy-nine uses of "Saxones." On the importance of the use of these terms in the vulgate, First Variant, and Wace – including the renaming of the island – see below "Postscript," and Chapters 3 and 5. See also Chapter 1, n. 150.

111   On the early British church, see Chapter 1, n. 110 and n. 94 above.

112   On Geoffrey's insistence that the Britons had their own archbishop and the importance of their not capitulating to Augustine and therefore to Canterbury, see Heal's discussion of Geoffrey and her extensive references on the early British church ("What Can King Lucius do for You? The Reformation and the Early English Church").

134   CHAPTER 2

Saxons persisted in depriving them of their country" (§188.187–93). Referring
to the Saxons, the Britons "detested" them, "despised" their beliefs, "shunning
them like dogs" (§188.193–95).

The Britons' refusal to capitulate to Augustine inspires King Edelbertus
of Kent to incite King Edelfridus of Northumbria, together with other Saxon
subkings ("et ceteros regulos Saxonum" §189.198) to gather an army to march
on Bangor and kill Dinoot; casualties are great on both sides, including the
martyrdom of the monks of Bangor. This situation spurs the Briton chiefs to
unite in making Caduan their king. However, when both sides were poised for
battle, "their friends interceded and reconciled them, agreeing that Edelfridus
should rule Britain north of the Humber and Caduan south of the river"
becoming "such good friends that they held all their possessions in common"
(§190.218–25).

This reconciliation, dividing of territory, and holding of possessions in
common has vast implications for the future of the island, as it sets the stage
for the co-rulership of the island for almost 300 years past the point of transfer of power according to Bedan chronology; however, Geoffrey mentions it
in a very off-hand manner, without fanfare. Although the implications are
wide-ranging, the cooperation and peace are short lived: in the following generation, the kings (Edelfridus and Caduan) each have a son and the sons are
raised together. However, when the sons return from their childhood home
in Brittany, Caduallo son of Caduan would like to grant Edwin (Edwinus) son
of Edelfridus permission to wear his Saxon crown at regular ceremonies in
Northumbria. Although Caduallo does not object, his nephew Brianus decries
the former perfidy of the Saxons and convinces Caduallo to deny this permission and wage war on the Saxons under Edwin. Brianus's speech is comprised
largely of a list of Saxon treacheries, permitting Geoffrey another opportunity
to remind the reader that despite the current peace, the Saxons are still Saxons
(§191.258–77).

Caduallo is chased from Britain, returning to Brittany. He and king Salomon
engage in a dialogue that Geoffrey again uses as a summation of Saxon per-
fidies. Salomon supplies Caduallo with ten thousand troops who cross back
to Britain and proceed to slaughter the men of Penda, king of the Mercians.
Caduallo gathers more Britons in order to advance north of the Humber
against Edwin, while Edwin gathers "all the subkings of the English" ("omnes
regulos Anglorum" §200.428).

Following a number of battles in which the Britons are victorious –
including Edwin's death at the battle of Hedfield (§197) – Oswi becomes king
of Northumbria after the death of his brother Oswald. Oswi, "by giving many
gifts of gold and silver to Caduallo, who now controlled the whole of Britain,

HISTORIA REGUM BRITANNIAE: PART 2   135

was granted peace and became his subject" (§200.458–60); it is worth noting
that in Geoffrey's version, Caduallo "who now controlled the whole of Britain"
(§200.459) wears the crown, and celebrates Whitsun in London together with
"all the kings of the English – except only Oswi" (§200.467–70). As is fitting in
such a scene with a head king and subservient leaders of all groups, the implication is that Oswi is the vassal and Caduallo the liege lord, which is certainly
not what Bede narrates.[113]

In keeping with Caduallo's superiority in this picture, Peanda, king of Mercia
seeks Caduallo's permission to attack Oswi whom he claims has "singlehand-
edly disturbed the peace of the kingdom"; not knowing what to do, Caduallo
consults his advisers, and Margadud, king of the Demetae, argues that it would
be wiser to not let the Saxons live in peace among them but rather he should
not hesitate "to allow Peanda to attack Oswi, so that they will wipe each other
out in civil war and disappear from [our] island" (200.488–90). Oswi offers
Peanda "countless royal ornaments" to call off the attack but Peanda persists
and is ultimately killed. Peanda's son Wulfred, "who allied himself with the
Mercian leaders Eba and Edbert to rebel against Oswi ... eventually made
peace with him on Caduallo's orders" (§201.500–3). Oswi is never heard about
again in Geoffrey's text.

After reigning forty-eight years as the "most noble and mighty king of the
Britons" – and apparently a peacemaker, according to Geoffrey – Caduallo
(Cadwallon/Cædualla) dies and is succeeded by his son Cadualadrus
(Cadwaladr/Cadwallader), whom according to Geoffrey, "Bede calls Chedualla
the Younger" (§202.513–14).[114] In the context of explaining Cadwallader's ill-
ness following twelve years of peace (reminiscent of Arthur's twelve-year

---

113   Oswy/Oswi/Oswiu (c. 612–670, king of Mercia 642–670, king of Northumbria 655–70),
      was the last of seven Bretwaldas listed by Bede in his famous list of the kings who held
      the overlordship over the Saxon kingdoms (*HE*, ii.5). On the Bretwaldas in Bede see
      Patrick Wormald, "Bede, the *Bretwaldas* and the Origins of the *Gens Anglorum*," in *Ideal
      and Reality in Frankish and Anglo-Saxon Society*, ed. Wormald (Oxford: Oxford University
      Press, 1983), 99–129, and Barbara Yorke, "The Bretwaldas and the origins of overlordship
      in Anglo-Saxon England," in *Early Medieval Studies in Memory of Patrick Wormald*, ed.
      Steven Baxter, Catherine Karkov, Janet L. Nelson, and David Pelteret, Studies in Early
      Medieval Britain (Aldershot: Ashgate 2009; repr. London: Routledge, 2017), 81–96; see also
      F. M. Stenton, *Anglo-Saxon England*, 204, and Rebecca Thomas who argues that due to
      Geoffrey's reinterpretations, his "Cadwallon thus has a far firmer grip on events in Mercia
      than Bede's Oswiu" ("Geoffrey of Monmouth and the English Past," in *A Companion to
      Geoffrey of Monmouth*, 105–28).
114   It makes sense that Geoffrey would name Bede here – although for such a minor note as
      a variant on a name – because he has been writing of early English kings which at least
      some of his readers would have known from Bede's narrative (although they might not
      have been aware at the time of the divergences between Bede and Geoffrey).

136   CHAPTER 2

peace), Geoffrey makes an aside to note that Cadwallader's mother was Peanda's paternal sister "but by a different mother, belonging to the noble line of the Gewissei" (§202.516–18).[115] This piece of information is dropped in passing, with no hint at the importance of this indicator of, at the least, royal assimilation between the Britons and the Saxons, though as we have already seen, the Briton Caduallo and Saxon Edwin were raised together at the court of Cadfan ap Iago.[116] Instead, Geoffrey passes immediately to civil strife, famine and plague, all of which cause Cadwallader to flee to Armorica seeking the aid of King Alain.

The king's lamentation is the last speech in the *HRB*. Geoffrey sounds one last time the theme of God's wrath to punish the Britons putting high melodrama in Cadwallader's mouth:

> Come back, Romans, come back, Scots and Picts, come back, ravenous Saxons; see, Britain lies at your mercy, uninhabited because of God's anger, when you could never make it so. We have been driven out not by your bravery, but by the power of the highest King, against which we have never ceased to offend. (§203.541–44)

According to Geoffrey, Britain was nearly devoid of its original population (save "a few whom death had spared in the regions of Wales" §204.547–48), or of any population at all, except a few Saxons who survived the plague. In an almost humorous aside, he adds that "those Saxons who survived when the dreadful plague was over announced, as was their unfailing custom, to their fellow-countrymen in Germany that, if they came as immigrants, they could easily occupy the island, devoid as it was of its inhabitants" (§204.550–53). The ensuing description indicates that Geoffrey would probably have subscribed to the modern "vast immigration" theory of the Saxon takeover, at all levels of society, not just elites, military, etc.:[117]

---

115 For more on this relationship narrated in the vulgate, that Caduallo, after making peace with Peanda, married the latter's sister with whom he had Cadwallader, see Chapter 3, n. 123.

116 On Cadfan, see n. 34 above. Le Saux comments that in Wace's *Brut*, "Cadwallan, though, is no Brutus, and certainly no Arthur" and that his marriage to Penda's sister "marks the beginning of an irreversible assimilation process between Britons and Saxons, which makes Cadwallader's renunciation of the British throne rather less momentous than it could seem" (*Companion*, 149). On Wace's portrayal and uses of Caduallo (Cadwallo), see Chapter 5, n. 253.

117 On theories of the Saxon arrival and population of the island, see Chapter 1, nn. 96–101 above.

HISTORIA REGUM BRITANNIAE: PART 2

> On receiving the news, that wicked people ass[e]mbled a vast crowd of men and women, landed in Northumbria and filled the empty tracts of land from Scotland to Cornwall. There were no natives to stop them, save a few remaining Britons living in the remote forests of Wales. This marked the end of British power in the island and the beginning of English rule. (§204.553–59)

This would appear to be a final ending yet there is a bit more. Cadwallader plans to return to Britain, but an angelic voice stops him, advising him to abandon the plan, as the Britons would not regain control over the island until the time Merlin prophesied to Arthur (§205.563–66). After Cadwallader's death in 689 (one of the few years provided by Geoffrey), Ivor and Yni assemble a fleet, land in Britain and subject the Saxons to sixty-nine years of "savage incursions" but ultimately to no avail: the Britons were no longer called Britons but Welsh, they fought among themselves, while the Saxons "acted more wisely, living in peace and harmony" eventually occupying all of Loegria, ruled by one king, Athelstan.

This is the three-hundred year gap to which Leckie refers (though it is closer to two hundred and fifty years), surmising that the unaccounted for years between 758 (sixty-nine years past Cadwallader's death) and the reign of Athelstan (924–39) imply shared rule over the island.[118] Although Leckie is right in calling attention to this gap and pointing out its problematic nature – highlighting the issue of the passage of dominion itself because it affords an extremely rich and useful barometer for exploring Geoffrey's possible motivations – the "gap" is more ambiguous than Leckie implies and the narrative in which it is couched is brief in the extreme, as if Geoffrey has already expended all of his available energy creating kings, and on the earlier part of the text. He has run out of both time and kings.

4 **Postscript: Geoffrey's Ideas on Multiple Ethnicities, Nationalities, Allegiances – including His Prejudices Interwoven with Origin Stories as Part of His Endeavor to Negotiate Identities**

In her masterful essay on Scotland before 1100, in the context of speculation on Pictish identity, Katherine Forsyth gives a broad overview of competing identities and allegiances in northern England, which can serve up to a point

---

118 Leckie, *Passage*, 54; see also the Introduction, n. 53 above. The Latin text for §204.550–59 appears in Chapter 1, n. 146.

138 CHAPTER 2

as a foundation for our discussion of Geoffrey's participation in what Forsyth terms "anti-Anglo-Saxon ideology" and other issues of identity.[119] Beginning with Bede in whose writing "historians can trace ... a distinctly anti-British stance,"[120] Forsyth proposes that

119 Katherine Forsyth, "Origins: Scotland to 1100," in *Scotland: A History*, ed. Jenny Wormald (Oxford: Oxford University Press, 2005), 1–38, here at 11. Referring to Arthur's possible portrayal as an anti-pagan crusader and the Saxons as symbols of paganhood in general, Siân Echard notes that a number of scholars have found similarities between Geoffrey's anti-Saxon program and the preaching of the crusades, including Geraldine Heng (*Empire of Magic*), Robert Stein (*Reality Fictions*), and Lawrence Warner, adding that "while other kings in the Christian era ... perform such pious deeds as rebuilding churches, Arthur is the first to be figured as an anti-pagan crusader" (Echard, *The Arthur of Medieval Latin Literature: The Development and Dissemination of the Arthurian Legend in Medieval Latin*, Cardiff: University of Wales Press, 2011, cited at 55, and n. 53). On the other hand, Warner writes that instead of following Bede, Gildas, and others who posited the Britons as the new Israelites, that is, as the chosen people, Geoffrey has written the Israelites out of "the story" altogether, focusing not on a chosen people with regard to a return to Jerusalem and the west's regaining of the Holy Land, but on the west's quest for Troy, the Trojans replacing the Israelites ("Geoffrey of Monmouth and the De-Judaized Crusade," *Parergon* 21.1 [2004]: 19–37). For another perspective on the chosen people or the "New Israel" *topos*, see Conor O'Brien who argues against scholars who view "references to the New Israel becoming a *topos* in the historiography of the Anglo-Saxons, Visigoths, and Irish, among others, as well as that of the Franks" ("Chosen Peoples and New Israels in the Early Medieval West," *Speculum* 95.4 [2020]: 987–1009, 987). His recent article "builds on the scholarship of the past generation, which increasingly questioned the validity of the New Israel topos (988)...[questioning] the entire validity of applying to the early Middle Ages the idea of ethnic election, a post-Reformation development in Christian political thinking" (989), arguing rather that "texts, like Alcuin's *Life of Willibrord*, which utilize the language of 'chosenness' and references to Old Testament Israel to describe contemporary peoples, were not trumpeting the exclusive divine favor of one ethnic group, but that, in fact, they were asserting participation in the universal church" (988). See also George Molyneaux who rejects the assumption that the early English (Germanic settlers) saw themselves as God's elect: "The English could see themselves as a Christian people, and thus among God's chosen, but they do not appear to have claimed to have been the beneficiaries of a more particularist form of divine election" ("Did the English Really Think they were God's Elect in the Anglo-Saxon Period?" *Journal of Ecclesiastical History* 65.4 [2014]: 721–37, 721). It is doubtful, however, that Geoffrey was arguing ecclesiastical issues by writing the Israelites out of his text, but rather against Saxon claims to lands, cultural superiority, and political hegemony over the Britons.

120 See for example K. H. Jackson, "On the Northern British Section in Nennius," in *Celt and Saxon: Studies in the Early British Border*, ed. N. K. Chadwick (Cambridge: Cambridge University Press, 1963), 20–62, and Chapter 1, n. 75 above. Cf. Thomas Charles-Edwards who argues that Bede displays "no national antipathy" against the Britons, observing that while "there may be some truth" in the opinion that "Bede's judgments upon the Britons are coloured, presumably by ethnic antipathy or political opposition ... if so, it was well submerged" ("Bede, The Irish and the Britons, *Celtica* 15 (1983): 42–52, here at 48 and 43).

HISTORIA REGUM BRITANNIAE: PART 2   139

He may have been at pains to recognize the distinctness of the Pictish *gens*, of whom he was more approving. Perhaps a key reason may be that, as Bede wrote, Picts faced Angles across the Forth. A little over a generation earlier, the Brittonic continuum had been breached by invading Germanic-speakers. With the old lines severed, those on either side had begun to develop along divergent lines. These redefinitions were part of a much wider process, for it was in this period that the various peoples of Britain, both incomer and native, were forging new ethnic identities for themselves. The disparate Germanic tribes who had settled in eastern Britain were beginning for the first time to view themselves all as "English," even though they remained politically divided.

Focusing on the Picts and speculating on how they may have viewed themselves and how others may have viewed them – with admittedly little evidence to go on – Forsyth continues that "perhaps in opposition to this [new tendency for Germanic tribes to begin to view themselves as 'English']:

an anti-Anglo-Saxon ideology seems to have begun to bind together the different British speaking polities of the west, and across the Irish Sea a new unifying "Gaelic" identity was being fostered among the kingdoms of the Irish. It may be that a distinctive "Pictish" identity, encompassing

---

Charles-Edwards argues that Bede's opinions stem "not from mere dislike of Britons as enemies of the English" but from the former's resistance to preaching the Gospel to the English, and their rebelliousness against the Romans, two areas in which Bede contrasts the Irish to the Britons, finding the former much more sympathetic. Charles-Edwards contends that whatever antipathy toward the Britons there is to be found in Bede comes not from the English historian but from his source, Gildas: "if he has a bias, it is of British manufacture" (45). See also Clare Stancliffe who comments that "one cannot but be struck by the slanted way in which Bede portrays [the Britons] in contrast to the English and the Irish"; she continues though, "in fairness to Bede, however, we need to balance all that we have said about his hostility to the Britons with an appreciation of the limits to this hostility." In reference to Bede's treatment of [bishop] Ninian, "a most reverend and holy many of the British people" ("Nynia episcopo reuerntissimo et sanctissimo uiro de natione Brettonum" *HE*,iii.4; Stancliffe's translation), we see that what "Bede – or his informant – is doing is bestowing impeccable Christian credentials on Ninian at a time when being 'British' was virtually synonymous with being 'heretical' in the eyes of many English churchmen ... Ninian, like Alban, receives this highest of all accolades from Bede." But in the last analysis, Stancliffe concludes that men such as Ninian and Alban "remain isolated figures in his *Ecclesiastical History*; and when Bede generalises from individual to people in his history, it is Cadwallon, not Ninian, who typifies the Britons" (*Bede and the Britons: Fourteenth Whithorn Lecture, 17th September 2005*, Whithorn: The Friends of the Whithorn Trust, 2007, cited at 40–41). For additional information and perspectives, see Chapter 6, n. 71 below.

140   CHAPTER 2

all the Brittonic territory north of the Forth, was being forged at the same
time for similar reasons. In the scant documentary record, we can trace
the metamorphosis of the old tribal affiliations into territorial identities.
The contemporary sources refer to "the men of Fife," "the men of the
Hebrides," "the men of Orkney," "the men of Moray." These regional identities were strong and endured throughout the early medieval period, yet,
transcending them we see what might well have been an entirely new
concept: a sense of common "Pictishness," an identity which in some way
united these people and distinguished them from their neighbours the
Gaels, the Angles, and even the Britons, an identity which, following
the Latin sources of the time, we label "Pictish," but, ironically, for which
the Pictish word has not survived.[121]

While one can envisage Geoffrey's participation in the developing "anti-Anglo-
Saxon ideology," it is more difficult to see him as a proponent of any sort of
"pan-Celticism" as he tends to see peoples separately and does not appear to
promote solidarity among the Celtic peoples. It would also appear that in the
Historia he lumps together the different regional groups of the "men of the
north" mentioned by Forsyth when he identifies many of them simply as Picts
(or as Scots; it is never completely clear in Geoffrey's text).[122]

There is no question that in Geoffrey's construction of early British history,
he invokes groups of insular peoples, but he views many of them unfavorably as
the enemies of the Britons, with the Saxons at the top of the list, though often
with the Picts and the Scots not far behind; in addition, he appears ambivalent toward the Romans.[123] While he mentions those peoples "openly" – that
is by name, rather than obliquely or metaphorically as he refers to the French
through references to the Gauls (as Arthur's adversaries). He may also be referring to the Normans – and by extension the "Norman English" – even more
obliquely through the figure of Arthur as the model of effective leadership. As

---

121   Forsyth, "Origins: Scotland to 1100," 10–11.
122   Sims-Williams warns against assigning "pan-Celtic" sentiment to this early period, as
      tempting as that might be ("Celtomania and Celtoscepticism," *Cambrian Medieval Celtic
      Studies* 36 (1998): 1–36).
123   Sims-Williams argues that Geoffrey's work sits squarely within two primary aspects of the
      Welsh historical tradition, the desire to promote the myth of the unity of Britain, and a
      vision of history as oppression (within which the history of Britain is but a series of con-
      quests) ("Some functions of origin stories"). In Geoffrey's view, by extension, all peoples
      other than the Britons who claimed to be the first to have arrived, were often considered
      enemies, or at the least, competitors.

usual with Geoffrey, there is an almost infinite richness of possibilities to be found in the ambiguities of his narrative.[124]

In terms of Geoffrey's attempts to deal with competing identities in the vulgate *Historia* which is informed by "the politics of cultural nationalism,"[125] there is at least one nagging question to be addressed: Why does Geoffrey mount such a virulent opposition to the Saxons (of the sixth through the ninth centuries) if the English – the "ethnic" English populace, that is, not the "Norman English" aristocracy – were so submerged (or even oppressed) in the early twelfth century when he was writing?[126] In other words, what forces, circumstances, cultural views and expectations was he reacting against? Perhaps the ethnic English were not as submerged/repressed/dominated by the "Norman English" as scholars have assumed (and has been recounted by the Anglo-Saxon Chronicle)?[127] Although there are no simple answers to these questions, it is difficult to believe that Geoffrey's anti-Saxon sentiment and rhetoric derived solely from earlier Welsh tradition: he must have had more contemporary or topical, pressing motivation(s) than, for example, reaction to Anglo-Norman/English criticism of the Welsh and others as barbarians.[128] Michael Faletra in fact argues that Geoffrey's *Historia* may have ultimately been intended to support Norman political aims throughout the island, including in Wales, and that "it is to William of Malmesbury's *Gesta Regum Anglorum* that the *Historia* ... responds most directly, and it is in the proto-nationalist, pro-Norman, anti-Welsh tradition of the *Gesta Regum* that Geoffrey's work should most appropriately be considered."[129] Faletra contends that although

---

124 See Sjoerd Levelt's essay devoted exclusively to the *Historia*'s ambiguity, "'This book, attractively composed to form a consecutive and orderly narrative': The Ambiguity of Geoffrey of Monmouth's *Historia regum Britannie*," in *The Medieval Chronicle II: Proceedings of the 2nd International Conference on the Medieval Chronicle, Driebergen/Utrecht 16–21 July 1999*, ed. Erik Kooper, Costerus New Series 144 (Amersterdam: Rodopi, 2002), 130–43.

125 Gillingham, "The Context and Purposes," 21.

126 See, for example, Stephen Baxter, "Lordship and Labour," in *A Social History of England, 900–1200*, ed. Julia C. Crick and Elisabeth Van Houts (Cambridge: Cambridge University Press, 2011), 98–114, and the very useful, wide-ranging "Introduction," 1–13.

127 See in particular the Peterborough MS. for the year 1137 (Swanton ed. and trans., 263–66). On the myth of the "Norman Yoke," which apparently entered into English discourse early in the 17th century, see Christopher Hill, *Intellectual Origins of the English Revolution – Revisited* (Oxford: Oxford University Press, rev. ed. 2001), esp. pp. 361–65.

128 See esp. nn. 71 and 75 above.

129 Taking partial exception to John Gillingham's assertion that "Geoffrey was a Welshman whose object was to secure cultural respectability for his own nation" ("Context and Purposes," 20, paraphrasing Geoffrey Barrow, "Wales and Scotland in the Middle Ages," *Welsh History Review* 10.3 (1981): 302–19, 305), Faletra recognizes that Gillingham's study "presents Geoffrey as keenly aware of the political situation in twelfth-century Britain"

142   CHAPTER 2

Geoffrey "certainly does not engage in the same type of vehement moralized Othering of the Britons as William does," Geoffrey represents the Britons nonetheless "less as the stigmatized Other than as the paradoxically glorified subjects of incipient colonization." In Faletra's view, ultimately "the *Historia* accomplishes much the same purpose through its strategic use of polysemicity as the *Gesta* does through its investigative thoroughness: they both legitimate Norman colonization of Wales by creating and perpetuating textual myths of the innate defeatedness – and the inevitable defeatability – of the British people." Granted, Geoffrey's patrons were highly placed and highly visible members of the Anglo-Norman aristocracy,[130] it is difficult to believe that all the civil strife narrated in the *Historia*,[131] Arthur's moderated imperialism, and the Britons' defeat at the hands of the unyielding and intolerant Saxons were meant to signal to the aristocracy the legitimacy of their imperialistic goals and not serve as a warning to the possibility of a fall, just as Rome – and Arthur – fell when they overreached beyond moderated and tolerant rule.

But neither the suggestion of Geoffrey offering potential support for Anglo-Norman colonization or that of a warning for the Anglo-Norman aristocracy against internecine warfare goes far enough to explain the specific phenomenon of Geoffrey's virtually unremitting animosity toward the Saxons, but perhaps the following suggestion from Rees Davies does, or at least, it will take us a bit further.

As Davies points out, on the one hand, that is, on the level of overt programmatic political policy, "for at least the first century after the Norman conquest of England, royal policy towards Scotland, Wales and Ireland may, therefore, be

---

("Narrating the Matter of Britain," 62). See also idem, *Wales and the Medieval Colonial Imagination*, and Martin B. Shichtman and Laurie A. Finke, "Profiting from the Past."

130   On Geoffrey's patrons (real or "fabricated"), see Paul Dalton, "Topical Concerns," Jaakko Tahkokallio, *The Anglo-Norman Historical Canon: Publishing and Manuscript Culture*, Cambridge: Cambridge University Press, 2019), esp. 48–80, J. Blacker, *The Faces of Time*, esp. 160–67 (1994); Fiona Tolhurst, *Geoffrey of Monmouth and the Translation of Female Kingship*, esp. 19–51; on the multiple dedications, see Julia C. Crick, *The Historia Regum Britannie of Geoffrey of Monmouth, IV: Dissemination and Reception in the Later Middle Ages* (Cambridge: D. S. Brewer, 1991), esp. 113–120.

131   On the *Historia* as a warning against the destructive dangers of conflict as seen through lengthy passages such as those on Belinus and Brennius, Maximianus, Locrinus, Lear, and the seemingly endless battles between the Britons and the Saxons, see Paul Dalton, "Topical Concerns," Jane Zatta, "Translating the *Historia*: The Ideological Transformation of the *Historia Regum Britannie* in the Twelfth Century Vernacular Chronicles," *Arthuriana* 8.4 (1998): 148–61, esp. 151, 156; Chapter 1, n. 39, and Blacker, *Faces of Time*, esp. Chapter 3.

HISTORIA REGUM BRITANNIAE: PART 2

broadly characterized as reactive, responding (often reluctantly and belatedly) to threats and invitations but rarely initiating action, least of all action which might be construed as a policy of royal conquest."[132] However, on the other hand, in the years following the initial military conquest of England by members of the Norman aristocracy in the mid-eleventh century, there was a steady stream of English colonists into Wales, Scotland, and Ireland which naturally had a tremendous impact on those areas beyond "simply" the military conquest. Drawing attention to the subject of English settlement – or to use a more pointed term, colonization – of Wales, Scotland and Ireland in the twelfth and thirteenth centuries, Davies underscores what could be, for our purposes here, a very logical explanation of contributing factors in Geoffrey of Monmouth's antipathy toward the "Saxons":[133]

> if we had not been seduced to such a degree by what has been called (in a different context) "the myth of the Normans," we might take a rather different view of what happened in the British Isles [in the twelfth and thirteenth centuries]. We might view it less as a "Norman conquest" ..., more as the second tidal wave of Anglo-Saxon or English colonization. The first came in the early Middle Ages as soldier-colonists penetrated into the eastern lowlands of Wales and anglicized much of the eastern lowlands of what we know as southern Scotland. The second wave appears to have started in the late eleventh century and flowed more or less strongly over parts of lowland Wales, Ireland and Scotland for almost two centuries ... Thus the peoples who settled in the lowlands of Wales were overwhelmingly English, not Norman or Flemish. It was "Saxons" ... whom Gilbert Fitz Richard of Clare brought "to fill the land" of Ceredigion in the early twelfth century; it is English personal- and field-names which predominate in the earliest land-deeds for "Norman" Wales in districts such as Brecon, Glamorgan and Gower.[134]

---

132 Davies, *Domination & Conquest*, 69.
133 See also G. W. S. Barrow, *The Anglo-Norman Era in Scottish History* (Oxford: Clarendon Press, 1980), 6; Wendy Davies, *Wales in the Early Middle Ages* (Leicester: Leicester University Press, 1982), 113, 195; and John Gillingham, "A Second Tidal Wave? The Historiography of English Colonization of Ireland, Scotland and Wales in the Twelfth and Thirteenth Centuries," in *Historiographical Approaches to Medieval Colonization of East Central Europe*, ed. J. Piskorski (Boulder, CO: University of Colorado Press, 2003), 303–27.
134 R. R. Davies, *Domination and Conquest: The experience of Ireland, Scotland and Wales 1100–1300* (Cambridge: Cambridge University Press, 1990), 12.

144   CHAPTER 2

If we assume for the purposes of argument that Geoffrey's sympathies lay in the narrowest sense with the Welsh – though in Geoffrey's case, it is admittedly hazardous to assume anything – his antipathy toward the Saxons could stem in part from a form of xenophobia toward "invading foreigners" but also a reaction toward occupiers who did not seek to be co-inhabitants with the "Britons" but who wished to be in charge, to dominate (rather than assimilate – a point to which we will return below), and who had the power of the crown on their side, the English crown requiring subservience, particularly of the Welsh who were both less prosperous and less territorially ambitious – or territorially successful – than the Scots.[135]

It will be useful to return to the Picts, as they are targets of less of Geoffrey's animosity than the Saxons or the Scots, and the case of the Picts may also point up attitudes Geoffrey seemed to have about identities in general. First, in terms

---

135   On Geoffrey's pro-Welsh leanings or bias, see in particular John Gillingham, "Context and Purposes." It should be noted that Wales had been subject to more significant land-grabbing by William the Conqueror and Norman barons than had Scotland: " he gave [his barons] a relatively free hand to acquire as much land as they could at the expense of the Welsh" but his authority remained paramount; "his march through south Wales to St Davids in 1081 demonstrated to Welsh prince and Norman baron that his authority in Wales brooked no limits or opposition" (Davies, *Domination & Conquest*, 70); for a later period, William of Malmesbury comments that "the Welsh were in constant revolt, and King Henry [I] maintained pressure on them by frequent expeditions until they surrendered" (*GRA* v.401). With respect to Scotland Archibald Duncan contends that "[in] contrast [to] the long Anglo-Welsh struggle" it appeared that "what the English king needed [from Scotland] ... was peace (by fear or friendship) with the Scottish king; [he] did not need conquest of the provinces of Scotland ... Henry I, Henry II and his sons showed no very active desire to reduce the Scottish king to a client status" (A. A. M. Duncan, *Scotland: The Making of the Kingdom*, Edinburgh: Oliver & Boyd, 1975, 254–55). On King David's aspirations as well as his successes in creating a "Scoto-Northumbrian" realm (though not the independence of Scotland itself), see Richard Oram, *Domination and Lordship: Scotland 1070–1230* (Edinburgh: Edinburgh University Press, 2006; reprinted with corrections 2011), chapter 3, "Building the Scoto-Northumbrian Realm, 1136–57," 74–114; Keith J. Stringer, *The Reign of Stephen: Kingship, Warfare and Government in Twelfth-Century England* (London: Routledge, 1993), 35–36; G. W. S. Barrow, *David I of Scotland (1124–1153): The Balance of New and Old*, The Stenton Lecture 1984 (Reading: University of Reading, 1985), 18; and Dauvit Broun, *Scottish Independence and the Idea of Britain: From the Picts to Alexander III*, esp. 1–34; see also n. 144 below. For a different perspective on the very complex perceptions in – and about – medieval Wales in an earlier period, see Lindy Brady whose study argues for seeing the Welsh March from the fifth century through the Norman Conquest as an "Anglo-Welsh cultural zone," an area of largely peaceful interactions, and thus a reconsideration of the belief that interactions between those groups were largely adversarial (*Writing the Welsh Borderlands in Anglo-Saxon England*, Manchester: Manchester University Press, 2017).

HISTORIA REGUM BRITANNIAE: PART 2   145

of animosity, in some instances, Geoffrey even appears ambivalent toward the Picts, mixing surprisingly a bit of positivity in with the hostility. The Picts are first mentioned in the context of an origin-story in section 70. During the reign of Marius, a Pictish king named Rodric arrives from Scythia with a large fleet, lands in the north of "Alba"[136] and proceeds to ravage the area – Geoffrey does not state who was living there at the time. Marius gathers his people and defeats Rodric in several battles, eventually killing him. He does allow however the defeated people to live in the part of "Alba" called Caithness, which was deserted at the time, having been "uninhabited and uncultivated for many years" (§70.380–82), implication being that it had at one time been inhabited and cultivated. In a story borrowed from Bede, Geoffrey then reports that since the Picts had no women with them, they asked the Britons for their daughters and female relatives; the Britons were appalled and refused. The Picts then went to Ireland, came back with women, with whom they propagated. On that note, Geoffrey concludes: "But enough of the Picts, since it is not my intention to write either their history or that of the Scots, who are descended from them and the Irish" (§70.386–88).

The second mention of the Picts occurs as the Britons rely on the Picts who help Fulgentius defeat the Romans (§74.22–26), or at least that is the implication; Fulgentius sails to Scythia in the hopes of getting aid from the Picts and he is eventually victorious. More ambiguity then ensues: Carausius (in Roman history, a Menapian soldier from Belgic Gaul who declared himself Roman Emperor of Britain in c.286), in Geoffrey a Briton of humble origins, persuades the Roman Senate to give him command of a fleet so that he might protect the northeastern coast of Britain. He tells the Britons that if they make him king, he will kill or expel the Romans and rid the island of barbarians – presumably anyone who is not a Briton, but no group is specified. Carausius kills the Briton king, Bassianus, who had been betrayed by the Picts brought to the island by Fulgentius, makes himself king, gives the Picts a home in Alba, "where they have remained ever since, mixed with the British" (§75.54–62). The phrase "cum Britonibus mixti" is itself ambiguous; it can mean "intermingled," "living among" or "assimilated," as where the Scots are referred to several sections earlier as descendants of the Picts and the Irish. Thus the Picts are equally saviors, traitors, and progenitors, or at the least, co-countrymen with the Britons. As unsavory as they are at times, though, in Geoffrey's vulgate, the Picts can't hold

---

136   On Geoffrey's use of the toponym "Alba," see Alex Woolf, "Geoffrey of Monmouth and the Picts," in *Bile ós Chrannaibh: A Festschrift for William Gillies*, ed. William McLeod, et al (Ceann Drochaid, Perthshire: Clann Tuirc, 2010), 439–50, 440.

146   CHAPTER 2

a candle to the Saxons when it comes to perfidy and evoking animosity on the part of the author.

With respect to the Scots, Alex Woolf writes that Geoffrey "appears to share the view that the Scots of his own day were the product of assimilation and inter-marriage between the Picts and the Gaels of an earlier age espoused by contemporary scholars such as Geoffrey Barrow and Dauvit Broun, whose use of the term 'Picto-Scottish kingdom' to describe the cultural identity of Alba between the late ninth and the early twelfth century lays particular emphasis on this mixed heritage in the process of Scottish ethnogenesis."[137] In other words, Geoffrey expresses a very different view of the Scots in relation to the Picts than his contemporary Henry of Huntingdon – whom Woolf views as the "apparent target" of the *HRB* and who may be the source of the theory that the Picts disappeared as victims of genocide (rather than through intermarriage and complete assimilation).[138] In addition, Woolf sees Geoffrey as having perhaps special knowledge of the Scots, or "at least interest in the northern political scene."[139] This view runs contrary to Tatlock's, for example, that Geoffrey expressed nothing but contempt for the Scots, a position, while extreme, has some merit since the Scots so often seemed to be brought in by Geoffrey as the second half of a matched set with the Picts, that is, often mentioned in the same breath derogatorily as ravagers.[140] It is not impossible that

---

137   "Geoffrey of Monmouth and the Picts," 439. Though see Broun for a different view more recently, in "The Origins of Scotland," where he writes that "if we want to understand how Scotland got its name, and what this signifies, we need to wipe the old story of a 'Scoto-Pictish union' from our minds and look afresh at the issue" (93).

138   "Geoffrey of Monmouth and the Picts," 439.

139   "Geoffrey of Monmouth and the Picts," 440.

140   Although current scholars tend to dismiss Tatlock's views as "old-fashioned" (if they even entertain them), the latter encourages us to keep the issue of Geoffrey's prejudices – however we may interpret them – in mind, even if we don't share the interpretations. Tatlock writes, "the people of Scotland are treated with less respect than any other; the Welsh and even the English are represented favorably once or twice, the Scots only with indifference or contempt" (*Legendary History of Britain*, 18). He concludes that "from the appearance of things Scottish in the *Historia* one would fancy the author a man of the word with somewhat scholarly tastes and with Anglo-Norman sympathies," and "at the very end, the Saxons are praised as wiser than the Welsh, keeping peace and cultivating the country. This merely shows that Geoffrey loved not the English more but the Welsh less. His attitude to the English all through is that of a Celt who stood in with the Normans; who hated and despised the stronger and more barbarous conquerors of the Britons, and despised them the more when in their turn they were conquered. But here as elsewhere his lack of tenderness for the Welsh makes one believe him a Breton" (*Legendary History*,

HISTORIA REGUM BRITANNIAE: PART 2   147

these opposing views could both be illuminating, pointing out a what appears as a deep-seated animosity, which may in fact stem from "political envy."

Woolf notes that Geoffrey mentions a tripartite division in the north, supported by Arthur, who restores to Auguselus the kingship of the Scots, to Urianus the "scepter of the Moravians" and restores Loth to the "consulate" of Lothian and its associated provinces, suggesting that this tripartite division "would seem to reflect quite realistically the situation pertaining in the early twelfth century when Moray retained its own king and when Lothian and neighbouring provinces, such as Teviotdale and Clydesdale, were held by a cadet of the royal house."[141] Is it possible that Geoffrey is, in part, championing the Britons – that is, as metaphor for the Welsh – as a separate people from the Scots since the former were not able to pursue an equivalent to the latter's expansionism vis-à-vis the English while Geoffrey was alive?[142] Although King Malcolm of Scotland became William the Conqueror's vassal in 1072, "there was no Scottish Hastings, and the Normans attempted neither to dislodge the native dynasty nor to take over the country,"[143] at least from 1072 until the death of the last of the Conqueror's sons in 1135, which put Scotland into a different relationship with England than Wales – and later with Europe, through Queen Margaret – more connected, more privileged, more prosperous – during the

---

18–19). Estimations such as Tatlock's tend to take the text at face value, a very different approach from that of more modern critics who, as Lawrence Warner has remarked, have been setting aside more traditional views on Geoffrey's *Historia*, bound and determined to find "subversion" in his work ["The desire to find themes counter to the dominant ones of the *Historia*, or 'mischief,' or 'subversiveness,' permeates modern scholarship," "Geoffrey of Monmouth and the De-Judaized Crusade," here 36 n. 55].)

141   "Geoffrey of Monmouth and the Picts," 441. On the kings of Moray and holdings (and rulers) of neighboring provinces, see A. A. M. Duncan, *The Kingship of the Scots, 842–1292* (Edinburgh: Edinburgh University Press, 2002), chapter 4, and Richard Oram, *David I: The King who Made Scotland* (Stroud: Tempus, 2004), 39–48 and 59–72.

142   On Scottish expansionism in the early twelfth century and the complex subject of the Welsh and the Irish as secondary powers to the Norman English (and perceptions of their peoples), certainly with respect to the Scots, see n. 135 above, and nn. 144–45 below, and Rees Davies, "Presidential Address: The Peoples of Britain and Ireland, 1100–1400. II. Names, Boundaries and Regnal Solidarities," *Transactions of the Royal Historical Society*, Sixth Series, 5 (1995): 1–20.

143   G. W. S. Barrow, "Anglo-French Influences," in *Who are the Scots? and The Scottish Nation*, ed. Gordon Menzies (Edinburgh: Edinburgh University Press, 2002; orig. pub. in *Who are the Scots?*, London: BBC, 1971 (51–65), 85–97, here 85).

148   CHAPTER 2

time Geoffrey was writing,[144] which might have led to feelings of resentment
in Geoffrey toward the Scots.[145]

144   At least the primary royal figure, King David I of Scotland (1124–53), could have been
       the object of envy, having been raised at the English court, and knighted by Henry I; he
       participated in the English succession struggles by supporting his niece, Matilda's, claim
       to the throne, and claimed Cumberland, Westmorland, and Northumberland on behalf
       of his son, Earl Henry. Except for the brutal campaign which ended at the Battle of the
       Standard in 1138, David's reign was fairly peaceful, while the king enjoyed a very posi-
       tive reputation for administrative and church reform. William of Malmesbury writes of
       David that he was "a young man of more courtly disposition than the rest, he had from
       boyhood been polished by familiar intercourse with the English ['nostrorum conuictu et
       familiaritate limatus'], and rubbed off all the barbarian gaucherie of Scottish manners"
       (*GRA* v.400). Perhaps while at the same time resenting David's influence not shared by
       Welsh princes, Geoffrey could have modeled Arthur on him as well as on Henry I, or as
       a Welsh counterpoint to those two monarchs, respectively king of Scots and king of the
       Anglo-Norman *regnum*; in terms of further models for Arthur, Edwin Pace carries further
       Tatlock's suggestion of Athelstan as a possible model for Arthur (*Legendary History*, 307),
       citing the former's illegitimate birth, that both succeeded a sovereign who died on cam-
       paign, both dominated the island of Britain through a decisive battle "that utterly routed
       their foes," and that they both "could claim descent from a long line of kings" ("Breton
       Origins," 76–78). Cf. Edward J. Cowan who posits that Geoffrey admired David (though
       not the Scots in general), knowing "very well as did his contemporaries, that the king
       who came closest to fulfilling the role of Cadwallader or Cynan or Arthur, or whoever
       was to unite the Celtic peoples and restore them to their former grandeur, was David, *rex
       Scottorum*. Of that splendid vision, Scot, Briton, Morayman, Lothanier or Norman could
       be a part, if he adhered to the king of the Scots" ("Myth and Identity in Early Medieval
       Scotland," 132). For a variety of perspectives on David I's role in early twelfth-century
       British politics and his presentation by chroniclers, including his biographer and contem-
       porary of Geoffrey of Monmouth, Aelred of Rievaulx, see Judith A. Green, "David I and
       Henry I," *Scottish Historical Review* 75 (1996): 1–19, Joanna Huntington, "David of Scotland:
       'Vir tam necessarius mundo'," in *Saints' Cults in the Celtic World*, ed. Steve Boardman, John
       Reuben Davies, Eila Williamson, Studies in Celtic History 25 (Woodbridge: Boydell, 2009),
       130–45, Keith Stringer, "King David I (1124–53): The Scottish Occupation of Northern
       England," *Medieval History* 4 (1994): 51–61, and G. W. S. Barrow, "King David, Earl Henry
       and Cumbria," CWAAS (Cumberland and Westmoreland Antiquarian and Archeological
       Society) 99 (1999): 117–27; and Richard Oram, *David I: The King who made Scotland*,
       Tempus Scottish Monarchs (Stroud: Tempus, 2004), esp. 167–89.
145   Even as early as the 1130s, Scotland with its Anglo-French nobility was "as much a part of
       this complex transnational aristocratic structure as anywhere else, where families were
       not just 'English' but also 'French' and 'Scottish'" (Melissa Pollock, review of Richard Oram
       Domination and Lordship, *HER*, 128.531[2013]: 408–9, here 409). According to Pollock,
       Oram, to whose arguments she takes exception in this instance, "follows a trend in Scottish
       history that continues to assume that Scotland was not directly involved in any meaning-
       ful sense with the Continent" (410); see Richard D. Oram, *Domination and Lordship*. In
       terms of Scotland's "integration" into English hegemony, Davies writes, "As for Scotland,
       its history in the early twelfth century showed clearly that effective political tutelage and
       a deep aristocratic penetration could be achieved without military confrontation, let

HISTORIA REGUM BRITANNIAE: PART 2   149

In conclusion, Geoffrey does not seem to want to admit – or at least portray – the concept of multiple simultaneous ethnicities, nationalities, or allegiances, except most narrowly in the case of the Scots whom he simply declares descended from the Picts and the Irish, which is not exactly multiple simultaneous ethnicities, but the closest Geoffrey comes to it. For Geoffrey, each group is distinct, separate, and most relationships are adversarial; in Geoffrey's world, although character does matter and sometimes individuals transcend their groups, individuals often seem branded, or even trapped by their ethnic or group identities, and that these groups are often pitted one against the other. On one level, Geoffrey's efforts to distinguish one group from another are not unlike the efforts or habits of other historians, for example, William of Jumièges or Orderic Vitalis, who always distinguished *Normanni* from *Franci*. Perhaps it would be impossible for those writers to entertain the modern possibility that today Normans might also consider themselves French or that English might also consider themselves British, though Keith Stringer suggests that "the concept of 'simultaneously held identities' [was not] entirely alien to twelfth-century pundits."[146] Granted, issues of identities are invariably complex and identities – with their elements of language, lineage, shared goals, etc. – are not mutually exclusive arenas; in addition, we have to recognize that there is a difference between an individual having mixed simultaneous identities, and groups intermingling or assimilating. Nonetheless, Geoffrey does not appear to have embraced mixed identities or mixed allegiances – at least not honorable ones (for Geoffrey, mixed allegiances often meant betrayal). However, Geoffrey's impulses to draw mutually exclusive groups may have had more to do with the fact that he was constructing a symbolic text, with an almost archetypal network of groups who represented ideas and not necessarily historical "realities," than that he was unaware of or incapable of adjusting to the concept of "simultaneously held identities" in individuals, or ethnic interpenetration, or mutual understanding among groups.

But then again, perhaps the latter – principally ethnic mixing and mutual understanding – was part of Geoffrey's goal, though as usual, he wasn't too

---

    alone conquest" (*Domination and Conquest*, 24). On the relationships between Scottish and French families in the twelfth century, see Martin Aurell, *L'Empire des Plantagenêt*, and M. A. Pollock, *Scotland, England and France after the Loss of Normandy, 1204–1296: 'Auld Amitié'* (Woodbridge: Boydell, 2015), Introduction 1–10.

146 On the fluidity of identities in Insular and Continental medieval historiography, going beyond the Normans as a starting point, see Stringer's tremendously useful Prologue to *The Normans and the "Norman Edge": Peoples, Polities and Identities on the Frontiers of Medieval Europe*, ed. Keith J. Stringer and Andrew Jotischky (Abingdon, Oxon; New York: Routledge, 2019), 1–27.

150   CHAPTER 2

clear about it. It is also tempting to view a link between 1) Geoffrey's animosity toward the Saxons; 2) the tendency for the Saxons to not seek to assimilate but to separate themselves giving at least the illusion that they considered themselves culturally superior to other insular groups; and 3) Geoffrey's desire to buy "cultural respectability" (to borrow Gillingham's term) for the Britons, and by extension for the Welsh, wishing to avoid the sensation of being "second-class" – or even "third-class" – citizens after the English, and the Normans.

It is in studies of languages in Britain that one finds the greatest evidence of non-assimilation by the early English. Huw Pryce points out that Gerald of Wales rejects Geoffrey's etymology for why the Welsh were called Welsh – "a name which owes to their leader Gualo, or to queen Galaes or to their decline [into barbarism]" (§208. 592–4) – instead writing in the *Descriptio Kambriae* that "the Anglo-Saxons, 'because in their language they call all that is alien Welsh (*Wallicum*), also called the peoples alien to them Welsh (*Walenses*)'." Pryce notes that "both Geoffrey and Gerald share an assumption that there was something pejorative about the Latin terms *Wallia* and *Walenses* (and variants thereof) ... and thus point up two related issues: the abandonment of a 'British' vocabulary, and the adoption in its stead of a vocabulary derived from Old English *W(e)alas*." Pryce concludes however that "the adoption by Cambro-Latin writers of English terms for Wales and its people is, therefore, probably best understood in terms, not of cultural domination, but of a wider dynamic of cultural interaction and adaptation in twelfth-century Wales."[147]

Nonetheless, it is difficult to ignore the phenomenon of cultural domination, because this adaptation went in the direction of the Welsh adapting to the English and not the reverse, according to other scholars. While Brian Ward-Perkins expresses recognition that for purposes of discussion Geoffrey is painting "deliberately a very generalized picture [which] does not preclude moments of political friendship ... and some cultural interchange," in large part the strong sense of difference on the part of the early English, is seen in the fact that

> the Germanic invaders absorbed very little of the native culture of Britain; and, by an act of supreme arrogance, they even termed the Britons '*wealas*', or 'foreigners', in their own island. The Anglo-Saxons learned to speak neither Latin nor Brittonic (the native Celtic vernacular of the Britons) ...

---

147   Huw Pryce, "British or Welsh? National Identity in Twelfth-Century Wales," cited at 785 and 801.

their failure, or refusal, to absorb any of the speech of the Britons into their wider language is quite remarkable.[148]

Margaret Gelling comes to a similar conclusion, stating that although "primitive Welsh place-names which were adopted and preserved by English speakers provide the only firm positive evidence for extended peaceful coexistence between the two peoples" yet in the last analysis, "the Old English language ... was remarkably immune to Welsh influence."[149] While Gelling seeks to explain this by positing that both groups were farmers and already had vocabulary which suited them, without the need to borrow, the isolation of the languages argues for a lack of assimilation – which is in fact what Wace says as we shall see in Chapter 5 – very unlike that of other European peoples, and certainly not the Normans whom it has been observed "often opted for a strategy of assimilation with the native communities with which they interacted," and that ultimately they "adapted themselves out of existence."[150] Ward-Perkins contends that "Anglo-Saxon Britain is undoubtedly a particularly extreme case of cultural domination ... unlike the Franks and the Rus, the Anglo-Saxons remained very Anglo-Saxon. In absorbing huge numbers of Britons into their ranks, they adopted remarkably little from them."[151] Working from a different vantage point, Elizabeth Tyler's work brings her to a similar conclusion. Her study on texts associated with the early English royal dynasties from the time of Alfred the Great to the Norman Conquest also contributes to an image of expressly cultivated English distinctiveness from the Britons. By tracing their origins back to the Germanic gods and biblical figures while avoiding Trojan origins, the English were "expressing their deliberately maintained separateness from other European dynasties, both Continental and Welsh," signaling an effort to disassociate themselves from the "legacy of the Roman Empire and then Frankish dominance."[152]

Although all generalizations will have exceptions, the broad pattern of behavior suggested by Ward-Perkins may serve to provide a further possible explanation of Geoffrey's animosity toward the Saxons:

---

148 Ward-Perkins, "Why did the Anglo-Saxons not become more British?" 514.

149 Margaret Gelling, "Why Aren't We Speaking Welsh?", *Anglo-Saxon Studies in Archaeology and History* 6 (1993): 51–56, cited here at 56.

150 *Crusading and Pilgrimage in the Norman World*, ed. Kathryn Hurlock and Paul Oldfield (Woodbridge: Boydell, 2015), Introduction, p. 3; Hurlock and Oldfield cite R. Allen Brown on the extent to which the Normans adapted/assimilated (R. Allen Brown, *The Normans and the Norman Conquest*, Woodbridge: Boydell, 1985, p. 25).

151 Ward-Perkins, "Why did the Anglo-Saxons not become more British?" 526.

152 Elizabeth Tyler, "Trojans in Anglo-Saxon England: Precedent without Descent," 2 and 20.

152 CHAPTER 2

it has often been observed, and the experience of post-Roman Britain confirms the observation, that the amount of borrowing between one culture and another is determined not only by the amount of contact between the two, but also by the perceived status that each culture has in the eyes of the other.[153]

If Geoffrey had been sensitive to perceptions of being considered of a group not sufficiently worthy of mingling with, on many levels a "second class" – or "third class" – citizen (to borrow a modern term), the Welsh secondary to the English, and then later, tertiary to the Normans, it may have fed an unfortunate animosity to the Saxon ancestors.[154]

In turn, Wace may have picked up on Geoffrey's animosities – it would have been very difficult not to – and being a Jerseyman, a small-town boy who eventually made it to Paris to be educated and trained as a *magister*, to eventually know three king Henries, he may have had some sympathy toward feelings of cultural, if not personal, inferiority. Perhaps his empathy gave him additional impetus to include the legend of the Round Table. As we will see further on in Chapter 5 – after our examination of the pro-English treatment of Geoffrey in the First Variant in Chapter 3 – Wace, as usual, tries to see all sides and eschew partisanship – either pro-British or pro-Saxon – whether for practical reasons or loftier ones: with his introduction of the Round Table, and its intermingling of individuals from many cultures without the need of interpreters, no language is supreme and none is inferior, and by extension, no group is supreme and none is inferior (that the king himself is a Briton is of course not without significance), although admittedly, all those at the Table are of a high rank. At the Round Table, each member is specifically named, complete with regional identity, so that each maintains individual identity while at the same time participating as an equal in the larger group. Perhaps the Jerseyman Wace was

---

153   Ward-Perkins, "Why did the Anglo-Saxons not become more British?" 530.

154   Of course, Geoffrey was not the only one who expressed animosity toward groups other than his own (whichever group that may have been). William of Malmesbury tars the Bretons with the same brush as the Britons, referring to the Bretons as the *Britones transmarinos*: "The Bretons, whom as a young man he [Henry I] had had as his neighbours in the castles of Domfront and Mont-Saint-Michel, he used to bring into his service for money. As a race they are penniless at home, and happy to earn the rewards of a laborious life elsewhere at the expense of strangers. Pay them, and they will throw justice and kinship to the winds, and not refuse to fight even in a civil war; and the more you give, the readier they will be to follow wherever you lead. Henry knew this habit of theirs, and if ever he needed mercenary troops, spent a great deal on Bretons ["spent," lit., "lost" or "wasted" *multa perdebat in Britones*], taking a short lease of that faithless people's faith in return for coin" (*GRA* v.402).

trying to use the court of Arthur, the great equalizer, to promote the idea of multiple identities – multiple among different individuals but also multiple within a single individual, thinking of bi-lingual and tri-lingual patrons – to counteract the lure of linguistic chauvinism and separatism. Through 1) the negative example of the Saxons who appear as a major symbol of separatist pull and cultural domination in the *Brut*; 2) the questionable actions of the early Trojans and Britons, vis-à-vis the aboriginal giants, and others; and 3) the positive example of the Round Table, Wace offers a message of tolerance and equanimity for men and women of all ranks and groups, particularly for the primarily French-speaking ruling class which doubtless enjoyed many advantages over the native English and British: Wace's message may well be that everyone's linguistic heritage and culture are important – in an ideal world there would be no place for feelings of cultural superiority, certainly not as a justification of privilege and power to the detriment of others.

CHAPTER 3

The First Variant Version

1 Introduction

In his article on the "erasure" of Wales in medieval English culture, Simon Meecham-Jones establishes a number of useful paradigms that can be equally illuminating for a study of the First Variant (hereafter FV) and Wace's *Brut* as they are for Geoffrey, Gildas, and Bede. He writes:

> The representation of Wales in Medieval English culture was created as, and has remained, a discourse shaped from the repetition of (often artful) forgettings and historical errors, repeated to sustain complex and sometimes mutually contradictory ideological agendas. In the medieval period, these forgettings and errors had become crystalized into a consensus of accepted albeit contradictory, propositions, significantly derived and certainly sustained by the texts of three of the most talented and influential mythmakers of the medieval period – Gildas, Bede, and Geoffrey of Monmouth. The four central elements of this consensus might be classified as the discourse of Britishness, the discourse of authority, discourse of peripherality, and the discourse of unequal value.[1]

Both the FV redactor and Wace also participated in these discourses, though most frequently discussing what they painted as conflicts between the Britons and the Saxons, not really touching upon the contemporary situations in Wales or the Welsh marches. Meecham-Jones continues:

> Whether the erasure of Wales resulted from indifference, ignorance, or an aversion fostered by the perceptions of Welsh "otherness" (for which we might blame Giraldus Cambrensis and Walter Map, amongst others) or perceived Welsh inferiority (for which Gillingham lays the blame on William of Malmesbury), it is remarkable how accurately the literary

---

1 "Where was Wales? The Erasure of Wales in Medieval English Culture," in *Authority and Subjugation in Writing of Medieval Wales*, idem and Ruth Kennedy, ed. (London: Palgrave Macmillan, 2008), 27–55, cited at p. 27.

record mimics the political development of the relationship between England and Wales.[2]

I would like to look at the other side of this issue: while I am not arguing that the literary record never mimics political developments, this can also be seen the other way around, that political developments can be supported by textual communities, and can often be led, shaped, or informed by them. These texts not only reflected dominant ideologies but also contributed to their creation and perpetuation by rationalizing and sanctifying them for not only the ruling elites but also for others in either the clerical, monastic, or lay audiences, whether Latin-speaking/listening/reading or strictly conversant in the vernacular.[3]

This chapter will follow the structure of the preceding chapter, with the comparison of the FV to the vulgate focusing on the selected critical junctures of these texts, while querying in what ways this text may have informed the political or cultural environment of its audience: the foundation myth, including the description of Britain; the *adventus Saxonum*; Arthur; the stages of the passage of dominion, including the conversion of the English; and the final passage of dominion. We will engage the four discourses set out by Meecham-Jones: 1) Britishness, 2) authority, 3) peripherality (or marginalization), and 4) unequal value, or to use another term, cultural imperialism. It will be important to take up both stylistic differences – largely in general terms – and political differences in more specific terms with a view toward getting a greater sense of the intersections and divergences of these two texts. However, because Geoffrey's vulgate text is so rich and various, it would be impossible for any single study to draw comparisons comprehensively between the majority of the figures, such as the numerous kings who "predate" the Romans, kings most likely manufactured by Geoffrey to bolster up his portrayal of the glorious past of the Britons, preceding and during the Roman occupation. Thus, much remains for scholars

---

2   Meecham-Jones, "Where was Wales?" 47.

3   Although it is easy to fall into the pattern of thinking that identity is monolithic – especially since Geoffrey of Monmouth and other medieval writers tended to act as if that were so – it is not. On identity in contemporary Wales as an excellent example, including consideration of Denis Balsom's influential "three Wales model" and his efforts to map the complex relationships between place, identity, class, cultural attachment, and political affiliation, see Daniel John Evans "Welshness in 'British Wales': negotiating national identity at the margins," *Nations and Nationalism: Journal of the Association for the Study of Ethnicity and Nationalism* 25.1 (2019): 167–190, and Denis Balsom, "The Three-Wales Model" in J. Osmond (ed.), *The National Question Again: Welsh Political Identity in the 1980s* (Llandysul: Gomer Press, 1985), 1–17. Of the elements of "place, identity, class, cultural attachment, and political affiliation," perhaps only political affiliation is too anachronistic for our purposes.

156   CHAPTER 3

of historical writing, political ideologies, and literary recastings of the legendary history of Britain, now that editions, revised editions, and translations are
becoming more available.[4]

Before entering into the analysis proper, it should be pointed out that there
are two major perspectives on the dating and authorship of the First Variant:
1) the minority view that the First Variant preceded the vulgate text – that it
was a draft, seized upon and exploited by Geoffrey of Monmouth, and that the
latter's vulgate was a rewriting of the former; and 2) the majority view, that the
First Variant was a recasting of the vulgate, with the primary aim of bringing
the narrative of the early history of England back into the largely pro-English
Bedan orbit. As is the case with any literary or historical debate, scholars' arguments don't necessarily fall neatly into one or the other "camp," but nonetheless these "camps" are important to keep in mind when setting the First Variant
into a workable context. A wealth of detail can be brought to bear, but again,
many of the details can be viewed from either perspective: for example, in general, in the FV, the trappings of wealth, generosity, splendor, and the cultural
capital those elements of life among the elite entail, are missing from the FV.
One could surmise that either Geoffrey added those elements to appeal to the
growing interest in romance themes on the part of the royal and aristocratic
Anglo-Norman lay audience or that the FV redactor suppressed them in deference to a more ecclesiastical audience.[5] This may well be a simplistic reduction

---

4   As Oliver Padel observes while trying to "redress the balance" between more frequent schol-
    arly attention paid to Brittany than to Cornwall in the vulgate, "the *History of the Kings of
    Britain* is so closely packed with material of every kind that anyone who reads it with a partic-
    ular interest will be able to pick out items of note," Geoffrey's work is profoundly rich and it is
    impossible to do justice to all factors in each passage ("Geoffrey of Monmouth and Cornwall,"
    16–17). That said, upon close examination, the First Variant version reads as if it were much
    less "tightly packed" than the vulgate, the latter with its over 900 names (Reeve, ed, lii) and
    107 kings (on the number of kings [and queens], see Chapter 1, n. 4). While comparisons
    of isolated corresponding passages tend to bear this out, only a systematic concordance of
    each text might begin to provide more concrete, comprehensive support for this assertion.
    Providing such a concordance is, however, beyond the scope of this study.
5   See n. 24 below on Diana Greenway's reflections on Geoffrey's audience, and that of the First
    Variant; see also Susan M. Johns on the relationship between growing female literary patron-
    age in the twelfth century, Geoffrey's largely (though not exclusively) positive portrayal of
    women, and the appeal of many aspects of his text to royal lay audiences (*Noblewomen,
    Aristocracy and Power in the Twelfth-Century Anglo-Norman Realm*, Manchester University
    Press, 2003, 40–43) and Fiona Tolhurst among others (see nn. 22 and 79 below). Although he
    doesn't address issues concerning the First Variant version per se, Jaakko Tahkokallio's recent
    study on "publication" and early dissemination of Geoffrey of Monmouth's *Historia* (as well
    as William of Malmesbury's *Gesta Regum* and Henry of Huntingdon's *Historia Anglorum*)
    provides novel and useful insights on the heterogeneity of audiences in the first half of the
    twelfth century (*The Anglo-Norman Historical Canon*, esp. 66–76); see also Blacker, *Faces of*

THE FIRST VARIANT VERSION

of the enormous complexities posed by these two texts, but nonetheless a useful one, at least for the purposes of discussion.[6]

As Neil Wright remarks, the language used by the FV redactor is a crucial factor in revealing that the FV bears "the stamp of a mind other than Geoffrey's."[7] There is no question that we have two versions, similar in "story line" but in many places very different in vision, and language in others. It is not a question of miscopying or needing to expand the number of copies. We have two very different texts, as we will also see in the following chapter on Wace who often tried to incorporate major points from each, reconciling them with varied levels of success. The goal here is to present as many points of comparison and divergence as possible to help readers come to their own conclusions as to the relationship between these two texts. As Barbara Herrnstein Smith posited forty years ago in her work on narrativity: once the variables, from major events to the smallest of semantic markers, are rearranged in response to political, social, linguistic, and even metrical functions and expectations, we no longer have different versions of the same story, but actually different stories.[8]

2   Dating and Authorship of the First Variant Version

One might almost say that the First Variant version of Geoffrey of Monmouth's *Historia Regum Britanniae* has suffered neglect in recent years in inverse proportion to the attention scholars have lavished on Geoffrey of Monmouth's vulgate version, and yet it is a very important text for the growing Galfridian tradition. As Alan MacColl has observed, on the other hand, the First Variant,

---

Time, 135–47 (1994; rev. e-book, Intro. to Chapter 2, "Patronage and Social Function") and 160–67 (1994; rev. e-book, Geoffrey of Monmouth section, Chapter 2).

6   See Wright ed. for detailed arguments against the FV authorship by Geoffrey himself, Wiliam of Malmesbury, Henry of Huntingdon, or Wace (*The Historia Regum Britannie II*, lxx–lxvi); although Hammer's edition of the Variant was not particularly favorably reviewed in its presentation of the text, he too expressed the opinion that the Variant followed the vulgate, stating that "in the person of the unknown redactor ... [the Variant] adds a new chronicler, who though inspired by Geoffrey, refused to reproduce him slavishly ... instead prefer[ing] to handle Geoffrey's text boldly by adding new material which he thought of interest and contracting his author's text as his fancy dictated" (Hammer, ed., 19–20). Since I am arguing below that the FV was a revision of the vulgate and not vice versa, I am using the word "redactor" for the FV author; my use of the pronoun "he" is for simplicity's sake (rather than "he/she") and in no way implies that I am dismissing the possibility that the redactor was a woman. See Warren for her use of "redactors" plural (*History on the Edge*, 72 ff.).

7   Wright ed., II, lxv.

8   "Narrative Versions, Narrative Theories," *Critical Inquiry* 7.1 (1980): 213–36.

158 CHAPTER 3

"had an influence on English historiography out of all proportion to the tiny number of its surviving manuscript witnesses."[9] The First Variant has often been considered Wace's main source for, the *Roman de Brut*, the latter forming the basis for the British section of the prose *Brut*, which itself was "the first truly comprehensive history of England in the vernacular" becoming the "most widely copied secular text of the late Middle Ages in England, and between the fourteenth and early sixteenth centuries it was the standard history of England."[10]

---

9   "Meaning of 'Britain' in Medieval and Early Modern England," 253. On the current count of ten First Variant manuscripts, see nn. 10 and 21 below. On manuscripts of the vulgate *Historia*, see Jakko Tahkokallio, who counts nearly 80 manuscripts of the vulgate before *c.*1210, and states that "the count of surviving manuscripts runs to 225 at the moment" ("Early Manuscript Dissemination" in *A Companion to Geoffrey of Monmouth*, 155–80, cited at 155; see also his n. 1, 155) and idem "Update to the List of Manuscripts of Geoffrey of Monmouth's *Historia regum Britanniae*," *Arthurian Literature* 32 (2015), 187–203, as well as Reeve, ed., xxxii–l, and vii–viii, n. 5; Julia C. Crick, *The Historia Regum Britannie of Geoffrey of Monmouth, IV: Dissemination and Reception in the Later Middle Ages* (Cambridge: D. S. Brewer, 1991), 14–15, 98, 175, 214–17; and additional sources in n. 21 below.

10   MacColl, "Meaning of 'Britain'," 254. Contemporary neglect of the First Variant is in part due to the very practical circumstance that no English translation had appeared until recently (or possibly a translation in any language). This has now been remedied by David W. Burchmore's English translation with facing page Latin text. Based on Wright's edition, Burchmore's text has approximately 200 emendations, 20% of which are spelling differences in proper names; while Wright concludes after lengthy textual comparisons (see his introduction) that "aHR seem to preserve the better text of the First Variant, being closer to the vulgate text and the Variant's other sources" (ed. II, cxiii), his edition, with R as a base MS (Paris, Bibliothèque de l'Arsenal 982), "does not contain vulgate or other interpolations of the sort that disfigure Jacob Hammer's edition" (ed., II, cxv), and he also uses the group DES "to correct obvious errors in R" particularly in §§149–208 (ed., II, cxv); for an exception, see n. 52 below on DES's correction of Brutus's parentage using the vulgate (§6), which is less authentic than the FV version from aHR (following Landolfus closely) which gives Brutus as Aeneas' grandson and not great-grandson. In preparing his version of Wright's text, Burchmore has "not felt bound by [Wright's] preference for the readings of *aHR* over those in *DES*" (430), and thus the majority of his emendations are readings from DES (see Wright, ed., II, lxxviii–xci and cxxii, for the list of the eight known manuscripts he collated, and n. 21 below on the two new manuscript witnesses discovered after he published his edition). I am grateful to Dr. Burchmore for having shared his text and translation with me in advance of publication (*The History of the Kings of Britain: The First Variant Version*, ed. and trans. David W. Burchmore, Dumbarton Oaks Medieval Library 57, Cambridge, MA: Harvard University Press, 2019). In addition to Burchmore's welcome addition to Galfridian studies, this chapter owes a tremendous debt to Neil Wright's exemplary edition accompanied by a substantial Introduction (II, xi–cxvi) and copious variants throughout, as well as to Leckie's *Passage of Dominion* which contains a sustained and detailed examination of this text's narrative focusing on periodization (Leckie, *Passage of Dominion*, 101–17). In terms of extended discussions (as opposed to

THE FIRST VARIANT VERSION   159

As noted by Wright, Robert Caldwell was the first to address the question of the date of the First Variant. The first of his two articles was devoted primarily to the interrelationship of the FV and the *Roman de Brut* of Wace; here Caldwell argued that Wace had drawn principally on the FV, though the second half of the *Brut*, especially the section dealing with Arthur, was based primarily on the vulgate; regarding authorship, Caldwell accepted Jacob Hammer's implication that the Variant version was not produced by Geoffrey but rejected Hammer's "ill-founded assertion that it was demonstrably the work of a Welshman" and regarding dating, Caldwell concluded that the Variant was in circulation before Wace finished his *Brut* in 1155.[11] In his second article, Caldwell changed his stance on the dating and proposed that the absence of certain material from the vulgate and the presence of material drawn from Bede and Landolfus Sagax indicated that the FV came first, and that the vulgate was a reworking of

---

passing references), Fiona Tolhurst's analyses must also be mentioned here (*Geoffrey of Monmouth and the Feminist Origins of the Arthurian Legend*, esp. 25–6, 77–9, 81, 111–12, 158 n. 6, 158–9 n. 10, and 160 n. 23, and *Geoffrey of Monmouth and the Translation of Female Kingship*, esp. 133–88 devoted to the First Variant and Wace's *Brut*), as well as Michelle Warren's *History on the Edge*, esp. chap. 3, 60–82 (60–76 devoted primarily to the FV). In 1951 Jacob Hammer published (in "seriously mangled form," according to Wright, ed., II, xi) a text of the *Historia* which differed in numerous ways from that which before had been regarded as the standard version *Geoffrey of Monmouth: Historia Regum Britanniae. A Variant Version edited from manuscripts*, ed. Jacob Hammer (Cambridge, MA: Medieval Academy of America, 1951); Hammer dubbed the latter the "vulgate," a term which has stuck, and the other, the "First Variant" version ("First" because he had discovered yet another version, which he was editing at the time of his death [H. D. Emanuel, "Geoffrey of Monmouth's *Historia Regum Britanniae*: a Second Variant Version," *Medium Ævum* 35 (1966): 103–11]). Wright notes that "there has thus far been no consensus of opinion on such fundamental issues as exactly how the text of this Variant relates to that of the vulgate" (ed., II, xvi) and sets about to fill in many of the gaps after summarizing the various hypotheses (ed., II, xi–xvi). See also R. William Leckie, Jr., *The Passage of Dominion*, esp. pp. 26–28, 102–13, 115–17, 119. In this book, I have used Wright's edition of the FV, and largely Burchmore's translation, taking care to be sure that any emendations Burchmore has made to Wright's edition do not substantially affect his translation (because they might then no longer correspond to Wright's edition that I am citing). Any changes I might make to the translations will be signaled as such in the notes, stating that they are my translations, since I do not always agree with Burchmore. See also Paul Russell, Review of *History of the Kings of Britain. The First Variant Version*, by ed. and trans. David W. Burchmore, *North American Journal of Celtic Studies*, 4.2 (2020): 237–41 and Ben Guy, Review of *History of the Kings of Britain. The First Variant Version*, ed. and trans. David W. Burchmore, *The Journal of Medieval Latin* 32 (2022): 300–07.

11   Robert A. Caldwell, "Wace's *Roman de Brut* and the *Variant Version* of Geoffrey of Monmouth's *Historia Regum Britanniae*," *Speculum* 31 (1956): 675–82, 675 and 682; Wright ed., II, cited at xiii; Hammer, ed., 19. See also Wright's analysis of the scholarship devoted to these questions (ed., II, xi–xvi).

160   CHAPTER 3

the FV.[12] Pierre Gallais rejected this idea: in his efforts to save Wace from the label of "compilateur," which he found demeaning to the French poet's originality, Gallais argued that Wace's *Brut* was the original upon which the FV was based, Wace having used the vulgate, the latter composed between 1138–1150 and the FV therefore after 1155.[13]

Hans-Erich Keller has advocated a return to Caldwell's original position, though with qualifications.[14] Based on an examination of place names in the FV and the *Brut*, Keller held that Caldwell had been correct in supposing that the FV predated the *Brut*. Elaborating on a different suggestion made by Caldwell, Keller identified the vulgate and the FV with the two sources referred

---

12   "The use of sources in the *Variant* and vulgate versions of the *Historia Regum Britanniae* and the question of the order of the versions," *BBIAS* 9 (1957), 123–4. Wright expresses the regret that this article was only published as an abstract that did not permit Caldwell to fully develop his arguments (ed., II, xiii, n. 11). Burchmore notes that while neither the whole article was published nor was another article, "The Vulgate and Variant Versions of the *Historia Regum Britanniae*," referred to in *PMLA* 73 (1958), p. 4, the original typescripts were donated by Caldwell's daughter, Dr. Elizabeth Kaplan, in 2008, and are now preserved in the Elwyn B. Robinson Department of Special Collections at the Chester Fritz Library of the University of North Dakota, Grand Forks (trans., xxiv, n. 7). Burchmore also cites a virtually unknown article by Caldwell, where the latter argues that the *liber vetusissimus* was the First Variant (though not explicitly identifying it with Gaimar's "good book of Oxford") – and that it had not only been given to Geoffrey by Archdeacon Walter ostensibly to "revise and polish and publish" but written by Walter in Latin, not in "the British tongue" as Geoffrey had claimed ("Geoffrey of Monmouth, Prince of Liars," *North Dakota Quarterly* 39 (1963): 46–51, cited at 51) (Burchmore, trans. xiv, n. 25). See n. 16 below on Ian Short's discussion of Gaimar's epilogue, with special reference to two of four main sources – Walter Espec's book borrowed from Robert of Gloucester to be translated from the Welsh, and the "good book of Oxford" belonging to Walter Archdeacon of Oxford, which had material not in the book(s) "belonging to the Welsh."

13   Pierre Gallais, "La *Variant Version* de l'*Historia Regum Britanniae* et le *Brut* de Wace," *Romania* 87 (1966): 1–32. See Wright who notes a striking circumstance (to be elaborated on in the following chapter on Wace), that "not a single one of the numerous passages and details unique to Wace's poem" are found in those FV MSS (ed., II, civ). This would strongly suggest that it is virtually impossible, or at the least, highly unlikely, for the FV to have been based on the *Roman de Brut*. It is quite possible that Wace may thus have used a conflate manuscript of the vulgate and FV which is no longer extant – similar to MS. c (Cardiff, South Glamorgan Central Library, 2.6.11), which according to Wright (ed., II, cv) is First Variant in §§5–108 and §§178–208, though even in those sections, it is heavily interpolated with vulgate passages, and largely vulgate elsewhere – but he also may have incorporated material, such as on the Round Table, he heard in oral versions, or obtained from other written sources we no longer have (see for example Chapter 5, n. 7 below). On Wace's use of multiple sources – including oral sources – for the *Roman de Rou*, for example, see Chapter 5, n. 255.

14   "Wace et Geoffrey de Monmouth: problème de la chronologie des sources," *Romania* 98 (1977): 379–89.

THE FIRST VARIANT VERSION   161

to by Gaimar – the vulgate with "le livre Walter Espac" (6448) and the FV with "le bon livre dë Oxeford/ki fust Walter l'arcediaen" (ll 6464–65).[15] Following this line of reasoning, Keller concluded that the source of the *HRB* was not the "liber vetustissimus" belonging to the Welsh in the possession of Walter archdeacon of Oxford as Geoffrey had claimed, but instead the FV, that is, "le bon livre dë Oxeford," written before 1138 and possibly by Archdeacon Walter himself – a suggestion which Wright soundly rejects as "wild speculation."[16]

---

15 All references here are to Ian Short's recent edition of the *Estoire des Engleis*, which has supplanted Bell's (*L'Estoire des Engleis by Geffrei Gaimar*, ed. Alexander Bell, Anglo-Norman Text Society 14–16, Oxford: Basil Blackwell, 1960; repr. New York: Johnson Reprint Corp., 1971). According to Gaimar, in the epilogue of the *Estoire des Engleis*, his patron Constance Fitz Gilbert, borrowed from Walter Espec a book (a historical narrative) which Robert, earl of Gloucester, "had had translated ... in accordance with the books belonging to the Welsh that they had in their possession on the subject of the kings of Britain" (Short, ed. and trans., ll. 6449–52, trans. p. 349; cf. Short, "Gaimar's Epilogue," 341), a historical narrative which many scholars might assume to be Geoffrey's *Historia* which Geoffrey dedicated to Robert (at least according to the most widely found dedication in the majority of manuscripts; see Crick, *The Historia Regum Britannie of Geoffrey of Monmouth, IV: Dissemination and Reception*, 118–19).

16 Ed., II, xvi. Wright demonstrates that the FV must have been an adaptation of the vulgate – and not the other way around – a conclusion shared by Leckie (*Passage*, 25–8, 102–9) and the majority of scholars; David Burchmore disagrees, however, following Caldwell and Keller, arguing that the "good book of Oxford" preceded the vulgate (identifying the "good book" with the First Variant) and was actually written by Archdeacon Walter of Oxford (not to be confused with Walter Espec), to be borrowed later by his clerk or *magister* in his household, Geoffrey of Monmouth, whom the Archdeacon permitted to revise and make it "his own" (trans., xv–xix). Although Wright demonstrates that much of Keller's formulation remains in the realm of conjecture – especially the idea that the FV preceded the vulgate, and that Archdeacon Walter was the author of the FV – Ian Short's recent work on Gaimar shows that Walter Espec's book, which Gaimar says the latter borrowed from Robert of Gloucester (quite possibly a copy of Geoffrey's vulgate) was Gaimar's primary source for the early period but that the poet made corrections based on supplementary material which he found in "the good book of Oxford" belonging to Archdeacon Walter – though it bears pointing out that Gaimar says "belonging" to Archdeacon Walter, which does not necessarily imply authorship, "ki fust Walter l'arcedaien" (l. 6465). That Gaimar may have used the "good book of Oxford" to supplement his other source raises the possibility that "the good book of Oxford" was of similar biases to the FV – since it had material not in the book(s) "belonging to the Welsh" (and that Robert of Gloucester had requested be translated into Latin), as Gaimar characterizes the source he associates with Robert of Gloucester (Gaimar, *Estoire*: "added to it the supplementary material that the Welsh had omitted," ll. 6460–61; trans. Short, p. 351), enabling Gaimar to bring the material from the vulgate more into line with the account of early English history in the ASC, Gaimar's predominant source, as well as with Bedan tradition. Short – who does not openly comment on the FV per se – suggests tantalizingly, yet with wise caution: "At all events, Gaimar's two separate books of overlapping historical material stand in clear contrast to Geoffrey of Monmouth's single [alleged] source, Archdeacon Walter's *liber vetustissimus*. And what

162   CHAPTER 3

The most recent advocate for Caldwell's arguments that the First Variant preceded the vulgate, and that the former was indeed "le bon livre dë Oxeford," and authored by Walter archdeacon of Oxford, is David Burchmore, who suggests further that Walter permitted Geoffrey to adapt the FV and then take credit of authorship (of the revised vulgate) because given Walter's position as a "respected member of the royal administration," he might not have wanted to publish

> under his own name an alternative history in which the Britons ruled the island through the late seventh century and hoped one day to rule again. The work risked controversy not so much for the legend of Trojan origins (which the Normans had embraced as well), or the fabulous exploits of Arthur (for which there was an eager audience), but because it systematically contradicted the canonical version of English history set forth

---

is surely equally, if not more, significant is that Gaimar fails to make any mention at all of Geoffrey of Monmouth – almost as if his name was not yet, when the *Estoire des Engleis* was composed in 1136–37, attached to the Welsh historical tradition represented by archdeacon Walter's and by Earl Robert's books. The temptation here to conjecture is difficult to resist: might these two texts have formed a pre-Geoffrey of Monmouth historical corpus to which Gaimar had access independently of Geoffrey? This in turn poses further questions: what could the relationship have been between these two texts and between them and Geoffrey of Monmouth, and when and how did Geoffrey come (if indeed he did) to appropriate them? To these and to similar speculative questions I leave it to others to provide what answers they will" ("Gaimar's Epilogue," 340). To Short's questions, I would like to add another: could Geoffrey have issued a "pre-publication" copy of the *HRB* – to which the FV redactor had already reacted, recasting as he saw fit, before Gaimar was writing in the late 1130s, such that Gaimar had access to both the vulgate and the First Variant – the latter being the recasting of a pre-publication copy of Geoffrey's text? For example, we know that Henry of Huntingdon wrote numerous versions of his *Historia Anglorum* between *c.*1133 and *c.*1155 (*The History of the English People 1000–1154*, trans. Greenway, xix, n. 5). On the other hand, if we follow Paul Dalton's dating of *c.*1141–*c.*1150 for Gaimar's original or for a possibly revised copy (presumably of the now-lost *Estoire des Bretuns* as well as the *Estoire des Engleis*, "The Date of Geoffrey Gaimar's *Estoire*," 38–39), that would have given Gaimar enough time to have used both the vulgate and the FV, the FV having been written between 1138 (the most often postulated date of Geoffrey's *Historia*; cf. Reeve's conjecture, *c.*1123–Jan. 1139, ed., p. vii) and the early 1150s (dating of the FV per Wright, ed., ii, lxx). Nevertheless, while this is a fascinating set of questions that beg to be solved – including the nature of the "liber vetustissimus" whose existence Gaimar would seem to corroborate when he mentions Robert of Gloucester's desire to have an ancient book belonging to the Welsh translated for him – quite possibly what Geoffrey refers to as the ancient book "in the British tongue" he alleges was given to him by Archdeacon Walter – I am compelled to embrace both Short's enthusiasms and cautionary notes, leaving future discoveries of the textual history of these works to others.

THE FIRST VARIANT VERSION   163

by Bede and the Anglo-Saxon Chronicle and accepted by establishment
historians such as William of Malmesbury and Henry of Huntingdon.[17]

Despite the passion of Burchmore's arguments – which have their rightful
place in this debate which has yet to be resolved (and may never be, to all
scholars' satisfaction), despite Burchmore's apparent belief in the possibility of its "resolution" – there are at least two ironies here: first, that Geoffrey
produced a text much more "alternative" than the First Variant whose appearance in public Archdeacon Walter was allegedly worried about although he
ostensibly wrote the narrative nonetheless; and second, the FV can be demonstrated to be considerably more "respectful" of the Bedan framework than
Burchmore's discussion admits.[18]

Since the main purpose of the FV appears to have been to couch the
Galfridian material in a more "English-friendly" framework, another interesting question is who would have wanted this, other than fellow historians;[19]

---

17   Burchmore, trans., xix–xx.
18   Burchmore may be too optimistic when he writes "the resolution of this question is central
      to understanding the nature of Geoffrey's unique contribution to medieval historiogra-
      phy and the development of Arthurian literature. If the Variant came first, then its author
      deserves much of the credit for the content and organization of Geoffrey's work, while
      Geoffrey's principal accomplishment was to supply the further narrative elaboration and
      rhetorical polish that ensured its widespread impact and enduring popularity" (trans.,
      ix). In addition to Burchmore's optimism that this debate can actually be solved without
      extensive textual analysis – and perhaps not even then – is the thorny problem of "con-
      tent" which varies widely between these two texts. Perhaps what they share is structure/
      organization as Burchmore notes, but it is difficult for me to say, at least according to my
      reading of these texts, that they share "content" since their political, ethnic, and religious
      perspectives are so very different – unless one defines "content" strictly as characters and
      events without necessarily considering the portrayal of those characters or the narrator's
      attitude(s) toward those events. For example, while Burchmore acknowledges that the
      vulgate "heightens the anti-Saxon rhetoric" (trans., xxii), he doesn't appear to attach, how-
      ever, any particular political importance to those narrative "alterations." In terms of which
      text came first – and we may ultimately be facing a "chicken-and-egg" scenario – it makes
      far greater sense to me that the FV redactor would tone down, for example, Geoffrey's
      vitriol against the Saxons to make the FV text conform more closely to English historical
      production – which was the dominant school of historiographical thought at the time –
      rather than Geoffrey taking the FV's much more neutral, often undramatic prose of the FV
      and infusing it with vitriol, thereby transforming Walter's pro-English text (if Walter were
      indeed the author) into a counter-cultural manifesto.
19   If we can judge from Gaimar's reliance on the ASC for his *Estoire des Engleis*, there were
      at least a handful of members of the Anglo-Norman aristocracy who were interested in
      English history, though it is not yet clear how many would have been interested in an
      English perspective rather than a British perspective. On Gaimar's political motivations
      in response to audience expectations, see Paul Dalton, "The Date of Geoffrey Gaimar's

164   CHAPTER 3

it appears unlikely (or perhaps only remotely possible) that Geoffrey's more outlandishly pro-British vulgate was a recasting of the FV.[20] My discussion of the First Variant below is therefore based on the premise that some version of the *Historia* ("some version" meaning as represented by a particular manuscript witness available to the FV redactor, but not necessarily still extant)[21]

Estoire des Engleis, the Connections of his Patrons, and the Politics of Stephen's Reign," and idem, "Geoffrei Gaimar's *Estoire des Engleis*, Peacemaking, and the 'Twelfth-Century Revival of the English Nation'"; J. Blacker, "'Dame Custance la gentil': Gaimar's Portrait of a Lady and her Books"; Emma Bérat, "The Patron and her Clerk: Multilingualism and Cultural Transition," *New Medieval Literatures* 12 (2010): 23–45; and John Gillingham, "Kingship, Chivalry and Love. Political and Cultural values in the Earliest History Written in French: Geoffrey Gaimar's *Estoire des Engleis*," and idem, "'Gaimar, the Prose *Brut* and the Making of English History," in *L'Histoire et les nouveaux publics dans l'Europe médiévale*, ed. Jean-Philippe Genet (Paris: Publications de la Sorbonne, 1997, 165–76; repr. in *The English in the Twelfth Century*, 113–22). On the publication circle of Geoffrey's history and how it intersects with Gaimar, his work and patrons, see J. Tahkokallio, *The Anglo-Norman Historical Canon*, 57–60.

20   Leckie concurs that FV was a revision of the vulgate: "Before Geoffrey's *Historia* forced the twelfth century to reassess the entire matter [the role of the Britons in the early history of Britain], writers had little reason to take the Britons seriously into account, and they certainly had no cause to modify English traditions regarding the importance attached to Hengist and Horsa. The efforts at accommodation found in the First Variant presuppose an earlier version of the *Historia*, one which created a challenge to conventional thinking" (*Passage*, 26–27). While also accepting the dominant view that the vulgate preceded the FV, Michelle Warren reads a more significant reflection of Welsh interests into the FV, based in part on the later dissemination of manuscripts in Wales; she admits though that "although these thirteenth- and fourteenth-century manuscripts do not testify directly to twelfth-century copying in Wales" one can infer that "they do show that this *Historia* circulated there and that it appealed to Welsh readers" (*History on the Edge*, 61). She does not reject Leckie's arguments that the FV is largely Anglo-centric, maintaining that due to their status as both conquered peoples in Britain, the Welsh and the English "could envision the value of arguments based on liberty rather than on territorial possession" and that thus they shared views "on the Insular colonial past that are largely compatible" (62). On the dissemination of the FV, see Crick, *IV: Dissemination*, 197–98, 214–15, and Wright ed., II, lxxviii–cxiv.

21   For further information on the manuscripts, see Julia C. Crick, *The Historia Regum Britannie of Geoffrey of Monmouth, III: A Summary Catalogue of the Manuscripts* (Cambridge: D. S. Brewer, 1989), 173–99 (including details on First Variant, Second Variant mss and conflate vulgate and variant mss); and Michael D. Reeve "The Transmission of the *Historia Regum Britanniae*," 102. Burchmore reports two further FV witnesses that have come to light since Wright published his edition in 1988: Lawrence, University of Kansas, Kenneth Spencer Research Library MS. 9/1:A22, a fragment from the second half of the twelfth century, and fourteenth-century Trinity College Dublin MS. 11500 (trans., 427, 429–30 and 432 nn. 2–3). On the former, see Tahkokallio, "Update to the List of Manuscripts," 187 and on the latter, idem, "Early Manuscript Dissemination," 155 n. 1. See also Georgia Henley on fourteenth-century MS Dublin, Trinity College 11500 in "Transnational book traffic in the

THE FIRST VARIANT VERSION 165

provided the basis for the FV, and that major differences (other than stylistic, but many of those could be included as well) originate from a desire to pull the material back into the Bedan orbit.[22]

In general, the primary stylistic tendencies in the FV relative to the vulgate – I will discuss the major political differences below, beginning in the next section on the Description of Britain – first noted by Hammer, and commented on by Gallais and others as well as nuanced by Wright, though interpreted often differently, include: 1) a penchant for biblical phraseology;[23] 2) a greater

---

Irish Sea zone. A new witness to the First Variant version of Geoffrey of Monmouth's *De gestis Britonum*" (*North American Journal of Celtic Studies* 4.2 (2020): 131–62.

22   Tolhurst notes the FV redactor's use of Bede has broad implications, marking him "as someone whose historiographical orientation, unlike Geoffrey of Monmouth's, is pro-English in addition to being pro-Welsh" (*Geoffrey of Monmouth and the Translation of Female Kingship*, 135). On the pro-English perspective of the FV, see Leckie, *Passage*, 106–107; on the pro-Welsh, see Michelle Warren, *History on the Edge*, 71–76. In an original discussion of this important but relatively little-known text, Tolhurst adds a further perspective, stating that in addition to the "undermining" of Galfridian historiography, the First Variant redactor's revision of Geoffrey's text, while "only partial ... has palpable consequences: it decreases the narrative or historical significance of all but one of Geoffrey's good female figures while villainizing the female figures that commit moral wrongs, regardless of their individual circumstances," thereby also undermining "the concept of female kingship as well as the positive presentation of female figures that makes female kingship so attractive in the Galfridian account of the British past" (*Female Kingship*, 135–36, 134).

23   The subject of biblical phrasing – like so many aspects of Galfridian scholarship – is vastly complex and can be interpreted in numerous ways. Professing more interest in the "imprint" biblical language had on the *HRB* than on motifs and modeling on biblical figures, Jacob Hammer provides an extensive list of phrases which he found to have echoed biblical passages; however, a fair number of these appear rather commonplace and thus not overwhelmingly indicative of biblical "imprint," such as Geoffrey's use of *bellatores enim viri* to describe Octa and Ebissa (taken directly from the *HB*) which Hammer says is found frequently in the Bible (either as *bellatores viri* or *viri bellatores*) ("Geoffrey of Monmouth's Use of the Bible in the *Historia Regum Britanniae*," *Bulletin of the John Rylands Library* 30.2 (1946): 293–311, here 304). In the introduction to his edition of the (First) Variant, Hammer also provides a short list of biblical phrases, but for some readers, the list of "biblical expressions absent in the vulgate" may not be sufficient to support Hammer's assertion of a "fondness for biblical phraseology" evinced by the Variant (ed., 9–10, here 10). Wright provides an extensive list of classical and biblical phrases (ed. II, xxiii–xxvi, the biblical esp. n. 30 on xxiii–xxiv, classical nn. 31–36 on xxiv–xxv), some of which overlaps with Hammer's, but not the majority by any means. Wright also cautions though that "too much should not, at this stage, be made of these biblical and Classical allusions unique to the Variant, since other such echoes and quotations of the Bible and Classical authors are either shared by both texts or found solely in the vulgate; and, indeed, such borrowings are characteristic of Geoffrey's literary technique. It must be noted, however, that these independent echoes constitute an important element of the different handling in the Variant of material common to both texts" (ed., II, xvi–xxvii).

166   CHAPTER 3

number of classical references; 3) more (and often banal) repetitiousness; 3) a
tendency to curtail or even eliminate speeches – though some are expanded
and others completely altered; 4) the elimination of personal authorial/
narratorial information, commentary, and most editorializing; and 5) an overall effort to reduce bombast and "tone down or omit unpleasant details."[24]

On the element of biblical resonances in the *HRB*, see also Paul Feurherd, *Geoffrey von Monmouth und das alte Testament mit Berücksichtigung der Historia Britonum des Nennius*, Inaugural-Dissertation, Friedrichs-Universität Halle-Wittenberg (Halle, 1915).

24   Wright ed., II, xi; Hammer, ed., *VV*, 8–12. Wright also notes what he characterizes as a "preference for non-Galfridian vocabulary," providing a list on p. lxv. Although Gallais based
his analysis solely on the Arthurian section of Wace's *Brut* and the FV, and concluded that
the FV was based on the *Brut*, on the level of vocabulary, he comments that it would be
possible to create a dictionary of synonyms based on the differences between the vulgate
and the FV ("La Variant Version," 7–8, n. 1), adding that the FV "élimine ou altère presque
tout ce qui exprime la personnalité de Geoffrey," 8, n. 1). Burchmore's argument that the FV
preceded the vulgate (though not Wace) is also based on stylistic grounds: "More importantly, the Variant is thoroughly inferior in style to the Vulgate – which raises the obvious
question why anyone, working within Geoffrey's own lifetime, would completely rewrite
the text in such a way as to make it *worse* rather than *better*. ... In moments of heightened
action, the Variant often shifts abruptly between the past and present tenses (sometimes
within a single sentence); the Vulgate uses the historical present more sparingly and
with greater consistency. ... On the larger scale of narrative the Vulgate is consistently an
improvement over the Variant. Battle scenes are more vivid, dramatic and suspenseful.
Direct speeches are more eloquent and contribute more effectively to the motivation of
the characters. Placing the two versions side by side, and comparing them sentence by
sentence, leaves me convinced that the Variant was the earlier draft" (unpub. draft Intro.,
5–6; this passage does not appear in the published text and translation volume exactly
as it appears here, but sections of it can be found in the Introduction; see for example,
xiv). I remain more convinced on political and thematic grounds that the FV is the revision, than I am swayed by evaluations of relative aesthetic value (e.g. stylistically "better"
vs. "worse"). The nature of audiences might also come into play as suggested by Diana
Greenway: "An oral context, too, though remote from the schools, is the environment in
which we should place Geoffrey of Monmouth's *HRB* and its variant versions. If Geoffrey's
vulgate was intended primarily for reading aloud to a lay audience, it seems likely that
the First Variant was a version modified for ecclesiastical ears" (Review of Wright's ed.
of the FV and Alexander Nequam's *Speculum Speculationum*, ed. Rodney M. Thompson,
Albion 22.1 [1990]: 102–4, here 104). It seems more plausible that pro-British sentiment,
more vehement speeches and violent battle scenes, and more elaborate love scenes,
would be toned down in favor of more "acceptable," that is, more traditional pro-Saxon
views, less florid rhetoric, with more biblical references and sympathy for ecclesiastical
concerns rather than the other way around, but ultimately, more research is needed to
move this debate forward (if it can indeed be eventually resolved satisfactorily). Although
it is the only manuscript to do so and thus not conclusive, the redactor of a *codex mixtus*
of the First and Second Variants ("the latter being used extensively from §61," Wright,
ed., II, lxxix), MS. a, Aberystwyth, N L W, 13210 (early 13th century) refers to that copy as
ostensibly a variant version, that is, with the phrase "correcta et abbreuiata" ("Explicit

THE FIRST VARIANT VERSION   167

3   The Description of Britain and the Foundation Myth

Wright provides a helpful division of the FV into ten categories to facilitate
comparison with the vulgate, as well as providing a block diagram showing the
number of chapters in each of the ten categories.[25] The opening chapter of the
FV, § 5, is one of only five chapters which contain information unique to the FV
and traceable to known sources (category I); only 2% of the 208 chapters fall
into this category, which demonstrates that the FV-redactor rarely made radical departures from the general outline, at least not with respect to the "topics"
of the majority of the sections, but in terms of tone and perspective, there were
definitely changes.[26]

---

hystoria Brittonum correcta et abbreuiata," fol. 64rb after §208); see Daniel Huws and
Brynley F. Roberts, "Another Manuscript of the Variant Version of the 'Historia Regum
Brittaniae," *BBSIA* 25 (1973), 147–52, here at 150; Julia Crick, *Summary Catalogue of the
Manuscripts*, 4; Wright, ed., II, lxxviii. We can't know of course if the redactor considered
the manuscript he was working on "corrected and abbreviated" because it was made up
of multiple versions – FV and SV – or whether he considered it "corrected and abbreviated" relative to the vulgate version only. For descriptions of the Second Variant which,
although significantly shortened, remains closer to the vulgate than the First Variant, see
Crick, *Dissemination*, 15–16, and Hywel D. Emanuel, "Geoffrey of Monmouth's *Historia
Regum Britannie*: A Second Variant Version." Jacob Hammer was preparing an edition of
the Second Variant at the time of his death; Emmanuel sought to complete Hammer's
work, but he too died before he could complete an edition.

25   Wright's ten categories, subdivided into three groups (total of 208 chapters) are:
        Group I: A: chapters containing material common to vulgate and Variant, and cast in
        similar style (6 chapters, i.e., Merlin's Prophecies, 3%); **B:** chapters containing material
        common to vulgate and Variant, but with differences of style and diction (159 chapters,
        76%); **C:** chapters containing material common to both texts but in less full form in the
        FV (118 chs., 57%); **D:** chapters common to both texts, but found in extremely brief form
        in the FV (20 chs., 10%); it should be noted that some of the chapters in this category over-
        lap with those in H, because chapters lacking speeches, for example, are much shorter
        in comparison to their "counterparts" in the vulgate; **E:** chapters containing a speech or
        speeches common to both texts, but found in fuller form in the FV (10 chs., 5%); **F:** chap-
        ters (or material contained in that chapter) common to both texts, but found in a differ-
        ent order in the FV (16 chs., 8%); **Group II: G:** entire chapters found only in the vulgate
        (9 chs., 4%); **H:** chapters some of whose material is found only in the vulgate (48 chs.,
        23%); **Group III: I:** chapters containing material found only in the FV, and drawn from
        a recognizable source (5 chs., 2%); **J:** chapters containing material found only in the FV
        (sources unknown) (20 chs., 10) (see Wright, ed., II, xvi–lxxiii; Table I, xviii).
26   In the other category containing information unique to the FV (J), with the difference
        that here the information cannot be traced to sources, there are 20 chapters (Wright,
        ed., xviii–xix) or 10% of the text, and thus more extensive than those chapters which are
        unique but whose sources can be traced; in total, then, approximately 12% of the FV is
        unique, relative to the vulgate. It is worth noting that section J also contains the greatest
        concentration of political differences in the narrative threads, concentrated primarily in

168   CHAPTER 3

The case of §5 is also unusual in that it is the only chapter in the FV which is
almost completely different from that of the vulgate; in addition, in the FV, §5
is the opening chapter, since the FV redactor has eliminated §§1–3/4[27] of the

---

1) the narratives of the renaming of the Island (§§186–87); 2) details of Augustine's conversion of the English (§188) and the martyrdom of the monks of Bangor (§189); 3) the
plague that drove the Britons from the island (§203); 4) English rule under King Athelstan
(§204); 5) the ultimate fate of the Britons (§207); and 6) the reference in the colophon to
the author of the *Historia* as Geoffrey Arthur (§208), all to be discussed below.

27   Six of the eight FV manuscripts do not contain the prefatory chapters §§1–3/4 (Wright,
     ed., II, lxxviii–xci). With respect to the vulgate, the designation "§§1–3/4" stems from the
     fact that some manuscripts of the *HRB* contain §4 while others do not. On those that
     contain § 4 – that is, the dedication added to Waleran of Meulan in MSS which contain
     the dedication to Robert in §3 – see Crick, *Dissemination IV*, 185. A single MS contains a
     double dedication to Stephen (in § 3) and Robert (in §4), Bern Burgerbibliothek MS. 568
     (for which see Wright's edition, *The Historia Regum Britannie of Geoffrey of Monmouth I:
     A single-manuscript edition from Bern, Burgerbibliothek, MS. 568*, Cambridge: D. S. Brewer,
     1984, xiii–xiv, and Crick, *Dissemination IV*, 180–81). It is also noteworthy that the FV
     manuscripts do not contain either the preface or the dedication to Merlin's Prophecies
     (§§109–110) though Exeter MS. 3514 has added them back in (Wright ed., II, lxxxiv: "later
     in the thirteenth century, Exeter 3514 received an extensive series of additions (written
     in a number of hands) which were so placed as to surround the original book," lxxxii);
     see also David Dumville who reports that MS. c adds the initial dedications in §§1–3
     from the vulgate text ("The Origins of the *C*-Text of the Variant Version of the *Historia
     Regum Britannie*," *Bulletin of the Board of Celtic Studies* 26, 1974–76: 315–22, 318 n. 5). That
     as a general rule, the FV redactor has omitted the preamble and the letter to Alexander
     of Lincoln may well indicate that he was not as interested in the contemporary topical
     potential of the book of *Prophecies* than he was in either prophecy itself or in convey-
     ing the "gist" of the *Historia* in terms of "textual fidelity". See Paul Dalton who proposes
     that the "fact that the *Prophecies* was written at the behest of Alexander, a close relative
     of the bishop (Nigel of Ely) said to have uncovered a plot in 1137 to hand the government
     of England to the Scots, is of major significance in determining its meaning and purpose
     and those of the *Historia* as a whole" ("The Topical Concerns of Geoffrey of Monmouth,"
     696). Unlike some of the vulgate manuscripts, twelfth-century anonymous commentar-
     ies, and the Anglo-Norman verse Prophecies, for example, in the Prophecies proper, FV
     manuscripts also do not appear to have the "Vae tibi Neustria" prophecy which possibly
     alludes to the burial of Henry I (Henry "the Lion"), intimating that the Normans would
     finally suffer defeat and be dispersed from English soil; FV MS E., Exeter 3514, however
     has a variant of this prophecy as a gloss to the Prophecies (Hammer, "Bref commentaire,"
     113–17, esp. 116 note); see also Hammer, ed., *Variant Version*, 126, note to l. 88, on the pos-
     sibility of this prophecy in glosses in MS c Cardiff South Glamorgan Central Library 2.611
     (according to Crick III: Summary Catalogue, 89, and Wright, ed., II, lxxix–lxxx a FV with
     vulgate conflate): "*Vae tibi, Nestria, quoniam in te cerebrum leonis effundetur et dissipa-
     tis membris a marino solo eliminabitur*," and also as marginalia in MS. D Dublin, Trinity
     College 515 (E.5.12): "*Vae tibi, Neustria, quia in te cerebrum leonis effundetur*" (Hammer, ed.,
     126 n for l. 88); see also Hywel D. Emanuel, who proposes that "most of the manuscripts
     of the SV [Second Variant] have the additional sentence: "*Ve tibi Neustria quia cerebrum
     leonis in te effundetur, dilaceratisque membris a patria solo eliminabitur*," but he does

THE FIRST VARIANT VERSION   169

vulgate which contain the dedication(s) and other authorial references; the
vulgate MSS which contain §§1–3 but in which the name of the dedicatee
is missing from §3, still mention the "liber vetustissimus" as the source and
Archdeacon Walter in that connection, which ultimately is also a form of personal information.[28]

That §5 is the opening chapter of the FV, and that it is the only chapter
which is so extensively different from the vulgate, is crucial to our overall
understanding of the text because the opening chapter sets the tone for the
entire work, and, as observed in Chapter 1, the nature of the description of
Britain reveals how each author conceived of the island, his attitude toward
the realm(s), and thus toward those whose political agendas and ideologies
he wished to promote. According to Wright, the major differences between
the vulgate and the FV versions of the description of Britain stem from the
fact that Geoffrey "draws freely" from Gildas's *De Excidio* whereas when the
First Variant redactor borrows from Bede's *Historia Ecclesiastica* he borrows

---

not specify which manuscripts (of the fifteen he knew and the three more reported by
Crick, *Dissemination*, 181–98) he designates as "most" ("A Second Variant Version," 109).
On the vulgate manuscripts which have this interpolation – considered by some scholars to be an early interpolation, by others a late one – see Reeve, "The Transmission,"
102, 109; H. L. D. Ward, *Catalogue of Romances in the Department of Manuscripts in
the British Museum*, 3 vols. (vol. 3 J. A. Herbert) (London: Longmans, 1883–1910), vol. I
(1883), 208–9; Wright, ed., I, xi, n. 10; and Carolyn Eckhardt, "The Date of the 'Prophetia
Merlini' Commentary in MSS. Cotton Claudius B VII and Bibliothèque Nationale Fonds
Latin 6233," *Notes and Queries*, n.s. 23 (1976):146–47 and eadem, ed., *The Prophetia Merlini
of Geoffrey of Monmouth: A Fifteenth-Century English Commentary*, Speculum Anniversary
Monographs 8 (Cambridge, MA: Medieval Academy of America, 1982), esp. 1–15, an introduction to the *Prophetia* and commentary traditions. On the implications of this proph-
ecy and its inclusion in Alexandrine versions of the Anglo-Norman verse Prophecies of
Merlin and in John of Cornwall's mid-twelfth-century Latin commentary (*c.*1153–54), see
Anglo-Norman Verse Prophecies of Merlin, ed. and trans. J. Blacker (Dallas, TX: Scriptorium,
2005; rev. ed. of "The Anglo-Norman Verse Prophecies of Merlin," *Arthuriana* 15.1 [2005]:
1–125), 21–22 n. 34, and eadem "Where Wace Feared to Tread: Latin Commentaries on
Merlin's Prophecies in the Reign of Henry II," *Arthuriana* 6.1 (1996): 36–52, esp. 39–41, 43,
46–47 nn. 5–6, and nn. 24–28 on 49–50, and on the twelfth-century anonymous commentaries, Jacob Hammer, "A Commentary on the *Prophetia Merlini* (Geoffrey of Monmouth's
Historia Regum Britanniae, Book VII)," *Speculum* 10 (1935): 3–30 and idem, "A Commentary
on the *Prophetia Merlini* (Geoffrey of Monmouth's *Historia Regum Britanniae*, Book VII)
(Continuation)," *Speculum* 15 (1940): 409–31. The text in the earliest extant twelfth-century
commentary (without glosses) reads: "*Vae tibi, Neustria, quoniam in te cerebrum leonis
effundetur et dissipatis membris a nativo solo eliminabitur*" ("Woe unto you, Normandy, for
in you the brain of the lion will be poured forth and with parts scattered from native soil,
will be banished," Blacker "Latin Commentaries," 40).

28   On the acephalous manuscripts, including those of the First Variant, see Crick,
Dissemination IV, p. 117, n. 36. On the "nameless" dedications, see also Crick, 117–20.

170   CHAPTER 3

"practically verbatim."[29] However, Geoffrey whose description is roughly the length of Gildas's, further idealizes the early part of the description of the *locus amoenus* as found in Gildas.[30] The First Variant, while borrowing a few phrases almost word-for-word from Bede, cuts a great deal of the extended content, even cutting from Geoffrey as we shall see below.

In comparison with the First Variant, the distinguishing features of Geoffrey's description of Britain[31] are 1) the sole use of the name Britannia, not as a term from a former era, but as a contemporary one, and as referring to the entire island; 2) the elements which make the island sound like an earthly paradise including vast green pastures, ample fish, honey, and three "noble rivers ... on which foreign goods can be brought in by boat from every land"; 3) the change in tone occurring about two-thirds of the way through with the description of the once-thriving 28 cities, not all of which continued in the same glorious condition; 4) the naming of the five peoples who have inhabited Britain, including the Normans; 5) how the pride of the Britons brought about their fall through divine retribution, which visited upon them the Picts, the Scots, and then the Saxons:

Vulgate §5

Britannia, insularum optima, in occidentali occeano inter Galliam et Hiberniam sita, octingenta milia in longum, ducenta vero in latum continens, quicquid mortalium usui congruit indeficenti fertilitate ministrat. Omni etenim genere metalli fecunda, campos late pansos habet, colles quoque praepollenti culturae aptos, in quibus frugum diuersitates ubertate glebae temporibus suis proueniunt. Habet et nemora uniuersis ferarum generibus repleta, quorum in saltibus et alternandis animalium pastibus gramina conueniunt et aduolantibus apibus flores diuerborum colorum mella distribuunt. Habet etiam prata sub aeriis montibus amoeno situ uirentia, in quibus fontes lucidi, per nitidos riuos leni murmure manantes, pignus suauis soporis in ripis accubantibus irritant. Porro lacubus atque piscosis fluuiis irrigua est et absque meridianae plagae

---

29   Wright, ed., II, xlii.
30   For example, the superlative in the vulgate, "it supplies all human needs with its boundless productivity" (§5.26; "quicquid mortalium usui congruit indeficenti fertilitate ministrat"); Michael Winterbottom, ed. and tr. *Gildas. The Ruin of Britain and Other Works*, 16–17 for the translation, and 89–90 for the original. See also M. Winterbottom, "The Preface of Gildas' *De Excidio*," Transactions of the Honourable Society of Cymmorodorion (1974–5): 277–87.
31   See Chapter 1 on Geoffrey's description of Britain in the context of Gildas, Bede, Henry of Huntingdon, and William of Malmesbury.

THE FIRST VARIANT VERSION

171

freto, quo ad Gallias nauigatur, tria nobilia flumina, Tamensis uidelicet et Sabrinae nec non et Humbri, uelut tria brachia extendit, quibus transmarina commercia ex uniuersis nationibus eidem nauigio feruntur. Bis denis etiam bisque quarternis ciuitatibus olim decorata erat, quarum quaedam dirutis moeniis in desertis locis squalescunt, quaedam uero adhuc integrae templa sanctorum cum turribus perpulera proceritate erecta continent, in quibus religiosi coetus uirorum ad mulierum obsequium Deo iuxta Chritianam traditionem praestant. Postremo quinque inhabitatur populis, Normannis uidelicet atque Britannis, Saxonibus, Pictis, et Scotis;[32] ex quibus Britones olim ante ceteros a mari usque ad mare

---

32 Geoffrey largely (if not exclusively) uses "Scoti" to refer to the Scots, not to the Irish, whereas "*Scotti* in Bede always means the Irish race whether in Scotland or Ireland" (*HE*, ed., 16, n. 1); Wright points out that William of Rennes also uses "Scoti" to refer to the Scots (as opposed to the Irish) as does Geoffrey (*The Historia Regum Britannie of Geoffrey of Monmouth, V. Gesta Regum Britannie*, ed. and trans. Neil Wright, Woodbridge, D. S. Brewer, 1991, xiv, n. 24). What is not completely clear , however, are the reasons behind Wright's decision in his translation of the vulgate in Reeve's edition 16 years after his edition of the *GRB*, to apparently to translate Geoffrey's "Scotti" as occasionally "Irish"; the usage of *Scotti* in Gildas is also considered to refer to the Irish as is the usage in the *Historia Brittonum* (Thomas D. O'Sullivan, *The De Excidio of Gildas: Its Authenticity and Date*, Leiden: E. J. Brill, 1978, 24 and Bart Jaski, "'We are all of the Greeks in our Origin': New Perspectives on the Irish Origin Legend," *Cambrian Medieval Celtic Studies* 46 (2003): 1–53, 7 [for HB]). It is possible that Bede wished to establish or emphasize an early connection between the Irish and the Scots, though the simplest explanation may be that "the name Scotia originally designated Ireland" (Cowan, "Myth and Identity in Early Medieval Scotland," 130). What is clearer though is that Geoffrey did not choose to make that connection between the Irish and the Scots either extensively or to emphasize it – not seeking to demonstrate that the Picts, Scots, and Britons shared a common ancestry – as he remarks in the passage where he recounts how the Picts went to Ireland to seek wives since the Britons rebuffed them, by implication "rightly" refusing to marry their daughters "to such people" (§70. 382–83). In an authorial aside, Geoffrey adds, drawing a distinction between the Picts and the Irish, and the Scots who descended from them both: "But enough of the Picts, since it is not my intention to write either their history or that of the Scots, who are descended from them and the Irish" (§70. 386–88; "Sed haec hactenus, cum non proposuerim tractare historiam eorum siue Scotorum qui ex illis et Hibernensibus originem duxerunt"). The First Variant redactor follows Geoffrey in using the term *Scoti* to refer to the descendants of the Irish and Picts though without ever explicitly describing the descent; in his rendition of this same passage, the FV redactor omits, as he often does, the metanarrative comment, in this case about not devoting time to the history of the Picts and Scots and simply tells that the Picts sought wives in Ireland and then settled in Britain: "Transuentes igitur in Hyberniam duxerunt de populo illo uxores ex quibus ora soboles in magnam multitudinem creuerunt; et exinde Picti Britanniam incoluerunt"; "Passing over therefore to Ireland, they took wives from that people and with their offspring they multiplied in great numbers; and after that the Picts lived in Britain", §70.3). Among the vast number of studies on the early accounts of the mythical origins of the

insederunt donec ultione diuina propter ipsorum superbiam supeue-
niente Pictis et Saxonibus cesserunt. Qualiter uero et unde applicuerunt
restat nunc perarare ut in subsequentibus explicabitur. (Reeve, ed., 7)

Britain, the best of islands, lies in the western ocean between France and
Ireland; eight hundred miles long by two hundred miles wide, it supplies
all human needs with its boundless productivity. Rich in metals of every
kind, it has broad pastures and hills suitable for successful agriculture, in
whose rich soil various crops can be harvested in their season. It has all
kinds of wild beasts in its forest, and in its glades grow not only grasses
suitable for rotating the pasture of animals, but flowers of various colours
which attract bees to fly to them and gather honey. It has green meadows
pleasantly situated beneath lofty mountains, where clear streams flow in
silver rivulets and softly murmur, offering the assurance of gentle sleep to
those who lie by their banks. Moreover, it is watered by lakes and streams,
full of fish, and apart from the straits to the south, which allow one to sail
to France, it stretches out, like three arms three noble rivers, the Thames,
the Severn and the Humber, on which foreign goods can be brought in by
boat from every land. It was once graced with twenty-eight cities, some
of which lie deserted in lonely spots, their walls tumbled down, while
others are still thriving and contain holy churches with towers rising to a
fine height, in which devout communities of men and women serve God
according to the Christian tradition. It is finally inhabited by five peoples,
the Normans, the Britons, the Saxons, the Picts and the Scots; of these the
Britons once occupied it from shore to shore before the others, until their
pride brought divine retribution down upon them and they gave way to
the Picts and the Saxons. It remains now to relate how they landed and
from where, as will soon be explained. (Wright, tr., 6)

The contrast with the First Variant is immediately apparent, as the praise of the
plenty is less fulsome, the commentary of disappointment and disillusionment

Irish and Scots (and sometimes Picts), see in addition to sources mentioned elsewhere,
Colin Breen, "Maritime Connections: Landscape and Lordship among the Gaelic Atlantic
Seaboard of Scotland and the North of Ireland during the Middle Ages," *Journal of the
North Atlantic* 12.1 (2019): 3–15, https://doi.org/10.3721/037.012.sp202; Edward J. Cowan,
"Myth and Identity in Early Medieval Scotland"; Dauvit Broun, *The Irish Identity of the
Kingdom of the Scots: From the Picts to Alexander III* and idem, *Scottish Independence and
the Idea of Britain*; Ewan Campbell, "Were the Scots Irish?"; Molly Miller, "Matriliny by
Treaty: The Pictish Foundation-Legend"; and Patrick Wormald, "The Emergence of the
Regnum Scottorum: a Carolingian Hegemony?"

THE FIRST VARIANT VERSION   173

regarding more recent events is absent, and other details important in the vulgate narrative are omitted:

First Variant §5
Britannia insularum optima quondam Albion nuncupata est: in occidentali occeano inter Galliam et Hyberniam sita octingenta milia passuum in
longum, ducenta uero in latum continens. Terra opima frugibus et arbo-
ribus et alendis apta pecoribus ac iumentis; uineas etiam quibusdam in
locis germinans set et auium ferax terra, fluuiis quoque multum piscosis
ac fontibus preclara copiosis. Habet et fontes salinarum, habet et fontes
calidos, uenis quoque metallorum eris ferri plumbi et argenti fecunda.
Eratque quondam ciuitatibus nobilissimis .xx. et .viii. insignita. Insula
hec Britones et Pictos et Scottos incolas recepit. Britones autem a quibus
nomen accepit in primis a mari usque ad mare totam isulam insederunt;
qui de tractu Armenicano ut fertur Britanniam aduecti sunt. Qualiter
uero et unde uel ubi applicuerunt restat calamo perarare sequendo ueterum hystorias qui a Bruto usque ad Cadwaladrum filium Cadwalonis
actus omnium continue et ex ordine texuerunt.

Britain, the best of islands, was once named Albion: it lies in the western
ocean between France and Ireland, eight hundred miles long and two
hundred miles wide. A land rich with fruit and trees and commodious
to raising sheep and livestock; even in some places sprouting grapevines,
but also rich with birds, and rivers too with abundant fish and renowned
for its abundant springs. It has both salt and warm springs, and is rich
in veins of copper, iron, lead, and silver metals. It was once noted for
twenty-eight most noble cities. This island received as residents the
Britons, the Picts, and the Scots. The Britons from whom it derived its
name once held the whole island from sea to sea; they sailed, as it was
reported, to Britain from Armorica. It remains to relate how they landed
and where, following the histories of the ancients from Brutus up to
Cadwaladr son of Cadwalonis, all the acts continuously and in order.[33]

---

33   Wright, ed., II, p. 1. All translations of the FV are from Burchmore unless otherwise indi-
      cated, using chapter numbers with his subdivisions (subdivisions required by the press),
      as in "§104.4" for example. As mentioned above, Wright does not use line numbers or
      subdivision numbers, or book numbers, in his FV edition; Burchmore also uses the chap-
      ter divisions Wright uses from Faral's 1939 edition of the vulgate (as well as reintroducing
      book numbers). I have not used any book numbers from any of the Galfridian texts. This
      translation of §5 is mine.

174   CHAPTER 3

As noted by Wright with respect to §5 in the FV, "all the Gildas-derived[34] material [in the vulgate *Historia*] from *quicquid mortalium usui congruit* ["it supplies all human needs"] to *traditionem praestant* ["serve (God according to the
Christian) tradition"] is replaced by a shorter passage copied almost word for
word from [Bede's] *Historia Ecclesiastica* 1.1."[35] Based on a detailed comparison of a number of passages elsewhere in the vulgate and FV, though, Wright
concludes that the FV "despite omissions, retained the Gildas-based passages
of the vulgate more often than it suppressed them," most often cutting what
might have seemed to the FV redactor as bombast, omitting much "rhetorical
writing and characteristic Gildasian imagery and vocabulary."[36]

Interestingly, although the First Variant redactor borrowed from Bede's first
paragraph,[37] he appears to have cut out more from Bede's complete passage

---

34   Whether we characterize these phrases as "Gildas-derived" or perhaps "Gildas-inspired,"
        Gildas does not have this particular superlative passage found in Geoffrey, "quicquid mor-
        talium usui congruit indeficienti fertilitate ministrat" (§5.26; "it supplies all human needs
        with its boundless productivity"), though the final part of Gildas's "preamble" (*DEB* 1–3.,
        pp. 87–90), devoted to geography and made up of one long rambling sentence (*DEB*, 3.1–4,
        pp. 89–90) certainly has echoes of a *locus amoenus* theme: "To water it, the island has clear
        fountains, whose constant flow drives before it pebbles white as snow, and brilliant rivers
        that glide with gentle murmur, guaranteeing sweet sleep for those who lie on their banks,
        and lakes flowing over with a cold rush of living water" (3.4, p. 17; "... fontibus lucidis
        crebris undis niveas veluti glareas pellentibus, pernitidisque rivis leni murmure serpenti-
        bus ipsorumque in ripis accubantibus suavis soporis pignus praetendentibus, et lacubus
        frigidum aquae torrentem vivae exundantibus irrigua," p. 90). See also N. J. Higham, "Old
        Light on the Dark Age Landscape: The Description of Britain in the *De Excidio Britanniae*
        of Gildas," *Journal of Historical Geography* 17.4 (1991): 361–72.
35   "Geoffrey of Monmouth and Gildas," 25.
36   "Geoffrey of Monmouth and Gildas," 26.
37   In the historical introduction to his edition of Bede's *HE* (with R. A. B. Mynors), Bertram
        Colgrave comments that book I contains little original material. For example, the first
        chapter (which consists of the description of Britain and little else) is "a mosaic of
        quotations from Pliny, Gildas, Solinus and Orosius, together with a sentence from the
        Hexaemeron of St. Basil" (ed., xxxi); see also 14–15 n. 1. Wright provides the follow-
        ing phrases as the principal borrowings made by the First Variant redactor from Bede,
        Historia Ecclesiastica 1.1: "Britannia oceani insula, cui quondam Albion nomen fuit, ...
        per milia pasuum .dccc. in boream longa, latitudinis habet milia.cc. ... Opima frugibus
        atque arboribus insula, et alendis apta pecoribus ac iumentis, uineas etiam quibusdam in
        locis germinans, sed et auium ferax terra marique generis diuersi, fluuiis quoque multum
        piscosis et fontibus praeclara copiosis ... Habet fontes salinarum, habet et fontes cali-
        dos, ... etiam uenis metallorum, aeris ferri plumbi et argenti, fecunda ... Erat et ciuitatibus
        quondam .xx. et viii. nobilissimis insignita ... In primis autem insula Brettones solum, a
        quibus nomen accepit, incolas habuit; qui de tractu Armoricano, ut fertur, Britanniam
        aduecti australes sibi partes illius uindicarunt" (Wright, ed., II, xliii) ("Britain, once called
        Albion, is an island in the ocean ... extends 800 miles to the north, and is two hundred
        miles broad ... The island is rich in crops and in trees, and has good pasturage for cattle

THE FIRST VARIANT VERSION   175

than from Geoffrey's (though what he cuts out from Geoffrey – to be discussed below – is nonetheless significant). From Bede's description of Britain, which is substantially longer than either that of the vulgate or FV, the First Variant redactor eliminated numerous details including 1) the length of the nights in winter and the days in summer; 2) the five languages spoken on the island (English, British, Irish, Pictish, and Latin); 3) the background of the Picts and the Irish (even though English is mentioned here in the FV as one of the five languages, the Saxons or Angles as peoples are not mentioned);[38] 4) the lack of serpents in Ireland; and 5) that the Irish "formed the third nation in Britain in addition to the Britons and the Picts" (*HE*, i. 1, 21).

In terms of the peoples of the island, first we should note that the FV redactor follows Geoffrey in using "Scoti" to refer to the Scots rather than to the Irish[39] as in Bede, and as we will see below, the redactor embraces Geoffrey's position that the Scots and Picts were enemies of the Britons, but he accomplishes this with less gusto, i.e., less enthusiasm and certainly less anger than in the vulgate where the Scots and Picts function as a "matched set" of enemies of the Britons and who appear almost as if on cue to harass the Britons.[40] Although it would have been chronologically impossible for Gildas or Bede to have mentioned the Normans as one of the invading peoples, it is noteworthy that the FV

---

    and beasts of burden. It also produces vines in certain districts, and has plenty of both land- and waterfowl of various kinds. It is remarkable too for its rivers, which abound in fish ... and for copious springs ... The land possesses salt springs and warm springs ... [the land also has] rich veins of metal, copper, iron, lead, and silver ... The country was once famous for its twenty-eight noble cities ... To begin with, the inhabitants of the island were all Britons, from whom it receives its name; they sailed to Britain, so it is said, from the land of Armorica, and appropriated to themselves the southern part of it" (translation from Colgrave and Mynors, ed. and trans., pp. 15, 17).

38   According to Bede's editors, his famous division of the invading peoples into Angles, Saxons, and Jutes (1.15, 50) is "perhaps his most important contribution to the history of the invasion" (ed., p. 50 n. 1), though he inevitably referred to the whole complex of invaders as the "gens Anglorum".

39   See n. 32 above.

40   We shouldn't necessarily be surprised by Geoffrey's portrayal of the Scots and Picts as enemies of the Britons, rather than as co-occupiers, since "Gildas's portrayal of them [as well as of the Saxons] is both impersonal and relentlessly hostile" (Peter Turner, "Identity in Gildas's *De Excidio et Conquestu Britanniae*," *Cambrian Medieval Celtic Studies* 58 (2009): 29–48, here 38). See also Alheydis Plassam who points out that Gildas refers to the Irish and Picts as "overseas nations," who appear to "owe their existence, in Gildas's eyes, merely to the fact that God wants to punish His disobedient people, the Britons," not original "inhabitants" like the Britons; for Gildas, "compared with these almost subhuman peoples [Irish, Picts, and Saxons], the negative attributes of the Britons are almost trivial" ("Gildas and the Negative Image of the Cymry," *Cambrian Medieval Celtic Studies* 41 (2001): 1–15, here 11 and 10).

176   CHAPTER 3

redactor does not; it is also significant that only Geoffrey mentions the Saxons as a people who inhabited Britain, and in addition it is not surprising that he mentions them disparagingly.

The First Variant redactor however, could certainly have named the Saxons but he chose not to,[41] focusing on those peoples who were later more closely associated with the Britons as Celtic, non-Saxon peoples, but whom Geoffrey nonetheless cast as enemies due to their early history as invaders.[42] In Geoffrey's *Historia*, particularly the Saxons are set up from the very beginning as enemies of the peace, destroyers of the *locus amoenus* whom the Britons

---

41   Interpreting this material somewhat differently, Warren observes that the latter part of the FV's opening description "narrows the *Historia's* historiographical focus" restricting the population "to the conquering and unconquered Britons, overlooking their conquerors [the Saxons/English] until absolutely necessary"; additionally, she posits that the redactor(s) in this opening description "(drawing from Bede) resurrect the genealogical multiplicity that Geoffrey carefully trimmed, asserting that the Britons originated in Armorica" (63), i.e., that they were not native but rather the island's earliest settlers (*HE*, I.i, p. 16; Bede also writes that in the beginning, all the inhabitants of Britain were Britons: "in primis autem insula Brettones solum"). For Geoffrey, the Britons were both descended from Trojans, from a far-away land, but also native, since apparently the giants were not considered fully human peoples, and thus were "written off" as not native people, but rather of the same rank as animals. Thus, Geoffrey would need to suppress the Armorican connection here in order to stress the native, but the FV redactor, not having the same agenda as Geoffrey, does not, nor does the FV-redactor try to openly reconcile the Britons both as Trojans and as native.

42   While I do not find it inconsistent that Geoffrey would play both ends against the middle with regard to the Normans – that is, both tarring the Normans with the same brush as the Saxons, as invaders and colonizers as argued by John Gillingham ("The Context and Purposes") and others (see esp. Warren who sees Geoffrey as a "border intellectual," reading in his history "both support for and subversion of Norman rule" [Lisa Lampert Weissig, *Medieval Literature and Postcolonial Studies*, Postcolonial Literary Studies, Edinburgh: Edinburgh University Press, 2010, cited at 44) – while at the same time advising the Anglo-Norman ruling elite to avoid internecine conflict in order to remain peacefully in power, as argued by Paul Dalton and others (see Chapter 1, n. 39) – the following suggestions offered by Fiona Tolhurst to explain Geoffrey's inclusion of the Normans in his description of Britain are certainly possible: 1) that by putting the Normans at the head of the list, Geoffrey is following Dudo of Saint-Quentin in "presenting the Normans as God's chosen people, the 'new Israelites'"; 2) by pairing the Normans and the Britons toward the head of the list, Geoffrey associates the two peoples' common (Trojan) ancestry, making "the Norman Conquest less culturally disruptive than the invasions of the Saxons and the Danes"; and 3) that the "Normans' position signals both their current possession of dominion over Britain and their advanced civilization, the Britons' position their former and perhaps future domination as well as their formerly great civilization, the Saxons' position their military success despite their status as non-Christians, and the Picts' and Scots' lowly positions their crushing defeats by Roman and Briton troops as well as their supposed barbarity" (*Geoffrey of Monmouth and the Translation of Female Kingship*, 57).

THE FIRST VARIANT VERSION 177

were unable to ultimately withstand. In this initial section in the vulgate, the Normans as well are associated with the Saxons as occupiers, though they are never mentioned again by name as a people.[43]

The group of occupiers who are surprisingly not mentioned as such by those writers who give lists of inhabitants of Britain – that is, Bede, Geoffrey, or the First Variant redactor (or by William of Malmesbury or Henry of Huntingdon for that matter) – is the Romans.[44] This is a surprising silence in this context since as Peter Turner comments with respect to Gildas's *De Excidio*, the Romans "are not bit players; we receive more information about them than about any other foreign group," a situation which is even more pronounced in the vulgate *Historia*, given the relative length of that work.[45] In a provocative study on identity in the Late Antique world as seen through Gildas's *De Excidio*, Turner claims that Gildas's view of the Romans is "overwhelming[ly] positive,"[46] particularly after their conversion to Christianity, the latter always being distinguished from the Britons who were according to a proverb, "cowardly in war and faithless in peace" (*DEB*, §6.2, 18; "ita ut in proverbium ... nec in bello

---

43 "Normannia" is found in §155.302 and §156.348 in connection with Bedevere, Arthur's cupbearer whom the monarch makes duke of Normandy.

44 In a passage which sets the tone for a largely positive portrayal, William of Malmesbury mentions the Romans in the first chapter of his *Gesta Regum Anglorum* (though he does not present strictly speaking a description of Britain): "Romani Britanniam, per Iulium Cesarem in Latias leges iurare compulsam, magna dignatione coluere, ut et in annalibus legere et in ueterum edifitiorum uestigiis est uidere" (*GR*, I.i, 16; "The Romans, having under Julius Caesar compelled Britain to accept the rule of Rome, held it in high regard, as we can read in the annals and see for ourselves in the remains of ancient buildings," I.i, 17). Following his account of the physical geography of Britain, and a list of the twenty-eight cities in "the time of the Romans and the Britons" (*HA*, 1.3, 15), Henry of Huntingdon contextualizes the coming of the Romans in a substantially less sanguine manner than William, including them in his list of the five plagues (reminiscent of the OT ten plagues of Egypt; see Greenway, ed. and trans., lix and n. 13; see also Chapter 1, n. 86 above, where this passage is cited). While observing that Henry was pursuing the idea of divine vengeance inflicted on a "faithless people," an idea "adumbrated in both Gildas and Bede and based on Old Testament models," Greenway comments that Henry "even sees through the 'Norman myth' to the self-destructive force within" (ed. and trans., lix); cf. Nancy Partner's discussion of the plagues though without reference to biblical precedents (*Serious Entertainments*, 22–5). The Danes appear in Henry's list, as they are a more prominent focus in the English historiographical tradition than they are in the Galfridian.

45 Turner, "Identity in Gildas's *De Excidio et Conquestu Britanniae*," 38.

46 Turner notes that "even the outright condemnation of the persecutions at §9.2 produces no general attack on the Romans themselves" (Turner, "Identity in Gildas's *De Excidio et Conquestu Britanniae*," 41); cf. Plassmann who distinguishes between Gildas's praise for Roman military prowess and his criticism for administrative offenses, including the brutality of the local governors ("Gildas and the Negative Image," 7).

178   CHAPTER 3

fortes sint nec in pace fideles," p. 91); Gildas celebrates the Romans for their
"efficiency, vigour, and bravery," in turn a "complete contrast with the Saxons
who are, from the outset, 'hated by man and God'" ("deo hominibusque invisi,"
DEB §23.1, ·p. 97).[47] Turner concludes that through using the Old Testament
principally in his analogy between the Britons and the Hebrews – the latter
who were albeit declared to be God's chosen people, had a history marked
by infighting, rebellion, and flight (*DEB* §19.3, for example) – Gildas was able
"to locate [Britain's] identity in the very disunity that plagued the island."[48]
Turner argues furthermore that the vision Gildas suggested was "highly ethno-
centric and had a clear moral function"; his "total suppression of regional identities was a call to national unity; his insistence on the eternal separation of
Britons and Romans was an admonition and a challenge to the pretensions of
regional rulers."[49] However, we need to avoid thinking of this "call to national
unity," as being evidence of a "pan-Celtic" sense of identity: Gildas's enthusi-
astic account of the Roman army's campaign on behalf of the Britons against
the Picts and Irish in chs. 14–17 illustrates instead a unity among the Britons
against outsiders – in this case the Picts and the Irish – which it certainly was
in Geoffrey's vulgate *Historia*.[50]

   It is also possible that Gildas, Bede, Geoffrey and the First Variant chose not
to list the Romans in their opening descriptions of the island, which they could
have done either neutrally as inhabitants or negatively as occupiers, in order
later in their texts to be better able to 1) establish Rome on a par with Troy as

---

47   Turner, "Identity in Gildas's *De Excidio et Conquestu Britanniae*," 41.
48   Turner, "Identity in Gildas's *De Excidio et Conquestu Britanniae*," 38.
49   Turner, "Identity in Gildas's *De Excidio et Conquestu Britanniae*," 41, 43.
50   At the stage at which Gildas is writing, the Picts and Irish (as well as the Scots in Geoffrey
     and First Variant) are presented as enemies of the Britons and not yet perceived as com-
     patriots when viewed in contrast to the Saxons. On the very complex later (perhaps even
     modern) development of "pan-Celtic" sentiment, see especially Patrick Sims-Williams,
     "Celtomania and Celtoscepticism," and idem, "Celtic Civilization: Continuity or Coinci-
     dence?" *Cambrian Medieval Celtic Studies* 64 (2012): 1–45. Cf. Edward Cowan who writes,
     in reference to the tenth-century Pictish Chronicle, "The Picts and the Scots are given a
     common Scythian origin which splices them into the children of Israel stories ... descen-
     dants not only of Japheth and Noah ... [but also] of the Trojans. A conscious effort had
     been made to demonstrate that Picts, Scot and Britons shared a common ancestry; they
     were of one race. Such myths also constitute a remarkable manifestation of pan-Celticism.
     That Pan-Celticism became a reality when Scots, Picts, the men of the north, Strathclyde
     Britons and Dublin Norse allied under the fortuitously named Constantine against
     Athelstan at Brunanburh in 937. But myth is not necessarily a defence against the mighty,
     as Scottish history was to demonstrate so often; they were defeated" ("Myth and Identity
     in Early Medieval Scotland,"123–24). On the Battle of Brunanburh (and the poem by that
     name included in the ASC for 937), see the Introduction, n. 47.

THE FIRST VARIANT VERSION   179

part of the foundation narratives; 2) acknowledge the contribution of Roman civilization to each of their aspiring political entities; 3) not risk offending the papal see through negative portrayals of Rome; 4) not undermine clerical culture; 5) not provoke hostilities with the Holy Roman Empire; and 6) establish further links to the Mediterranean crusading enterprise. While it is impossible to conclude with certainty the validity of any of these possibilities, it remains odd that the Romans are not included in any of the aforementioned descriptions of Britain and her inhabitants.

In addition, the First Variant redactor borrows from Bede the element that the Britons first migrated to the island from Armorica, a statement that contradicts the vulgate's Trojan origin story, in which the last battle the Trojans fight before leaving Gaul was near Tours where Turnus is buried (§20.436–437). The mention of Armorica in FV §5 appears to be strictly a borrowing from Bede's description of Britain: there is no reference to Armorica in the pertinent chapters of the FV where this section of the narrative is elaborated (§§17–20); the Trojans set sail for Britain from Aquitaine as in the vulgate text.[51]

Perhaps not surprisingly therefore, the most important change in the First Variant's description of Britain relative to the vulgate is the lack of mention of the Saxons in the list of inhabitants of the island; the FV redactor follows Bede again here, as well as later in the text, where the Saxons will be portrayed as important victors, not inevitable and regrettable conquerors. As a related consequence, the FV redactor, while naming the Picts and the Scots along with the Britons as inhabitants of the island, leaves out Geoffrey's reference to the Picts as a dual part of divine punishment (Picts and Scots are almost inseparable in the vulgate) along with the Saxons, whom God visits upon the Britons for their pride. In §5, Geoffrey emphasizes that the Britons were the first settlers, and he gradually integrates them into the history of the island as original peoples. The FV redactor does not name the Britons as the first settlers, and the aspect of indigeneity – once the giants are gone – is much less important in the FV, if at all.

---

51   In one of his numerous attempts to reconcile the First Variant and the vulgate (see Ch. 5 below), Wace has the Trojans head for Brittany, naming the mouth of the Loire as the Trojans' point of landing after having left Spain on their way to Brittany (ll. 793–800); however, Brittany itself is not the site of their last Continental campaign before sailing to Britain. Thus, Wace makes a partial nod to the suggestion in the FV's description of Britain while at the same time following the major outline of the narrative in the FV §§17–20 and in the vulgate where the Trojans leave for Britain from Aquitaine (where Geoffrey has apparently located the mouth of the Loire; Tatlock, *Legendary History*, 98).

180 CHAPTER 3

The remainder of the foundation narrative – §§6–22 – contains relatively few changes in the FV with respect to the vulgate. However, the most notable changes are:

1) In §6, the redactors of FV MSS DES claim two Silvii: a) Silvius Postumus (as found in Landolfus) – that is, Ascanius's half-brother born after Aeneas's death (from the union with Aeneas's second wife, Lavinia) – and b) Silvius, Ascanius's son, and father of Brutus (with Lavinia's niece) as reported in the vulgate; DES though still presents Brutus as Aeneas's *great-grandson* as in the vulgate, the son of Silvius, who was the son of Ascanius (having made a correction based on a vulgate MS or MSS "and perhaps also because of the difficulty that Postumus who was supposedly the progenitor of the Roman royal dynasty, is later killed by his son Brutus in aHR's text"); MSS aHR however report Brutus as Aeneas's *grandson* (from Silvius Postumus with Lavinia's niece, with no direct descendance from Ascanius);[52]

---

52 Wright, ed., II, c–ci, cited at c. Interestingly, in the vulgate text, in §54, Julius Caesar remarks on common ancestry of the Romans and the Britons: "Nobis Aeneas post destructionem Troiae primus pater fuit, illis autem Brutus, quem Silvius Ascanii filii Aeneae filius progenuit" (§54.7–9; "After the sack of Troy our first ancestor was Aeneas, theirs Brutus, whose father was Silvius, son of Aeneas's son Ascanius"), that is, that Brutus was the son of Silvius, son of Ascanius, and thus Aeneas's great-grandson, just as in vulgate §6 (ci). However, in all manuscripts of the FV, in §54, Caesar also appears to connect the ancestors of the Romans and the ancestors of the Trojans, but the birth order is different: "Nobis Eneas post destructionem Troie primus pater fuit, *illis autem Brutus, Siluii Enee filius*" ("For us [the Romans], Aeneas was the first father after the destruction of Troy, for them [the Trojans] *theirs was Brutus, the son of Silvius Aeneas*" (my emphasis and translation). Wright comments that this is not clear, though most likely it means that Brutus is represented as the son of Silvius Aeneas, the fourth king of the Latins – following Ascanius's heir, Silvius Postumus, third king of the Latins; Wright concludes that "it seems then that aHR's internally more consistent version is the original [FV version], while DES contain a (vulgate) interpolation in §6" (ci). Wace has the two Silvii as well in his narrative of Brutus's parentage (ll. 107–135), probably having used "a text of the DES-type," according to Wright (ed., II, civ, and Weiss, trans., 5, n. 3); Wace however, gives Brutus as *great-grandson* of Aeneas (as in the vulgate), son of Ascanius's son Silvius who "bore his uncle's name, but didn't live or last very long" (113–14). This second Silvius – Ascanius's son, not Silvius Postumus, who was Ascanius's half-brother, half because Ascanius's mother was Creusa, not Lavinia (though Wace calls Silvius Postumus, Ascanius's half-brother, his brother "sun frere," rather than half-brother (108); FV does as well §6) – "secretly loved" Lavinia's niece, who gives birth to Brutus. Wace's presentation leads Wright to consider that the FV may have been itself revised before Wace began working, or that Wace may have used a conflate FV manuscript possibly a predecessor of the group DES-type, rather than a vulgate text independently (ed., II, civ); on this possibility, see also Chapter 5, n. 7. See also Chapter 6, n. 26, on the Munich *Brut's* presentation of a FV version of Brutus's parentage, in FV §6.

THE FIRST VARIANT VERSION 181

2) in §15, when Innogen, the daughter of King Pandrasus is married to Brutus, and they set sail for the land promised by the goddess Diana, Innogen's tears at leaving her family and home are missing, as are Brutus's reassurances;

3) in §16, when the Trojans arrive at the isle of Leogetia, a number of details are missing, including that Brutus sends 300 men to investigate the island;

4) §17, the description of Brutus's lack of certainty as to whether Diana's speech was part of a dream or whether she had actually been there is missing; the description of Corineus is missing as is the explanation of how his name was the origin of the adjective "Cornish";

5) §20, when the Trojans fight the Gauls, after great butchery inflicted by the Britons, victory is achieved: in the vulgate, Brutus makes the decision himself to sail for Britain, but then tells his men so that they can prepare to board the ships and leave; in the FV, he gathers his men more formally in an assembly – as if perhaps either to emphasize or give the illusion that they participated in the decision, and tells them of the decision; the FV furnishes the geographic detail of Totnes being located at the mouth of the River Dart;

6) section §21 is one of 7 chapters in Wright's category F (chapters containing material often common to the vulgate and FV, but in different order), since in the FV, the wrestling match between Corineus and Gogmagog occurs before the Trojans begin to settle the land, rather than after as in the vulgate; in the vulgate, the detail that Corineus could have had his choice of which region to pick but he preferred Cornwall (in the FV, he is simply assigned the western region); the reference to the Trojans' language as "crooked Greek" in the vulgate is missing in the FV;

7) §22 – the narrative of how Lud built walls around New Troy which he commanded be named Kaerlud or Lud's city, and the mighty argument which ensued between him and his brother, Nennius, since the latter wanted the memory of Troy to continue to be reflected in the name, is missing from the FV; Geoffrey's final remark that he won't retell the whole story because Gildas has already done it better is also missing from the FV, as are the majority of Geoffrey's narratorial interventions.[53]

Thus we see the FV's elimination of emotions for dramatic effect , which often happens in that text – here, Innogen's tears and Brutus's reassurances; the removal of Geoffrey's narrative reflections/interventions; the elimination of the vulgate's images of the Trojans tilling the land and settling in, as if they had

---

53   This narrative is also elaborated on by Wace in such a way that further suggests he either had the FV and the vulgate to hand or a conflate version.

182 CHAPTER 3

always been there (§21.458–59 "in a short time, the country appeared to have been occupied for many years");[54] and less attention paid to the language spoken by the Trojans, that is, no reference harkening back to the Trojans' Greek origins (vulgate §21.461–62: "the language of his people, previously known as Trojan or 'crooked Greek', was henceforth called British"; FV §21: "the language of the people, which had previously been known as Trojan was called British"). In the FV, thus, the connection to the Trojans and their Greek origins is less cemented by details than in the vulgate, again demonstrating a shift in priorities.[55] Perhaps because the Saxons did not consider themselves descended from the Trojans,[56] the Trojan connection to the Britons is less important to the FV redactor than to Geoffrey, for whose narrative agenda that connection was central to the Britons' identity.

4 *Adventus Saxonum*

Although the narrative of the *adventus Saxonum* itself is roughly comparable in the FV with that of the vulgate, a fair bit of the preparation for that section in the two texts is disparate, particularly the portrayals of the Britons' plight at the time of the Romans' departure. By eliminating the two speeches of Archbishop Guithelinus, the first in London presented in §90 and the second

---

54 See Sylvia Huot's study of giants in *Outsiders* (esp. 27–68) on the discounting of giants as less than human; see also Chapter 5 below on what is in effect Wace's portrayal of the slaughter of the giants as a form of medieval ethnic cleansing.

55 On "crooked Greek" see Sara Harris, *The Linguistic Past in Twelfth-Century Britain*, Cambridge Studies in Medieval Literature 100 (Cambridge: Cambridge University Press, 2017), p. 209, n. 17. Michael Curley comments that "a deeper knowledge [of Welsh] might be inferred from [Geoffrey's] clever (and possibly tongue in cheek) etymology of the Welsh word for their own language, *Cymraeg*. ... If this *jeu d'esprit* [Geoffrey's claim that the Trojan language was called "Crooked Greek"] is his own invention rather than common 'academic folk etymology,' as Brynley Roberts believes" it demonstrates "Geoffrey's awareness of two Welsh words, *cam*, 'crooked,' and *Groeg*, 'Greek'" and "perhaps more importantly, knowledge of Welsh initial consonantal mutation (lenition) that would cause the consonantal G to be dropped from *Groeg* when the prefix cam was attached" to form the word "*camroeg*, close enough for Geoffrey" to *Cymraeg*. Curley conjectures that it was either an "insider's joke" or "already an established etymology whose linguistic basis was well known" (Michael J. Curley, *Geoffrey of Monmouth*, Twayne's English Authors Series 509, New York: Twayne, 1994, 11–12). Again, in light of Warren's arguments in favor of pro-Welsh leanings of the FV redactor, one wonders if the vulgate manuscript used by the redactor(s) did not have this reference to *curuum Graecum* in it (§21.462), and if it did, why the redactor(s) didn't include it. See also Chapter 5 for Wace's interpretation of this element, given his fascination for etymology.

56 See the Introduction, n. 10, especially Susan Reynolds's "Medieval 'Origines gentium'."

THE FIRST VARIANT VERSION 183

again in §92, together with the response of Aldroenus, leader of Brittany, the
FV redactor basically takes the stuffing out of the vulgate account. In the vulgate, Guithelinus's first speech is meant to shame the Britons into defending
themselves, rather than asking the Romans to defend them against their enemies, explaining that the Romans are ready to give up their role as defenders
of Britain:

> Will you always rely on the help of others? Will you not take up shields,
> swords and spears against robbers who would be no braver than you,
> were it not for your slothful laziness? The Romans have grown tired of
> the unremitting travel they must endure to fight your enemies for you.
> They prefer to forgo all the tribute you pay them rather than to continue
> being exhausted like this on land and sea (*HRB*, §90.37–42).[57]

And Guithelinus's second speech, this time having arrived in Armorica to
enlist the aid of Aldroenus of Brittany:

> The Romans have turned their backs on us and refused all help. With
> nowhere else to turn, we ask you to take pity on us and we beg you for
> your protection to save from barbarian invasion a kingdom which you
> will inherit (*HRB*, §92.101–2).

Aldroenus replies, rather grudgingly:

> There was once a time when I would not have refused to take retain if it
> were offered; no other country was in my opinion more fertile, while it
> enjoyed peace and tranquility. But now that it is prey to misfortune, it has
> been cheapened and become hateful both to me and to other chiefs … Yet
> since my fathers' fathers had a claim on your island, I entrust you to my
> brother Constantinus with two thousand knights so that with God's help
> he can free your country from barbarian attack and assume its crown …
> I can say nothing of committing more, since the French threaten to attack
> us daily (*HRB*, §92.109–12; 119–22; 125–26).[58]

---

57   "Eritne ergo spes uestra semper in alieno tutamine, et non instruetis manus uestras peltis,
      ensibus, hastis in latrones nequaquam uobis fortiores si segnitia et torpor beasset? Iam
      taedet Romanos tam assidui itineris quo uexantur ut pro uobis cum hostibus congredian-
      tur. Prius omne tributum quod soluitis amittere praeeligunt quam hoc modo diutius terra
      et ponto fatigari" (§90.37–42).

58   "Olim tempus erat quo non negarem insulam Britanniae recipere si quis eam largiretur;
      non enim existimo alteram patriam fertiliorem fuisse dum pace et tranquilitate frueretur.

184   CHAPTER 3

In the FV, Guithelinus's two speeches are missing, eliminating yet another chance to both pity and blame the Britons for their inability to fight off the invading Picts and Scots in the era before the Romans' departure. Of Aldroenus's reaction to the archbishop's visit, the FV redactor writes:

> Upon seeing a man of such reverence, Aldroenus received him with honor, and learning the reason for his visit he was saddened and mournful about the persecution of his relatives and their country, and he promised to bring such relief as he could. He gave to him his warlike brother Constantine and two thousand soldiers from those chosen by the Britons. (FV, §92.2)[59]

In broad outline, the upshot is the same – the Britons receive the help of two thousand soldiers under the command of Constantine – but the FV narrator completely passes up the chance to berate the Britons and heighten the tension and suspense with angry rhetoric, including a jab at the French.[60]

In terms of the *adventus* itself which takes place very soon after the departure of the Romans, whereas in Bede and Henry of Huntingdon, Vortigern invites the Saxons, and the *HB* where the Saxons come as exiles, uninvited (§31) but Vortigern "receives" them and later dies "without honour" (§48) as a result, and in Gildas, Vortigern "the ill-fated tyrant" "admits" the Saxons (§§23–24), in both the vulgate and the FV, the Saxons arrive as exiles, uninvited (§98),

---

At nunc, quoniam infortunia acesserunt, uilior facta est et michi et ceteris principibus odiosa ... At tamen, quoniam ius in insulam aui et attaui mei habuerunt, trado tibi Constantinum fratrem meum et duo milia militum ut si Deus permiserit patriam a barbarica irruptione liberet et sese diademate illus insigniat ...; nam de ampliori numero commilitionum tacendum censeo, com inquietudo Gallorum cotidie immineat" (§92.109–12; 119–22; 125–26).

59   Qui uiso tante reuerencie uiro excepit illum cum honore cognitaque sui aduentus causa, tristis ac mestus de pesecutione agnatorum et patrie, subsidium se ferre quale posset promisit. Tradiditque sibi Constantinum fratrem suum bellicosum et duo milia militum ex electis Britonibus (FV, §92.2).

60   The intermediate section 91 between Guithelinus's speeches and Aldroenus's reply is also considerably shorter in the FV than the vulgate, the FV narrator conveying the disaster without the poetic imagery containing the pity for the Britons, and minus Geoffrey's editorial comments (vulgate: "Alas for the divine retribution upon their previous sins! Alas for so many warlike knights through Maximianus' madness! ... So it goes when defence of a realm is left to farmers ... the wretched people were torn apart by their enemies like lambs by wolves" §91.70–71; 74–75; 77–78; FV "Those who were thrown to the ground the enemies pursued as they were fleeing; while pursuing they killed them; they handed some of them over to prison in chains; and such a slaughter was made as had never been made before" §91.3).

THE FIRST VARIANT VERSION   185

though Geoffrey's approach to the Saxons is very different from that of the
FV redactor; in fact, the latter's approach toward the Saxons could almost be
characterized as anodyne in comparison with Geoffrey's frequent vituperation
in the vulgate, though in this early portion of the text, Geoffrey's animosity
toward the Saxons has not yet reached its zenith.[61]

In general, the narratives of the initial landing are parallel, except for the
fact that in the vulgate, Hengist and Horsa ask for titles as well as for land.
Vortigern refuses the titles – although he has just finished saying he would
refuse them nothing – claiming that he does not know them well enough,
and even if he did, it would go against the wishes of his nobles (§99.314–23).
In the FV, after helping Vortigern dispatch his enemies the Picts in the North,
Hengist also asks for a fortified city or castle, but Vortigern refuses, again saying it would go against the wishes of his nobles. He does agree however to
let the Saxon leaders send to their homeland for reinforcements. By trimming
this short dialogue about titles and granting of a fortified city or castle, the FV
redactor has made Hengist and Horsa seem less grasping. Vortigern ultimately
agrees to give Hengist enough land to build his own castle himself, though no
titles (FV, §99.6).

Geoffrey places the paragraph on the arrival of St. Germanus at the opening of section §101, between the end of §100 which narrates the marriage
of Vortigern and Hengist's daughter Ronwen (whom Vortigern met for the
first time at the castle Hengist built himself with a "thong" of land, in Saxon

---

61   See esp. the Postscript to Chapter 2 and also nn. 138–39 below on Brian's speech which is
      a notable example of the vulgate's vilifying of the Saxons, found in a passage completely
      absent from the FV. Even in passages where the differences are subtle, they are evident:
      for example, in §§104–105 (discussed more fully below) which recount the treachery of
      the "night of the long knives" in both texts, in the vulgate Geoffrey states in both sec-
      tions that the Britons were unsuspecting having been tricked into coming on May Day
      to negotiate peace with the Saxons; he refers to the pagans as "wolves attacking shep-
      herdless sheep" (§105.496–97) whereas the FV redactor says "they were being slaughtered
      like sheep" (§105.1) referring to the Britons without adjectives or other labels for the
      Saxons; Geoffrey tells where the Britons were given a Christian burial near an histori-
      cally important monastery (§104.470–73), increasing their humanity and the pathos of
      their deaths, as well as contrasting the Christian Britons with the pagan Saxon betrayers,
      and that the victory went to the Saxons, increasing the Britons' victimhood. The FV does
      not contain the mention of the burial, nor are the Saxons labeled as betrayers, though
      the FV mentions Hengist's treachery more than once. At the end of §105, following the
      Saxons' land-grab (which differs, depending on the historian/text, see the Introduction),
      the vulgate and the FV each relate that Vortigern fled the Saxons, the "nefandam gentem."
      As seen throughout this chapter, the FV's approach toward the Saxons is fairly anodyne
      compared to Geoffrey's.

"Thancaster" §99.335–37)[62] and the statement regarding the anger the union engendered in the king's three sons, Vortimer, Katigern, and Paschent (§100, 365–68), and preceding Hengist's speech to Vortigern about becoming his advisor, now that he is the latter's father-in-law (§101.378–83). Geoffrey's focus in the Germanus passage is strictly on the eradication of the Pelagian heresy, and how St. Germanus set Christian worship in Britain to rights again; albeit brief, given its placement in the midst of narratives of strife caused by this marriage, the section stands out as a pious interlude. The remainder of §101 is devoted to the arrival of Octa, Ebissa and even more Saxons, until the Britons rebel, remove Vortigern from the throne, and drive the Saxons from the land, under the command of Vortimer, who is revered for his victory in four battles. In the vulgate, §102 – except for the opening sentence which relates Vortimer's restoration to his subjects of their possessions, and St. Germanus's inspiration to rebuild churches – is devoted to Ronwena's poisoning of Vortimer.

In the FV, §101 contains no mention of St. Germanus – the FV apparently compacts or economizes Germanus's arrival in vulgate §101 into the one lengthier and more tumultuous narrative of §102. In the FV, §101 is devoted solely to the Britons' rebellion precipitated by the unfortunate marriage of Vortigern and Ronwen and the influx of Saxons, in which Saxon treachery is feared but even more fearsome is being overrun by Saxons who were mixing – and presumably intermarrying – with Christians. It is important to note though that the vulgate strikes an even more xenophobic note than the FV: the latter mentions the elements of "mixing," the fear engendered, and not being able to tell pagans from Christians; the FV does not however mention intermarriage, nor the interdiction by Christian law.[63] In the vulgate we read:

> Pagans ought not to communicate or mix with Christians, as it was forbidden by Christian law; moreover so many of them had arrived that his subjects feared them; no one knew who was pagan and who Christian, since the pagans had married their daughters and relatives. With such

---

62   On the FV's slightly compressed version of this etymology, and Wace's changes, see Chapter 5, n. 43 and Chapter 6, n. 96.

63   "Quod cum uidissent Britones, timentes prodicionem dixerunt regi nimium se indulgere atque credere Saxonibus paganis, in tantum ut fere iam totam terram cooperirent mixti cum christianis; nec erat iam facile dinoscere qui forent pagani, qui christiani. Insuper tanta multitudo emerserat ut omnibus essent terrori" (Wright ed., §101, p. 93; "When the Britons had seen this, fearing treachery they said to the king that he indulged and trusted the pagan Saxons excessively, to the point that they had already overwhelmed nearly the whole land, mixed with the Christians; it was not easy now to discern who were the pagans and who the Christians. On top of that, such a crowd had arrived that they were a terror to everyone" §101.4).

THE FIRST VARIANT VERSION 187

objections, they urged the king to expel them lest they get the upper hand over his subjects by some act of treachery.[64]

Again, Geoffrey's text evinces more animus toward the Saxons than does the FV redactor, and also takes more opportunities to emphasize how Christian the isle of Britain was before the coming of the Saxons.[65]

---

64   "Non enim debebant pagani Christianis communicare nec intromitti, quia Christiana lex prohibebat; insuper tanta multitudo aduenerat ita ut ciuibus terrori essent; iam nesciebatur quis paganus esset, quis Christianus, quia pagani filias et consanguineas eorum sibi associauerant. Talia obicientes, dissuadebant regi retinere illos, ne in proditione aliqua ciues supergrederentur," §101.391–96).

65   Geoffrey first mentions Christianity when he discusses the arrival of Christianity in Britain in §72. He describes the pagan church as it existed in Britain before the coming of Christianity, which he says was bought to Britain during the reign of King Lucius in the second century AD. In the FV, Wright places §72 under category B, "chapters containing material common to vulgate and Variant, but with differences of style and diction (159 chapters, 76%)" (see n. 25 above). Thus the FV version of the coming of Christianity to Britain is largely similar to that of the vulgate, but the final paragraph of §77 which covers the Diocletian persecution is greatly abbreviated (falling under Wright's category D, "chapters common to both texts, but found in extremely brief form in the FV (20 chs., 10%)". In Geoffrey's §72, Gildas is flattered (per usual) with the mention of the victory of Aurelius Ambrosius in the book written by Gildas; this is at least a plug for the glory of that leader of the Britons; more importantly for our understanding of the political perspectives of the FV, no such mention of the glory of the Britons is made in FV §72 where the book of Gildas is mentioned. According to Geoffrey in §77, Christianity flourished until the reign of Asclepiodotus, when the Diocletian persecutions began; Geoffrey writes that God saved Britain from a complete eradication of Christianity through the burning of scriptures and the executions of "faithful congregations" by providing the enlightenment of holy martrys ("magnificauit igitur misericordiam suam nobis Deus, qui gratuito munere persecutionis tempore, ne penitus crassa atrae noctis caligine populous Britonum offuscaretur, clarissimas lampades sanctorum martirum ei accendit" §77.108–111). Geoffrey uses far more details both of the persecutions and the martrys God sent to enlighten and save the Britons than the skeletal details provided by the FV redactor, without the Galfridian flourishes such as "Among the men and women who stood firm in Christ's army were the martyrs Alban of Verolamium, and Julius and Aaron, citizens of Caerleon. Alban, burning with the virtue of love, first concealed in his home his confessor Amphibalus, who was being pursued by persecutors and was about to be caught, and then faced impending death by exchanging clothes with him thus imitating, Christ, who laid down his life for his flock; the other two, after enduring frightful bodily torture, swiftly ascended to Jerusalem's splendid gates with the trophy of martyrdom" (§77. 114–121). The FV redactor, summing up his 4-sentence §77 – how Asclepiodotus took the crown with the people's consent; ruled the land for ten years in peace and justice; the Diocletian persecution began against the Christians – writes: "Coming therefore all the way to Britain [Maximianus Herculius] with his awful inquisition, after the bishops and the priests were slaughtered, along with countless numbers of people, among others there suffered Saint Alban of Verulamium, and also Julius and Aaron, citizens of the City

188   CHAPTER 3

In the FV, following the Britons' victory over the Saxons, §102 opens with Vortimer's restoration of property. Then St. Germanus (lit. "holy bishop") who had come with Lupus of Troyes sent by the pope in Rome directs the renewal of demolished churches, and the re-establishment of the Christian faith. The FV redactor then adds an original sentence to ostensibly enhance the vulgate's reference to the restoration of the true faith:

> ut uerbo predicacionis et luce ewangelii gens que errorum tenebris et ignorantie a statu fidei suscepte deciderat, iterum eorum admonitionibus Deo per omnia cooperante corroboraretur et ecclesie catholice redderetur (§102).

> by the word of preaching and the light of the gospel, the people who had sunk to the darkness of their errors and ignorance from the height of the faith they had received were again strengthened by admonitions of those men and were returned to the Catholic church, with God helping in all things.[66]

In addition to the emphatic references to the "word of preaching" and the "light of the gospel", the placement of the expanded Germanus passage both makes it seem more natural – Germanus was helping Vortimer, and while he was at it, he rid the land of the Pelagian heresy. However, this arrangement also highlights by contrast Ronwen's treachery since the latter episode follows directly upon the Germanus episode:[67]

---

of Legions" (§77.3). Some of the basic details of the persecution are relayed, but not as fulsomely as in the vulgate, and certainly without the passion. In light of the tendency toward religious perspective in the FV (relative to the vulgate which is heavily secular in tone), this may seem odd, but not in light of the fact that this persecution happened on the "Britons' watch" (before the firm establishment and conversion of the Saxons), though not through their fault. In a brief passage on Ascleiodotus's reign, Wace recounts that Diocletian sent Maximianus "par cruelté e par enjurie, / Pur tuz les crestïens destruire / Ki aveient abatement / Ultre Mon Geu vers occident" (5581–84) "with cruelty and injustice, to destroy all the Christians who lived past Montgieu toward the West," but he says no more about this (see Weiss's identification of "Mon Geu" as the Saint Bernard Pass, trans., 73, n. 2). See also Chapter 5, and Chapter 6, n. 199 on Wace's treatment of the Pelagian heresy (which he never names, but refers to the consequences, blaming them on the Saxons).

66   My translation.

67   The vulgate does refer to Ronwen's treachery in similar terms, though there it is the mention of Vortimer's good deeds that incited envy in Ronwen and that then set the stage for treachery, rather than being preceded by a scene of religious renewal: "But his [Vortimer's] good deeds stirred up the envy of the Devil, who entered the heart of his step-mother Ronwein and moved her to plot his murder" (*HRB*, §102.415–16; "Sed bonitati eius inuidit

THE FIRST VARIANT VERSION   189

> Postquam ergo restituta est fides Christi per totum regnum Britannie ad
> integrum hostesque deleti qui et fidem et populum inpugnabant, inui-
> dia dyaboli qui Ronwen nouercam Uortimerii ad hoc nephas instigauit
> ueneno periit Uortimerius. (FV, §102)

> After that, once the faith of Christ was restored to wholeness through-
> out the entire kingdom of Britain, and the enemies were destroyed who
> had attacked both the faith and the people, Vortimer died of poison from
> the envy of the devil, who incited Ronwen, Vortimer's stepmother, to this
> wicked deed. (§102)[68]

Each text includes the Britons' fear that treachery will follow the influx
of pagans (*HRB*, §101.389–90 and FV, §101), which functions as a presage in
both texts, as very soon afterwards, Hengist resorts to "unheard-of treachery"
(*HRB*, §104.459). The so-called "night of the long knives" – where the leaders
of the Britons are treacherously massacred by Hengist and the Saxons at what
was supposed to have been peace talks requested by the Saxons and agreed to
by the Britons – is first "reported" in the *HB* (chs. 45–46); Hengist orders the
Saxons to hide knives in their boots and slaughter the unarmed Britons upon
his signal. In *HB*, 300 Britons are killed, Vortigern begs for his life and cedes
"several districts, namely Essex and Sussex, together with Middlesex and other
districts that they chose and designated" (*HB*, ch. 46, p. 32).

   Geoffrey includes a passage more elaborate than that found in his only probable source for these events, the *HB* (it is not included by Bede, Gildas, or Henry
of Huntingdon in either the *HA* or the *EW*) and is echoed by the FV redactor
(§§104–5) who also writes of "unprecedented treachery"[69] on Hengist's part,
though FV omits or adjusts some suggestive details:

1)   in the vulgate, around 460 barons and earls are killed; they are later
     "interred and given Christian burial by Eldadus not far from Kaercaradoc,
     now called Salisbury, in a cemetery beside the monastery which abbot
     Ambrius founded long ago" (*HRB*, §104.470–73); no burial is related in the
     FV, Christian or otherwise;

2)   in the vulgate, the districts ceded by Vortigern are not named; in the FV,
     Vortigern is made to swear that he will hand over "all the cities and camps
     and fortresses of the kingdom";

---

   ilico Diabolus, qui in corde Ronwein nouercae suae ingressus incitauit eam ut neci ipsius
   immineret").

68   My translation.
69   "noua prodicione usus," Wright ed., II, §104, p. 96; Burchmore trans., §104.1.

190   CHAPTER 3

3)   in both texts, the Saxons then proceed to capture London, York, Lincoln, and Winchester, while Vortigern retreats to Wales, "not knowing what he would do against the terrible barbarians"[70] ("inscius quid contra nefandam gentem ageret," *HRB*, §105.498).

The two most outstanding differences in the FV in this episode are, first, the elimination of the mention of Christian burial for the Britons, a point of honor for Geoffrey who seeks to underscore the early establishment – and practice – of Christianity in Britain well before Augustine's conversion of the Saxons.[71] Second, while it did not serve Geoffrey's purpose to enumerate the regions/districts Vortigern cedes to the Saxons, as in the *Historia Brittonum*, the FV, on the other hand, also declines to name the districts, but makes the point that Vortigern was forced to swear that he would hand over *every* city, fort, and camp in the kingdom. In the FV thus, the Saxon victory is more easily seen as universal – they were victorious *everywhere* – an important point for the more pro-Saxon FV redactor, even though the victory was a result of treachery.

5   King Arthur

Some of the most revealing discrepancies in Arthur's portrayal between the vulgate and the FV are: 1) the battle of Bath; 2) plenary court at Pentecost and Arthur's crown wearing at Carleon; 3) Arthur's interactions with the Roman emperor Lucius Hiberius; 4) the battle against the Romans at Seisia; and 5) the final battle at Camlann. In general, the trappings of wealth, generosity, splendor, and the cultural capital that those elements of life among the elite entail, are missing from the FV. In the perhaps insoluble debate over which text came first, either Geoffrey added those details to the FV/first version to suit the royal lay audience and the growing interest in romance narratives, or the FV redactor suppressed them in deference to a more "ecclesiastical" audience.

In the FV, Arthur's portrait in §143 contains less fulsome praise, and the tone is less slanted toward Arthur's generosity; it would appear that the portrait is

---

70   Wright translates "nefandem gentem" as "terrible barbarians" whereas Burchmore uses "the wicked people" ("not knowing what he could do against the wicked people", "ignorans quid sibi agendum foret contra nefandam gentem," FV, §105.3), choices of modern English vocabulary that illustrate even in themselves differently weighted perspectives.

71   Interestingly, although the FV has a reputation for greater championing of church issues and piety, the narrative of the coming of Christianity to Britain is somewhat less poignant or pointed in the FV than in the vulgate, as is certainly FV §77. See n. 65 above.

THE FIRST VARIANT VERSION
191

more neutral than in the vulgate.[72] The vulgate reads – with lines in italics which are missing from the FV:

> He was a youth of fifteen, of great promise and generosity, whose innate goodness ensured that he was loved by almost everybody. As newly-crowned king, he displayed his customary open-handedness. *Such a crowd of knights flocked to him that he ran out of gifts. Yet a man who combines an upright character with natural generosity may be out of pocket for a short time, but will never be the victim of lasting poverty.* Arthur who was both upright and generous, decided on war against the Saxons, to use their wealth to reward his household retainers. *Right was on his side as he should have been ruler of the entire island by lawful inheritance.* He gathered his younger subjects and set off for York. At this news, Colgrimus gathered the Saxons, Scots and Picts to meet him with a great host by the river Duglas where they fought a battle damaging to both sides. Arthur, however, was the victor, pursuing the retreating Colgrimus, and when he entered York, subjecting him to a siege. (§143.9–23)

Not only does the FV eliminate the authorial aside about generosity, but it also eliminates the two comments that Arthur had right on his side and that he was the legitimate ruler of the entire island ("commonebat etiam id rectitudo, cum tocius insulae monarchiam debuerat hereditario iure optinere," *HRB*, §143.16–18). It does say he was "welcomed and accepted by the people and the leaders of the entire kingdom," but that is more vague and thus more

---

72   Although Gillingham is right in commenting that Arthur is a military figure, "a warrior-king, a figure from an heroic age, endowed with some overtones of chivalry to bring him up to date" ("Context and Purposes," 37), I disagree that Arthur is "in no sense a paradigm of good civilian kingship" (37), since I find that Geoffrey's portrait is much more "civilized" than Gillingham deems it, especially in comparison with Gormund; this aspect of Arthur's "civilization" is established by Geoffrey from the beginning, admittedly with an imperialistic streak added along the way, and little emphasis on administrative concerns; see Chapter 2 on Geoffrey's Arthur and Chapter 5 on Wace's comparisons of Arthur with Gormund. Nonetheless, we need to keep in mind Gillingham's excellent emphasis on ambiguity, seen for example in his comment that "The *History* (*HRB*) is particularly susceptible of myriad interpretations since it is shot through and through with ambiguity. In one of its most famous passages, for example, we are told that at the battle of Camblann, 'Arthur was mortally wounded and was thence taken to the Isle of Avalon to have his wounds healed'" ("Context and Purposes," 19). Although the FV redactor may not have specifically tried to avoid ambiguity relative to Arthur, he does diminish the grandeur of the latter, as seen in cut or trimmed speeches, for example.

192   CHAPTER 3

open to interpretation whereas the status of "heredetario iure" reported by the
vulgate is neither vague nor open to interpretation:

> Arthur was then fifteen years old, a youth of great strength and bold-
> ness and generosity; for that reason he was welcomed and accepted by
> the people and the leaders of the entire kingdom. After he was invested
> with the royal insignia, he soon decided to attack the Saxons, through
> whom both his father and his uncle had died by treachery, and through
> whom the whole land had been thrown into confusion. Therefore, after
> assembling his army he went to York. But when Colgrin, who was ruling
> the Saxons after Octa and Eosa, heard that a new king of the Britons had
> arisen, he came against Arthur with a great multitude of his Saxons and
> Scots and Picts, and once they joined in battle next to the River Duglas, a
> large part of both their armies was struck down, with victory favoring the
> Britons in the end and Colgrin fleeing in disgrace. (FV, §143.1)

However, the FV does remind the reader/listening audience that Arthur's
father and uncle had died by treachery at the hands of the Saxons, and that
the "whole land had been thrown into confusion" by the behavior of the latter
("per quos et pater et patruus eius dolo perierant, per quos etiam tota terra
turbata erat" §143).[73]

Arthur's stature is also diminished – or de-dramatized – in the FV through
its shortening of the monarch's speech at the battle of Bath (§146).[74] Arthur's

---

73 Michelle Warren observes that "while Geoffrey goes on to emphasize that Arthur exer-
    cises authority by right of inheritance ('hereditario jure'), the First Variant immediately
    describes his preparations for a de facto demonstration in battle (137–38). The battle itself
    exacts revenge for damaged kin ..." She goes on to point out that "with the elimination of
    further speeches (which explain the battle's royal and Christian justifications in Geoffrey's
    Historia), family vengeance alone justifies the war." She concludes more broadly though
    that in the FV "these revisions support the logic of counterconquest, wherein a subju-
    gated people like the Welsh justifiably make war against those who steal their ancestral
    lands" (*History on the Edge*, 73). Although Warren argues that "the First Variant's recon-
    quest of the Briton past thus subtly sustains the political conquest of Welsh sovereignty in
    the present" and that "these post-colonial efforts hold out the promise of colonial rever-
    sal, in both narrative and politics" (72), I find the FV's de-emphasis of Arthur's generosity,
    grandeur, and legal right to govern by heredity to be more indicative of an Anglocentric
    emphasis than of a pro-Welsh bias and anticolonial perspectives.

74 As is typical of the FV redactor's methods (being an "an enemy of long speeches and
    rhetoric in general," as Wright observes, "Geoffrey of Monmouth and Gildas," 30), in close
    proximity to the Bath section (§146), the FV redactor also eliminates Uther's speech at
    the battle of St. Alban's (§141), relating the gist in the third person, but without mak-
    ing the Saxons sound dishonorable as Geoffrey does, and without the drama of Uther's

THE FIRST VARIANT VERSION   193

40-word speech from the vulgate, which contains a reference to the faithless-
ness of the Saxons and a call to arms, is eliminated by the FV redactor, as is
Archbishop (of Caerleon) Dubricius's speech also exhorting the Britons to
"defend their land and fellow-countrymen, whose expulsion by the treacherous pagans will be a reproach against [them] forever" if they fail to protect
them (*HRB*, §146.89–92 and §147.96–105). The FV redactor also eliminates the
passage where Arthur cries out to Mary – whose image is emblazoned on his
shield – and kills 470 of the enemy single-handedly, with his sword, Caliburnus.
The vulgate passage:

> Abstracto ergo Caliburno gladio, nomen sanctae Mariae proclamat et
> sese cito impetu infra densas hostium acies immisit. Quemcumque
> attingebat Deum inuocando solo ictu perimebat, nec requieuit impetum
> suum facere donec quadrigentos septuaginta uiros solo Caliburno gladio
> peremit. (§147.125–28)[75]

The changes in the FV could be considered subtle but they do affect Arthur's
portrayal and the message of the larger sections. Following the descriptions
of Caliburnus, Pridwen, and Ron (Arthur's shield and lance), the FV does
not repeat the name of Caliburnus, nor does the king cry out to Mary or God
(though it is said her image was "imprinted" *impressa* upon it):

---

declarations about honor: "When the Saxons saw this [that the Britons under Uther's
command were demolishing the fortifications], and realized they were poorly protected,
marching forth at dawn from the city to the open field they challenged the Britons to battle. Without delay the Saxons were defeated ... Thereupon King Uther arose with such joy
that, jumping from the wagon, not protesting about his infirmity, and dissolved in laugh-
ter as if he were healthy and strong, he cheered his men and would have rushed to pursue
the fleeing Saxons, if he men had not advised against this so that his infirmity would not
overcome him more seriously" (FV, §141.1–2). In the vulgate, having been brought to the
battle on a bier and the Saxons having declared it "beneath their dignity to fight someone who was half-dead already" (§141.566–67), Uther exclaims "laughing out loud ... in
happy tones: 'The villains called me a king half-dead, because I lay sick on a litter. And so
I was. Yet I prefer conquering them when half-dead to being beaten when hale and hearty,
and having to endure a long life thereafter. It is better to die with honour than to live in
shame'" (§141.588–93). The FV also eliminates Archbishop Dubricius's 100-word speech to
inspire the Britons at Bath (§147.96–105). On Bath (*pagum Badonis*) and Badon Hill, see
Chapter 1, n. 76, Chapter 2, nn. 16 and 46–49, and Chapter 5, nn. 66 and 71.

75   "Unsheathing his sword Caliburnus, he called out the name of St Mary and swiftly hurled
himself upon the dense ranks of the enemy. As he called on God, he killed any man he
touched with a single blow and pressed forward until with Caliburnus alone he had laid
low four hundred and seventy men" (§147.125–28).

194   CHAPTER 3

> Boldly ascending the mountain after them [the fleeing Saxons], and
> shouting to his men with a loud voice, after a short while Arthur gained
> the summit of the mountain and scattered the enemy's foundations right
> and left. More than four hundred fell in that first assault, as much from
> Arthur as from his men.(§147.2)[76]

The key phrase here is *tam ab Arthuro quam a suis illo – as much from Arthur as
from his own* [*men*] – which forces Arthur to share the glory of the killing with
his soldiers, thereby reducing his stature, or at the least, taking him out of the
concentrated spotlight.

There are two particularly conspicuous omissions from the sections on the
plenary court at Pentecost and Arthur's crown wearing at Carleon: 1) from the
list of attendees, the fourteen named "men of no lesser rank" ("non minoris
dignitatis heroes," *HRB*, §156. 339–40), almost all of whose names begin with
"Map" or "Mab" are missing from the FV (though the vulgate's comment "and
many others too numerous to name" is reproduced approximately, but without any specific names, "in addition there came heroes of great fame whom it
would be tedious to enumerate or name" (§156.5);[77] 2) neither of the vulgate's
two now famous passages about love as an inspiration to both knights and
ladies are included by the FV redactor, not surprisingly as the redactor seems
to have eschewed many if not all trappings of courtly culture.

In the FV, following the comment that the Britons followed the ancient
Trojan custom whereby the men dined separately from the women, the narrative passes directly to the field games, in a vaguely perfunctory fashion:

---

76   "Arthuro itaque post eos montem uiriliter ascendente atque suos magnanima uoce incla-
     mante montis cacumen post paululum adeptus est atque dextra leuaque hostium phalan-
     ges strauit. Plusquam .cccc. tam ab Arthuro quam a suis illo primo impetu ceciderunt ..."
     (FV, §147). Cf. Warren's almost opposite interpretation of Arthur's stature as portrayed in
     this scene: "While Geoffrey's Arthur begins is attack in anger after watching his men fail,
     in the First Variant Arthur courageously climbs the hill immediately after the description
     of the Saxons's defensive position [141]. He exhibits no emotion, and the narrator does
     not mention any prior skirmishes. Arthur then shouts general encouragement to his men
     without mentioning God or Mary, and achieves victory quickly through the strength of
     his right hand ["dextra"] instead of with Caliburn. By substituting Arthur's body for the
     sword, redactors create a powerful giant-hero, equal in himself to an entire army" (*History
     on the Edge*, 74).

77   The absence of Welsh names here is noticeably inconsistent with the pro-Welsh sym-
     pathies on the part of the FV redactor(s), as argued by Warren (*History on the Edge*, esp.
     60–76), although we can't always expect texts to be consistent. On the use of Welsh names
     in Geoffrey of Monmouth, see Michael Faletra, "Narrating the Matter of Britain," and
     Karen Janulak, *Geoffrey of Monmouth*.

THE FIRST VARIANT VERSION 195

Finally, refreshed by the ceremonial feast, various individuals organized various games and spread themselves over the fields and meadows outside the city. Some spent that day pleasantly with boxing gloves, some with wooden swords, some with dice and various games, and in this way the three remaining days of the festivities were finished. On the fourth day, honors were distributed. (FV, §157.3–4)

In the vulgate, the following passage – omitted in the FV – sets the scene for the elegance of Britain:

> After they had been seated according to their rank, Kaius the steward, dressed in ermine, and with him a thousand nobles similarly attired, served them courses. Opposite, a thousand men dressed in vair followed Beduerus the butler, similarly attired, offering various drinks of every sort in goblets. In the queen's palace numerous attendants in various liveries were also doing service and performing their roles; if I were to describe it all in detail, my history would become too wordy. So noble was Britain then that it surpassed other kingdoms in its stores of wealth, the ostentation of its dress and the sophistication of its inhabitants. All its doughty knights wore clothes and armour of a single colour. Its elegant ladies, similarly dressed, spurned the love of any man who had not proved himself three times in battle. So the ladies were chaste and better women, whilst the knights conducted themselves more virtuously for the sake of their love. (*HRB*, §157.377–91)

Thus, in the FV, the number of servers – all nobles – for the men's group, their attire, that they were offered more than one kind of drink; that the same scene was playing out among the women; and the narrator's aside that the book would be too long of the whole scene were described in complete detail, are all missing. The vulgate's comment on the elegance and nobility of Britain is also lacking, as are the details on love as an incentive to efficiency and prowess in battle.

In the vulgate, following the passage on elegance and love as an incentive to enhanced military activities, the narration moves on to the games, but not without a second even more pointed reference to the role of sexuality and seduction in the efficient production of military prowess:

> When at last they had had their fill at the banquets, they separated to visit the fields outside the city and indulge in varied sports. The knights exercised on horseback, feigning battle. The ladies, watching them from

196   CHAPTER 3

the battlements, playfully fanned the flames in the knights' hearts into furious passion. Then they peacefully passed the remainder of the day in various games, some contending with boxing gloves, some with spears. (§157.392–95)

The FV's lack of references to – and thus lack of valorization of – dedicated flirting – albeit with the implication that chastity could be useful in and of itself, but also as an incentive to further prowess – supports Diana Greenway's suggestion that the FV was prepared with an ecclesiastical, or certainly more sedate or prudish, audience in mind, than Geoffrey's.[78] Similarly, although the narrative use of women's attentions in this way cannot necessarily be construed as feminist per se, Fiona Tolhurst argues that the suppression of female roles in the FV fits a broader pattern of focusing on male-associated and ecclesiastical values, and significantly de-emphasizes the active role of women characters in that version, thereby generally devaluing female power, a process which she refers to as the "Variant-redactor's ecclesiasticization of a secular, feminist text" (i.e., the vulgate *Historia*).[79] In addition, the symbolic capital of the courtiers' scenes of opulence and love may have been either too "dangerous," or simply not the central interest for the FV redactor. It should be noted as well that the FV redactor has also eliminated here (as often happens) all narratorial asides, including those references to the length of the book, and the value of chastity.[80]

---

78   See n. 24 above.

79   A sub-heading of Tolhurst's Chapter 3 "Undermining and Degrading Female Kingship in the First Variant and Wace's *Roman de Brut*" (133–88) in *Geoffrey of Monmouth and the Translation of Female Kingship*, p. 134. See her detailed comparative analyses of numerous female figures in the vulgate and FV (*Geoffrey of Monmouth and the Translation of Female Kingship*, esp. 134–49), and in Wace who she sees as following the FV in the devaluing – and sometimes villainizing – female characters 154–55; see also n. 22 above, Chapter 5, nn. 44–45 below. Lori J. Walters expresses views similar to those of Tolhurst in this context, Tolhurst citing the former's view that "another means of accounting for the conflicting images of women in the *roman de Brut* [sic] is Eleanor of Aquitaine herself" (153) (Walters, "Wace and the Genesis of Vernacular Authority," in *"Li premerains vers": Essays in Honor of Keith Busby*, ed. Catherine M. Jones and Logan E. Whalen, Amsterdam and New York: Rodopi, 2011, 507–16). Cf. interpretations in Chapter 5 regarding Wace's treatment of female figures.

80   Tolhurst also points out that the FV redactor "essentially ... removes most of the passages in which Geoffrey expresses his personal values" (*Translation of Female Kingship*, 135). Although this would indeed appear to be the FV redactor's intent, we need to keep in mind that narratorial asides do not always reflect an author's personal views but may be a *topos* used by the author to create a particular persona. On the creation of authorial personas, see especially Peter Damian-Grint, *The New Historians of the Twelfth-Century*

THE FIRST VARIANT VERSION   197

As part of the FV redactor's relentless pattern of reducing Arthur's personal glory – or tempering Geoffrey's aggrandizement of the king – we find the Roman emperor Lucius Hiberius's letter handed to Arthur at the end of the Whitsun four days of festivities by the twelve elders holding olive branches. In the FV, the end of the speech is more pointed and more threatening. Instead of the vulgate's:

> The senate has decreed that redress must be sought for the insults you have heaped upon it; therefore I set the middle of August next year as the time by which you are ordered to appear in Rome, to satisfy your masters and accept the sentence they will justly hand down. Otherwise I shall enter your territory in person and take steps to recover with the sword whatever you in your frenzy have stolen from the republic. (*HRB*, §158.426–31)

we find:

> Therefore because you were not afraid to provoke the dignity of Rome by such an excess of offenses, the Senate accuses you and calls you on the charge against the majesty of Rome and summons you so that, in the middle of August next year, you may answer to the Roman Senate for these and all other things of which you are accused. However, if I am sent by the Senate across the Alps with the Roman army, I will come and take possession of the regions that you pride yourself in having seized and restore them to Roman authority against your will. Then I will find you in whatever place you are hidden and take you bound in chains back to Rome with me. (FV, §158.3–4)

In addition to this excellent example of typical syntactic redundancy (without apparent drama intended) in the FV[81] – in this passage, the word "Senate" appears three times – the FV redactor adds the threat that the emperor will seek out Arthur and bring him back to Rome as a prisoner or slave in chains. This added threat can be read in at least two ways: as an image of slavery or complete subservience which ironically elevates Arthur above his "masters"

Renaissance, and David Hult, "Author/Narrator/Speaker: The Voice of Authority in Chrétien's *Charrete*" in *Discourses of Authority in Medieval and Renaissance Literature*, ed. Kevin Brownlee and Walter Stephens (Hanover, NH and London: University Press of New England, 1989), 76–96 (notes, 267–69).

81   As noted by Wright, the FV redactor both abbreviates but also elaborates, his style of *amplificatio* often including what modern critics would probably find as unnecessary redundancy (ed., II, lxiii–lxiv). My translation.

198   CHAPTER 3

since he eventually is poised to conquer Rome before he is called back to
England by Mordred's treachery; or the threat can be seen to demean the
king as an allusion to the growing English disdain for the British taking of
slaves in war.[82]

In a notable rearrangement of several sections preceding the battle of
Siesia against the Romans – a battle which appears downplayed in the FV in
comparison with the vulgate – the shuffling around of various elements plus
the addition of new ones creates a very different picture from that of the vulgate.[83] In the FV's rearrangement of 159–164b,[84] the FV redactor eliminates
Hoel's speech that falls in the vulgate in §160, following Arthur's response
to Lucius's letter. By eliminating Hoel's speech, the FV redactor suppresses a
key opportunity for one of Arthur's most trusted supporters – and king of the
Amorican Britons – to remind the convened nobles of the prophecies of the
Sibyls that three rulers of the Britons will also rule Rome, the first two being
"principes Beli et Constantinum" (*HRB*, §160.495). While it is true that in the
vulgate immediately preceding Hoel's speech, Arthur reminds the crowd that

82   Gillingham, "Conquering the Barbarians," 46–47. Of course, other possibilities also exist
      including that Rome's threats are meant to elevate Rome's stature as the papal seat and
      thus presenting all ecclesiastical matters as superior to lay governance.
83   With respect to descriptions of battles in the FV, Wright observes: "Another type of
      material sometimes absent from the Variant consists of battle-descriptions and related
      passages (as in §§10, 37, 91, 166, 170, 171, and 174); this point should not, however, be over-
      emphasised, as the Variant does contain other such passages, often indeed stylistically
      different and as vigorous as their counterparts in the vulgate" (ed., II, xli) and "com-
      pare, for instance, the treatment of the battle between Aurelius and Hengist in Variant
      and vulgate, §123" (II, xli, n. 48). Wright also notes that among only 16 (of 208) chapters
      where events – or the chapters themselves – are out of order, we have two outstand-
      ing clusters: 159–164b (the reaction of Arthur and the Britons to the Romans' demands
      and the preparations for the battle against the Romans at Siesia) and 184–87 (Gormund's
      depredations and their effects). Le Saux writes that for the first cluster, since Geoffrey
      recounts the events in chronological order, the "overall effect" is one of a "build-up to the
      Roman campaign, with the successive speeches of Arthur, Hoel and Angusel providing a
      thrice-repeated justification of the British refusal to pay tribute to Rome in terms which
      are historical, moral and emotional"; the Variant version with fewer speeches which are
      scattered rather than concentrated in Arthur's council scene (vulgate §§159, 160 and 161)
      and events out of order, seems more detached and "the stress is shifted from the justifica-
      tion of the campaign to the presentation of the opponents' forces" (*Companion*, 96–97).
84   The rearrangement of 159–164b (numbering derived from the vulgate, and based on
      Wright's edition of the FV), together with some new content, is as follows in the FV: 159,
      [160 is missing, that is, Hoel's speech], 162a [an original paragraph on the council debate
      as part of the decision-making process], 163, 164a, 161 [an original paragraph containing
      Arthur's request for aid plus Auguselus's speech changed from the vulgate], 162b, and
      164b. See also Wright's chart, II, xxxvii, noting however that in the chart he uses "i" and "ii"
      in place of "a" and "b," as found in the text itself.

THE FIRST VARIANT VERSION   199

Belinus occupied Rome and Helena's sons Constantine and Maximianus each
ruled Rome – and thus there is a slight discrepancy between what Arthur says
and Hoel's narrative – in Hoel's speech Arthur is named directly as the third
Briton who will wear the crown of Rome: "You now stand before us as the
third to whom that high title has been vouchsafed" (§160.496–97). Hoel urges
Arthur to claim what is rightfully his, for the sake of the Britons' honor and of
Arthur's. This over 300-word speech in the vulgate is replaced by an 8-word
sentence in the First Variant in 162b to the effect that Duke Hoel promised
Arthur 10,000 men.

The FV redactor relocates the speech by the king of Albany, Auguselus,
in §161 (which should have followed Hoel's now-missing speech in vulgate §160) and replaces it (and Hoel's speech) with an original paragraph
which outlines the collective administrative response to Lucius's letter (section §162a); Auguselus's speech appears in §161, right after a second unique
paragraph entailing Arthur's request for aid from his nobles, which is another
passage marked by a more administrative tenor.

The changes in Auguselus's speech are themselves revealing of the FV's tendency to sanitize Geoffrey's text, rendering it less epic and more administrative. The vulgate version reads:

> As soon as I realised that my lord's desires were as he said, my heart
> felt greater joy than I can tell here and now. I count as nothing all the
> campaigns we have waged against so many mighty kings as long as the
> Romans and Germans [*Germani*] remain unpunished and the harm they
> have inflicted on our countrymen in the past goes unavenged. Now that
> we have permission to fight them, I am overjoyed and long for the day
> of battle, thirsting for their blood as if I had been denied water for three
> days. When I see that dawn, how sweet will be the wounds I give and
> receive when we exchange blows! Death itself will be sweet, as long as
> I die avenging our forefathers, preserving our freedom and securing the
> fame of our king. Let us attack these effeminates [*semiuiros*] and never
> relent until we have won a welcome victory and deprived the vanquished
> of their titles. I shall provide two thousand armed knights for our army,
> and foot soldiers besides. (*HRB*, §161.504–18)

The FV version:

> Right now there is need for however many of us are under your author-
> ity to prepare with all our strength and spirit to exalt and magnify the
> honor of your majesty. For nothing before this could have more readily

won me over than a confrontation with the Romans, which if it had not been voluntarily offered, would have been wished for by us all. Indeed, who could ever endure without hatred their arrogance and the yoke of servitude imposed on free men, when such a despicable race and cowardly rabble demand that so many men, strong in military power and accustomed to warlike behavior, be summoned before their tribunals and that an accounting be rendered for old taxes which, if they were ever paid by our predecessors, were more extorted than received, by a certain violence and unjust exaction from our people who, as it happened, were not then strong enough to resist. Therefore let us attack these half-men, so that we may secure liberty for ourselves and other peoples and, after we achieve victory, we may thoroughly enjoy their riches, the overabundance of which makes them so insolent. So that you will know, my lord king, that my actions conform to my words, I will accompany your campaign with two thousand cavalry, excluding the foot soldiers who are not easily counted, and if it pleases you I will lead the attack against the Roman eagles. And after the Romans are defeated and we have been enriched with their wealth, we must attack the still rebellious Germans, to the point where the whole Cisalpine region shall lay open before you. (FV, §161.2–4)

In addition to the verbosity of the FV version, the passage is marked by a more vituperative yet at the same time bureaucratic tone created both by the less personal rhetoric (only three uses of the first-person singular pronoun [or verb associated with the first-person] as opposed to eight in the vulgate) and the mention of the Romans' exaction of an accounting of back taxes which is a primary reason given in this speech to fight the Romans, in addition to the "hatred of their arrogance and the yoke of servitude." In the FV's version of Auguselus's speech, the goal is the securing of liberty, not vengeance; another goal is becoming enriched with the Romans' wealth – but that wealth is itself notably criticized "the overabundance of which makes them so insolent," couched in language reminiscent of a sermon – rather than the spilling of blood, as expressed by Auguselus with gusto in the vulgate; and there is no mention of the harm inflicted by the Romans and the Germans, and thus we hear less thirst for vengeance against the Romans and the Germans – perhaps due to the Germans being countrymen of the Saxons, toward whom the FV redactor is more sympathetic than Geoffrey. The theme of "dulce et decorum est pro patria mori" is greatly reduced and weakened by the FV redactor, as Auguselus gives reasons and justifications, often in a preachy tone, for the conflict rather than exclaiming his bloodlust. The FV's Auguselus sounds more rational, and

THE FIRST VARIANT VERSION   201

therefore less angry toward the enemies – though an energetic note is certainly
sounded in favor of liberty – whereas in the vulgate, he sounds more passionate and impatient for the bloodletting.

In the FV, the other original paragraph (in §162a) has a perfunctory ring
as well, sounding not unlike a committee report, as if the redactor used it to
smooth over his revisions and wanted to emphasize the collective aspect of the
decision-making process;[85] nevertheless, it does serve to restore a bit of dignity
to Arthur, with its final description of the "uirorum quoque bellatorum incom-
parabilem dignitatem atque diuiciarum ammirabilem copiam":[86]

> After these and other things like them were explained by the king, it
> pleased all who were there and they praised his decision. When they
> returned to the Roman ambassadors, they delivered the response which,
> after the king had spoken, had been debated in council and also commit-
> ted to writing; once the document was signed, the ambassadors returned
> to Rome as soon as possible, where they described the steadfast courage
> of the Britons and the measured response of King Arthur in everything,
> the incomparable dignity of the warlike men and the astonishing abun-
> dance of riches. (FV, §162a)

It is not clear why the FV redactor sought to underplay the lead up to – and
the battle itself – against the Romans at Siesia, but that is indeed the effect
of the numerous abbreviations and changes within that portion of the narrative. At the very least, the FV sounds summative, perfunctory, and administra-
tive/bureaucratic: the FV redactor appears to have less "at stake" than Geoffrey
in presenting the Britons at one of their most vibrant moments – not to mention justifiably rebellious – and the Romans at their most grasping, and unde-
servedly so, at least according to the vulgate.[87] Among the missing chapters,
events or descriptions in the FV are:[88]

---

85   In the vulgate, Arthur does receive the pledges of support from his regional leaders, but
      there is no "council debate" or explicit mention of a signed or sealed document to that
      effect (§162.519–20).
86   The whole of FV §162a (p. 154) reads: "Hec et his similia rege prosequente placuit omni-
      bus qui aderant et collaudauerunt eius senteniam. Reuerisque ad Romanorum legatos
      responderunt eis que in concione rege dictante collata fuerant atque scripto mandau-
      erunt; cartisque signatis Romam quantocius regrediuntur narrantes Britonum con-
      stantem audaciam atque regis Arthuri modestam per omnia responsionem, *uirorum
      quoque bellatorum incomparabilem dignitatem atque diuiciarum ammirabilem copiam*"
      (my emphasis). Burchmore's translation.
87   See n. 83 above.
88   See also n. 84 on the rearrangement of §§159–164b.

202   CHAPTER 3

1) §160 Hoel's speech (with only one clause in 162b, regarding the number
of troops promised)

2) §166 details of Gawain's battle with the Romans (e.g., the younger
Britons do not egg on Gawain to create a distraction in the Romans' camp
to provide a pretext for battle)

3) §170 Roman battle positions at Siesia and a catalogue of their leaders:
in the FV, following Lucius's speech to the Roman troops, and a sentence
very similar to the vulgate's report of common consent and an oath of
support, instead of the 200–word description of the battalions and their
leaders as in the vulgate, the FV sums up thus:

> Once they were armed and had their troops in order, they approached
> the valley mentioned before; there they stared at the enemy occupying
> the whole valley to the left and right (FV, §170.4).

4) §171 details of initial clashes at Siesia – among the characters not
named in this section in the FV are:
  a) the king of Spain and Lucius Catellus (Romans);
  b) the king of Scotland and the duke of Cornwall (Britons);
  c) Gerinus and Boso (Britons);
  d) king of the Parthians (on the side of the Romans);
  e) the Danish king, Aschillus (on the side of the Britons);
  f) the king of Libya (on the side of the Romans).
  [Bedevere is killed and Kaius wounded (both texts)]

5) §173 list of casualties among the Britons

6) §174 further details of fighting at Siesia (see below)
and

7) §175, the authorial comment on the justice of the Britons' victory at
Siesia.

In FV §174, Arthur's angry, exasperated speech to both reproach and inspire the
troops is missing the rhetorical appeal to the ancestors ("mementote auorum
uestrorum"), and the appeal to freedom ("mementote libertatis uestrae"), as
well as the injunction "What are you doing, men? Why are you letting these
women[89] get away unharmed? Let none of them escape with their lives" ... "Let
no one escape alive, not one." The vulgate reads:

---

89   Although in the vulgate *HRB*, Arthur is certainly not consistently a figure of chivalry
      and courtesy as often seen later in romance, it is difficult to think that literally "women"
      was meant here, rather than "cowards" or "semiuiri" (lit. "half-men"), a term used in

THE FIRST VARIANT VERSION   203

Quid facitis, uiri? Vt quid muliebres permittitis illaesos abire? Ne abscedat ullus uiuus. Mementote dexterarum uestrarum, uae tot proeliis
exercitatae terdena regna potestati meae subdiderunt. Mementote auorum uestrorum, quos Romani dum fortiores errant tributarios fecerunt.
Mementote libertatis uestrae, quam semiuiri isti et uobis debiliores
demere affectant. Ne abeat ullus uiuus, ne abeat. Quid facitis? (§174.
423–28)[90]

In addition to draining some of the vulgate's rhetorical power created by the
triple repetition of the word "mementote" by using it only twice, and by removing the ring composition of the opening and closing "Quid facitis?" the FV
redactor makes further choices which change the tone and the impact of this
speech. In the FV, in place of the reference to the ancestors and the heightened
impatience in tone, Arthur tries to shame his troops by pointing out how he
would never abandon them, so why are they abandoning him?:

Utquid fugitis? Quid pertimescitis? Ne abscedat ullus uestrum! Ecce dux
uester, qui ad certamen uos adduxi, paratus, si forte contingat, pro uobis
occumbere; nec, dum uita comes fuerit, uos uel campum hunc relin-
quam donec triumpho potitus hostes fuge aut dedicioni hodie compel-
lam. Mementote dextrarum uestrarum que tot preliis exercitate omnibus
aduersariis usquemodo preualuerunt. Mementote libertatis uestre quam
sibi subdere affectant semiuiri isti. (§174)

Why do you run away? What are you afraid of? Do not withdraw, any of
you! Here is your leader, [I] who led you to the battle, ready to die for you,
should that happen; while life is with me, I will not abandon you or this
field of battle until, once victory is achieved, this day I drive the enemy to
flight or surrender. Remember your right hands, which, tested in so many
battles, have up to now prevailed against all adversaries. Remember your
liberty which these half-men want to make subject to themselves. (§174)[91]

Auguselus's speech (§161.515, and translated there by Wright as "effeminates") as well as
further on in this speech.

90   "What are you doing, men? Why are you letting these women get away unharmed? Let
none of them escape with their lives. Think of your sword-hands, which have endured
so many battles and subjected thirty kingdoms to my power. Think of your forefathers,
whom the Romans, when they were mightier, forced to pay tribute. Think of your freedom, which these half-men, weaker than yourselves, wish to take away. Let not one escape
alive, not one. What are you doing?" (vulgate, Wright, trans.)

91   My translation. Burchmore gives "Be mindful" for both the occurrences of "Mementote,"
whereas Wright in the vulgate has "Think of," each probably wanting the verb in English
to take "of" in order to fit with the Latin genitive forms which follow.

204   CHAPTER 3

In the FV, the speech uses arguments that are less magisterial, and also that do not employ the best psychology: Arthur directly accuses his men of cowardice and tells them basically that he is better than they are. The FV also eliminates Arthur's reminder that his troops have conquered thirty kingdoms for him – Geoffrey would never miss such an opportunity to advertise! Following the speech, the FV also eliminates details including the comment that both sides fought so hard it was as if the battle had just begun and equating Arthur and the Roman emperor in stature and stamina (*HRB*, §174. 441–47), yet another missed opportunity to aggrandize Arthur.[92]

At the end of the Arthurian section, the FV redactor hits the major high points of the battle of Camlann, but without the pathos or the poetry. For example, in the vulgate, Arthur meets Mordred – and the Saxons, Irish, Scots and Picts – after marching to Winchester on the third day; Arthur has 60,000 troops remaining from his old army whom he formed into six groups "each comprising six thousand, six hundred and sixty-six warriors" (§178.50–52) to whom he assigns leaders, organizing the remainder under his command; his own army is divided into nine columns each with a right and a left wing, "urging them to kill the disloyal thieves who, at the behest of a traitor, had come to Britain from foreign kingdoms to steal their titles" (§178.57–60), calling them "thieves" and also "barbarians" ("diuersos ... barbaros" §178.60). In the FV, none of these epic hyperbolic figures of the Britons' army divisions remain, nor do the enemy armies "in the very bitter fighting that ensued, almost all the commanders on either side were killed, along with their soldiers" (*HRB*, §178. 74–75), nor the labeling of the Britons' enemies as "barbarians"; what does remain in the FV is the summary of the outcome (after the naming of Mordred's leaders who fell, as in the vulgate), including Mordred's death, the deaths of "many thousands of their men" (FV, §178.3) and the compellingly ambiguous mortal wounding of Arthur and his voyage to Avalon for his wounds to be healed ("ad sananda uulnera sua," *HRB*, §178.82; FV, §178.3).

6   Stages of the Passage of Dominion

This next-to-final section incorporates the various stages of the passage, from the involvement of Gormund, Augustine's conversion of the English, up to Cadwallader's decisions, and the final comments by Geoffrey regarding his

---

92   With all these missed opportunities to accentuate Arthur's grandeur, it is not surprising that §174 falls under Wright's category D, sections that are "very much shorter" in the FV than in the vulgate (Wright ed., II, xxviii–xxix).

THE FIRST VARIANT VERSION   205

historian colleagues in the vulgate's epilogue (which will be treated separately
later in the chapter). These stages form a pattern – in the elements they retain
of the vulgate, those which are rejected, and those which are reordered – a pattern which can aid in an overall understanding of the primary goals of FV in
relation to the vulgate.

Of the 20 chapters (or roughly 10%) of the FV identified by Wright as containing material unique to that version, with sources not as yet identified, not
quite half occur toward the end of the text and deal with the eventual Saxon
takeover.[93] Of particular note are:

---

93   Perhaps not uncoincidentally, Geoffrey's most significant linguistic borrowings from
      Bede – and his greatest thematic divergences – come in the last twenty chapters of the
      vulgate, that is from the mission of Augustine to the death of Cadwallader ("Geoffrey of
      Monmouth and Bede," 34). The sections of the FV in Wright's category J, which also con-
      tain those last twenty chapters (indicated in bold below) – material unique to the FV, and
      of unknown sources (see also n. 26 above) – are as follows:
          §39   description of the marshy nature of Britain
          §43   details of the battles of Brennius and Belinus against the Romans
          §46   description of Ireland and details of its colonization
          §72   details of the conversion of Lucius and the British
          §94   details of Vortigern's part in the coronation of Constans
          §101   details of Vortimer's third victory over the English (explaining its occurrence in
                 Kent)
          §130   details of Merlin's transporting of the Giant's Ring (by spell rather than by phys-
                 ical means)
          §137   details of Uther's infatuation for Igerna (in FV their liaison is inspired by the
                 devil, and compared w/ David & Bathsheba); reflections on the effects of love
                 missing
          §145   Arthur requires the English to leave behind their arms before retiring from
                 Britain to the Continent
          §146   the English, as a consequence unarmed, seize weapons from the British
                 population
          §161   Arthur's request for aid from his nobles
          §164   Arthur entrusts the interpretation of his dream to God
          §172   greater emphasis on the paganism of some of the peoples subject to Rome
          §§186–87 Loegria renamed Anglia after the English; creation of an unspecified num-
                 ber of English kings
          §188   details of Augustine's conversion of the English
          §189   details of the martyrdom of the monks of Bangor
          §203   details of the plague that drove the British from the island
          §204   details of English rule under Athelstan
          §207   details of the ultimate fate of the British
          §208   reference in the colophon to the author of the *Historia* as Geoffrey Arthur.
      Regarding those last 20 chapters, §§184–87 (§185 is missing from the FV, and §187 is also
      missing except for one clause found in §186[i]) treat the devastation of Britain wrought
      by Gormund, the clerics and population fleeing. In the vulgate, Geoffrey's main source

206   CHAPTER 3

1)   the description of Ireland in §46 and a number of details of its coloni-
     zation (including its prosperity after colonization): Geoffrey refers to
     the thirty ships filled with men and women encountered by Guirguint
     (Belinus's son) after he defeated the Danes and set about returning to
     southern Britain via the Orkneys as Basques driven out of Spain (though
     the FV does say they are from Spain); Guirguint grants them Ireland which
     was at the time of Guirguint's victory over the Danes "devoid of inhabit-
     ants" whereas the FV redactor makes the point that those peoples – who
     are not identified as Basques in that text – settled Ireland; Guirguint is
     buried in Carleon (no mention of his having built a fair amount of it as in
     the vulgate §46.254–55);

2)   in §130 in the vulgate, Merlin mocks the men's efforts at moving the
     stones through physical means, commenting at the end, following
     Aurelius's command to set up the giant's ring, he "obeyed and erected
     them round the cemetery exactly as they had stood on mount Killaraus
     in Ireland, so proving the superiority of brains over brawn" "ingeniumque
     uirtuti praeualere comprobauit" (§130.298) – in the FV, the comment
     about brains over brawn is omitted, but at the beginning of the passage,
     Merlin declares to the men "that you will understand that native ability
     of the spirit prevails over strength of the body, watch how this structure
     of stones, which did not yield to your strength, will now be brought down
     by our machinations more easily than you can imagine" (§130.4; "Ut
     sciatis animi ingenium preualere fortitudini corporis, ecce lapidum hec
     structura, que uestris uiribus non cessit, leuius quam credi potest nostri
     iam machinacionibus deponetur" §130); while *ingenium* is repeated, the
     mentioning of the spirit *animi* has a more religious overtone, albeit in
     combination with "machinacionibus"; and

3)   more notably §137, in the vulgate, Uther's passion for Igerne is cel-
     ebrated, humored and aided such that "commanserunt deinder pariter
     non minimo amore ligati" "they remained together thereafter, united by
     no little passion" (§138.534–36)[94] – in the FV, the redactor comments on

---

     for §§179–87 is Gildas 27–36; particularly noteworthy is §185, whose tone is very typical
     of Gildas. On Geoffrey's use of Gildas, see Wright, "Geoffrey of Monmouth and Gildas
     Revisited." For which sources Geoffrey used and where, see Reeve, ed., lviii–lix.

94   Siân Echard rightly points out that the Bern MS. contains an anomalous reading, "cum
     minimo amore" "with little love": "Commanserunt deinde partier cum minimo amore
     ligati progenueruntque filium et filiam," whereas the dominant reading is "non minimo
     amore," or "by no little love". She adds that the FV omits the issue of love, underscoring
     instead the legitimacy of the marriage "The king and queen Igerna celebrated their mar-
     riage legitimately and magnificently" ("Nuptiis igitur legittime atque magnifice celebratis

THE FIRST VARIANT VERSION

207

the love having been inspired by the devil, and compares it to David and Bathsheba "respexisset rex tamquam Dauid in Bersabee, subito Sathana mediante" (§137) while the scene of consummation is much shorter than in the vulgate, though the FV redactor does add, instead of naming their two children Arthur and Anna, he just names Arthur, but on a positive note: "the same night Igerna conceived that celebrated Arthur who, after he grew to manhood, shone throughout the whole world for his goodness" (§137.11) ("conceptit enim nocte Igerna celeberimum illum Arthurum qui postquam adultus est probitate sua toto orbe enituit" §137).

The differences in §§184–87, the passages which contain the nucleus of the passage of dominion, are as follows:[95]

HRB (vulgate):

§184 – devastation of Britain: the Saxons send for the African king, Gormund who was at that time subduing Ireland; he brings 160,000 troops; he captures and burns Cirencester and the surrounding countryside (and beyond)

§185 – narratorial aside decrying the "slothful race" of the Britons who are divided by civil strife and thus incapable of defending their land, and how their descendants "will regret it one day": this passage largely based on Gildas's views has no parallel in the FV, presumably since the redactor did not share those regrets (in addition to avoiding authorial asides in general)

§186(a) – having "laid waste almost the entire island," Gormund gives the "largest portion of it, called Loegria," to the Saxons; the remaining Britons retreat to Cornwall and Wales

§186(b) – the priests retreat to Wales and to Brittany; the churches of the two provinces of Loegria and Northumbria have "lost their entire congregations"

§187(a) – the British lose the crown

§187(b) – but the Saxons do not become "masters" of the island either, as related in the FV: three British kings rule alongside three English kings

---

commanserunt pariter rex et regina Igerna"; Wright ed., II, §138). She doesn't note, however, the FV's reference to David and Bathsheba (§137), which serves to complete the picture of the illegitimacy of the love, but the legitimacy of the marriage (*Arthurian Narrative in the Latin Tradition*, 55, n. 53).

95   I am basing this schema on Wright ed., II, xxxvii, with the addition of "a" and "b" to more clearly illustrate the changes made by the FV in the events and their order; for sections 185–187, neither Reeve (vulgate) nor Wright (FV) uses "a" and "b" in this cluster in the presentation of the texts (Wright does use the designations "a" and "b" in the FV for the cluster 162a, 163, 164a, 161, 162b, 164b, discussed above in the context of the events leading up to the battle of Siesia; see also nn. 83–84). For this cluster in the FV, Wright uses slashes in the presentation of the text (but not in his chart): 184/6, 186/7; in the chart, he uses (i) and (ii) as in 186 (ii), 186 (i), 187 (i) and 187 (ii). However, since Reeve does not use the "a" and "b" designations, I have put them in parentheses.

208   CHAPTER 3

FV:

§184 – devastation of Britain: the Saxons send for the African king, Gormund who was at that time subduing Ireland; he brings 160,000 troops; he captures and burns Cirencester and the surrounding countryside (and beyond)

[§185] – narratorial aside (which makes up the whole section in the vulgate) missing from the FV

§186b – "the bishops fled from their sees" and "as many of the monks and the nuns and all the people as could escape the sword of the Africans" ... "the land was emptied of all its splendor" – a less detailed but broader portrait of Gormund's devastation than in the vulgate; this section varies from the one in *HRB* and is combined with §184

§186a – having "laid waste almost the entire island," Gormund gives the "largest portion of it, called Loegria," to the Saxons; henceforth the island is named England, after the Angles – with no explanation regarding how the Saxons became Angles, nor any explanation of the renaming of the island;[96] the remaining Britons retreat to Cornwall and Wales

§187a – missing from the FV except for one rather vague clause adapted from vulgate §187(b) – that is, Geoffrey's declaration of three kings each ruling the Britons and the Saxons – which sets up a parity of governance – is replaced by the following statement which sets up a parity of aggression, but not of governance: "and they continued like this for a long while [fighting back and forth], such that neither could the Saxons prevail over them [the Britons] nor they over the Saxons" ("et sic diu perseuerauere ut nec Saxones in illos, nec illi in Saxones preualerent" FV, §186/7);

§187(b) – "entirely absent from the Variant text, which has a different passage at this point":[97] the passage to which Wright refers is made up of one sentence, preparing the way for Augustine's mission [since it was that in the time of Ethelbert, Augustine arrived, as told in §188], a sentence which can be seen to contrast "the apparent stability of the English kingdoms" against the backdrop of the "barbarism of the Britons":[98] "Creati sunt interea plurimi

---

96   Perhaps the FV redactor's reference to the Angles is simply following Bede who reports in the context of Augustine's arrival, that it was "about 150 years after the coming of the *Angles* to Britain" (*HE*, 1.23). Wace tries to rectify the oversight of not defining who the Angles were (never being too comfortable with undefined terms), as well as the confusion about the dating of Athelstan's reign; see Chapter 5, n. 198. See also Leckie, *Passage*, 104–5 and Wright, ed., II, lxxix–lx, and n. 103 below. On Wace's expanded role for Gormund and its impact on his portrayal of King Arthur, see J. Blacker, "Arthur and Gormund: Conquest, Domination and Assimilation in Wace's *Roman de Brut*."

97   Wright, ed., II, xxxvii.

98   See Leckie who writes, "The redactor clearly associates political fragmentation with the advent of Anglo-Saxon rule but makes no mention of any attendant disorder. Instead of

THE FIRST VARIANT VERSION 209

reges Anglorum Saxonum qui in diuersis partibus Loegrie regnauerunt; inter quos fuit Edelbertus rex Cancie, uir illustris et magne pietatis" (FV, 186/7; "Meanwhile many kings of the Anglo-Saxons were created, who ruled in diverse parts of Loegria; among them was Ethelbert, king of Kent, a famous man of great piety").[99]

Although Leckie rightly places a good deal of weight on the FV's version of the passage of dominion with its renaming of the island immediately after Gormund's Donation in 186/7,[100] the renaming itself is accomplished with relatively little fanfare, especially the transformation of the Saxons into Angles, and then into "Anglo-Saxons"; even the last sentence in 187(b) which slips in the remark that *numerous* kings were established among the "Anglo-Saxons" – implying that the latter's dominion was more widespread than that of the Britons, and thus that there were already the beginnings of an imbalance of power – unlike Geoffrey's three Briton kings who ruled alongside three Saxon kings – is very understated, almost perfunctory, and it also contradicts the statement just preceding about how no one side dominated or prevailed.[101]

---

balancing the methods of government, he juxtaposes the barbarism of the Britons and the apparent stability of the English kingdoms. Æthelbert is said to have been one of the English rulers, and mention of his name provides a transition to Augustine's mission" (*Passage*, 105). It would appear, though, that the redactor's view of early English "political fragmentation" may not have been as straightforward as Leckie argues.

99 Burchmore, trans., §187.3.
100 See esp. *Passage*, 104–8.
101 Keeping in mind that in the FV, the broader details of Gormund's devastation – including the plundering and razing of monasteries and churches, and the flight of priests and bishops taking relics of their saints – are told without any specific names though in §186b attached to the end of §184 – the following comparison shows the major differences between the vulgate and the FV surrounding Gormund's Donation and its aftermath, about which the FV declares in the last sentence preceding §186/7: "et desolata est terra ab omni specie sua, maxime Loegria que pars Britannie melior extiterat" (§184/6; "and the land was robbed of all its splendor, especially Loegria, *which had become the better part of Britain*" my translation and emphasis). This latter phrasing could be construed as more favorable to the land controlled by the Saxons, and by extension, to the Saxons themselves – "the better part" (qualitative) rather than "the larger part" (quantitative) as in the vulgate (§186.156–57) – than the lands remaining to the Britons:

Vulgate §186.154–69: "Postquam autem ut praedictum est infaustus tyrannus cum innumerabilibus Affricanorum milibus totam fere insulam uastauit, maiorem partem eius, quae Leogria uocabatur, praebuit Saxonibus, quorum proditione applicuerat. Secesserunt itaque Britonum reliquiae in occidentalibus regni partibus, Cornubiam uidelicet atque Gualias, unde crebras et ferales irruptiones incessanter hostibus fecerunt. Tunc igitur archipraesules Theonus Lundoniensis et Tadioceus Eboracensis, cum omnes ecclesias sibi subditas usque ad humum destructas uidissent, cum omnibus ordinatis qui in tanto discrimine superfuerant diffugierunt ad tutamina nemorum in Gualiis cum reliquiis sanctorum, timentes ne barbarorum irruptione delerentur tot et tantorum ueterum sacra ossa si ipsa in imminenti periculo desererent et sese instanti martyrio offerrent. Plures etiam Armoricanam Britanniam magno nauigio petiuerunt, ita ut tota ecclesia duarum prouinciarum, Loegriae uidelicet et Northamhimbriae, a conuentibus suis desolaretur. Sed haec alias referam, cum librum de exulatione eorum transtulero."

Vulgate §186: "When, as I have said, that ill-omened usurper and his countless thousands of Africans had laid waste almost the entire island, he gave *the largest portion* of it, called Loegria, to the Saxons, *through whose treachery he had landed. The remnants of the Britons* had retreated to Cornwall and Wales, *the western parts of the kingdom,* from where they continued to launch frequent **damaging** incursions. *It was then that the archbishops of London and York, Theonus and Tadioceus, seeing that all the churches subject to them had been razed to the ground, fled to the safety of the Welsh forests along with all the priests who had survived the danger; with them they took the relics of the saints, fearful that the holy bones of so many ancient sages would be destroyed if they abandoned them in such peril by embracing their own imminent martyrdom. More priests sailed in a great fleet to Brittany, with the result that the churches of the two provinces of Loegria and Northumbria lost their entire congregations. But I shall relate their story elsewhere, when I translate the book about their exile.*"

Vulgate §187.170–75: "Amiserunt deinde Britones regni diadema multi temporibus et insulae monarchiam nec pristinam dignitatem recuperare nitebantur; immo partem illam patriae quae eis adhuc remanserat non uni regi sed tribus tyrannis subditam ciuilibus proeliis saepissime uastabant. Sed nec Saxones diadema insulae adhuc adepti sunt, qui tribus etiam regibus subditi quandoque sibi ipsi quandoque Britonibus inquietationem inferebant.

Vulgate §187: "Then for a long time the British lost the royal crown and control over the island; *nor did they strive to recover it, but continually laid waste the area they still held, since it was ruled not by one king, but by three usurpers. Nor yet did the Saxons become masters of the island, as they too were subject to three kings and warred sometimes against each other and sometimes against the Britons.*" [§188 begins the narrative on the arrival of Augustine.]

FV §186/7: Postquam infaustus ille tyrannus totam regionem illam deuastauit, Saxonibus tenendam dimisit atque ad Gallias cum Ysembarto transiuit. Hinc Angli Saxones vocati sunt qui Loegriam possederunt et ab eis Anglia terra postmodum dicta est. Britonibus enim fugatis ac dispersis amisit terra nomen Britannie sicque Angli in ea super reliquias Britonum regnare ceperunt et Britones regni dyadema in perpetuum amiserunt nec postea pristinam dignitatem recuperare potuerunt. Secesserant itaque eorum reliquie partim in Cornubiitam, partim in Guallias, ubi nemoribus obtecti in montibus et speluncis cum feris degentes longo tempore delituerunt donec reuocata audacia irrupciones in Anglos Saxones crebras facere conati sunt et sic diu perseuerauere ut nec Saxones in illos, nec illi in Saxones preualerent. Creati sunt interea plurimi reges Anglorum Saxonum qui in diuersis partibus Loegrie regnauerunt; inter quos fuit Edelbertus rex Cancie, uir illustris et magne pietatis.

FV §186/7: "After that ill-omened tyrant devastated that region, he left it to be held by the Saxons and crossed over to Gaul with Ysembertus. *Henceforth the Saxons were called English who possessed Loegria, and from them the land was afterward called England.* The Britons having fled and dispersed, *the land lost the name of Britain and thus the English in it began to rule over the remnants of the Britons*, and the Britons lost the crown of the kingdom, nor were they able to regain it for a long time afterward. Thus the remnants of them had withdrawn partly into Cornwall, partly into Wales, *where they hid for a long while,*

THE FIRST VARIANT VERSION   211

The FV redactor doesn't follow Bede exactly – Bede who would appear to place the passage to Saxon power much earlier. But actually the "passage of dominion" in Bede is a "non-event," occurring as if wordlessly at some point between the battle of Mount Badon "about 44 years" (*HE*, I. 16) after the arrival of the Saxons, the Pelagian heresy, and the mission of Augustine, the mission which Bede dates to around 150 years after the coming of the Angles (*Anglorum*, English) to Britain (*HE*, I. xxiii).[102] Nevertheless, the FV redactor does seem to want to counter the vulgate's stretching out of Britons' shared dominion with the "Anglo-Saxons" up until the reign of Athelstan with the more traditional, English-authored understandings (including those of the ASC and Bede), though his attempt is confused and awkward at best, as can be seen in §§186/7.[103]

> *passing their time among the wild beasts, concealed among the mountains in forests and caves until, recalling their courage,* they attempted to make repeated attacks against the Anglo-Saxons; and they continued like this for a long while, *so that neither could the Saxons prevail over them nor they over the Saxons. Meanwhile many kings of the Anglo-Saxons were created, who reigned in different parts of Loegria. Among them was Ethelbert the king of Kent, a famous man and one of great piety"* (Burchmore's translation §§186/187.1, 3, my emphasis). [§188 begins the narrative on the arrival of Augustine.]

102   Bede reports the Britons' victory at Mount Badon, but then does not elaborate on subsequent developments regarding secular leadership, instead inserting an account of Germanus's efforts to stem the spread of Pelagianism (*HE*, 1.17–21, pp. 54–66). He returns to the period after Mount Badon following the account of Germanus, but even so, his focus is on Insular Christianity, turning to Augustine's mission, preceded by remarks on the Britons' refusal to aid in the Christianization of the English. See Leckie, among others, *Passage*, 13–14. On Bede's use of "Anglorum" as a collective term (but not of the Angles as a specific group per se) referring to the arrival in *HE* I.xxiii, see Michael Richter, "Bede's *Angli*: Angles or English?"

103   The FV does seem to use a form of "Anglo-Saxons" occasionally: §44 "postea Saxones Angli, Belnesgata appellaverunt" "which the Anglo-Saxons later called Billingsgate" and §198 "in totum Saxonum Anglorum genus debachatus est" "[Cadwallon] vented his fury against the whole Anglo-Saxon race." On the subject of the shared dominion, Wace tries to rectify the confusion of this situation – the Saxons prevailed; the Saxons didn't prevail – as well. See Leckie, 109–17 who argues that in Wace, "the reign of Keredic/Cariz marks the passage of dominion," (109–10); he also elaborates on many of the nuances of Wace's presentation and attempts at reconciliation of the various versions he found in his sources. See also Gioia Paradisi, who asserts that Wace primarily connects Gormund's conquest of the land and handing it to the Saxons with the passage (*Le Passioni della storia*, 233–41) and Le Saux who disagrees, proposing that Wace "creates a transitional period during which we sympathise totally neither with the Britons nor with their hereditary enemy" and that since the "English are not yet civilised" and are "therefore unable to truly assume dominion over the land handed over to them by Gurmund," concluding that for Wace, "the passage of dominion is the consequence of Augustine's activities, rather than of Gurmund's" (*Companion*, cited at 147–48).

212   CHAPTER 3

Granted, they are not anywhere near each other physically in the narratives, the sections on the Christianization of Britain (§72) and the conversion of the English (§188–89) are most effectively analyzed as a set piece.[104] To begin with the Christianization, while the FV often lives up to its reputation for a greater championing of church issues and piety, the narrative of the coming of Christianity to Britain is virtually identical to that of the vulgate, except for a few differences, including the following: first, in Geoffrey's vulgate, the passage is more extensive than Bede's (*HE*, I.iv),[105] while the section in the FV falls somewhere in between the two in length. In the vulgate, at Lucius's request, the pontiff sends two religious instructors, Faganus and Duvianus, who preached, anointed, and "brought him [King Lucius] to Christ" (§72.407–9). Thus, in the vulgate, Lucius instigates the Christianization by seeking conversion himself; then "the people of his country immediately flocked from all quarters to follow their king's example, and were cleansed from the same font and restored to the kingdom of heaven" (*HRB*, §72.409–11). The Christianization is thus made an image of unity as well.

In a rare passage focused on administrative matters, Geoffrey then relates the beginning of monastic communities in Britain, how "when the blessed teachers had eradicated paganism from nearly the whole island, they rededicated to the One God and his saints the temples which had been built to honour many gods, and they filled them with various communities of men in clerical orders" (§72.411–14), specifically noting how the twenty-eight previously idolatrous priests were transformed into Christian bishops. The three high priests who had presided over London, York, and Caerleon are subsequently transformed into archbishops; he recounts how the diocese of Deira and Scotland were subject to the metropolitan of York, Loegria and Cornwall to London, and Kambria (*Kambria, id est Gualia*) under Caerleon (*HRB*, §72.416–26). In closing the section, Geoffrey relates that "when at last everything had been reorganized, the priests returned to Rome to obtain from his holiness the pope confirmation of all they had achieved. With it they came back to Britain, accompanied by many others, whose teaching, shortly after they arrived, strengthened the British people's faith in Christ," adding in a characteristic authorial aside, "Their

---

104   See also n. 65 above on the coming of Christianity in the context of the Diocletian persecution(s).

105   In Bede, the section has four sentences: two for the dating of the crowning of Marcus Antoninus Verus as emperor (156, AD; the fourteenth after Augustus); one to explain who Lucius was and why he wrote to Elutherius; and the fourth to say that Lucius's "pious request was quickly granted and the Britons preserved the faith which they had received, inviolate and entire, in peace and quiet, until the time of the Emperor Diocletian" (*HE*, I.iv).

THE FIRST VARIANT VERSION   213

names and acts can be found in the book which Gildas wrote about the victory of Aurelius Ambrosius. I saw no need to repeat in my inferior style what he had narrated in so distinguished a work" (*HRB*, §72.427–33).

The passage in the FV is very similar except that the latter adds the detail that Lucius was the "first of all of the kings of the Britons to yearn for the name of Christ" and, the detail that the people Faganus and Duvianus had taught and converted "despis[ed] the idols and [went about] breaking them to pieces one by one" (§72.4); in addition the FV adds details regarding the idolatrous practices of the twenty-eight priests and three archpriests "who burned incense to the gods according to the heathen custom and obtained omens from offerings of sheep" before they were converted to bishops and archbishops (§72.5). The FV redactor also replaces Geoffrey's more fulsome aside about Gildas[106] with the simpler, less flattering comment that "their acts will be found clearly set forth in the book that Gildas the historian composed" (§72.8) ("quorum actus in libro quem Gyldas hystoriographus composuit lucide scripti reperiuntur," end of §72).

While the versions of §72 are very similar, the same is not true for the vulgate's and FV's portrayals of Augustine's mission to convert the English (§§188–89). A close examination of these two versions reveals two clearly different political agendas, and in addition, the FV appears to be divided in its loyalties:

Vulgate
[§188] At this time the blessed pope Gregory sent Augustine to Britain to preach God's word to the English,[107] who, *blinded by their pagan beliefs, had completely destroyed Christianity in the part of the island they occupied. It still flourished in the British part, never having wavered since it was introduced in pope Eleutherius' time.* When Augustine landed, he found in their province seven bishoprics and an archbishopric, occupied by most holy incumbents, and many monasteries in which the Lord's flock observed the regular life. Amongst them was a *most noble house* in the

---

106 More than likely *HB*, since Gildas does not mention these events (Felicity Heal, "What Can King Lucius do for You? The Reformation and the Early English Church," 595). In *HB* ch. 22, we read one long sentence making up this section: "Lucius, the British king, received baptism, with all the underkings of the British nation, 167 years after the coming of Christ, after a legation had been sent by the Roman emperor and by Eucharistus, the Roman Pope" (Morris, ed. and trans., 23). Heal notes that "Bede's story was supported by Nennius, though he offered slightly different dates, misnamed the pope and had under-kings being baptized with Lucius" ("King Lucius," 595).

107 One of Geoffrey's only uses of the term "Anglis" rather than "Saxones" ("ut Anglis uerbum Dei praedicaret" (§188.176–77).

214   CHAPTER 3

city of Bangor, which had so many monks that, although it was divided
into seven subunits, each with its own prior, none of them comprised
less than three hundred monks, who all sustained themselves with their
own labour. Their abbot, named Dinoot, was *impressively* well instructed
in the liberal arts. To Augustine's request for the submission of the British
bishops and his suggestion that they should share in his efforts to convert the English, *Dinoot replied with various objections to the effect that
they owed no obedience to him, since they had their own archbishop, nor did
they preach to their enemies, since the Saxons insisted on depriving them
of their country; and for that reason the British detested them, despising*
[§189] *their faith and beliefs and shunning them like dogs.* Edelbertus, king
of Kent, indignant that the Britons had refused to submit to Augustine
and had rejected his preaching, incited Edelfridus, king of Northumbria,
and the other Saxon subkings to collect a great army and go to the city of
Bangor to kill Dinoot and the other priests who had slighted them. They
obeyed, assembled a huge army, and entered the province of the British,
came to Leicester, where Brochmail, its earl, awaited them. Countless
monks and hermits had also gathered there from various British provinces, and particularly from Bangor, to pray for the salvation of their
people. Edelfridus, the Northumbrian king, attacked Brochmail, who,
resisting with inferior numbers, finally fled and abandoned the city, but
only after inflicting heavy losses on the enemy. After the city was captured, Edelfridus learned the reason why the monks were there and
ordered them to be slaughtered first, so that *one thousand*, two hundred
of them were martyred that very day and won their place in the kingdom of heaven. Next the Saxon despot marched on Bangor. When they
heard of his fury, British chiefs came from all sides, including Bledericus,
duke of Cornwall, and Margadud and Caduanus, kings of the Demetaie
and Venedoti; a battle was fought, in which Edelfridus was wounded and
put to flight *and no fewer than ten thousand and sixty-six of his men were
killed.* On the British side there fell Bledericus, duke of Cornwall, *who had
been their overall commander*.

First Variant[108]

[§187] Among them [the many kings of England] was Ethelbert king
of Kent, a famous man of great piety, [§188] in whose time the blessed

---

108   Since I am citing Burchmore's English translation, we have his presentation of the last
       sentence of §187 as running into the start of §188. Also, Wright gives "Edelbertus" whereas
       Burchmore has "Athelbrictus," one of the more radical spelling emendations he provides
       (from DES, rather than R).

THE FIRST VARIANT VERSION 215

Augustine was sent to England by the blessed Roman Pope Gregory to preach the word of life to the English, *who were driven away by the Christian British and still persisted in their pagan ways. Coming then to Kent, Augustine was graciously received by King Ethelbert, and with his permission and consent, preached the word of God to the English people and marked them with the sign of the faith. Not long after that, King Ethelbert himself, along with others, followed in the sacrament of baptism. Once Christianity had been accepted by the English in Kent, the faith of Jesus Christ was spread all the way to the borders of the Britons.* Arriving there, Augustine found in the province that the Britons held at that time seven bishops and one archbishop and many abbeys in which the Lord's flock held holy orders. Among them was an abbot named Dinoot, steeped in the liberal arts,[109] governing almost two thousand monks in the city of Bangor. Divided among various houses, they acquired their sustenance through the labor of their own hands, and divided it in seven parts *each according to one's need,* and no part contained less than three hundred monks. *When Augustine insisted that they ought to submit themselves to him, as the bishop and primate of the whole realm,* and should join with him in the common task of converting the English people, they all refused, bishops and abbots alike, stating that they owed him no submission, and did not wish to speak with their enemies for him, *because their kingdom and language and priesthood and customs were entirely different; especially since that accursed nation was hateful to them, inasmuch as it had violently expelled them from their proper home, and still continued to use force against them. Indeed, they said, they did not wish to communicate with the English any more than with dogs. Moreover, they had put their own archbishop and primate in command, and a king with the crown of his kingdom, whom they preferred to obey according to the law of God. Finally, because they had received the grace of baptism earlier, it seemed unworthy and would be against the custom of the church for them to be made subordinate in any way to late-coming and uncivilized enemies.* [§189] When Ethelbert, the King of Kent, heard that the Britons refused to submit to Augustine and spurned his preaching, he took it very badly[110] and sent to King Ethelfrith of the Northumbrians and other lesser kings of the Saxons, asking them to gather an army and come to the city of Bangor

---

109 Wright R "Dinoot nomine liberalibus artibus *inbutus*" (§188); Burchmore DES "Dinoot nomine, liberalibus artibus *eruditus*" (§188.2).

110 Wright R "ut audiuit Britones *dedignantes* subiectionem facere Augustino et predicacionem eius spernere, *grauissime* ferens" (and *grauissime* cR) (§189); Burchmore DES "ut audivit Britones *indignantes* subiectionem facere Augustino et praedicationem eius spernere, *graviter* ferens" (§189.1).

216 CHAPTER 3

to destroy Abbot Dinoot along with the rest of those who scorned the preaching of Augustine. Quickly obeying the orders of the king, they led forward a great army[111] and, making for the province of the Britons, they came to Chester, where Brochmail, the commander of that city, was waiting for their arrival with his own army. Opposing them with a smaller number of soldiers, as the English savagely pressed forward he lost his army and turned to flight. And so, after the city was captured by Ethelfrith, *the citizens and the commoners who had shut themselves inside because of their fear came running out to beg for their safety*. Monks and hermits also came to that city, very many religious men from the various provinces of the Britons and mostly from Bangor, to intercede for the safety of their people in the presence of King Ethelfrith and the other lesser kings. *When the terrible and deadly barbarians understood why they had come, just like herds of sheep in their pens they slaughtered* as many as *two thousand* two hundred of them without mercy, and made martyrs of the faithful. When they advanced farther in order to attack the city of Bangor and complete the ongoing massacre, the leaders of the Britons heard of their madness and came together as one, namely Bledric the Duke of Cornwall and Margadud the King of the Demetians, and also Cadvan King of the Venedotians. After they joined in battle, with God's help they drove that same Ethelfrith away in flight, wounded, *and wiped out nearly his whole army*. On the side of the Britons Duke Bledric was also killed.

The vulgate is strongly pro-Briton, as expected; from the beginning Augustine arrives *in Britanniam* whereas in the FV he arrives *in Angliam*. In the first sentence, we read that the Saxons (English) "had completely destroyed Christianity in the part of the island they occupied" which emphasizes that their dominion is not universal; further emphasis is added by the following sentence to the effect that Christianity "still flourished in the British part," accompanied by an additional reminder of the era when Christianity was established in Britain, that is, in the time of pope Elutherius, significantly before the arrival of the Saxons, two aspects which are suppressed in the FV; as Leckie summarizes, in the vulgate it is the Saxons who need spiritual guidance, not the Britons.[112] The superlative nobility of the house of Bangor (*in ciuitate Bangor quaedam nobilissima*) is coupled with a superlative – worthy of wonder – used for Dinoot's learning (*miro modo liberalibus artibus eruditus*). The Britons hold firm that they "do not preach to their enemies" (*nec suam praedicationem*

---

111 Wright R "exercitum *grandem*" (§189); Burchmore DS "exercitum *magnum*" (§189.2).
112 *Passage*, 105–7.

THE FIRST VARIANT VERSION   217

inimicis suis) – the reader is clear that the Saxons are not only cohabitants
of the island but also enemies. As if the point could possibly be missed by
the audience, the vulgate narrator adds that with respect to the Saxons "for
that reason [the Saxons' having pushed the Britons out of their own land] the
British detested them, despising their faith and beliefs and shunning them like
dogs" (§188–89.193–95; "unde eos summo habebant odio fidemque et religio-
nem eorum pro nichilo habebant nec in aliquo Anglis magis quam canibus
communicabant").[113] Surprisingly, the vulgate narrator gives a smaller number of "one thousand, two hundred" martyrs following the battle at Bangor
whereas the FV narrator gives "two thousand, two hundred," thereby expanding the number of martyrs among the Britons. Not surprisingly, in the vulgate
a precise figure is given for Edelfridus's troops killed "no fewer than ten thousand and sixty-six" where the FV gives "and wiped out nearly his whole army."
Geoffrey has also suppressed the doctrinal issues reported by Bede (e.g, dating
of Easter) and through that suppression and emphasis on the Britons as prac-
ticing Christians long before Augustine's arrival, Geoffrey gives the impression
of Augustine's visit as gratuitous at best;[114] however, the FV also suppresses the
doctrinal issues, though Augustine is seen in a more positive light.

What we are characterizing as the FV's ambivalence lies primarily in the
tension between the apparent sympathy for the Saxons at the opening of section §188 and the sympathy for the Britons at the close of the section. At the
beginning of §188 in the FV, Kent takes center stage as the most outstanding
arena for the introduction of Christianity among the English, thereby associating Christianity on the island with Canterbury, and of course Augustine
with Canterbury as well, who became the first Archbishop of Canterbury in
597 – but this also implies that Christianity was not widespread at all in Kent,
reminiscent of the vulgate's sweeping statement that the Saxon pagans "had
completely destroyed Christianity in the part of the island they occupied"
(though Geoffrey does not specify geography in his passage).[115] In the FV,

---

113 The FV uses similar language for the Saxons in this context, thus giving the impression of
     ambivalence, or perhaps simply careless copying of the master text (?) but it is difficult
     to believe that a scribe/redactor could be this careless as to characterize so negatively a
     people usually treated well in the narrative: "gens illa maledicta illis foret exosa, utpote
     quae de propriis sedibus illos violenter eiecerat, et adhuc eis vim inferre perseverarent.
     Neque enim aiebant Anglis magis quam canibus communicare velle" (FV §188).
114 Leckie characterizes the slaughter of the monks at Chester as "the awful consequence of a
     jurisdictional dispute initiated by a meddlesome prelate" (*Passage*, 106). This is certainly
     the impression Wace gives; see Blacker "Why such a Fishy Tale?"
115 The Bedan tradition places Kent, Canterbury, and Ethelbert front and center for the con-
     version narrative and the founding of the English church, from a much more positive per-
     spective (celebrating the birth of the English church) than Geoffrey's narrative, of course.

218   CHAPTER 3

King Ethelbert is converted, then the English people, so that "the faith of Jesus Christ was spread all the way to the borders of the Britons." There are at least two further implications of this geographic information: 1) that Christianity was not practiced by any Britons who may have been living outside of their own kingdom (regions), for example, in Mercia, Kent, Northumbria or elsewhere,[116] and 2) that at the time of Augustine's arrival, Christianity was confined to the realm of the Britons – which implies that the Saxons were uniformly pagans, itself an unusual statement on the part of the FV redactor, and possibly an ambivalent one.

In fact, the contrast between the kingdoms of the Britons and the Saxons is a key element in this passage in the FV. First, Augustine insists that he be considered "bishop and primate of the *whole* realm," a status not even suggested in the vulgate; in fact, the latter text does not confer an official rank on Augustine for any part of the kingdom, stating only that pope Gregory sent him. Second, FV relates that the Britons will not submit to Augustine's authority "because their kingdom and language and priesthood and customs were entirely different"; stated this way, the reason sounds quite legitimate, that it would in fact have been inappropriate for the Britons to have complied with Augustine's request/demand, which is part of the ambiguity of the passage, revealing possibly an ambivalence on the part of the FV redactor, that is, a stronger sympathy for the Britons than seen elsewhere in the text; one might have on the contrary expected the First Variant redactor to have sided with Bede in this context, being appalled by the behavior of the Britons toward Augustine (regardless of their justifications) (*HE*, ii.2, pp. 138–142).[117]

---

116   We can't expect the FV redactor to have known with any certainty how widespread the Britons were at this time (or in the preceding centuries or subsequently for that matter). On the contemporary debate on population patterns in sub-Roman Britain and through the seventh and eighth centuries, see Chapter 1, nn. 98–101.

117   "Thus the prophecy of the holy Bishop Augustine was fulfilled, although he had long been translated to the heavenly kingdom, namely that those heretics [the Britons] would also suffer the vengeance of temporal death because they had despised the offer of everlasting salvation [through helping Augustine preach to the Saxons] ("Sicque completum est presagium sancti pontificis Augustini, quamuis ipso iam multo ante tempore ad caelestia regna sublato, ut etiam temporalis interitus ultione / sentirent perfidi, quod oblata sibi perpetuae salutis consilia spreuerant" *HE*, ii.2, pp. 140–43). Colgrave and Minors remark "while Bede is always friendly toward the Irish and Picts, this story in which he shows no sympathy for the slaughtered monks reflects his deep sense of the sin of the Britons in refusing to have any dealings with their Saxon fellow Christians. The story is also possibly told as an example of Augustine's prophetic powers. The gift of prophecy together with the power to work miracles both had their place in the Life of the typical saint" (142, n. 1).

THE FIRST VARIANT VERSION 219

Third, the following statement in the FV (end of §188) is highly complex: "it would be *against the custom of the church* for them [the Britons] to be made subordinate in any way to late-coming and uncivilized enemies": a) "against the custom of the church" implies at least against the custom of the British church, if not of the whole church, and while this speech is uttered by abbots and bishops of the Britons, it is an eloquent justification by the FV redactor on their behalf; b) the modifier "late-coming" referring to the Saxons (*posteris*), chronologically prioritizes the Britons both with respect to religion as well as to territorial dominion, another bit of "evidence" in support of the Britons' position and refusal to cooperate with Augustine; and c) the phrase "uncivilized enemies" (*barbaris inimicis*) applied to the Saxons on the part of the FV redactor is also surprising.

One might anticipate this type of derogatory description from Geoffrey, but not from the FV redactor, especially if one expects the latter to be pro-Saxon exclusively, and thus the description introduces the aspect of ambiguity or ambivalence. The sense of pity for the British monks is further reinforced by the comment "When the *terrible and deadly barbarians* [*diri et funesti barbari*] understood why they had come, just like herds of sheep in their pens they slaughtered [*ouium greges in caulas ... trucidauerunt*] as many as two thousand two hundred of them without mercy, and made martyrs of the faithful" (§189.3). It is of course possible that the FV redactor was more sympathetic to the fate of the slaughtered Christians at the hands of pagan barbarians – and thus increased the number of those martyred from one thousand to two thousand – because those who were slaughtered were monks, rather than because they were Britons.[118]

7 Cadwallader and the Final Passage

Although the FV redactor tends to shorten or eliminate speeches, Cadwallader's lament as he heads to Brittany following the plague which followed the famine differs significantly from that of the vulgate in its expansion, almost doubling the length:

---

118   Neil Wright notes that in the vulgate and FV, the Bangor monks are not killed during the battle "but slaughtered in cold blood after it – their death being more emotively portrayed as martyrdom." He goes on to comment, though, that probably because "monasticism is not altogether favourably treated in the *Historia*" Geoffrey did not "lay greater emphasis on the martyrdom – unlike the author of the first Variant Version" ("Geoffrey of Monmouth and Bede," 39 and n. 33).

220 CHAPTER 3

Vulgate

Woe to us sinners for the terrible crimes with which we never ceased to offend God when we had time to repent. His mighty retribution is upon us, to uproot from our native soil us whom neither the Romans once nor later the Scots, the Picts or the deceitful treachery of the Saxons could drive out. In vain have we so often recovered our native land from them, since it was not God's will that we should reign there for ever. When the one true Judge saw that we would never renounce our sins and that no one could drive our people from its kingdom, he sent his wrath to punish our foolishness, and now we abandon our home in droves. *Come back Romans, come back, Scots and Picts, come back ravenous Saxons*; see, Britain lies at your mercy, uninhabited because of God's anger, when you could never make it so. We have been driven out not by your bravery, but by the power of the highest King, against which we have never ceased to offend. (*HRB*, §203.532–41)

First Variant

Woe to us wretches and sinners, who suffer this tribulation and dispersion because of our tremendous sins, by which we offended God; *we have lost both our people and our country*. We must greatly fear that after this we might lose our heavenly homeland and be deprived of our eternal inheritance. *Lord, take pity on us; mercifully allow a time and place of repentance*. Do not become exceedingly angry so that, although we lose our earthly and immediate inheritance, we shall not be completely deprived of that which all good men you have chosen in this life strive to attain. The power of your vengeance banishes us from our country, we whom neither the Romans of old nor any stronger race could root out. Truly we have sinned beyond measure *before you and your angels*, and are unworthy that we should, once we turn to repentance, inhabit the lands that we lived in. We are banished by the lash of your anger because we, your most worthless servants, scorned the indulgence of your mercy when it was allowed. We now experience the severity of the Judge, we who, when we had the time, did not want to turn our eyes to our [heavenly] paternity. In vain did we so often, with your help, fight against the enemy for our land and so often, with you granting [it], regain it after being expelled, if you had once decided in this way to extirpate our entire race from the land of the living. *But be appeased, we beg you, about our evil, and turn our sorrow into joy so that, snatched from the peril of death, while we live, we might serve you, our Lord God, forever*. And so *let* the Romans *return, let* the Scots and the Picts *return, let* the faithless Saxons and the rest *return,*

THE FIRST VARIANT VERSION   221

> to whom Britain lies open, the island they did not empty, being emptied
> by the wrath of God. It is not the strength of those others who banish us,
> but the anger and power of the supreme King. (§203)

As noted above, Wright has remarked that the "Latin vocabulary of the Variant
version bears the stamp of a mind other than Geoffrey's"; one can go further to
suggest that the attitudes and goals also bear the "stamp of a different mind"
which can be seen through a comparison of these two passages, one of which is
intended to be a revision of the other, but whose tone – and possibly function –
is so dissimilar.[119] In the vulgate, Cadwallader's lament is just that, a lament,
filled with a good measure of bitterness reminiscent of Gildas's exasperation
with the Britons. The theme of God's wrath is central, and Cadwallader is angry
that the Britons have brought the wrath of God upon themselves. The perspective is political, with the "deceitful treachery" of the Saxons at the beginning
and the "ravenous" Saxons at the end as a reminder of the most despised enemy
of the Britons (for Geoffrey). The first time the Romans, Scots, Picts and Saxons
are named, it is in the context of those who could not drive out the Britons,
despite the latter's sinfulness. The second time they are mentioned, it is with
direct address – as if Cadwallader dares these peoples to return, to take Britain
who lies at their mercy. In both texts' versions of Cadwallader's speech, it is
clear that the foreigners have been neither brave nor strong enough to empty
the island, but that has occurred through the wrath of God.

In the FV, Cadwallader's speech is less of a lament and more of a prayer:
although Cadwallader is seen to lament the Britons' sinfulness as in the vulgate,
in the FV the rhetorical structures of prayer dominate, such that Cadwaladr
appears less as a king or a political leader than a priest. The tone resembles
that of the Psalms: "Lord take pity on us; let us pass mercifully through this
time ... we have sinned before you and your angels ... But be appeased we
beg you ... and turn our sorrow into joy ... living for you, our Lord God, whose
servants we must be, we shall serve forever ..." In keeping with this tone is
Cadwallader's preoccupation with eternal salvation, never mentioned in the
vulgate, but mentioned twice in the FV where salvation appears paramount
to earthly glory.[120] The first time the Romans are mentioned it is they alone,

---

119   Wright, ed., II, lxv. The translation of the FV §203 is my own.
120   While it is possible that the FV redactor included references to eternal salvation as an
       allusion to Caedwalla's saintliness borrowed from Bede (if the FV redactor had even been
       aware that Geoffrey's Cadwallader was a conflate character with significant "borrowings"
       from Bede), it is more likely that the preoccupation with the salvation of the Britons' souls
       reflects the FV redactor's religious leanings, which were not shared by Geoffrey whose
       vulgate text is notably secular, as has often been pointed out by scholars including Flint

222   CHAPTER 3

and the Romans, Scots and Picts are mentioned once as a collective in the FV – unlike twice as a threesome in the vulgate – and exhorting, as if in a prophecy, rather than the dare or a threat as in the vulgate ("come back" *redite*); in the FV, the Saxons are only disparaged once as "faithless" (*perfidi*), not as "ravenous" (*ambrones Saxones*). The FV redactor has turned Cadwallader's largely political lament into a devotional piece, which suits the character less – the last reigning king of the Britons in the narrative – though the context of the plague and divine wrath remains largely the same.[121]

Not surprisingly, the end of the texts §§204–208 contains major similarities but also divergences, most notably the reordering of the major events. While it is true that much of the vulgate's §207 is recounted in different language and with different perspectives in FV's §204, the rearrangement is also very telling:

Vulgate

§204 more Saxons come following the plague;

§205 Cadwallader learns of his fate; angelic voice ("vox angelica") commands Cadwallader to "go to pope Sergius in Rome, where, after doing penance, he would be numbered among the saints. It said that through his blessing the British people would one day recover the island, when the prescribed time came [as Merlin had told Arthur], but that this would not happen before the British removed Cadualadrus' body from Rome and brought it to Britain; only then would they recover their lost kingdom, after the discovery of the bodies of the other saints which had been hidden from the invading pagans," §205.566–72);

§206 Alan consults books of prophecies, those uttered by the eagle at Shaftesbury, by the Sybil and by Merlin; he advises Cadwallader to do what the angelic voice had told him; after appointing Ivor and Yni to look after the Britons, Cadwallader goes to Rome where he dies soon after;

§207 Ivor and Yni's 69-yr. "rally" and Britons' subsequent failure, criticism of Britons now called the Welsh, Athelstan crowned;

§208 Geoffrey's "threat" to colleagues wishing to write on this material.

("Parody and its Purpose"), Hanning (*Vision of History in Early Britain*, esp. 126–30, 135–36, 142, 171), C. N. L. Brooke ("Geoffrey of Monmouth as an Historian") and Kelli Robertson, "Geoffrey of Monmouth and the Translation of Insular Historiography," *Arthuriana* 8.4 (1998): 42–57.

121   As frequently noted, the FV redactor is less interested than Geoffrey in the "divine vengeance paradigm" as Paul Dalton calls it ("The Topical Concerns of Geoffrey of Monmouth," 696).

THE FIRST VARIANT VERSION   223

First Variant

§204 Cadwallader leaves for Brittany and more Saxons arrive, Athelstan the first among the English to wear their crown;

§205 "vox divina" relates Merlin's prediction;

§206 Alan consults books about the prophecies of the eagle, the Sibyl, and Merlin; Alan recommends that Cadwallader follow the advice of the divine voice; Pope Sergius blesses Cadwallader in Rome and the latter dies;

§207 Ivor and "his nephew" [Yni]'s 48-ryr. "rally" and Britons' subsequent failure; Britons renamed Welsh;

§208 naming of Geoffrey as author.

In both texts, section 204 recounts Cadwallader's voyage to Brittany and the gracious welcome he was given by King Alan, Salomon's nephew. After eleven years the plague ceased, and the Saxons did not hesitate to announce, "as was their unfailing custom, to their fellow-countrymen in Germany that, if they came as immigrants, they could easily occupy the island, devoid as it was of its inhabitants" (*HRB*, §204.551–53). Both texts relate that the Saxons landed in Northumbria

> and filled the empty tracts of land from Scotland to Cornwall. There were no natives to stop them, save a few remaining Britons living in the remote forests of Wales. This marked the end of British power in the island and the beginning of English rule. (*HRB*, §204.555–59)

Here, though, following a different "closing" sentence, the FV adds a unique passage:[122]

> From that time the power of the Britons ceased and the English began to rule the whole kingdom. After Athelstan was made king, the first among them who wore the crown, maintaining peace and concord among themselves like brothers they cultivated the fields, rebuilt the cities and towns, and, appointing magistrates and rulers in the cities, they handed

---

122   In the vulgate, Athelstan is mentioned in a half sentence in §207: "thus, with British lordship overthrown, they [the Saxons *Saxones*] came to rule all Loegria, led by Athelstan, who was the first of them to wear its crown" ("et sic abiecto dominio Britonum iam toti Loegriae imperauerant duce Adelstano, qui primus inter eos diadema portauit," *HRB*, §207.596–97). On this reference to Athelstan in the FV's unique passage, Burchmore argues that "the Variant is here projecting into the future, not (*pace* Leckie and Wright) erroneously making Athelstan a contemporary of Cadwallader" (trans., 487 n. to §204.4).

down the laws they had brought from their own land to be followed by their subjects; dividing up the dukedoms and honors among themselves exactly as the Britons had held them before, they lived in that desirable land with the greatest peace and security. (§204.3–4)[123]

This unique passage in FV §204 contains an idyllic tableau in which Athelstan is made first king of all the English, and the latter are able to maintain peace, a very important point especially given how it follows the passages decrying the Britons' inability to live in peace. In addition, nowhere in the vulgate does it say that the English used the laws they brought with them from their native land, nor does it say that they divided up the "dukedoms" (*ducatus*) in the same manner as the Britons; the FV thereby suggests that the Saxons' form of government was a combination of Saxon and Briton customs. However, the vulgate does contain comments about the Saxons' prosperity, in §207, in the same breath as the crowning of Athelstan toward the very end of the text.

While it is true that much of the vulgate's §207 is recounted in different language and with different perspectives in the FV in §204, again the rearrangement is significant. In §204, the FV redactor has included Athelstan and the Saxons' tilling of the fields in the same time frame as King Alan of Brittany – which in a way makes the scenes with King Alan a secondary focus – whereas Geoffrey's emphasis is on Alan and the Britons' final crisis in Brittany. The FV redactor has also inserted a new "fact" that Britain had been "deserted and empty" for eleven years following the plague, and that the Saxons have yet again sent for more of their countrymen from Germany, which harkens back to the beginning of the *adventus Saxonum*. In that way, the FV redactor makes Britain sound forlorn and pitiful and in need of saving by the Saxons, and by extension, that the arrival of the Saxons was both a blessing and an "achievement." The narrative loop back to the beginning of the Saxon arrival on the island continues as the Britons are again chased into the woods and mountains, inhabiting only Wales and Cornwall; Northumbria is named as the landing site, and the "entire land from Albany to Cornwall" is occupied by the Saxons. Athelstan is crowned king of all the kingdom; this narrative then is followed by the narrative on Cadwallader – who has almost become secondary like King Alan – and his holy decision and death, before the "next conclusion" in §§207–8.

The FV continues in §205 to relate that while the English grew in strength and numbers, Cadwallader grew sad and sought the advice of King Alan as to how to be restored to his former power. After receiving the advice, "as he

---

123   For the full text of FV §§ 204–6 in Burchmore's translation, see his pp. 417, 419, and 421.

THE FIRST VARIANT VERSION 225

was preparing his fleet, a divine voice thundered at him to stop what he had begun," since the prophecy held that the English would hold Britain until "that time came which Merlin had predicted" (§205.1–2). The divine voice continues to explain that Cadwallader should "hurry to Pope Sergius in Rome where, after doing penance, he would be received among the blessed." Furthermore, the Britons would only – "according to the merit of their faith" – regain Britain in the future, "when the fated time should be completed" (§205.2). This time would only occur after the Britons had brought Cadwallader's remains from Rome back to Britain.

In §206 in the FV, Alan consults writings about the prophecy of the Eagle at Shaftsbury, as well as the verses of Merlin and the Sybil, and finding them to be in agreement with the revelation Cadwallader had received, he advises Cadwallader to appoint his son Ivor "or his nephew" to govern the Britons so that "their race would not altogether perish or lose its freedom through barbarian attacks" (§206.2). Soon after, Cadwallader renounces the world, and receives blessing from the pope, passing from this world 20th, April 689.[124]

In FV §207, Ivor goes to Wales, assembles the Britons from the caves and forests where they had been hiding, and "vigorously" fights the Saxons for forty-eight years. After Ivor's death, the Britons can no longer resist the Saxons because of their internal strife, and divine retribution that caused them to abandon "all their battles in defeat" (§207.2). The FV narrator then explains that

> Tunc autem Britones sunt appellati Gwalenses siue a Gwalone duce eorum siue a Galaes regina siue a barbarie uocabulum trahentes. Degenerati autem a Brittanica nobilitate Gualenses qui in parte boreali Anglie remanserunt numquam postea Loegriam uel ceteras australes partes recuperauerunt. (§207)

---

124   The FV redactor maintains Geoffrey's conflation of the historical King Cadwaladr (Cadwallader) of Gwynedd (d. 682) with the English king, Caedwalla of Wessex, who died in Rome in 689. When Geoffrey introduces Cadwaladr in §202, he cites Bede – the only time he mentions the historian by name – saying that Bede called Cadwaladr "Chedualla the Younger," thereby giving the figure who for Geoffrey was the last British king, a half-English royal pedigree, his mother having been "Peanda's paternal sister, but by a different mother, belonging to the noble line of the Gewissei" (*HRB*, §202.513–14, 516–18). See Wright , "Geoffrey of Monmouth and Bede" (here 50–52) who suggests that "Geoffrey's literary aim may have been to define this [messianic] role more precisely by ascribing Caedwalla's saintly death in Rome to Cadwaladr, the last King of Britain – since, according to Geoffrey, the Britons would not recover the island until Cadwaladr's bones had been returned to Britain [§205.569–571]" ("Geoffrey of Monmouth and Bede," 50). In §202, the FV redactor neither cites Bede nor does he provide the attribution of "Chedualla the Younger" as "proof" of Cadwallader's pedigree.

226   CHAPTER 3

At that time, however, the Britons were called the Welsh, taking the word either from their leader Gwalonus, or from Queen Galaes, or from their barbarism.[125] But those Britons who stayed behind in the northern part of England, now degenerated from the British nation,[126] never recovered Loegria or the other parts in the south.

In terms of the narrative proper (before the final section §208 containing the "dedicatory" epilogue), the major discrepancy in §§204–7 – other than "Ivor *or* his nephew" which the vulgate has more succinctly as "his son Ivor *and* his nephew Yni," an error which suggests that the FV redactor really didn't understand or wasn't paying too close attention to what he was copying, and the ordering

---

125 *A barbarie*, which Wright translates in the vulgate as "decline," a more complimentary term than "barbarism" (*HRB*, §207.594); see Chapter 2, n. 39 for the Latin text of this passage in *HRB*. I am retaining "barbarism" here (in agreement with Burchmore) because I find it in keeping with the general tone of the FV with reference to the Britons (except in isolated instances such as the slaughter of the monks of Bangor where the FV redactors sympathies are with the Britons/monks). On the twelfth-century perception of British societies as barbarous, see Chapter 1, n. 71, as well as Judith Weiss, "'History' in Anglo-Norman Romance: The Presentation of the Pre-Conquest Past," in *The Long Twelfth-Century View of the Anglo-Saxon Past*, ed. Martin Brett and David Woodman, Studies in Early Medieval Britain and Ireland (London and New York: Routledge, 2015), 275–87, and David Crouch, *The Chivalric Turn: Conduct and Hegemony in Europe before 1300* (Oxford: Oxford University Press, 2019).

126 My translation. According to Wright's variants (ed., II, 192), MS. P agrees with MSS DES in reading "Sed illi Britones qui in parte boreali Anglie remanserunt a lingua Britannica [DE] [Britannica lingua PS] degenerati numquam Loegriam ..." ("But those Britons who stayed behind in the northern part of England, having degenerated from the British tongue, never [regained] Loegria ...," Burchmore §207.2). MSS aR read "Degenerati autem a Britannica nobilitate Guallenses qui in parte boriali Anglie remanserunt numquam postea Loegriam ..." which more closely resembles the FV text as edited by Wright (and which I have translated here as "the British nation" rather than using Burchmore's translation from PDES, since it makes more sense to me than the comment about the language); a variant in MS c does not use the phrase about language either, eliminating both the language and the "nobility" ("nobilitate") reading simply "Degenerati autem Britanni qui in parte boriali insule remanserunt numquam postea Loegriam [...]" ("But those Britons degenerated who remained in the northern parts of the island [and] never recovered Loegria ..." my translation) which is also closer to Wright's text and to the vulgate. There does not seem to have been agreement on the part of the FV redactors/scribes as to who or what degenerated – the language or the people / nation; see Wright, FV, ed., II, cxi, and Burchmore who has in general "dispensed with the now-superseded readings of P" (trans., 431), but included readings from the newly discovered MS. T (unknown to Wright); in this instance, T has the "language" reading "a lingua Britannica degenerati" (trans., note for §207.2, 440).

THE FIRST VARIANT VERSION   227

of the section contents – is of course the material on Athelstan contained in
the unique passage in §204. First, the placement of the material on Athelstan
is intentional: coming at the end of §204 – that is, at the end of the principal
section that relates Cadwallader's self-imposed, but very necessary, exile, and
the image of the 11-year waste land of Britain "dreadful and overgrown, its cities deserted and empty for eleven years, with no inhabitants except for a few
Britons" simultaneously being "unpleasant for the Saxons and also the Angles,
because they were dying in it without pause" (§204.1) – Athelstan's is a success
story in comparison with all the turmoil and Cadwallader's sorrow. Thus, in the
FV, Athelstan's crowning precedes Cadwallader's memory of his lost kingdom,
and his death, stealing the Briton king's thunder and undercutting the pathos
of the ending.

One could argue that the path cleared for Athelstan by internecine warfare
among the Britons, and the plague, was an easy one: the FV narrator remarks
that after Britain was repeopled by new inhabitants from Germany, they met
with no resistance:

> nor was anyone left over who might hinder them, or abide in that empty
> place except for a few remnants of the Britons, who either survived
> and escaped the plague just mentioned, or were born afterward. They
> inhabited the hidden recesses of the woods, abiding only in Wales and in
> Cornwall. (§204.3)

Athelstan is the first to wear the crown – by implication of a united Britain
though this is not explicitly stated. That the English followed the same governmental structures on the local level (dukedoms) as the Britons does not
diminish Athelstan's success, rather it would appear to enhance it, nor does
the fact that the FV redactor has telescoped nearly 300 years seem to diminish
the ruler's success. What is important is the peace and prosperity, creating an
image not unlike that of King Arthur's twelve-year peace, except with the latter, there were portents of future misfortune.

In the transition at the opening of §205, one reads

> And since a great length of time had passed and the English people, as we
> said, had strengthened and increased, when Cadwallader recalled his lost
> kingdom, now cleansed of the contamination mentioned before. (§205.1)

We don't have specific details about the time line – the "great length of time"
(*magnum temporis spacium*), so we can't know if the FV redactor thought
Athelstan was still on the throne when Cadwallader grew wistful about

228   CHAPTER 3

regaining his lost kingdom.[127] Nonetheless, Athelstan's appearance on the scene is mentioned by the FV redactor as an achievement, and not as a necessary evil, as seen in the vulgate, where he is mentioned in §207 (not §204), following the narrative of a 69-year "rally" led by the Britons, and where even after that, the Welsh, "unworthy successors to the noble Britons" never recovered control of the island, but "kept constantly massacring the foreigners or each other" (*HRB*, §207.599–600).

Although Leckie may go too far in claiming that Geoffrey opens up a 300-year window of shared British and Saxon control over the island when he remains silent concerning the details of the nature of rulership during the years between the plague in Cadwallader's reign[128] and Athelstan's coronation in 927, nonetheless the FV tries to not leave any room for doubt: by soldering Athelstan's reign onto the end of the plague, there is no room for disputing who was in charge of the island, or for going back, although the exact chronology remains ambiguous and certainly dubious, given the centuries that in fact separated these rulers.

In addition, although the FV redactor perhaps unwittingly repeats Geoffrey's conflation of Cadwallader and Caedwalla – which Geoffrey accomplished in order to make the former more saintly, and by so doing, on a certain level, raise him above Athelstan's stature as not only a king but a saintly messianic figure – the FV redactor unlike Geoffrey docs not cite Bede, and thus uses less emphasis or justification for the stature of this figure.[129] That the FV redactor relates Ivor's return to the island in such an off-hand, non-dramatic manner – Ivor or "his nephew"! – also reducing Geoffrey's 69-year rally led by Ivor and the Britons to 48 years, further serves to water-down the drama of §207, and while not being as Anglo-centrically celebratory as §204, one does not have the impression that the redactor feels any sorrow or bitterness regarding how things turned out for the Britons.[130]

---

127   Interestingly, the vulgate maintains that there was "a short time" which passed, "in which the English grew stronger" as Cadwallader remembered his kingdom "now free of the plague" (*HRB*, §205.560–62), but that precedes the coming of Athelstan in the vulgate, whereas in the FV, the "great length of time" follows Athelstan's reign – or perhaps interrupts it – with the narrative of Cadwallader; the chronology of the FV is too vague to determine with any certainty.

128   There is thought to have been two devastating plagues during Cadwallader's reign, the first in 664 and the second in 682. Though little is known of his reign, it is generally accepted that he died during the second of the plagues.

129   See n. 124 above on Geoffrey's possible goals in conflating those two figures.

130   We have no way of knowing whether the FV redactor toned down (relative to Athelstan) his portrayal of Cadwallader because he may have been afraid of prophecies possibly circulating which alluded to a contemporary Cadwallader and Conan overthrowing

THE FIRST VARIANT VERSION   229

In addition to the "second conclusion" (in FV that is, in §§207–8), numerous
other details serve to put the nail in the Britons' coffin, as if that were really
necessary. In §206, the FV redactor waters down the vulgate's version of Alan's
directive to Cadwallader, that the latter should

> "obey what had been ordained by God, give up Britain and do what the
> angelic voice had told him; but he should send his son Ivor and nephew
> Yni to the island to rule the surviving Britons, so that the people descended
> from their ancient race should not lose their freedom because of barbar-
> ian invasion" ("suggessit Cadualadro ut diuinae dispensationi pareret et
> Britannia postposita quod angelicus ei praeceperat monitus perficieret,
> filium autem suum Iuor ac Yni nepotem suum ad reliquias Britonum reg-
> endas in insulam dirigeret, nec *gens antiquo genere* illorum edita liber-
> tatem barbarica irruptione amitteret," my emphasis, *HRB*, §206.580–82).

> FV: "in order to comply with divine providence and bring to fulfillment
> what had been revealed to him from heaven, he should direct his son Ivor
> or his nephew into Britain to govern the remnants of the Britons, so that
> their race [*gens eorum*] would not altogether perish or lose its freedom
> through barbarian attacks" (§206.2)

For the FV redactor, the Britons are no longer an "ancient people" – *antiquo
genere*: there is little or no concern for their descendants, and the phrase "his
son Ivor or his nephew" is certainly not as dramatic as Alan's directive in the
vulgate, nor are Cadwallader's progeny seen as a united front – sending the one
or the other, whoever might be available at the time of departure will do in a
pinch! The "remnants of the Britons" – *Britonum reliquias* – is not exactly a flattering description either. In other words, even in cases where the "gist" is nearly
the same – which, as it turns out, is not true at the end of the texts – the events

---

the English through an alliance of the Welsh, Bretons, and Scots – as the dissolution
of Norman power is alluded to in the "Vae tibi Neustria" ["Woe unto you, Normandy"]
prophecy, interpolation or glosses, found in some vulgate manuscripts and commentaries; see Paul Dalton who writes, "when the *Prophecies* was doubtless circulating, and possibly revised, four things gave its message even greater credence: Welsh risings led in part
by a prince named Cadwaladr, Scottish invasions commanded by a king descended from
the Anglo-Saxon monarchs that penetrated deep into English territory, the uncovering
of a plot among native Englishmen to kill all the Normans and hand the kingdom to the
Scots, and the existence of a Breton duke named Conan ... In their [the *Prophecies*'] depiction of the overthrow of the Normans by an alliance – led by Cadwaladr and Conan – of
the Welsh, Bretons, and Scots and the restoration of British sovereignty, they projected a
terrifying picture of what was soon to come" ("Topical Concerns," 701) and n. 27 above.

230   CHAPTER 3

and speeches are not invested with the same pathos or concern for the Britons
by the FV redactor as they are by Geoffrey in the vulgate text.[131]

In addition to the rearrangement of events in §§204–208, the last two sections of the vulgate and the FV contain disparities and raise further questions,
particularly about the FV redactor's motivations. Italics set off the primary textual differences:

> *Vulgate §207: Ivor and Yni* assembled a fleet, gathered as many men as
> they could and, having landed in *Britain*, subjected the *English* to savage
> incursions for *sixty-nine years*. All was in vain, however, since the once
> proud race had been so weakened by plague, famine and their habitual
> strife that they could not ward off their foes. As their culture ebbed,
> they were no longer called Britons, but Welsh, a name which owes its
> origin to their leader Gualo, or to queen Galaes or to their decline. *The
> Saxons acted more wisely, living in peace and harmony, tilling the fields and
> rebuilding the cities and towns; thus, with British lordship overthrown, they
> came to rule all Loegria, led by Athelstan, who was the first of them to wear
> its crown. The Welsh, unworthy successors to the noble Britons,* never again
> recovered mastery over the whole island, but squabbling pettily amongst
> themselves and sometimes with the Saxons, kept constantly massacring
> thc foreigners or each other.
>
> *§208:* The Welsh kings who succeeded one another from then on I leave
> as subject-matter to my contemporary, *Caradoc of Llancarfan,* and the
> *Saxon kings to William of Malmesbury and Henry of Huntingdon; however,
> I forbid them to write about the kings of the Britons since they do not pos-
> sess the book in British which Walter, archdeacon of Oxford, brought from
> Brittany,*[132] *and whose truthful account of their history* I have here been at
> pains in honour of those British rulers to *translate into Latin.*
>
> FV *§207: Ivor,* however, *came to Wales* with twelve ships and, after he
> assembled the remnants of the Britons *from the caves and the forests,*
> along with the multitude that he had brought with him, he immediately
> decided to attack the *Saxons,* and he fought against them vigorously for
> *forty eight years.* But after Ivor departed from this life, *because of their
> internal strife* the Britons could not resist the Saxons in any way. *For divine*

---

131   On the portrayal of the status of the Britons in the FV, cf. Warren who writes, "in the First
       Variant, then, the Britons are simply overwhelmed by the multitudes of the enemy; they
       never lose their status as a prestigious ethnic group" (*History on the Edge,* 69).

132   See n. 135 below.

THE FIRST VARIANT VERSION   231

retribution was visited upon the Britons to such a degree that they aban-
doned all their battles in defeat. At that time, however, the Britons were
called the Welsh, taking the word either from their leader Gwalonus, or
from Queen Galaes, or from their *barbarism. But those Britons who stayed*
behind in the northern part of England [*in parte boreali Anglie*], *having*
degenerated from the nation / people of Britain, never recovered Loegria
or the other parts in the south.[133]

§208: But I, *Geoffrey Arthur of Monmouth,* who took pains to translate
this history of the Britons from *their language into ours,* leave the deeds
and fortunes of the *kings who ruled the Welsh* from that time on to be written by those who follow me.

The major disparities are: in this context Geoffrey does not mention "divine
retribution," but rather gives a list of the Britons' failings and unfortunate
events (plague, famine, and continual strife); in the vulgate, Ivor and Yni land
in Britain, whereas in the FV, only Ivor lands and it is said to be in Wales; the
FV appears to identify more than Geoffrey with Latin as "our" language; in the
vulgate 208, Geoffrey enumerates who can continue his work and who cannot, whereas the FV redactor simply says "those who follow him" can carry on;
Geoffrey again reiterates his claim of Walter Archdeacon of Oxford's role in pro-
curing the "liber uetustissimus" whereas the FV redactor says nothing on this
subject; in the FV, the redactor uses a phrase found in some vulgate manuscripts
in the prologues, comprised of Geoffrey's "self-styled" Monemutensis with his
"byname" Arthur, "by which he is distinguished in charter attestations."[134]

Finally, Geoffrey's famous and pointed epilogue (§208) in which he leaves
to his contemporary, Caradoc of Llancarfan, the subject matter of the Welsh
kings; to William of Malmesbury and Henry of Huntingdon the Saxon kings;

---

133 My translation. For the last sentence, Burchmore's text reads "Sed illi Britones qui in parte
     boreali Angliae remanserunt, *a lingua Britannica degenerati,* numquam Loegriam vel
     ceteras australes partes recuperaverunt" which he translates as "But those Britons who
     stayed behind in the northern part of England, *having degenerated from the British tongue,*
     never recovered Loegria or the other parts in the south" (§207.2); it should also be men-
     tioned that "lingua" can be another way of saying "race, people"; see n. 126 on the question
     of who or what degenerated as reported in the different manuscripts. In addition, it is
     curious that the redactor, after having just said that the Britons were henceforth called
     "Welsh" would, two sentences later, refers to the group as "Britons," unless he is making
     a distinction between the Britons of the north, and the Welsh of Wales. He also distin-
     guishes the south from Loegria, which Geoffrey does not do in this context.
134 On this and other monikers used in MS prologues, see Crick, *IV: Dissemination and*
     Reception, 122–133, cited here at 126. See also Padel, "Geoffrey of Monmouth and Cornwall,"
     esp. 1–4 and Wright ed., II, liii on the First Variant's use of this "full name."

232 CHAPTER 3

and forbids them to write about the kings of the Britons because he is the only one in possession of the "quondam Britannici sermonis librum uetustissimum" (Prologue) which Walter archdeacon of Oxford brought from "Britannia"[135] in the FV is reduced to

> But I, Geoffrey Arthur of Monmouth, who took pains to translate this history of the Britons from their language into ours, leave the deeds and fortunes of the kings who succeeded in Wales from that time on to be written by my successors. (§208)

Narratorial asides are extremely rare in the FV, and this one, other than the name Geoffrey Arthur of Monmouth, gives little "personal" information away. It is much more a standard passing of the baton than Geoffrey's epilogue, and certainly not a threat to contemporary competitors, nor does the FV redactor evince any sort of proprietary relationship with his text.

8   Conclusion

Although we can easily say that the First Variant is without question a separate version of the *HRB*, it is more difficult to clearly identify its national and civic agendas, than it is to suggest possibilities for Geoffrey's vulgate, in part because the FV is a more neutral, seemingly less engaged, text.

We have seen in this chapter a range of approaches to the Galfridian material – again working from the premise that the FV is a revision and not the other way around. In §5, which contains the description of Britain, the FV redactor has direct recourse to Bede, yet uses far fewer details. As noted above, in the FV, the praise of island's abundance is less fulsome, Geoffrey's commentary (relying chiefly on Gildas for this section) of disappointment and disillusionment regarding more recent events is absent, and other details important in the vulgate narrative are omitted, the most important being mention of the Saxons as one of the invading peoples. The First Variant redactor could certainly have named the Saxons but he chose not to, perhaps in order to avoid

---

135   "cum non habeant librum illum Britannici sermonis quem Waltrus Oxenefordensis archidiaconus ex Britannia aduexit" (*HRB*, §208.604–6). Wright translates *Britannia* here as "Brittany" for reasons that are not altogether clear, perhaps following the logic that Geoffrey claims here that Walter must have brought the book from Brittany rather than bringing him the book from Britain since he was already *in* Britain.

THE FIRST VARIANT VERSION   233

his primary source's – the vulgate's – disparaging remarks about that group,[136] whom Geoffrey sets up as enemies from the beginning of his history. In the vulgate, the narrator doesn't have a kind thing to say about the Saxons until the end, when he declares that "the Saxons acted more wisely, living in peace and harmony, tilling the fields and rebuilding the cities and towns; thus with British lordship overthrown, they came to rule all Loegria, led by Athelstan, who was the first of them to wear its crown" (*HRB*, §207.594–97).[137]

With regard to the Saxons, it bears mentioning that Brian's speech to Cadwallon, in response to the king's question as to why he was weeping, is completely absent from the FV (though even the vulgate Bern redactor tones it down); Wright remarks that this passage is the "locus classicus" of Geoffrey's vitriol against the Saxons, referring to the speech as a "catalogue of English perfidy":[138]

> I must weep constantly, I and the British people, who have been harried by barbarian attack since the time of Malgo and have never yet found a leader to restore their former glory. And now you allow what little honour they have left to be undermined, since Saxon newcomers, who have always betrayed us, are set to wear a crown in the kingdom they share with us. Moreover, emboldened by the royal title, they will gain greater repute in their native land and will soon be able to invite their fellow-countrymen

---

136   In the FV, the use of disparaging language toward the Saxons is extremely rare. Notable exceptions are in the context of the "night of the long knives" (§104–5) and the slaughter of the monks of Bangor (§189).

137   But even in this miniature idyllic scene – which in Geoffrey's text forms a set piece with the *locus amoenus* that was Britain "in the beginning" – Geoffrey doesn't miss an opportunity to drive home the finality of Saxon domination.

138   "Geoffrey of Monmouth and Bede," 42 n. 40. Apparently the Bern MS. has a number of references where the negative views of the Saxons are "toned down." See Wright's discussion of the various changes in Bern and his conclusion that "the Bern text represents an attempt by an unknown scribe partially to exonerate the English and to suggest that their take-over of the island, if bloody was at least not illegitimate" (Wright, ed., I, lvilix, cited here at lix); see also Hammer who claims that [the passages provided by Wright] represent "an attempt to whitewash the Saxons" ("Remarks on the Sources and Textual History of Geoffrey of Monmouth's 'Historia Regum Britanniae' with an Excursus on the 'Chronica Polonorum' of Wincenty Kadlubek (Magister Vincentius)," *Bulletin of the Polish Institute of Arts and Sciences in America* 2.2 (1944): 500–64, cited at 525–26). Bern may also be atypical (without familiarity with the majority of the manuscripts, I cannot say for certain) in its addition on Arthur's fate: with some finality, Bern adds, "Anima eius in pace quiescat" [§178, last line; "May his soul rest in peace"] to which Wright responds "clearly, this version has no time for the Breton hope that Arthur would return, but records unequivocally that the national hero was dead" (ed., I, lix).

234   CHAPTER 3

to come and banish our people. Since they have always been traitors and never keep their word, I think we should not honour but destroy them. When Vortigern first received them, they stayed here under a pretence of peace, allegedly to fight on the side of our people, but, once they were able to reveal their wickedness, they repaid good with evil, betraying Vortigern and slaughtering his subjects. Then they betrayed Aurelius Ambrosius, whom they poisoned at their feast, despite the solemn vows they had made. They also betrayed Arthur when they abandoned their obligations and fought on Modred's side against him. Finally they pretended to be loyal to king Kareticus, yet summoned against him Gormundus, king of the Africans, through whose intervention our countrymen lost their land and the king was ingloriously banished. (*HRB*, §191.258–77)[139]

In the vulgate, the themes of dishonor, lying, betrayal, barbarism, treachery, and murder are piled on against the Saxons, as if in a last attempt to sound the alarm while the Britons still have a chance to prevail.

While the Picts are mentioned as one of three peoples to have inhabited Britain (§5) the FV redactor leaves out Geoffrey's reference to the Picts as a dual part of divine punishment (Picts and Scots) along with the Saxons, whom God visits upon the Britons for their pride, though the Picts take on that role later in §204, in Cadwallader's lament/prayer. As seen above, although the Scots and Picts figure in the FV, they are not as a general rule as "villainous" as in Geoffrey's vulgate.

Although the FV redactor leans toward Bede's views in general his borrowings are not slavish: he borrows from Bede the element that the Britons first

---

139   "Flendum michi est gentique Britonum perpetue, quae a tempore Malgonis barbarorum irruptione uexata nondum talem adepta est principem qui eam ad pristinam dignitatem reduceret. Adhuc etiam id tantillum honoris quod ei remanebat te patiente minuitur, cum aduenae Saxones, qui semper proditores eius extiterunt, in uno cum illa regno diademate insigniri incipiant. Nomine etenim regis elati, famosiores per patriam ex qua uenerunt efficientur citiusque conciues suos inuitare poterunt, qui genus nostrum exterminare insistent. Consueuerunt namque proditionem semper facere nec ulli firmam fidem tenere; unde a nobis opprimendos esse, non exaltandos censerem. Cum ipsos primo rex Vortegirnus retinuit, sub umbra pacis remanserunt quasi pro patria pugnaturi, sed cum nequitiam suam manifestare quiuerunt malum pro bono reddentes prodiderunt eum populumque regni saeua clade affecerunt. Prodiderunt deinde Aurelium Ambrosium, cui post horribilia sacramenta una cum eo conuiuantes uenenum potare dederunt. Prodiderunt quoque Arturum quando cum Modredo nepote suo, postposito iure quo obligati fuerant, contra illum dimicuerunt. Postremo, Karetico regi fidem mentientes, Gormundum Affricanorum regem super ipsum conduxerunt, cuius inquietatione et patria ciuibus erepta est et praedictus rex indecenter explusus" (§191.258–77).

THE FIRST VARIANT VERSION   235

migrated to the island from Armorica, a statement that contradicts the vulgate's Trojan origin story, in which the last battle the Trojans fight before leaving Gaul was near Tours where Turnus is buried (§20.436–437). However, the mention of Armorica in the FV appears to be strictly a borrowing from Bede's description of Britain and is not supported elsewhere in the text: there are no further references to Armorica in the pertinent chapters of the FV where this section of the narrative is elaborated (§§17–20); the Trojans set sail for Britain from Aquitaine as in the vulgate text.[140]

It is unsupported borrowings like these or fuzziness of detail such as Cadwallader's "son Ivor or his nephew" that suggest either the FV redactor was not too well versed in the material he was conveying or did not feel a great stake in arguing particular points – except for establishing the Saxons as the fated victors over the Britons.

The FV redactor appears to show less enthusiasm for Arthur than one might expect from an early text narrating the life of that king. The king's generosity is understated, as are his prowess in battle, as well as his stature as a rival of the Roman emperor. In fact, the lack of enthusiasm for the battle of Siesia tends to undercut Arthur in the FV, which was an opportunity to show the king at his most glorious before the fall. Even Arthur's demise is related in rather rushed fashion.

In the sections on Augustine's conversion of the English, we see more clearly the FV redactor's ambivalence toward the Saxons. At the opening of the narrative, the king of Kent is introduced, unlike in the vulgate; Canterbury is thus brought center stage. Yet toward the end of the passage, a definite sympathy comes through for the British monks slaughtered at Chester, though as suggested above, this sympathy may be more due to their status as monks and not because they were Britons.

Perhaps the clearest glimpse of the FV redactor's sympathies in general – or his leanings – can be seen in Cadwallader's lament, which the FV redactor turns into a long prayer whose tone echoes the Psalms – a rare instance where not only does the FV redactor not eliminate a speech, but he actually makes

---

140   In one of his numerous attempts to reconcile the First Variant and the vulgate (see Ch. 5 below), Wace has the Trojans head for Brittany, naming the mouth of the Loire as the Trojans' point of landing after having left Spain on their way to Brittany (ll. 793–800); however, Brittany itself is not the site of their last Continental campaign before sailing to Britain. Thus, Wace makes a partial nod to the suggestion in the FV's description of Britain while at the same time following the major outline of the narrative in the FV §§17–20 and in the vulgate where the Trojans leave for Britain from Aquitaine (where Geoffrey has apparently located the mouth of the Loire; Tatlock, *Legendary History*, 98).

one longer.[141] By delivering that speech – or uttering that prayer – the figure of Cadwallader takes on an even more saintly air than Geoffrey gives him through his conflation of the Welsh messianic figure of the last British king with Bede's English saint Cadwaella. In the FV, Cadwallader is framed at further remove from the politically charged nature and goals of those who wrote of the Welsh messianic figure: it is more important for the FV redactor to demonstrate piety and the power of prayer than to illustrate the saving of any particular people(s) on the political level. While the FV redactor does seem to have a separate identity in mind for the English and the "others," which is perhaps why he does not overtly seek to appropriate the Britons' myth of Trojan descent for the English – though as to whether the redactor chose to distinguish the English from the Britons by underplaying the Trojan ancestry myth for the latter is open to conjecture.

In closing, although she is writing about thirteenth century historians, Susan Reynolds's remarks on definitions of origins and their importance to many groups are useful for us here in distinguishing between the visions of Geoffrey of Monmouth, for whom descent was vitally important, and the FV redactor, for whom it seems less so:

> In the thirteenth century, the loss of Normandy and failures in war evoked xenophobia, while the 'community of the realm' was further consolidated by frequent and increasingly large meetings of parliaments. In 1295 Edward I evidently thought he could awaken useful patriotic indignation by telling parliament that the king of France had the detestable plan of wiping the English language from the earth. Despite the common association of language, people and descent, English writers of the thirteenth century do not seem to have expressed any sense of regnal solidarity through a regnal descent myth. Perhaps the claims which successive kings made to overlordship of Wales, Scotland, and Ireland, as well as to inherited fiefs in France, inhibited their subjects from writing in such terms. Such claims may, however, explain how it was that the English felt able to appropriate the Britons' myth of Trojan descent, thus apparently claiming a single ancestry for all the inhabitants of Britain, inside and outside the kingdom of England itself. Their neighbours, however, were defiantly conscious of being distinct peoples. Bishop Bernard (d. 1148) of St David's in Wales pointed out to the pope that his people differed from

---

141 The speeches which are significantly different (and longer) in the FV are those of Hengist (§121), Gorlois (§136), Auguselus (§161), and Cadwallader (§203) (Wright, ed., II, xxx).

THE FIRST VARIANT VERSION   237

those of Canterbury in nation, languages, laws and manners, judgements and customs.[142]

The analogy in Reynolds' statement about thirteenth-century historians isn't perfect in our context since the FV redactor does not seem interested in the Saxons appropriating the Britons' myth of Trojan descent, yet it highlights that the FV redactor does demonstrate an awareness of the importance of the differences in customs between the Saxons and the Britons. As mentioned above, the FV redactor inserts a sentence not found in the vulgate narrative of Augustine's conversion of the English, apparently justifying the Britons' refusal to preach to the English in virtually the same terms as Bishop Bernard's – which may in fact have been a commonplace – i.e., that the Britons did not wish to speak to their enemies on behalf of Augustine's mission "because their kingdom and language and priesthood and customs were entirely different" (FV, §188.3).

On the other hand, Michelle Warren asserts that, at least in the case of the Britons in Britain and the Armorican Britons, i.e., the Bretons, the FV redactor suppresses not only the differences between those groups, but also what they have in common, stating that "when Cadwallo seeks assistance from the Armorican Britons, redactors suppress his lengthy oral history of the two groups' common ancestry" (§182) but also "when Conanus requests Briton women for Armorica, redactors eliminate his warning against becoming *commixti* with the Armoricans" (§77), as if to imply that the FV redactor may have not had strict objections to assimilation.[143] Thus we have a message of minimizing the relationship between the Britons in Britain and the Britons on the continent – as if they were not connected at any time – while at the same time demonstrating a lack of concern for the blending of the two. In addition, as seen in FV §207, the redactor would appear to be making a distinction between the "Britons of the North," the Welsh, and possibly the Britons "of the South," while designating Loegria – by process of elimination – as the Saxon strongholds (kingdoms) of the east. Although these distinctions are made in only one place in the text, this might be an interpretive avenue worthy of pursuing in future studies.

For now, though, in my reading of the text, I find so many mixed messages, so many seemingly unintended or unresolved contradictions, that the text tends to defy interpretations, unlike Geoffrey's vulgate which permits, and encourages, simultaneous multiple interpretations, as seen in the richness of

---

142 "Medieval *Origines Gentium* and the Community of the Realm," 385.
143 *History on the Edge*, 68–69.

contemporary scholarship on Geoffrey. Suffice it to say that the FV does not share Geoffrey's pro-Briton stance, and that in its absence, what remains is at least a veneer of pro-English sentiment. An investigation of Wace's attempts to reconcile divergent readings in the *Historia* material may bring more clearly to the fore the FV's political agenda, or perhaps serve to further underscore the largely non-committal tenor of the First Variant.

CHAPTER 4

Wace's *Roman de Brut*, Part 1

Gaimar's Estoire des Engleis

1 Introduction

Until fairly recently, Wace's *Roman de Brut* was one of the most often cited but least well known vernacular chronicles of the twelfth century; when looking at the scholarship on Wace's *Brut* as a whole, the vast majority of references to the work are focused very narrowly on two points: Wace's introduction of the Round Table to the Arthurian corpus and Laȝamon's claim that Wace presented the *Brut* to Eleanor of Aquitaine.[1] Although studies – older as well as newer – at least partially devoted to the *Brut* have taken up such issues as Wace's treatment of the Trojans, his portrayal of Arthur, Gormund, and other quasi-historical figures such as Lear (in addition to lexical issues and

---

1 In preparing my *Wace: An Analytical Bibliography* (2008), where I and my collaborator, Glyn Burgess, intended to report on all items ever written on Wace's life, career, and five poems (and we came quite close, having only been unable to find around a dozen books, theses or articles), I was astounded to see that scores of items beyond the roughly 500 items (not including editions and translations) we included, contained only one or two lines about the *Brut*, and that, very often just a mention of the Round Table (those items with only passing references were not included). For the substantive studies, see the *Bibliography*, especially items by Damian-Grint, Le Saux, Paradisi, Mathey-Maille, Laura Ashe, Baumgartner, Weiss, Leckie, Blacker, Houck, Finke and Shichtman, Michelle Warren, and more recently since publication of the *Bibliography*, especially unpublished PhD thesis and articles by Francesco Di Lella (see Chapter 6, n. 2 below), Margaret Lamont, "Becoming English: Ronwenne's Wassail, Language, and National Identity in the Middle English Prose *Brut*," *Studies in Philology* 107.3 (2010): 283–309, and Fiona Tolhurst, *Geoffrey of Monmouth and the Translation of Female Kingship* and *Geoffrey of Monmouth and the Feminist Origins of the Arthurian Legend*, and other studies referenced below, published after 2007/2008. I have no intention here of engaging the question of whether Wace presented the *Brut* to Eleanor, but simply to point out that it is very often mentioned as one of Wace's *Brut*'s two "claims to fame" along with the Round Table. On Wace and Eleanor specifically, see especially Karen Broadhurst who questions not Henry II's patronage of Latin writing, but his and Eleanor's joint patronage of vernacular literature ("Henry II of England and Eleanor of Aquitaine: patrons of Literature in England?" *Viator* 27 (1996): 53–84). See also Fiona Tolhurst who writes "[Broadhurst] debunks the myth of Eleanor's patronage of courtly literature" ("What ever Happened to Eleanor? Reflections of Eleanor of Aquitaine in Wace's *Roman de Brut* and Lawman's *Brut*," in *Eleanor of Aquitaine: Lord and Lady*, ed. Bonnie Wheeler and John Carmi Parsons, New Middle Ages (New York: Palgrave Macmillan, 2003), 319–36, here 320).

© KONINKLIJKE BRILL NV, LEIDEN, 2024 | DOI:10.1163/9789004691889_006

240   CHAPTER 4

manuscript studies), the work's version of the description of Britain, the Trojan foundation myth, the *adventus Saxonum*, and Arthur's reign and the passage of dominion to the Saxons as an interrelated network of narratives, have yet to be studied in any detail within the context of the cultural visions and motivations seen in Latin and French textual precedents.

The current study is meant in part to address that gap, including questions as to the relationship between Wace's *Brut* and the vulgate *Historia* and FV,[2] to what extent he tries to reconcile Galfridian chronological structures with those found in Bede and the Anglo-Saxon Chronicles, and to what extent, and in what ways – including his emphasis on the evolution of language – Wace invents his own particular blend of historiographical traditions.

Alan MacColl has argued recently that whereas Geoffrey's emphasis was on the downfall of the Britons and the moral failings which contributed to it, "Wace showed little interest in the first of these themes and none at all in the second"; according to MacColl, what interested Wace was the "'passage of dominion' and the change of name from Britain to England." Although MacColl may go too far when assigning a certain Anglo-centric perspective to Wace, as when he writes that "through its influence on vernacular English historiography, Wace's *Roman de Brut* seems to have played a key part in promoting the idea that 'Britain' was merely another name for the actual kingdom of England," the Norman writer assuredly does not filter the Galfridian material through the same pro-Briton lens as Geoffrey, and in the touches he shares with the First Variant, one finds more fascination than dismay in Wace in the face of the "Anglo-Saxon achievement."[3] At the same time, through his

---

2   I agree with Laurence Mathey-Maille who maintains that Wace used the vulgate and the First Variant in fairly equal measures, whenever the material suited his vision, adding material from other sources including oral sources as well, that "Wace ne privilégie pas forcément la *Variant Version* ... il puise, tour à tour ou simultanément, dans l'un ou l'autre des textes, au gré de choix toujours conscients et signifiants" ("De la Vulgate à la Variant Version de l'*Historia regum Britannie*: Le *Roman de Brut* de Wace à l'épreuve du texte source," in *L'Historia regum Britannie et les "Bruts" en Europe*, *1*, 129–39, cited at 131). See also Françoise Le Saux who argues that "Wace did not accord a privileged status to the vulgate text" which is "confirmed by an overview of the *Roman* as a whole"; she goes on to state that the "Variant text is used to the apparent exclusion of the vulgate in almost 50% of the chapters following §118" concluding that "the usual pattern for the remaining material is the merging of the information and/or presentation of the two *Historia* texts, frequently accompanied by authorial adaptation" (*Companion*, 92). Cf. Chapter 5, n. 7 below on Wright's views of the distribution of these two sources in Wace's *Brut*, which I find convincing in many of its details, though I tend to view the distribution more evenly balanced or more frequently alternating than he does.

3   Alan MacColl, "The Meaning of 'Britain' in Medieval and Early Modern England," 256. MacColl goes further to propose that "Wace's equation of Britain and England was different

WACE'S ROMAN DE BRUT, PART 1   241

portrayal of Arthur as the civilizer – as a person, in his role as king, and via the
Round Table – Wace stands out as the first French vernacular champion of the
Britons, a perspective on Wace which may not have been recognized or articu-
lated as such heretofore.

2 Setting the Stage: Gaimar's *Estoire des Engleis*

Although perhaps somewhat unorthodox, I would like to open my discussions
of Wace's *Roman de Brut* (1155) with a comparative analysis of points in the
narrative where the *Brut* intersects with Arthurian or other British historical
elements in Gaimar's *Estoire des Engleis*; this approach may appear atypical,
if only because the latter work ostensibly "covers" a very different era than the
Brut.[4] However, since it is possible that Gaimar's now lost *Estoire des Bretuns*
may have been a source for the *Brut* – though there is no way to prove this
one way or the other – a comparison of key intersections and key divergences
between the *Estoire des Engleis* and the *Roman de Brut* raises important questions about Wace's perspectives and goals.[5]

---

from the earlier tradition according to which 'Britannia' and 'Albion' were the old names for
a greater 'Anglia' comprising the whole island" but rather instead "Wace's England was the
actual kingdom of England, not some larger realm of English aspiration" (256). However, the
idea that Wace viewed Britain as synonymous with England – that is, territorially confined
to just England – is belied by Arthur's imperialist ambitions in the *Roman de Brut*, ambitions that appear to subsume Scotland, and certainly Ireland. One needs to remember that
Arthur's imperialist ambitions in the *Brut* are profoundly complicated as well: fundamentally
one has two binary situations: on the one hand, Arthur is a Briton, seeking to fight and conquer, among other foreign peoples, the Saxons – a goal of which Geoffrey would also have
approved – but on the other hand, those regions/kingdoms which could be construed as
more closely allied with the Britons – i.e., the Scots and the Irish – end up being subsumed
just as the Britons will be by the Saxons at the end of the "story."

4   For references on (and discussions of) Gaimar's work, perspectives, and patrons, in addition to
what follows, see Chapter 1, nn. 5, 19, 84, and Chapter 2, n. 75, and Chapter 3, nn. 15–16, and 19.
5   It has often been assumed that Gaimar's lost *Estoire des Bretuns* – which the scribe of MS.
R (Short's base MS, London BL Royal 13. A. xxi, early fourteenth century) alludes to in the
Estoire des Engleis (ll. 1–4) – was somehow lost precisely because it was supplanted in each
of the four MSS (from the late twelfth through the early fourteenth centuries) containing the
Estoire des Engleis by Wace's *Brut*, stimulating speculation by some scholars that the latter
poem was simply more interesting or better written; see for example, M. Dominica Legge,
Anglo-Norman Literature and its Background, Oxford: Oxford University Press, 1963, 30 and
277. Citing Tatlock's surmise that the *Estoire des Bretuns* was an epitome (*Legendary History
of Britain*, 456), Short speculates that Gaimar's version may not have been retained since it
may have been significantly shorter than Wace's and that compilers may have sought more

242   CHAPTER 4

Of Gaimar, Ian Short has written that "instead of 'helping the Normans
to become more English,' as if it were a stark alternative, vernacular historiography was contributing to a form of multiculturalism that enabled
the many different ethnicities that constituted English society to assimilate at their own pace and in their own time."[6] The approaches of Gaimar
and Wace toward the competing ethnicities they treat in their texts reveal
not only these authors' perspectives on their material, but may also be a
window onto how they thought that the different groups – the Britons,
Picts, Saxons (from many regions), and Danes[7] – may have seen themselves

---

    fulsome versions, Gaimar's "concision and brevity in the 1130s [leaving] the door wide open
for Wace's eloquent prolixity in the 1150s" ("What was Gaimar's *Estoire des Bretuns*?" *Cultura
Neolatina* 71 (2011): 147–49, cited at 149). In addition, we shouldn't forget Wace's role as the
"civilizer "of Arthur, and in turn Arthur as the civilizer/champion of the "barbarians," transforming the "barbarians" into respectable populations, as respectable as the English. In this
context, might it not also be possible that the *Brut* may have been more popular – at least
with compilers of manuscripts – because, even though Wace made efforts in the *Brut* to reconcile Geoffrey's views of English history with those of Bede, the Norman poet was more
sympathetic to the Briton-oriented history presented by Geoffrey of Monmouth than to the
more Anglocentric view which might have been expressed by Gaimar, that is, if we can haz-
ard a guess as to what the general point of view of the *Estoire des Bretuns* might have been,
judging by the Anglocentricity of the *Estoire des Engleis*, Arthur perhaps not being as glorious, no Round Table, etc. On the Anglocentricity of the *Estoire des Engleis*, see R. R. Davies,
"The Matter of Britain," esp. 12–13; notably, "Even Norman power and the abuse of it – though
it clearly haunts and worries William of Malmesbury and deepens Henry of Huntingdon's
moralizing gloom – is barely allowed by Gaimar to interrupt the flow of an essentially English
story" (12) and "Geffrei Gaimar – his French name, his Norman patrons, and his use of the
French language notwithstanding – likewise seemed to have no doubts where his ethnic loyalties lay. 'According to the customs of us English' is one of the phrases he lets drop, and his
remarkable portrait of William Rufus as a world-conquering, Arthur-imitating figure is seen
as predicting the victory of the English" (13, and n. 27, giving ll. 4991 and 6298 in Bell, ed.; see
Short, ed., 4996, "solum la lai de nos Engleis" "According to our English customs"). On the
MSS, see Ian Short, ed., xvii–xxii and note to ll. 1–4, p. 357, and Bell, ed., xv–xviii. On the extent
to which Gaimar may have followed Geoffrey in the lost *Estoire des Bretuns*, see Ian Short,
"What was Gaimar's *Estoire des Bretuns*?".

6 Short, ed. and trans., Introduction, xlix, and citing R. H. C. Davis, *The Normans and their Myth*,
    126–27.

7 Short: "Anglo-Scandinavian integration within the Danelaw had already been achieved,
    whereas the new, multi-ethnic Anglo-Norman English, even though they were already call-
    ing themselves English by the 1130s, were to retain some sense of cultural separateness
    right through to the fifteenth century" (Introduction, ed., xlix; also Short, "*Tam Angli quam
    Franci*"); cf. Gillingham, "Henry of Huntingdon and the Twelfth-Century Revival of the
    English Nation." Noting with respect for Short's reassessment of the question of "Englishness"
    following the Norman Conquest in "*Tam Angli*" and elsewhere, Gillingham comments, "for
    a thoroughly positive view of the cultural and linguistic melting-pot, see Short 'Patrons and
    Polyglots' (244–9)" ("Henry of Huntingdon," 124 n. 4). Gillingham adds that "by this date

WACE'S ROMAN DE BRUT, PART 1   243

as well.[8] Short maintains that "historiography was, in this respect, a tool for a continual process of rearticulating and redefining a wide range of continuities" and that Gaimar "looked for, and found, common ground on which to foster mutual understanding and respect, and peaceful cohabitation, between peoples of different cultures in Anglo-Norman England ... his advocacy of the peaceful resolution of conflict is a thread which runs unbroken throughout his narrative." Gaimar's extant history was indeed, "as Hugh Thomas reminds us, a conciliatory history of the English."[9] Although Rees Davies's view of Gaimar's Anglocentricity in the *Estoire des Engleis* does not necessarily argue for hostility or non-conciliatory arguments or positions on Gaimar's part, it provides a crucial counterpoint from which to consider Gaimar's history.[10]

3   The Prologue to the *Estoire des Engleis*

As Lesley Johnson posits in her analysis of the Anglo-Norman (verse) *Description of England*, "twelfth-century writers tried to mediate between alternative images of the insular past, and to give it a shape,"[11] and Gaimar's

---

[*c*.1140] people like Gaimar, Constance FitzGilbert, Henry [of Huntingdon] and Bishop Alexander [of Lincoln] were at home with the English past. The post-Conquest traumas had faded. Now English history was felt less as a catastrophe and rather more as the history of an increasingly civilised people ...," adding however the crucial point which underscores the important, painful and problematic aspect of self-identity of the English when weighed against the "Britons": "as Henry's account of the Battle of the Standard indicates, the self-identification of the English as civilised rested in part upon a negative perception of 'Celtic' society" (Gillingham, "Henry of Huntingdon," cited at 124, n. 4 and 141). See also Chapter 2, nn. 71 and 75 on perceptions of the Britons as barbarians.

8   On the evolving uses of ethnic names and definitions of identities in Britain, particularly in the early Middle Ages, see especially Walter Pohl, "Ethnic Names and Identities in the British Isles: A Comparative Perspective," in *The Anglo-Saxons from the Migration Period to the Eight Century: An Ethnographic Perspective*, ed. John Hines (Woodbridge: Boydell, 1997), 7–32, and the discussion following, centering largely on the debate concerning the role of biological elements versus that of social mechanisms in defining ethnicity as a concept or ethnicities as phenomena (32–40).

9   Short, ed. and trans., xlix. Thomas, *The English and the Normans*, 65, 361.

10   Davies, "The Matter of Britain" and n. 5 above.

11   Johnson, "The Anglo-Norman *Description of England*: An Introduction," 24. The Anglo-Norman verse *Description of England*, which may have been written as early as 1139 but before the end of the twelfth century (Johnson, 11), as found in Gaimar and Wace MSS D and L (see also n. 17 below), functions "as an overview of Insular history, in the form of a historiographical mnemonic ... [covering] events from the destruction of Troy to those of the reign of Henry II" (Johnson, 27). She finds that one outstanding difference between that text and Gaimar's *Estoire* is that the *Description* affords no early role to

244   CHAPTER 4

Estoire des Engleis is no exception; in fact Gaimar's text as a whole, beyond
a comparison with the Anglo-Norman *Description*, may be one of the more
inventive "mediations" extant due to a number of original interpretations of
English history, including Mordred's "donation," the lumping together of the
British peoples as all Britons while at the same time not associating the Britons
with the Welsh,[12] and the sometimes ambiguous but largely sympathetic role
afforded the Danes, as seen in the "courtly interlude" of Haveloc the Dane, but
also in support for King Cnut's claims of prior sovereignty over England before
the Saxons ever arrived.[13] In fact, John Gillingham states that "one of Gaimar's

---

the Danes (nor does Wace's *Brut*) and sticks closely to the traditional narrative of the
adventus Saxonum as initiated by Hengist and Horsa. The discrepancies Johnson finds
between the descriptions of the passage of dominion in Gaimar – "the movement from
a land governed by English kings to one ruled by a single king is recorded in the narrative, but this complex process is further complicated by Gaimar's account of the history
of Danish kings in this country too" – Wace (who emphasizes Gormund's Donation, to
be discussed below), and the Anglo-Norman *Description*, pertain primarily to the latter
text's insistence on the Heptarchy (not in Gaimar or Wace) and its suggestion that the
establishment of the Saxons' power "can be summed up in a neat, synchronous arrangement in which the Heptarchy is succeeded by a unified realm" (26). According to Johnson,
the "passage" in Gaimar is from "English kings" to a "single [English] king, rather than a
transition from the Britons to the Saxons, which is plausible given Gaimar's emphasis on
the English, his inclusion of the Danes into the mix, as well as the fact that we are reading
the *Estoire des Engleis* as his only extant text; I refer below to the "Briton to Saxon passage
of dominion" in Gaimar as a "non-event" because the Britons have been left out (in the
Estoire des Engleis), not unlike in Bede (though with different preoccupations), but unlike
in Geoffrey, the FV, and Wace (however, see n. 25 below). See also Peter Damian-Grint
who examined Bell's hypothesis that the *Description* and the Royal *Brut* may have had the
same author, and finding it plausible, concluded that both texts may well date from the
twelfth-century ("Redating the Royal *Brut* Fragment," *Medium Aevum* 65.2 (1996): 280–85;
Bell, ed., "*Description*," 36–37).

12   See n. 24 below.
13   Ian Short writes that Alexander Bell (ed.) has "convincingly shown, between these two
points, the twilight of the Arthurian world and the beginnings of the Saxon domination,
Gaimar has inserted, into what we may assume was the first draft of his history, an interlude in romance mode on Haveloc the Dane [ll. 37 or 41 to 818]" (Short, ed. and trans., note
to lines 1–4, 357). Short argues that it makes sense that Gaimar would want to provide
evidence early on in his narrative to shore up the passage on King Cnut's claim (4315–24)
that the Danes had settled in England, enjoying sovereignty there before the Saxons came
(Short, ed., 357). On Gaimar's potential goals for the courtly aspects of the Haveloc episode, among other goals, see also Blacker, *Faces of Time*, 86–88, 91, 171–72, 231 n. 199 (1994);
Scott Kleinman, "The Legend of Havelok the Dane and the Historiography of East Anglia,"
Studies in Philology 100 (2003): 245–77; *Le Lai d'Haveloc and Gaimar's Haveloc Episode*,
ed. Alexander Bell (Manchester: The University of Manchester Press, 1925) and idem,
"Gaimar's Early 'Danish' Kings," *PMLA* 65 (1950): 601–40, esp. 634–40; Dalton, "Geffrei
Gaimar," 431–35; A. R. Press, "The Precocious Courtesy of Geoffrey Gaimar," in *Court and*

WACE'S ROMAN DE BRUT, PART 1   245

recurring themes [...], the notion of an ancestral right which the Danish kings claimed to have to the throne of England" is "one of the most memorable features of Gaimar's history. "[14] Although the emphasis here in this discussion is on the elements of the history of the Britons, and not Gaimar's history of the English, it is important to note before proceeding that the Norman Conquest would appear to be treated as "casually" as Gaimar treats the passage of dominion from the Britons to the Saxons, that is, the latter being explained by Gaimar as a natural progression of immigration and settlement, rather than the result of dramatic events such as Gormund's Donation.[15] On the Norman Conquest, Short remarks that the "Danish bias gives way to a pro-English stance in Gaimar's post-Conquest sections," but a pro-English stance that ironically minimizes the English defeat at Hastings and does not demonize the Normans: "indeed, Gaimar seems to view the Conquest as little more than a legitimate change of dynasty, effected with minimum disruption, certainly not as a military, social and cultural cataclysm."[16]

The prologue of Gaimar's *Estoire des Engleis* (1–36)[17] contains what might be construed as a description of Britain, but not "from the beginning" as in

---

  Poet. Selected Proceedings of the Third Congress of the International Courtly Literature Society 1980, ed. Glyn S. Burgess (Liverpool: Francis Cairns, 1981), 267–76; and Elizabeth Freeman, "Geffrei Gaimar, Vernacular Historiography, and the Assertion of Authority," *Studies in Philology* 93.2 (1996): 188–206, esp. 193–96, 199–200.

14 Gillingham, "Gaimar, the Prose *Brut* and the Making of English History," in *The English in the Twelfth Century*, 113–22, cited at 119). Cf. Emily Winkler who takes an opposing view, arguing that "Gaimar dismisses eighth-century Danish claims to rule in Britain as entirely irrelevant," finding that on the whole "Gaimar does not in fact, have a bias in favour of the Danes" (*Royal Responsibility in Anglo-Norman Historical Writing*, Oxford: Oxford University Press, 2017, 178). See also n. 23 below.

15 On Gaimar's "non" passage of dominion from the Britons to the Saxons, see lines 28–32, as well as n. 11 above and nn. 21 and 23 below.

16 Short, ed. and trans., xliv and 429–30, note to l. 5342. See also R. H. C. Davis who comments that "the most remarkable feature of [Gaimar's] work is the treatment of the Norman Conquest, which he somehow manages both to describe and to pass over with studied casualness" (*The Normans and their Myth*, 127). With these seemingly tolerant views of the Danes, the pro-English tenor of the text, as well as the apparent acceptance of the Norman overlords as a natural consequence of political progress, Gaimar would seem to be echoing – or embracing? – the "melting-pot" scenario referred to above in n. 8. See also Elizabeth Freeman who writes that "Anglo-Norman England was a society of coexisting, competing and mutually-enhancing literary cultures" ("Geffrei Gaimar," 189).

17 Bell believed the prologue was authentic, defending it against critics who thought it was not, but he preferred to refer to it as a connecting piece between the book which preceded and the *Estoire des Engleis* rather than as a "prologue" to the latter text ("The 'Prologue' to Gaimar," *Modern Language Review* 15.2 (1920): 170–75). It is extant in three of the four MSS: R (see n. 5 above), D (Durham Cathedral Library C. iv. 27, late twelfth or early thirteenth c.)

246   CHAPTER 4

Bede whose description also includes the richness of the island's flora and
fauna, or Geoffrey with his list of the five peoples who had conquered Britain
(except the Romans).[18] Gaimar's opening description is more historical and
political than natural or geographic, and provides an outline of a very specific
time frame (though no years are given), when compared for example with the
descriptions of Britain in Bede, Henry of Huntingdon, and Geoffrey: that is,
from the defeat of the descendants of Arthur and Constantine through the
changing of the name of the island.

As Leckie notes, the opening passage or prologue, has both a "retrospective
and anticipatory function"[19] and is unique both in terms of content and perspective. It can be divided into four sections:

1)   the reminiscence of what was recounted in a previous volume, and how
      Constantine held Britain after Arthur (1–6);
2)   how things went badly for the Britons after the reigns of Constantine,
      Arthur, and Yvain because the Saxon foreigners came in droves and
      steadily, led by Cerdiz (Cerdic), to whom Mordred gave the land between
      the Humber River and Caithness, while others "in addition seized and
      occupied all the land over which Hengest had previously ruled" (7–16);
3)   how the Britons, as well as the Scots, Picts, Galwegians (Gallovidians),
      and Cumbrians experienced strife (17–22);
4)   how the island became known as England since so many English had
      come (from German lands), while Arthur's kinsmen continued to wage
      war on them (23–36):

> *Çaenarere el livre bien devant –*
> *si vus en estes remembrant –*

---

and L (Lincoln Cathedral Library 104, late thirteenth c.) (but not in H, London College of
Arms Arundel XIV, early fourteenth c.). D and L have a different first two lines ("Oïd avez
cumfaitement / Costentin ot cest casement, / E cum Yvain ...") which do not refer to the
Estoire des Bretuns (and lack R's 3–4), a circumstance which Short concludes indicates
that the first four lines of R in which a previous volume is referred to were scribal rather
than authorial in origin. Although extant in only one MS, lines 1–4 in R remain nonetheless important because they refer both to the previous book and to Arthur (Short, ed. and
trans., note to ll. 3–4).

18   The Anglo-Norman *Description* derives primarily from Henry of Huntingdon's description
      at the opening of his *Historia Anglorum*, though the latter contains echoes of Bede which
      also carry over to the *Description* to a more limited extent (Johnson, "The Anglo-Norman
      Description of England," 17–23).

19   *Passage of Dominion*, 80. Short refers to ll. 1–36 as the "transition passage-cum-prologue"
      to emphasize its two main functions: a transition from the *Estoire des Bretuns* to the
      Estoire des Engleis, and an introductory passage to the latter text (ed. and trans., 357).

WACE'S ROMAN DE BRUT, PART 1

avez oï comfaitement
Costentin tint après Artur tenement,   (4)
e com Iwein [re]fu feit reis
de Muref e de Löeneis.
mes de ço veit mult malement:
mort sunt tut lur meillur parent.   (8)
Li Seisne se sunt espanduz,
ki od Certiz furent venuz;
dés Humbre tresk'en Cateneis
doné lur out Modret li reis,   (12)
si unt saisi e [tut] purpris
la terre que ja tint Hengis;
cele claimant en heritage,
car Hengis est de lur linage.   (16)
Este vus ci [un'] acheson
dunt en travail entrent Breton,
si funt Escoz e les Pictais,
li Gawaleis e li Combreis: (20)
tel guere funt la gent estraigne
en grant dolur entra Bretaigne.
Li Angleis tuzjurs acreisseient
car de ultremer sovent venaient: (24)
cil de Seissoigne e de Alemaigne
s'ajust[ei]ent a lur compaigne;
pur dan Hengis lur ancessur
les altres firent d'els seignur;   (28)
tuzjurs sicom il conqera[i]ent,
des Engleis la reconuissaient:
la terre k'il vont conquerant
si l'apel[ei]ent Engeland.   (32)
Este vus ci un'acheson
parquei Bretaigne perdi son nun.
E les nevoz Artur regnerent
ki encontre Engleis guereierent.   (36)

You have, if you recall, already heard, in the previous volume, how Constantine ruled over this domain in succession to Arthur, and how, in his turn, Yvain was crowned king of Moray and Lothian. The situation, however, turns out badly, for the foremost members of their family are killed, and the Saxons who had arrived with Cerdic continued to expand their territory. King Mordred had

248   CHAPTER 4

ceded them all the land between the River Humber and Caithness, and they
in addition seized and occupied all the land over which Hengest had previously ruled and which they, as descendants of Hengest, claim as their rightful
inheritance. One explanation for the increasing difficulties encountered by the
Britons – and, by the same token, the Scots, the Picts, the Galwegians, and the
Cumbrians – is that Britain entered a period of such hardship as a result of
ever greater incursions by foreign armies. The numbers of the English kept on
increasing as, time and again, they arrived from overseas, and their ranks were
swelled by invaders from Saxony and Germany. [26]

On account of lord Hengest having been their ancestor, the Britons[20]
accepted them as their overlords. As the conquests increased, they more and
more acknowledged the land under conquest as being that of the English, and
therefore called it England.[21] This is one explanation of why Britain lost its
name. Arthur's kinsmen succeeded to the throne and continued to wage war
on the English. [36][22]

This prologue contains a number of surprising features:

1. The information that Mordred actually ceded – rather than promised – to
    the Saxons all the land from the Humber to Caithness appears for the first
    time in historical narrative – in Gaimar;[23] the steady stream of newcom-

---

20   Although the pronouns in lines 27–28 are ambiguous, Short's reading that the Britons
     accepted "les autres" as descendants of Hengist and Horsa – which thus granted "les
     autres" legitimacy – is plausible since the newer immigrants from Saxony and Germany
     were also willing to accept as their overlords those who came before them from those
     regions and had already established themselves, since they all shared Hengist as an
     ancestor. Lines 9–16 also support the reading that the continually arriving Saxons were
     the descendants of Hengist referred to in line 28, not the Britons, but that the Britons –
     according to Gaimar – ultimately accepted the new invaders as overlords since they were
     descendants of Hengist and Horsa. See also n. 24 below.

21   This is the only place in the *Estoire* (l. 32) where the term "Engeland" is used to desig-
     nate England. Short comments that "this neologism is made to replace the term *Bretaine*,
     and in so doing acts as a signal of the passage of dominion from the native Britons to
     the incoming Anglo-Saxons" (note to l. 32, p. 358). See also his note to l. 41 (p. 359), and
     Gaimar's explanation for the word *Engleis* (ll. 847–54) contained only in MS. R (ll. 831–54).
     On the similarities between Gaimar's account of the name change and that of the First
     Variant, see Leckie, *Passage*, 78–86. Cf. Wormald "Engla Lond." However, even if this
     renaming does signal the passage of dominion, we still have the problem of reconciling
     Cnut's claim of the Danes' prior sovereignty, and Gaimar's apparent support of the notion
     that they settled the islands before the Saxons. See n. 26 below.

22   All citations from and translations of the *Estoire des Engleis* are Short's, unless otherwise
     indicated.

23   Gaimar may have interpreted Mordred's donation as a "real" event, based on the passage
     in the *HRB* where Geoffrey tells that Mordred had *promised* the Saxon leader Chelricus
     (Cheldric) the territory from the Humber River to the northernmost tip of Scotland, plus

WACE'S ROMAN DE BRUT, PART 1 249

ers also took over the lands that Hengist had once ruled (Kent and environs), which means, taken literally, that Gaimar considered the Saxons, following Mordred's "donation," to have had dominion over Scotland and southeast England;[24]

much of Kent, in exchange for military support against Arthur: "That most foul traitor Modred had sent the Saxon leader Chelricus to Germany to collect there as many men as he could and sail back with them as quickly as possible. In return, Modred had promised him all the island from the river Humber to Scotland and as much of Kent as Hengest and Horsa had occupied in Vortigern's time. Chelricus had carried out his mission, returned with eight hundred ships full of armed pagans and now agreed formally to obey the traitor as if he were his king" (*HRB* §177.10–15). Gaimar's text assumes the accomplishment of the transfer of lands, though that does not appear to have been Geoffrey's intention (nor that of the First Variant redactor, since that text has the same passage as Geoffrey's, in similar language, FV §177). In terms of the "logic" of the larger Arthurian narrative in Geoffrey, since Arthur kills Mordred at the battle of Camlann, the latter would not have had the opportunity to cede or donate lands, even if he had taken control of them when he usurped Arthur's throne while the king was fighting the Romans in Gaul, regardless of Mordred's promise and Cheldric's having kept his end of the bargain. In addition to Gaimar's apparent confusion of Geoffrey's later (non-datable) Cheldric (*HRB*, §177) with the earlier 6th-c. Cerdic (actual king of Wessex 514–39) (in *HRB*, §101, Cherdic, arrived after Hengist and Horsa, at Vortigern's behest; ASC 495, roughly 45 years after Hengist and Horsa), he reiterates the kernel of the story later in the *Estoire*: Danish king Cnut explains to Edmund that it is *he* who has the stronger claim to England, having descended from Danr (who was king nearly one thousand years before Cerdic, and who "held the land in chief from God," 4317–21) whereas Edmund is descended from Cerdic: "It was Mordred who granted Cerdic his fief; he never held it in chief, and your family is descended from him" (4322–24); in the end, Cnut offers peace, suggesting they divide the land in two between them. On Gaimar's confusion of Cheldric and Cerdic, and this very strange sequences of events and its adaptation by Richard of Devizes in the late twelfth century, see John Gillingham, "Richard of Devizes and 'a rising tide of nonsense': How Cerdic met King Arthur," in *The Long Twelfth-Century View of the Anglo-Saxon Past*, ed. Martin Brett, David A. Woodman (London: Routledge, 2015), 141–56; see also Short, ed., note to lines 4317–30, p. 415, and Bell's "Gaimar's Early 'Danish' Kings," 627–29. Although we may well construe Mordred's having met Cerdic as "nonsense" (as well as Arthur's battle against Cerdic, which also surely seems to be "nonsense"), as Leckie points out, Gaimar sought to establish "a direct causal link between Modred's treachery and English domination" (*Passage of Dominion*, 81). In Leckie's view, Gaimar rejects Gildas's and Geoffrey's depiction of the mid-sixth century as "a time of relative stability when the Britons held the Saxons in check," placing the start of the passage of dominion in the time of Constantine, marked by Mordred's donation (*Passage*, 82). On the other hand, this would seem to contradict the "non-passage" of dominion recounted in Gaimar's prologue ll. 28–32 where it is just a shift in populations which marks the passage, not the donation of lands on anyone's part (but contradictions do of course occur in many texts, Gaimar's being no exception).

24 Gaimar appears to have considered all the Saxons to have been descendants of Hengist and Horsa, including the immigrants who came over from Germany with Cerdic who, according to Richard of Devizes, were descended from the sons of the Briton King

250   CHAPTER 4

2. While there is virtually no narrative in the *Estoire des Engleis* describing
    the end of Arthurian dominion,[25] Gaimar seems to be sympathetic to the
    Britons here, which is surprising given that the bulk of the *Estoire* is told
    almost entirely from the vantage point of the English, with periods of
    apparent support for the Danish claims.[26] Among the signs of possible
    sympathy toward the Britons are:

Ebraucus who had traveled to Germany and settled there. Richard maintained that "their descendants were those Angles and Saxons who in later times, led by Horsa and Hengist, by conquering Britain recovered the inheritance of their fathers"; as Gillingham further observes, "despite the fact that neither Hengest nor Horsa figure in the West Saxon genealogical tradition" ("Richard of Devizes and 'a rising tide of nonsense'," cited at 150 and 148, n. 38). Gillingham posits that "there is much [in Richard's texts] which suggests that Richard read Gaimar, and then set about creating a drastic and dramatic clarification of the rather confused references to Cerdics which he had found in the *Estoire des Engleis*" (148).

25   Whether Gaimar recounted the *adventus Saxonum* in its more traditional Bedan form, which gives primacy to Kent not to the West Saxons, at – or toward – the end of the now lost *Estoire des Bretuns*, we will never know. However, it is surprisingly absent here at this stage of the narrative, due in part to his treatment of the role of the Danes in the early history of England, his non-traditional emphasis on the arrival of Cerdic and his son Cynric in 495 (as opposed to Hengist and Horsa in the longships, etc., mid-fifth century), and his different presentation of Gormund's role in the late ninth century (see also n. 39 below). It is possible that Gaimar gave Cerdic "pride of place" since he was the first documented king of Wessex (reigned 519–34) and he had landed in Hampshire (in around 494), where Gaimar's patrons held lands (as well as in Lincolnshire); Cerdic defeated the local British king and added the isle of Wight to his territories. Regardless of his motivations, it is clear that Gaimar gives primacy to the West Saxon origin myth over that of Kent. On the multiple origin legends of the Germanic settlers, and their appearance in the Anglo-Saxon Chronicles, and the "Anglian collection" of royal genealogies, see Barbara Yorke, "Anglo-Saxon Origin Legends," and David Dumville, "The Anglian Collection of Royal Genealogies and Regnal Lines," *Anglo-Saxon England* 5 (1976): 23–50.

26   One major aspect of the *Estoire* that may argue against an assessment of solely Anglocentric bias in the *Estoire des Engleis* would be Gaimar's treatment of the Danes, which is not only interestingly inconsistent, but also more often favorable. While at times Gaimar portrays the Danes as typical marauding villains, referring to them as being "de mult mal eire" (3470; "by disposition exceedingly evil") and having other negative characteristics (e.g., the *felon Daneis*, 3123, 3533), he also appears to present them, in the early sections of the *Estoire* at least, as the rightful claimants to control over the island, having settled and cultivated the land before the Saxons. According to Short, by inserting the Haveloc episode immediately after the prologue (at either 37 or 41–818), Gaimar seeks to "establish an early Danish presence in England prior to any Saxon conquests" which "can hardly be seen as a politically neutral invention on Gaimar's part," adding that "when recounting the first Danish incursions in 787, [Gaimar] goes out of his way to recall earlier settlements by the Danes and their claims to rightful inheritance (2065–86)" and "when Cnut negotiates with Edmund Ironside, he is even more explicit in his claims of prior settlement (4513–24)" (ed. and trans., note 37, p. 358). Short characterizes Gaimar's attitude toward the Danes as "ambivalent but unusually tolerant ... in general" and finds his "pro-English

WACE'S ROMAN DE BRUT, PART 1 251

a) the narrator's comment that the numbers of the English kept growing does not seem to be reported with joy, and

b) the Britons are said to have undergone great hardship – but this possible sympathy toward the Britons as it turns out does not appear
to carry over to Arthur since Gaimar remarks that the Danes hated
Arthur and fought with Mordred against him;[27]

3. Gaimar puts the Scots, the Picts, the Galwegians (li Gawaleis; Galloway,
Scotland, 20) and the Cumbrians[28] in the same category as the Britons,

---

stance" less consistent than others have. See ed., Introduction, xliii, on this ambivalence
and the idea of "a Danish claim to the English throne based on prior sovereignty"; cf. Susan
Crane who writes that Gaimar "reworks the Danish invasions into a success story of intermarriage and international alliance" ("Anglo-Norman Cultures in England, 1066–1460,"
in *The Cambridge History of Medieval English Literature*, ed. David Wallace, Cambridge:
Cambridge University Press, 1999, 35–60, cited at 40), and Gillingham who characterizes
the idea of the Danish claim to dominion in England as "one of the most memorable
features of Gaimar's history" ("Gaimar, the Prose *Brut* and the Making of English History,"
119). It should be kept in mind, as Catherine Croizy-Naquet notes, that according to Dudo
of St. Quentin and others, Rou and his followers left Denmark, settled in and founded
Normandy (911), and that their descendants conquered England in the following century
(Catherine Croizy-Naquet, "L'*Estoire des Engleis* de Geiffrei Gaimar, ou comment faire
mémoire du passé," in *Le Passé à l'épreuve du présent: appropriations et usages du passé
au Moyen Âge à la Renaissance*, ed. Pierre Chastang, Mythes, Critique et Histoire (Paris:
Presses de l'Université Paris-Sorbonne, 2008, 61–74, p. 69). On Gaimar's possible motives
for this favorable treatment of the Danes, see also Paul Dalton, "The Date," and J. Blacker,
Faces, 171–72 (1994).

27 Gaimar does add though, immediately following the prologue and just before the start the
Havecoc interpolation, that the Danes hated Arthur's Britons because they (the Danes)
had had relatives who had died in the battles Arthur waged against Mordred, whom
Arthur also killed subsequently (37–40; "Meis li Daneis mult les häeient / pur lur parenz ki
morz estaient /es batailles kë Artur fist / contre Modret k'il puis oscist"). In Gaimar's eyes,
this would further support the Danes' claims to prior dominion, though why the Danes
would have sided with Mordred against Arthur in the first place remains a mystery. This
information of Danish participation in the battles between Arthur and Mordred – and
also the fact that it is "battles" plural, not the single one at Camlann with which Arthur
and Mordred are most frequently associated – may be unique to Gaimar (as a written
source, and may have circulated only orally), since he is introducing the Danes into the
history of the island well in advance of their actual arrival toward the end of the eighth
century. See Short, ed. and trans., note to l. 37.

28 Gaimar continues this association of the Scots, Picts, Galwegians, and Cumbrians – and
by extension and implication, the Britons – from the "early British history" section further
into his history. We see the same phrase with reference to tenth-century Athelstan (Aprés
un an, ne mains ne plus, / a Bruneswerce out le desus / sur les Escoz e sur Combreis, sur
Gawaleis e sur Picteis; ... (3521–24; "He severely plundered the country, and after a year,
neither more nor less, he got the better of the Scots, Cumbrians, Galwegians, and Picts at
Brunanburh [in 937]"). After Edgar's death (k. 959–75), and his eldest son Edward's short

252   CHAPTER 4

that is, in contrast to the English, who were descended from the Saxons and others from Germany. However he does not openly identify the Welsh with the Britons as Geoffrey of Monmouth does at the end of the *Historia*;[29]

4.   On the other hand, despite the "othering" of the Britons, and their "association" with the Scots, Picts, Galwegians (Gawaleis in 20, not the Waleis in 4117), and the Cumbrians, Gaimar does not appear to use the identifying pronouns "we" or "us" for any of the groups for whom or about whom he writes.[30]

Keeping in mind Rees Davies's arguments that Gaimar's text is largely Anglo-centric, it is possible that Gaimar's lumping together of the Scots, Picts, Galwegians, and Cumbrians is connected to his seeing Britain as just an earlier stage of England, British history as just an earlier stage of English history, rather than seeing those peoples as legitimate groups, coexisting with the English. Dauvit Broun comments that "it was inevitable … that Geoffrey of Monmouth's glorious British past should be identified by English historians

---

reign (k. 975–78), Aethelred, Edward's half-brother, came to the throne with the help of his mother Queen Aelfthryth (whom Gaimar suggests had her stepson Edward the Martyr killed for that purpose, ll. 4009–43; on the tradition of Aelfryth's possible complicity, see Pauline Stafford, "Aelfryth," in *The Wiley Blackwell Encyclopedia of Anglo-Saxon England*, ed. Michael Lapidge, John Blair, Simon Keynes, and Donald Scragg, Chichester and New York: John Wiley and Sons, 2nd ed., 2014, 11–12). According to Gaimar, Aethelred was also challenged by his elder brother, Edmund, who was in turn supported by the Welsh (4105–12). About Aethelred, Gaimar adds that "The Scots and the Picts, the Cumbrians as well as the Welsh would not deign to have Aethelred as their overlord, and never had the slightest intention of serving him" ("e les Escoz et les Pictais/[e] les Waleis e les Cumbreis/ne deignouent de lui tenir / ne n'urent soing de lui servir," 4116–20), as if the Welsh have now replaced the Galwegians in his thinking of the triad of Scots, Picts, and Galwegians, as peoples along with the Britons who were subjugated by the arrival of more and more Saxons (as stated in the prologue, ll. 17–20) and who are shown here (4116–20) to not capitulate to/cooperate with Aethelred; see Paul Dalton "Geffrei Gaimar's *Estoire des Engleis*," 440–41, and also Short, note to line 20, p. 357, on the form *Gawaleis*.

29   Cf. Short, ed. and trans., who asserts that Gaimar makes the identification of the Britons with the Welsh early in the text, stating with respect to the slaughter of the monks at Chester "ASC (E) confirms Gaimar's figure of 200 priests killed, though it specifies that they were there to pray for the Welsh army (Gaimar's *Bretuns* of l. 1084), not to bury them" (note to line 1087, pp. 370–71).

30   On Gaimar's patron, Constance fitz Gilbert, who with her husband Ralph, were members of an old Lincolnshire family, see Chapter 1, n. 19, and Chapter 3, nn. 15–16, and 19, and n. 5 above; on the family connections both aristocratic and religious, see Short, ed. and trans., xxvii–xxix, and within the context of broader issues of patronage particularly by women in the first half of the twelfth century in England, see Susan M. Johns, *Noblewomen, Aristocracy and Power in the Twelfth-Century Anglo-Norman Realm*, 37–39, 42–43.

WACE'S ROMAN DE BRUT, PART 1

as part of England's history. This is also reflected in how Gaimar's *Estoire des Engleis* was read."[31] Elizabeth Freeman puts forward another plausible reading or explanation of Gaimar's apparent lack of identification with any one group: "For Britons, Saxons, Danes, or Normans – the honored territory of rightfulness remained possible for all. This suggests that the 'right' ideal was not ethnically or culturally specific"; citing William Sayers view that Gaimar's "support and sympathy are for each new dynasty once established and legitimized on the throne,"[32] Freeman concludes her observation that "once a king – any king – succeeded rightfully and legally to the crown, Gaimar invariably supported the status quo."[33] Regardless of whether or not Gaimar was that much of a historiographical chameleon as it were, it is clear that he was both anxious to authorize his work with frequent references to "li livre" – the ASC[34] – while at the same time synthesizing as much evidence/material as he saw fit for his public's consumption.

4   The Foundation Myth, the *Adventus Saxonum*, and the Passage of Dominion

Although Gaimar does include some details – confused as they are – of his version of the *adventus Saxonum* in his presentation of early British history in the *Estoire des Engleis*, the latter does not contain any version of either the

---

31   *Scottish Independence and the Idea of Britain*, 42. The fact that Gaimar's *Estoire* is preceded by Wace's *Brut* in the four manuscripts in which it was found, and followed in two by Jordan Fantosme's chronicle of the Anglo-Scottish war of 1173–74 (*Jordan Fantosme's Chronicle*, ed. and trans. R. C. Johnston, Oxford: Clarendon Press, 1980) has prompted Peter Damian-Grint to propose that these three texts formed "a complete composite history of Britain" for audiences of the early thirteenth century (*The New Historians*, 51). On the MSS, see nn. 5 and 17 above, and also Ian Short, ed. and trans., xvii–xxv and note to ll. 1–4, p. 357, and Bell, ed., xv–xviii.

32   W. J. S. Sayers, *The Beginnings and Early Development of Old French Historiography (1100–1274)* (Berkeley: University of California Press, 1967), 190–91.

33   Freeman, "Geffrei Gaimar," 200.

34   See Short, ed. and trans., "The annal for 966 ... marks the end of Gaimar's dependence on the ASC as a sole source, but intermittent use of it continues into the rest of his narrative" (note for line 3586, p. 401). Short also notes "that Gaimar wished his history to be regarded as authoritative ... is abundantly clear from the careful and detailed references in his epilogue documenting his numerous written sources, their provenance, and their pedigree" (xv); see also Damian-Grint, *The New Historians*, 49–53, 114–15, 132–33. On Gaimar's use of the ASC as authorization, particularly following his use of oral sources, see Freeman, "Geffrei Gaimar," 190–91, 194.

254   CHAPTER 4

Trojan or Saxon foundation myths to speak of,[35] even though he may have seen an earlier version of MS. F of the Anglo-Saxon Chronicle(s) containing a Latin preface on the coming of the Trojans to the island.[36] As far as the *adventus* is concerned, in the main narrative of the *Estoire des Engleis* (819–54), in the year 495, Cerdic lands with his fleet, together with his son Cynric; a genealogy follows, from their time back to Hengest and Horsa, followed by a brief explanation of the origins of the West Saxons, the South Saxons, the East Saxons and the Middle Saxons,[37] and again how the English took their name from "the country named Angle" ("nez del païs di Ange ad nun, / Engleis tuz les apela hom" 853–54).[38] Cerdic fights a war of twenty-four years before achieving "any

---

35   Though of course he may have done that in the lost *Estoire des Bretuns*, but it is worth not-
      ing here that there are no references to that sort of material in the *Estoire des Engleis*. For
      non-exhaustive lists of sources on the Trojan foundation myth, see Chapter 1, n. 40, and
      Chapter 5, n. 5 below. On the underpinnings of identities which may be gleaned from the
      multiple Saxon foundation myths, see for example, Barbara Yorke, "Political and Ethnic
      Identity: A Case Study of Anglo-Saxon Practice," in *Social Identity in Early Medieval Britain*,
      ed. William O. Frazer and Andrew Tyrell (London and New York: Leicester University
      Press, 2000), 69–90, and eadem, "Anglo-Saxon Origin Legends"; Stephen J. Harris, *Race
      and Ethnicity in Anglo Saxon Literature* (London and New York: Routledge, 2003), esp.
      Chap. Five, "Woden and Troy," 131–56, 237–43.

36   Pauline Stafford's insistence on using the plural "Chronicles," arguing that each of the
      recensions is unique and contains a narrative told from a unique perspective is espe-
      cially useful for our purposes ("The Anglo-Saxon Chronicles, Identity and the Making of
      England," *The Haskins Society Journal* 19 (2008): 28–50). As Stafford notes "F's new preface
      on Trojan origins was not added to the genealogical one, which A and G shared. Rather
      it was an addition to the preface which we now find in D and E ... derived from Bede's
      Historia Ecclesiastica ... D and E's preface was probably that which once stood at the
      beginning of the most famous of the lost vernacular chronicles, the so-called Northern
      Recension" (42). Short has demonstrated that Gaimar used "an independent copy of the
      Northern Recension" (ed. and trans., xv, n. 24), which Stafford describes as "largely the
      result of the collation of Alfred's chronicle with two other major sources: Bede's *HE*, and a
      Latin chronicle produced almost certainly at York *c.* AD 800, perhaps in part by Alcuin ...
      From Bede, they [the compilers] took a much extended story of conversion, and probably
      a new preface. That preface tells of the arrival on the island of Britain of Picts, Britons and
      Scots; and it is paralleled by a much augmented entry under the year 449, which tells of
      the arrival of Angles, Saxons and Jutes" (43). As we discuss below, Gaimar however, clouds
      matters by confusing the Cerdic who landed, according to the ASC, roughly 45 years after
      the first wave of Saxons, and the king who supposedly "received" Mordred's "donation"
      many years later (see nn. 24 above and 38 below).

37   Reminiscent of a passage in Bede, though without mention of specifics on those who
      originated in "the land between the kingdoms of the Jutes and the Saxons, which is called
      Angulus" from whence came "the East Angles, the Middle Angles, the Mercians, and all
      the Northumbrian race" (1.15).

38   In this passage about Cerdic's landing, Gaimar calls Cerdic "l'altre Certiz" (822) which
      Short translates as the "second Cerdic." However, the chronology and circumstances

WACE'S ROMAN DE BRUT, PART 1   255

victory of significance over the Britons" ("Vint e quatre anz dura la guere / ainz
ke Certiz poüst conquere / sur les Bretons gueres de chose" 855–57).

In Gaimar, Cerdic is also associated with the first of three "sieges" of
Cirencester, wherein one finds Gaimar's reference to fire having been brought
by sparrows, leading to its capture;[39] subsequently, Cerdic and his men

---

associated with "each" Cerdic, that is, the Cerdic in the prologue l. 10 and the one here
at l. 822 – the circumstances of the first mention in the prologue being the landing c.495
(ASC) and the second, the full narrative of Cerdic's landing – suggests that the two Cerdics
are one in the same – as if the author or scribe had forgotten that the prologue is meant to
sketch out events to come in the main narrative – rather than a second king by the same
name ("Donc out de la Nativité / ben pres de cinc cenz anz passé – / n'iert ke [sul] cinc anz
a dire" 819–21) ["At that time, very nearly five hundred years had passed since the birth of
Christ; indeed the date was only five years short of that number"]. John Gillingham notes
that, in addition, Gaimar appears to have conflated Geoffrey's Chelric (HRB §177.10–15) –
the Saxon warlord to whom Mordred promised the said lands in exchange for his military
help for Arthur's return from Gaul and final battle with Mordred, a much later circumstance (though impossible to date) – with the much earlier king Cerdic who landed c.495
("Richard of Devizes and 'a rising tide of nonsense,'" 147).

39 Geoffrey of Monmouth describes a siege of Cirencester, but led by Gormund the African
king (HRB, §184) during the reign of the legendary Briton king Keredic in the late sixth
century (not datable) and under very different circumstances, including the missing detail of the sparrows which Gaimar provides (the "incendiary bird motif," as it is
sometimes referred to; on this motif, see Helen M. Cam, "The Legend of the Incendiary
Birds," English Historical Review 31.121 (1916): 98–101, esp. p. 100, and A. H. Krappe, "The
Sparrows of Cirencester," Modern Philology 23 (1925–26): 7–16); Wace as well associates
the sparrows with Gormund's siege of Cirencester (the Galfridian Gormund) (approx. late
sixth century, though not datable as such) (13589–604). In addition, in Gaimar's Estoire,
there are at least two (if not three) sieges of Cirencestre: one full-blown siege ll. 855–72
(that of the "incendiary bird motif" wherein Cerdic captures the city and burns it down),
one taking of the town ll. 993–94, and Gormund's (the second "Gurmund") occupation of Cirencester ll. 3240–58 (though not completely described as a siege). In Gaimar
(3069–3232), the first Gormund ("Gurmund"), is an historical Danish king of East Anglia,
at first an enemy but then later converted to Christianity by Alfred (ASC 875, 878, 890) and
has nothing to do with the Galfridian narrative of Gormund, Cirencester, or the "incendiary birds"; the second "Gurmund" is also a Danish king (legendary), who at Cirencester
"expelled a large number of unfortunate people from their land" at the end of his army's
occupation of that city (Estoire 3233–40), apparently in the late ninth century (if we can
judge by correspondences with the ASC which records a Danish raiding-army wintering
in Cirencester in 879); although with altered context, Gaimar's second Danish "Gurmund"
is also associated with France (though without the epic hero Isembard attached to him)
(ASC "the land of the Franks" (see Short, note to line 3292); see also Blacker on Gaimar's
two Danish Guthrums (one historical, one legendary), the second Gaimar associating with France and the French legend ("Arthur and Gormund," 267). Mordred's "donation" makes up part of the island's territorial history in the Estoire, but the Galfridian
Gormund's "donation" of Loegria to the Saxons does not, most likely because of its role
in the Galfridian framework. See also Short on a "particularly obscure passage" on the

256   CHAPTER 4

"pursued their conquest right up to the Severn, killing all the most prominent Britons, and from the sea where they had originally landed they took possession of the whole country and the kingdom as far as the Severn, and they drove the Britons out" (867–72). In the *Estoire*, Cerdic is thus afforded a much greater role in the *adventus Saxonum* and the eventual routing of the Britons than he is in the Bedan tradition – where one finds emphasis on the Kentish legend of the arrival of Hengist and Horsa in the long ships – or in the Galfridian tradition, based on the Trojan myth.[40] As Leckie notes, by making Cerdic more central than Hengist – though Gaimar mentions Hengist as an important ancestor of all Saxon-related groups – Gaimar "depicts the Germanic conquest of Britain as essentially a West Saxon achievement,"[41] appearing perhaps unintentionally in the process to demote Kent and the East Saxons, though he does not openly disparage the latter and other Saxon groups.

As seen in Chapters One, Two, and Three, both Geoffrey and the First Variant redactor assign great importance to Gormund's predations and his handing over of Loegria to the Saxons, set in the late sixth century, shortly before Augustine is sent on his mission by Rome to convert the Saxons. Despite the disaster that Geoffrey portrays, he goes on to imply that nearly 300 years of shared Briton-Saxon rule follow Gormund's Donation, whereas the First Variant redactor signals the changing of the island's name and thus the taking on of a strictly English identity almost immediately following the Donation, the Donation having a very large and not regrettable role in the making of the English nation. Since neither the near namesakes Guthrum – king of East Anglia and baptized Adelstan (Athelstan)[42] as example to the East Anglians by St. Augustine – or the Danish king, "Gurmund" in Gaimar's text bear more

---

destiny of Gormund's troops after his death (the second "Gurmund"), which Alexander Bell (ed., *L'Estoire*, 247–48) viewed as Gaimar's "attempts to reconcile elements from the Gormund legend with the text of ASC 892" (Short, ed., note to ll. 3399–3409, p. 398).

40   On the Kentish legend of Hengist and Horsa and a compelling comparison of how the Anglo-Saxon Chronicles and the *Historia Brittonum* present virtually identical events with a different slant, the former "for the benefit of an English audience," and the latter "for a British audience," see Nicholas Brooks, "The Creation and Early Structure of the Kingdom of Kent," in *The Origins of Anglo-Saxon Kingdoms*, ed. Steven Bassett (London and New York: Leicester University Press, 1989), 55–74, cited here at 63. On the recurrent structural patterns in many English origin myth narratives, see Patrick Sims-Williams, "The Settlement of England in Bede and the Chronicle."

41   *Passage of Dominion*, 86.

42   This Adelstan/Athelstan is the third of four figures in the *Estoire* of that name: 1) Adelstan, that is Ealhstan bishop of Sherborne 2257; 2) Adelstan, Athelstan king of Kent 2388, 2479, 2480; 3) Adelstan, Athelstan baptismal name of Guthrum, king of East Anglia 3220, 3380; and 4) Adelstan, Athelstan king of England (who wore the crown of a united England in the early tenth century) 3513.

than a weak resemblance to the Galfridian Gormund, it is not surprising that Gaimar does not mark the passage of dominion from the Britons to the Saxons following Gormund's Donation of Loegria to the Saxons – since the latter is literally a "non-event" in the *Estoire*. In fact, Gaimar does not follow the First Variant redactor either in this case by dramatically marking the passage at all, let alone placing it following Gormund's Donation. Instead, as we've seen in the prologue, Gaimar refers to the growing number of descendants of Hengist and how the swell of population from the Saxon lands came to influence the name of the land of "Engeland" (l. 32). Rather than a dramatic event, such as Gormund's Donation, Gaimar claims that a gradual but relentless influx of the foreign population effected the passage of dominion, as if imperceptibly, until it was impossible to not notice.[43]

In terms of "highlights" of early British history in the *Estoire*, while the earlier coming of Christianity to Britain (from at least the third century) receives no attention from Gaimar, he does devote a few lines to Augustine's arrival to convert the English (597 AD), which he says he found in the written record as having occurred "six hundred and five years" after the birth of Jesus (1021–22). Although he provides no details of the Britons' resistance to the prelate from either a British or English perspective, he does write a few lines about Mellitus and Justin, the two bishops ordained by Augustine. Gaimar remarks that the prelate created and maintained peace, having "given a firm undertaking, in the form of a prophecy, that 'any Britons in this country who deliberately

---

43   In the context of his genealogical aside on four of the seven kingdoms of the Heptarchy – interrupting his narrative on Cerdic – Gaimar explains how the English, *les Engleis*, got their name, again dominating largely by press of population, but regardless of the mechanisms of their arrival, ultimately all "descendants of this royal line" could be traced back to Woden: "Beldeg was of Woden's stock, and from this line Horsa and Hengest were born. From this same line came the peoples who were subsequently called the West Saxons, the South Saxons, the East Saxons, and the Middle Saxons. But because Hengest and Horsa, and after their deaths Cerdic, who came here to this country and frequently made war here, were descendants of this royal line, these people and their noblemen, in addition to those who had been born in the country named Angle ["nez del païs ki Ange ad nun" 853], were all called English" (Short, ed. and trans., ll. 840–54). See also nn. 20 and 24–26 on Gaimar's various portrayals of English descent, and also Yorke who comments that "it would appear that by the time Bede wrote descent from Woden was a *sine qua non* for any family that wished to be considered as royal," as it was for the royal house of Kent in the *Historia Ecclesiastica* ("Anglo-Saxon Origin Myths," 27). While acknowledging Leckie's view that Gaimar seems to give primacy to the West Saxons in terms of the *adventus* via Cerdic, the passage noted above suggests as well that Gaimar saw all the English, regardless of who initially effected the *adventus*, as coming from the same stock, thus at least metaphorically presenting a "united front" in contrast to – or against, depending on one's perspective – the Britons and other groups on the island.

258 CHAPTER 4

break the truce will perish at the hands of the Saxons.' Thus the prophecy was accomplished and well and truly fulfilled" (1095–1102). Gaimar's portrayal of Augustine's mission is very minimalistic, certainly in comparison with at least three other approaches: 1) Bede's lengthy narrative devoted to the prelate (*HE* i.22–23–ii.4) and anti-Briton rhetoric; 2) Geoffrey's obvious distaste for what he viewed as Augustine's arrogance (§§188–89); and 3) Wace's ridiculing of the archbishop based on Dorchester legends (as will be seen below).

5   The Epilogue to the *Estoire des Engleis*

Although Gaimar does not mention Arthur or the Arthurian kingdom by name beyond the prologue, the longer epilogue refers to a network of sources, two in particular which pertain to Arthurian material, including "Walter Espec's book" borrowed from Robert of Gloucester which Robert allegedly had translated into Latin from the Welsh (and quite possibly an early draft of the *Historia Regum Britanniae*) and "the good book of Oxford," as well as the Washingborough book (a copy of the ASC, which he also calls the Winchester History) (though not Arthurian of course).[44] The shorter epilogue which Short prints as an Appendix is very conventional and does not contain references either to sources or to patrons of his own work, unlike the numerous details in the longer epilogue. He speculates that Gaimar may have written the longer epilogue with its plethora of details in response to objections to an earlier version, though he concludes that "there are no grounds for postulating that the shorter epilogue [with its sole mention of Queen Adeliza who commissioned a commemorative volume on King Henry I and its elimination of Constance fitz Gilbert, Walter Espec, Walter archdeacon of Oxford, and Robert of Gloucester] pre-dates the longer."[45] While these textual mysteries cannot be solved here, it remains without question that Gaimar's *Estoire des Engleis* presents at the very least a fascinating window onto the beginnings of vernacular historical writing and patronage in England in the first half of the twelfth century.

---

44   See Chapter 3, nn. 12, and 15–16 for discussions of these references as well as their relation to Geoffrey's vulgate and the First Variant. On the Washingborough book, see Short, "Gaimar's Epilogue and Geoffrey of Monmouth's *Liber vetustissimus*," esp. 328–33.

45   Short, ed. and trans., Appendix, 354–55. In addition to the references in the notes cited above, for Short's discussion of the two epilogues with reference to Gaimar's possible revisions and reissuing of his *Estoire*, see the Introduction (to Short's edition) where he asks, "Might an amplified and more explicit epilogue have perhaps been thought necessary to explain and justify the second edition that we postulate?" (xxx–xxxi, cited at xxx).

CHAPTER 5

Wace's *Roman de Brut*, Part 2

1   Wace's *Roman de Brut*: Organization of the Chapter

The discussion of this long, complex verse narrative will be broken down into several sections:

2 Foundation myth
   2.1   The Britons settle the land
   2.2   The giants
   2.3   The importance of language and the changing of names
   2.4   Brittany and the theme of ethnic separatism
3 The *Adventus Saxonum*
4 King Arthur
   4.1   Introduction
      4.1.1   Birth and rise to power
      4.1.2   Arthur's battles
         4.1.2.1   Arthur and the Scots
         4.1.2.2   The beginning of Arthur's foreign conquests
      4.1.3   The founding of the Round Table and more foreign conquests
      4.1.4   Organization and governance; Arthur's Plenary Court
      4.1.5   The Roman campaign and its context
      4.1.6   Arthur's last battle: The Battle of Camlann
         4.1.6.1   The "Breton Hope"
5 Gormund's donation and the passage of dominion; Gormund and Arthur as leaders
6 Augustine's conversion of the English
7 Cadwallader and the "Final Days"
8 Conclusion: The role of language, ethnic/cultural separatism, and the characterization of Arthur as insider/outsider, barbarian and civilizer

2   Foundation Myth

2.1   *The Britons Settle the Land*

If we can judge by preservation of the text, Wace's *Roman de Brut* appears to have been significantly more popular than Gaimar's *Estoire des Bretuns*, which

---

© KONINKLIJKE BRILL NV, LEIDEN, 2024 | DOI:10.1163/9789004691889_007

260   CHAPTER 5

has not yet been discovered, having been apparently eclipsed by the *Brut* in each of the four MSS where the *Estoire des Engleis* is found; the count of *Brut* manuscripts is currently nineteen complete or nearly complete copies, plus fifteen incomplete copies that survive either as extracts or as manuscript fragments, the most extensive preservation of an Old French historical narrative of the twelfth century.[1]

The *Brut* opens with an 8-line prologue declaring Wace's authorship and setting forth the general topic at hand: a history of the kings of England and their ancestors and descendants; the geographical description of the island with which Gildas, the *Historia Brittonum*, Bede, Henry of Huntingdon's *HA*, and the *HRB* all begin (with variations) is absent.[2] It is worth noting that Wace uses the word "Engleterre" already in line 4, although his primary focus for the

---

1   For full details of all the manuscripts known to him, see Ivor Arnold's account in *Le Roman de Brut de Wace*, 2 vols. (Paris: Société des anciens textes français, 1938–40), I, vii–xiv; for a more recent list (though without full manuscript details), see *Wace's Roman de Brut: A History of the British: Text and Translation*, trans. Judith Weiss (Exeter: University of Exeter Press, 1999; 2nd ed. 2002), 2nd ed., xxvii–xxviii [Weiss uses Arnold's edition in facing page (though without his extensive variants), but with numerous emendations to the text, all of which are recorded, in addition to her own notes on her translation and on the presentation of the text], and Appendix 1 below. The most recent manuscript discovery is that of a fragment containing an apparently not-too-faithful rendition of roughly the Arthurian section, ll. 9049–13680 (with lacunae) on the dorse (verso) of roll London, College of Arms 12/45A, a roll also containing a newly discovered anonymous *Brut*; see Ian Short, "Un *Roman de Brut* anglo-normand inédit," *Romania* 126 (2008): 273–95, and Appendix 2, n. 1, below. With the caveat that this list cannot be exhaustive (and noting that other resources will be referenced by topic), for additional interpretations of characteristics of some of the major manuscripts, see esp. Le Saux, *Companion*, 85–94 and eadem, "On Capitalization in Some Early Manuscripts of Wace's *Roman de Brut*," in *Arthurian Studies in Honour of P.J. C. Field*, ed. Bonnie Wheeler, Arthurian Studies 57 (Woodbridge: Boydell and Brewer, 2004), 29–47; Jane Bliss and Judith Weiss, "The 'J' Manuscript of Wace's *Brut*," *Medium Aevum* 81 (2012): 222–48; and Judith Weiss, "The Text of Wace's *Brut* and How it is Treated by its Earliest Manuscripts," in *L'Historia regum Britannie et les "Bruts" en Europe, II: Production, circulation, réception*, 83–101. Although Wace's *Brut* is often considered an Anglo-Norman text, Wace was a Norman and wrote in a "Norman-based *Schriftsprache*" (on Wace's language, Ian Short, private communication). Cf. Dean and Boulton's invaluable compendium, item 2: "Composed by a Norman, this poem of 14866 lines belongs to Anglo-Norman literature by its content, its influence, and the number of its Anglo-Norman manuscripts" (*Anglo-Norman Literature: A Guide to Texts and Manuscripts*, 2).

2   It may have been easier for Wace to eliminate the description of the English countryside – though by doing so, he also eliminates any list of the peoples who occupied the island – than for Bede or Geoffrey for example, not being nostalgically tied to the "homeland"; this is not to say that that the *Brut* is devoid of images of natural beauty and abundance, but that an introductory tone-setting description is absent. For suggestive analyses of romantic pastoralism and the role of the English countryside in the formation of English and/or British identity, see especially David Lowenthal, "The Island Garden: English Landscape and British Identity," in *History, Nationhood and the Question of Britain*, ed. Helen Brocklehurst and Robert Phillips (Houndmills and New York: Palgrave Macmillan, 2004), 137–48 and Christine Berberich,

WACE'S ROMAN DE BRUT, PART 2   261

work is a history of the Britons, and he often uses "Bretaine" as well, at times apparently interchangeably.[3] His history of the Britons is though, not surprisingly, first a history of kings (and their immediate supporters or enemies), and very secondarily a social history, with the social aspect almost always revolving around the leaders, though issues of group identity, assimilation and separation are seen beyond the elites (as for example, the influence of the Round Table can be seen more broadly).

The contents of the *Brut* itself fall into roughly six topic areas:

1. Aeneas's flight to the founding of New Troy in Britain (9–1250) (Prologue 1–8);
2. Brutus's reign, his descendants' reign through the death of Belinus (who defeated Rome with his brother, Brennius) (1251–3240);
3. Settling of Ireland by Pantelous and his people, the arrival of the Romans, through the Romans' departure (3241–6258);
4. Start of the house of Constantine, death of Constant at the hands of the Picts, who make Vortigern king, arrival of Hengist and Horsa through the conception of Arthur and defeat and death of Octa and Eosa (6259–9004);
5. Death of Uther and succession of Arthur, Arthur's reign and conquests, Morvid helps the Britons defeat the Romans, Mordred usurps the throne and Arthur returns to Britain, through his last battle (9005–13298);
6. The reigns of Constantine, Cunan, Vortipore and Malgo; Gormund's invasion, the siege of Cirencester, and the Donation; Augustine's conversion of the English and the slaughter of the monks at Bangor; Cadwan and Elfrid share the kingdom (the former south of the Humber and the latter north of the Humber), followed by conflicts between their sons Chadwalein (Caduallo/Cadwallo, next to last king of Britain) and Edwin, wars with the Saxons; the famine; through the death of Cadwallader last king of Britain; Yvor and Yni cross the sea back to Britain from Brittany, and rule the Britons who now live in Wales and are called Welsh; Athelstan the first Englishman to rule all England except Wales and Cornwall (13299–14858) (Epilogue 14859–66).[4]

"'I Was Meditating about England': The Importance of Rural England for the Construction of 'Englishness'," in *History, Nationhood and the Question of Britain*, 375–85.

3   Cf. Alan MacColl: "Wace omitted Geoffrey's opening description of Britain, supplying instead his own introduction, which instructs us to read what follows as the history of England. He will explain, he says, 'who they were, and whence they came, who once upon a time were the rulers of England (Engleterre).' The result is a reorientation of the whole narrative" ("The Meaning of 'Britain' in Medieval and Early Modern England," 255–56).

4   This schema differs from Thorpe's thematic divisions of Geoffrey's *Historia* (see opening pages of Chapter 2 above) in that Thorpe divides his section four "The House of Constantine" into two parts, thereby creating sections four and six, separated by section five containing the Prophecies of Merlin. Since the *Brut* does not contain the Prophecies of Merlin, I have not

262   CHAPTER 5

Thus, the narrative proper begins with a description of Aeneas's flight from Troy, and a reminder of Helen's capture by Paris and the Greeks' destruction of Troy as their revenge; the entire Trojan section (11–1250, Aeneas's flight to the founding of New Troy) is told in extraordinary detail, and without an overview of the history and geography of the island, which tends to put even more focus on the Trojans and their role.[5] Although we will never know what Gaimar's treatment of the Trojans and the early Britons might have been in the *Estoire des Bretuns*, we can say that the Wace's approach toward the evolution of places, peoples, and languages was very different from Gaimar's, judging from the latter's description in the prologue of the *Estoire des Engleis* of how England became England, and how her inhabitants became English. Broadly speaking, Gaimar asserts the "overwhelm by numbers" theory of the transition from the Britons to the Anglo-Saxons in his prologue, but elsewhere he uses political markers such as the arrival of Cerdic and his battles against the Britons, whereas Wace tends to create more a picture of interweaving of populations, metamorphosis, and assimilation, sometimes conveyed in his etymological passages – though this is not consistently the case by any means.[6]

---

followed Thorpe. See nn. 55, 160, and 178 below on Wace's inclusion of other isolated prophecies and his omission of the book of Merlin's Prophecies.

5   Among the sources on the Trojans and Wace, including on *translatio imperii* and the Trojan foundation myth, see especially Françoise Le Saux, *Companion*, 102–10; despite the amount of detail, according to Le Saux, Wace tends to suppress references to the Trojans' violence (*Companion*, 280); Douglas Kelly, "The Trojans in the Writings of Wace and Benoît de Sainte-Maure," in *People and Texts: Relationships in Medieval Literature: Studies Presented to Erik Kooper*, ed. Thea Summerfield and Keith Busby, Costerus New Series 166 (Amsterdam and New York: Rodopi, 2007), 123–41; Dominique Boutet, "De la *translatio imperii* à la *finis saeculi*: progrès et decadence dans la pensée de l'histoire au Moyen Age," in *Progrès, reaction, decadence dans l'occident médiéval*, ed. Emmanuèle Baugartner and Laurence Harf-Lancner (Geneva: Droz, 2003), 37–48; Laurence Mathey-Maille, "Mythe troyen et histoire romaine: de Geoffrey de Monmouth au *Brut* de Wace," in *Entre fiction et histoire: Troie et Rome au Moyen Age*, ed. Emmanuèle Baumgartner and Laurence Harf-Lancner (Paris: Presses de la Sorbonne Nouvelle, 1997), 113–25; Hélène Tétrel, "Trojan Origins and the Use of the *Aeneid* and Related Sources in the Old Icelandic *Brut*," *The Journal of English and Germanic Philology* 109.4 (2010): 490–514, esp. 497, 499, 503–4, 508; and Carol Bubon Kearns, "The Influence of the Trojan Myth on National Identity as Shaped in the Frankish and British Trojan-origin myths and the *Roman de Brut* and the *Roman de Troie*," upub. Ph.D. dissertation, University of Florida 2002, esp. chapters 2 and 3.

6   Wace's emphasis on the evolution of language as seen here in the foundation myth section, on similar material in 3739–90, and elsewhere in the *Brut*, stands in contrast to Gaimar's overall approach which emphasizes less metamorphosis and evolution – he certainly doesn't share Wace's fascination for etymology – while calling attention to more disjunctive changes such as political landmarks (though rarely with chronology); see also Lesley Johnson who notes the ways that Wace uses etymological discourse to emphasize both political and

WACE'S ROMAN DE BRUT, PART 2   263

Although my emphasis here is on the effects – and potential goals – of the composite of details in the *Brut*, and not on the strict identification of sources, it is important to point out Neil Wright's findings that Wace, whose *Brut* is our "earliest witness to the First Variant version," used the vulgate text "extensively in the second half of his poem" while "in the first half ... he employed the vulgate very seldom, relying almost exclusively on the First Variant."[7] The

cultural continuities and discontinuities ("Etymologies, Genealogies, and Nationalities (again)," in *Concepts of National Identity in the Middle Ages*, ed. Simon Forde, Lesley Johnson, and Alan V. Murray, Leeds Texts and Monographs, new series 14 (Leeds: School of English, University of Leeds, 1995), 125–36; on language change in Wace's *Brut*, see also Margaret Lamont, "When are Saxons 'Ænglisc'? Language and Readerly Identity in Laȝamon's *Brut*," in *Reading Laȝamon's Brut*, esp. pp. 300–2. On the importance of metamorphosis, evolution of language and groups, and naming including place names in Wace, see Douglas Kelly, "The Trojans in the Writings of Wace and Benoît de Sainte-Maure," and Joanna Bellis, "Mapping the National Narrative: Place-Name Etymology in Laȝamon's *Brut* and its Sources," in *Reading Laȝamon's Brut*, 321–42. Bellis argues that for Geoffrey, Wace, and Laȝamon, "etymologizing the landscape was a means of giving Britain a glorious and self-authenticating history, independently from their problematic sources" (321), finding that "Laȝamon in particular relates to the national myth very differently from Wace, his source, identifying with the conquered rather than the conquerors, history's losers rather than its victors"; according to Bellis, unlike Wace, who used etymologies as "certifiers of the veracity of his account" Laȝamon's "etymological truth-claims function more as elegies for the erosion of the glory of the national myth, and as prophecies for its ultimate reinstatement" (322); Bellis also suggests that in Wace "etymology is not static but fluid, an unfinished and developing story rather than a closed master narrative," (336) but adds that "Wace's employment of the etymological truth-claim is not to [as Michelle Warren has put it] 'recuperate defeated legitimacies' but to 'remember old forms only in order to complete history's linear progression and thereby the historian's conquest of the past'" (*History on the Edge*, 156, cited by Bellis on 336); while for some scholars admittedly, the idea of "complet[ing] history's linear progression" might sound more like an indication of a codification of the past rather than the fluidity and evolving movement Bellis seeks to convey, each of these perspectives is valuable. More specifically on Wace's fascination for etymology, see Laurence Mathey-Maille, "La pratique de l'étymologie dans le *Roman de Brut* de Wace," in *"Plaist vos oïr bone cançon vallant": mélanges de langue et de littérature médiévales offerts à François Suard*, ed. Dominique Boutet, Marie-Madeleine Castellani, François Ferrand and Aimé Petit, Université Charles de Gaulle – Lille 3, Collection Travaux et Recherches, 2 vols. (Lille: SEGES, 1999), II, 579–86, eadem, "L'Étymologie dans le *Roman de Rou* de Wace," in *"De sens rassis": Essays in Honor of Rupert T. Pickens*, ed. Keith Busby, Bernard Guidot, and Logan Whalen, Faux Titre 259, (Amsterdam and New York: Rodopi, 2005), 403–14, and on the connections between etymology and geography in Wace's chronicles, eadem, "La géographie anglo-normande dans le *Roman de Brut* et le *Roman de Rou* de Wace," in *Troisième journée d'études anglo-normandes. Adaptation, parodie et autres emplois*, ed. Michel Zink (Paris: Académie des inscriptions et belles-lettres, 2014), 45–54.

7 FV ed., II, cii.; cf. Laurence Mathey-Maille who argues against strictly dividing the *Brut*'s two main sources into vulgate toward the end and FV toward the beginning (I express my agreement with her, Chapter 4, n. 2 above). However useful Wright's generalization may be when we want to think of the text in its broader outlines, though, it does not always hold true,

264   CHAPTER 5

first section of the work, from Aeneas's travels to Italy to the founding of New
Troy (11–1250), traces the wanderings of the Trojans, who, under Brutus's leadership, choose to become migrants to a foreign land, to take their chances
on a better but unknown future, rather than creating potentially unending
enmity with the Greeks. Soon after their departure from Greece, they come to
a deserted island, where Brutus dreams of the goddess Diana, who foretells of
the island of Albion, beyond France, across the sea. They continue, and when
they reach Spain:

La troverent a un rivage	There, along the banks of a river, they found
Des Troïens de lur lignage	Trojans from their line,
Quatre granz generaciuns,	Four whole generations,
Que Antenor, uns des barons	Whom Antenor, one of the barons
Amena de Troie fuitis	Brought from Troy as fugitives
Quant li Greu les orent conquis.	When the Greeks had defeated them.[8]

(773–78)

---

as Wright himself demonstrates, if we are envisaging Wace using a "pure" vulgate text and
a "pure" First Variant, switching back and forth at will. More plausible, based on Wright's
meticulous work on the FV MSS, and intersections with Wace, is that, "Wace's poem points
to the revised First Variant text represented by group-DES already being in existence by 1155,
but in a more complete form than is found in the extant witnesses" (civ), the "more complete
form" being what Wright refers to as Wace's "source text (w)". Wright nuances the discussion by adding that "the combined evidence of c [Cardiff Library, South Glamorgan Central
Library, 2.611]....., a conflate vulgate [§107–77, §§209–end] and First Variant MS – with FV
in §§5–108, and §§178–208 only, and even in those sections heavily conflated with the vul-
gate] and Wace's source text (w) thus shows that by 1155 the First Variant version had already
been revised at least twice" (cxiv); Wright also concludes that "MS c, therefore, agrees now
with DES, now with aHR" (cv), which makes it all the more difficult – if not impossible – to
pin down definitively which version Wace used, though we can still talk about readings that
are more prevalent in vulgate MSS and which are FV-related. Thus Wace's source may have
been a First Variant manuscript with significant vulgate sections or interpolations, and most
likely, without any identifying attribution (see Chapter 3, n. 13 above), since it is difficult to
believe that he used two different manuscripts simultaneously; see also Chapter 3, nn. 52–53,
on Wace's version of Brutus's parentage which resembles the vulgate (Brutus was Aeneas's
great-grandson) (not the FV aHR where Brutus was Aeneas's grandson), and the possibility of
his having used "a text of the DES-type," i.e., a FV with vulgate "corrections" in places (Wright,
ed., II, civ). In general, Wace ultimately arranged his details from the interlacing of what he
had before him, and mixed in oral sources, among others. As in the case of many Latin historical texts of his era, Wace's *Roman de Brut* was a work of synthesis.

8   All citations of Wace's *Brut* are from Arnold's edition; the translations are mine, unless otherwise indicated.

Many of these other Trojans join Brutus, for the remainder of the voyage, along with their leader, Corineus, who was "mult granz, / Hardiz e forz come gaianz" (781–82; "very tall, bold, and strong as a giant"), a fortuitous combination of qualities, as one sees later in the Trojans' encounter with the giants in Britain. Up until this point, Wace uses many more "personal" details than Gaimar, drawing a more intimate portrait, including for example Brutus's friendship with Corineus. In general terms, except for the large "asides" which do touch on the growing thematic of love – the story of Haveloc the Dane, Buern Bucecarle, and Edgar and Elstrid – Gaimar's narrative is more reminiscent of annals than Wace's.[9]

Accompanied by Corineus, Brutus and the Trojans make their way toward Brittany; here Wace adds one of his typical toponymic references, that it wasn't yet called Brittany but Armorica (795–96), already signaling his interest in transitions and marking of transitions through changing of place names. Brutus and his group land where the Loire meets the sea. Interestingly, the First Variant redactor borrows from Bede's description of England the element that the Britons first migrated to the island from Armorica, a statement that contradicts the vulgate's Trojan origin story, in which the last battle the Trojans fight before leaving Gaul was near Tours where Turnus is buried (Bede,

---

9 Some might find Wace's text more reminiscent of romance, but I tend to agree with Le Saux who writes that "the prevailing tone is more epic than courtly," echoing Hans-Erich Keller, "Wace continue bien plus la tradition des chansons de geste ... qu'il n'est le précurseur de la littérature courtoise" (*Companion*, 80 and n. 2) (Keller, *Étude descriptive sur le vocabulaire de Wace*, Deutsche Akademie der Wissenschaften zu Berlin, Veröffentlichungen des Instituts für Romanische Sprachwissenschaft 7, Berlin: Akademie-Verlag, 1953, 14). In my view, while the tone may be epic, the text itself is historiographical, or was at least intended to be considered as history. For various perspectives on how to classify this text, see Peter Damian-Grint on the largely historical intent of the text, including a very useful review of scholarship on this subject (*New Historians*, 53–56); see also Laurence Mathey-Maille, "De l'*Historia Regum Britanniae* de Geoffroy de Monmouth au *Roman de Brut* de Wace: la naissance du roman," in *Le Travail sur le modèle*, ed. Danielle Buschinger, Médiévales 16 (Amiens: Presses du Centre d'Études Médiévales, 2002), 5–10, who postulates that the *Brut* "vacille entre la geste, l'historiographie et le roman" (7) and concludes that it should be called a "roman historique" (10); see also eadem, "Le *Roman de Brut* de Wace: une œuvre inclassable?" in *L'Œuvre inclassable: Actes édités par Marianne Bouchardon and Michèle Guéret-Laferté* (Actes du colloque 18) (Rouen: University of Rouen, CÉRÉdI, 2016), 1–6 http://ceredi.labos.univ-rouen.fr/public/?l-oeuvre-inclassable.html. On Wace's view of historical writing as an "inexact science" given that historians can never locate the exact "truth" of events, and also must portray what they find though the imperfect medium of language, see my "Le rôle de la *persona* – ou la voix auctoriale – dans la *Conception Nostre Dame*, le *Roman de Brut* et le *Roman de Rou* de Wace," in *Le Style de Wace: Actes du colloque de la* SERAM, *Jersey juillet 2019*, ed. Denis Hüe, Françoise Laurent, Michel Vital Le Bossé and Laurence Mathey-Maille (Orléans: Éditions Paradigme, 2020), 51–71, esp. 69–71 and n. 34.

HE 1.436–437). This particular mention of Armorica in the FV appears to be strictly a borrowing from Bede's introductory description: that is, there is no reference to Armorica in the pertinent chapters of the FV where this section of the narrative is elaborated (§§17–20); there, the Trojans set sail for Britain from Aquitaine as in the vulgate text.

In one of what appears to us to be Wace's numerous attempts to reconcile the First Variant and the vulgate – whether he found those two versions either not readily distinguishable in a mixed/conflate manuscript such as the Cardiff MS., or more obviously separate in two physically different sources, we can never know – Wace has the Trojans *head* for Brittany, naming the geographical point "where the Loire meets the sea" as the Trojans' point of landing after having left Spain on their way to Brittany (793–800). However, in the *Brut*, Brittany itself is not the site of the Trojans' last Continental campaign before sailing to Britain, nor does the narrative show them spending any time there. Thus, Wace makes a partial nod to the suggestion in the FV's description of Britain while at the same time following the major outline of the narrative in FV §§17–20, which in this instance mirrors the vulgate where the Trojans leave for Britain from Aquitaine, not Brittany.[10]

In the vulgate, following their defeat of the Poitevins, the Trojans "ravaged almost all Aquitaine in this way" (*HRB*, 19.394–95), "hacking and killing" (§20.442–43), and proceed to set up camp on the spot where Brutus will eventually build Tours – the vulgate says "according to Homer" (*HRB*, §19. 396) – named after the valiant Turnus, Brutus's nephew, who is ultimately buried there after the Trojans' defeat of the French (*Galli* – Gauls) (§20.433–34, 436–37); for this information, the First Variant version is almost identical to the vulgate (§19–20). On the other hand, with his characteristic thoroughness, Wace opens a parentheses, and instead of saying that Brutus had a camp built where the Trojans waited for two days for the Poitevin king Guffarius to bring French reinforcements (*les Franceis*), Wace shows that the very beginnings of construction of the city has started – Brutus instructs that a castle be built on top of the hill – the poet adding that "it was through the work of these people that Tours first came into being, Tours the city, which is still there today" (941–43; "Par l'ovrainne de cele gent / Out Turs primes comencement, / Turs la cité, ki encor dure"); in Wace Brutus and his troops remain there waiting twelve days (not two).

---

10   Where Geoffrey has apparently located the mouth of the Loire (Tatlock, *Legendary History*, 98).

WACE'S ROMAN DE BRUT, PART 2 267

Following the battle of Tours and the defeat of the French, the Trojans leave for Britain, where they find no inhabitants except giants;[11] in the *Brut*, "En cele ille gaianz aveit, / Nule gent altre n'i maneit (1063–4; "There were giants on this island; no one else lived there").[12] Wace, true to form, tells us that he cannot provide us with all the names of the giants because he only knows one of them, Gogmagog, their leader (1067–68).[13] Wace proceeds to recount Corineus's

11　In Reeve's critical edition of the vulgate, we read "quae a nemine, exceptis paucis gigantibus, inhabitatur" (§21.453–54; "it had no inhabitants save for a few giants," i.e., not strictly speaking humans). In Wright's edition based on the Bern MS., the "giants" are initially referred to as "gigantic humans" ("que a nemine exceptis paucis hominibus gigantibus," §21), but then later as giants, Gogmagog having the stature of twelve cubits (cf. Reeve, ed., §21.470). The initial variant in the Bern MS. implies that the original inhabitants were people – discounted though they were – bearing numerous implications for their eventual elimination in Wace's *Brut*.

12　While the phrase "nule gent altre" might imply that Wace considered the giants *genz*, that is people, it is also possible to read this line as "No group other than the giants lived there," guaranteeing that the Britons would become the native people; however, since giants were not often perceived as people, why they needed to be eliminated is unclear unless to remove any competition at all for resources; on the complexities of the portrayals of giants, their "humanity" as well as their "inhumanity" and marginalization, see Huot, *Outsiders*, 1–25. Weiss translates 1064 as "No one else lived there" (p. 29).

13　Wace's thoroughness, his penchant for filling in details, and his love of lists, all fall under the category of what Brian Woledge terms "Wace's love of precision" ("Notes on Wace's Vocabulary," *Modern Language Review* 46.1 (1951): 16–30, cited at 26); similarly, M. Malkiel Jirmounsky points out, that in the *Brut*, "motifs are often developed through concrete details, often painstakingly, in such a way that 'toutes les possibilités sont énumérées' ('all eventualities are listed')" ("Essai des analyses des procédés littéraires de Wace," *Revue des Langues Romanes* 63 (1925–26): 261–96, 269, cited in *Wace, The Hagiographical Works: The Conception Nostre Dame and the Lives of St Margaret and St Nicholas,* Jean Blacker, Glyn S. Burgess (trans.), and Amy V. Ogden, Studies in Medieval and Reformation Traditions 169, Text and Sources 3 (Leiden: Brill, 2013), 48); see also Weiss, xx–xxi; and cf. Alex Delusier, "L'Illusion stylisque du réalisme dans le *Roman de Brut* de Wace," Academia, 2020 https://www.academia.edu/43191879/Lillusion_stylis tique_du_r%C3%A9alisme_dans_le_Roman_de_Brut_de_Wace. On Wace's use of the "ne sai *topos*" in the *Brut* and the *Rou*, see esp. Danièle James-Raoul, *La Parole empêchée dans la littérature arthurienne* (Paris: Honoré Champion, 1997), 281–82; Penny Eley and Philip E. Bennett who observe that "statements beginning 'ne sai' are in fact the commonest form of authorial /narratorial intervention in the *Rou* as a whole" ("The Battle of Hastings according to Gaimar, Wace and Benoît: Rhetoric and Politics," *Nottingham Medieval Studies* 43 (1999): 47–78, 68 n. 52); and Peter Damian-Grint, who suggests that in the *Rou* in particular, Wace "somewhat perversely appears to base his explicit authorisation very largely, indeed almost exclusively on claiming ignorance," associating ignorance and even silence with being truthful, as if using a "'silence rather than untruth' topos" ("Truth, Trust and Evidence in the Anglo-Norman *Estoire*," *Anglo-Norman Studies XVIII. Proceedings of the Battle Conference 1995*, ed. Christopher Harper-Bill, Woodbridge: Boydell and Brewer, 1996, 63–78, cited at 74–75). On these and other topoi, see also Jean Blacker,

268   CHAPTER 5

single combat with Gogmagog, ending in the latter's defeat, as he fell to his death into the ocean off Cornwall; here Wace follows the FV ("Locus ergo ille nomen ex casu illius sortitus est usque in presentem diem"; That spot is named after his fall even to the present day, §21.3), without naming the spot ("Since then that place had the name of the giant who fell headlong there"; 1167–68 "Li leus out puis le nun e a / Del gaiant qu'illuec trebucha" 1167–68). The vulgate refers to the place by name as "Gogmagog's Leap" ("Locus autem ille, nomen ex praecipitatione gigantis adeptus, Saltus Goemagog usque in praesentem diem uocatur," "The place took its name from the giant's plunge and is still called Goemagog's Leap," §21.487–89).[14]

2.2   The Giants

Wace however makes a radical departure from all his sources (that is, those sources of which we are aware), when he reports the elimination of all the giants. The vulgate reports that all giants were chased into caves except Goemagog (§21.456–57) prior to Brutus's partitioning of the land; then Goemagog arrives with twenty giants, whom the Trojans kill and Corineus fights Goemagog. The material is similar in the First Variant, except that the partitioning of the land takes place after the single combat. In Wace, there is no report of chasing of the giants into caves; the twenty giants accompany Gogmagog out of caves and are killed.

However, Wace goes even further, presenting what could be viewed as a genocide, a situation which at least for modern readers does not add prestige to the Trojans' "civilized profile," nor engender sympathy for the Britons when they become the colonized later in the text. Immediately after Gogmagog's fall, Wace writes "Quant la terre fud neïee / Des gaianz e de lur lignee" (1169–70; "When the land was cleansed of the giants and their line").[15] If "e de lur lignee"

"Narrative Decisions and Revisions in the *Roman de Rou*," in *Maistre Wace: A Celebration, Proceedings of the Colloquium held in Jersey 10–12 September 2004*, ed. Glyn S. Burgess and Judith Weiss (St. Helier: Société Jersiaise, 2006), 55–71.

14   Since Wace is so fascinated by names, it is likely that if he had seen the name of the place in his source, he would have included it; it may not have been in his source, nor had he heard it in a legend.

15   Interestingly, one manuscript avoids the genocide image altogether, as lines 1169–70 are missing in H (Paris, BnF fr. 1450, 13th c., an unusual MS containing four complete and one fragment of Chrétien's romances and the First Continuation of the *Perceval* interpolated between lines 9798 and 9799 of the *Brut*); in MS. G lines 1169–70 are missing altogether, while G adds more details in twenty-two lines between 1168 and 1169, narrating how the giants were chased into the mountains and were slaughtered there, such that not one was left standing "Onc ne lor eschapa un pié" ("Not a single one survived"; the twenty-first line added by G, Arnold ed., I, p. 66; see Weiss, p. 30, n. 6). Other MSS have similar renditions

WACE'S ROMAN DE BRUT, PART 2   269

were not added, we might be able to interpret the killing of the giants as referring to the twenty who had accompanied Gogmagog, but the thoroughness of the line being wiped out is inescapable: there were no more giants hiding anywhere who could reproduce and carry their line forward. Once this cleansing has taken place, the Trojans who have now become Britons, have also become ersatz natives, as if they were the original inhabitants; the slate has been – quite literally – wiped clean.[16]

That a quasi-idyllic passage on the partitioning of the land, cultivation, building of towns, naming, defining of languages should follow immediately upon an account of what amounts to ethnic cleansing is even more ironic, and certainly less easy to justify for modern sensibilities, but for Wace, this is a passage where the importance is not that of renewal or prosperity of the land (although those are important), but of native status, or original birth: since the giants were not considered legitimate inhabitants, i.e., worthy of Britain, because they were not "really people" – after all, Diana had promised Brutus and the Trojans an

---

     of what has been reported by Arnold and retained by Weiss (though the latter does not note the variants here): 1169: where Arnold and Weiss both have "neïee", C has "finee" [When the land was *finished* with the giants, and their lineage]; S has "delivree" [When the land was *delivered* from the giants and their lineage]; and J, A, and KG have variations of "neïee" – "nesiee," neie," and "nestoiee" respectively, R having "vuidée" "emptied" (variants for line 1169, Arnold ed., I, p. 66). For a chart of the codices containing the *Brut* (and other texts), see Appendix 1 below; see also Chapter 6, n. 14 on the Royal *Brut* (MS. B) which reports that Brutus's people killed nineteen of the twenty giants they encountered except "Geomagog," who soon perishes at the hands of Corineus at "Gogmagog's Leap," saying nothing about any others (994–1000).

16   At the risk of oversimplifying, it can be said that giants in this period were not ordinarily considered fully human beings, although they were often depicted as having human or human-like features. Nonetheless, the complete wiping out of any group presented as an acceptable practice is disconcerting at the least, certainly for modern sensibilities. Sylvia Huot writes that "the elimination of giants, in short, is essential to the process of establishing civilization and furthering God's plan, whether in the Holy Land or in Britain. Whereas Britain under the giants remained in a state of wilderness, Brutus and his men divide it up, according to a system of feudal government, build cities, and 'improve' the land through agricultural management. Tellingly, neither Geoffrey of Monmouth nor Wace addressed the question of where the British giants came from or how they might have lived before the arrival of the Trojan settlers" (*Outsiders*, 37–38). On images of the monstrous and the role of monsters in Galfridian material, see Jeffrey Cohen, *Of Giants*, esp. 39–61, Sylvia Huot, *Outsiders*, 37, 42–43, 65–66, 70–74, and 141–42. Especially pertinent to remember is Cohen's observation with regard to Geoffrey but it certainly holds for Wace here, that "the irony, of course, is that the Celtic ('British') peoples whose history Geoffrey is writing stand exactly in this aboriginal position to the Anglo-Saxons who 'settle' the island – that is, in the preconquest account of English history, the Celts occupy the place of the Galfridian giants, the invading Germanic tribes that of the glorified British" (34–35).

270 CHAPTER 5

empty island. As Barbara Yorke has observed as a general pattern among more "innocent" origin legends ("innocent," that is, in which mixed groups tried to justify their unity of origin, not where one completely eliminated the other), "what origin legends did in essence was provide a new start ... the mongrel nature of new regimes was disguised by a myth of common origins in which old identities could be conveniently subsumed."[17] However, Wace goes further, and rather than having the giants and their progeny subsumed into the general population, he makes sure they are all wiped out; Wace uses the past participle "neïee" which means "washed away, wiped out, drowned" or "cleansed".[18] It is as if in Wace, the Trojans wanted to make sure that they had firmly established themselves, bringing civilization to Britain, taking no chances that members of an anterior group remained to make claims or compete for natural resources.[19] For Wace it was essential that the Britons be the first peoples of the island, and that they only displaced non-human mythical creatures.[20]

---

17   "Anglo-Saxon Origin Legends," 15–16.

18   Though see manuscript variants in n. 15 above.

19   For a text meant on some levels to foster sympathy for a downtrodden group, i.e., the Britons, this passage as it stands in the *Brut* is regrettably reminiscent of the mythology surrounding Columbus's "discovery" of the Americas, which substantially if not completely discounts the Indigenous populations. Although the Indigenous in the West Indies were not wiped out through a calculated program of genocide, the North American Indigenous populations often did not fare much better, for numerous reasons; see Dunbar-Ortiz, *An Indigenous Peoples' History of the United States*, esp. pp. 45–55 on the myth of "the pristine wilderness" and Ania Loomba, *Colonialism/Postcolonialism*, esp. pp. 115–17. Perhaps because Michelle Warren's characterization of Geoffrey's *Historia* as a portrayal of "the forgotten empire of a marginalized people in reaction to an urgently present colonial dynamic" (*History on the Edge*, 116 ff.) is often so fitting, we are surprised to see references to what amounts to genocide and ethnic separatism perpetrated by the Britons earlier in the narrative, that is, before the stage where they themselves are exterminated or driven out, depending on which narrative one refers to.

20   Though as we see below, there is another context in which the Britons are not innocent in the realm of colonizing others, when they completely displace the native Bretons, to become the "legitimate" Bretons, i.e., the first Britons to inhabit Brittany. Nonetheless, it was very important to Wace that the Britons be the first group to inhabit Albion because to him, native primacy had a stronger claim to political domination than the claims of outsiders. This position is admittedly complicated, however, by the fact that Wace was a Norman historian writing for the Anglo-Norman, Anglo-Angevin elite(s), that the Normans were relative parvenus in mid-twelfth-century England, conquering parvenus at that, who imposed many aspects of their linguistic, political and social culture upon the English (British and those of Germanic descent alike), expecting and demanding compliance, if not assimilation. There is an additional connection between native primacy and Wace's Normanness: in the *Roman de Rou*, Wace makes a point to talk about his origins, telling his audience that he was from the isle of Jersey, that he was educated in Caen, and that he continued his studies in [the île de] France before beginning his career as a writer

(III, 5297–5312). That he would enumerate the steps in his biographical journey suggests that his origins are essential to his perception of his relationship to his craft and to the world. Wace was an island boy made good, come to the big city as a step in his training, and eventually making his way to the biggest city, the center of civilization (though here again this is tricky because Wace rarely has a good word to say about the French in either the *Brut* or the *Rou*). He was apparently very conscious of his insular origins, and perhaps his sensitivity toward the marginalized and innocent victims is in part due to his sense of origins, a possible pride in originary status, while at the same time inalterably an outsider looking in. In addition, in the *Rou*, Wace shows a clear preference for the rights of eldest sons, particularly those of Robert Curthose, whom Wace viewed as wrongly disinherited by his brother, Henry I. While a preference for primogeniture as a criterion for inheritance can be seen on the one hand as an aristocratic attitude, it can also be read as a preference for the person who "got there first" (as in the case of Robert; among other sources, see Françoise Le Saux, "'La geste des trois fils Guillaume': Henry I in Wace's *Roman de Rou*," *Reading Medieval Studies* 12, 2008: 191–207, and Charity Urbanski, *Writing History for the King, Writing History for the King: Henry II and the Politics of Vernacular Historiography*, Ithaca, NY and London: Cornell University Press, 2013, 211). On Wace's self-revelations in the *Rou*, see Blacker, "Narrative Decisions and Revisions in the *Roman de Rou*," in *Maistre Wace: A Celebration,* ed. Burgess and Weiss, 55–71, and eadem "Le rôle de la *persona* – ou la voix auctoriale – dans la *Conception Nostre Dame*, le *Roman de Brut* et le *Roman de Rou*"). For differing perspectives, see David Hult who argues that "authorial self-consciousness in [medieval] texts entails neither self-depiction nor self-expression of a personal kind ... especially when such expression is taken to be an end in itself. I do not mean to say that statements of individual condition are excluded but that they ... can take the form of a justification for the act of writing; a statement about where the materials were found and sometimes how; a mention of artistic criterial; or an address to the author's patron ... Authorial naming is not biographical as we use the term; as a literary act, it performs a function within the broader context of literary transmission. By naming himself, the author identifies, justifies, and distinguishes his work from that of others." Hult goes on to say specifically about Wace that "Wace's statements about this own poverty evoke the larger question of the economic constraints governing the production of literary and historical works, aspects of patronage, and even the moral virtue known as *largesse*" ("Author/Narrator/Speaker: The Voice of Authority in Chrétien's *Charrete*," 80). Although Peter Damian-Grint would like to qualify Hult's remarks regarding the conventionality of authorial self-consciousness by adding that "nevertheless, the different ways in which authorial interjections are used do reflect different modes of authorial presence" and can be useful particularly to historians for that reason ("Truth, Trust and Evidence in the Anglo-Norman *Estoire*," 65), he expresses both the view that many of Wace's self-revelations may be set-pieces used to "authorize" his work, while underscoring their importance and utility nonetheless as a possible window onto audience expectations in the period: "There is in fact no evidence that Wace is any more independent and critical than any other twelfth-century historian. His highly self-conscious self-presentation as a scholar who carefully weighs up the credibility of different sources is in fact a literary *topos*: its value lies not in the information it gives us about his methods (which is non-existent), but in the clear picture it draws of what an intelligent – and successful writer thought a vernacular historian *ought* to look like. We have no direct information about audience attitudes towards *estoires*; but the self-image that Wace projects

272   CHAPTER 5

2.3   *The Importance of Language, and the Changing of Names*
After the opening couplet on the completion of the ridding the land of giants
(1169–70), the closing section of the foundation story contains a passage with
an idyllic scene of prosperity, followed by Brutus's naming the land after himself, and Corinee after Corineus; Wace says he doesn't know by what error it
was subsequently called Cornwall, but he adds, in his usual thoroughness, an
extra clarification "Del nun qu'el out premierement / Tient encor le comencement" (1187–88; "It still retains the beginning of the name it had at first"). This
early passage (to be discussed more fully below) also contains a presage of
Gormund's Donation, one of many details not found in this form or at this
early stage in either of his principal sources:[21]

---

provides us with abundant circumstantial evidence as to what they might have been
expecting" ("Propaganda and *essample* in Benoît de Sainte-Maure's *Chronique des ducs de
Normandie*," *Medieval Chronicle IV*, ed. Erik Simon Kooper, Amsterdam and Atlanta, GA:
Rodopi, 2006, 39–52, cited at 49).

21   In fact, Wace often elaborates significantly on any toponymics his sources provide. His
earlier etymological and toponymic passage about New Troy is no exception, expanding
substantially on both the vulgate and FV (§22) which mention that Brutus named the
new city New Troy which it "retained" "for a long time until it was eventually corrupted
to Trinovantum" (*HRB*, I, §22.493–95; for the Latin regarding the "corruption," see n. 77
below); but, both Wace and the FV omit the vulgate's reference in §22 to Lud's brothers,
Nennius and Cassibelanus (§22.496–501). Both the vulgate and the FV mention Lud and
his two brothers later: in the vulgate §53 for the second time, and for the first time in
the FV (§53); when Wace reprises later the material on King Lud, as well as the different
names for London, he does mention the two brothers (3737–38), but more importantly,
he adds further etymological and toponymic details (3757–90) not found in the vulgate
or the First Variant (either in §22 or §53), and not found either in the *Brut* ll. 1201–46. The
following later passage from Wace (as compared with the minimal passages in the vulgate
and FV) contains a typical example of this kind of expansion in the *Brut* (relative to his
two main sources) on the theme of changing cultures and languages:
      Vulgate: Later it was renamed Kaerlud, a name afterwards corrupted to Kaerlundein;
as time passed and languages changed, it was called Lundene and then Lundres when
foreigners landed and conquered the country. When Lud died, his body was buried there
beside the gate which is still named after him, Porhlud in British and Ludgate in English
(§53.375–81).
      First Variant: It was later called Kaerlud after him, but then became Kaerlondem
through corruption of the name. As time passed, through alteration of the language it
was called Lundene, and after that Lundres by the arrival of strangers who altered the
native language to their own. When Lud finally died, his body was buried* in that city
next to the gate which is still known from his name as Portlud in British and Ludesgata in
Saxon [lit. *Saxonice*, in the language of the Saxons] (FV §53.2–3; *Burchmore has "hidden"
for "reconditum").
      Wace: The "reprise" (3757–90) follows, containing details not in the initial narrative on
the naming of Trinovant (1217–46): "Up until his time, and long before, / London was called
Trinovant, / But because of Lud, who honored it greatly / And spent much time there, /

La parole e li nuns dura	The language and the name lasted
Tant que Gormund i ariva;	Until the time when Gormund came;
Gormund en chaça les Bretuns	Gormund chased away the Britons
Si la livra as Saissuns[22]	He gave it [the land] to the Saxons
Qui d'Angle Angleis apelé erent,	Who, from Angles, were called English,
Ki Engletere l'apelerent;	Who called it England;
Tuz les Bretuns si eissillierent,	They exiled all the Britons,
Que unches puis ne redrescerent.	Who never again rose up.

(1193–1200)

As noted in Chapters 1 and 2, Geoffrey's vulgate does not contain a statement of how the English came to be called English, nor does the passage of dominion occur this early chronologically (late seventh century) nor this radically;

It was called Kaerlud. / Then foreign men came / Who did not know the language, / They said 'Londoin' for 'Lud'. / Then came the Angles and the Saxons / Who recorrupted ["recorumpurent"] the name in turn, / Naming 'Londoin' 'Lundene' / And they used 'Londene' for a long time. / Next the Normans came and then the French, / Who did not know how to speak English/ Nor how to say 'Londene' / Thus they said it as best they could. / They called 'Londene' 'Londres' / Thus keeping it in their language [lit., Thus they kept their word [for it]. / Through alterations and changes / In the languages of the foreign peoples, / Who often conquered the land, / Often lost, often taken, / The names of towns have changed, / Either lengthened or shortened; / One can find very few, / As I hear and understand, / Which have completely kept the name / They had in the beginning. / When the good king Lud died, / He was buried in London / Next to a gate, which was called / For him 'Porlud,' in the British language. / The English altered the word / And called it 'Ludgate'" (3757–90). Among the details Wace adds to the meager references in his sources is an extra stage or layer in the renaming process, "Lud" to "Londoin" effected by certain unspecified foreigners – whether Angles or Saxons is not clear – and the additional clarification that it was the Normans and the French who also changed the name to "Londres," "keeping it in their language." It is worth noting that Wace names the Normans and the French here as two different groups of French speakers (independent of his sources – though Geoffrey in §5 names the Normans as one of the five peoples who had conquered Britain); this may possibly in part be explained by the fact that Wace was a Norman (Jerseyman) by birth. See also Rupert T. Pickens who argues that cultural differences are often more important than political ones in the *Roman de Rou* and the Bayeux tapestry; that is, it is often more important that the Normans and the French are opposed to the English, rather than distinctions between the Normans and the French ("Implications of Being 'French' in Twelfth-Century England," in *"Chançon legiere a chanter": Essays in Old French Literature in Honor of Samuel N. Rosenberg*, ed. Karen Fresco and Wendy Pfeffer (Birmingham, AL: Summa Publications, 2007), 373–86, esp. 380–82).

22 Although Weiss retains "a uns Saissuns" (lit., "to a Saxon") from Arnold, it makes more sense to me to use the variant from CSH, "as Saissuns" ("to the Saxons") (Weiss, p. 30; Arnold, I, p. 67). See "Lu regne ad as Sednes duné," l. 13637, from the passage (cited below, 13631–40) where the transfer actually takes place "in real time" (rather than the "presage").

274 CHAPTER 5

in the First Variant, a statement similar to Wace's occurs much later in the text (§186/7), and is not presaged as it is here. Wace does repeat the result of Gormund's Donation at roughly the same place in the narrative as it is recounted for the only time in the FV, including a repetition of the changing of names. But the repetition contains an original expansion as well (13641–662) in the detail that the English "wished to keep their customs; they did not want to take up another language" (13659–660; "Cil voldrent tenir lur usage;/Ne voldrent prendre altre language"). This suggestion that the English did not want to mix culturally with the Britons might not be stated as directly in Wace's sources. It also goes further than what he says about the Normans and the French who spoke English "as best they could" but ultimately kept "Londres" in their own language, without the stronger comment that they wanted to retain their own customs as well, with the implication that the "Normans and French" kept their name for London out of a lack of linguistic talent, rather than ill will.[23]

This early stage in the *Brut* is critical for Wace to expand on his sources in the area of lexicon, since language will be one of his most essential themes in the evolutionary narrative he is assembling, as well as the mixing – or non-mixing – of cultures. In the context of studies of early medieval Britain, as well as later medieval and modern perceptions, William Frazer calls attention to certain "structuring principles within which societies organize their social identities" which "help to constitute both the way modern scholars think about early medieval Britain" but also how "early medieval people's perceptions of themselves" may have been constructed. To the "structuring principles" Frazer lists (and his list was surely not meant to be exhaustive, nor categorically confining) – "ethnicity, nationalism, social location, subjectivity/personhood, political organization (e.g. legal definitions), kinship, the human body, gender, age, groups, proximity/regionality, memory and ideological systems (e.g. spirituality and religious belief)"[24] – I would like to add language, for as Benedict Anderson writes, "there is a special type of contemporaneous community which language alone suggests."[25]

---

23   "Norman vindrent puis e Franceis, /Ki ne sourent parler Engleis, / Ne Londene nomer ne sourent / Ainz distrent si come dire pourent, / Londene unt Londres nomee/ Si unt lur parole guardee" (3769–74; "Next the Normans came and then the French, / Who did not know how to speak English/ Nor how to say 'Londene' /Thus they said it as best they could. / They called 'Londene' 'Londres' / Thus keeping it in their language [lit., Thus they kept their [own] word [for it]"); see also n. 21 above and n. 199 below.

24   William O. Frazer, "Introduction," in *Social Identity in Early Medieval Britain*, ed. idem and Andrew Tyrell (London and New York: Leicester University Press, 2000), 1–22, cited at 6.

25   *Imagined Communities*, 132.

In a recent study on Jersey Norman French, Mari Jones notes that

> although one of the purposes of language is to allow speakers to communicate, the act of using one linguistic variety rather than another immediately serves to ally speakers to a given speech community or to distance themselves from it. A language, therefore, often carries a symbolic force as an emblem of groupness, a focus of ethnic allegiance and belonging, on a par with other symbols, such as a flag or a national anthem ... this ability to confer a sense of belonging, and to distinguish a sense of 'sameness' and 'otherness,' has led commentators ... to debate whether identity should be judged to constitute a distinct major function of language.[26]

Our purpose is not to debate the competing purposes of language, but to underscore the symbiotic relationship between language and identity.

For the Norman poet Wace, whom Jones points out has himself become over time an identifying symbol and source of pride in Jersey up to the present day, a symbol used to raise the profile of Jèrrais, the French dialect still spoken today on Wace's native island, language is central to identity, and this centrality is seen especially in the *Roman de Brut*. The most common form of emphasis on language in the *Brut* is etymologies, a subset of which are toponymics. As Laurence Mathey-Maille points out, in the *Brut*'s roughly 15,000 lines, between 250–300 lines are devoted to explanations of the origins of words or place names.[27] While mathematically speaking, this is a small percentage, in terms of narrative fabric, it is more significant than the percentage itself might indicate since in the *Brut*, some sort of these explanations accompanies nearly every major set of events. In addition, most often, these etymologies are not found in Wace's two major sources – or at least not nearly to the same extent or frequency – Geoffrey of Monmouth's *Historia Regum Britanniae* and the First Variant version.

In the *Brut*, there are essentially three forms of naming: first, through express socio-political will of the rulers; second, by evolution or as Wace puts it "corruption" over time; and third, through mispronunciation by ruling foreigners, which can be considered simply a sub-category of evolution, often a result of colonization. As an example of conscious name-changing handed down from the top, we see that Brutus names the entire land after himself, and even goes so far as to rename the entire people after himself:

---

26 Mari C. Jones, "Identity Planning in an Obsolescent Variety: The Case of Jersey Norman French," *Anthropological Linguistics* 50.3–4 (2008): 249–65, cited at 249.

27 Mathey-Maille, "La pratique de l'étymologie," 580.

La terre aveit nun Albion,	The land was called Albion,
Mais Brutus li chanja sun nun,	But Brutus changed its name,
De Bruto, sun nun, nun li mist,	After Brutus, his name, he gave the name,
E Bretainne apeler la fist;	And he called the land Britain;
Les Troïens, ses compainuns	His companions, the Trojans
Apela, de Bruto, Bretuns.	He called Britons, after Brutus.
(1175–80)	

All three categories of name-changing can be seen in this passage that describes how Brutus named New Troy, his capital on the Thames, in this, the first time this material is presented (not the reprise in 3757–90):[28]

Pensa sei que cité fereit	He thought to himself that he would make a city
E Troie renovelereit.[29]	And rebuild Troy.
Quant il out quis leu covenable	When he had found a suitable place
E aaisiez e delitable,	Convenient and delightful,
Sa cité fist desur Tamise;	He had his city built on the Thames;
Mult fud bien faite e bien asise.	It was very well done and well situated.
Pur ses anceisors remembrer	To remember his ancestors
La fist Troie Nove apeler;	He had it called New Troy;
Puis ala li nuns corumpant,	Then the name was corrupted,
Si l'apela l'om Trinovant;	It was called Trinovant;
Mais qui le nom guarde, si trove	But he who looks at the name, finds
Que Trinovant est Troie Nove,	That Trinovant is New Troy,
Que bien pert par corruptiun	Which appears easily through the corruption
Faite la compositiun.[30]	Done to the name.
Por Lud, un rei ki mult l'ama	For Lud, a king who loved it very much
E logement i conversa,	And had his lodgings there,
Fu puis numee Kaerlu.	It was later named "Kaerlu."

---

28 The reprise is cited in n. 21 above, in a different context, in English translation only.

29 Weiss restores P's "que" in l. 1218: E que Troie renovelereit.

30 Following this line, Weiss restores a couplet from MS. P (London, British Library Additional 45103) (though printed in brackets and not counted in the line numbering; p. 32): ["Urb est latins, citez romanz, / Cestre est engleis, kaer bretanz"] ["'Urbs' is [the word for city] in Latin, 'citez' in French, 'chester' in English, 'kaer' in British"].

WACE'S ROMAN DE BRUT, PART 2

Puis unt cest nun Lud corumpu	Then the name was corrupted from Lud
Si distrent pur Lud Lodoïn;	One said "Lodoïn" for Lud;
Pur Lodoïn a la parfin	In the end, for Lud, "Lodoïn"
Londenë en engleis dist l'um	"Londenë" one said in English
E nus or Lundres l'apelum.[31]	And we now call it "Lundres."
Par plusurs granz destruiemenz	Through numerous great acts of destruction
Que unt fait alienes genz	Done by foreign peoples
Ki a terre unt sovent eüe,	Who often held the land,
Sovent prise, sovent perdue,	Often took it, often lost it,
Sunt les viles, sunt les contrees	The towns, the regions,
Tutes or altrement nomees	All are now named differently
Qui li anceisor nes nomerent	Than the ancestors named them
Ki premierement les fonderent.	Who first founded them.
(1217–46)[32]	

Wace tells us that in order to remember his ancestors, Brutus wanted to "renew" Troy by naming his capital in the new land "New Troy."[33] We then learn that over time the name was "corrupted" to "Trinovant" and then again to "Troie Nove." Later it was called "Kaerlu" or "City of Lud" in the tongue of the Britons, this being a conscious, planned renaming. Later, the name became "Lodoïn" which the English corrupted to "Londenë" (perhaps through mispronunciation?) and we "nus" – the French speakers in Wace's audience in France and England – call it "Londres" (again, with a different pronunciation). The goal of this passage is to explain that the majority of the changes in names were not necessarily conscious – that through great destruction, taking and losing of lands, names were completely changed, and none remains the same as the first founding ancestors gave them. However, although not all changes

---

31 It is important to note that Wace identifies himself with the French speakers here.

32 That the name New Troy became "corrupted" to "Trinovant" is reminiscent of one of the few details in the vulgate and FV ("Condidit itaque ciuitatem ibidem eamque Troiam Nouam uocauit. Ea, hoc nomine multis postmodum temporibus appellata, tandem per corruptionem uocabuli postmodum Trinouantum dicta fuit" §22.495–96; "There he founded a city which he called New Troy. It retained this name for a long time until it was eventually corrupted to Trinovantum"; FV "Condidit itaque ibidem ciuitatem eamqaue Nouam Troiam uocat; que postmodum per corruptionem uocabuli Trinouantum dicta est" §22; "He built a city there and called it New Troy, which was later called Trinovantum through corruption of the name" §22.2) (see nn. 21 and 23 above).

33 For a survey on this identification of London, see John Clark, "Trinovantum – the evolution of a legend."

were necessarily conscious ones, resulting from administrative decisions, they nonetheless carry political importance, as new colonizers move in, and earlier populations are taken over. In fact, later in this chapter, I suggest that Wace likely proposed the Round Table with ideological intent – rather than simply as a vestige of folklore or participation in the new "courtly" mode – in part as a model of governance to mitigate the negative aspects of linguistic solidarity and cultural pride, that is, to argue against social divisions brought about by an excess of linguistic or cultural chauvinism.

2.4   *Shifting Identities: Brittany and the Theme of Ethnic Separatism*
Passages emphasizing the cyclical nature of history and the constancy of change may suggest, as Margaret Lamont states, that "implicitly, no one group is fully 'native' in the *Roman de Brut*, because the history is layered with languages and cultures that change over time whether or not they are mixed with other cultures. Thus 'Trojan' becomes 'British' ... identity shifts, and later arrivals might, too, shift from foreigners to inhabitants."[34] While Wace may be trying to stay impartial in recounting all these changes and shifts, and while he may succeed up to a point, he is also condemning certain cultural and political behaviors – such as the catastrophic devastation allegedly wrought by Gormund followed by a diaspora – and endorsing others, including King Arthur's tolerance and encouraging of multiple identities at the Round Table. Because there seems to be very little voluntary intermixing or tolerance between cultures in the *Brut* – except by Arthur's orders – the disturbing references to genocide, diaspora, and expressions of ethnic separatism make the lessons of the Round Table all the more important.

Toward the end of the third section of the text, not long before the Romans leave Britain and the Saxons arrive, there are further images not of genocide – technically speaking since men were killed but not women and children – but of a violent refusal to mix cultures, a refusal which prefigures the Saxons' attitudes toward the Britons and their language, in the scenes surrounding the Roman senator Maximien's (Maximianus) gift of Brittany to Cunan (in Wace) (Conan, Conanus Meriadocus). The background to this story in the vulgate (and very similarly in the FV) is that Conan should have inherited the isle of Britain instead, from his uncle, Octavius, but Octavius had given the throne of Britain to Maximien in the hopes of future glory; Maximien had proven his mettle by seizing Brittany, thinking he could later seize all of Gaul and become emperor of Rome. Maximien makes peace with the angry Cunan and together they slaughter all the male Franks (Gauls), leaving only women

---

34   Lamont, "Becoming English," 291.

WACE'S ROMAN DE BRUT, PART 2 279

(and presumably children, though none are mentioned) as survivors (§§84–87); their goal was to eventually pacify "the captured kingdom and fill it with a British population" (§86.348–50).[35] In order to avoid the Britons' intermarrying with the Frankish women, Cunan sends for 11,000 noblewomen and 60,000 peasant women from Britain as wives (v, §88), including Ursula, daughter of Dionotus, king of Cornwall.

Wace does not report the slaughter of all the male Franks but in the face of the advance of Maximien's army, 15,000 are killed and the rest threatened with extinction, and are thus forced into exile, fleeing Brittany for their lives, leaving the Frankish women and children behind, who ultimately also fled, "Thus the land was emptied and left entirely to the Britons" ("Issi fu la terre vuidiee / E as Bretuns tute laissiee" 5965–66), according to Maximien's plan:

"Des païsanz la vuiderum

E des Bretuns la poplerum,
Si sera, quant ele ert poplee,
La menor Bretaine nomee.
Ne vuil que altre gent i maine,

Pur nos Bretuns sera Bretaine."
      (5937–42)[36]

"We will empty the land of the local inhabitants
And we will people it with Britons,
When it is peopled,
It will be called 'Little Britain.'
I don't want any other people remaining,
It will be Little Britain for us Britons."

---

35 On the silence of the Merovingian and Carolingian sources on this genocide, see Jean-Christophe Cassard, "Le génocide originel. Armoricains et Bretons dans l'historiographie bretonne médiévale," *Annales de Bretagne et des pays de l'ouest*, 90.3 (1983): 415–27. For a recent and thorough reconsideration of the question of British migration in Armorica, with extensive references including a substantial number of French sources, see Caroline Brett, "Soldiers, Saints, and States? The Breton Migrations Revisited," *Cambrian Medieval Celtic Studies* 61 (2011): 1–56; for emphasis on archaeological evidence, see also Pierre Roland Giot, Philippe Guignon, and Bernard Merdrignac, *Les premiers Bretons d'Armorique* (Rennes: Presses Universitaires de Rennes, 2003; published simultaneously in English as *The British Settlement of Brittany: The First Bretons in Armorica*, Stroud: Tempus 2003). The classic study of early Brittany from an historical (as opposed to mythical) perspective remains Léon Fleuriot, *Les Origines des la Bretagne* (Paris: Payot, 1980); see also Nora K. Chadwick, "The Colonization of Brittany from Celtic Britain," *Proceedings of the British Academy* 51 (1965): 235–99, esp. 262–70; T. M. Charles-Edwards, *Wales and the Britons 350–1064* (Oxford: Oxford University Press, 2013), 56–74 ("The Origins of Brittany"); and Dermot Fahy, "When did Britons become Bretons?: A Note on the Foundation of Brittany," *The Welsh History Review* 2 (1964–65): 111–24.

36 Whether this Galfridian-type narrative is based on an early Breton origin myth is not clear, but the effect is the same: the "original" people (the Franks, in this case) are replaced with

280 CHAPTER 5

In the *Brut*, Maximien has 100,000 peasants brought from Britain, in order to "people" Brittany, wanting to give them wives but not Frenchwomen:

Ne lur volt pas doner Franceises,	He didn't want to give them Frenchwomen,
Ne pur force, ne pur richeises,	Neither by force, or gifts,
Ne lur lignage entremeller	Nor to mix their lineages
Ne lur terres acomuner.	Nor to hold their lands in common.

    (6009–12)

He sends to king Dionot "who was in charge of England" (6014; "Ki aveit en guarde Engleterre")[37] for his daughter, Ursula, and marriageable girls, of whom Dionot gathered 11,000.

Wace combines the basic outlines of the Galfridian story of the British Ursula and her marriageable companions (many of whom protested the marriages but had not sworn oaths of virginity) with the legend of St. Ursula and the 11,000 virgins martyred by the Huns;[38] thus Wace's presentation of this situation involves greater pathos for the shipwreck of the women and their subsequent martyrdom at the hands of the barbarians Wanis, king of Hungary and Melga, king of Scythia, than we see in Geoffrey (and the First Variant, which resembles the *Historia* here).

However, it is important to note that neither Geoffrey nor Wace report an alternative tradition which may have circulated early orally but was found written in Breton chronicles of the later Middle Ages. In the Breton version, the immigrants who came with Cunan took native wives as spouses (perhaps since the female Britons originally sent for had been lost at sea?). However, they had the native women's tongues cut out so that they could not transmit their own language to their descendants, an act that besides being spectacularly inhumane is a radical form of cultural genocide, legendary or not.[39]

---

    a new "original" people, who as time goes on, become considered natives. In line 5942, the similarities to a few modern-day unfortunate xenophobic slogans are hardly inescapable.

37   Weiss restores MS. P's ordering of this line: "Ki en guarde aveit Engleterre" (p. 152, n. 1). According to the vulgate, Maximianus had put Dionotus, king of Cornwall, in charge of England during his absence (§87.369–70); the FV has the same, except that Dionotus is duke of Cornwall ("ducem Cornubiae") rather than king (§87).

38   Margaret Houck, *Sources of the Roman de Brut of Wace*, University of California Publications in English, 5 (Berkeley and Los Angeles: University of California Press, 1941), 161–356, here 247–50. In Geoffrey, Wanis is king of the Huns and Melga of the Picts, but the eleven thousand young women ("noblemen's daughters," §88.374) are not portrayed as martyred virgins.

39   On this Breton legend reported in later chronicles, see Bernard Merdrignac, "Conan Meriadoc," in *Celtic Culture: An Historical Encyclopedia*, ed. Koch. II, 473–75, here 474.

3   The *Adventus Saxonum*

Unlike Gaimar in the *Estoire des Engleis* who mentions Hengist and Horsa as ancestors but emphasizes the coming of Cerdic and his son Cynric fifty years later as apparently the most memorable arrival of future conquering Germanic invaders, Wace follows the general outline of the Bedan tradition seen in Geoffrey and the *Historia Brittonum*, foregrounding the coming of Hengist and Horsa as the beginning of the arrival of the Saxons.[40] In Wace, the three boats are small (naceles 6704) and the lords of these foreigners with "handsome faces and fine bodies" ("genz estranges .../ Od bels viaires, od gent cors" 6706–8) are of great height, their language foreign ("Dui frere de grant estature / E d'une estrange parleüre," 6709–10). Wace may be the only author who mentions the foreignness of the language immediately.

In the *Brut*, when Vortigern asks why they have come, Hengist replies in a speech following the general outline of the *HRB*, with two variations: in the vulgate (§98), Hengist declares that their purpose is to offer their service to the king or to other lords, followed by the explanation that whenever there is overpopulation at home, all those over the age of fifteen draw lots and those who lose, must leave; also in the vulgate only, Hengist and Horsa say they are descended from dukes;[41] in the *Brut*, no mention is made of the offer of service or the descent from dukes, but the fertility of the Saxons is elaborated on at length, including with hyperbolic statements such as "Kar enfanz plus espés

---

40   Bede: Vortigern invites the Saxons ("tunc Anglorum siue Saxonum gens, invitata a rege praefato," "At that time the race of Angles or Saxons, invited by Vortigern ..." 1.15); Gildas: here Vortigern does not exactly invite the Saxons, but they are "admitted" (or "let in") by the "ill-fated tyrant" to fight other barbarians (English, p. 98; "igitur intromissi in insulam barbari" ... "infausto tyranno" §23, 5 and 4); *HB*: a mixed picture, in that originally, the Saxons come as exiles, uninvited, arriving purely by chance (ch. 31) but in ch. 48, Vortigern was "hated for his sin, because he received the English people, by all men of his own nation ..." and he "wandered from place to place until at last his heart broke, and died without honour" (English, p. 33, although "propter susceptionem populi Saxonici" [p. 73] "for the reception of the Saxon people" does not necessarily mean "invited"); Geoffrey: Saxons come as exiles, uninvited, arrive purely by chance (§98.248–54); First Variant: Saxons come as exiles, uninvited, arrive purely by chance (§98. 1–2); Henry of Huntingdon, *HA*: "The race of Saxons, or English, invited by the above-mentioned king [Vortigern], came to Britain in three long ships, in the year of grace 449, during the reign of Marcian and Valentinian, whose imperial rule lasted seven years, and in the twentyfourth [sic] year after the kingdom of the Franks had begun, whose first king was Faramund" (11.1); Henry of Huntingdon, *EW*: Vortigern "called in the English only to be betrayed by them" (§8, p. 111).

41   The FV does not contain the offer of service, nor the statement that they are descended from dukes.

282   CHAPTER 5

i naissent / Que ces bestes qui as chans paissent" (6761–62; "For children are
born thicker and faster there than beasts grazing in the fields").[42]

Although in the *Brut*, Vortigern does not invite the Saxons, once they have
arrived, he offers to pay them handsomely for military support against the
Picts and the Scots, to which they readily consent. Having provided the support, Hengist persuades Vortigern to provide him and his men with a fortress,
which in the vulgate takes its name "from the string with which it had been
measured out": "for it was later called in British Kaercarrei, and in English
Thanccastre, or Castrum Corrigiae in Latin" ("dictum namque fuit postmodum Britannice Kaercarrei, Saxonice uero Thanccastre, quod Latino sermone
Castrum Corrigiae appellamus" *HRB* §99. 335–37). The First Variant has a similar etymology, though somewhat compressed, while Wace eliminates the mention of Latin but elaborates, adding the French term for the castle ("Chastel de
cureie en rumanz"; 6921 "Chastel de cureie" in French).[43]

Other divergences from his two sources go beyond Wace's fascination with
languages, adding extra nefarious details about the Saxons, though eliminating the vulgate's comment that "Pagans ought not to communicate or mix

---

42   The comment on beasts and children, absent from the vulgate, echoes the following in
      the FV: "Indeed our land is more fruitful in its plenty of men for begetting children than
      of other animals, although in its own way it is by no means diminished in its popula-
      tion of wild beasts and its abundance of resources" (§98.4) ("Est enim terra nostra fecun-
      dior hominum procreandorum ubertate quam ceterorum animalium, licet ipsa quoque
      ferarum habundancia atque diuiciarum copia in suo genere nequaquam fraudetur" §98).

43   First Variant: "Quod edificatum traxit nomen ex corrigia: Saxonice Thancastre, Britannice
      uero Caercarrei, quod Latino uerbo 'Castrum corigie' sonat" (§99, "The building took its
      name from the thong: in Saxon 'Thancastre,' in British 'Kaercarrei,' which in Latin means
      'Castle of the Thong'; my trans.). Five *Brut* MSS (PHKRN) have four more lines between
      6925 and 6926, an etymological "interpolation" rejected by Arnold "on the grounds that
      it was very unlikely Wace would have thought Wancaster [sic] was Lancaster" (Weiss, 174
      n. 6, reporting Arnold ed., II, 804–5). However, Weiss has not transcribed the variants as
      Arnold has them: Premierement ot nun Thwancastre / Or l'apelent plusurs Lancastre / Qui
      (P Si) ne sevent pas l'achaisun / Dunt Thwancastre ot primes cest nun [N De Wancastre
      ot pris] (Arnold, ed., I, 367; "First it was called Thwancastre, but some later called it
      Lancaster. They don't know why Thwancastre was its first name "). Arnold comments (ed.,
      II, 805) that the castle in question must have been Caistor near Grimsby, in the medieval
      period Thongcaster (citing Eilert Ekwall, *The Concise Oxford Dictionary of Place Names*
      [Clarendon, 4th ed. 1966], *s. v.* Thong, 444; Arnold, ed., II, 805) (see also Weiss, 175, n. 1, on
      Caistor). Weiss uses "Wancastre" in place of "Thwancastre" (6917, 6919, and 6925) as seen
      in PD (and N, in the "interpolation") (according to Arnold's variants (ed., I, 367). Given
      that Wace often reports errors others have made in pronunciation, spelling, etc., it is not
      implausible that the comment about some calling the castle Lancaster may actually have
      been his reporting an error which some had made because they didn't know why it was
      first called "Thwancastre." For further details, see Chapter 6, n. 96.

WACE'S ROMAN DE BRUT, PART 2   283

with Christians, as it was forbidden by Christian law" (§101.391–92) (a comment also eliminated by the First Variant). However all three texts say that so
many Saxons had arrived that it was growing impossible to tell who was pagan
and who was Christian, the vulgate adding "since the pagans had married their
daughters and relatives" (§101.394–95: "quia pagani filias et consanguineas
eorum sibi associauerant"). Before being poisoned by Ronwen (Ronwenne) –
Hengist's daughter, Vortigern's wife – for whom he had given Hengist the
province of Kent as a dowry – and his stepmother – Vortimer and the Britons
rebel against Vortigern, forcing the Saxons to flee. At that time, St. Germanus
of Auxerre came with Lupus of Troyes to preach to the British; according to
the vulgate and First Variant, because of the Pelagian heresy (§101, FV §102)
(though both the vulgate and the FV add also due to the Saxons), but according
to Wace, to rebuild the churches and reestablish order since "God's law" was
"poorly observed because Hengist had corrupted it" ("E pur la lei Deu anuntier /
Ki malement esteit tenue, / Pur Henguist ki l'out corumpue," 7136–38). Thus in
effect Wace blames the after-effects of the Pelagian heresy exclusively on the
Saxons, with no mention of the heresy itself.

Wace uses two additional sets of events to further portray the Saxons
negatively: Vortigern's love – and lust – for Ronwen, and the "night of the
long knives." In her comprehensive feminist reading of characterization in
Geoffrey's vulgate, the First Variant, and Wace's *Brut*, Fiona Tolhurst traces the
transformation of Ronwen, from Geoffrey's fairly neutral, non-condemnatory
version, to Wace's development of the "Variant-redactor's version that both
sexualizes and villainize Ronwen as part of a pagan conspiracy [wherein]
Wace continues the process of transforming a loyal daughter into a servant
of the Devil (*HRB* 99.299–105.498; *FV* 100.1–102.24)."[44] As in the First Variant,
Wace emphasizes Ronwen's "alluring body," turning Ronwen from recipient
of the kiss as in Geoffrey, to bestower of the kiss, and thus the figure of the

---

44   Tolhurst finds this presentation equally "in keeping with Wace's heavy-handed moraliz-
      ing throughout his Vortiger [sic] sequence" (*Geoffrey of Monmouth and the Translation of
      Female Kingship*, 163). For an overview of Wace's portrayal of women and a very useful
      listing of the ninety-eight female characters he has identified in Wace's five works (three
      of whom, the Virgin Mary, and the goddesses Minerva and Diana, appear in multiple
      texts), see Glyn S. Burgess, "Women in the Works of Wace," in *Maistre Wace: A Celebration*,
      91–106. More specifically for the *Brut*, see Gemma Wheeler, "Rewriting the Past: Women
      in Wace's *Roman de Brut*," *Reading Medieval Studies* 37 (2011): 59–77, and Laurence
      Mathey-Maille, "Figures de femmes dans le *Roman de Brut* de Wace," in *Désir n'a repos:
      hommage à Danielle Bohler*, ed. Florence Bouchet and Danièle James-Raoul (Pessac:
      Presses Universitaires de Bordeaux, 2015), 415–26.

284   CHAPTER 5

temptress is unavoidable.[45] However, while acknowledging Tolhurst's assessment of "Wace's tendency to translate potentially evil female characters into truly evil ones" (the goddess Diana, and Lear's daughters Gornille and Regau, for example), for our purposes in this case, Wace's villainization of Ronwen is more, or at least equally, a part of his negative portrayal of the Saxons – his *Brut* is significantly more Briton-slanted than is the First Variant – than it is of women per se, if the blaming of the aftermath of the Pelagian heresy on Hengist is any indication.

Ronwen's treachery as "wicked stepmother" in murdering Vortigern's son, Vortimer, is followed as if it were a set piece, by the "night of the long knives"; in Geoffrey, this treachery is "unheard of" (noua proditione usus, §104.459–60; the same in the First Variant §104.1, trans. Burchmore "unprecedented") while in Wace, the character of Hengist is modified and emphasized, rather than the treachery itself: Hengist has a "wicked heart," and sends a treacherous message to the king asking for a peace parley, which he had no intention of keeping peaceful, which Wace relates a bit further on ("Henguist, qui out le quer felun, / Manda al rei par traïsun / Que pais e trives lur dunassent / E entretant a els parlassent" 7207–10). In the vulgate and FV, Vortigern suggests that Hengist and the Saxons – who claim to desire peace – should meet on May 1, and Hengist should bring with him very few retainers. Wace follows suit, but adds that Hengist suggests that neither side bring any weapons, lest a fight break out (7225), this last detail making the treachery even deeper since they all agree to forgo weapons, and Hengist proceeds to order all his men to put a long knife in one of their boots (7233–34). At the parley, while the Britons are defenseless, Hengist yells, "Grab your knives!" ("Nim eure sexes!" 7237)[46] and four hundred and sixty Britons are slaughtered on the spot; the FV does not give a figure but both the vulgate and Wace do (7256–57, §104.470). Wace also gives a figure for the number of Saxons killed by the Briton Eldulf, count of Gloucester: 70 men killed by him alone (7267).

After narrating the slaughter, in the vulgate and First Variant, the Saxons are seen as reluctant to kill Vortigern but instead extort him into surrendering his cities and castles in exchange for his life: they take London, York, Lincoln and Winchester, laying waste to "all regions" (§105.489–95); the FV is virtually identical, minus the phrase about laying waste ("quasque prouincias deuastantes" *HRB* §105.495). After giving the Saxons London, Winchester, Lincoln, York, and Chichester, Wace adds that before fleeing to Wales, and in order to "release

---

45   *Geoffrey of Monmouth and the Translation of Female Kingship*, 163. See the First Variant §100 and the *Brut*, 6987.

46   *HRB* §104.462, "Nimet oure saxas!"; FV "Nimet eowre seaxas!"

WACE'S ROMAN DE BRUT, PART 2   285

himself from [any further] ransom, and get out of prison" (7291–92; "Pur qui-
tance de raençun / E pur eissir de la prison"), Vortigern gave the Saxons "en
feu" – in fee – (7294) the regions of Sussex, Essex, and Middlesex "because they
adjoined Kent" (7295) – the element of being "in fee" implying that the Saxons
would continue to be Vortigern's vassals, though this status of Saxon fealty to
Vortigern or other Briton rulers is not mentioned again in the remainder of the
Brut narrative.[47]

In addition, Wace provides a false etymology for those regions: so that the
English would never be reminded of this treachery by their ancestors, or be
reproached for it, they apparently kept the "sex" suffix in the names of those
regions – although the regions were named years after the treachery – but they
ended up changing the word they used for knives:

Engleis le repruvier oïrent	The English heard themselves reproached
De la traïsun que cil firent,	About the treason they committed,
La fin de la parole osterent,	So they removed the end of the word,
Les nuns des cultels tresturnerent,	They transformed the name for "knives,"
Pur oblier la desonur	To forget the dishonor
Que fait orent lur anceisur.	That their ancestors had done.
(7303–8)	

Wace would appear to give this etymology not only to explain the change in
the English word for knives from "saxas" (though he does not provide the new
word, despite his passion for etymology), but also to acknowledge the hideous-
ness of the treachery, and the English people's wish to avoid reminders of the
guilt of their ancestors, and thus by association, their own guilt, adding an
extra layer of rebuke to the narratives in the vulgate and First Variant.[48]

---

47   In §46, the *Historia Brittonum* reports that Vortigern "to save his life, he ceded several
     districts, namely Essex and Sussex, † together with Middlesex and other districts that
     [the Saxons] chose and designated†" (see Chapter 1, n. 65 regarding the dagger symbols).
     The *HB* does not mention the element of holding the land in fee, nor does it contain the
     false etymology. This innovation on Wace's part has historical and political implications –
     many of which are likely anachronistic from his own time – and is certainly worthy of
     further investigation by specialists in early English landholding customs and transitions
     to the feudal system in England, topics which are beyond the scope of this study.
48   See also Tatlock, *Legendary History*, 386 n. 24, on a similar incident – at which Saxons
     drew large knives not from their boots but from under their cloaks in order to slaughter
     Thuringians at a peaceful conference – as reported by the tenth-century Saxon chronicler,
     Widukind of Corvey, in the *Annales de Witonia* (*Annales Monastici*, Rolls Ser., II. 34–5).

286   CHAPTER 5

Wace's portrayals are not always consistent either with his sources' portrayals or internally consistent within his own poem (a point to which we will
return later). At times, Wace's presentation of the Saxons as enemy invaders
is more tempered than Geoffrey's which often borders on vitriol, perhaps not
surprising since the Latin historian apparently identified himself with the
Britons – or at least he demonstrates more empathy for the Britons (except
when he is railing against their disunity in an authorial aside as in §203, where
he has Cadwallader's speech echo his own words). For example, Geoffrey uses
the term "barbarian"[49] at the earliest opportunity to identify Hengist as he
settles in at Vortigern's court: "Paruerunt ilico barbari et foedere confirmato in
curia ipsius remanserunt" (§98.291; "The barbarians instantly agreed, signed
a treaty and stayed in his court"); the FV also uses "barbari" but includes a bit
of flattering description regarding the Saxons' prowess in warfare: "Paruerunt
barbari et federe firmato curiam repleuerunt proceribus et ualidis uiris et ad
bellum strenue edoctis ..." (§98; "The barbarians complied, and once a treaty
was confirmed, they filled the court with nobles and robust men and those
vigorously trained in warfare ..." [my trans.]).

Wace takes a different approach than the vulgate, and goes further with the
"flattery" than the FV, having already mentioned the Saxons' physical beauty,
especially the two brothers' physical beauty, in glowing terms earlier in the
text, here emphasizing the whole group's nobility in terms which would soon
form part of the French courtly lexicon: "Issi sunt li Saisne remés, / E al sec
unt traites lur nés; / Sempres fu la curt replenie / De mult gente bachelerie"
(6813–16; "Thus the Saxons stayed and put their ships in dry-dock; at once the
court was filled with many fine young men").[50]

    Tatlock notes that "these large knives, 'quibus hodie Angli utuntur,'" were favorites with
    the Saxons, and according to some (says Widukind) from them the Saxons got their name,
    'cultelli enim nostra lingua sahs dicuntur'" (386, n. 24).

49   He is certainly not using the term to mean "non-Roman" but is employing it with full
    pejorative vigor. On the use of the term in multiple guises, see Shami Ghosh, *Writing
    the Barbarian: Studies in Early Medieval Historical Narrative*, The Early Middle Ages 24
    (Leiden: Brill, 2015), Introduction, 1–38, esp. 3, n. 8, and Gillingham, "Conquering the
    Barbarians: War and Chivalry in Britain and Ireland," *The English in the Twelfth Century*,
    41–58 (orig. pub. in *The Haskins Society Journal* 4, 1992 [Boydell, 1993], 67–84).

50   When Hengist and Horsa first arrived, Wace had written: "Li reis esguarda les dous freres /
    As cors bien faiz, as faces cleres, / Ki plus grant erent e plus bel / Que tuit li altre juvencel"
    (6723–26; "The king looked at the two brothers with their well built bodies, and shining
    faces; they were taller and more handsome than all the other youths"). Although this posi-
    tive description could be interpreted as faint praise, that is, that Hengist and Horsa were
    taller and more handsome than the other young men in attendance, "li altre juvencel"
    (and perhaps the latter were not particularly fair and strapping), one can also read the
    four lines – and "li altre" – as high praise, as Weiss has in her translation, where she reads

4   King Arthur

4.1   *Introduction*

Wace's development of Arthur, both as "barbarian" king and great civilizer – whose court now includes the Round Table in its earliest written manifestation[51] – transcends in scope even the portrayals in the vulgate and First Variant, although the latter two texts deal more extensively with Arthur than any preceding extant narratives. Intimately tied up in this portrayal are Wace's – and his contemporaries' – views of barbarism and civilization, native populations and foreigners, colonizers and colonized, symbiotically entwined binaries that can be separated only for the purposes of discussion. Although like most writers Wace is not completely consistent in any of his portrayals, as noted above, there are certain patterns that emerge and often reflect the tensions within, and among, these different groups.

In light of increasing anti-British sentiment on the part of Geoffrey's contemporaries,[52] it becomes all the more imperative to see as one of Wace's

---

"li altre" not as all the other young men who happened to be in attendance at the time, but all other young men in general: "The king observed the two brothers, with their shapely bodies and fine faces, who were taller and more handsome than *all other young men*" (our emphasis). On Wace's tendency to render more acceptable, to "neutralize" or "depoliticize" the enemy through terms of praise, see J. Blacker, "Transformations of a Theme: The Depoliticization of the Arthurian World in the *Roman de Brut*." As mentioned above, by "depoliticization," I do not mean that Wace's *Brut* is devoid of political content (as some may have construed my meaning in their reading of the 1988 article), but rather that he tends to praise those fighting on the "other side" – such as Julius and Lucius Caesar – as well as the "heroes" of his narrative, through the use of what might be termed "reflex praise" or automatic praise, out of what could appear to be simple politeness, perhaps as part of the growing courtly ethic. See also Chapter 6, n. 91.

51   See nn. 111–112 below. For other aspects of Wace's king Arthur, see Véronique Zara, "The Historical Figure of Arthur in Wace's *Roman de Brut*," *Arthuriana* 18.2 (2008): 17–30 (Lagniappe Festschrift in Honor of Norris J. Lacy).

52   While these ideas may have circulated among "ordinary" people on many levels of society, they were also promulgated in the highest circles, among very visible writers and other intellectuals, including William of Malmesbury, Richard of Hexham, John of Salisbury, and Gerald de Barri, to name only a few; see esp. John Gillingham, "The Beginnings of British Imperialism." Gillingham argues in fact that Geoffrey's colleague, with whom he may have felt in competition (see Chapter 1 on Geoffrey's epilogue), William of Malmesbury, was the first medieval writer to reincorporate the Roman view of barbarism – the principal criterion being civilized behavior – into his own, thereby creating a polarity of civilized vs. uncivilized to parallel that of Christian vs. pagan, as well as the "perception of the Celtic peoples as barbarians" (9); see Chapter 2, n. 71. As Gillingham notes, the "perception of Celtic societies as barbarous obviously functioned in part as an ideology of conquest," suggesting that "the greater significance of the imperialist outlook was the barrier it set up between the conqueror and the conquered – a barrier which inhibited assimilation" (17).

primary goals not only inclusion but also redemption. He not only sought to write a history of the native peoples (setting aside the giants for the time being) which his colleagues would take seriously as an integrated part of the history of the island, but he also sought to redeem those peoples in the face of growing disapproval, even scorn, on the part of many in the "Anglo-Saxon" dominant group. Particularly for his portrayal of Arthur, Wace goes further than Geoffrey and the First Variant redactor toward a portrait of redeemed and redeemer, civilized and civilizer.

The Arthurian section of this chapter will be divided as follows: 1) birth and rise to power; 2) Arthur's battles within the isle of Britain and the beginning of the foreign conquests; 3) Arthur's marriage and court, including the Round Table; 4) foreign conquests; 5) defeat of the Romans; and 6) return to Britain to fight the usurper, Mordred, and his "final" battle.

4.1.1   Birth and Rise to Power

Although Arthur is not given special talents at birth by elves as he is in Laȝamon's *Brut*,[53] in Wace's poem, Arthur's conception and birth are symbolically important, because of who his parents are, his unusual conception, and also his father's legacy.[54] Other than the relocating of the Giants' Ring from Ireland to Stonhenge, Arthur's conception is the only other set of circumstances where Merlin's preternatural powers are invoked.[55] At Uther Pendragon's coronation feast, he sees his host's wife, Ygerne "the most beautiful woman in Britain" (*HRB*, §137.455–56), dance and is overcome with lust for her. After confessing this situation to one of his knights, Ulfin of Ricaradoc, the latter counsels the king to summon Merlin, who proceeds to offer herbs to change the king's appearance to that of the count Gorlois, Ygerne's husband, so that she will be deceived and sleep with him, thereby satisfying his great passion. During that night of lovemaking, Arthur is conceived; Gorlois is killed

---

53   On the role of elves in Laȝamon's *Brut*, see Jordan Church, "'The Play of Elves': Supernatural Peripheries and Disrupted Kingship in Layamon's *Brut*," *Philament* 24.1 (2018): 15–32; http://www.philamentjournal.com.

54   In terms of Arthur's conception and birth, Wace follows the general outlines of the vulgate and FV, without outstanding departures.

55   Merlin's prophetic powers are not at issue here, as they are almost exclusively confined to the book of Prophecies in both the vulgate and the FV, though Wace does not include them. For a discussion of possible reasons for Wace's refusal to include the Prophecies, see J. Blacker, "'Ne vuil sun livre translater': Wace's Omission of Merlin's Prophecies from the *Roman de Brut*," in *Anglo-Norman Anniversary Essays*, ed. Ian Short, Anglo-Norman Text Society Occasional Publications Series 2 (London: ANTS, 1993), 49–59.

WACE'S ROMAN DE BRUT, PART 2   289

in battle – which Uther regrets, but then he is free to marry Ygerne.[56] Geoffrey comments that there was "no little passion" in their marriage, but both the First Variant redactor and Wace refrain from commenting on the love in Uther and Ygerne's marriage: it is enough that Arthur was conceived that first night.[57]

In terms of the symbolism of Arthur's conception, Denis Hüe proposes that the conception is constructed based on a very archaic heroic savior motif in the Indo-European tradition, wherein Arthur is made to conform simultaneously to three requirements: 1) that the hero represent new blood, yet be of noble lineage; 2) that he be the son of a king, yet a bastard; and 3) that he be born of an adulterous yet faithful mother.[58] It is not necessary though, as Hüe points out, that Wace seek to reconcile the mythical and the legendary with the historical, forsaking some of the former elements in order to reinforce belief in the latter, because they can – and do – all coexist simultaneously; in fact the power of the myths which intersect with Arthur, the "political" figure, are inseparable from him as leader and historical artifact.[59]

I would like to expand the symbolic paradigm from the Galfridian material – with Wace's additions – beginning with Arthur's conception, to include the following elements, each of which points to Arthur's status as insider or outsider,

---

56 Denis Hüe argues that Wace casts doubt on Ygerne's loyalty to Gorlois; the fact that Wace also has Gorlois leave the banquet brusquely (similarly to his sources), makes him look like the villain of the scene, more brutal than the king, as if to make Uther and Ygerne appear to be the correct couple ("Les Variantes de la séduction: autour de la naissance d'Arthur," in *Le Roman de Brut entre mythe et histoire: actes du colloque, Bagnoles de l'Orne, septembre 2001*, ed. Claude Letellier and Denis Hüe, Medievalia 47 (Orleans: Paradigme, 2003), 67–88). On a contradictory note though, which undermines a uniform picture of Uther's nobility of spirit, Wace adds that Uther *appeared to regret* Gorlois's death – at least he said he did – as that had not been his intent, but few believed him: "Del cunte li pesa, ce dist, / Ki ert ocis, pas nel volsist. / Mult le plainst, mult le regreta, / A ses baruns s'en coruça; / Semblant fist que mult l'en pesast, / Mais poi i out qui ço quidast" (8797–8802; "It weighed on him, he said, that the count was killed, he hadn't wanted that. He bemoaned it a lot, he grieved him greatly; he was angry with his barons. He gave the impression that it weighed on him greatly, but there were few who believed that").

57 *HRB* §138.535: non minimo amore legati "united by no little passion." See Weiss, trans., 233, n. 1, and Tolhurst on this union of the king and queen as "partners in love and power rather than spouses out of political necessity" (*Feminist Origins*, 23, and 149, n. 35).

58 Hüe, "Les Variantes de la séduction," 68–69. See also on these points, D. Boutet, *Charlemagne et Arthur* (Campion, 1992), and J. Grisward, "UterPendragon, Arthur, et l'idéologie royale des Indo-européens," in *Le Moyen Âge aujourd'hui, Europe*, 654, 1983, 111–120 (repr. in D. Hüe, *Fils sans père, études sur le Merlin de Robert de Boron*, Medievalia 35, Orleans: Paradigme, 2000, 103–13).

59 Again, I am defining "historical artifact" as an element of a text or cultural remnant *believed* to be true, that is, *believed* to have existed in "actual history" without necessarily any scientific corroboration.

290 CHAPTER 5

and sometimes as both, each of these statuses contributing to his plasticity as a literary/historical figure across eras and genres of historiographical or romance narrative:

1) illegitimate son – outsider (Merlin's use of herbs and other forms of deception to disguise Uther);
2) son of a king and future queen – insider;
3) inherits the throne thus, by extension, through magical means – outsider;[60]
4) earns the right to be king through his own seemingly transcendental prowess – characterized as the "greatest king" (and other superlatives) – insider;
5) belongs to a "barbarian group" when seen from the perspective of the soon-to-be-dominant group, the Saxons (Angles, mentioned in some texts, in the eleventh hour) – outsider;
6) functions as a civilizer through his founding of the Round Table which carries socio-linguistic as well as socio-political connotations – insider;
7) member of a colonizing group and a colonized group, conqueror and conquered – insider and outsider;
8) dies but doesn't – human and messianic figure, "Breton hope" – both within the human realm and outside it (the consummate insider/outsider).

As a ruler, Arthur had an exemplary model in his father, Uther, who is reported to have marched through Northumberland into Scotland, after having dispatched Octa and Eosa to London as prisoners (*HRB* §137), in a consolidation of power which lead to peace and stability; Wace relates, "never before had a king ever established such great peace throughout the kingdom as he did" ("Par tut le regne tel pais mist / Unches reis ainz si grant ne fist" 8549–50).[61] Following the events leading up to Arthur's conception, Wace remarks that Uther "reigned a long time, safe and sound and peacefully" (8823–24; "Uther regna bien lungement, / Sains e salfs e paisiblement"). Upon the king's victory over Octa and Eosa where the two Saxons are eventually killed, he falls ill and dies soon after, his only drinking well having been poisoned by men sent by the Saxons (§§141–42), men who, Wace interjects in keeping with his fascination

---

60 Absent from the Galfridian material, the motif of the test of Arthur pulling the sword from the stone in order to prove his descendance from the regal line apparently enters the written tradition in Robert de Boron's late twelfth-early thirteenth century, *Roman de Merlin*; see Rosemary Morris, *The Character of King Arthur*, 36–49.

61 In l. 8824, Weiss restores "*n'i* fist" from MS. P, p. 214 n. 4. Although this can be read as referring to just the north country and what later became Scotland ("De Northumberlande en Escoce," 8543), it can also be interpreted as an image of maintaining peace throughout the kingdom of the Britons, "par tut le regne." Geoffrey sets Octa (c. 500–543, king of Kent) and his kinsman Eosa in an earlier time to make them rivals of Uther, apparently without mention of their connection to the kingdom of Kent.

WACE'S ROMAN DE BRUT, PART 2   291

with language, "knew how to speak many languages" (8970; "Ki parler sorent maint langage"), suggesting that they had the skills to overhear and understand everything at Uther's court.

Upon Uther's death, Arthur is crowned by acclamation of the bishops and barons. In the opening section on his reign, Geoffrey emphasizes Arthur's generosity as his most noteworthy characteristic even as a fifteen-year-old youth:

> of great promise and generosity, whose innate goodness ensured that he was loved by almost everybody. As newly-crowned king, he displayed his customary open handedness. Such a crowd of knights flocked to him that he ran out of gifts. (*HRB* §143.9–12)

Geoffrey then proceeds to comment in general (perhaps providing a well known proverb, or common saying from the time?) on how an upright and generous man, even if he's "out-of-pocket" from time to time, if he's careful, will never be poor for long.[62] He declares Arthur an upright and generous man ("quia in illo probitas largitionem comitabatur," §143.15), who almost immediately proceeds to decide on war against the Saxons, being practical deciding also "to use their wealth to reward his household retainers" (§143.16), since "right was on his side as he should have been ruler of the entire island by lawful inheritance" (§143.16–18).[63]

Wace departs from both the vulgate and the First Variant: he eliminates the proverb on poverty, and the declaration that right was on Arthur's side in his decision to fight the Saxons. Wace uses the First Variant's rationale – that the Saxons had killed his father and uncle and generally wreaked havoc on the island (9037–38) – but adds that soon after becoming king, Arthur swore an oath through his own free will ("De sun gré fist un serement," 9034) that "the

---

62   "Sed cui naturalis inest largitio cum probitate, licet ad tempus indigeat, nullatenus tamen continua paupertas ei nocebit" (§143.13–14).

63   In a much shorter introduction to Arthur's reign, the FV eliminates the proverb on generosity and poverty, as well as the notion that Arthur would use the Saxons' wealth to pay his own retainers. More importantly, there is no mention of right being on Arthur's side in his decision to fight the Saxons since he was the rightful heir of the entire island ("Et erat tunc Arthurus .xv. annorum iuuenis, magne uirtutis et audacie atque largitatis: unde poupulo ac principibus tocius regni gratus et acceptus erat. Insignibus itaque regiis iniciatus mox Saxones inuadere decreuit per quos et pater et patruus eius dolo perierant, per quos etiam tota terra turbata erat," FV §143; "Arthur was then fifteen years old, a youth of great strength and boldness and generosity; for that reason he had been welcomed and accepted by the people and the leaders of the entire kingdom. As soon as he was invested with the royal insignia, he decided to attack the Saxons, through whom both his father and his uncle had died by treachery, and through whom the whole land had been disrupted" [my translation]).

292   CHAPTER 5

Saxons would never have peace as long as they were in the land with him"
(9035–36; "Que ja Saisne pais ne avrunt / Tant cum el regne od li serunt");[64]
Wace does mention Arthur's drive to collect mercenaries, but not that they will
be paid with spoils taken from the Saxons (though perhaps Wace's audience
might have assumed such, and there was no need to make that detail explicit).
Wace also dedicates a 20-line passage to Arthur's gift-giving at court, later in
the narrative in the context of the Round Table (10601–620).[65]

4.1.2   Arthur's Battles

In the vulgate *Historia*, no sooner does Arthur decide to fight the Saxons than
his battles – based broadly but not slavishly on the twelve originally outlined
in the *Historia Brittonum* – begin.[66] Much has been written about these battles,
scholars most often trying to locate them – or deny their existence – in historical geography, but for our purposes, what remains most important are Wace's
choices, which he used and which he didn't.[67] Not surprisingly, the narrator of
HB declares all of Arthur's battles victorious. The sole exception is the battle of
Camlann – which is not mentioned in *HB* – where Mordred does fall but Arthur
is fatally wounded, which occurs much later in the Galfridian narratives.[68]

     Geoffrey has apparently reduced the number of battles from twelve to four
or five – depending on how one counts – all of which he associates with well

---

64   Weiss restores the reading from MS. P, "*nen* avrunt" (p. 226 n. 5).
65   Ten manuscripts do not contain these lines, and some or all of the lines occur in four
       others but with a different placement (Arnold, II, 555 and Weiss, 266, n. 2). In Wace's
       gift-giving section, he eliminates Geoffrey's mention of the ecclesiastical administrative
       gifts of abbeys, bishoprics, and archbishoprics (*HRB*, §157.402–3).
66   See Chapter 1, n. 76 for more details (including spellings) and the citation on the twelve
       battles in the *HB*, and for a variety of perspectives on these battles, their possible loca-
       tions, their fictitious nature or historical plausibility (varying based on the authors' per-
       spectives as to whether Arthur is historical or not, and if historical, a northern leader of
       Strathclyde or a southerner). See also Appendix 3 as an illustration of the variations on
       the battles among the texts in question, and the note on the "river Duglas."
67   Breeze who argues for Arthur's historicity as a leader of Strathclyde, characterizes one
       of the earliest catalogues of the battles by John Leland (1503?–52), antiquary to Henry
       VIII, as "a tarpit for the unwary"; one might be tempted to apply this turn of phrase more
       broadly as well ("The Historical Arthur").
68   The battle of Camlann appears in writing for the first time in the tenth-century *Annales
       Cambriae* for the year 537 (Morris, ed., 85). In the vulgate: "Sed et inclitus ille rex Arturus
       letaliter uulneratus est; qui illinc ad sananda ulnera sua in insulam Auallonis euectus
       Constantino cognito suo et filio Cadoris ducis Cornubiade diadema Britanniae conces-
       sit anno ab incarnatione Domini .dxlii." (§178.81–84; The illustrious king Arthur too was
       mortally wounded; he was taken away to the island of Avallon to have his wounds tended,
       and, in the year of Our Lord 542, handed over Britain's crown to his relative Constantinus,
       son of Cador duke of Cornwall). On the ambiguity of this famous passage, which contains
       one of Geoffrey's rare dates, see Chapter 2, n. 63. The First Variant follows Geoffrey here;
       Wace departs by including a passage on the "Breton hope" (to be discussed below).

WACE'S ROMAN DE BRUT, PART 2   293

known sites,[69] rather than being as vague as HB (though there still remains some vagueness, as to whether, for example, Geoffrey intended the battle of York and the one at the river Duglas to be one and the same):[70]

1) at the river Duglas;
2) York, where Arthur subjects Colgrinus to a "siege";
3) battle of Lincoln, "on a hill between two rivers in the province of Lindsey" (§145.59–60);
4) battle of Celidon Wood;
5) battle of the *pagum Badonis* (Geoffrey's Bath);[71]
6) battle of Dumbarton;[72]
7) battle at the "river Camblan" (§178.46).

---

69 Geoffrey, having "little special knowledge" of the north (Tatlock, *Legendary History*, 22), was possibly loath to become involved in efforts by his colleagues (such as Henry of Huntingdon or William of Malmesbury) to identify the vague places named as Arthur's battle sites in the *Historia Brittonum* – the most vague being the four battles at the "river Duglas" without any further specificity – and thus he elected to place at well known sites the few battles he does describe; see also Breeze, "The Historical Arthur and Sixth-Century Scotland," 160.

70 Tatlock identifies the first battle at the river Duglas to be the same as the battle of York, i.e., Arthur's first battle against the Saxons, the unidentifiable *fluuium Duglas* "south of but evidently not far from York" (*Legendary History*, 22). If one identifies the battle of the *fluuium Duglas* with that of York as Tatlock does – and one "downgrades" the sieges at Dumbarton, Thanet and Loch Lomond, to below the status of "battles" – then there are only four battles, reduced from the twelve in the *Historia Brittonum*. On the other hand, the First Variant would appear to treat the battles at the river Duglas and York as two separate events, as well as the sieges of Dumbarton and Loch Lomond as having the weight of two battles, thus bringing the total of battles in the FV to seven (rather than four or five). In the FV, the isle of Thanet is not mentioned in §148 as a refuge for the Saxons following the siege of Dumbarton, but rather in §101 in the context of the Saxons' fleeing the onslaught of the Britons after the latter had deposed Vortigern and made Vortimer their king.

71 On Geoffrey's identification of "Badonicus Mons" or "Mons Badonis" with Bath, see Tatlock, *Legendary History*, 47 and n. 190 where he states, "Of course the earlier historians' Mons Badonicus or Badonis Mons can have no connection with the English name Bath; but that would not trouble Geoffrey." But in Geoffrey, the battle of Bath comes earlier than Arthur's twelfth (and final) battle at Mount Badon in *HB*.

72 The battle of Dumbarton is barely described; the major part of the section in which it is mentioned is devoted to Cador duke of Cornwall, whom Arthur ordered to pursue the Saxons elsewhere while the king goes on ahead to Scotland (§148.133–35). Besides his intention to save Hoel who is ill in Dumbarton (§148.136–37), the only time we hear of Arthur's involvement at Dumbarton is at the beginning of the next section, where we learn that Dumbarton ("Alclud") has been freed from barbarian attack ("Alclud, quam Arturus a barbarica oppression liberauerat," §149.148–49). Those Saxons who survive Cador's onslaught, retreat to the isle of Thanet, and thus Thanet from the *HB* is given a nod, but as in the First Variant (though there without the mention of Hengist, §101), in the *HB*, Thanet is mentioned in the context of Vortimer's having driven Hengist, Horsa, and his people to the isle of Thanet (*HB* 43). On Thanet, see Chapter 1, n. 118, and n. 140 below.

294   CHAPTER 5

In broad outline, Wace follows the First Variant – including a siege at Loch Lomond – with Arthur laying siege to Colgrin at "a pass near the river Duglas" ("Dejuste l'eue de Duglas / S'entrevindrent a un trespas," 9049–50), and then chasing him to York, where he again lays siege.[73] The next battle is that of Lincoln ("Nichole"), followed by that of Celidon Wood. In Wace, the main battle is that of Bath, followed by the routing of the Scots at Loch Lomond, with "Camble" (13253)[74] as almost an afterthought, following Arthur's international conquests as in the vulgate and FV (see below under "Breton hope") making a total of seven battles in the *Brut* (unless one conflates those of "the river Duglas" and York, which would then yield six).

Two of these battles are particularly worthy of note: Bath and Loch Lomond. The battle of Badon Hill, absent in Wace as in Geoffrey and FV, is not the last of Arthur's battles in the early part of his career as it is in the *HB*, but its "equivalent" (in stature), Bath, falls roughly mid-way through the "national" battles and cements the king's relationship with the Virgin Mary. It should be remembered that Wace was an important participant in the growth of Marian devotion in England as well as in Normandy, as the author of the *Conception Nostre Dame* (*c.*1130–40), written at the height of the English revival of the feast of the Conception and contemporaneous with the first French resistance – that of St. Bernard – to including the feast of the Conception in the regular liturgical calendar; the *Conception*, based primarily on apocryphal sources, made up of four shorter poems on the conception, birth, life, death and Assumption of the Virgin Mary, is essentially the earliest cycle on the Virgin in the vernacular.[75] Given Wace's literary efforts as part of a larger movement to spread the devotion to Mary and fill in the gaps in the public's knowledge – particularly

---

73   Since the "river Duglas" (whose precise location relative to authentic geography is unknown) and York are perceived by Wace to be nearby each other, it is possible that he considered these two sieges/battles as one. See also Appendix 3.

74   See Weiss, 333, n. 1 on the names for Camlann.

75   On the growing cult of the Virgin in England and Normandy, and Wace's literary participation, see *Wace, The Hagiographical Works*, 13–56 (Introduction to the *Conception Nostre Dame*); see also Rita Beyers, "La Conception Nostre Dame de Wace: premier poème narrative sur la Vierge en ancien français," in *Serta devota in memoriam Guillelmi Lourdaux. Pars posteriora: Cultura medievalis*, ed. Werner Verbeke, Marcel Haverals, Raphaël De Keyser and Jean Goossens, 2 vols., Medievalia Lovaniensia, series 1, 21 (Leuven: Leuven University Press, 1992–95), II, 359–400, Mary Clayton, *The Cult of the Virgin Mary in Anglo-Saxon England*, Cambridge Studies in Anglo-Saxon England 2 (Cambridge: Cambridge University Press, 1990), and Richard Southern, "The English Origins of the 'Miracles of the Virgin," *Medieval and Renaissance Studies* 4 (1958): 176–216. On St. Bernard's resistance (on theological grounds), see Marielle Lamy, *L'Immaculée Conception. Étapes et enjeux d'une controverse au Moyen Âge (XIIᵉ–XVᵉ siècles)*, Collection des Études Augustiniennes: Moyen Âge et Temps Modernes 35 (Turnhout: Brepols, 2000), esp. 43–45.

WACE'S ROMAN DE BRUT, PART 2   295

genealogical gaps not addressed in the Bible – it is not surprising that Wace makes original references to the Virgin in the *Brut*, including amplifying Arthur's active devotion to her.

In the *Brut*, there are five references to Mary: two used as a dating mechanism,[76] the shield, the invocation at the battle of Bath, and Hoel's foundation of a chapel in her name on the isle of Tombelaine to commemorate his daughter Helene's life and death, in the channel to the north of Mont-Saint-Michel (11602–6).[77] Mary is only mentioned alone in the vulgate in two references: the first, the image of Mary on Arthur's shield (§147.109–10), and the second to Arthur having involved Mary at the battle of Bath (in the invocation, §147.125); the FV contains only the shield reference (§147.1), without the invocation.[78]

Briefly, regarding the invocation, as Rosemary Morris points out, Arthur's invocation of Mary appears as a sort of battle cry,[79] and is a combination of the Norman battle cry seen in the *Roman de Rou* – "Deus aie!" ("May God help us!") – and Mary's name, forming the cry "Deus aie, sainte Marie" ("May God help us, Holy Mary!").[80] Those familiar with Wace's corpus will not be surprised that he has taken this opportunity to turn a third-person report of what Arthur exclaimed into direct address providing the exclamation itself, since the use of dialogue is one of the hallmarks of his literary techniques.[81] Although Arthur's battle cry appears only once in the *Brut*, it is not insignificant that Wace capitalized on a reference to Mary to create a cry that he might have hoped would rival Charlemagne's "Monjoie" (although as Morris adds, it apparently did not catch on!).

---

76   Julius Caesar had come from Rome into France "Seissante anz ainz que Jesu Crist / De Seinte Marie nasquist" (3827–28, "Sixty years before Jesus Christ was born of the Virgin Mary" [lit. "saint/holy," my translation; Weiss gives simply "Mary" here]) and for Cadwallader's death, "Set cenz anz un meins puis que Crist / En sainte Marie char prist" (14837–38, "Seven hundred minus one year after Christ's incarnation in the Virgin Mary," my translation; Weiss restores DL's "and one" "e un," rather than P's "un meins" "minus one"). While Arnold's text has 699 and Weiss's 701, neither version agrees with the vulgate and the FV which both have 689 years (*HRB* §206.585–6 and §206.3).

77   Neither in the vulgate (§165.107–9) nor in the FV (§165) is this new chapel dedicated to the Virgin.

78   In the First Variant, Arthur dons his golden helmet, and Pridwen his shield "on which the image of Saint Mary was imprinted to invoke her memory" at the major battle of Bath as in the vulgate and the *Brut* (FV, §147.1).

79   Morris, *The Character of King Arthur*, 128.

80   "Avant s'en passe si s'escrie, / 'Deus aïe, sainte Marie!'" (9341–42; "Pushing onward, he cries, 'May God help us, Holy Mary!'").

81   M. Malkiel Jirmounsky, "Essai d'analyse des procédés littéraires de Wace," and Le Saux, *Companion*, esp. 102–7.

296   CHAPTER 5

Regarding the shield, regardless of which side one falls on the issue of King Arthur's historicity – with the two main "camps" being, at the risk of oversimplifying: 1) those who believe that Arthur has a basis in historical fact and was later mythologized, or 2) those who believe that he was originally a mythical figure who later became historicized[82] – it remains clear that, as Rosemary Morris observes, "early sources are much confused as to the nature of the image which Arthur bore on his shield."[83] In the ninth century, the *Historia Brittonum* relates that Arthur carried an image of the Virgin Mary on his shoulders ("super humeros suos")[84] into the eighth battle at Guinnion Fort for three days and three nights. The *Annales Cambriae* report that in AD 516, Arthur carried the Cross on his shoulders into the Battle of Badon.[85] In the twelfth century, William of Malmesbury continues the reference to shoulders – which may have originated in early translations from the Old Welsh of the word "scuit" "shield" often confused with "scuid" "shoulder";[86] in the *Gesta Regum Anglorum*, "at length at the siege of Mount Badon, relying on the image of our Lord's Mother which he had fastened on his arms, [Arthur] attacked nine hundred of the enemy single-handed, and routed them with incredible slaughter" (1.8.2).[87] In fact, Arthur has greater success recorded by William in this context than by Geoffrey, the First Variant redactor or Wace.[88]

Around a decade after William was writing, Geoffrey of Monmouth made what is apparently the first literary reference to a religious figure on a shield (more specifically than William's "armis suis"), emphasizing the shield on the shoulder and not the shoulders themselves: in the *Historia Regum Britanniae* (vulgate as well as the First Variant), Arthur carries an image of the Virgin on his shield into the battle of Bath (the most important battle in the Galfridian

---

82   For surveys on these two "camps," with nuances, see N. J. Higham, *King Arthur: Mythmaking and History*, esp. 10–37, and Thomas Green, *Concepts of Arthur*, esp. 7–44.

83   Morris, *The Character of King Arthur*, 127.

84   Ch. 56; see also Field, "Arthur's Battles," 23.

85   *Annales Cambriae* (Morris, ed., 85).

86   See also Peter Field, "Arthur's Battles," 15, nn. 82–83.

87   This is one of two places William mentions Arthur, the first being as the "warlike" Arthur who aids Vortigern's successor Ambrosius, "the sole surviving Roman," to fight off the "barbarian menace" ("intumescentes barbaros" 1.8.2), and the second where he says that the tomb of Arthur had still not yet been found although his nephew Walwein's had been (III.287.1). It is in the context of the first reference that William remarks that the Britons have told "many wild tales" with Arthur as their hero, but that given his exploits, he deserves discussion in "reliable history" rather than in "false and dreaming fable" (1.8.2 "dignus plane non quem fallaces somniarent fabulae sed ueraces predicarent historiae").

88   In the vulgate, Arthur kills four hundred seventy (147.128), FV "more than four hundred fell in that first assault, as much from Arthur as from his men" (147), Wace, "he killed four hundred alone, more than were killed by his own army (9355–56).

WACE'S ROMAN DE BRUT, PART 2 297

material for this portion of Arthur's career, but not the last battle as Badon Hill is in *HB*).[89] Roughly twenty years later, in his mid-twelfth-century verse translation and adaptation of the Galfridian material, Wace makes an editorial decision to introduce further precision into this question of just where the image of Mary was: rather than "on" the shield which could mean either "on the outside" or "on the inside," Wace specifically declares the image to be "on the inside" – "Dedenz l'escu"[90] – thereby transforming the symbol from one of public display to one of private devotion. This distinction was a vital one for Wace since Arthur's connection to Mary would ensure that monarch's association with the growing cult of the Virgin in twelfth-century England and Normandy, and thus, by extension, for the Anglo-Norman ruling house.

While Geoffrey was apparently the first to associate a religious figure with a weapon (albeit a defensive weapon), Wace transforms the image from public to private, or more precisely, he renders the less-precise phrasing of "on the shield" unambiguous, with "dedenz l'escu," so his audience does not have to wonder where the image was. Arthur had this image painted on the inside of the shield "pur enur e pur remembrance," "for honor and memory/remembrance."

With the image of Mary on the outside of the shield, the enemy would see her image; if Arthur were not leading the charge, some of his soldiers might also see it. In battle, on the outside of the shield, the image of Mary serves as

---

89   Vulgate: "humeris quoque suis clipeum uocabulo Pridwen, in quo imago sanctae Mariae Dei genitricis inpicta ipsum in memoriam ipsius saepissime reuocabat" (§147.108–10). While the first part of Wright's translation is not in question, "and shouldered his shield called Pridwen, on which was depicted Mary, the Holy Mother of God," he translates the last phrase "in memoriam ipsius saepissime reuocabat" as "to keep her memory always before his eyes" which suggests that Arthur could actually *see* the image while in battle, though without indicating the exact location of the image, an interpretation that might take Geoffrey a bit far; cf. Peter Field, "Arthur's Battles," who states that Geoffrey has transformed the image "into a painting on the inside of Arthur's shield" (31, n. 83). Regarding the translations of Geoffrey, however, Thorpe's more open-ended translation might be preferable "which forced him to be thinking perpetually of her," leaving more vague (in keeping with the Latin) the question of the location of the image, whether on the outside of the shield or the inside. The First Variant reads "humeris clipeum uocabulo Pridwen, in quo sancte Marie ymago impressa sui memoriam dabat" (§147; "and on his shoulder the shield called Pridwen, on which the image of Saint Mary was imprinted to invoke her memory" §147.1). See also Gerard J. Brault, *Early Blazon: Heraldic Terminology in the Twelfth and Thirteenth Centuries with Special Reference to Arthurian Literature* (Woodbridge: Boydell, 1997, 2nd ed.), 24.

90   Dedenz l'escu fu par maistrie   Inside the shield, there was skillfully
       De ma dame sainte Marie   Portrayed and painted the likeness
       Purtraite e peinte la semblance,   Of my Lady Holy Mary
       Pur enur e pur remembrance.   For [the sake of] honor and remembrance.
            (9293–96)

298   CHAPTER 5

an identifier – the bearer is a Christian – and possibly as a tool of conversion. For readers of the Latin texts, the image of Mary on the outside of the shield or on the shoulders also serves as an historical marker, quite possibly to reinforce Arthur's historicity: Mary was there, Mary was real, Arthur was there with Mary, therefore Arthur was real – and really there.

With Mary inside the shield, Wace also bestows Arthur with historical veracity, just as would have been conveyed if he had retained the designation "on the shield." However – and though this may be placing too much weight on the one word "dedenz" – with Wace's textual and polemic participation in the growing cult of Mary, it makes sense that he wanted to go much further than his sources by emphasizing the personal connection Arthur had with Mary. Henry ɪɪ's father, Henry ɪ was a very strong supporter of the practice of the feast of the Conception in mid-twelfth-century England, and it would have been to Henry ɪɪ's advantage – having just come to the throne the year before Wace presented him (possibly) and Eleanor (the latter according to Laȝamon) with the *Brut* – to be portrayed as a supporter of Mary through association with Arthur (and Henry's predecessor, William the Conqueror). Arthur holds his shield with Mary facing him, protecting him, interceding for him, reminding him of the greater good. In Wace's *Brut*, at the Battle of Bath, Arthur dons his father's golden helmet with a dragon painted on top, and carries his sword, Caliburne, his lance Ron, and his shield Pridwen, making a glorious pubic display, but with the private display of Mary, for his eyes only, at least during the fighting.

Wace's influence in this regard can be seen in later works as well. For example, in Laȝamon's *Brut* (*c.*1200), at the Battle of Bath, Arthur's accouterments are the same, with the image of Mary painted on the inside of the shield, but the phrasing for Mary is different, "on the inner side engraved in lines of red gold a noble likeness of the Mother of God."[91] In Laȝamon, Mary's role as Jesus's mother is accentuated but she is not named by her given name, and thus, in a way, the reference is less personal than in Wace. In the *De Instructione Principis* (*On the Instruction of a Prince*) (*c.*1223), Gerald of Wales preserves the specific reference to the interior of the shield, refers to Mary by her title (thus another less personal reference than in Wace), but adds an interesting devotional element for Arthur, including a bit of publicity for Glastonbury and its connection with Arthur preceding the reference to the shield:

---

91   *Layamon's Arthur. The Arthurian Section of Layamon's Brut* (*lines 9299–14297*), ed. and
        trans. W. R. J. Barron and S. Carole Weinberg (Harlow: Longman, 1989; rev. ed. Exeter:
        Exeter University Press, Exeter Medieval English Texts and Studies, 2001), 69.

The memory of the famous Arthur, king of the Britons, is not to be suppressed, which the histories of the famous monastery of Glastonbury praise greatly, and of which he was the distinguished and generous patron and a magnificent supporter in his day. Truly he loved the church of St Mary the mother of God at Glastonbury more than all other churches in his kingdom and he promoted it before the others with far greater devotion. In the time when the warlike man lived, he caused to be painted on the inside of his shield a picture of the Blessed Virgin, so that in battle he would always have it before his eyes; and whose feet, whenever he found himself in the turning point of a battle, he was accustomed to kiss with the greatest devotion.[92]

For Peter of Langtoft writing his Chronicle nearly one hundred years after Wace, as well, Mary is mentioned by name, and her image is inside the shield, so that "Arthur ne l'oublye" ("Arthur doesn't forget her").[93]

For Wace, given Mary's stature and growing influence or presence at all levels of society, it is not surprising that he would want to associate King Arthur with her, to emphasize quite possibly the personal nature of belief and faith, upon which he comments especially in the *Assomption* section of the *Conception Nostre Dame*. In the later romance tradition, Arthur is most often brought down by his faith and trust in earthly women, but in the *Brut*, it would appear that he has faith that he will be saved by Mary, if not in this life, then surely in the next.

After invoking Mary at the battle of Bath, and killing four hundred Saxons alone, Arthur delegates the final touches to Cador, sending him after the Saxons who have fled to Mount Tiegnwic, near the river Teign,[94] while the king heads on to Scotland. The Scots, upon hearing that Arthur will join the fray (they had been rebelling against Arthur), set off for Moray, where the king follows them.[95]

---

92 Trans. Scott McLetchie, 1994, Internet Medieval Sourcebook (no line numbers), https://sourcebooks.fordham.edu/source/1223gerald-arthurtomb.asp.

93 Thomas Wright, Public Record Office, 1866, no line numbers, p. 152.

94 Weiss notes that the vulgate has the Saxons flee to the Isle of Thanet at this point in the text (§148.145); the First Variant does not specify any location (§148), whereas Wace shifts the scene to the West Country and introduces a river and a mountain (Weiss, 237, n. 1).

95 The vulgate says they fled to "Mureif" (§149.149), while the FV has "Mireif ciuitatem Albanie" (§149; Murielf MS. H). Wace follows the latter at this one juncture – but not elsewhere, see n. 108 below – stating that Moray is a city (9417), rather than "eandem prouinciam" as in the vulgate (§149.151). The *HB* redactor describes the "stagnum Lumonoy" under the category of wonders of the world, "de Mirabilius Britanniae"; although Geoffrey appears to identify this site with Loch Lomond, as do the FV redactor (§149; see

300   CHAPTER 5

4.1.2.1   *Arthur and the Scots*

The battle of Loch Lomond is noteworthy on a number of levels, besides being
Arthur's last domestic battle before turning to foreign conquests. Perhaps for
modern audiences the ferocity with which Arthur fights the Scots is in stark
contrast to his private devotion to Mary or his generosity for which he was
reputed since his youth, but in the *Brut*, his ferocity, in fact cruelty, is an inte-
gral part of the larger picture. In the vulgate, Arthur blockades the Scots and
Picts at Loch Lomond, starving them out after two weeks, "until they died in
their thousands" ("tanta afflixit fame ut ad milia morerentur," §149.159–60).
The Irish king, Gillamurius, comes to their aid with a great host, only to be
"mercilessly cut down and forced to sail home" (§149.160–62), and "once victorious, [Arthur] redirected his attention to the Scots and Picts and began wiping
them out with utter ruthlessness" (§149.164–66; "Potius illico uictoria, uacauit
iterum delere gentem Scotorum atque Pictorum, incommutabili saeuitiae
indulgens"). The First Variant redactor tones down the cruelty, replacing the
phrase "incommutabili saeuitiae indulgens" with the more low-key "perseue-
rauit Scotos et Pictos infestare" (§149.4, "[he] continued to harass the Scots
and Picts"). In each Latin version, bishops and other clergy come to Arthur
barefoot, carrying relics and church treasures, to beg him for mercy. They argue
that it is not necessary to kill the remaining survivors but if granted their lives,
they would gladly be slaves in perpetuity. In the vulgate, Arthur is moved to
tears upon hearing these pleas (§149.174); in the FV, which tends to introduce
the factor of religion more frequently than the vulgate, the clergy add that the
survivors would continue to worship God as Christians while bearing the yoke
of slavery, and Arthur is moved to pardon them, but without tears.

In the *Brut*, the tableau at Loch Lomond differs significantly from its two
main written sources.[96] First, in this scene, Wace has eliminated the Picts,
deviating from both the vulgate and First Variant; in fact, the Picts figure in the
Brut far less frequently than in the vulgate or the FV where they are almost a
matched set with the Scots, particularly in Geoffrey's text where the Scots are

---

Burchmore, n. to §149.2, p. 473) and Wace (9425), it is not in Moray, as Weiss notes (237,
n. 2). Geoffrey adds to *HB*'s marvels the eagles who nest on the rocks in the Loch and the
portents their cries announce upon their yearly return ("which every year used to gather
to mark with loud cries any marvel about to occur in the kingdom" §149.156–57); FV follows the vulgate on the open-ended subject of portents, but Wace adds a sinister note,
saying that from what he has heard, the eagles would gather, fight among themselves and
shriek, and this announced portents of great destruction ("grant destructiun," 9440) in
the days when "wicked people used to come to lay Scotland waste," "Quant males genz
venir soleient / Ki Escoce guaster deveient" (9433–34).

96   It is impossible to know with any certainty whether Wace relied on oral sources for his
Loch Lomond passage or if he relied on his own invention.

WACE'S ROMAN DE BRUT, PART 2   301

rarely mentioned without the Picts (a situation to which we will return later in the chapter).[97] Second, Wace expands the narrative on the blockade to starve out the Scots:

Tant les assailli e guarda,	He so severely attacked and restrained,
Tant les destrainst e afama,	Oppressed and starved them so much,
A vinz, a cenz e a milliers,	That by the twenties, hundreds and thousands,
Chaeient morz par les graviers.	They fell dead on the shores.
(9451–54)	

Although Wace may have done this for purely poetic effect, it is nonetheless noteworthy, for it is followed by Arthur's making short work of the Irish king, Gillamarus, chasing him and his troops back to their ships, forcing them to depart, before turning back to the lake where he left the Scots.

Here, Wace adds no more about Arthur's resumption of the slaughter of the Scots (as in the vulgate) – in Wace, Arthur may be a barbarian king, but he is no butcher (as will be seen below in the contrast between Arthur and Gormund). Instead, Wace moves on directly to the two pleas for mercy without describing any more killing and death; in his text, the second plea is original and far more complex than that of his sources which only have the one plea. In the vulgate and First Variant, the plea is reported in the third person, delivered by bishops and other clergy – thus "official" representatives of the people, more learned, and of higher social status. Wace devotes four lines to this third-person plea from the clergy, but then adds a forty-five-line speech that becomes the focal point of the passage (9477–9520). The speech is made by Scottish women – not from the noble elites but simply women – who plead for the remaining men, women, and children to be spared.[98]

Not only does Wace achieve significant dramatic effect by adding this speech on the part of Scottish women, but also the contents of the speech are remarkably complex, as if to display contemporary negotiating tactics in addition to the contents of the arguments themselves,[99] including criticism of

---

97   For approximate tallies of occurrences of these groups by name in the vulgate, FV, and Wace, see the Conclusion of this chapter.

98   On Wace's use of direct address in the *Brut*, see Le Saux, *Companion*, 106–7, 134–37, and 140.

99   Wace is known for his interest in warfare and sea battles, so it is not unreasonable to think that negotiating tactics and other forms of diplomacy also fascinated him. On Wace's penchant for military vocabulary and war narratives, as well as his expertise, see Matthew Bennett, "The Uses and Abuses of Wace's *Roman de Rou*," in *Maistre Wace*, 31–40,

302   CHAPTER 5

Arthur, criticism of the Saxons, and the importance of Christian solidarity. The
women ask Arthur – apparently not expecting any reply, except that he cease
ravaging the Scots and recognize the validity of their arguments.[100]

The stages of the speech are 1) why have you destroyed the land?; 2) why
destroy the land further?; 3) if you don't have mercy on the men, then have
mercy on the women and children; 4) we have already paid sufficient penalty
when the Saxons came – we didn't invite in the Saxons who ravaged our land;
5) "if we harbored them, they harmed us even more" (9495–96; Si nus les avum
hebergiez, / Tant nus unt il plus damagiez); 6) they seized our property and sent
it home to their lands; 7) we had no one to defend us; 8) they had the power, we
endured it; 9) the Saxons were heathen and we [the Scots] Christians 10) "They
did us wrong; you do worse still" (9509; Mal nus unt fait, tu nus faiz pis); 11) no
honor or fame will come to you by killing those who ask for mercy; 12) you
have conquered us but let us live; 13) we are Christians like you; 14) "No matter
where it is, give us land!" (9514; "Quel part que seit, terre nus livre!"); 15) we are
willing to be slaves if we can continue to live, and as Christians, since "we hold
the [same] faith you do" (9518; "Nus tenum la lei que tu tiens"); 16) Christianity
will be brought low if this land is destroyed; and 17) we are willing to be slaves
if we can continue to live, and as Christians.

---

and idem, "Wace and Warfare," in *Anglo-Norman Studies XI: Proceedings of the Battle
Conference, 1988*, ed. R. Allen Brown (Woodbridge: Boydell Press, 1989), 37–57, and on his
familiarity with seagoing vessels and navigating military maneuvers on water, as well as
maritime vocabulary in general, see William Sayers, "A Norse Etymology for Luff, 'Weather
Edge of a Sail'," *American Neptune* 66:1 (2001): 25–38 and idem, "Arthur's Embarkation
for Gaul in a Fresh Translation of Wace's *Roman de Brut*," *Romance Notes* 46.2 (2006):
143–56. See also Elisabeth van Houts, "Wace as Historian," in *Family Trees and the Roots
of Politics: The Prosopography of Britain and France from the Tenth to the Twelfth Century*,
ed. K. S. B. Keats-Rohan (Cambridge: Boydell, 1997), 103–32 (repr. in E. M. C. van Houts,
History and Family Traditions in England and the Continent, 1000–1200, Aldershot,
Ashgate, 1999, 103–32, and in *The History of the Norman People: Wace's Roman de Rou*,
trans. Glyn S. Burgess, Woodbridge, Boydell, 2004, xxxv–lxii). On the related topic of the
ocean voyages leading up to and involved in the Norman Conquest, see also Elisabeth van
Houts, "The Ship List of William the Conqueror," in *Anglo-Norman Studies X: Proceedings
of the Battle Conference 1987*, ed. R. A. Brown (Woodbridge, Boydell, 1988), 159–93 (repr. in
E. M. C. van Houts, *History and Family Traditions in England and the Continent, 1000–1200*,
Aldershot, Ashgate, 1999, 159–83), and Matthew Bennett, "Poetry as History? The 'Roman
de Rou' of Wace as a Source for the Norman Conquest," in *Anglo-Norman Studies V:
Proceedings of the Battle Conference 1982*, ed. R. Allen Brown (Woodbridge, Boydell, 1983),
21–39.

100   In the vulgate, Geoffrey constructs the passage so that the clergy tell Arthur that the people and land have been ravaged enough, that there was no need to kill every last one, and
that if need be, they would live in slavery if they had to, if granted a small portion of their
country (§149.169–75).

WACE'S ROMAN DE BRUT, PART 2

303

The arguments can be broken down into four topic groups: First, demanding Arthur's justifications for what he has done, if only as a rhetorical ploy. Second, the defenselessness of the Scots is accentuated, in the face of the Saxons and now before Arthur as well – the Scots are victims, and not of their own doing; this argument acts as a veiled reminder of Vortigern's having invited the Saxons, as seen in Bede, but it is not clear how many in Wace's audience – unless "professional" historians – might have been aware of Bede's presentation of the *adventus Saxonum*, unless that version had already passed into legend, reaching beyond those who were able to read Gildas and Bede.[101] Furthermore, the Scots are victims of the Saxons just as the Britons, and thus the Scots and the Britons may have more in common than they might have otherwise thought; in other words, the Scottish women seek to set up at least a "psychic" alliance between the Scots and the Britons.[102] Third, that Christians should form a community, not fight one another, and that the result of Christians fighting Christians would be destruction of the whole land. Lastly, the Scots would be willing to hold any land at all – a more conciliatory position than in the vulgate *Historia* where the clergy ask on their behalf that they specifically be allowed to keep a portion of *their own* lands ("sineret illos portiunculam habere patriae, perpetuae seruitutis iugum ultro gestauros" §149.172–73, "if he let them keep a small portion of their country, they would willingly bear the yoke of slavery for ever")[103] – and live, even as slaves.

This passage also serves to draw the Scots closer to Arthur and the Britons, if only as two parts of a larger community of Christians, if not as British, or at least as non-Saxons. Here Wace appears to attempt to mitigate the previously adversarial position the Scots held vis-à-vis the Britons – as a traditional enemy of the Britons in the *HRB*[104] – as if to say that it's better to band together

---

101 It needs to be remembered as Colgrave and Mynors point out, "though Bede incorporates the tradition related by Gildas about the coming of the Angles and Saxons, he makes certain significant changes. Gildas leaves the story vague but Bede provides a name for Gildas' 'superbus tyrannus.' The name Vortigern is apparently a title meaning 'chief lord' of which Gildas' phrase may perhaps be a latinization" (ed. *Historia Ecclesiastica*, p. 48, n. 2).

102 See n. 108 below.

103 Thorpe treats this passage somewhat differently: "He should allow them to have some small tract of land for their own" (IX.6, p. 219). This implies that they could keep some land for themselves, for their own use, without accentuating who had held the land previously, that it had been "their own." Cf. Michael Faletra, "The bishops also asked that Arthur allow the besieged to have some little plot of land of their own, seeing that they would be bearing the yoke of servitude anyway" (trans., §149, p. 169).

104 Seen for example in §91 where "foul crowds of Scots, Picts, Norsemen, Danes and other allies" (§91.59–62) ravage the land of the Britons following the departure of the Romans,

304   CHAPTER 5

as enemies of the Saxons, than to fight each other. Through this speech, Wace reminds his audience yet again of the Saxons' perfidy: according to the Scottish women, when the Scots took them in and protected them, the Saxons treated them even more poorly; this is another anti-Saxon element, but also one which draws "victim" cultures together.

In addition, due to Arthur's conquest, in broad terms, a colonial situation is established, whereby the Scots are essentially the colonized and the Britons the colonizers (although the analogy does not work perfectly since, in the text, Arthur's "peoples" had no explicitly articulated plans to settle the region).[105] Arthur's status is increased since it is now up to him as victor – albeit potentially a fellow Briton[106] – not only to grant the Scots mercy but also to give them permission to live on the land(s) they formerly held.[107]

---

as well as Cadwallader's final lament: "Woe to us sinners ... His mighty retribution is upon us, to uproot from our native soil us whom neither the Romans once nor later the Scots, the Picts or the deceitful treachery of the Saxons could drive out" (§203.532, 534–36).

105 Technically speaking, the situation involving Arthur and the Scots in this instance might more properly be called one of "lordship" and not "colonization," but I am invoking a colonial situation to emphasize the absolute nature of domination by conquest, those in power vs. those not. In a particularly useful study on the distinctions between the terms "lordship" and "colony" in the Middle Ages, focusing on medieval Ireland but having much broader implications, R. R. Davies points out that the terms cannot be used interchangeably for a number of reasons, primarily that "colony" connotes a more dependent relationship than "lordship" does, "it is the governmental dependence which is perhaps even more clearly the hallmark of colonial status" ("Lordship or Colony?" in *The English in Medieval Ireland: proceedings of the first joint meeting of the Royal Irish Academy and the British Academy, Dublin, 1982*, ed. James Lydon (Dublin: Royal Irish Academy, 1984), 142–60, cited here at 152). In addition, "colonisation included the cultivation of new land and in some degree the displacement of the native population" (151); see n. 108 below. See also M. I. Finley who warns against historians (this can be applied more broadly to many fields of scholarship) embroiling themselves "by their retention of loose usage in many complicated contexts" ("Colonies – An Attempt at a Typology," *Transactions of the Royal Historical Society* 26 (1976): 167–88, cited at 169). See also Loomba's discussion of the distinction between administrative colonialism and settler colonialism (*Colonialism/Postcolonialism*, 22–25).

106 On the modernist assumption of "fellow Celt" feeling, see Patrick Sims-Williams who claims that "self-conscious Celtic solidarity cannot be traced back beyond the modern period" ... and that any proposed alliances of Scots, Irish, and Welsh leaders were based primarily on "common grievance against the English rather than their ethnic kinship" ("Celtomania," 11). See also Matthew Hammond, "Ethnicity and the Writing of Medieval Scottish History," 17.

107 With respect to the relationships between the British territories/kingdoms and England in the Galfridian material and how Geoffrey's goals as he was writing during the reign of Stephen may have been received by the Anglo-Norman elites, Alan MacColl proposes that "if the history of Geoffrey's Britannia is to be read primarily as a warning of the dangers facing England at the time the work was written, the interpretative emphasis is shifted away from imperial and expansionist concerns to the governance of England itself ... In

WACE'S ROMAN DE BRUT, PART 2 305

In the *Brut*, following the speech of the Scottish women, Arthur shows compassion (though without tears) and spares all the living Scots and their progeny; he "spared them life and limb, he received their homage and left them alone" (9525–26; "Vie e membre lur parduna, / Lur humages prist sis laissa"), one of his many acts of magnanimity which balances out his fierceness in battle. In perhaps a nod to the "psychic" alliance proposed by the Scottish women – material unique in the *Brut* – peace is restored, the Scots are no longer enemies of the Britons, and Arthur divides Scotland among three highly born British lords.[108]

After Arthur distributes rulership over the three divisions of territories north of the Humber, Wace declares that:

Quant Artur out sa terre assise	When Arthur had established his realm,
E part tut out bone justise,	And had established justice throughout,
E tut sun regne out restoré	And had restored his whole kingdom,
En l'ancïene digneté.	To its former dignity.
(9641–44)	

---

the early years of Stephen's reign (1135–54), one imagines that Geoffrey and his intended audience would have been less interested in dreams of a pan-Britannic empire than in the immediate problems of ensuring stable government and securing England against Welsh rebellion and incursions by the Scots" ("The Meaning of 'Britain' in Medieval and Early Modern England," 252).

108   It is possible that Wace meant this to be more than a "psychic" alliance, as it seems to presage for example, Arthur's trust in the Scottish king Angusel (albeit one of his barons) as he places the latter at the head of his first battalion in preparation for war with the Emperor Lucius (12358–59). Although Wace follows the vulgate (§152.201–5) and FV (§152.2 "Uranium sceptro Murefensium insigniuit") in Arthur's dividing the land north of the Humber into three parts, restoring ancestral rights of rulership as they were before the Saxon incursions – Scotland to be ruled by Angusel, Lothian to be ruled by Loth, and Moray to be ruled by Urien (Moray seen in Wace here as a region not a town, l. 9632, Urien "Cil ki sire ert de Mureifens") – he deemphasizes that the Scots had once been enemies of the Britons, and appears to construct a melding of sorts, albeit with Arthur as king over all (9614–40). However, this "melding of sorts" is all the more complicated because if Arthur is giving ancestral lands to high-born British lords who had previously ruled territories north of the Humber, who were the peoples they supposedly ruled? Britons? Those who eventually became Scots? Probably not the Scots as Geoffrey perceived them, i.e., as invading enemies nearly as pernicious as the Saxons. This is not an answerable question since we have no way of telling who Wace thought those people were, nor can we address definitively the extent of anachronism in the *Brut*. We also don't know to what extent Wace may have taken into consideration the multi-layered complexities between the era the Galfridian material is supposedly referring to and Wace's own lifetime. See the Conclusion to this chapter for more reflections on these issues.

306   CHAPTER 5

Arthur takes Guinevere as his queen. Where the vulgate has one sentence
regarding Guinevere's superlative beauty, her noble Roman ancestry, and having been brought up at the court of duke Cador, Wace uses fourteen lines and
adds the following details: that she was *curteise*, the location of Cador's court
was in Cornwall, she was brought up as befitted a close kinswoman of the duke,
that Cador's mother had been Roman, she had a noble countenance, her manners were perfect, and she was generous and well spoken, that Arthur loved
her deeply, but they produced neither an heir nor other children (9645–58).[109]

---

109   Genuevre prist, sin fist reïne,   He took Guenievere and made her his queen,
      Une cuinte e noble meschine;   A gracious and noble maiden;
      Bele esteit e curteise e gente,   She was beautiful and courtly and well born,
      E as noble Romains parente;   And from noble Roman stock;
      Cador la nurri richement   Cador brought her up richly
      En Cornoaille lungement,   In Cornwall, for a long time,
      Cume sa cusine prochainne;   As his close cousin;
      E sa mere resteit romaine.   And his mother had been Roman.
      Mult fu de grant afaitement   She was of high breeding
      E de noble cuntienement,   And of noble behavior,
      Mult fu large e buene parliere,   She was a generous and a good speaker,
      Artur l'ama mult e tint chiere;   Arthur loved her very much and held her dear;
      Mais entr'els dous n'orent nul eir   But between the two of them they did not
                                                   have an heir
      Ne ne porent emfant aveir.   They were not able to have children.
           (9645–58)

Wace adds the detail about no heirs or other children (Weiss, 243, n. 6), in his characteristic thoroughness. Guinevere's ability to speak well fits in with Wace's preoccupation with
languages, their origins, vocabulary and diction in general. For further discussion of Wace's
presentation of Guinevere, see esp. Charlotte A. T. Wulf, "A Comparative Study of Wace's
Guenevere in the Twelfth Century," in *Arthurian Romance and Gender; masculin/féminin
dans le roman arthurien medieval; Geschlechterrolen in mittelalterlichen Artusroman*, ed.
Friedrich Wolfzettel (Amsterdam and Atlanta, GA: Rodopi, 1995), 66–78, and eadem,
"The Coronation of Arthur and Guenevere in Geoffrey of Monmouth's *Historia regum
Britanniae*, Wace's *Roman de Brut*, and Lawman's *Brut*," in *Reading Laȝamon's Brut*,
229–51. Although there is no extended discussion of Wace's presentation of Guinevere
per se, Fiona Tolhurst's chapter "Undermining and Degrading Female Kingship in the
First Variant and Wace's *Roman de Brut*," provides illuminating analogies nonetheless
(*Geoffrey of Monmouth and the Translation of Female Kingship*, 133–88, esp. pp. 155–88),
finding that "Wace's manner of translating this story [of Octaves's daughter] confirms
that, although he develops the roles of Galfridian females, he generally grants them less
political power and historical significance than Geoffrey does. As a result, female figures
in the *roman de Brut* [sic] conform to traditional gender roles while their Galfridian coun-
terparts do not" (188).

WACE'S ROMAN DE BRUT, PART 2   307

4.1.2.2   *The Beginning of Arthur's Foreign Conquests*
When springtime had returned,[110] Arthur had his fleet prepare to sail to Ireland, which, as in the vulgate, he conquered easily as the Irish were "defenseless"; Wace adds the detail that the Irish did not know how to shoot bows, which the Britons had, and did (9684–87). As in Scotland, Irish King Gillomar "did homage to Arthur and his domain was returned to him" (9699–9700; "Mais cil fist a Artur humage / Si prist de lui sun heritage"), giving hostages as a guarantee of yearly payment of tribute. After conquering Ireland, Arthur heads to Iceland "par tut volt aver seinnurie" (9707; "For he wanted to have dominion over everything").

After Arthur conquers Iceland, Gonvais king of Orkney, Doldani king of Gotland, and Rummaret of Wenelande,[111] having heard of Arthur's conquests, come to him offering many gifts and willingness to be among his barons. Arthur agrees, returns to his ships and returns to England, and is welcomed with great joy. It is at this juncture – during the twelve years' peace – that Wace inserts two narratives on the Round Table, not found in his two Latin sources, and about which he says the Britons told "mainte fable" (9751–52):[112] 1) the first

---

110   See below for a discussion of Arthur's foreign conquests in the comparative context of Gormund's predations and Arthur's brand of imperialism. Although Arthur's "empire" never existed in real terms, in terms of its literary/historical portrayal in the *Brut*, it most closely parallels the suggestion made by Michael Hardt and Antonio Negri regarding the Roman Empire which they found dissimilar to modern European colonialism, "since imperial Rome was also loosely incorporated into its subject states rather than [having] controlled them directly" (Ania Loomba, *Colonialism/Postcolonialism*, cited at 10). Hardt and Negri compare the "new Empire" (or "new order," a vastly complex and disputed concept in and of itself, whose analysis is beyond the scope of our study) to Rome, arguing that "contemporary Empire is 'imperial not imperialist' because it does not consist of powerful nations that aim to 'invade, destroy and subsume subject countries within the sovereignty' as the old powers did but rather to absorb them into [a] new national network" (Michael Hardt and Antonio Negri, *Empire*, Cambridge, MA and London: Harvard University Press, 2000, 182, cited within Loomba, 10). This is what Arthur's "empire" attempted to do – not to "destroy and subsume" but to "annex" into a new "network," with as little political and cultural interference as possible, according to Wace.

111   The mysterious Rummaret (Romarec) of Weneland has occasioned a number of studies; see for example Houck, *Sources*, 257–59; Ernest C. York, "Wace's 'Wenelande': Identification and Speculation," *Romance Notes* 22.1 (1981): 112–18; William Sayers, "Rummaret de Wenelande: A Geographical Note to Wace's *Brut*," *Romance Philology* 18 (1964): 46–53; Hans-Erich Keller, "Les Conquêtes du roi Arthur en Thulé," *Cahiers de Civilisation Médiévale* 23 (1980): 29–35; and Arthur C. L. Brown, "The Round Table Before Wace," *Studies and Notes in Philology and Literature* 7 (1900): 183–205 (repr. Boston: Atheneum, 1900), esp. 201 and n. 1.

112   Many (too numerous to list here) have considered Wace's phrase "Dunt Bretuns dient mainte fable" to refer to the Bretons, which is possible, but not necessarily preferable to

308   CHAPTER 5

narrative is the relatively short passage on the foundation of the institution of
the Round Table (9747–60); 2) and the second, the much longer, more complex
narrative on the court festivities on the occasion of Arthur's coronation, which
by extension implies how the social organization created and maintained by
the institution of the Round Table functioned in "real time" (10197–622).

4.1.3   The Founding of the Round Table and More Foreign Conquests

The description of the Round Table itself and its purpose falls in the middle of
a passage composed of sixteen lines on Arthur's nobility (9730–46), fourteen
on the Round Table itself (9747–60), closed by twenty-six lines on why the best
knights and leaders from all around came to Arthur's court (9761–87).[113] With

---

the Britons; Weiss agrees that the French term "Bretons" here refers to the Britons, but
chooses "British" for her translation (p. 245). Probably the most well-known recent work
on the Round Table is Beate Schmolke-Hasselmann, "The Round Table: Ideal, Fiction,
Reality," *Arthurian Literature* 2 (1982): 41–75; see also Maurice Delbouille, "Le Témoignage
de Wace sur la légende arthurienne," *Romania* 74 (1953): 172–99, and Tatlock, *Legendary
History*, 471–72, 474–75. Schmolke-Hasselmann agrees with the latter two scholars that no
"Round Table was ever associated with King Arthur before Wace," supported by evidence
including that "not one of the numerous references to the Arthurian legend before the
middle of the twelfth century mentions the Round Table. Nor is it present in the earliest
iconographic material – the famous Modena archivolt and the mosaics in Southern Italy"
("The Round Table," 43 and nn. 5, 8, and 9 (43–44)); cf. Arthur C. L. Brown, "The Round
Table Before Wace."

113   At this moment in the narrative, we find the famous passage on the "aventures" that took
place during the twelve-year peace:

En cele grant pais ke jo di,	In this time of great peace I am talking about,
Ne sai si vus l'avez oï,	I don't know if you've heard about it,
Furent les merveilles pruvees	Wondrous events happened
E les aventures truvees	And adventures transpired
Ki d'Artur sunt tant recuntees	Which are told so much about Arthur
Ke a fable sunt aturnees.	That they have turned into fables.
Ne tut mençunge, ne tut veir,	Neither wholly lies, nor wholly truth,
Tut folie ne tut saveir.*	Neither all folly, nor all wisdom.
Tant unt li cunteür cunté	The tale-tellers told so much
E li fableür tant flablé	And the fablers fabled so much
Pur lur cuntes enbeleter,	In order to embellish their tales
Que tut unt fait fable sembler.	That they made them all seem like fables.
(9787–98)	

*(For this line, Weiss restores a reading from MS. P: *Ne* tut folie ne tut saveir.) MS. H
(BnF fr. 1450) inserts after l. 9798 six texts, five of which are Chrétien's romances, as if
to offer examples or proof of the "aventures" (*Erec et Enide, Perceval*, anonymous First
Continuation [of the *Perceval*], *Cligès, Yvain*, and *Lancelot* [frag.]); Wace's text resumes

WACE'S ROMAN DE BRUT, PART 2 309

the stage set regarding Arthur's nobility, the Round Table comes at the exact juncture where Wace needs to explain how Arthur will arrange his knights and how he will maintain the peace when each nobleman is just as noble as the next, but might invariably think himself superior. It is as if Arthur created the Round Table to prevent social disintegration caused by personal narcissism:

Pur les nobles baruns qu'il out,	For his noble barons
Dunt chescuns mieldre ester quidout,	Each of whom thought he was better,
Chescuns se teneit al meillur,	Each one held himself to be the best,
Ne nuls n'en saveit le peiur,	No one knew who was the worst,
Fist Artur la Roünde Table	Arthur had the Round Table made,
Dunt Bretun dient mainte fable.	About which the Britons tell many tales.
Illuec seeient li vassal	There the vassals sat,
Tuit chevalment e tuit egal;	All as leaders and all equal;
A la table egalment seeient	They were all seated equally at the table
E egalement servi esteient;	And they were served equally;
Nul d'els ne se poeit vanter	None among them could brag
Qu'il seïst plus halt de sun per,	That he was higher than his peer,
Tuit esteient assis meain,	They were all seated at the main table,
Ne n'i avait nul de forain.	There was no one on the outside.[114]
(9747–60)	

Political and social equality are paramount here. In the next part of the passage, the social finery and conformity among those from within Gaul – and Britain – is stressed and presages the elegance of the festivities and the scope of the guest-list at Arthur's crown-wearing later in the text: "No one was considered courtly – whether Scot, Briton, Frenchman, Norman, Angevin, Fleming, Burgundian or Lorrainer – whoever held his fief, from the West as far

---

after this very lengthy interpolation at l. 9799 and continues to the end, l. 14866 (see Appendix 1). It needs to be pointed out that a "fable" in Old French can mean not only a fable, but also a story, fiction, tale, lie, or falsehood.

114   Line 9754 "leaders" from the expression "tenir terre chevalment" referring to tenants-in-chief, that is, those who held lands directly from the king and thus were of high rank (at the time Wace was writing). For further details on the egalitarian seating arrangement, see Félix Lecoy, "*Meain* et *Forain* dans le *Roman de Brut*," *Romania* 86 (1965): 118–22.

310   CHAPTER 5

as Muntgieu,[115] if he did not go to Arthur's court and stay with him and wear the livery, heraldic device and armor in the fashion of those who served at Arthur's court" (9761–72).[116] Linguistic equality is even more in evidence in the lengthy passage on the festivities at Arthur's plenary court and coronation, to be discussed below.

In terms of the arrangement of the narrative of the *Brut*, the passage on the foundation of the Round Table is bracketed by Arthur's overseas conquests: first, of Ireland and Iceland which precede the founding of the Round Table; the founding is then followed by Arthur's conquest of Norway and Denmark, and finally France before taking a break to celebrate his coronation at Carleon – after spending nine years in France, that is. Since Wace's passage on the coronation festivities (and the social functioning of the Round Table, though without naming the Round Table itself at those festivities) is considerably longer than that of his sources (neither of which contain the Round Table, of course), one has the impression that perhaps the social refinement at the court and promoted by the Round Table itself was meant to somehow balance out what is basically an imperialistic land grab on Arthur's part.

Wace does not miss out on telling us how much Arthur wanted to conquer as many lands as he could. When Loth sees that he will lose his right to Norway to Riculf (a Norwegian baron), Loth appeals to Arthur who promises to give Norway to Loth; Arthur enters the country by force and "inflict[s] great damage on the land" (9839). After forcing Norway to surrender, and placing Loth in charge "on the condition that Loth held it from him and acknowledged him as overlord" (9885–86), Arthur crosses into Denmark where king Aschil enters into an agreement with him to become his man and so that he held the whole kingdom in Arthur's name. Then, because, although:

Artur fu liez del grant esploit	Arthur was happy with this great exploit
E del conquest que il faiseit.	And the great conquest[s] he had made.
Ne li pout mie encor suffire.	[But] it wasn't yet enough for him.
(9887–89)	

---

115   The Great St. Bernard Pass, the third highest pass and one of the oldest in the Western Alps, in terms of usage. This location is also found in the *Rou*; see *The History of the Norman People: Wace's Roman de Rou*, trans. Glyn S. Burgess, 247.

116   "N'esteit pas tenuz pur curteis/ Escot ne Bretun ne Franceis, / Normant, Angevin ne Flamenc / Ne Burguinun ne Lochrenc, / De ki que il tenist sun feu, / Des occident jesqu'a Muntgeu, / Ki a la curt Artur n'alout / E ki do lui ne sujurnout, / E ki n'en aveit vesteüre / E cunuissance e armeüre / A la guise que cil teneient / Ki a la curt Artur serveient."

WACE'S ROMAN DE BRUT, PART 2   311

Arthur brings with him to France the best Danish archers and knights – adding
these details to the vulgate, of Arthur's more "civilized" comportment: Arthur
takes Flanders and Boulogne, but makes his men behave wisely, "sagement fist
sa gent cunduire" because he didn't want the land destroyed, "ne volt pas la
terre destruire" (9897–98); in the vulgate, "Arthur sailed to Gaul, marshalled his
forces and began to ravage the entire country" ("nauigauit Arturus ad Gallias
factique turmis patriam undique uastare incepit," §155.250–51).[117]

As if to continue to balance Arthur's land-lust with a more civilized set of
behaviors – especially after the rather violent "performance" in Norway – Wace
emphasizes Arthur's "civilized" approach to his conquest of France. In preparations to fight Frollo, the Roman provincial lord, where Geoffrey states that
even the Gallic soldiers went over to Arthur's side due to the king's generosity,
Wace adds they did so, partly because of the king's "clever words" ("sun cuintement parler" 9949), his *noblesce*, out of fear but also for refuge (9951–52).[118]
After Frollo's defeat, Arthur's troops blockade Paris. After a month, to avoid
his people's starvation, Frollo challenges Arthur to single combat; this detail
is retained from either the vulgate or FV, but Wace adds the detail of women
and children begging Frollo to give in and ask Arthur for peace (9989–90),
reminiscent of the speech of the Scottish women, though this time related in
the third person and in only two lines. Interestingly, in the vulgate, it is Frollo
who requests the single combat, and his request is due to the fact that he pre-
fers to rely on his own strength against Arthur since his army is significantly
out-manned, whereas in the *Brut*, Frollo makes the request to save the people
of Paris, so that the city would not be destroyed no matter who won the combat; thus, even the Roman enemy – not forgetting that Frollo is the Roman
tribune ruling Gaul – is more "civilized" in the *Brut* than in the two primary
Latin sources.[119]

With all of France conquered, Arthur spends nine years in his new lands.
Wace adds to Geoffrey (and the FV) the detail that Arthur, at the beginning of
the nine years, rewards the older men with wages and gifts, sending them back
to their home lands (presumably in Britain), while keeping the younger and
unmarried men with him since they sought out further conquests (10133–42).
At the end of the nine years, in the vulgate, before returning, Arthur gives
Normandy to his butler Bedevere and Anjou to his steward Kay, "and many

---

117   While the FV tones down the vulgate's "uastare" ("ravage" or "lay waste") with "infestare"
       ("harass," §155), it does not contain the tempering details Wace has added.
118   "Li Franceis a lui se turnoent, / Cil ki poeient e osoent / Tant pur sun cuintement parler, /
       Tant pur sun largement duner, / Tant pur la noblesce de lui, / Tant pur poür, tant pur refui"
       (9947–52).
119   This is in keeping with Wace's habit of providing at least a few redeeming qualities for
       nearly all enemies. See Chapter 6, n. 91.

312   CHAPTER 5

other regions to noble men of is retinue" (§155.301–3) (FV §155.9: "he was generous in giving other honors to many according to their merit and dignity of birth"). Wace adds the specifics "Flanders to Holdin, Le Mans to his cousin Borel, Boulogne to Ligier and Pontif to Richier" (10163–66),[120] followed by a unique passage of rejoicing upon Arthur's return (10171–96).

4.1.4   Organization and Governance; Arthur's Plenary Court

Before entering into the discussion of the details of the plenary court, we need to bear in mind the importance of ceremony in the description of Arthur's coronation and festivities at his plenary court, an importance which cannot be overstated. In his review of Malcolm Vale's *The Princely Court: Medieval Courts and Culture in North West Europe, 1270–1380*, Maurice Keen expresses the following assessment that appears as applicable to the mid-twelfth century when Wace was writing as to the late thirteenth to fourteenth centuries of which Vale writes:

> the secular elements in the developing ritual and style of the courts' *grans festes* are what are most striking, as Vale observes them: the tourneying, gaming and hunting, the banqueting at marriages and the heraldic display of funerals, the collective chivalrous vows. French, as the predominant language of culture through the north west European region, facilitated simultaneously the exchange of ideas and fashions between courts and their competition as magnetic poles of power. Conspicuous consumption, lavish gift giving, generous patronage of the arts and of artificers in the interests of display were essential to courtly living. Consumption needed to be conspicuous, and the cultivation of noble tastes, manners and pastimes needed to be visible and organized if courts were to discharge their function, of giving body to the dynastic political ideology of which they are an expression.[121]

---

120   MSS PSHABKGRN omit ll. 10165–66; Arnold supplies the couplet (on Boulogne and "Puntif," that is, Pontif) from D (presumably, since D is the MS he used for verses 12000–14866 [end], whereas he used P for 1–11999); Weiss notes that none of these four men appear in *HRB* at this juncture, though Borel, Holdin, and Ligier appear soon after in §156 (257, n. 1), Richier (Richerius) appearing in §§166–67; Pontif is identified as Ponthieu (see *Roman de Rou*, trans. Burgess, 2004, 391). For an analysis of Arnold's editorial principles, see J. Blacker, "Will the Real *Brut* Please Stand Up? Wace's *Roman de Brut* in Anglo-Norman and Continental Manuscripts," in *Text: An Interdisciplinary Annual of Textual Studies* 9, ed. D. C. Greetham and W. Speed Hill (Ann Arbor: The University of Michigan Press, 1996), 175–86.

121   Keen, *English Historical Review* 117.473 (2002): 903–5, here 904.

In Wace's *Roman de Brut*, completed in 1155, and, according to Laʒamon's Middle-English *Brut* chronicle (*c.*1205), offered to Henry Plantagenet's queen Eleanor of Aquitaine, we find what must be the earliest detailed tableaux of ceremonial gift-giving and court festivities in French, applied anachronistically back to the reign of King Arthur of Britain, six hundred years before Wace's time. Any discussion of the historical implications of these celebration tableaux and their roles in creation of the twelfth-century social imaginary though has a bit of a chicken-and-the-egg aspect to it: that is, do the tableaux reflect a growing sociocultural reality already in existence at the time Wace was writing, or were they meant to serve a more prescriptive role as a template of the desired ideals as envisaged by the author, his patrons and audience? The truth most likely lies somewhere in between.[122]

---

122   In general, I find Karen Broadhurst's arguments persuasive, expressing skepticism – or at the very least, hesitancy – toward assuming any direct connection between treatments expressed in literary and historical texts and any potential wishes of Henry and Eleanor, particularly the popular belief that "Henry II also used vernacular literature in order to connect himself favorably with the legendary King Arthur" which "does not pass scrutiny" ("Henry II of England and Eleanor of Aquitaine: Patrons of Literature in French?" 68–69); of all the evidence examined by Broadhurst regarding numerous works which may mention in passing the two royals or may allude to them, the most compelling direct connections of patronage are between Henry and the Norman histories of Wace (the *Roman de Rou*) and Benoît de Sainte-Maure (*Chronique des ducs de Normandie*), which supports Ulrich Broich's thesis that "in general Henry was interested in literature that was important for the strengthening of his position as a ruler, the stabilizing of the stately order, and the defense of his foreign and domestic policy" (68; see also Walter F. Schirmer and Ulrich Broich, *Studien zum literarischen Patron am England des 12. Jahrhunderts*, Wissenschaftliche Abhandlungen der Arbeitsgemeinschaft für Forschung des Landes Nordrhein-Westfalen 23 (Cologne: Springer Fachmedien Wiesbaden, 1962), 92, 200). Broadhurst concludes that because "the demonstrable patronage of vernacular literature by Henry II and Eleanor of Aquitaine was severely limited": "Unfortunately, we must therefore revise the image often portrayed by scholars of the influential connection between literature in French and this king and queen of England. As John Benton has noted: 'The danger of tentative conclusions growing with repetition into positive assertions is so great that there may be value in reminding the reader of what we do not know'" (84; Benton, "The Evidence for Andreas Capellanus Re-Examined Again," *Studies in Philology* 59 (1962):471–78, 78); see also Ian Short, "Patrons and Polyglots," and John Gillingham, "The Cultivation of History, Legend, and Courtesy at the Court of Henry II," in *Writers in the Reign of Henry II*, 25–52. Cf. Charity Urbanski, *Writing History for the King*. About his own views, particularly with respect to the paucity of Latin patronage at the court of Henry and Eleanor, Gillingham remarks: "My sceptical approach to the role of this king and queen does not, of course imply that in cultural terms the period was not a remarkable one. To quote Ian Short: 'It would [nonetheless] be only a slight exaggeration to conclude that for a short space of history, the courts of Henry I and Henry II and the Anglo-Norman baronage and Church had presided over a literary and intellectual efflorescence of remarkable brightness'" (Gillingham, "Cultivation of History," 39

The passages in question occur in the *Brut* between the time of Arthur's coronation at Caerleon (not his initial coronation at Silchester upon his father Utherpandragon's death, vulgate and FV §143 and *Brut*, 9011–12), and the arrival of the Roman ambassadors with the threats from the emperor Lucius Hiberius.[123] The court festivities which accompany this ceremonial coronation come toward the end of this principal section of Arthurian narrative in the *Brut* – the main events of which are Arthur's succession, the Battle of Bath (often considered synonymous with Badon Hill) and the ultimate defeat of the Saxons, Arthur's marriage to Guinevere, and his foreign campaigns, including his conquest of Gaul (France). The description of the Round Table, appearing for the first time in Wace's *Brut*, comes about one third of the way through the Arthurian section; the narrative of the Round Table further establishes a tone of a more outwardly cohesive political organization than that seen in the vulgate and First Variant material. Just as the founding of the Round Table is bracketed by Arthur's foreign conquests – Ireland and Iceland preceding, and Norway, Denmark, and Gaul following – the subsection involving the plenary court, its ceremonies and celebrations, is likewise bracketed by conquest scenarios: the conquest of Gaul/France and the arrival of the Romans, as if to provide this time an illustration of the sophistication of the court by association with France, as well as the effects of the Round Table (although it is not mentioned by name) and as a preliminary to Arthur's greatest potential conquest: that of the Roman Empire.

---

and Ian Short, "Language and Literature," in *A Companion to the Anglo-Norman World*, ed. Christopher Harper-Bill and Elisabeth van Houts, Woodbridge: Boydell, 2002, 191–213, 212.) However, my main goal here is to consider the social climate and metaphoric implications of Wace's *Brut* and his Galfridian sources, without assigning specific interests to the monarchy. That said, we shouldn't forget Wace's mentions of Henry's having granted him a prebend ("une provende") in Bayeux, quite possibly in "payment" for the *Brut*, adding "and many other gifts" (*Roman de Rou*, iii, 170–75). Although he doesn't address the subject of royal patronage per se, Christopher Berard argues (similarly to Urbanski, but with respect to the Arthurian material rather than the history of the Normans and the Conquest) that Henry might have found Wace's fashioning – after himself – of Arthur as a *roi-chevalier* "very much in [his] interest," given that the Plantagenet king was without royal parentage on his father's side: "emphasizing nobility of character and deeds as the principal qualities of a good king seems to have been how Henry's writer compensated for his lack of royal paternity," suggesting that "Wace made Arthur into a legitimizing predecessor for Henry II as Geoffrey of Monmouth had done a generation earlier for the successors of Henry I" (*Arthurianism in Early Plantagenet England*, 45).

123   In this section of the *Brut*, Wace has used primarily Geoffrey's vulgate; see Chapter 2, n. 2 and n. 7 above on general patterns of Wace's use of the vulgate and First Variant.

The timing of the arrival of the Roman ambassadors is also critical in the sense that some of the most influential men in the known world are gathered in one place – the most notable from Arthur's kingdom and foreign leaders and dignitaries. When the Roman ambassadors arrive, if all had not already been assembled, at least a royal assembly of those nearest to Arthur would have needed to have been called in order to confront the new challenge; as Timothy Reuter notes in his study of assembly politics in Western Europe from the eighth century to the twelfth, "An audience was required, and assemblies provided it. It was here that ambassadors were formally received and formally given leave to return to their masters ... If they happened to turn up when no assembly was scheduled, they might well be asked to wait until one was."[124]

In broad outline, Geoffrey's narrative of the plenary court and its ceremonies (§§156–57) can be summed up as follows: following Arthur's victory over Frollo in Gaul, as Whitsuntide approaches, the king returns to England, summons his barons to a plenary court, and prepares for a crown-wearing ceremony; the beauty of Caerleon's location and the city's wealth provide the ideal setting for this meeting of the court; messengers deliver invitations (i.e., summonses), to bishops, archbishops, and barons from across Arthur's realm and kings from overseas territories, including a large Welsh contingent recognizable from their names beginning with *map* (or *mab*); a notably large train of accouterments, mules and horses accompany the invitees. The Primate of Britain, Archbishop Dubricius who had legally crowned Arthur at Silchester upon the death of Utherpendragon presides over the crown-placing ceremony, accompanied by two other archbishops and the four kings of Albany, Cornwall, Demetia, and Venedotia; from another direction are led the queen and the consorts of the four kings, with four white doves according to custom, into the church of the dedicated virgins. Once the procession is over, organ music is played and choirs sing while knights circulate between the two churches, and mass is celebrated in both. The king and queen change into lighter regalia; it is said that according to the ancient custom of Troy, the king dines with the men and the queen with the women; when all are seated according to their rank, a thousand noblemen clad in ermine and led by Kay the Seneschal bring the food; the same number clad in minever led by Bedevere the cupbearer "offering various drinks of every sort in goblets" (§157.381–82); innumerable servants dressed in varying liveries were performing their duties in the queen's hall.

---

124 "Assembly Politics in Western Europe from the eighth century to the twelfth," in *The Medieval World*, ed. Peter Linehan, Janet L. Nelson, and Marios Costambeys (London: Routledge, 2001), 432–50, here 441.

316   CHAPTER 5

Next comes the famous passage which explains that by that time:

> So noble was Britain then that it surpassed other kingdoms in stores of
> wealth, the ostentation of its dress and the sophistication of its inhabit-
> ants. All its doughty knights wore clothes and armour of a single colour.
> Its elegant ladies, similarly dressed, spurned the love of any man who had
> not proved himself three times in battle. So the ladies were chaste and
> better women, whilst the knights conducted themselves more virtuously
> for the sake of their love. (§157.385–91)

After eating, all go out to the fields for games; Arthur gives an immense prize
to each of those who win in their chosen category. The festivities last for three
days and on the fourth, all those who had served Arthur receive a gift of a city,
castle, archbishopric or other landed possessions. Dubricius resigns the office
of archbishop of Caerleon (and concomitantly the roles of Primate of Britain
and Papal Legate), and David, uncle of King Arthur, is consecrated in his place;
Arthur distributes benefices among the clergy. Twelve senior men come as
messengers from Rome and the next chapter in the saga begins.

Although not all details where Wace's *Brut* diverges from his sources carry
equal weight, the main discrepancies in the narrative of the plenary court and
festivities are noteworthy. In the *Brut*, Wace more openly emphasizes Arthur's
wealth, that after Arthur "had given his barons fiefs and made all his close
friends rich" (10171–72; "Quant il out ses baruns feufez / E fait riches tuz ses
privez") – he crossed to England in April. Here follows a 25-line passage unique
to Wace, on the general rejoicing upon Arthur's return, primarily demonstrated by kissing: husbands and wives, sons and daughters, fathers and moth-
ers, cousins and neighbors embraced, lovers kissed, Wace adding that the latter
did more when they had the chance! (10171–96); several lines are devoted to
describing conversations of passers-by with those returning from war. Arthur
gives still further rewards to his barons, and then Arthur, in order to "display
his wealth and spread his fame[125] took counsel and was advised to assemble his barons at Pentecost, in summer, and then have himself be crowned"
(10197–204). In other words, the decision to hold a crown-wearing was made
collectively, not by Arthur alone.[126]

---

125   "E pur faire de sei parler" (10200), lit. "to have himself talked about." "Artur enura tuz les
      suens, / Mult ama e duna as buens. / Pur ses richeises demustrer / E pur faire de sei parler, /
      Prist conseil si li fu loé / Qu'a la Pentecuste en esté / Feïst sun barnage assembler / E dunc
      se feïst coruner" (10197–10204).
126   In the *Historia*, after Arthur has spent nine peaceful years in Gaul, he gives Normandy
      to Bedevere, Anjou to Kay, and other provinces to noblemen who had served him.

WACE'S ROMAN DE BRUT, PART 2   317

Although in the *Historia*, the display of prosperity was an incentive in calling the plenary court, it appears that Wace is more direct about that factor than Geoffrey, for whom the sanctity of the ceremony and the role of the clergy are more important.[127] Geoffrey's physical description of Caerleon relies on the element of the gold-painted gables of its roofs (§156.317), as it does in the FV, while all three both liken the city to Rome. Wace goes further, though, adding to Caerleon's geographical situation, details of the wealth of fish and game in the environs, two churches, both prestigious, and adds at this juncture that Caerleon was the seat of an archbishop, together with "noble priests" and canons who, among other things, helped Arthur by interpreting portents; Wace comments "Bon ert a cel tens Karlion, / Ne fist puis se empeirer non" (10235–36; "At that time, Caerlion was in good shape; it has done nothing but deteriorate since then").[128] Regarding the learned men, Wace summarizes with less precision Geoffrey's details that Caerleon "also possessed a college of two hundred scholars, skilled in astronomy and other sciences, who attentively studied the paths of the stars and accurately predicted to the king the portentous events that were to come" (§156.322–25), saying that "there were many powerful clergy, and very learned canons who knew about astronomy; they concerned themselves with the stars and often said to King Arthur how the works he wished to perform would come to pass" (10228–234).[129]

Geoffrey's guest list can be divided into six categories: 1) the kings of the realms of Britain (Scotland, Moray, North Wales, South Wales, and Cornwall); 2) the archbishops of three metropolitan sees of London, York, and Caerleon (though the only one mentioned by name is Dubricius, archbishop of Caerleon); 3) the leading men from the ten principal cities of Gloucester, Worcester, Salisbury, Warwick, Leicester, Chester, Canterbury, Bath, Dorchester, and Oxford; 4) rulers from Wales; 5) kings of the foreign regions or countries conquered by Arthur (Ireland, Iceland, Gotland, the Orkneys, Norway, and Denmark); and 6) rulers

---

       Arthur alone decides to hold a crown-wearing during the feast of Whitsuntide; he explains his plan to the members of his court and they suggest Caerleon as the best site (§155.304–§156.306–12).

127   In fact, Wace omits a passage from the vulgate on the gifts of bishoprics and archbishoprics (§158.404–11). In the FV, the passage of ecclesiastical gift-giving is at the end of §157 (§157.5); it presents an almost identical narrative to that in the vulgate in that the names and offices are the same but some of the phrasing is different.

128   John Gillingham remarks that, in locating Arthur's court in Wales at Caerleon, Geoffrey "seems to be more Welsh even than the Welsh ... [since] the earlier Welsh tradition seems to have placed it in Cornwall" ("Context and Purposes," 25).

129   "Mult i aveit riche clergied, / E chanuines de grant clergie / Ki saveient d'astronomie; / Des esteiles s'entremeteient, / Al rei Artur suvent diseient / Cumfaitement li avendreit / Des ovres que faire vuleit."

318   CHAPTER 5

from Gaul, as well as Bedevere and Kaius and the twelve peers of France.[130]
Wace's guest list of all those summoned (or invited) by King Arthur is very
close to Geoffrey's;[131] in the French poem, however, the names at times appear
in a different order, most likely to produce better rhymes; further examination could conceivably reveal a political subtext in Wace's reordering, though
perhaps not as radical as the "de-Welshing" seen in the First Variant's omission
of all names beginning with *Map* (or *Mab*), the Welsh prefix meaning "son"
(roughly 20% of the named attendees). Importantly, Wace does not remove
those names but merely translates *Map* or *Mab* by *fiz*.[132] In addition, Wace
includes the mention of the three archbishops – and only Dubricius by name –
a bit further on than Geoffrey does (after the names of the earls representing
important cities and the Welsh rulers, rather than after the kings of different
regions/kingdoms of Britain), whereas the First Variant redactor omits those
references altogether from the plenary court passage, which is somewhat odd
since the First Variant redactor tends to be more interested in ecclesiastical
matters than Geoffrey.

Wace also adds what could be called "courtly touches" such as the comment that Angusel, king of Scotland was dressed handsomely and Urien, king
of Moray, and calling the son of Owain, courtly (10249–50, 10251), the hero of
poems by the Welsh historico-legendary poet-prophet Taliesin.[133] While wrap-
ping up the passage on invitees, Wace puts in a plug for the French: "Hoel [from
Brittany] and all those from France had noble bearing, fine weapons, handsome clothes, beautiful trappings and well fed steeds" (10323–26; "Hoels et
tuit cil de vers France / Furent de noble cuntenance,/ De beles armes, de bels
dras, / De bels lorains, de chevals gras"). Wace may well have shared William
of Malmesbury's view of civilization "in socio-economic as well as in cultural

---

130   These divisions are adapted from those of Erik Kooper, "Guests of the Court: An Unnoticed
      List of Arthurian Names (British Library, Add. 6113), in *Li premerains vers: Essays in Honor
      of Keith Busby*, ed. Catherine M. Jones and Logan Whalen, (Amsterdam and New York:
      Rodopi, 2011), 223–34, here 224–25.
131   With some exceptions. Weiss notes that Wace adds "Guergint, count of Hereford" (10259)
      (259 n. 2) though she does not mention in the context of additions the somewhat anoma-
      lous "Margoïd" (10278), which may also be unique, though likely a distortion of "Masgoit"
      in the name "Gorbonian Masgoit" embedded in the list of "Map" names (*HRB*, §156.342;
      this name does not appear in the FV since none of the "Map" names appear in that text).
      Wace divides "Kinlit(h) Mapneton" into two figures, "Kinlint" and "Neton" (10281).
132   Cf. Kooper who argues that Wace also "de–Welshes" the guest list by using *fiz* instead of
      map/mab, but this is not the case since *fiz* means "son" in Old French.
133   Weiss, 259, n. 1; Roberts, "Geoffrey of Monmouth," in *Arthur of the Welsh*, 109.

WACE'S ROMAN DE BRUT, PART 2

terms"; as John Gillingham has observed, the latter considered that it was "French culture, not Christianity alone, which made the English civilised."[134]

Before the ceremonies themselves, Wace inserts what appears to be a unique passage (10337–58), outlining the heightened activity associated with preparing the court for the ceremonies and later for the feasts. The passage deals primarily with finding lodgings for the guests (or creating lodgings through the use of tents), and while not highly specific, it provides a picture probably designed to convey the industry and organization involved in this endeavor, if not the scale; Wace's comment that it seemed like a fair ("feire semblast" 10358) underscores this universally peacetime activity, for all levels of society.

The descriptions of the ceremony itself – or ceremonies, since the king and the queen were apparently crowned separately[135] – are somewhat vague in each text, though Geoffrey includes that Dubricius was accompanied by "a choir of clergy of all stations [who] sang before him" (§157.363–64; with wondrous melodies "miris modulationibus"). Perhaps neither Geoffrey nor Wace had attended a crown-wearing but if they had, they did not provide many details. Interestingly, though, Martin Biddle notes that

> we have no record of the sequence of ceremonies which attended a crown-wearing in Norman England, but it probably involved the appearing of the crowned king to a wider audience than could be present in the church itself … in public procession between the residence, where the crown had been placed on the king's head and the church, and back again, but it may also have been a ceremony in itself.[136]

Both the *Historia* and the *Brut* contain the passage on the first meal which follows the crown-wearing, where it is said that "the Britons used to observe the

---

134 "Context and Purposes," 6.

135 The queen's coronation is not explicitly narrated in the vulgate, FV or Wace; in the vulgate *Historia* we read, "when at last the religious services in each church were over, the king and queen removed their crowns and put on lighter robes" (§157.372–74), and in the *Brut*, "when the service was over, and the last words of the mass sung, the king took off his crown, the one he had worn in church; he put on a lighter one, and the queen did the same. They took off the weightier robes and put on lesser, lighter ones" (10437–44; "Quant li servise fu finez / E Ite missa est chantez, / Li reis ad sa curune ostee / Qu'il aveit el mustier portee; / Une curune menur prist, / E la reïne ensement fist; / Jus mistrent les gra300aturs, / Plus legiers pristrent e menurs"). As Weiss notes, the "Ite" signals permission to leave at the end of the mass ("literally: Go, the mass [is ended]") (263, n. 2).

136 "Seasonal Festivals and Residence: Winchester, Westminster and Gloucester in the Tenth Twelfth Centuries," in *Anglo-Norman Studies VIII: Proceedings of the Battle Conference 1985*, ed. R. Allen Brown (Woodbridge, Suffolk: Boydell, 1986), 51–63, here 62.

320   CHAPTER 5

old Trojan custom that men and women should celebrate feastdays separately"
(§157.375–77). Geoffrey and Wace each emphasize the scale of the endeavor,
at least for the men: Kay is accompanied by 1,000 noblemen clad in ermine
serving the food to the king's group while Bedevere is accompanied by 1,000
clad in minever (Wace has ermine for all) serving the drinks; unless the correspondence of servers to guests was one-to-one or similarly small, one can
only imagine the number of invitees if there were 2,000 servers! The queen
had innumerable servants as well dressed in appropriate liveries. In the subsequent equally famous passage, the audience learns that no knight no matter
how nobly born could expect to win the love of a lady if he had not proven
himself three times in battle, hence in the *Brut*, "the knights were more worthy
[for it], and did better in the fray; the ladies, too, were the better and lived a
more chaste life" (10517–20; "Li chevalier mielz en valeient / E en estur mielz
en faiseient, / E les dames meillur esteient / E plus chastement en viveient").
To this picture of sophistication and courtesy on the part of the nobility, Wace
adds: "Even the poor peasants were more courtly and brave than knights in
other kingdoms, and so too were the women" (10499–502; "Plus erent curteis e
vaillant / Neïs li povre païsant / Que chevalier en altres regnes, / E altresi erent
les femes"). Not surprisingly, the First Variant, which often cuts material from
the vulgate, is extremely sparing here: there is one short phrase on Arthur's
generosity, five sentences on the crown-wearing, one sentence on the men dining separately from the women, and one sentence on the three days of games
and celebrations, with no details of scale or even hints of gallantry and its role
as a social facilitator (§157).

Three more divergences in the *Brut* are worthy of note: first, there is a 46-line
passage found in approximately one-third[137] of the extant 34 manuscripts and

---

137   Brackets indicate a passage found in a minority of the manuscripts; MSS PDLFHABNT
       lack ll. 10543–588. See Weiss, 266, nn. 1 and 2 and Arnold, ed., II, 553, 555 for the manu-
       scripts that omit some of these lines but also include some, as well as for the manuscripts
       missing ll. 11601–620, cited in n. 140 below; see also Jane Bliss and Judith Weiss, "The 'J'
       Manuscript of Wace's *Brut*," esp. 225. Although neither Weiss nor Arnold note this specific
       detail in their texts, apparently MS. K (the Guiot MS., BnF fr. 794) has "cymbes" in line
       10552 rather than "timbes," that is "cymbals" rather than "tambourines" (*La Partie arthu-
       rienne du Roman de Brut de Wace*, ed. I. D. O. Arnold and M. M. Pelan, Paris: Klincksieck,
       1962, l. 2006 [in the *Partie arthurienne*, the passage in question is numbered 1997–2040]):

       [Mult out a la curt jugleürs,   There were many minstrels at the court,
       Chanteürs, estrumenteürs;   Singers, instrumentalists;
       Mult peüssiez oïr chançuns,   You could have heard many songs,
       Rotruenges e novels suns,   *Routrouenges* and new melodies,
       Vïeleüres, lais de notes,   Music for the *vïèle*, lays with melodies,

Lais de vïeles, lais de rotes,	Lays for the *vièle*, lays on rotes,
Lais de harpes, lais de frestels,	Lays for harps, lays for flutes,
Lires, tympes e chalemels, 10550	Lyres, drums, and shawms,
Symphonies, psalteriuns,	Hurdy-gurdies, psalteries,
Monacordes, timbes, coruns.	Monochords, tambourines/cymbals, and *chorons*.
Assez i out tresgeteürs;	There were plenty of magicians;
Joeresses e jugleürs;	Female minstrels and male;
Li un dient contes e fables,	Some told stories and tales,
Alquant demandent dez e tables.	Others asked for dice and backgammon.
Tels i ad juent al hasart,	There are some who play games of chance,
Ço est un gieu de male part;	That's a game of evil nature;
As eschecs juent li plusur	Most play chess
U a la mine u al grainnur. 10560	Or at dice or something better.
Dui e dui al gieu s'acompainnent,	Two by two they join the game,
Li un perdent, li un guaainnent,	Some lose, others win,
Cil envient qui le plus getent,	Some envy those who make the most throws,
As altres dient qu'il i metent;	They tell the others what they would do;
Sur gauges empruntent deniers,	They borrow money against pledges,
Unze pur duze volentiers;	Gladly taking eleven for twelve [on the loan];
Guages dunent, guages saisissent,	They give pledges, they seize pledges,
Guages prenent, guages plevissent,	They take them, they promise them,
Suvent jurent, suvent s'afichent,	They often curse, often asserting their honesty,
Suvent boisent e suvent trichent; 10570	They often deceive, they often cheat;
Mult estrivent, mult se curucent,	They fight a lot, they get angry a lot,
Suvent mescuntent, suvent grucent;	They often miscount, they often complain;
Dous e dous getent e puis quernes,	Two and two they throw and then double fours,
Ambesas e le tiers e ternes,	Double aces and threes and double threes,
A la fïee getent quines,	Sooner or later they throw fives,
A la fïee getent sines;	Sometimes sixes;
Sis, cinc, quatre, trei, dous e as	Six, five, four, three, two and ace
Unt a plusurs toleit lur dras.	Have taken clothes off many.
Buen espeir ad ki les dez tient;	Those holding the dice have high hopes;
Quant sis compainz les ad si crient. 10580	When their companions have them they shout.
Assez suvent noisent e crient;	They often make noise and shout.
Li un as altres suvent dient:	Some often say to the others:
"Vus me boisiez, defors getez,	"You're cheating me, throw them out,
Crollez la main, hochez les dez!	Shake your hand, scatter the dice!
Jo l'envi avant vostre get!	I am raising the bid before you throw!
Querez deniers, mettez, jo met!"	If you're looking for money, put some down, I am!"
Tels i puet aseeir vestuz	You can see many who sit down clothed
Ki al partir s'en lieve nuz.]	Who when leaving get up naked.

322   CHAPTER 5

fragments of the poem (19 complete or nearly complete copies, and 15 incomplete copies that survive either as extracts or as manuscript fragments).[138] This passage has no parallel in the *Historia* (vulgate or Variant); Geoffrey mentions field games including throwing of rocks and javelins, and dice in passing, in the context of the knights excelling and the ladies watching from the ramparts. Wace adds a list of the types of entertainers, songs, musical instruments, and games involving betting; revealing perhaps where his sympathies lay (there are a number of references to gambling losses in the *Roman de Rou* and hoping for more financial support from patrons),[139] much emphasis is put on the gambling, including dialogue.

The second textual divergence is also an addition to the narrative of the fourth day following the three days of festivities: an expansion of two lines in Geoffrey into twenty-two on Arthur's gift-giving to those who came from foreign lands, from among his "finest possessions" – including horses, jewels, greyhounds, birds, silver and gold from his treasury – with the verb "duna" ("he gave") having a prominent place through the rhetorical device of *anaphora*, widely used by Wace for lyrical emphasis.[140] No one appears to go away

---

     Joseph Harris and Karl Reichl comment that "this passage with its profusion of instruments is typical of similar descriptions in the literature of the High and Late Middle Ages" but at the same time they observe that Wace's passage "is the earliest of its kind and also one which contains a number of technical terms that have given rise to some musicological and philological dispute"; for further discussion of the terms referring both to instruments and performers, see esp. 166–68 and 175 of their Chapter 5 "Performance and Performers" in *Medieval Oral Literature*, ed. Karl Reichl, De Gruyter Lexikon (Berlin and Boston: De Gruyter, 2012), 141–202. With reference to the gambling section of this passage, Rhiannon Purdie notes that "dicing is often depicted as a disreputable, lower-class occupation, but this is more symbolic of its moral status than of the social realities of dice playing," and that "what is clear is that Wace felt he could rely on a thorough knowledge of these dicing tricks in his courtly audience" ("Dice-games and the Blasphemy of Prediction," in *Medieval Futures: Attitudes to the Future in the Middle Ages*, ed. J. A. Burrow and Ian P. Wei, Woodbridge: Boydell and Brewer, 2000, 167–84, cited at 174 and 175).

138   I am grateful to Professor Short for this phrasing of the manuscript count of the *Roman de Brut* (see Appendix 1).

139   On Wace's references in the *Roman de Rou* to what appear to have been gambling debts, and the need for remuneration (though not necessarily due to the gambling debts, but support for his work), see Blacker, *Faces of Time*, 37–40 (1994).

140   A cels ki d'altre terre esteient,   To those who were from foreign lands,

       Ki pur amur al rei veneient,   Who came for love of the king,

       Duna cupes, duna destriers,   He gave cups and chargers,

       Duna de ses aveirs plus chiers. 10600   He gave gifts from his finest possessions.

       [Duna deduiz, duna joiels,   He gave objects of amusement, he gave jewels,

       Duna levriers, duna oisels,   He gave hares, he gave birds,

empty-handed. In Wace's text more so than Geoffrey's, Arthur's coffers appear bottomless: he gives lands seemingly without restraint to the native faithful, and innumerable luxury items to foreigners, which they can take back home with them, further spreading Arthur's fame and reputation for generosity, a cardinal medieval virtue.

As mentioned briefly above, the third major divergence involves an important omission in the *Brut*, however. On the fourth day, the *Brut* relates how Arthur gave lands to those (from Britain) who served him, including towns and castles, bishoprics and abbeys. However, there are no details regarding the ecclesiastical gifts, whereas in the *Historia*, Dubricius resigns his post as Archbishop of the City of Legions (as well as those associated titles of Primate of Britain and Papal Legate), and Arthur consecrates as Archbishop his uncle, David, "whose life was a model of goodness for all his pupils" (§158.406). In addition, in the *Historia*, Geoffrey names specifically other prelates to whom Arthur distributes benefices (§158), as does the First Variant (§158) where Teliaus, priest of Llandaff, replaces Archbishop Samson of Dol (with "support of" Hoel

Duna peliçuns, duna dras,	He gave pelicans, he gave clothes,
Duna cupes, duna hanas,	He gave cups, he gave chalices,
Duna palies, duna anels,	He gave embroidered silks, he gave rings,
Duna blialz, duna mantels,	He gave tunics, he gave cloaks,
Duna lances, duna espees,	He gave lances, he gave swords,
Duna saietes barbelees.	He gave barbed arrows.
Duna cuivres, duna escuz,	He gave quivers, he gave shields,
Ars e espiez bien esmoluz, 10610	Bows and swords well sharpened,
Duna lieparz e duna urs,	He gave leopards and he gave bears,
Seles, lorains e chaceürs.	Saddles, bridles and hunting horses.
Duna haubercs, duna destriers,	He gave hauberks, he gave chargers,
Duna helmes, duna deniers,	He gave helmets, he gave money,
Duna argent e duna or,	He gave silver and he gave gold,
Duna le mielz de sun tresor.	He gave the best out of his treasury.
N'i out hume qui rien valsist	There wasn't a man who was worth anything
Qui d'altre terre a lui venist	Who came to him from another land
Cui li reis ne dunast tel dun	To whom the king did not give such a gift
Qui enur fust a tel barun.] 10620	That it gave that baron honor.

Lines 10601–620 are missing in MSS PDLCFHABNT; as Weiss notes, "some or all of these [lines] occur in MSS KEGJ (though displaced), ORS and Hague (10589–601 omitted; 10602–3 are replaced with two very similar lines)" (trans., 266, n. 2); at line 10599, DLCK have "deniers" (coins, money) and not "destriers" (chargers, war horses) (Arnold, ed., II, 555). On Wace's use of *anaphora*, of which the above is an excellent example, *enumeratio*, and *isocolon*, as well as his "judicious use of direct speech and dialogue" in the *Brut*, see Le Saux (*Companion*, 104–7, cited at 104) as well as Jirmounsky, "Essai d'analyse des procédés littéraires de Wace."

324   CHAPTER 5

duke of the Armoricans, "annitente Hoelo *duce Armoricanorum*," FV §157.5);
vulgate, with "full support of" Hoel, king of the Armorican Britons, "annitente
Hoelo *rege Armoricanorum Britonum*," §158.408). Through the two significant
additions to the festivities and omission of the ecclesiastical benefices, Wace
further increases his emphasis on the secular ceremonies, and the growing
interest in worldly largesse, without the "distraction" of ecclesiastical largesse.

The events surrounding Arthur's plenary court in the *Brut* and the *Historia*
have symbolic importance and implications on a number of levels, starting
with the historical: 1) they remind us that although we as moderns are for the
most part used to continuously functioning governments, in the Middle Ages,
at least until the end of the twelfth century, secular government did not meet
frequently and business (legislation, resolution of disputes, military planning, consultation about the state of the realm, etc.) was conducted primarily through occasional assemblies, with the regnal assemblies being the most
important and broadly attended;[141] 2) the scale of the festivities accompanying
the crown-wearing in particular signals the immense symbolic as well as literal
capital associated with those events; as Timothy Reuter points out, "Celebrating
church feasts does not in itself imply a large gathering; but crown-wearings
almost certainly do – there is not much point in wearing your crown among
a small circle of close friends, immediate family and the local bishop";[142] 3) in
describing a crown-wearing at Arthur's time, Geoffrey of Monmouth attempts
to push the celebration – and indeed the institution of centralized kingship –
back hundreds of years prior to the time he is writing; as Martin Biddle has
observed with respect to crown-wearing in earlier periods, "if ... crown-wearing
had been a regular aspect of the pre-Conquest feasts [Easter, Whitsun, and
Christmas], it seems improbable that this would have been ignored by the
author of the *Vita Ædwardi* and unknown to William of Malmesbury [who
associates crown-wearings at the three Christian feasts with the reign of
William the Conqueror]";[143] 4) since the time of William I and William II (the
latter who was particularly known for lavish displays, including the new hall he
had built at Westminster in 1097–99 "on a quite exceptional scale"),[144] the practice of large assemblies at regular crown-wearings had fallen off, quite possibly
due to the immense expense; that crown-wearings became smaller and less
elaborate is suggested by Henry I's later practice, "for few of the houses where
only one of the feasts was celebrated can have been large enough to cope with

---

141   Reuter, "Assembly Politics," 433, 440.
142   Reuter, "Assembly Politics," 434. See also Finke and Shichtman, "Symbolic Capital."
143   Biddle, "Seasonal Festivals and Residence," 58 and n. 35.
144   Biddle, "Seasonal Festivals and Residence," 59.

WACE'S ROMAN DE BRUT, PART 2   325

the kind of gathering described by William of Malmesbury and the annal for 1086 [entry in the Anglo-Saxon Chronicle]."[145]

As a consequence, it is quite possible that Geoffrey and Wace were harking back to the "glory days" of fuller celebrations, suggesting the ceremonies and festivities at Arthur's plenary court as a model for their contemporary King Stephen (1135–54) and into the future, for Henry II (1154–89). In addition, as Gillingam notes, for Geoffrey, the choice of Caerleon as Arthur's seat and the emphasis on the crown-wearing carries additional historical implications, since "as seems most likely, Morgan resumed the ancestral title [of king, in the Welsh revolt] in the euphoria of 1136–7, then when Geoffrey was writing the later sections of his History, there was once again a king in South Wales, a British king at Caerleon." Furthermore, "if the Welsh were now allies of Robert of Gloucester [that is, as supporter of the royal claimant Matilda in her war against Stephen of Blois], then might not Geoffrey's counter-history now have the extra advantage of being politically convenient to his patron?"[146]

As scholars have recently shown regarding fantasies of Troy,[147] the Arthurian social imaginary – in which each Arthurian text participates in its own specific ways – provides glorious connections with the past as well as a framework for socialization and identity for the future. If we apply Charles Taylor's term "social imaginary," that is, simply "the way ... contemporaries imagine the societies they inhabit and sustain" to the Arthurian scenes highlighted here, we find the following picture or self-image of the society portrayed, whether that picture be aimed at combatting the image of the Britons and Welsh as barbarians, promoting the French connections of the Anglo-Norman Anglo-Angevin aristocracy, or melding the ancient British past within the English contemporary society: what we see is 1) a socially cohesive, highly organized society where the most visible nucleus is those in power at the top – yet Wace adds universalizing details to the effect that even poor peasants model themselves upon the sophistication of those at the top and by extension possibly enjoy a decent level of existence (a sort of medieval top-down theory, a psychic if not material "something for everyone"); 2) a society that recognizes quality both in terms of leadership and material goods, and seeks to perpetuate that level of quality, gaining status through association with wealth, and a large part of whose identity is based on that status; 3) a system which cannot function

---

145   Biddle, "Seasonal Festivals and Residence," 57.
146   Gillingham, "Context and Purposes," 36, 37. On Morgan ap Owain, see also p. 98 in Gillingham, "The Foundations of a Disunited Kingdom," 93–109 (*The English in the Twelfth Century*).
147   See Chapter 1, nn. 40 and 95, and n. 5 above.

solely on warfare but which must recharge through the social connectivity of games, music, and spectacle in necessary times of peace; 4) a system which values symbols of power and which is creative enough to invent traditions to sustain them and create respect for them; and lastly 5) a society that cultivates texts in order to preserve those traditions, while simultaneously entertaining and inculcating a belief system, at least aspects of which allegedly dated back to the Trojans. Here Wace apparently shares Geoffrey's perspective, that "not only that the Britons had a long and heroic history of migration and successful war, but that they had long been civilised."[148]

4.1.5   The Roman Campaign and Its Context

It is immediately following these scenes of gift-giving, both of luxury goods and lands, that the Roman ambassadors arrive, demanding the full attention of the court. For Wace, the juxtaposition of the narrative preceding the arrival of the Roman ambassadors and the scene of their arrival carries even weightier implications than in the vulgate or the First Variant because the latter two texts do not contain the *Brut*'s implementation of the Round Table as an instrument of social organization and the expansion on the ceremonies of Arthur's crown-wearing, further illustrating the high level of civilization that the Britons had attained by the time of Arthur's reign. The Romans come as representatives of Rome's imperial glory, which Arthur and his kingdom now demonstrably rival. In addition, Arthur's barons have no intention of permitting Arthur to pay tribute to Rome, even if that had been his choice.

Wace has increased the stakes for Arthur and the Britons: not only has Arthur effectively annexed both Scotland and Ireland, but he has also subdued Norway, Iceland, Denmark, and brought France into his orbit. He then has the foresight to establish the Round Table where all barons – and thus regions – are equal, where everyone understands the same language without having to assimilate and learn it, losing touch with their original cultures.[149] Establishing the Round Table puts Arthur – and by extension, the Britons – in

---

148   Gillingham, "Context and Purposes," 30.

149   Given Wace's fascination with language, it is interesting that he does not mention explicitly in which language all these different barons from many lands communicated at the Table – a form of Brittonic, keeping in mind the ancient setting? The *lingua franca* of Anglo-Norman French, thinking of the twelfth century and the medium of Wace's poem? The possibility of everyone understanding the same language at the Round Table has prompted lighthearted joking among scholars in recent years (at conferences) based on the "universal translators" of science fiction film and television, but in all seriousness, if in the *Brut* all attendees learned the same language in order to communicate at Arthur's Round Table, the emphasis has not been on their abandoning their original languages and cultures in order to do so.

WACE'S ROMAN DE BRUT, PART 2   327

a morally superior position to the Romans, who, at least according to the legendary history of Britain, had never treated provincials – or foreigners – of
any rank as equals.[150]

In the vulgate, the events leading up to Arthur's Roman campaign are as follows, their order as important as their content:

> §158: as a preamble, following the reading of the Romans' letter, Cador
> tells the group he is grateful to God for sending the Romans, since he
> had feared the Britons would become soft from years of peace, gaming,
> lovemaking, etc.;
> §159: Arthur in council expresses his views regarding the Roman
> ultimatum;
> §160: Hoel makes a speech supporting Arthur;
> §161: King Angusel of Scotland promises his support; wants to punish the
> Germans and "effeminate" Romans [*semiuiros* 161.515]; other kings pledge
> support: 183,200 knights and countless footsoldiers;
> §162(a): Arthur accepts their offers, giving instructions; catalogue of
> British forces;
> §162(b): Now that Arthur is sure of his countrymen's support, he dis-
> misses the Roman ambassadors;
> §163: Lucius prepares for war; catalogue of Roman forces, 400,160 strong
> §164(a): beginning of August, Roman troops set out for Britain;
> §164(b): Arthur entrusts Guinevere to Mordred, sails to Normandy; en
> route, he has a prophetic dream.

The order is chronological, with the emphasis on the Britons' united front
together with their comrades in other countries and regions, and on the necessity of the Romans paying tribute, not the Britons.

In the First Variant, the order of events and speeches differs. In addition,
there are other significant changes of content as well as form:

> §158: as a preamble, following the reading of the Romans' letter, Cador
> tells the group he is grateful to God for sending the Romans, since he
> had feared the Britons would become soft from years of peace, gaming,
> lovemaking, etc.;

---

150   Cf. Le Saux who sees the vulgate as painting the Britons as morally and militarily superior
      to the Romans, whereas she finds this portrayal of British superiority "strongly attenu-
      ated" in the FV, which may have appealed to Wace (*Companion*, 89–90). See n. 155 below
      on use of parentheses around sections designated with "a" and "b" for vulgate *HRB*.

328   CHAPTER 5

§159: Arthur in council expresses his views regarding the starkly unacceptable Roman ultimatum (speech in different form, though);

§160: – missing –

§162a: dismissal of Roman ambassadors;[151]

§163: Lucius prepares for war; catalogue of Roman forces, 400,160 strong

§164a: at the beginning of August, Roman troops set out for Britain (combined with §163 above);

§161: King Angusel of Scotland's speech (with different introduction and form), including suggestion they invade Germany – "we must attack the still-rebellious Germans" [§161.4] – after conquering Rome; refers to Romans as *semiuiros*;

§162b: catalogue of British Forces (incl. one sentence from vulg. §160); 120,000 from the islands, Norway and Denmark plus 80,000 cavalry from Gallic provinces, and from Britain 60,000 cavalry in addition to foot soldiers;

§164b: Arthur entrusts Guinevere to Mordred, sails to Normandy; en route, he has a prophetic dream.[152]

In addition to stylistic differences, the First Variant eliminates a very important speech, that of Hoel, one of Arthur's primary allies since he is head of the Armorican Britons; next, it separates the other two speeches, those of Arthur and Angusel, with the effect that, unlike in the vulgate, we don't see the solidarity of Arthur's allies, but rather that solidarity is broken up – or interrupted by – the Romans' reactions to Arthur's counter-ultimatum and the Romans'

---

151   In his edition of the First Variant, Wright provides a list of sections for the vulgate (II, xxxvi–xxxvii) where 162(i) ("i" is the designation in his list, not as in the edited text itself, where it is labeled as 162a) contains the catalogue of British forces and 162(ii) the dismissal of the Roman ambassadors, which correctly follows the order in the vulgate narrative itself, both in his edition of the Bern MS. and in Reeve's edition. However, in the list for the FV (II, xxxvii), there is a mislabelling: he gives "162(ii)" [162b] – labelled as containing the dismissal of the Roman ambassadors – as the section which follows the "absent 160," whereas in the text as he edits it, we in fact have 162a–containing the dismissal of the Roman ambassadors – following directly after "absent 160"; in the First Variant text itself, 162b (actually containing the list of troops) follows 161 later on. In the list above, I have corrected the section titles – using lower case letters rather than small romans – to represent the text as Wright edits it, not representing the labeling of the sections as they appear in his list (II, xxxvii). In other words, Wright's list indicates that for the FV, §162a comes after 159 – which it does – but labelled as containing the catalogue of British forces – which it does not. In his edition of the FV, coming after 159, 162a contains Arthur's dismissal of the Roman ambassadors.

152   Burchmore's text follows this order except that since he uses book numbers (whereas Wright does not), Book IX ends with §164a and Book X begins with §161 (without interruption).

WACE'S ROMAN DE BRUT, PART 2   329

subsequent preparations for war. In addition, in the First Variant and the vulgate, the Romans are said to have over 400,000 troops; in the vulgate the Britons are counted at 183,200, and in the First Variant, while the Britons have greater numbers than in the vulgate, the count is more vague, in that there are 120,000 from the neighboring lands and islands (Ireland, Iceland, Gotland, the Orkneys, Norway, and Denmark) (without specifying how many are cavalry and how many foot soldiers), plus 80,000 cavalry from Gaul and 60,000 cavalry from Britain, plus an unspecified number of foot soldiers.[153]

As Le Saux notes, Wace follows the First Variant's general organizational pattern, supplementing with material from the vulgate.[154] However, in addition, Wace – who never marches in lock step with his sources – adds still more details found in neither of the two main known sources. The narrative pattern in the *Brut* for Arthur's Roman campaign is as follows:[155]

> 158: as a preamble, following the reading of the Romans' letter, Cador tells the group he is grateful to God for sending the Romans, since he had feared the Britons would become soft from years of peace, gaming, lovemaking, etc., but Wace adds Walwein's speech lauding lovemaking and other peacetime activities;
> 159: Arthur's speech;
> 160: Hoel's speech is put back in – a critical speech containing the Sybil's prophecy that Arthur will be the third Briton to wear the crown of Rome (as in the vulgate);

---

153 Though not necessarily intended to imply that the Romans outnumbered the Britons "by over two to one" (Le Saux, *Companion*, 98). Le Saux observes that "it is possible that the absence of precise figures [in Wace] for Arthur's army may be due to the Variant text used by Wace, as one of the manuscript-witnesses collated by Wright [R, Paris, Bibliothèque de l'Arsenal 982] omits the last sentence of Variant §162b which states the total strength of the British army" (*Companion*, 98 and n. 40). That missing sentence however refers to the troops coming in from Britain alone, not the total army to be led by Arthur ("Ex ipsa Britannia .lx. milia equitum preter pedites connumerati sunt," §162.b; "From Britain itself, sixty thousand mounted soldiers in addition to foot soldiers were counted in the total" [my trans.]). It should be noted, though, that in the *Brut*, on the eve of the battle, spies for the Britons observed Lucius's army encamped, and assessed it relative to Arthur's as "four against one" ("Cuntre un hume aveit cil quatre," 11635).

154 *Companion*, 98.

155 In §158, each of the two Latin texts has a short speech by Cador, lord of Cornwall, condemning sloth and exhorting Arthur and his men to battle. As noted above in Chapter 2, n. 95, since Reeve does not use the designations "a" and "b" for sections, I have placed those designations in parentheses. Although in Wace there are neither numbers nor "a" and "b," I have used both (with parentheses for "a" and "b") in order for the correspondences to the vulgate and FV to be clearer.

330   CHAPTER 5

161: Angusel's speech and declaration that they will cross into *Lorraine and* Germany, "so that no country remains on this side of the mountains which is not yours" he tells Arthur – "we shall seize everything, whether rightly or wrongly" – a notably very controversial phrase, at least for modern audiences. Wace goes less far in his condemnation of the Romans – he doesn't call them *semiuiros* as in vulgate or FV, but he goes further on the importance of the conquest as both vengeance and world domination;
162(a): Arthur will demand tribute, not give it – he dispatches the ambassadors; Roman ambassadors praise Arthur to Lucius;
163: Roman preparations;
162(b): British preparations – no precise figure of troops given;
164(a): Romans depart for Britain, and Arthur leaves Mordred in charge;
164(b): Arthur departs; the narrative of his dream.

In Wace, Arthur's speech is expanded at the beginning with increased emphasis on the credit Arthur gives his barons, with encouraging inclusive expressions such as "companions in prosperity and companions in adversity ... if I have lost or conquered, whether one or the other, you've endured both with me ... Through you and through your support, I have had many victories " (10781–82, 10785–86, 10789–90; "Compainun de prosperité / E compainun d'adversité ... Si jo ai perdu ou cunquis, / L'un e l'altre avez od mei pris ... Par vus e par vostre adjutorie / Ai jo eü mainte victorie"). The central section is both expanded and vaguer, the latter because Wace refers to "the emperor" whereas in the vulgate and the FV, the Caesars are each named, Lucius and Julius (§159).

The justifications for the Britons' upcoming war preparations are roughly comparable in the three texts, except that Wace expands the vulgate's proverbial declaration "what is obtained by force of arms is never the rightful possession of the aggressor" (§159. 461–62; "Nichil enim quod ut et uiolentia acquiritur iuste ab ullo possidetur qui uiolentiam intulit") and the FV redactor's revision "but what is stolen away by violence from a free people, it is lawful to restore it, returning it to its original condition and status at any time" (§159, my trans.; "Quod autem uiolencia a populo libero subreptum est licet aliquando redintegrari et ad pristinum statum duci")[156] by adding references to the emo-

---

156   Arthur:

"Mais force n'est mie dreiture	"But force is never righteousness,
Ainz est orguil e desmesure.	It is pride and excess.
L'um ne tient mie ço a dreit	One does not hold rightly
Que l'um ad a force toleit.	What one has taken by force.
Bien nus leist par dreit ço tenir	We are allowed to hold by rights
Qu'il solent a force tolir." (10829–34)	What [others] are used to taking from us by force."

WACE'S ROMAN DE BRUT, PART 2   331

tional toll the Roman domination took on the Britons, that is, how the Romans "have shamed us with the harm and losses, the disgrace, suffering and fear they inflicted on our ancestors" (10835–38). In the *Brut*, these ideas are repeated similarly further on in Arthur's speech in the context of how the Romans had exacted tribute in the past and thus they demand it again, thinking it is their right (10847–50). As in the vulgate and the First Variant, in the *Brut*, Arthur rehearses the vexed history of the Romans and the Britons beginning with [Julius] Caesar's conquest, stating that since Caesar's Romans wanted tribute from the early Britons, now Rome wants it from Arthur and his generation. Arthur reminds his men of Belinus's and Brennius's defeat of Rome, as well as of Constantine king of the Britons who held Rome and Maximianus king of Britain who conquered France and Germany and then Rome.

However, while echoing the Arthur of the vulgate and FV, Wace's Arthur gets more swept up in the moment showing his more military and imperialistic side, perhaps surprising some in modern audiences who may be more used to the *roi fainéant* of the French verse romances or the seemingly never-ending chivalry associated with Arthur in the prose romances.[157] In the explanation that the Britons owe no tribute to Rome but that rather it is the Romans who owe them, and perhaps forgetting that he has just made the pronouncement that those who take lands and possessions by force do not deserve them (unless in order to right a wrong, i.e., to restore previously stolen lands), the gist of which is "what is taken by force is not justly held" ("L'um ne tient mie ço a dreit / Que l'um ad a force toleit" 10831–32), Arthur gives this advice: "may he have all, he who can [defeat the other], there is no other justice" (10893–94; "Or

---

157   With reference to Geoffrey's *Historia*, Helen Fulton observes that Arthur with respect to military matters "is the exact opposite of the *roi fainéant*, 'do-nothing king,' of later French romance, being constantly in motion, constantly in the thick of every battle" although "Arthur is no tyrant: he constantly seeks, and listens to, the advice of his counselors, retreating from battle or making truces on their advice. Even in peacetime, Arthur knows how to behave" ("History and Myth: Geoffrey of Monmouth's *Historia Regum Britanniae*," in *A Companion to Arthurian Literature*, ed. eadem, Blackwell Companions to Literature and Culture 58 (Oxford and Malden, MA: Wiley-Blackwell, 2009), 44–57, here 52. On the theme of Arthur as the *roi fainéant* in Old French romance (particularly striking in Chrétien's *Roman de Perceval*), see esp. Barbara Nelson Sargent-Baur, *Dux Bellorum/Rex Militarum*/roi fainéant: La Transformation d'Arthur au XIIe siècle," *Le Moyen Age: Revue d'Histoire et de Philologie* 90.3–4 (1984): 357–73 (repr. as *Dux Bellorum/Rex Militarum/roi fainéant*: The Transformations of Arthur in the Twelfth Century," in *King Arthur: A Casebook*, ed. Edward D. Kennedy (New York: Garland, 1996), 29–43; and "From Heroic King to *Roi fainéant*: Arthur of Romance," in *The Encyclopedia of Medieval Literature in Britain*, ed. Siân Echard, Richard Rouse, and Jacqueline A. Fay (Hoboken, NJ: John Wiley, 2017), 178–82.

332   CHAPTER 5

ait tut ki aver le puet; / Altre dreiture n'i estuet").[158] Referring to the emperor,
Wace's Arthur adds, "Quant jo chalenz e il chalenge, / Ki tut purra prendre, si
prenge!" (10903–4; "If I and he both lay claim, then he who will be able to take
it all, may he seize it!"). Thus, in Arthur's speech in the *Brut*, the "might makes
right" argument that has been rejected with respect to the Romans – for the
Romans, might does not make right – has just been adopted for the Britons.

Wace includes Hoel's speech because eliminating it would have removed –
as we can see in the First Variant – an important reference to the Sibyl's prophecy of the third British king to rule Rome: first Belinus, then Constantine[159]
and then Arthur, making Arthur the fulfillment of the Sibyl's prophecy, adding
significantly to Arthur's prestige.[160] In Wace, Hoel's speech also forms part of

---

158   Cf. Michelle Warren who does not see this as a contradiction or an application of the
       same principle to one group but not to another. She argues interestingly that "Arthur
       does not make this counterargument to legitimate Briton right; rather the comparison
       ridicules the reasoning [on the part of the Romans] that tenure derives from historical
       precedent" (*History on the Edge*, 165). She adds in conclusion that "avoiding references to
       courts or history, the Arthurian response to Roman imperialism argues that claims will be
       defended and prosecuted solely through force" (165).
159   Constantine I, son of Constantius (king of Britain) and Helen daughter of Coel, who in
       the *Historia* conquered Rome "and subsequently gaining control over the whole world"
       (§80.163–64 "adiuit Romam subiugauitque illam sibi et postmodum monarchiam totius
       mundi optinuit"). In the Galfridian material, not to be confused either with Constantine II
       (brother of Aldroenus, king of Brittany), Arthur's grandfather, king of Britain and founder
       of the House of Constantine, or Constantine III whom Geoffrey made to be Arthur's suc-
       cessor, the last king of the Britons; it is possible that Geoffrey, departing from Gildas's
       account, transformed the king of Dumnonia in sub-Roman Britain into the successor to
       Arthur. In addition, not to be confused with the historical Flavius Claudius Constantinus
       (Constantine III), a Roman general who declared himself Western Roman Emperor in
       Britannia in 407 and also established himself in Gaul.
160   While Wace elected to not include a translation of Merlin's Prophecies from the *Historia*
       (vulgate and First Variant), stating that he was concerned to not misstep by mistranslat-
       ing, he did include the isolated prophecy by Taliesin (ll. 4855–76) predicting the coming
       of Jesus Christ (not in either the vulgate or the FV) – so that the Britons were the first in
       the world to have heard the announcement of the birth of the Messiah – as well as Diana's
       prophecy to the Trojans about the remote and uninhabited isle of Britain reserved just for
       them, and the Sibyl's prophecy in Hoel's speech. On Wace's reluctance to include Merlin's
       Prophecies in the *Brut*, which not only circulated separately from the *Historia* but are
       found in almost identical form in the vulgate and FV manuscript witnesses, see J. Blacker,
       "'Ne vuil sun livre translater'"; on Taliesin, a Welsh poet generally considered to be histori-
       cal (6th c.), see Le Saux, *Companion* 116–17, who conjectures that Wace took the passage
       in question from an oral source, and also Tatlock, who says the figure is found only twice
       before Wace, in *HB* and Geoffrey's *Vita Merlini*, but apparently not the prophecy of the
       coming of the Messiah (*Legendary History*, 469). John Matthews also notes, that "Taliesin
       is said by the Jersey poet Wace, to have made a similar prophecy (though here we are in
       mythic time again, since Taliesin lived long after the birth of Christ)" (*Taliesin: The Last*

WACE'S ROMAN DE BRUT, PART 2   333

a set piece – the three speeches grouped together representing the input of
Arthur and the council – a very important element in Arthur's characterization
as an efficient leader, and not a tyrant.

The third major difference between the two Latin sources' presentation
of the push up to the Roman campaign and Wace's is the latter's inclusion of
Auguselus's urging to take Germany after conquering Rome, plus then adding, on his own, the region of Lorraine. In the vulgate, the reference to the
Germans[161] is that they thus far "remain unpunished" along with the Romans
for the harm they did to the Britons in the past (§161.507–8), and Auguselus
looks forward to vengeance "death itself will be sweet as long as I die aveng-
ing our forefathers, preserving our freedom and securing the fame of our
king" (§161.513–15). In the FV, Auguselus wants to punish "the still rebellious
Germans" and expand Arthur's territory to include the whole Cisalpine region
("tota terra Cisalpina"). Wace goes further, retaining the reference to take
Germany – without explicit justification, but by implication that after taking
the city of Rome, they should proceed to the empire's northern holdings –
adding Lorraine to Auguselus's territorial wish-list, echoing the FV's emphasis
on world conquest.[162] However, Auguselus's recommendations "to seize everything" are immediately followed by the remark, "whether rightly or wrongly"
(11035; "Tut prendrum a dreit e a tort"). This remark, in its blatant endorse-
ment of territorial appropriation for its own sake undermines – and not just for
modern audiences – the somewhat higher moral tenor of the arguments from
Arthur and Hoel, who although endorsing violence, appear to be doing so in
the name of righting historical wrongs and liberty for the Britons.[163]

    Celtic Shaman, trans. John Matthews with Caitlín Matthews, 2nd ed., Rochester, VT: Inner
    Traditions, 2002).

161   The only other mentions of *Germani* are in the passage (§43.171, 178) where Belinus and
    Brennius "divide and conquer," Belinus remaining with the Britons to fight the *Germani*
    and Brennius taking his army to "punish the Romans for breaking their word" (§43.176–77).
    No overt connection is made to the homeland of the Saxons.

162   Le Saux views this as a sea-change: no longer is it a question of conquering Rome but of
    world conquest (*Companion*, 98).

163   Weiss comments that Wace's addition of Angusel's exhortation to take everything *a dreit
    e a tort* ("rightly or wrongly", "at all costs") was "an important issue in later Arthurian lit-
    erature like the alliterative *Morte Arthure*" (277, n. 1) (Angusel is Wace's spelling). See also
    Michelle Warren who sees Angusel's speech as "the strongest statement yet [in the *Brut*]
    of legitimizing force" (*History on the Edge*, 165). In fact, she goes as far as to characterize
    Wace's view in general as "resolutely expansionist" wherein "coercive boundary formation
    leads to peace and greater wealth," an assertion which rings true in a number of contexts;
    however, her more sanguine perspective on the First Variant redactor's more idealistic
    view of warfare when compared with Wace is perhaps too generous: "Whereas the First

334   CHAPTER 5

Following the wrenching interlude of Arthur's single combat against the
giant of Mont-Saint-Michel which serves on one level as an intricate build-up
to Arthur's penultimate battle, that is, the Roman campaign,[164] Wace adds the
detail that the chapel Hoel had built on Helen's gravesite ("Tumbe Eleine,"
"Eleine's tomb") was dedicated to the Virgin Mary (11602–3), and that Arthur
as the ever-efficient general leads his troops toward Autun, putting his
faith in God.

Although Wace devotes nearly 10% of the entire narrative of the *Brut* to the
Roman campaign (11609–13030, that is, 1421 lines out of 14,866 relative to 5%
of the vulgate, §§166–76, or eleven chapters out of 208), and fills it with many
scenes of combat, spying, and two dramatic speeches – one by Arthur and one
by Lucius – the Roman campaign may seem anticlimactic or perhaps gratuitous
to modern readers, for several reasons: 1) although Arthur has actually gained
in stature – he acts more removed like a modern general than a medieval epic
soldier, except for his one outstanding battle scene (12887–932) – emphasis in
the French poem shifts to his nephew, Walwein (Gauvain) who is sent as a messenger to Lucius as well as fighting in battles;[165] 2) more of the battle action is
carried by Arthur's individual knights – such as Cador and Borel, Richier and
Bedevere – rather than by the king himself, and thus there is less emphasis on
the kingdom as a political unit, causing at least a modern audience to perhaps

---

    Variant's pervasive valuation of force derives primarily from the ideology of liberty, in the
    Roman de Brut force sustains colonialist domination" (*History on the Edge*, 170).

164   On this episode, focusing primarily on the themes and implications of rape and cannibal-
    ism (at the opening of the narrative, when faced with a contingent of attacking Bretons,
    the monster is seen to "either [sink] their boats with great boulders or [kill] some with
    various weapons, capturing the majority and eating them alive" §165.35–37; *semiuiuos*,
    lit. "half-alive"), see especially Heng, *Empire of Magic*, 19, 20, 35–51; Laurie Finke and
    Martin Shichtman, "The Mont St. Michel Giant: Sexual Violence and Imperialism in the
    Chronicles of Wace and Laȝamon"; and Hwanhee Park, "Arthur and the Mont St. Michel
    Giant in Laȝamon's *Brut*: Exposing the Fragility of Kingship," *Arthuriana* 26.1 (2016): 5–21.
    Although Warren points out that in his rendition, Wace "is apparently the first to turn
    the episode toward rape" he is "also alone (along with the redactor of the prose *Merlin*
    [428–32]) in overlooking cannibalism"; it should be noted though that the FV redactor
    also omitted that aspect of the giant's characterization, saying only that "the knights of
    that region [Brittany] had followed but accomplished nothing against the giant" (§165.1).
    In addition, Warren reads the Mont-Saint-Michel episode in territorial terms, accentuat-
    ing Arthur's assertion of jurisdiction over the Mont in his victory over the giant (regret-
    tably too late to save Helen, Hoel's niece, who died under the giant's weight following the
    rape); the Mont was territory which had been contested in Wace's time, since, follow-
    ing Henry I's death: its inhabitants sided with Matilda and those of nearby Avranches in
    Normandy with Stephen (*History on the Edge*, 165–67).

165   Le Saux, *Companion*, 138–39.

WACE'S ROMAN DE BRUT, PART 2

lose sight of the political stakes involved;[166] 3) Lucius is at times portrayed in a positive light which at least for modern audiences undermines the pathos of this villain;[167] and 4) there are no administrative "results" that come out of

---

166 There are of course exceptions, where Wace reminds us of the stakes, the importance of military conquest, and the importance of Britain's status, such as in the passage full of lyrical repetition, where Walwein describes for Lucius how Rome first won France and how the Britons took her back, and how Lucius should give up now, as Arthur forbids him to advance:

"Par nus te mandë e defent,	Through us he orders you and forbids you,
Que sache tuit comunement,	May all have common knowledge of it,
Que en France tun pied ne mettes	That you do not set foot in France
Ne de France ne t'entremettes.	Nor do you concern yourself with France,
France tient e France tendra,	He holds France and will hold France.
Cume sue la defendra.	He will defend her as his own.
Ço te mande que rien n'i prenges	He orders you to take nothing from it
E si tu sur lui la chalenges,	And if you claim her from him,
Par bataille seit chalengee	It will be challenged by battle
E par bataille deraisnee.	And by battle vindicated.
Romain par bataille la pristrent	The Romans took it through battle
E par bataille la cunquistrent,	And by battle they conquered it,
E il l'a par bataille eüe	And he had it through battle
E par bataille l'ad tenue;	And he held it by battle;
Par bataille reseit pruvé	It will be once again be shown by battle
Kin deit aver la poësté.	Who should have it through strength.
Demain, seinz altre demurance,	Tomorrow, without further delay,
Vien, si tu vuels desrainer France;	Come, if you want to claim France,
Ou tu t'en va, si t'en repaire,	Or go, go back,
Returne t'en, n'a ci que faire!	Return, you have nothing more to do here!
Nus avum pris, tu as perdu."	We have won, you have lost."
(11713–33)	

167 See n. 50 above referring to one of Wace's techniques I refer to elsewhere as "reflex praise," that is, automatic painting of any important figure such as Julius Caesar, or in the following case, Lucius – regardless of his or her status vis-à-vis the heroes of the narrative – in often glowing terms:

Lucius fud d'Espaine nez,	Lucius was born in Spain,
Des Romeins bien enparentez;	Of well connected Romans;
Anz aveit de bone juvente	He was still fairly youthful,
Meins de quarante e plus de trente;	Less than forty but more than thirty years old;
Hardiz ert e de grant curage,	He was bold and of great courage,
Fait aveit ja maint vasselage;	He had already performed many brave deeds;
Pur sa force e pur sa valur	On account of his strength and his valor
L'aveit l'um fait empereür.	They made him emperor.
(12451–58)	

336 CHAPTER 5

the campaign, that is, the "administrative circle" is not closed:[168] for example, no legates are sent to the Round Table or to Arthur's realm in any capacity, no tributes are paid to Arthur, nor is Arthur's territory increased, as the Britons never make it to Germany and Lorraine as Angusel had hoped.

Although in Wace, Arthur appears to be left with little except for "psychic gratification" – "Arthur was joyful and glad that he had tamed the arrogance of Rome" (12977–78; "Arthur se fist joius e lié, / Que l'orguil de Rome ot pleissié") – it must be remembered that, thanks to Arthur, Britain is no longer under threat from Rome, nor beholden to the Empire in any way. In the vulgate, Arthur "took pity on his enemies, ordering the locals to bury them, and he sent Lucius' body to the senate together with a message that this was all the tribute that Britain needed to pay" (§176.476–78). This ironic remark is reinforced by Wace who repeats that Arthur treated the body of the emperor with great honor but expands the message sent back to Rome along with the body (on a bier), rendering it more surly and further asserting Arthur's prerogative: he "informed the Romans that he owed them no other tribute from Britain which he governed, and whoever would demand tribute from him, he would send them back in the same way" (12987–94).[169]

Following the burials across France of Arthur's elite warriors, including Bedevere, Kay, and Walwein, the king heads toward Rome, only to turn back before crossing the Alps, having learned of Mordred's treachery. Thus, however one assesses the extent of the positive outcome of Arthur's Roman campaign – aborted before full conquest was achieved, as Arthur audibly regrets, "lamenting the perjury of Mordred, who made him abandon a great conquest" (13050–51; "Del parjurie Modred pleinant, / Ki turné l'ot de grant cunquest") – the victory was only partial and short-lived at that.

---

168 Admittedly, since Arthur never makes it to Rome, turning back to rescue Britain from the usurper Mordred, it is impossible that the administrative circle be closed, i.e., that Rome formally become a territory of Britain; the Romans' breaking of their promise to pay tribute after they were overtaken by Belinus and Brennius (2906–18; 3145–56) is never set right, but at least the Britons will not pay tribute to the Romans, as threatened by Lucius. Without the administrative circle closed, Wace apparently did not choose to invent a role for the Romans in Britain at this point, though his introduction of the Round Table indicates that he was not completely averse to inserting original material into his history of the Britons.

169 "Le cors fist de l'empereür / Prendre e guarder a grant enur; / A Rome en biere l'enveia / E a cels de Rome manda / Que de Bretaine qu'il teneit / Altre treü ne lur deveit, / E qui treü li requerreit / Altretel li enveereit."

WACE'S ROMAN DE BRUT, PART 2 337

4.1.6   Arthur's Last Battle: The Battle of Camlann

Before Arthur's last battle starts, Wace reports "Mordred's Donation" to Cheldric, in different terms than Gaimar had at the opening of his *Estoire des Engleis*.[170] Wace writes that Mordred – whom he does not refer to as king, unlike Gaimar – in exchange for "eight hundred well-equipped ships, all loaded with knights" (13057–58) promises to Cheldric all the land from the Humber to Scotland, and all that Hengest had held in Kent when Vortigern had married his daughter, Rowena;[171] in Gaimar, the Saxons themselves seized and occupied the land Hengest had previously held in Kent, since the latter was not strictly speaking part of Mordred's Donation in Gaimar's narrative. Whether Wace actually believed that Cheldric in fact took possession of all those lands promised by Mordred, as Gaimar appears to have done (though not for the Kent portion) – Mordred, who ruled but for an instant, and did not have the authority to promise the lands, much less "give" them, as perhaps indicated by Wace's refusal to refer to Mordred as king – is unclear, but what is clear is that Wace has taken the mention of the lands involved in "expanded Donation" from the First Variant and the vulgate, but not necessarily the idea of any fulfilled promise that Cheldric in fact ever collected on this "inheritance," as portrayed in Gaimar.

---

170 See Chapter 4, n. 23.

171 | Oit cent nefs bien aparaillies, | Eight hundred well-equipped ships, |
|---|---|
| Tutes de chevaliers chargies. | All loaded with knights. |
| E Modred lur ot graanté | And Mordred promised to them |
| E en eritage duné | And gave them as a heritage |
| Pur lur aïe e pur lur force | For their help and their strength |
| Del Humbre tut des qu'en Escoce, | [The lands] from the Humber right up to Scotland, |
| E ço que ot en Kent Henguist, | And all that Hengist had in Kent, |
| Quant Vortiger sa fille prist. | When Vortigern had taken his daughter in marriage. |

(13057–64)

Wace's use of the term "eritage" raises the question as to whether Wace thought the lands promised might have been heritable, that is, with the possibility of being passed down through generations – but that still does not mean that Mordred's Donation was ever more than a promise, that it was ever "collected on" by the Saxons, since the lands were not Mordred's to give though "duné" would suggest that at least Mordred *thought* they were his to give. See Chapter 4, n. 23 on Gaimar's presentation of Cnut's claim that the Danes had priority in England over the Saxons because Edmund was a descendent of Cerdic (whom Gaimar confuses with Chelric) who never held the lands in chief, and he (Cnut) was descended from Danr who "held the land in chief from God." As to whether Wace might have also wanted to establish, through this confused series of events, as Leckie points out for Gaimar, that there was "a direct causal link between Modred's treachery and English domination" (*Passage of Dominion*, 81), is less than likely, but not impossible.

338   CHAPTER 5

In the *Roman de Brut*, the battle of Camlann, albeit containing moments of pathos, is not accorded the same kind of narrative expansion upon sources that the Roman campaign is, nor the future sections on Gormond's Donation and the passage of dominion, being a little less than 300 lines in length.[172] The most outstanding features of this battle are:

1) Arthur mourns Walwein and Angusel who were killed along with many others when their ships were unloaded;

2) Mordred flees to Cornwall, Guinevere takes the veil, as Arthur besieges Winchester;

3) Mordred amasses 60,000 troops, having summoned pagans and Christians, Irish, Norwegians, Saxons, and Danes, and to "those men who hated Arthur, and who feared his service, he promised those who had no land who would serve in order to get land, he gave and promised and begged as a man does who needs to";[173]

4) At "Camble" in the land of Cornwall, with many losses on each side, "the plain was covered with the dead and bloody with the blood of the dying; there perished the flower of youth, whom Arthur brought up well and gathered from many lands, and those of the Round Table, who were so praised throughout the world. Modret was slain in the battle, and the great majority of his men, and the flower of Arthur's people, both the strongest and the best";[174]

5) Whereas both the vulgate and the FV state that Arthur was mortally wounded, but (ironically) taken away to Avalon to have his wounds "tended"/ "healed" (vulgate, "ad sananda uulnera sua," §179.282; FV §178, "ad sananda uulnera sua"), Wace openly plants the seed of doubt regarding Arthur's death;

---

172   Le Saux, *Companion*, 141. On this battle in the *Brut*, and its implications including Arthur's death tale (or non-death tale), primarily in the Galfridian (including Wace) and early Welsh traditions, see Le Saux, 141–44: Rosemary Morris, *The Character*, 130–39; Michael Faletra, "Narrating the Matter of Britain: Geoffrey of Monmouth and the Norman Colonization of Wales"; A. L. Brown, "Camlann and the Death of Arthur," *Folklore* 72.4 (1961): 612–21. See also the Introduction, n. 20, and nn. 175–177 below.

173   "Manda ces que Arthur haeient, /E qui sun servise cremeient, /Manda ces qui terre n'aveient, /Ki pur terre servir voleient; /Duna e pramist e preia / Cumë huem fait ki busuin a" (13229–34).

174   "Grant fud de ambes parz la perte, / La plaine fud des morz cuverte / E del sanc des muranz sanglente. / Dunc peri la bele juvente / Que Arthur aveit grant nurrie / E de plusurs terres cuillie, / E cil de la Table Roünde / Dunt tel los ert par tut le munde; / Ocis fud Mordred en l'estur / E de sa gent tut li plusur, / E de la gent Arthur la flur / E li plus fort e li meillur" (13263–274). Both the vulgate and the FV give an itemized list of the fallen on both sides (§178).

WACE'S ROMAN DE BRUT, PART 2   339

6)   Wace is non-committal on Arthur's fate, but does state as do the vulgate
      and FV that in the year 542 he handed the crown on to Constantinus,
      son of Cador duke of Cornwall; Wace adds though as seen in the passage
      below, that Arthur surrendered his kingdom to his cousin, Constantinus,
      until his return (our emphasis), a point not made in either the vulgate or
      the FV.

4.1.6.1   *The "Breton Hope"*

Between the seed of doubt regarding Arthur's fate and his report of what is now
called "the Breton hope,"[175] Wace has firmly laid the groundwork – whether

---

175   Although in the scholarship, the "Breton hope" has traditionally been associated with
       the Bretons rather than with the Britons – or both – the ambiguity of Old French (and
       modern, for that matter) with respect to the adjective "breton" which can mean either
       "Briton" or "Breton" coupled with the fact that Wace is leaving things very open-ended,
       particularly here (and is often equivocal elsewhere), suggests the possibility that Wace
       could have meant either "Bretons" or "Britons" or perhaps both; Rachel Bromwich on
       this point writes: "Notwithstanding the ambiguity in Wace's use of the word 'Bretun', and
       the possibility that the reference to *li Bretun* and the Round Table may be an allusion to
       Insular rather than to Continental Britons, the reference to *li Bretun* in connection with
       the return of Arthur seems to be the latter" ("Brittany and the Arthurian Legend," 263; see
       also Houck, *Sources*, on the ambiguity of the term "Breton" in Wace, 255–56, who con-
       cludes that context suggests that except for the references to the taletellers fables about
       the Round Table and the expectation of Arthur's return, Wace's use of the term "Breton" in
       Old French refers to the insular Britons, not the Continental Britons, adding equivocally
       "or he may mean simply Britons as a whole, without thinking of any distinction between
       insular and continental," 256). In his *Epistola ad Warinum*, Henry of Huntingdon writes
       to "Warin the Breton," "Mortuum tamen fuisse Britones, parentes tui, negant. Et eum
       uenturum sollempniter expectant" (*HRA*, c.9, ed. and trans. Greenway; "But the Bretons,
       your ancestors, refuse to believe that he died. And they traditionally await his return,"
       trans. Greenway, p. 581; see also 580, n. 67 where she mentions that Wright suggests
       Henry included that information (not in Geoffrey) "because of its special relevance to
       his Breton addressee," "The place of Henry of Huntingdon's *Epistola ad Warinum*," 79; see
       Wright who also translates *Britones* as *Bretons* with regard to the hope of Arthur's return,
       "*Epistola ad Warinum*," §9, 112). As noted in other contexts, Diana Greenway writes that
       "the identity of Warin the Breton is unknown"; in addition to providing possible identities
       for that figure, she suggests "another alternative is that Henry was addressing a fictitious
       person, perhaps even a *Briton* rather than a Breton, invented to serve the purpose of justi-
       fying the epistolary form of this piece" (*HRA*, ed., 559, note 2). In addition to sources in n.
       20 in the Introduction above, on the Breton hope, see especially R. S. Loomis, "The Legend
       of Arthur's Survival," in idem, *Arthurian Literature in the Middle Ages: A Collaborative
       History* (Oxford: Clarendon Press, 1959), 64–71; Léon Fleuriot, "Le patriotisme britto-
       nique et l'histoire légendaire," in *Histoire littéraire et culturelle de la Bretagne*, ed. Jean
       Balclou and Yves Le Gallo (Paris: Champion, 1987), 105–19; and on Arthur's "afterlife" in
       Latin-language historical texts, pseudo-historical texts, and romances of the twelfth cen-
       tury, see Siân Echard, *Arthurian Narrative in the Latin Tradition*, Cambridge Studies in

340 CHAPTER 5

intentionally or not – for the question of Arthur's ultimate fate to be pulled
into the realm of vernacular historical writing, in addition to that of fictional
genres. Since the passage in the *Brut* is significantly more detailed than either
the allusion in William of Malmesbury's *Gesta Regum* or the reference in Henry
of Huntingdon's *Epistola ad Warinum*,[176] it merits citing in full:

Arthur, si la geste ne ment,	Arthur, if the narrative doesn't lie,
Fud el cors nafrez mortelment;	Was mortally wounded in his body;
En Avalon se fist porter	He had himself taken to Avalon
Pur ses plaies mediciner.	In order to have his wounds tended to.
Encore i est, Bretun l'atendent,	He is still there, the Britons await him,
Si cum il dient e entendent;	As they say and give one to understand;
De la vendra, encor puet vivre.	From there he will come, and he go on living.
Maistre Wace, ki fist cest livre,	Master Wace, who composed this book,
Ne volt plus dire de sa fin	Does not want to say any more about his end
Qu'en dist li prophetes Merlin;	Than the prophet Merlin said about it;
Merlin dist d'Arthur, si ot dreit,	Merlin said of Arthur, and he is right,
Que sa mort dutuse serreit.	That his death would be in doubt.
Li prophetes dist verité;	The prophet spoke the truth;
Tut tens en ad l'um puis duté,	Ever since then has one doubted,
E dutera, ço crei, tut dis,	And will doubt, I believe, for all time,
Se il est morz u il est vis.	Whether he is dead or alive.

Medieval Literature 36 (Cambridge: Cambridge University Press), esp. pp. 69–73, including William of Malmesbury's testimony "to the pre-Galfridian existence of the Breton
hope" (p. 69) and Giraldus Cambrensis's criticism of the "stupidities of the Britons [who]
thus assert that he is still alive," likening them to the Jews: "they anticipate his return
just as the Jews await their Messiah" (p. 73). Although he seems to go a bit farther in this
interpretation than the text would warrant, see Daniel Helbert who argues that Geoffrey
in the *HRB* actually "report(s) the Breton Hope" rather than simply planting the seed
through the ambiguity of Arthur's having been "mortally wounded" but also taken away
to Avalon to have his wounds tended ("'an Arður sculde ȝete cum': The Prophetic Hope in
Twelfth-Century Britain," *Arthuriana* 26.1: 77–107, cited at p. 86). He does write, however,
that Geoffrey was more "playful" with this idea in the *Vita Merlini* (86).

176 William of Malmesbury refers to the "old wives' tales" of Arthur's eventual return, though
not specifically to those spreading the tales: "Sed Arturis sepulchrum nusquam uisitur,
unde antiquas neniarum adhuc eum uenturum fabulatur" (*GRA*, iii.287.2–4; "Arthur's
grave, however, is nowhere to be found, whence come the traditional old wives' tales that
he may yet return").

WACE'S ROMAN DE BRUT, PART 2   341

Porter se fist en Avalun,	He had himself taken to Avalon,
Pur veir, puis l'Incarnation	In truth, since the Incarnation
Cinc cenz e quartante dous anz.	Five hundred and forty-two years.
Damage fud qu'il n'ot enfanz.	It is a shame he did not have children.
Al fiz Cador, a Costentin,	To Constantine, son of Cador,
De Cornuaille, sun cusin,	From Cornwall, his cousin,
Livra sun regne si li dist	He gave his kingdom, and told him
Qu'il fust reis tant qu'il revenist	That he be king until he returned.
(13275–98)[177]	

A number of elements are original here – that is, they are not found in either
the vulgate or the FV – making this report by Wace extraordinary:

1) Although the passage is ambiguous, Wace appears to assert that Arthur
   is still in Avalon, in addition to the fact that the Britons (or Bretons) still
   await his return and possible revival;

2) Wace says he will not pronounce judgment, any more than the prophet
   Merlin did;

3) Wace openly regrets that Arthur did not have children, as presumably,
   that would have made the succession clearer and more authoritative;

4) Arthur hands the crown to his cousin, Constantine, instructing him to
   take care of the kingdom until his return.

Points two and four are the most extraordinary of this very unusual passage.
It should be remembered that Wace declined to translate the book of Merlin's
Prophecies from his sources, because he claims to not have understood
them well enough to report on them properly.[178] Despite his omission of the
Prophecies, Wace still treats Merlin as an authority, and in the passage above,
as a convenient authority: Wace is able to remain non-committal on this doubt-
lessly politically sensitive matter – Arthur's eventual return – with Merlin as
a back-up. Furthermore, Wace finesses the topic by inserting a prophecy that
he claims to have heard from Merlin, to the effect that Arthur's end would
always be in doubt. Wace can thus remain certain about this uncertainty, with

---

177 It is noteworthy that in this passage, Weiss also translates "Bretons" as "Britons," leaving
     open the possibility that both the Bretons – as in the folk tradition – and the Britons
     awaited Arthur's return (333–34).

178 "Ne vuil sun livre translater / Quant jo nel sai interpreter; / Nule rien dire ne vuldreie / Que
     si ne fust cum jo dirreie" (7539–42; "I do not wish to translate his book, since I do not know
     how to interpret it; I would not like to say anything, in case what I say does not happen"
     [lit. "In case it might not happen as I might say [it]"]). On Wace's refusal, see J. Blacker, "'Ne
     vuil sun livre translater'" and for the translated Prophecies inserted into four Wace MSS
     and found as well in three anonymous verse Bruts, see Anglo-Norman Verse Prophecies of
     Merlin, ed. and trans. eadem. Weiss restores the reading from MS. P for l. 7541: "Nule rien
     dire nen vuldreie" (p. 190, n. 1).

342   CHAPTER 5

impunity. Saying that Arthur gave Constantine the crown and kingdom for
safekeeping – temporarily – until his eventual return[179] – is a clever way for
Wace to avoid the subject of inheritance, a subject that he reinforces with his
regret that Arthur never had direct heirs.[180]

5   Gormund's Donation and the Passage of Dominion; Gormund and Arthur as Leaders

By relating that Arthur passed on his kingdom only temporarily, Wace finesses
the subject of the definitive passing on of Arthur's kingdom. Nonetheless,
Wace follows the vulgate and FV (with minor variations) through the short
reigns of Constantine, his nephew Cunan, Vortipor, Malgo, and Cariz (§184,
vulgate Kareticus, FV Carecius).

In the vulgate, following Arthur's "death" Constantinus subdues the Saxons,
butchers some of Mordred's sons, and dies four years later. Aurelius Conanus,
who showed "great promise" to rule the whole island except for his penchant
for civil strife, is succeeded by Vortiporius who puts down a Saxon rebellion,

---

179   At the end of §178, both the vulgate and the FV state that Arthur handed the kingdom over
       to his relative, Constantinus, son of Cador duke of Cornwall, but neither text mention
       until Arthur's "eventual return."

180   Legitimate inheritance was a very important subject for Wace. On his favoring (in the
       Roman de Rou) of Robert Curthose over Henry I whom he felt "stole" England from
       Robert – the eldest son who thus deserved to inherit the throne following the principle of
       primogeniture – see Elisabeth van Houts, "Latin and French as Languages of the Past in
       Normandy During the Reign of Henry II: Robert of Torigni, Stephen of Rouen and Wace,"
       in *Writers of the Reign of Henry II: Twelve Essays*, 53–78, esp. 61; William M. Aird, *Robert
       Curthose, Duke of Normandy c. 1050–1134* (Woodbridge: Boydell, 2008), 226–27; Blacker,
       Faces of Time, 117, 184–85 (1994), and new Introduction to the e-book, 32–33 n. 77; and
       Urbanski, *Writing History for the King*, 108–17, 210–11. For sources on how Wace's custom-
       ary efforts at impartiality may have been a source of displeasure for Henry II, possibly
       presenting too many versions of the Norman Conquest, for example, see Blacker, *Faces of
       Time*, new Introduction (revised electronic version, 2019). On the other hand, Wace's lack
       of impartiality in certain contexts, prompts Charity Urbanski to remark that "Wace might
       have been able to get away with a certain amount of discreet criticism of the royal lin-
       eage in the 1160s, but Henry would have been in no mood for Wace's defense of baronial
       power or his unpleasant reminders about the failings of his ancestors in the wake of such
       a large-scale rebellion [the war of 1173]" (*Writing History for the King*, 204). Urbanski also
       observes similarly that Wace was insufficiently impartial when treating Henry II's grand-
       father, Henry I, in his conflicts with Duke Robert Curthose; by defending Curthose as the
       first-born son against Henry I to the extent he did, Wace "effectively stated that the line of
       legitimate Norman dukes had ended with Robert and that Henry's usurpation [claim to
       rule Normandy] marked the beginning of a reign of impostors" (144).

then "becoming monarch of the entire kingdom, in the end [he] ruled his people well and in peace" (§182.113.14). Malgo succeeds him, a "mighty warrior" who "ruled the whole island as well as its six neighbours, Ireland, Iceland, Gotland, the Orkneys, Norway and Denmark, which he conquered in fierce battles" (§183.116–21).

As mentioned above, Wace considered Gormund's Donation – set in the late sixth century – the turning point in the passage of dominion, departing from Geoffrey who attributes substantial rule to the Britons for roughly another 300 years up to the reign of Athelstan in the tenth century. Wace's description of Gormund's conquest of the kingdom of Loegria[181] – depicting virtually total destruction precipitating a diaspora, together with the unwillingness of the Saxons to take on any of the religious, linguistic, and social customs of the native peoples – shows Gormund's conquest to be in many ways a model of military domination opposite from that of Arthur whose foreign conquests including Iceland, Norway and France left original cultures largely intact.[182] In Wace's *Brut*, in contrast with his own occasionally combative nature, imperialist goals, and devastating campaigns against the Scots and the Saxons, and in contrast with the unremitting destruction of Gormund's campaigns, King Arthur's respect for native cultures demonstrates a model of governance which values the rights of multiple groups to peacefully coexist, in essence, a form of political domination which requires neither annihilation nor cultural assimilation.

History and legend provide at least three figures whose names resemble Gormund, historical sources pointing to Vikings.[183] The first actually lived, the

---

181   According to Geoffrey, Brutus the eponymous founder of Britain had three sons: Locrinus, Albanactus and Kamber. Locrinus inherited Loegria (the central portion of the island, named after him, and later synonymous with England), Kamber received Wales and Albanactus, Scotland (*HRB*, §23.1–11).

182   By using the Gormund material as he does, Wace appears to contradict earlier implications of a more gradual evolution of peoples in Britain: if not the arrival of the Saxons (the *adventus Saxonum*), then at least the precipitating event of their eventual takeover was more akin to a cataclysmic event brought about by an enormous force of invaders, not the result of more widely spaced waves of invaders, nor of a gradual process of population change, or the arrival of a minority ruling elite. On the contemporary debate among historians, archeologists, anthropologists, and biologists seeking to define the actual nature of the *adventus Saxonum* and its effects upon the local populations, see for example Martin Grimmer, "Invasion, settlement or political conquest: changing representations of the arrival of the Anglo-Saxons in Britain," and the sources in Chapter 1, nn. 98–99.

183   For a concise summary of the historical and legendary precedents for the figure of Gormund, see Peter Rickard, *Britain in Medieval French Literature* (Cambridge: Cambridge University Press, 1956), 58–64. On the historical prototype of this very complex figure, the Viking Guthrum named in Asser's *Life of Alfred* (years 879–81, *Asserius de rebus gestis*

344   CHAPTER 5

historical Guthrum who raided England in the 860s and 870s, leader of the
Danish army that defeated Alfred and Ethelred in 871 and was later himself
defeated and converted to Christianity, receiving East Anglia in fief; before taking up the fief, he spent a year with his army in Cirencester (c.878). The second
was another leader of an army of Danes quite possibly with a similar name
who sailed from the Thames, wintered in Ghent, moved down the Somme
toward the end of 880, burning the abbeys of Saint-Riquier and Saint-Valéry,
and was driven back by Louis III of France at Saucourt in August 881.[184] This
second Viking leader was at times apparently fused with the first, and also later
transformed into an African king.[185] It is not so much the original means of
this transformation which can never be confirmed, but its uses, that concern
us here because whoever Gormund actually was, it is significant that Geoffrey,
the First Variant, and Wace chose the latter figure of African king in their histories of Britain. These three works also associate Gormund with the French

---

     Alfredi in *Asser's Life of King Alfred together with the Annals of St Neots*, ed. W. H. Stevenson,
     Oxford: Clarendon Press, 1904; repr. with introductory article by Dorothy Whitelock, 1959,
     47, pp. 35–6 and 56, pp. 45–7), in the Anglo-Saxon Chronicle and in Henry of Huntingdon
     (*HA*, v. 7–9, 35, ed. and trans. Diana Greenway, pp. 286–91, 336–37), see also *Geffrei Gaimar.*
     Estoire des Engleis, ed. and trans. Ian Short, note to lines 3240 ff., p. 395–96.

184   Rickard, *Britain in Medieval French Literature*, pp. 58–59. The Anglo-Saxon Chronicle
     names Guthrum and distinguishes between his army and a second army – or a section of
     the first that split off – presumably under the direction of another leader; this second army
     allegedly camped at Fulham then sailed to Ghent and later fought the Franks (875–78;
     879–82, *The Anglo-Saxon Chronicles*, ed. and trans. Michael Swanton, pp. 74–76; 76–77);
     see also nn. 117–20, pp. 250–51 in *Alfred the Great: Asser's Life of King Alfred and Other
     Contemporary Sources*, trans. Simon Keynes and Michael Lapidge (London: Penguin, 1983,
     2004). Guthrum spent twelve years ruling East Anglia as a Christian king, dying in 890;
     historical evidence does not support his having taken an army to the Continent during
     that time (Rickard, 59). Asser does not identify Gothrum as the leader of the second army
     (58–62, pp. 85–6, trans. Keynes and Lapidge), nor does Henry of Huntingdon identify him
     as head of the "nouum exercitum" ("the new army," v. 9, p. 290, *Historia Anglorum*, ed. and
     trans. Greenway).

185   Among the extensive literature on these fusions and transformations, see in particular
     Ferdinand Lot, "*Gormond et Isembard*. Recherches sur les fondements historiques de cette
     épopée," *Romania*, 27 (1898): 1–54, E. C. Southward, "Gormont roi d'Afrique," *Romania*, 69
     (1946–47): 103–12 and Ivor Arnold and Harry Lucas, "Le Personnage de Gormont dans
     la *Chanson de Gormont et Isembard*," in *Mélanges de philologie romane et de littérature
     médiévale offerts à Ernest Hoepffner par ses élèves et ses amis*, Publications de la Faculté
     des Lettres de l'Université de Strasbourg, 113 (Paris: Les Belles Lettres, 1949), 215–26. For
     perspectives on the implications of the protean changes of this character in the context of
     epic as historiography, see Joseph J. Duggan, "Medieval Epic as Popular Historiography," in
     Grundriss der Romanischen Literaturen des Mittelalters, XI.1, *Littérature historiographique
     des origines à 1500*, ed. Hans Ulrich Gumbrecht, Ursula Link-Heer, Peter-Michael Spangen-
     berg (Heidelberg: Carl Winter, 1986–87), 285–311, esp. 296 and 300.

noble, Isembard, though other resemblances with the fragmentary *Chanson de Gormont et Isembard* are few.[186]

In broad outline, in the Galfridian version initiated by Geoffrey and later adapted by the author of the First Variant and Wace, Gormund is a pagan African king, an eventual ally of the Saxons, who subdues Ireland in the sixth century, then sails to England, ravages the countryside, including Cirencester, and is there joined by Isembard, nephew of King Louis who renounces Christianity to gain Gormund's aid against his uncle; Gormund delivers Loegria to the Saxons and sails for France (though his battle against Louis is not contained in the Galfridian narrative). In the *chanson de geste* (dated to pre-1140) which may have been originally inspired by the invasion of Norsemen who burned down the abbey of St. Riquier in 881 and were defeated by Louis six months later at Saucourt-en-Vimeu, Gormund is said to be from the East – "d'Oriente" (line 69) and "Arabi/s" (lines 186, 443) – though Africa is not specifically mentioned per se; his men are referred to by the terms "pagans'"and "Saracens" as well as Turks, Persians and Arabs ("Turc e Persant e Arabi," line 433), though it is said there are Irish among them as well ("Ireis," lines 100, 282; "cil d'Irlande," 610). As John Tolan has pointed out, "for many western Europeans throughout the Middle Ages, Saracens were pagans, and pagans were Saracens: the two words become interchangeable," any group of non-Christians often being labeled "Saracens" as "the idolatrous other is an essential foil for Christian virtue."[187]

In the *chanson de geste* Gormund, leader of a pagan horde, is invited to France to wage war against the French king, by Isembard, a French noble who has offended King Louis and who is eager to wrest the throne from the monarch

---

186 *Gormont et Isembard. Fragment de chanson de geste du XIIᵉ siècle*, ed. Alphonse Bayot, CFMA (Paris: Honoré Champion, 1921). Resemblances are few, that is, between the *chanson* as it now exists in fragmentary form, and Geoffrey, the First Variant, and Wace. We will not speculate here regarding what might have been contained in the poem's missing beginning and end, and thus might have been known to twelfth-century historians. On Wace's and Geoffrey's sources with respect to the Gormund material, see Tatlock, *The Legendary History of Britain*, 45–46, 132, 135–38, 417, and Houck, *Sources*, 288–310 and 341–48. See also Jan de Vries, "La Chanson de *Gormont et Isembart'"* *Romania* 80 (1959): 34–62 and William C. Calin, *The Old French Epic of Revolt: Raoul de Cambrai, Renaud de Montauban, Gormond et Isembard*, (Geneva: E. Droz, 1962), 99–111.

187 *Saracens: Islam in the Medieval European Imagination* (New York: Columbia University Press, 2002), pp. 128–29. See also R. W. Southern, *Western Views of Islam in the Middle Ages* (Cambridge, MA: Harvard University Press, 1962), Norman A. Daniel, *Heroes and Saracens: An Interpretation of the Chansons de Geste* (Edinburgh: Edinburgh University Press, 1984), Paul Bancourt, *Les Musulmans dans les chansons de geste du cycle du roi*, 2 vols. (Aix-en-Provence: Université de Provence, 1982), and Sharon Kinoshita, *Medieval Boundaries: Rethinking Difference in Old French Literature* (Philadelphia: University of Pennsylvania Press, 2006).

346   CHAPTER 5

(who is also referred to as "emperor"). The battle which forms the focal part of
the fragmentary narrative (which appears to be missing both the beginning
and the end) between Gormund's army and Louis is set in north-east France,
near Cayeux; the battle of Saucourt-en-Vimeu is recorded in at least two Latin
chronicles, by Hariulf in the *Chronicon Centulense* (or the Chronicle of the
Abbey of St. Riquier), c.1088–1104, which contains parallels to the *chanson* but
in Latin prose, and by the *Annales Vedastini* (annals of St. Vaast, late ninth century) as the place where Louis III defeated an army of Vikings in 881.[188] In the
chanson, at the battle, Louis kills Gormund but is mortally wounded and dies
30 days later; since neither the beginning nor the end of the poem are extant,
we have no way of knowing if the narrative related Gormund's travel from
Britain to France – though there are said to be Irish in the "African's" army –
which would further link Geoffrey and Wace's Gormund with the character
of the epic.[189]

Despite the Danish associations played up by Gaimar, Geoffrey, the First
Variant and Wace give no hint of such connections. However, references to
Africa are not without literary precedent particularly in Geoffrey's *Historia*:[190]

---

188   Houck, *Sources of the Roman de Brut*, 293, 297; Hariulf, *Chronique de l'abbaye de Saint-
       Riquier (ve siècle – 1104)*, ed. Ferdinand Lot (Paris: Picard, 1894), III. 20, pp. 141, 143; III.
       22, p. 150; IV. 32, p. 264, and *Annales Vedastini* in *The Annals of Fulda: Ninth Century
       Histories, volume II*, trans. Timothy Reuter, Manchester Medieval Sources (Manchester:
       Manchester University Press, 1992), p. 90 (881) and n. 4; Manchester Medieval Sources
       Online (Manchester, 1992), online Dec. 2012, http://manchester.metapress.com/.

189   Roughly contemporaneous with Geoffrey's *Historia* and preceding Wace's *Brut* by about
       twenty years, Gaimar's *Estoire des Engleis* (c.1136 to 1137) contains two Gormunds – a
       "Godrum/Gudrun/Gudrum" thought to be Guthrum, Danish king of East Anglia, and a
       "rei Gurmunt," an epic Danish king, but with no signs of Isembard. In the *Estoire*, the first
       king mentioned wages war with other Danish leaders against Alfred is then converted to
       Christianity by Alfred (late ninth century) (lines 3069–3232). The second king Gormund
       ("Gurmunt") is leader of a Danish army at Chippenham, who winters in Cirencester with
       his army, destroys the town sending many into exile and in April of the following year
       (around 881?), installs garrisons in the region, summons the army at Fulham and pro-
       ceeds to lead a host of thousands including more than one hundred kings to France where
       he is defeated by Louis and dies (lines 3239–92). Gaimar maintains the two figures as of
       Viking origin, places emphasis on the conversion of the former, and makes no mention of
       Gormund's donation of Loegria to the Saxons in the sixth century by the latter. See also
       Chapter 4, n. 39.

190   Rickard speculates that the Welsh figure "Gormant ap Rica" in *Kulhwich and Olwen* may
       have given rise to the association of "ap Rica" with "Africa" for Geoffrey, and that this same
       substitution of Saracens for Vikings took place in the English legend of Horn; similar
       transformations can be observed in numerous *chansons de geste* (60–61 and nn. 2–3). See
       also Joseph Bédier, *Légendes épiques. Recherches sur la formation des chansons de geste*,
       4 vols., 3rd ed. (Paris: Honoré Champion, 1926–29), IV, 46–8.

WACE'S ROMAN DE BRUT, PART 2   347

in the book of Merlin's Prophecies, Merlin announces that Arabs and Africans
will dread the Boar of Cornwall (*Prophetiae*, 115);[191] also in the Prophecies, the
"sea wolf" along with the forests of Africa will raise up one of the most hated
of enemies, the "German worm" (*Prophetiae*, 112); the stones which formed the
Giants' Ring were brought from the remotest parts of Africa (§129.243–45); the
African king, Mustensar, and his army are among the foreign troops of Lucius
Hiberius (§163.4).

Although each of these images signals a sense of remoteness and formi-
dability, it is only the section on Gormund, African king, which is filled with
the "extraordinary loathing" reserved for Muslims in this period, as noted by
J. S. P. Tatlock.[192] The vitriol Geoffrey devotes to this figure – not including
the narrator's aside chastising the Britons for their continued civil war – is
reinforced by a description of nearly total annihilation. Following the razing
of Cirencester, with the Saxons as his allies, Gormund destroys surrounding
towns pushing the British ruler Kareticus back across the Severn, spreading
destruction eventually throughout the island:

> Mox, depopulans agros, ignem cumulauit in finitimas quasque ciuitates,
> qui non quieuit accensus donec cunctam paene superficiem insulae
> a mari usque ad mare exussit ita ut cunctae coloniae crebris arietibus
> omnesque coloni cum sacerdotibus ecclesiae mucronibus undique
> micantibus ac flammis crepitantibus simul humi sternerentur.
> Diffugiebant ergo reliquiae, tantis cladibus affectae, quocumque
> tutamen ipsis cedentibus patebat. (§184.135–41)

> Then, ravaging the fields, he heaped up against all the surrounding cities
> a fire which, once kindled, did not die down until it scorched almost the
> whole surface of the island from coast to coast, so that all the towns,
> along with their people and the priests of their churches, were laid in
> the dust by his relentless battering-rams, as blades flashed and flames
> crackled all around. The survivors, shocked by the catastrophe, fled to
> any place of safety they could find. (§184, p. 256)

The result of this destruction was nothing short of a diaspora to Wales and
Brittany, "ita ut tota ecclesia duarum prouinciarum, Leogriae uidelicet et

---

191   In his edition, Reeve does not use the designation "Liber VII/Book Seven" for the book
      of Prophecies (although the preceding and subsequent books are numbered VI and VIII
      respectively).

192   Tatlock, *Legendary History of Britain*, 138.

348

Northamhimbriae, a conuentibus suis desolaretur" (§186.167–68; "with the result that the churches of the two provinces of Loegria and Northumbria lost their entire congregations").

In the First Variant, the description of Gormund's predations is toned down somewhat in a passage less than half the length of that in Geoffrey's vulgate; part of this softening is achieved by the removal of Geoffrey's passionate aside to the Britons castigating them for their civil wars and thus their role in their own destruction (§185.141–54). Even without Geoffrey's editorializing, however, the phrasing in the First Variant has monumental qualities as in the following which echoes passages from the Pentateuch in its simplicity and sense of finality: "et desolata est terra ab omni specie sua, maxime Loegria que pars Britannie melior extiterat" (§184/86) ("and the land was robbed of all its splendor, especially Loegria, which had become the better part of Britain" [my trans.]).

In the passage immediately following, the First Variant adds yet another note of finality in declaring the changing of the name of the island, to follow upon the changing of the name of the Saxons to "Angli": "Hinc Angli Saxones uocati sunt qui Leogriam possederunt et ab eis Anglia terra postmodum dicta est" (§186/7) ("Henceforth, the Saxons who possessed Loegria were called 'Angles,' and because of them the land has been called 'Anglia' [England] ever since" [my trans.]). Geoffrey does not include this detail of the name change since that would not have served his purpose of illustrating shared British-Saxon power up until the tenth century. Thus, although the section in the First Variant reporting Gormund's Donation is shorter than in the vulgate, it may be seen as carrying greater weight in that Gormund's Donation is more significant for Saxon rule of the island, raising the stature of the latter group while diminishing that of the native Britons.

In his characteristic thoroughness, Wace adds details to his two *Historia* sources, both on Gormund's background and on the subject of the wake of Gormund's Donation; like the First Variant, he also eliminates Geoffrey's speech castigating the Britons, and moderates Gormund's characterization somewhat (thereby removing the vitriol aimed at this figure in the *HRB*).[193] Wace explains that Gormund is bold, rich, powerful, physically very brave, and from a great lineage (13385–88). In the *Brut*, Gormund is an African king, but the detail added is that he spurns his inheritance, leaving his inherited

---

193   Wace also adds the detail that Isembard is more specifically Louis's nephew who has been disinherited (lines 13521–22), as if to further explain or justify Isembard's rebellion. On other additions found in MS. J in particular (Paris, BnF fr. 1416), see Jane Bliss and Judith Weiss, "The 'J' Manuscript of Wace's *Brut*."

WACE'S ROMAN DE BRUT, PART 2 349

kingdom to one of his brothers, refusing to rule any kingdom he does not conquer himself (13394–400). He gathers a great fleet with 160,000 men, each of
them famous "tuz cuneüz e tut numez" (13406) and proceeds to defeat many
kings and conquer many lands en route to Ireland, where he quickly subdues
the population and names himself king, having achieved his goal of only ruling
a country that he had conquered, not inherited (13412–19). Up until this point
in the narrative, the portrayal is largely positive – as we have seen, Wace also
uses this rhetorical strategy earlier in the *Brut* with Julius Caesar in particular as if to make him a worthier opponent[194] – except for the remark which
repeats the gist of the passage which comes chronologically earlier in the narrative as a presage (1193–1200), that it was Gormund and his pagan horde who
caused the destruction through which Britain lost its name.[195]

However, soon things begin to turn downward in Gormund's portrayal.
The Saxons make peace with the Britons, but then they send for Gormund,
who enters into a pact with the Saxons to deliver them the land; Wace comments upon the logic of this arrangement since the Saxons were pagans like
Gormund, while the Britons were Christians. In an interesting note, Wace
adds that the Saxons led the Africans in the charge, giving the impression that
Gormund's Africanness is less a concern than his perceived "pagan" status,
and his collusion with the Saxons; in a way, in the *Brut*, the Saxons are on a
par with Gormund or even superior in their villainy (i.e., more a scourge than
the Saracens, who at this time were increasingly perceived as the traditional
enemies of Christendom in the epic tradition).

Wace's description of the devastation of the Gormund-Saxon attack is
graphic, certainly more detailed than in either the First Variant or the vulgate:

Saisne les Alfricans cunduient,	The Saxons led the Africans,
Maisuns ardent, viles destruient;	They burned houses, destroyed towns;
Les chevaliers e les vileins,	Knights and peasants,
Les clers, les muines, les nuneins,	Clerics, monks, nuns,

---

194 On Wace's relatively positive portrayal of Julius Caesar through the liberal use of ideal-
     ized courtly praise terminology, see J. Blacker, *The Faces of Time*, 97–99 (1994); see also
     nn. 50 and 167 above, and Catherine Croizy-Naquet, "César et le *romanz* au XIIe siècle,"
     Cahiers de Recherches Médiévales (special issue: *La Figure de Jules César au Moyen Âge et à
     la Renaissance*, 13, 2006): 39–49, esp. 39, 42–47, 49.

195 "In his time came the great flood of pagans and infidels whom Gormund brought by sea –
     you have certainly heard speak of them – who wrought the destruction through which
     Britain lost her name" (13379–84; "En sun tens vint la grant surverse / De paens e de gent
     adverse / Que Gurmunt amena par mer, / Bien en avez oï parler, / Ki firent la destruction /
     Dunt Bretaine perdi sun nun."

Batent e chacent e ocient;	They beat, drove away, and killed;
La lei Damnedeu cuntralient.	They opposed the law of God.
Mult veïssiez terre eissillier,	There you could see many lands laid waste,
Femmes hunir, humes percier,	Women dishonored, men pierced through,
Enfanz en berz esbüeler,	Children disemboweled in their cradles,
Aver saisir, preies mener,	Goods seized, spoils taken,
Turs abatre, viles ardeir.	Towers destroyed, towns burned.

(13477–87)

The mention of the diaspora functions as a presage of the decimation of the entire country. As the destruction continues, some of the Britons flee to Wales; those who could get ships sailed for Brittany, those who could not leave for Wales or get ships, stayed in Cornwall (13510–14).

Further destruction is described in detail in the narrative of Gormund's taking of Cirencester. This narrative appears to be a conflation of the vulgate *Historia* and First Variant versions of the siege of that city and Gaimar's narrative of Cerdric's use of the sparrow trick in the first of three sieges against that city related in the *Estoire des Engleis* (the "incendiary bird motif" as it has sometimes been called).[196] But in Wace it is not until Gormund has destroyed everything that he hands the land over to the Saxons as he promised:

Encore i perent les ruines	One can still see the ruins
E les deserz e les guastines	And waste land and wilderness
Que Gurmund fist en plusurs lieus	That Gormund wrought in many places
Pur tolir as Bretuns lur fieus.	In order to take their fiefs from the Britons.
Quant il ot guasté lu païs,	When he had laid waste to the country,

---

196   In the *Estoire des Engleis*, there are three sieges against Cirencester, though the first by Cerdric in the sixth century is more dramatic in its details than that of Gormund (who, in the *Estoire*, is a ninth-century figure contemporaneous with the historical Guthrum), and contains the stratagem of the sparrows not found in the *Historia* or First Variant (ll. 855–72; the second siege, ll. 993–94 by Ceawlin and Cutha ; and the third, ll. 3240–58 that of Gormund where a large number of the population are chased from the land, but without mention or graphic details of wide scale destruction and loss of life). See Short, ed. and trans., *Estoire des Engleis*, note to line 858, p. 368; Weiss, trans., *Roman de Brut*, p. 339, n. 2, and the resources in Chapter 4, nn. 38–39.

WACE'S ROMAN DE BRUT, PART 2   351

Les viles arses, l'aveir pris,	Burned towns and taken goods,
Lu regne ad as Sednes duné;	He gave the kingdom to the Saxons;
E il lur aveit afié	And he had promised them
A duner s'il le cunquereit	He would give it to them if he con-quered it
E il si fist, bien lur fist dreit.	And he did it, he truly did them justice.

    (13631–40)

To our modern sensibilities, it may be difficult to see how Wace perceives justice in these circumstances, but he does not miss this opportunity to note Gormund's faithfulness to his word, albeit to the perfidious Saxons. While Gormund is faithful, his mode of operations is one of destroy and conquer, set up by Wace as a model opposite to that of Arthur's more moderate methods of empire building.

Wace expands on the First Variant's remark that from then on, the land took the name of the Angles, probably trying to explain the abrupt introduction of this not-aforementioned group. Without using the proper name of "Angles," Wace implies that that is whom he is talking about: not exactly in so many words, he says that the Saxons took the name of Angles "after the line (people) who first received the land ... in order to remember their origins," thereby ostensibly identifying the Angles with the Saxons, saying that the Saxons were the Angles' descendants, rather than distinguishing them as two separate ethnic or cultural groups:

Cil unt la terre recuillie,	They [the Saxons] acquired the land
Ki mult l'aveient encovie.	Which they had so desired.
Pur un lignage dunt cil furent	After the line from which they came,
Ki la terres primes reçurent	[That is, those] who first received the land,
S'i firent Engleis apeler	They had themselves called "English"
Pur lur orine remenbrer,	In order to remember their origins,
E Englelande unt apelee	And they called "England"
La terre ki lur ert dunee.	The land which was given to them.

    (13641–48)

James Noble suggests another possibility: that Wace is drawing a distinction between the treacherous Saxons and the Angles, that is, between the Saxons who came first at the time of Vortigern, and the German settlers who arrived *after* Gormund's Donation, settlers who did not seek to destroy but rather to build themselves a new land, as Laȝamon has done in his *Brut* (c.1200), a text

352   CHAPTER 5

based largely on Wace though not without significant departures.[197] However, while this distinction may well hold true for Laȝamon, it does not seem to be the case for Wace's attempt to explain the First Variant's simple statement "Henceforth, the Saxons who possessed Loegria were called 'Angles,' and because of them the land has been called 'Anglia' [England] ever since" [my trans.]) ("Hinc Saxones Angli vocati sunt qui Leogriam possederunt et ab eis Anglia terra postmodum dicta est," FV, §§186/7), because it implies that the Saxons came first, and then the Angles. Since one of Wace's passions was etymology and toponymics, it is not unreasonable to think that he sought to justify the name "Engleterre" by saying the Saxons actually renamed themselves, and then their land in order to remember their ancestors, the Angles (13643–48), since it did not follow logically – to him – that the name "Engleterre" should derive directly from the words for Saxons, Old French "Sednes" or "Saissuns." Etymology aside, however, it would appear that Wace's additional explanation (13656–58 below) reflects a belief that these two peoples were either one in the same (from the beginning) or that somehow, they had evolved into one group, that the "new inhabitants" were simply more of the same groups as had come before, descendants but not distinct (but not Britons).[198]

---

197 "Layamon's Ambivalence Reconsidered," in *The Text and Tradition of Layamon's Brut*, ed. Françoise H. M. Le Saux (Cambridge: D. S. Brewer, 1994), 171–82 (pp. 180–82); see also Le Saux, *Layamon's Brut: The Poem and its Sources*, Arthurian Studies 19 (Cambridge: D. S. Brewer, 1989), pp. 174–75; *Layamon's Brut*, ed. G. L. Brook, R. F. Leslie, EETS, 2 vols. (Oxford: Early English Text Society, 1963), vol. 1, lines 1–8020; 1978, vol. 2, lines 8021–end.

198 Geoffrey does not mention a change in the territory's name, of course, since that would have undercut his efforts to illustrate shared custodianship of the island between the remaining Britons and the Saxons from the sixth to the ninth century (Leckie, *Passage of Dominion*, 105–11). The First Variant departs from the Galfridian version of shared power by showing a definitive Saxon takeover in the sixth century, more in line with Bede's chronology; the FV redactor explains how Britain was renamed and the Saxons were renamed as well (as cited above). Wace states that the name "Engleterre/England" came from the "Angle(s)/A(E)ngleis," who were later called "English"; he follows the First Variant's chronology but while saying that the Saxons were renamed Angles, he also implies that they had been Angles all along, that is, Saxons descended from Angles, stressing their origins (and perhaps unaware that they were originally two different peoples). In the last analysis, Wace seems to have had more linguistic rather than socio-political motives, needing to explain how one derived "Angleis" or "English" and "Engleterre" rather than using names which could have been derived from the words for "Saxon" (incl. "Saissuns"). Ultimately, in addition, following the tradition set forth by Gildas, pseudo-Nennius (*HB*), Geoffrey, and the First Variant redactor, Wace appears as well to have subscribed to the "mass extermination/exile" theory of the Saxon takeover, though not necessarily of the *adventus Saxonum*: "Tuz les Bretuns si eissillierent / Que unches puis ne redrescerent" (1199–1200; "They [the Saxons] exiled all the Britons, who never regained power"). In addition, he neither shared Bede's largely pro-English perspective (shared by his contemporaries

WACE'S ROMAN DE BRUT, PART 2   353

What is perhaps more important for our purposes here, though, in this renaming of a people is that according to Wace the Saxons – or Angles – did not choose to adopt the language or the customs of the native peoples.[199] They chose to maintain a barrier preventing assimilation – either their merging with the local peoples or vice versa – showing no interest in blending with any other groups which may have been there before their arrival. Additionally, the Saxons chose neither to assimilate with the native Britons nor to isolate themselves in peaceful coexistence; rather, they claimed the land as their own, imposing their culture and their language on the land or at the most extreme, driving the natives out. Wace is not describing linguistic coexistence here, but rather cultural domination, an attempt to privilege the autonomy of one group over that of another:

Des que Brutus de Troie vint	From the moment Brutus came from Troy
Tut tens Bretaine sun nun tint	Britain retained its name the whole time
Jesqu'al terme que jo vus di	Until the time I am telling you about
Que par Gurmund sun nun perdi	Which through Gormund it lost its name
Si ot novels abiteürs,	There were new inhabitants,

William of Malmesbury and Henry of Huntingdon, among others; see Gillingham, "Henry of Huntingdon") that the Saxon takeover was an "achievement" (i.e., that the Saxons were the agents of Britain's redemption), nor the two primary alternative models which modern archaeologists, anthropologists, and historians are currently debating to explain the Anglicization of England/Britain: 1) a gradual large-scale migration (or series of migrations) through which the Britons were outnumbered; or 2) the conquest of a minority elite – an elite similar to the Normans, but which did not eventually assimilate to the natives, unlike the Normans.

199   Wace apparently provides twelfth-century testimony for the idea that "the Germanic invaders absorbed very little of the native culture of Britain" (Ward-Perkins, "Why did the Anglo-Saxons not become more British?" 514). For a very different – if not completely opposite – perspective, see Jacqueline Burek who argues that Laȝamon demonstrates the Saxons' flexibility and interest in assimilation whereas the Britons' downfall was due in large part to their inflexibility and lack of interest in blending with cultures other than their own ("'Ure Bruttisce speche': Language, Culture and Conquest in Laȝamon's *Brut*," *Arthuriana* 26.1, 2016: 108–23). Although Burek doesn't discuss Bede, one hears Bedan echoes regarding the Britons' inflexibility, in religious contexts; Wace himself sounds a similar note, not with respect to inflexibility per se, but lack of interest in blending their culture with those of others as seen in his adaptation of Geoffrey's narrative of how the Britons did not want to intermingle with the natives in Brittany and insisted on sending for wives from Britain.

Novels reis e novels seignurs.	New kings and new lords.
Ci voldrent tenir lur usage;	They wanted to keep their customs;
Ne voldrent prendre altre language.	They didn't want to take on another language.
Les nuns des viles tresturnerent,	They changed the names of the towns
En lur language les nomerent.	And named them in their own language.

(13653–62)

While on the one hand this reference to "new inhabitants" comes in the context of the Saxons as descended from the Angles and now all are called English (though "new" also as opposed to the Britons), on the other hand it is difficult not to hear as well a reference to the coming of the Normans – yet another group that conquered Britain following the Romans, Saxons, and Vikings – although under the political and cultural domination of the Normans, the previous inhabitants were neither obliterated nor driven off either before or upon their arrival.[200]

Aside from Julius Caesar, the other most noteworthy conquering figure of the *Brut* is King Arthur. There are certainly obvious differences between

---

200   While there may be allusions to the arrival of the Normans, any parallels one may be tempted to draw must be nuanced, given the enormous complexity of cultural relations in England particularly in the century following the Conquest; see Hugh Thomas's study devoted to collective identities and assimilation in England in that period, *The English and the Normans*, esp. pp. 83–92. As Susan Crane has noted particularly with respect to the thriving British and English cultures in the face of the Norman invasion, and evidence of both multidirectional assimilation as well as preservation of native group values, "The conquerors and their followers were unquestionably bent on dominating the inhabitants of Britain, but this process was not entirely a matter of force, nor should the inhabitants' responding manoeuvres and successes be elided into a model of helpless subjection. The extent to which intermarriage, bilingualism and cultural adoptions came to characterize Norman rule sharply contrasts with the later British programme of empire-building and testifies both to the Normans' desire to make Britain their permanent home and to the conquered inhabitants' success at imposing themselves and their ways on the new arrivals" ("Anglo-Norman Cultures in England, 1066–1460," cited at 35); see also Short, "*Tam Angli quam Franci*" and Chapter 4, n. 7, as well as Chapter 2, nn. 72–74. By the same token, while acculturation can be an enriching experience for many groups, as Rees Davies has commented, "it can also be an insidiously destructive experience, especially for the minority or subservient culture and for the political and social order which is associated with it. This is particularly so when the intrusive culture is aligned, consciously or otherwise, with the ambitions of an acquisitive kingship and aristocracy, a centralizing church and a proselytizing and categorizing clerical élite. [...] This cultural challenge in its broadest sense is surely part of the essential context of the mentality of domination" (*Domination and Conquest*, 16).

Gormund, the African king, and Arthur, king of the Britons: 1) patterns of inheritance: Gormund declines his inheritance and sets off as an extremely powerful soldier of fortune, at the grave expense of other civilizations, whereas Arthur is born the son of a king but out of wedlock, and is destined to rule the land of his ancestors; 2) geographic origins (and in the twelfth-century context, linked with race): Arthur is a Briton and Gormund an African, associated with the Muslim Sahara or sub-Saharan Africa, insofar as they were conceived in the twelfth century; and 3) religion: Gormund is seen as pagan and Arthur is Christian.

Perhaps an even more important distinction, however, between these two figures which remains to be pointed out is the types of conquerors they are and the political and cultural situations they leave in their wake. First, it should be noted that, probably surprising to some in light of Arthur's subsequent romanticisation in later history and literature based largely on images of courtesy rather than valor in battle, in Wace's *Brut*, Arthur is no saint (except perhaps a warrior saint). In the *Brut*, despite his generosity, his founding of the Round Table (an element introduced by Wace), the twelve-year peace he is able to establish and maintain (seen in Wace's two major sources as well), Arthur is combative, albeit a worthy opponent, but also unabashedly land- and power-hungry. However, Arthur's brand of imperialism for the most part is not informed by a vision of cultural or moral superiority imposed by the conquerors on the conquered, unlike the form of imperialism practiced by Gormund and the Saxons which more closely conforms to the formulation that "a defining characteristic of imperial expansion is that the center must disparage the indigenous culture of peripheral groups."[201]

In the *Roman de Brut*, references to Arthur's combative nature include his swearing of an oath that "the Saxons would never have peace as long as they were in the land with him" (9035–36; "Que ja Saisne pais ne avrunt / Tant cum el regne od li serunt"); again against the arch-enemies, the Saxons, "never was such slaughter, such violent destruction, such torment and such suffering inflicted before upon the Saxons in a single day" (9175–78; "Unches si faite occisiun / Ne si laide destructiun / Ne tel besil ne tel dolur / Ne fu de Seisnes en un jur"); Arthur also vanquishes the Scots "because they had waged war against him and aided Cheldric" (9257–58; "Pur ço qu'il l'orent guereied / E a Cheldic orent aidied"); at Loch Lomond Arthur attacked the Scots "so severely, attacked and restrained, oppressed and starved them so much, that by the twenties, hundreds and thousands, they fell dead on the shores" (9451–54; "Tant les assailli e guarda, / Tant les destrainst e afama, / A vinz, a cenz e a milliers, / Chaeient

---

201 Michael Hechter, *Internal Colonialism*, 64.

356   CHAPTER 5

morz par les graviers"); and at the end of the Roman conflict, he had the body
of the emperor sent to Rome, declaring that he owed no more tribute than that
and "whoever would demand tribute from him, he would send him back in the
same way" (12994–95; "E qui treü li requerreit / Altretel li enveereit").

In addition, after conquering Ireland, Arthur goes to Iceland, and we have
another reference to his land-hunger:

La terre prist tute e cunquist	He took the whole land and conquered it
E a sei tute la suzmist;	And made it submit to him;
Par tut volt aver seinnurie.	He wanted to have dominion over everything.

(9705–07)

Gotland and the as-yet-unidentified Weneland quickly follow suit (9708–30).
Arthur then decides that he will proceed to conquer all of France: here Wace
tempers the situation, by not using the description found in the vulgate that
Arthur, when he learned of "kings of nations overseas [who] became very
frightened that he would attack and deprive them of their subjects" ... "he
exulted at being universally feared and decided to conquer all Europe" ("reges
transmarinorum regnorum nimius inuadebat timor ne inquietatione eius
oppressi nationes sibi subditas amitterant" ... "extollens se quia cunctis timori
erat, totam Europam sibi subdere affectat" §154.230–32, 235–36).[202] Before
heading to France, however, Arthur learns that his brother-in-law Loth, designated by the dying Norwegian king as his heir (since Loth was his nephew)

---

202   Although Arthur's "reputation for generosity and excellence" is also lauded in the vul-
       gate (§154.229–30), the passage in the First Variant is somewhat more flattering to Arthur,
       stating that in addition, he was accomplishing "greater things day after day" (§154.2) but
       appearing to emphasize his thoughts of his reputation above the fundamental acqui-
       sition of territory: "Fama quoque largitatis eius omnes terre principes superabat unde
       quibusdam amori, quibusdam timori erat, metuentes ne regna terrarum Europe probi-
       tate sua et donorum largitate sibi subiugaret. Arthurus igitur de die in diem in melius
       proficiens hanc eandem sentenciam et uoluntatem quam timebant in animo iam con-
       ceperat ut scilicet extra Britanniam se et gentem suam dilataret et nomen suum cunctis
       gentibus manifestaret et exaltaret" ("The fame of his generosity surpassed all the leaders
       of the land, so that he was loved by some and feared by others, dreading that he might
       conquer all the lands of Europe through his uprightness and the generosity of his gifts.
       Accordingly, while he was accomplishing greater things day after day, Arthur had already
       conceived in his own mind this same thought and desire which they feared, namely to
       extend himself and his people beyond Britain and to make his name known and praised
       by all peoples" §154.2).

has been denied sovereignty by the barons and citizenry. Arthur crosses the sea and inflicts great damage, plundering and burning houses and towns. After he has given Norway to Loth and the latter has sworn fealty, Arthur crosses to Denmark since, "La terre a sun ués cuveita" (9872) ("He desired the country for himself"). After conquering Denmark, which he did not damage due to the foresight of its king, Aschil who sought and obtained leniency,

Arthur fu liez del grant espleit	Arthur was happy about this great exploit
E del cunquest que il faiseit.	And the conquest he made.
Ne li pout mie encor suffire; ...	[But] it was not yet enough for him; ...
(9887–89)	

And as he said a bit earlier during the twelve years' peace, he would go to conquer France:

Par la bunté de sun curage	Because of the goodness of his disposition
E par le los de sun barnage	And because of the advice of his barony
E par la grant chevalerie	And because of the great chivalry
Qu'il out afaitee e nurrie,	Which he fostered and nourished
Dist Artur que mer passereit	Arthur said he would cross the sea
E tute France conquerreit;	And conquer all of France;
(9799–9804)	

Thus, in Wace's world view, since Arthur has right on his side, his combativeness and imperialistic tendencies are compatible with his nobility of disposition (and he probably appears less narcissistic than he might to modern audiences). It is important to note that while Arthur is no saint, he never descends to Gormund's level, that is, to an unremitting lust for power achieved through destruction: Arthur can be a magnanimous victor, showing leniency, especially when dealing with enemies of a lesser order than the Saxons. For example, after defeating the Scots at Loch Lomond, he yields to the Scotswomen's pleas for mercy, exacts only homage, and leaves them in peace (9465–9526). When conquering Flanders and Boulogne:

Sagement fist sa gent cunduire,	He made his men behave wisely,
Ne volt pas la terre destruire,	He did not want the land destroyed,
Viles ardeir ne robes prendre;	Towns burned, nor goods taken;

Tut fist veer e tut defendre	He forbid and prohibited them everything
Fors viande e beivre e provende,	Except meat, drink, and provisions,
E si l'um trove ki la vende,	And if anyone could find someone who was selling such,
A buens deniers seit achatee,	It should be bought with good money,
Ne seit toleite ne robee.	Neither confiscated nor pillaged.

  (9897–9904)

Perhaps as the ultimate gesture in order to protect both civilians and armies – as well as the civilization already flourishing – Arthur accepts Frollo's offer of single combat so that Paris and its people would not be destroyed (10009–10).

Unlike Gormund who consistently leaves destruction behind him and cannot be seen as a protector of civilization in any regard, Arthur – while a conquering figure collecting territories wherever he goes – for the most part makes certain that life in the conquered lands goes on as it did before the inhabitants were forced to pay fealty to him. As in both the vulgate and First Variant *Historia*, in the interim between the conquest of France and Arthur's return to his British kingdom to hold court at Caerleon, Wace portrays the king distributing lands to his best men: to Kay, Anjou and Angers, to Bedevere, Normandy, to Holdin, Flanders, among others (10133–10170). Even though this is a distribution of lands gained through conquest, what is absent is the destruction on a grand scale (remembering all the while that Arthur is not a pacifist), and particularly the changing of names. The changing of names so emphasized by Wace at the time of Gormund's donation is not an issue following Arthur's conquests: life continues as it always had, except that Arthur's men are in charge at least on some level. Unlike in the First Variant and in Wace where the loss of the name of Britain signals the triumph of the English, indicating a loss of cultural autonomy as well as political power, Arthur's conquests do not necessitate name changing, as if to say Wace presents a model for princes to show that political power and demands of fealty do not automatically entail cultural demise – either for the minority culture(s) or the majority – nor should they.[203]

Although we cannot conclude with any surety that this absence of changed names is indicative of a harmless policy – especially since having new lords in power almost inevitably entails changes and is not necessarily

---

203 For a particularly cogent discussion of the role of names and naming in the assertion of communal identity, cultural and political autonomy particularly within the sphere of medieval Britain, see Rees Davies, "Presidential Address: The Peoples of Britain and Ireland 1100–1400. II. Names, Boundaries and Regnal Solidarities."

innocuous – Wace nonetheless seems to be advocating peaceful coexistence, where neither group needs to assimilate to the other, where domination may be administrative but not cultural, if such a situation were possible, and not merely an ideal. Through examples of Gormund and Arthur, Wace seems to be saying that real power is in fact the restraint of power: that rulers must do what they need to do to maintain peace and continuity, but not in excess and not at the expense of cultural upheaval. As a Jerseyman, a native of an island which to this day has a distinct dialect and traditions, Wace seems to be advocating sensitivity to pre-existing traditions, the bringing about of change with as little threat to native populations as possible.

It is tempting to think that Wace was giving advice to the Norman princes, not just to avoid civil conflict, but also to endeavor to maintain as much continuity as possible for the English and British peoples. For Wace, Arthur as a symbol is not limited to a specific people, the Britons – as opposed to the Anglo-Saxons (or the Normans) – but rather he serves as a symbol of peaceful coexistence through moderated domination, a ruler who established the Round Table, where the linguistic "universal translator" is always "stuck in the 'on' position," a safe haven for peoples of multiple identities, where everyone is an "insider," and no one an "outsider." Perhaps this characterization contributed to Arthur's future literary grandeur and popularity, in addition to the elements of the Round Table and the twelve years' peace. If not, at least this more civilized, in fact, more tolerant civilizing model may have made it easier for Laȝamon to transform Arthur into an English king, since in Wace's *Brut*, while remaining rooted in "history" as a champion of the Britons, Arthur is already more than a vehicle of any single nationalist sentiment. On a more universal level, Wace's Arthur embodies a transcendental moderated ruler which any people might wish to have as its champion, its "once and future king."

6   Augustine's Conversion of the English

Chronologically falling between Gormund's Donation and the conclusion of the *Brut*, one finds Augustine's conversion of the English, a passage which cannot be further from Bede's honorable portrait of the prelate, or from his castigation of the Britons who refused to help evangelize the Anglo-Saxons, claiming that they shouldn't have to Christianize those who have tortured and tried to destroy them.

In her study of the sources of Wace's *Brut*, Margaret Houck devotes a chapter to St. Augustine's mission to convert the English, since in her view, there were only two sections in the poem where Wace made significant changes

360   CHAPTER 5

to material found in written sources: St. Augustine's mission and Gormund's Donation.[204] The focus here is on Wace's presentation of Augustine's mission, more specifically the narrative of the so-called "fish-tail miracle," a passage characterized by elements more reminiscent of fabliaux than of chronicles. I would like to suggest possible reasons behind not only Wace's largely unflattering picture of this saint, but also his inclusion of what are essentially racial slurs against the English, in his poem largely intended to introduce the English people and their past – as well as the Britons – if not glorify them for the Anglo-Norman, Anglo-Angevin ruling house of Henry Plantagenet.

Wace was not alone in using the saint's mission to serve his own narrative ends: there are significant differences among historical texts which treat this figure. In the *Historia Ecclesiastica* (*c.*725–31), Bede emphasizes successful conversions and ecclesiastical reforms, portraying Augustine as a well intentioned if often uninspired figure; in the *Historia Regum Britanniae*, Geoffrey of Monmouth portrays Augustine's mission as a hostile, gratuitous intrusion into the affairs of the British clergy, who had been Christians since the time of Pope Elutherius (though true to form, Geoffrey does not provide dates). Focusing on largely the same events as the vulgate *Historia*, the First Variant (*c.*1138–55) portrays the mission as a natural and necessary, albeit occasionally violent, outgrowth of Anglo-Saxon political dominance. In the *Gesta Pontificum* (*c.*1125–43), William of Malmesbury provides much the same pro-Anglo-Saxon view as Bede, emphasizing even more than Bede the holiness of the saint's miracles, and less the prelate's relative lack of administrative talent (1, 5–6, 184–85).[205] On this last point, the article on Augustine in the *Dictionary of National Biography* reads that, "Augustine does not seem to have been a man of great energy or decision" and that although he was a "zealous monk," his dealings with the Welsh clergy demonstrated a "decided want of tact and conciliatory power," expressing what is likely a prevalent modern view of this figure.[206] Thus, Wace did not find an unblemished, exalted figure in each of his sources, not even in the works of the saint's principal biographer, Goscelin of St. Bertin (d. 1097),[207] yet what Wace does with – or to – Augustine sets his narrative in a class by itself.

---

204   *Sources*, 261.

205   William of Malmesbury *Willelmi Malmesbiriensis Monachi Gesta Pontificum Anglorum, Libri quinque*, ed. N. E. S. A. Hamilton, Rolls Series 52 (London: Longman, 1870).

206   Leslie Stephen and Sidney Lee, ed. "St. Augustine of Canterbury," *Dictionary of National Biography*, 22 vols., 8 suppl. (London: Oxford University Press, 1937–39), 1, 727–29, cited here at 728–29.

207   Goscelin, *Vita S. Augustini, majus opusculum* (*Vita major*), *Acta Sanctorum* 19:6. Paris: Victor Palme, 1866. 26 May. 370–92.

In broad outline, the narrative of Augustine's mission runs as follows: as prior of Pope Gregory I's monastery of St. Andrew's in Rome, Augustine was sent by the pope, accompanied by forty monks, to preach the gospel in England. Upon his arrival in England in 597, Augustine was received favorably by the Saxon kings, in particular, Ethelbert, king of Kent; Ethelbert, whose wife Bertha, a member of the Frankish royal family and who was already a Christian, soon converted. The prelate was received less favorably by Dinoot, abbot of St. David's, who, on behalf of the British clergy, refused to accept the authority of Augustine as archbishop of Canterbury, or as he was consecrated by papal command, "archbishop of the English peoples." Quite possibly in keeping with Augustine's threat against the British that they would suffer if they did not submit, King Ethelfrid of Northumbria led a battle at Chester, which resulted in the slaughter of over 1200 monks from Bangor who had come to Chester to pray for the safety of the British forces. Thus, that "nation of heretics" as Bede called the Britons (*HE*, II, ii, 141) was brought under Augustine's control, thereby uniting British and Anglo-Saxon Christendom, though the tension between British and Roman Christianity continued for many decades.[208]

There are three central points of interest in Wace's narrative on St. Augustine: the fish-tail incident, the founding of Cerne Abbey, and the massacre of the Bangor monks at Chester. Tackling the third subject first, it is important to note that, like the vulgate and the First Variant, the *Brut* demonstrates that Augustine was unsuccessful in convincing the British clergy to aid in the conversion of the Anglo-Saxons, and especially in convincing them that their allegiance should be to his see at Canterbury, and not to their archbishop at Carleon.[209] Where the First Variant states matter-of-factly that the British had already established their own metropolitan (§188, but also earlier in §72), and where the vulgate justifies British primacy by dating British Christendom to the papacy of Elutherius (§§72 and 188.178–80), Wace states that the British see was established in Carleon by Rome; furthermore, the Britons were born Christians, as seven British bishops tell Augustine: "Nus sumes e avum esté / Cristïens de cristïens né" (13851–52; "We are and have been Christians born of Christians"), emphasizing the nature of the English as parvenus, "E cil sunt de paene gent / E cunverti sunt novelment" (13853–54; "And those are from a pagan people and newly converted"). Echoing the vulgate and First Variant,

---

208   C. Warren Hollister, *The Making of England, 55 b. c. to 1399,* 5th ed. (Lexington, MA: D.C. Heath, 1988), 39.

209   This inaccuracy regarding the existence of a British see at Caerleon was apparently invented by Geoffrey and perpetuated by Henry of Huntingdon and Wace, among others (Tatlock, *Legendary History,* 263 and n. 25).

362   CHAPTER 5

Wace writes that it seemed to Abbot Dinoot and his men a "vile chose" to preach to those who not only were parvenus – as if that weren't bad enough – but who had also chased the Britons off their own lands, "Ki de noz fieus chacié nus unt / E en noz fieus remanant sunt" (13859–60; "Who chased us from our domains and in our domains, remained as inhabitants").

While the Britons are portrayed as not overly tactful either, Wace justifies their stubbornness through arguments resembling those based on the principle of primogeniture: first-born, first-arrived have special privileges. However, Augustine appears less charitable than the Britons. After speaking with Dinoot, he couldn't take it anymore, "Saint Augustin n'i pot plus prendre" (13865), and sought out Ethelbert of Kent, and his kinsman, Ethelfrid of Northumberland. The use of plural verbs later in the verses, "Volent destruire mortelment / Ki ne lur portent reverence" (13878–79; "They wanted to bring mortal destruction to those who had no respect for them"), implies inclusion of Augustine in the group of those wishing to get revenge, since it was to him that the British clergy did not pay homage, not to the two kings. Wace attributes active collusion to Augustine, thereby siding with the vulgate *Historia* which lays blame for the slaughter at Chester squarely on the English. Although Wace says that the British defied Augustine, "pur hunte ... e pur vilté" (13884; "shamefully ... and with malice"), he adds a note not found in Bede, Geoffrey or the First Variant: after pointing out the martyrdom of 2200 innocent monks (Bede and Geoffrey give 1200 [*HE*, II.ii, 140; *HRB*, §189.209–10], Wace and the First Variant 2200 [13921 and §189.179]), Wace decries the slaughter, "Deus, quel dolor! Deus, quel pechié!" (13917; "Lord God, what sorrow! Lord God, what sin!), blaming by association Augustine along with the English kings and troops.

The narrative of the second of the three sections, Augustine's vision of God and discovery of a spring near Cerne, is much more reminiscent of the English and French hagiographic traditions than either the first or third sections. Unlike in the fish-tail episode where Augustine prays to God, in the Cerne passage, God appears and speaks directly to Augustine, expressing pleasure at what the prelate has thus far accomplished during his mission:

"Tien, dist il, tun purposement	"Keep to," He said, "your intention;
Si te cuntien seürement.	Thus, you will stay on a sure path.
Tu iés mis serfs et tu me pleis	You are my servant and you please me,
E bien me plaist ço que tu fais ...	And what you do pleases me ...
Tu troveras lu ciel overt	You shall find Heaven open
U cil entre ki bien me sert."	Where those enter who serve me well."

(13759–62), (67–68)

WACE'S ROMAN DE BRUT, PART 2 363

Wace follows William of Malmesbury and Goscelin in providing a Latin and Hebrew etymology for Cernel, "cerno" Latin for "I see," and "el" the Hebrew word for "God," to commemorate the site where Augustine saw God, and a spring flowed forth, the future site of Cerne Abbey, although the abbey is not mentioned by name.[210] As is typical of Wace, even more so than either of his primary sources for the *Brut*, the vulgate and First Variant *Historia*, he places an etymological passage at a crucial moment, as if initiation and commemoration cannot be accomplished without performing the ceremony of naming and explicating the name, not unlike a sort of linguistic baptism.

According to Wace, Augustine did not enjoy as much success as one might have thought, though he had some successes, "Saint Augustin mult s'esjoï / Del pueple ki s'i cunverti" (13699–700; "Saint Augustine was very happy about the people who were converted"). He had to expend considerable effort – "Saint Augustin mult se pena /E lungement i travailla" (13707–8) – to convert people of poor stock, "genz de put aire" (13705). He found the folk of Dorchester particularly wicked, "de male nature" (13719). They didn't care one whit about his sermons and attached rays' tails to the back of his vestments (13723–86). Augustine prays to God to mark those people with a perpetual sign so they would remember his dishonor, and God obliges by giving those people and all their descendants tails.[211]

---

210 On Hebrew etymology in Wace's *Brut*, see Michelle Warren, "Memory out of Line: Hebrew Etymology in the *Roman de Brut* and *Merlin*," *Modern Language Notes* 118.4 (2003): 989–1014.

211 I have added the italics below for emphasis:

Lez Dorecestre ot une gent,	Near Dorchester, there was a people,
Devers suth est prueceinement,	Toward the southern [side],
Saint Augustin lur sermuna	Saint Augustine preached to them
E la lei Deu lur anuncia.	And announced God's law to them.
Cil furent de male nature,	They were a bad breed,
De sun sermun ne orent cure;	They didn't care a bit for his speeches.
La u li Sainz lur sermunot	There where the saint preached to them
E de lur pru a els parlot,	And spoke to them about Christ,
A ses dras detriés li pendeient	On the back of his robes they hung
Cues de raies qu'il aveient;	Rays' tails that they had;
Od les *cues* l'en enveierent	They sent him away with the tails
E asez lunges le chacierent.	And chased him a rather long time.
E il pria nostre Seignur	And he prayed to our Lord
Que de cele grant desenur	That He, because of this great dishonor,
E de cele orrible avilance	And this horrible vileness
Ait en els signe e remembrance;	Make in them a sign and souvenir;
E il si orent veirement	And thus they had truly
E avrunt perpetuelment,	And will have in perpetuity,

364 CHAPTER 5

In the *Gesta Pontificum*, William of Malmesbury also provides the detail of rays' tails attached to Augustine's back, but William says nothing about a punishment. Instead, Augustine retreats to a quiet place where he has a vision of God, "in mentis oculo" (II, 184), and prophesies a change in the heart of the people. In William's account, the fountain springs up in direct connection with the irreverent folk of Dorset, so that they might be baptized. Proving Augustine right, the people repent and are baptized forthwith (II, 185).

Goscelin relates that the folk attached fish-tails to the vestments, without specifying what type of fish: "prominentes marinorum piscium caudas Sanctis appendisse" (*Vmaj*, 388). He also says in a vague way that it is a rumor – "Fama est" – that the folk were punished and that the unspecified punishment was borne by their descendants as well, a vagueness which possibly led Houck to conclude that the biographer knew more than he was telling.[212] Further on, Goscelin mentions that some nonbelievers suffered exposed flesh on their thighs and soles of their feet, as if goaded by an invisible fire, and when the fire of punishment turned into the fire of faith, they begged to be born again in Christ ("ardore poenali in ardorem fidei, omnes imploreant in Christo renasci," *Vmaj*, 388). In Wace's text, no one gets a second chance: those who play a dirty trick are made to pay forever, and in a corporeal way, just as the descendants of Bisclavret's wife in Marie de France's *lai* are forever noseless.[213]

In fact, the punishment of the Dorchester folk appears excessive. In Marie's *lai, Bisclavret*, Bisclavret's wife is punished for the sin of betrayal, including adultery, and while cruel, appears justifiable within the value system Marie has presented. However, in the *Brut*, for the naughty people of Dorchester to be physically disfigured now and in perpetuity for playing a practical joke seems extreme in its cruelty and pettiness, and makes one question Wace's motives

Kar trestuit cil ki l'escharnirent	Since all those who mocked him
E ki les *cues* li pendirent	Who hung tails on him
Furent *cué* e *cues* orent	Were tailed and had tails
E unkes puis perdre nes porent;	And they could not ever lose them;
Tuit cil unt puis esté *cué*	All those have since been tailed
Ki vindrent de cel parenté,	Who descended from that parentage,
Cué furent e *cué* sunt,	They were tailed and are tailed,
Cues orent e *cues* unt,	They had tails and have tails,
Cues unt detriés en la char	They have tails behind in the flesh
En remembrance de l'eschar	In remembrance of the mockery
Que il firent al Deu ami	That they made of the friend of God,
Ki des *cues* l'orent laidi. (13715–44)	[They] who defiled him with tails.

212 *Sources*, 268.

213 Marie de France, *Lais*, ed. Alfred Ewert (Oxford: Basil Blackwell, 1944; reissued with new Introduction and Bibliography, Glyn S. Burgess, London: Bristol Classical Texts, 1995).

for including this story, even if he did hear it during a possible trip to Cerne Abbey, one of the foreign holdings of St. Stephen's of Caen where Wace may have received his early education.[214]

Back to the fish for a moment. The thornback ray was likely a prized fish during Wace's time, since it shows up on English monastic diet rolls in the late 15th c. as a rare occurrence, served apparently as a delicacy, consumed not nearly as often as minnows, whiting, or herring for example.[215] The *raie bouclée* is still prized in France for the delicacy of its flesh, and would probably have been well known to the French in Wace's audience. Even so, Augustine was not served the fish as a delicacy but was rather decorated with dead tails, made possible by the hook-like thorns on the ray's back. What a convenient, self-contained – not to mention fragrant – way to play a joke on the prelate whose sermons were considered by most of the listeners in Wace's text at any rate, gratuitous at best, and threatening at worst, since he represented the need to capitulate to a foreign power. Yet it is ironic that Wace shows sympathy for the Bangor monks who also refused to capitulate while at the same time seemingly condemning the inhabitants of Dorchester.

While on one level this story is akin in structure to folktales which relate how the tiger got its stripes or the leopard its spots – with the obvious difference that the English do not have tails – the explanation of how the people of Dorchester came to have tails is not only racially derogatory but also odd in the context of a narrative on the mission of a saint and the first archbishop of Canterbury. We have to keep in mind that while the people are punished, it was Augustine who did not turn the other cheek but rather sought immediate retribution, appearing not much more righteous than the Dorchester pranksters.

---

214 According to Peter Rickard, "this legend attached itself firmly to Rochester in popular tradition," as seen in a Latin satire of the thirteenth century preserved in a fourteenth-century French manuscript which relates that as a result of their shameful treatment of St. Augustine, the inhabitants of Rochester have tails ("*Anglois coué* et *L'Anglois qui couve*," *French Studies* 7 (1953): 48–55, here 50 and 55 n. 19). While Rickard says that "some" of the *Brut* manuscripts give Rochester ("Roucestre," 13713, 13715) in place of Dorchester, according to Arnold, only one manuscript has such a substitution: MS. C, London, British Library Cotton Vitellius A. x.; MS. A, London, College of Arms Arundel XIV has "Excestre" in l. 13715 and MS. L, Lincoln, Cathedral Library 104 substitutes the following line for 13715: "Mugelingtune puis voleit estre". On "Mugelingtune," see Derek Brewer, "Englishmen With Tails: Laȝamon, 'Muggles' and a Transhistorical Ethnic Joke in English," *Medieval Heritage: Essays in Honour of Tadahiro Ikegami* (Tokyo: Yushodo, 1997), 3–15, here 9–13. See also James William Lloyd, "The West Country Adventures of Saint Augustine of Canterbury," *Folklore* 31 (2020): 413–34.

215 C. J. Bond, "Monastic Fisheries," *Medieval Fish, Fisheries and Fishponds in England*, 2 vols. ed. Michael Aston, BAR British Series 182 (i) (Oxford: BAR, 1988), I, 69–112, here 75.

366   CHAPTER 5

Just how widespread the legend of the tailed Englishmen was by Wace's time
is difficult to say, but it was apparently fairly common by the end of the twelfth
century. Although Wace assigns this fate to the people of Dorchester and their
descendants, Laȝamon complains that "English gentlefolk in foreign countries /
Because of that very deed go round with red faces, / And many a good man's
son when he is abroad, / Who never went anywhere near that place, is called
by everyone 'base'"; Rosamund Allen explains here that Laȝamon's use of the
word *cued* which she translates as "base" is a pun on *cué* "having a tail" and *qued*
"wicked, evil, sinful" (14768–72).[216] Peter Rickard notes that the phrase "Angli
caudati" is found in a Latin document possibly as early as 1163 and that Richard
of Devizes records that the taunt of "tailed" was flung at Richard I's crusaders
in Messina in October, 1190.[217] In an article on an early 15th-c. "Ballade contre
les Anglais," Paul Meyer refers to the insult of the tailed Englishmen as "the
insult most frequently addressed to the English" ("l'injure qu'on adresse le plus
habituellement aux Anglais") and explains that the origin of the insult is the
legendary curse placed on the inhabitants of Dorset by St. Augustine.[218]

Regardless of where Wace found the legend – it is worth the remembering that his *Brut* also contains the first written reference to Arthur's Round
Table which was likely legendary as well though much more positive – he did
use it. In this short passage, he portrays Augustine as the object of a trick, an
April fool, or as the French call it, a "poisson d'avril": the temptation to see a
connection between the French tradition of celebrating the day of fools by
attaching a paper fish to the back of the person being tricked and this legend
of St. Augustine is almost irresistible. But what did Wace seek to achieve in portraying the saint this way? Is Wace's presentation of Augustine's mission part of
Norman rulers' attempts to replace veneration of the English saints with veneration of Norman or French saints? Wace, who was well versed in hagiographical traditions having written saints' lives himself before beginning the *Roman
de Brut*, elected not to honor Augustine as Bede and Goscelin did with numerous accounts of miracles, including curing the sick and leprous, nor to use fish
symbolism as it was so often used in hagiographic texts, as symbolic of a source
of abundance and of God's caring provision for mankind. Perhaps Wace found
the "fish tail" story more in keeping with Geoffrey's negative assessment of the
saint, but Wace may have had other motivations as well.

On the whole, the three sections of Wace's presentation of Augustine's mission reflect many of his interests seen elsewhere in the *Brut* and in the *Roman*

---

216   Lawman, *Brut*, trans. Rosamund Allen (New York: St. Martin's, 1992), 464 n. to line 14772.
217   Rickard, "*Anglois coué*," 48.
218   "Ballade contre les Anglais," *Romania* 21 (1892): 50–52, cited here at 51 n. 2.

de Rou: the right of monks to military protection; the primacy of the first-born or first-arrived; the intimate connection between the name of a place, its function, and commemoration; and the importance of diplomacy and skillful rhetoric in general. In fact, these passages seem to be more about these ideas than they are about Augustine himself or the extent of his mission, for that matter.

Wace's modern readers are often left with the impression the historian was more interested in etymology, the places he valued, a variety of historical events and abstract values, than he was in creating a monolithic impression of an historical figure, or consistently arguing one particular side of a conflict or providing panegyric, and perhaps it is this aspect of his work that led nineteenth-century historians to consider Wace one of the most accurate of historians. Perhaps Wace's contemporary audience was comfortable with his eclectic approach, and in fact, expected it, since they were already used to medieval historical narratives, which often seem to us as containing, as V. H. Galbraith once noted, "just one thing after another."[219]

Houck seeks to explain the differences between Goscelin's, William's, and Wace's accounts of the fish-tail sequence by suggesting that because Goscelin, though French by birth, had lived in England for almost thirty years by the time he began writing his works on St. Augustine, he was more vague than Wace regarding the punishment of the inhabitants of Dorchester, and that William of Malmesbury's patriotism caused him to write of repentance rather than divine vengeance of ludicrous physical disfigurement.[220] This explanation does not seem likely, though, because even though it would have been more in keeping with the tenor of these the Latin monastic documents, whose goal it was to emphasize miracles of the saint, to refrain from ribald speculation, than for the vernacular chronicler, Wace probably had to be even more careful than Goscelin or William to not offend, since he was dependent on royal patronage, whereas Goscelin and William of Malmesbury were not. Then how can we explain why Wace was willing to offend in order to achieve his goals? Or was it his intention to offend, and if so, why?

While it is quite plausible that Wace could have associated the "fish-tail miracle" with an already current derisory ethnic joke in an effort to assert the superiority of the French at the expense of the English, as Derek Brewer suggests,[221] my instinct is that ethnic ridicule was not Wace's main goal, but rather the context (albeit, an unfortunate one) – or the pretext, now that he had his audience's

---

219   "Good Kings and Bad Kings in English History," *History* n.s. 30 (1945): 119–32, cited here at 119.

220   *Sources*, 272.

221   "Englishmen with Tails," 8.

368 CHAPTER 5

attention – for moral lessons. Wace was willing to risk offending everyone to convey a message disguised in metaphor, seeking to reach his audience more through metaphoric suggestion than through overt polemic.

In that light, the fish-tail miracle could serve as a warning to the Plantagenet house, parvenus par excellence: watch your back, do not expect to be accepted, do not seek to make fools of others or you will end up playing the fool, but also do not abuse your power; to high-ranking ecclesiastics, including possibly the archbishop of Canterbury: a warning to be reflective and not high-handed; to ordinary clergy: do not expect the crown to support you although you may be in the right by virtue of your vocation; to ordinary citizens: be careful of how you demonstrate your opinions for they may come back to haunt you.

On the other hand, it is certainly possible that Wace included the fish-tail miracle and conflated it with the legend of the tailed Englishmen for comic relief, or for a bit of mean-spirited fun aimed at the English members of his audience or at the English in general, though we should keep in mind that his audience included the Anglo-Angevin Henry II, and not the French king. Insulting the English for the sake of insulting the English is also not consonant with Wace's approach; his humor is often self-deprecatory, turned inward rather than outward. Even though long passages highlighting a single rhyme or a single word, such as the passage describing the gifts Arthur gave at his plenary court and containing 29 instances of the word *duna* ("he gave") in 18 lines (10599–616), are not uncommon in the *Brut*, it seems out of keeping with the formal register of the rest of the narrative for Wace to have tossed about so vigorously, playfully, the word *cué*, at the expense of the inhabitants of Dorchester and their progeny.

With all that said, even if we suspend our own expectations for a consistent high tone or correctness, Wace's rendition of the fishtail miracle stands as an odd moment, if not a distasteful one. No matter how one interprets that passage, it still remains quite a fishy tale.

7 Cadwallader and the "Final Days"

Following Geoffrey (§202) and the FV, Wace reports that Cadwallader reigned next after the 48-year reign of his father, Chadwalein, nephew of Penda, son of his sister ("Niés Peanda, fiz sa sorur," 14659), Penda having been king of Mercia, a Saxon, not a Briton.[222] Where Wace does diverge though is that in

---

222 On Geoffrey's mistaken conflation of Caedwalla king of Wessex and Cadwallader, king of Gwynned in Wales, c. 655–82, turning the amalgam into the last king of the Britons, see

the *Historia* §§202–3, the great famine is preceded by references to civil strife among the Britons and by Cadwallader's illness, whereas in Wace the references to civil strife and Cadwallader's illness (before the very end) are apparently missing, Wace choosing to focus on the famine and the plague.[223] In Geoffrey, Cadwallader laments Britain's troubles as punishment from God for their sins (§203), rather than as caused by the perpetual wars with the Romans, Picts, Irish, and Saxons, ending "with a bitter invitation to these latter to enjoy their unmerited gains."[224] In the FV, the narrator expands Cadwallader's lament, changing its tenor with Cadwallader praying for God's mercy on the Britons, demonstrating as earlier the FV redactor's interest in including many biblical borrowings and prayers, in keeping with the general religious tone of the text.[225]

Wace does not include the lament – since he does not seek to dwell on divine punishment of the Britons and snipe at enemies, or appeal to the deity – but rather he expands on the hardships of the plague followed by the famine where so many died that the living who were supposed to bury the dead instead had to be buried with them, providing a dramatic scene meant to evoke pity rather than either ethnic vitriol or biblical/pious reflection:[226]

Ne poeient pas fuisuner	Those living were not sufficient
Tuit li vif as morz enterrer;	To bury the dead;
Cil que le mort enterrer dut	Those who were supposed to bury the dead
Od le mort enterer estut.	Were buried with them.
(14689–692)	

      Weiss, note to l. 14653, on *HRB* §202 Cadwaladrus, FV Cadwalladrus: "This is Caedwalla king of Wessex (685–88), not British but English" (369, n. 2). See also Chapter 2, nn. 36–37 and Chapter 3, n. 124 above on Geoffrey's conflation and the FV's following as well.

223   See Weiss, trans., 369, nn. 3 and 5.

224   Wright, ed., II, xxxii.

225   Wright comments that while in the vulgate, "Cadwaladr's soliloquy takes the form of a lament ... in the Variant text, the speech retains this basic framework, but the addition of further elements of piety lend it more the character of a prayer ... Moreover, precisely these elements unique to the Variant contain, as Hammer noted in his apparatus, a plethora of biblical borrowings and allusions" (Hammer, ed., cited by Wright, ed., II, xxxii, n. 41).

226   Wace doesn't provide any explanation of who ultimately did the burying, but rather he relies on the drama of the description to carry the narrative.

370   CHAPTER 5

Wace relates that once many of the Britons had died and the land lay waste for
eleven years, the English (using here the term "English" rather than Saxons)
sent to Saxony for their kindred to come populate the land:

E li Engleis ki remés erent	And the English who remained
E de la famine eschaperent,	And who escaped the famine,
E plusur ki aprés nasquirent,	And many of those born after,
Si cum il porent mielz vesquirent.	Lived as best they could.
Que pur les viles restorer,	In order to restore the towns,
Que pur les terres laborer,	And work the lands,
Unt en Sessuine la mandé	They sent to Saxony
U lur anceisur furent né	Where their ancestors were born
Que od femmes e od enfanz,	That, with wives and with children,
Od meisnie e od serjanz	With households and servants
Vengent tuit esforceement,	They might all come in numbers,
Terres avrunt a leur talent.	They could have lands to their satisfaction.

   (14715–26)

Wace then gives examples of how they wished to take over but retain their own
customs:

Espessement e suvent vindrent;	They came abundantly and often;
Les custumes e les leis tindrent	They kept the customs and laws
Que lur anceisur ainz teneient	Which their ancestors had had
En la terre dunt il veneient.	In the land from which they came.
Les nuns, les lages, le language	The names, laws, language
Voldrent tenir de lur lignage;	They wanted to keep from their lineage;

   (14735–40)

This tendency toward parochialism pertains particularly to language, with
Wace commenting that in only in Wales was the proper British language still
spoken.[227] However, Wace reports that the counties, baronies, and lordships
were distributed by the English as the British had devised them, which on

---

227 "The areas in which the older British usage prevails are gradually reduced until only Wales
     remains (RDB, lines 14,751–6, p. 773). In the *Roman de Brut*, the geographic distribution of
     personal and place names mirrors the progress of Anglo-Saxon culture" (Leckie, *Passage
     of Dominion*, 114). See below for different perspectives on this phenomenon.

WACE'S ROMAN DE BRUT, PART 2   371

at least one level seems odd given the aforementioned English antipathy to British cultural customs and language:

Entre Gualeis uncore dure	The proper speech of the Britons
De dreit bretanz la parleüre.[228]	Still remains among the Welsh.
Les cuntez e les barunies,	The counties and the baronies,
Les cuntrees, les seigneuries	The regions, the lordships,
Tindrent issi e deviserent	They maintained them and arranged them
Cume Bretun les cumpasserent.	As the Britons had [originally] devised them.

(14751–56)

Following the FV, Wace mentions Athelstan as king at this time in order to place chronologically the re-arrival of the English; although he does not actually give dates for Athelstan's reign (924–940), he says the latter was the first to crowned king of all England except Wales and Cornwall (14757–60), relating the rumor that he may have been illegitimate, and also the story that his father, King Edward, gave the gift in Rome of the silver penny known as Peter's Pence, though crediting his ancestor Yne as the first to have made this gift.[229]

As Leckie points out, Wace is trying to reconcile the Galfridian tradition of nearly 300 years of joint rule between the Saxons and the Britons and the First Variant in which the Saxons take over from the time of Gormund's Donation and essentially rule the island from then on. Whereas the First Variant makes Cadwallader and Athelstan contemporaries, "unlike the anonymous redactor,

---

228   Weiss notes that Arnold supplies the couplet 14751–52 since it is missing from MSS DCSFJAPNT (it is not clear in Arnold from which MS specifically he supplied this couplet, though he lists a variant for 14751 from K; ed., II, 773).

229   See Houck, *Sources*, 252–3, who claims that Wace's statement about Yne (Ina, king of the West Saxons) as the originator of the payment of Peter's Pence is the first to be found in any chronicle before Wace's *Brut*, though it is found later in Roger of Wendover, Simeon of Durham and Matthew Paris (253); Henry of Huntingdon attributes its establishment to Offa of Mercia (Houck, 253) and William of Malmesbury to Aethelwulf (*GR*, ii, 113) though the author of the *De primo Saxonum adventu* in the first half of the 12th century attributes the inception to Ina (*Historia Anglorum*, Greenway ed., 247, n. 124). While it is quite possible that Wace gathered this information from oral sources as Houck suggests (253), he may also have been familiar with Simeon of Durham's Chronicle since it is possible he used some of its material on the Norman Conquest in his *Roman de Rou* a few years later (*Faces of Time*, 32 [1994] and *Rou*, Holden, ed. III, 112–114). See also F. M. Stenton, *Anglo-Saxon England*, 460 and 215, n. 1, and Rory Naismith and Francesca Tinti, "The Origins of Peter's Pence," *English Historical Review* 134.568 (2019): 521–52.

Wace knew full well the identity of the English king in question. Neither the Galfridian periodization nor the confusion surrounding Athelstan's dates were allowed to stand. To deal satisfactorily with both problems, Wace found it necessary to define Athelstan's importance to Insular history in considerable detail," first referring to Athelstan after the slaughter at Chester (in a passage without parallel in either the vulgate or FV),[230] and later, near the end of the *Brut*, skipping ahead nearly three hundred years from the seventh to the tenth century,[231] using Athelstan to "date" the final transition to English domination

---

230 Wace's first reference to Athelstan is actually to his having pushed the Britons back beyond the Tamar and the Wye, "at the time he reigned" – an essential phrase which demonstrates that Wace knew that Athelstan reigned in the tenth century, not in the seventh, although the passage in which his name appears does involve Cadwan and Margadud preparing to defend Bangor:

Mes Adelstan quand il regna	But when Athelstan reigned
Ultra Tambre les esluina.	He pushed them [the Britons] beyond the Tamar.
(13939–40)	
Mais Aedelstan tant les destreinst	But Athelstan pursued them so much
Que ultra Waie les enpeinst.	That he thrust them beyond the Wye.
(13945–46)	

The "les" here refers to the Britons of Athelstan's time, and perhaps was meant to create a parallel or a connection to the situation with Cadwan and Margadud, kings of South Wales and North Wales respectively, of a much earlier era; their colleague Bledric, another baron gathering troops to defend Bangor (after the slaughter of the Bangor monks at Chester) along with Cadwan and Margadud, Wace says, was lord of Cornwall and held Devonshire, "which the Britons held for a long time around path of the River Exe, from the spring from whence it came down to the sea" (13933–39; "Bledric de Cornuaille ert sire / E si teneit Devenesire; / Issi cum l'ewe d'Esse curt /) De la funteine u ele surt / Des qu'en la mer u el descent / Ço tindrent Bretun lungement; / Mes Adelstan quant il regna ..."). Weiss notes that "Arnold (II, p. 815) thinks the information about Athelstan [his supposed involvement with Cadwan, Margadud, and Bledric], absent in *HRB*, comes either from oral tradition or William of Malmesbury, *De Gestis*" (Weiss, p. 351, n. 2). William's passage concerns Athelstan having pushed the Western Britons ("who are called Cornish") out of Exeter: "he fixed the boundary of their territory at the river Tamar, just as he had fixed the boundary of the Northern British at the river Wye," thus placing Athelstan properly chronologically, as the king who "purged that city by sweeping out an infected race" (ii.134.6), though regrettably expressing very openly his anti-Briton views. This reporting by William is not universally accepted by current historians (i.e., that Athelstan had expelled the Cornish from Exeter, fixing the Cornish border at the River Tamar following his having fixed the border between England and Wales in the Hereford area at the River Wye), but at the least, the events recounted were to have transpired during Athelstan's reign in the early tenth century.

231 *Passage of Dominion*, 113–14.

WACE'S ROMAN DE BRUT, PART 2

after the plague, famine, and flight of the Britons and the influx of Saxons, the influx of Saxons being one of Wace's major ways of explaining the passage of all that time and how the Saxons finally took over. Although I don't agree with Leckie's assessment that Wace dealt with Athelstan "in considerable detail," I do see the Norman poet's Houdini-esque sleight of hand in trying to finesse and reconcile through the use of Athelstan ruler of a united England, the Galfridian version which was so favorable to the Britons and the FV which was much more favorable to the Saxons.

At the very end, following Geoffrey, though without the expression of bitter regrets, in Wace Cadwallader heads to Brittany but then wants to return to his homeland following the plague, only to be told by a divine voice that he must not return, but rather take a different voyage to the apostle in Rome, since the Britons would never regain the land until the time prophesied by Merlin:

Une voiz divine lui dist	A divine voice said to him
Laissast cel eire, altre en preïst; ...	That he must leave this path, and take another; ...
Engleis Bretaine aver deveient;	The English must have Britain;
Ja Bretun n'i recovereient	The Britons will not recover it
Jesqu'al tens que la prophecie	Until the time Merlin's prophecy
Que Merlin dist seit acumplie; ...	Says it may be accomplished; ...[232]
(14785–86); (14791–94)	

One final condition is set, though: that not until Cadwallader's remains, like relics of a saint, be returned to Britain, would the Britons be once again rulers of the whole land:

Ne ja ço estre ne purreit	Nor could this come to pass
Desi la que li tens vendreit	Until the time would come
Que les reliques de sun cors,	That his remains
De sepulture traites fors,	Be removed from his tomb,
Serreient de Rome aportees	And be brought from Rome
E en Bretaine presentees.	And presented in Britain.
(14795–800)	

---

232   Vulgate §205: "until the time came which Merlin had foretold to Arthur" ("antequam tempus illud venisset quod Merlinus Arturo prophetauerat" (§205.565–66); FV MSS DES omit the reference to Arthur.

374   CHAPTER 5

Cadwallader follows the instructions of the divine voice, but first bidding his son Yvor and his nephew Yni to cross into Wales to rule the Britons as their lords, lest they fall into dishonor for lack of a ruler. Cadwallader then travels to Rome, is absolved by the pope, falls ill, dies, and is buried honorably.

But Wace then again departs from the vulgate by forgoing much of Geoffrey's commentary in the penultimate section (§207): at the beginning of that section, Geoffrey bemoans the final demise of the Britons, decries the wisdom of the Saxons, and vilifies the unworthiness of the Welsh. In vulgate §208, Geoffrey issues his famous directives to his colleagues Caradoc of Llancarfan, that he write about the later kings of the Welsh, and that William of Malmesbury and Henry of Huntingdon should confine themselves to the Saxon kings but none should write about the early Britons "cum non habeant librum illum Britannici sermonis quem Walterus Oxenefordensis archidiaconus ex Britannia aduexit" (§208.604–6; "since they do not possess the book in British which Walter, archdeacon of Oxford, brought from Brittany"). Wace also eliminates the FV redactor's shortened version of §208[233] where the latter identifies "himself" as Galfridus Arthurus Monemutensis who took care to translate the history of the Britons into "our language." Instead, the Norman author identifies himself as Master Wace and gives the date of completion of the history as 1155, with a prayer for "our redemption" (14859–866).

8   Conclusion: The Role of Language, Ethnic/Cultural Separatism, and the Characterization of Arthur as Insider/Outsider, Barbarian and Civilizer

Although as noted above, Gaimar's *Estoire des Engleis* does not completely overlap with Wace's *Brut*, and in many respects, far from it, nonetheless, we have seen various points of comparison which support at least two opposing views of Gaimar's text: Ian Short's, that Gaimar was promoting an assimilationist perspective, a form of multiculturalism for his Anglo-Norman audience, while at the other end of the continuum, R. R. Davies's view that Gaimar was ultimately consistently pro-English – and that his no-longer-extant *Estoire des Bretuns* may have done so as well, which may have prompted manuscript compilers to

---

233   We need to remember that the vulgate does not mention Athelstan ruling a united England, until the penultimate sentence of §207, whereas the FV mentions Athelstan earlier, in §204 – in a unique passage – as if to get the audience used to idea of Athelstan's rule before the end of the text (see Chapter 3, nn. 122–23). The FV also has a milder version of the first part of §207; see Chapter 3 for the discussion of these concluding sections (§§204–8) in the FV.

prefer Wace's *Brut* with the Round Table, and a significant portion of the text devoted to Arthur, the insider/outsider, the civilizer of all groups including the British "barbarians" whom he transformed into respectable, courtly populations. Based on what we have of Gaimar, the Norman poet was likely more sympathetic to the Briton-oriented history of Geoffrey of Monmouth than to Anglo-focused texts such as the First Variant, with which Gaimar's extant history shares its pro-English leanings.

As we have seen, Wace was not particularly an advocate for the English, though he certainly did not demonize their predecessors as Geoffrey had. In terms of his having been less-than-sanguine in the face of various Saxon tendencies, Wace may be the only author up until the mid-twelfth century to observe that the Saxons sought to keep their own customs and their own language; neither Geoffrey nor the First Variant author makes this point (nor would it appear did Gaimar). Interestingly, regardless of how we choose to read Wace's observation – as praise of this tendency or criticism, or perhaps simply neutrality, as is often the case with Wace – Wace's testimony seems to support Bryan Ward-Perkins's appraisal that a strong sense of difference "on both sides of the English-Celtic divide, with a striking reluctance to acknowledge any reciprocal debts, seems to have been present from early Anglo-Saxon times. The Germanic invaders absorbed very little of the native culture of Britain ... only some thirty words in Old English are believed to derive from Brittonic."[234] Margaret Gelling suggests an alternative view for the "virtual absence in Old English of words borrowed from Welsh [which has] naturally been used as an argument against extensive contact between speakers of the two languages" – but Brittonic did not disappear because the Britons themselves did not disappear; the languages overlapped in England much longer than Wace implies. Gelling writes that the lack of borrowings from the original language group by the new settlers could indicate that the Saxons and the Britons had so much in common being both agrarian cultures that they didn't need to borrow words from one another: "words are borrowed when people encounter objects or concepts not catered for in their own vocabulary."[235]

On the other hand, if there had been a disproportionate number of settlers with respect to natives, this could have played a significant role in the "massive replacement of the general stock of British names by Old English toponyms" after the arrival of the Saxons.[236] In contrast, as Gelling observes, "the arrival of a Latin-speaking ruling class in the first century AD did not cause a

---

234 Ward-Perkins, "Why did the Anglo-Saxons not become more British?" 514.
235 Margaret Gelling, "Why Aren't We Speaking Welsh?", 56.
236 Gelling, "Why Aren't We Speaking Welsh?" 51.

376 CHAPTER 5

wholesale renaming of settlements: there are very few Latin items among the names recorded from Roman Britain"; the "same is true of the Norman conquerors at a later date: we have only a handful of French place-names in any area of England."[237] According to this model, the influx of Saxons was so great, that no one should be surprised that Old English became so dominant relative to Brittonic.

However, although the use of French in England apparently did not affect place-names, we can assume that the French language – and the associated French culture – enjoyed a more positive status in twelfth-century England than did Brittonic in the "Anglo-Saxon" age: for example, as John Gillingham comments, "in William of Malmesbury's eyes, the more 'Frenchified' England and the English became, the better."[238] French was the administrative language of England for at least two centuries after Wace wrote, but while it was the language of the conquering elite, it did not universally supplant English; in fact, there is evidence that by the middle of the twelfth century, many of the aristocracy if not the upper merchant class were becoming bilingual. Certainly, by the end of the century, French speakers in England thought of themselves as English and were rapidly assimilating.[239] In addition, except for place-names, French had a significantly greater influence on the English language than did Brittonic.[240]

The comparative social status of the two languages, Old English and Brittonic, from the seventh through the ninth centuries, was however different from that of French in England in the twelfth. Ward-Perkins writes:

> It has often been observed, and the experience of post-Roman Britain confirms the observation, that the amount of borrowing between one culture and another is determined, not only by the amount of contact between the two, but also by the perceived status that each culture has in the eyes of the other. When invaders find a native culture that they feel to be superior to their own, they borrow heavily and readily from it, as happened amongst the Franks in Romanized Gaul; but when, as in Britain, they find a culture that they, rightly or wrongly, perceive to be inferior, the story is very different.[241]

---

237 Gelling, "Why Aren't We Speaking Welsh?" 51.
238 ""The Beginnings of British Imperialism," 6.
239 Short, "*Tam Angli*," esp. 173–75.
240 William Rothwell, "Language and Governance in Medieval England," *Zeitschrift für französische Sprache und Literatur* 93 (1983): 258–70.
241 "Why did not the Anglo-Saxons become more British?" 530.

WACE'S ROMAN DE BRUT, PART 2   377

Use of the Old English word *weahl*, which originally meant "foreigner," later
"Briton, Welsh" and still later "slave," has led some scholars to say that the
Germanic settlers referred to the Britons as foreigners in their own land.[242] In
some early English law codes *wergild* – that is, legal monetary valuation of a
man's life as compensation for injury, death, or crime – was set at a lower rate
for the Welsh than for the English, indicating "the inferior social position of
the British" that reflected "standard Germanic practice in dealing with native
populations in the areas which they took over."[243]

As part of his effort to provide a glorious history for the Britons in competition with Bede who did the same for the Saxons, Geoffrey also sought to promote the Brittonic language. Kelli Robertson writes: "In order to write a history
that could address the past of the whole island, Geoffrey had to resurrect the
British language as a viable historical medium, one on a par with Latin, which
he does by giving it Trojan origins within his narrative."[244] Geoffrey's claim
of having a "very old book in the British tongue" was intended to support the
existence of a written history, to help dispel the growing view that the Britons
were simply barbarians.[245] It's not so much the secrets contained in Geoffrey's

---

242 Ward-Perkins, "Why did not the Anglo-Saxons become more British?" 514; Hugh Kearny,
     The British Isles: A History of Four Nations. 2nd ed. (Cambridge: Cambridge University
     Press, 2006), 82.

243 See Margaret Lindsay Faull, "Semantic Development of Old-English *Wealh*," *Leeds Studies
     in English* 8 (1975): 20–44, cited here at 21. From a different vantage point, Elizabeth Tyler's
     work on texts associated with the early English royal dynasties from the time of Alfred
     the Great to the Norman Conquest also contributes to an image of expressly cultivated
     English distinctiveness from the Britons ("Trojans in Anglo-Saxon England: Precedent
     without Descent"). According to Tyler, by tracing their origins back to Germanic gods
     and biblical figures while avoiding Trojan origins, the early English were "expressing their
     deliberately maintained separateness from other European dynasties, both continen-
     tal and Welsh" (2), signaling an effort to disassociate themselves from the "legacy of the
     Roman Empire and then Frankish dominance" (20).

244 Kelli Robertson, "Geoffrey of Monmouth and the Translation of Insular Historiography,"
     46–47. On the contrary, since Welsh had a vibrant and confident literary culture in the
     twelfth century, more so than English, Geoffrey may have wanted to point this out, rather
     than raising the status of Brittonic culture; see Ben Guy particularly on historical writ-
     ing, "Constantine, Helena, Maximus: on the appropriation of Roman history in medieval
     Wales, c. 800–1250," *Journal of Medieval History* 44.4 (2018): 381–405.

245 On William of Malmesbury as the "first English historian to adopt a new and contemptu-
     ous attitude to Celtic peoples," see John Gillingham, "Context and Purposes," esp. 27–29.
     On this growing negative view of the Celtic peoples in the twelfth century, see idem,
     "Conquering the Barbarians: War and Chivalry in Twelfth-Century Britain and Ireland,"
     also idem, "The Foundations of a Disunited Kingdom"; Robert Bartlett, *Gerald of Wales,
     1146–1223* (Oxford: Clarendon Press, 1982), esp. Chapter 6, "The Face of the Barbarian";

378   CHAPTER 5

source – whether spurious or not[246] – but its very existence in Brittonic that was meant to carry semantic weight. In this case, the linguistic medium was more important than the message – though the message was ultimately conveyed in the more universal medium of Latin.

Before evaluating Wace's treatment of the Scots, Picts, and Saxons (primarily) as arch-enemies as in the vulgate and more tempered in the FV, as discussed above in Chapter 1, it is worth keeping in mind that Geoffrey often mentions the Scots and the Picts as a "set," in the same breath, occasionally with the Norwegians and Danes (§§89.5 and 120.69) or with the Irish (Hibernenses; §203.541), depending on the context. Geoffrey rarely mentions the Scots alone, except in §137.442 where, after Uther's defeat of the Saxons at Mount Damen, the king "visited all the Scottish tribes and made than unruly people forget their savagery"; §151.192 in the context of Arthur's pardoning of the Scots near Loch Lomond (which Geoffrey does not mention by this name, although Wace gives an approximation, "l'estanc de Lumonoï" 9425);[247] and when he restores Auguselus to royal power over the Scots (§152.204). In very rare instances does Geoffrey say anything at all flattering or even moderated about these three groups, as in §207 where he says the Saxons were more practical than the Britons in terms of their handling of shared power, or where Arthur is ultimately lenient with the Scots at Loch Lomond; there is also the very neutral statement that he chooses not to write the history of either the Scots or the Picts (§70.387), though he does provide the "information" that the Scots were descended from the Irish and the Picts, appearing to share "the view that the Scots of his own day were the product of assimilation and

---

R. R. Davies, "The Peoples of Britain and Ireland, 1100–1400: II. Names, Boundaries and Regnal Solidarities."

246   See especially Ian Short, "Gaimar's Epilogue and Geoffrey of Monmouth's *Liber vetustissimus*," *Speculum* 69.2 (1994): 323–43.

247   In ch. 67, *HB* gives "stagnum Lumonoy" in the list of the "Wonders of Britain" [*de Mirabilibus Britanniae*]; see Weiss, trans. 237, n. 3. This lake is not to be confused with another lake belonging to the "wonders" described by Hoel in the Galfridian material and Wace, including another lake in Wales which the inhabitants call "Liliguan" or Lake Lliwan, described in *HB* 69, present in folklore but apparently now lost, §150). See Burchmore, trans., 474, n. to 150.2, on Liliguan referring to Lake Lliwan, Reeve, ed., lviii on Geoffrey's source(s) for the lakes, as well as nn. 95–96 above on Loch Lomond's erroneous placement in Moray by Geoffrey, FV, and Wace. See also Andrew J. Evans, John Nettleship, and Stephen Perry, "*Linn Liuan/Llynn Llyw*: The Wondrous Lake of the *Historia Brittonum's de Mirabilibus Britanniae* and *Culhwch ac Olwen*," *Folklore* 119 (2008): 295–318. The authors suggest that "the feature known variously as Linn Liuan/Llywan and Llynn Llyw was the area now occupied by Caldicot and the marshland up to Caerwent" (South Wales) and that "at least three potential whirlpools existed in this area until recently – and two, the Whirlyholes, were certainly sufficient to account for the dramatic wonder" (312).

WACE'S ROMAN DE BRUT, PART 2

intermarriage between the Picts and the Gael of an earlier age" with contemporary historians of our own age who lay "particular emphasis on this mixed heritage in the process of Scottish ethnogenesis" – though this view was not shared by Henry of Huntingdon who is "the earliest securely dated witness to the school of thought that presented the Picts as the victims of genocide," rather than attributing their disappearance to assimilation.[248]

In Geoffrey, the Scots are mentioned four times alone, nine times with the Picts alone, three times with either the Norwegians and Danes (§§89.5 and 120.69), or with the Saxons (§143.19), and there are nine references to the Picts alone. In general, the FV follows suit, with 8 references to the Scots and Picts together, four to the Scots alone and nine to the Picts alone. However, as we have seen in Chapter 3, the FV often does not repeat Geoffrey's vitriol, especially toward the Saxons, who appear in the vulgate much more often than the other enemies, and less often in general in the FV (79 references to the Saxons in the vulgate and 39 in the FV). This tempering is evident in isolated references but also in the fact that the FV redactor does not repeat Geoffrey's editorial remarks and asides, where the latter often vents his spleen, as it were. As we have seen earlier, the FV redactor also omits opportunities to praise the Britons, opportunities which Geoffrey never misses.

Although Wace does not eliminate mentions of the Scots and the Picts – 14 mentions for the Scots including 2 with the Picts and 2 with the Norwegians and Danes; 10 for the Picts; and 34 for the Saxons (in the case of the Saxons, though, they appear named roughly half as frequently in the *Brut* as in the vulgate, and roughly comparable to the FV for this group)[249] – with respect to his presentation of these groups, Wace tempers even further his portrayals in a number of ways: 1) by eliminating criticism in the form of negative adjectives – for the most part, though he maintains full references to the treachery of the night of the long knives (Saxons), and to the Saxons' paganism on numerous occasions, for example; 2) by eliminating the greater part of Brian's speech to Cadwallo on the continual treachery of the Saxons (vulgate §191) – the entire speech was eliminated by the FV, as discussed in Chapter 2;[250] 3) by shifting focus from the Saxons to the English by referring numerous times to the

---

248 Alex Woolf, "Geoffrey of Monmouth and the Picts," 439. See also Henry of Huntingdon, *Historia Anglorum*, I.8, 24–25; Woolf, *From Pictland to Alba*, 1–3; Dauvit Broun, *Scottish Independence and the Idea of Britain*, esp. chapter 2, and G. W. S. Barrow, *The Kingdom of the Scots* (Edinburgh: Edinburgh University Press, 2003, 2nd ed.).

249 I owe an enormous debt of gratitude to Dr. Yannick Mosset for having shared with me prior to publication his electronic transcription of the *Roman de Brut* in Arnold's edition. Nonetheless, the figures I provide in these types of tallies are approximate.

250 See also Weiss, 355, n. 1.

380   CHAPTER 5

English in a variety of contexts – 41 references to the English in Wace, 13 in
Geoffrey (in the vulgate, one reference to Henry I *regnum Anglorum* in the
prologue §3.20, the second to Dumwallo's establishing among the Britons
"the laws called Molmutine, which are still renowned even today among the
English" [§34.326–27], the third regarding Stonehenge, and the final 10 either
with reference to Augustine's conversion of the English or the final sections of
the text), and 9 uses by the First Variant; and 4) by making the Scots appear
on occasion a more sympathetic group, particularly in the long speech of the
Scottish women appealing to Arthur's mercy, to not kill any more than he had
already. Since items 1 and 4 have already been discussed in detail above, we will
focus here on 2 and 3, that is, on Brian's speech and on Wace's greatly increased
use of the term "Engleis" relative to his Latin sources.

Although his changes to Brian's speech (vulgate §191) are not as radical as
its complete removal by the FV redactor – a change Neil Wright considers
very significant in terms of the redactor's changing of focus/approach from
pro-British to more Anglocentric[251] – Wace does not mention the Saxons at
all in the speech, and certainly not in the scathing terms of Geoffrey's version.
Wace's treatment of Brian's speech is yet another example of how he compro-
mises either between his text and the vulgate, or his text and the First Variant;
here he deviates completely from the FV, but he is not nearly as extreme as
the vulgate.

In the context of Edwin's request to be crowned king north of the Humber –
as Cadwallo was king south – Brian is crying and Cadwallo asks why, in large
part because he needs advice regarding Edwin's request to wear a crown, as he
is inclined to give in:

"Brien, dist li reis, que as tu?	"Brian, asked the king, what's wrong?
Pur quei plures, qu'as tu eü?"	Why are you crying, what has hap-
	pened to you?"[252]
"Sire, dist il, jol vus dirrai:	"Sire, he replied, I will tell you:
Curusciez sui e grant doel ai	I am angry and have great sorrow
Que en nostre tens e par nus,	That in our time and because of us,
Dunt sui dolenz e curusçus,	About which I am sad and angry,

---

251   As noted in Chapter 3, Wright remarks that this passage is the "locus classicus" of
      Geoffrey's vitriol against the Saxons, referring to the speech as a "catalogue of English
      perfidy" ("Geoffrey of Monmouth and Bede," 42 n. 40). For the text (in English translation)
      of Geoffrey's speech by Brian and discussion of the Bern MS.'s changes in the vulgate, see
      Chapter 3, nn. 137–38.

252   Weiss restores MS. D's reading of "veü" instead of "eü" in l. 14078 (352, n. 6), which she has
      translated as "seen"; MSS LSA also have this reading (Arnold, 737).

Ad ceste terre honur perdue.	This land has lost its honor.
Grant hunte nus est avenue:	A great dishonor has come upon us:
Dous reis curunez volez faire,	You want to crown two kings.
A mal chief en puissiez vus traire,	You may come to a bad end,
De ço que uns reis sot tenir	Because one king should rule this land
E dunt l'un deit un rei servir."	And all should serve him."

(14077–88)

Upon hearing what Brian has to say, Cadwallo retracts his agreement to crown Edwin king as well. Edwin parts in anger, has himself crowned nonetheless, and many battles ensue. Edwin is eventually defeated by Cadwallo who has united with Penda, king of Mercia – which Wace points out was part of England (in case his audience is puzzled as to why the Mercian king helps Cadwallo).[253] In fact, as Weiss notes, "Stenton remarks that Cadwallon 'was the only British king of historic times who overthrew an English dynasty and the British peoples never found an equal leader.' In Bede, he is obviously a villain, while Edwin is virtuous" concluding that Geoffrey and Wace "are more neutral."[254] I agree with Weiss that Wace is definitely more neutral, but not that Geoffrey is, if one takes into account the remarks of Brian's speech in the vulgate, as well as all of Geoffrey's revisions regarding Edwin.

Another element of Wace's neutrality can be seen in his multiple references to the English, because roughly 42% of those references pertain to etymology and are new to Wace – primarily to changes in vocabulary though also pronunciations. Given that these are linguistic references, on the political level, they do not display favoritism to this group. Most of the remaining 19 or so

---

253 In the Galfridian version, which apparently contains a fair bit of revisionist history as far as Edwin is concerned (see Chapter 2, nn. 34–35, and 116), Edwin and Cadwallo were supposedly half-brothers, the narrative containing many details likely not found elsewhere, not all of which Wace repeats. In other versions, primarily the Anglo-Saxon Chronicle, Edwin, king of Northumbria initially prevailed over Cadwallon who was either defeated or went into exile, but eventually united with Penda and defeated Edwin at the Battle of Hatfield, c. 632–633. According to Stenton, Penda was not actually king when he joined forces with Cadwallo (as Wace states, and as he later became), but was "as yet merely a warlike noble of the Mercian royal house" before Hatfield (*Anglo-Saxon England*, 80). See also Julia Barrow, "Oswald and the Strong Man Armed," in *The Land of English Kin: Studies in Wessex and Anglo-Saxon England in Honour of Professor Barbara Yorke*, ed. Alexander James Langlands and Ryan Lavelle, Brill's Series on the Early Middle Ages 26 (Leiden: Brill, 2020), 183–96; Barbara Yorke, *Kings and Kingdoms of Early Anglo-Saxon England* (Milton Park, Abingdon: Taylor & Francis, 1990), esp. ch. 8, "Northumbria," 72–99; and N. J. Higham, *Kingdom of Northumbria: AD 350–1100* (Stroud, Gloucestershire: Sutton, 1993), 116.

254 Weiss, 363, n. 1. See also Stenton, *Anglo-Saxon England*, 81.

382   CHAPTER 5

references out of the 41, fall in the last 1200 lines of the poem: 1) Gormund's Donation; 2) Augustine's conversion of the English – interestingly, Wace claims Augustine converted the English *and* the Saxons (13813), the FV just the English (§188) (and the communal baptism is not mentioned at all by Geoffrey); 3) how the English became Cadwan's men (13965); 4) the turmoil between Edwin and Cadwallo, Penda and his family, and 5) of course, the final days where Athelstan becomes king of all the English (14758). Except for the changes Wace makes to the First Variant as discussed above, he tends to follow that text, though without the enthusiasm the FV redactor displays toward the "Anglo-Saxon achievement." Wace, as is often the case, is just trying to convey "the facts" without bias.[255]

Wace, as usual, tries to see all sides and eschew partisanship – either pro-British or pro-Saxon – whether for practical reasons or loftier ones: with his introduction of the Round Table, and its intermingling of individuals from many cultures without the need of interpreters, no language is supreme and none is inferior, and by extension, no group is supreme and none is inferior – that the king himself is a Briton is of course not without significance as is his multiple status, both outsider and insider, barbarian (to some) and civilizer (to the majority). At the Round Table, each member is specifically named, complete with regional identity, so that each maintains individual identity while at the same time participating as an equal in the larger group.

Perhaps Wace, the Jerseyman, was trying to use the court of Arthur, the great equalizer, to promote the idea of multiple identities – multiple among different individuals but also multiple within a single individual, thinking of bi-lingual and tri-lingual patrons – to counteract the lure of linguistic chauvinism and separatism. Through 1) the negative example of the Saxons who appear as a major symbol of separatist pull and cultural domination in the *Brut*; 2) the questionable actions of the early Trojans and Britons, and 3) the positive example of the Round Table, Wace offers a message of tolerance and equanimity for men and women of all ranks and groups, particularly for the primarily French-speaking ruling class which doubtless enjoyed many advantages over the native English and British populations: everyone's linguistic heritage and culture are important – in an ideal world there would be no place for feelings of cultural superiority, certainly not as a justification of privilege and power to the detriment of others.

---

255   This tendency is even more evident in his *Roman de Rou*, where he explains at various junctures how he found multiple versions in writing, and will provide them to his audience, as if to let them decide. The most well known of these passages with acknowledged multiple versions to ostensibly provide his audience as many facts as possible concerns Edward the Confessor's bequest to William of Normandy and the events surrounding the Norman Conquest; see Blacker, *Faces of Time*, rev. ed., new Introduction, 31–32 and n. 76.

CHAPTER 6

The Anonymous Verse *Brut* Tradition

1 General Introduction

As seen in Appendix 2, thus far we have discovered 16 early anonymous French verse versions of the Galfridian material: of those 16, 8 contain versions of Merlin's Prophecies (one octosyllabic, four decasyllabic, and three alexandrine), and the rest have various sections of the *Historia*; all of the manuscripts are Anglo-Norman, except two, and the majority of the texts date from the twelfth century, though they are found in manuscripts largely from the thirteenth and fourteenth century.[1] In this chapter we will examine five of these early anonymous French verse *Brut*s, chosen because they contain sections of the Galfridian material treated in this book, that is, either the foundation myths, the *adventus Saxonum*, Arthur's reign, or the passage of dominion, though each fragment rarely contains more than one of these sections.

The fragments to be discussed in this chapter are: 1) the early 13th c. Munich *Brut*; 2) the 12th–13th c. Royal *Brut*; 3) the late 13th c. College of Arms roll 12/45A;[2] 4) the mid 13th c. Harley *Brut* (BL, Harley 1605); and 5) the 14th-c.

---

1 See Appendix 2 for the anonymous French verse *Brut*s; on the dating of the texts themselves (not the manuscripts), see n. 2 below; regarding the count, see also n. 190 below. For further information on the early vernacular verse and later prose reception of Geoffrey of Monmouth, see J. Blacker, "The Anglo-Norman and Continental French Reception of Geoffrey of Monmouth's Corpus from the 12th to the 15th Centuries."

2 On this text which contains sufficient verse passages to be counted here, although it also has prose passages, see Olivier de Laborderie (who discovered the text), "'Ligne de reis': Culture historique, représentation du pouvoir royal et construction de la mémoire nationale en Angleterre à travers les généalogies royales en rouleau du milieu du 13e siècle au milieu du 15e siècle", unpublished PhD thesis, École des Hautes Études en Sciences Sociales, Paris, 2002, pp. 380–85 (revised version in *Histoire, mémoire et pouvoir: Les généalogies en rouleau des rois d'Angleterre (1250–1422)*, Bibliothèque d'histoire médiévale, 7, Paris, 2013); excerpts have been edited by Ian Short, "Un *Roman de Brut* anglo-normand inédit." Short observes that, given that the other anonymous verse versions are from the twelfth century (except for Egerton) and that the text he edits in this article also demonstrates older usages of language, it is also likely from the twelfth century (275); it has approximately 2500 lines, corresponding to lines 1293–8338 of Wace (with many lacunae), thus a significant reduction with respect to both the French poet's text and the Latin (275). See also Francesco Di Lella, "Il *Roll Brut* nel rotolo London, College of Arms, 12/45 A (prima parte)," *Critica del Testo* 22.1 (2019): 37–66; idem, "Il *Roll Brut* nel rotolo London, College of Arms, 12/45 A (seconda parte)," *Critica del Testo* 22.2 (2019): 61–83; and idem, "Il *Roman de Brut* in Inghilterra: Tradizione manoscritta e tradizioni letterarie," unpublished PhD thesis, Università di Roma "La Sapienza" and Université de la

---

© KONINKLIJKE BRILL NV, LEIDEN, 2024 | DOI:10.1163/9789004691889_008

384   CHAPTER 6

Egerton *Brut* (BL, Egerton 3028),[3] providing an analysis of selections from their
"alternative" versions of early British history, with short notes to the Bekker
fragment, Harley 4733, and Takamiya 115.[4] Although no identifying prologues
or epilogues are extant in any of these fragmentary texts to help us locate
in time and space their authors or audiences, their presentations of Arthur
among other aspects – for example, distinct echoes of the First Variant in
the Royal *Brut* – reveal nonetheless ideological transformations, including
Harley 1605's inclusion of the book of Merlin's Prophecies, thereby reinstating
(relative to Wace's omission that is) allusions to the Britons' future. The later
Egerton *Brut* – a form of abridgment of Wace's poem 88% of which is made
up of lines from Wace's *Brut* – emphasizes Arthur's dominance over Rome,
downplays Welsh and Britons' future roles, and reveals distinct anti-Scottish

---

Sorbonne, Rome and Paris, 2018, pp. 425–50. See also n. 74 below and Diana Tyson, "The Old
French *Brut* Rolls in the London College of Arms," in *Guerres, voyages et quêtes: Mélanges
offerts à Jean-Claude Faucon*, ed. Alain Labbé, Daniel W. Lacroix, and Danielle Quéruel (Paris:
Honoré Champion, 2000), 421–27.

3 The order of the texts discussed is based on the first section of the *Historia* they treat.
Thus: 1) Munich (begins with §5-); 2) Royal (§6-); 3) London College of Arms 12/45A (§23-);
4) Harley 1605 (§73-); and 5) Egerton (§65 -). Egerton is listed last since it is an outlier in the
sense that it is not a translation of a Galfridian text, but rather a form of abridgment of Wace's
Brut but with a number of different thematic and sociopolitical priorities (not a fragment of
Wace's text in my view; see nn. 5 and 174 below). However, Egerton 3028 provides very useful
points of comparison for the political programs of the other anonymous texts under consideration here.

4 In her essential article for these little-known texts (and Wace), Jane Zatta argues that "a comparison of similar episodes ... suggests that the vernacular *Bruts*, far from being mere translations, redeploy the Brut myth in order to redefine the respective roles of the monarch and
the nobility" and more specifically "the vernacular Anglo-Norman *Brut* chronicles inscribe
a relationship between monarch and subjects different than that seen in their source, one
which stresses not the role of the king in achieving an imperial destiny but rather the harm
that comes from kings who tend toward tyranny and the contribution of vassals who restrain
the power of the king," concluding that the "*Brut* chronicles differ from histories not in the
principle value they offer, that of participation in the national destiny, but in the rejection
of submission to an institutional authority as the means of achieving that end. ... They challenge the devaluation of the individual that characterizes the court histories and promote
and ideal of personal merit as the quality on which the legitimacy of lordship depends"
("Translating the *Historia*: The Ideological Transformation of the *Historia regum Britannie*
in Twelfth-Century Vernacular Chronicles," cited here at 149, 150, and 158). Although I have
different emphases here – rather on origins, ethnic identities, and inter-group struggles, and
less on the struggles of the Anglo-Norman nobility and the crown alluded to by Zatta as seen
through Geoffrey and his reception – Zatta's article is suggestive of a broad range of perspectives on these texts, departing from the source studies of earlier eras, to illuminate a number
of ideologies as frames of reference.

THE ANONYMOUS VERSE BRUT TRADITION

385

sentiment early in the reign of Edward II whose Scottish campaigns met with mixed success.[5]

Before proceeding to an analysis of the texts themselves, I need to point out, that while I am often comparing passages from the anonymous texts to Wace's *Brut* in order to highlight narrative strategies, differing uses of content from the Latin sources, and sometimes political perspectives, that does not mean that the anonymous authors had a copy of Wace available to them while composing, or if so, that they ever used it. Even the author of the Royal interpolation, whose text is inserted into a copy of Wace may not have had the whole of Wace's poem to hand when writing; perhaps only the assembling scribe did when inserting the section of the anonymous text into the Royal MS.'s *Brut* copy. Only Egerton obviously used Wace, as will be discussed below;

---

5   The Egerton text consists of 2914 lines, but as Ian Short notes, the excision of the first 8 folios implies at least a further 2000 lines now lost ("What was Gaimar's *Estoire des Bretuns?*", 149). Though nonetheless an anonymous *Brut* (for an opposing view, see n. 174 below), this 2914-line "epitome" 88% of whose lines are taken from Wace's 14866-line *Roman de Brut*, was likely "assembled" with its 337 original lines in the early fourteenth century for the illuminated manuscript in which it is found; it is *sui generis* in that it is a form of abridgment of Wace's *Brut* – with often very different intent – and not a "translation" of Geoffrey's *Historia*. See "An Anglo-Norman Metrical 'Brut' of the 14th Century (British Museum Ms Egerton 3028)," ed. Vivien Underwood, unpublished Ph.D. thesis, University of London, 1937, and J. Blacker, "Courtly Revision of Wace's *Roman de Brut* in British Library Egerton MS 3028," in *Courtly Arts and the Art of Courtliness: Selected Papers from the Eleventh Triennial Congress of the International Courtly Literature Society, University of Wisconsin-Madison, 29 July–4 August 2004*, ed. Keith Busby and Christopher Kleinhenz (Cambridge: D. S. Brewer, 2006), 237–58, Appendix A, 252–54; the more recently discovered long extract of Wace's *Brut* in College of Arms roll 12/45A (dorse) was not accounted for in the Appendix of this article (for details on this witness of Wace's text found on the reverse of the same roll where the text he edits is also found, see Short, "Un *Roman de Brut* anglo-normand inédit," esp. p. 274); now see below Appendix 1 for Wace manuscripts, and Appendix 2 for the anonymous verse *Brut*s. Egerton's unusual composition is noteworthy on many levels, not the least of which is that of material culture since "on every recto, there is a miniature, sixty-three in all, preceded by two to three lines which situate each miniature within the narrative; these verses preceding each miniature are all original non-Wace verses. In addition to the original lines preceding the miniatures, the Egerton scribe also used short passages to summarize material cut or to provide transitions between the Wace sections; these summative passages make up most of the remainder of the 12% of original lines" (Blacker, art. cit., here at 237); Egerton's assemblage also brings into relief the question of authorial voice, since so many of the lines are Wace's – "spoken" by the Norman poet – but then reassembled and illustrated to convey often a very different political and social program; the poem is not "by" Wace though we "hear" Wace at every turn (see the conclusion to the Egerton section below). On the miniatures themselves, see also Alison Stones, "The Egerton *Brut* and its Illustrations," in *Maistre Wace: A Celebration: Proceedings of the International Colloquium held in Jersey 10–12 September 2004*, ed. Glyn S. Burgess and Judith Weiss (St. Helier: Société Jersiaise, 2006), 167–76.

386 CHAPTER 6

others may not have ever seen or used Wace at all, likely being "independent productions."

2 Contextualizing the Anonymous Verse *Brut*s: Wace and Authorial Voice

In examining a variety of early verse *Brut*s including Wace's, we will inevitably encounter the question of multiple versions of an "original story." While the situation of the multiple *Brut*s which each in some way are based on written traditions and in some contexts, on one specific text, Geoffrey of Monmouth's *Historia Regum Britanniae* and/or the First Variant, is not completely analogous to that of a folk tale such as Cinderella whose multiple retellings are not consistently rooted in a textual tradition, there are parallels in the sense that the medieval authors of the *Brut*s appear to have had an ur-story in mind, that is, a story of the early kings of Britain, that existed beyond the texts containing it, a sort of Platonic ideal they were all trying to reach.[6] Nevertheless, even though the authors may have conceived of some larger scheme beyond their individual tellings, I will focus here on those individual tellings, but not exclusively through the lens of "versions," since when we say versions, we tend to fall into the "what is added, what is missing" mode. We can see from these different *Brut*s that the authors took separate paths and did not necessarily view their texts in relation to one another, if they were even aware of the other texts – other than "originals" they may have had in front of them. For the purposes of discussion, however, it may be simpler to call these renditions "versions," although I think ultimately, they are each separate stories. As Barbara Herrnstein Smith posited more than thirty years ago in her work on narrativity: once the variables from major events to the smallest of semantic markers, are rearranged in response to political, social, linguistic, and even metrical functions and expectations, we no longer have different versions of the same story, but actually different stories.[7]

We should also keep in mind the role of the "author-function" and the ways our perceptions of authorial voice can affect our reading of these texts, taking Michel Foucault's proposition that the "'author-function' … is not formed

---

6   One can look at this a different way, using Geoffrey of Vinsauf's concept of a "vital core," that is, the "telling" must contain elements without which the story would be unrecognizable. See n. 12 below.

7   "Narrative Versions, Narrative Theories."

THE ANONYMOUS VERSE BRUT TRADITION 387

through the simple attribution of a discourse to an individual [but rather] it results from a complex operation whose purpose is to construct the rational entity we call an author," and that it is an entity which is essentially a "projection of our own way of handling texts."[8] Following Foucault, we will put the emphasis here on how we as readers construct in our minds an anonymous author – what we're looking for in terms of authorial voice, what kinds of assumptions we make about an anonymous author – rather than concentrating on identifying the anonymous author, a task which often preoccupies scholars working with anonymous authorship.

Keeping in mind our input into perceptions of authorial voice, I also want to continue to explore – beyond the focus on Wace in Chapter 5 – the elements that make us hear Wace's voice as so distinctive: is Wace more "modern" than the others – and what do we mean by "modern"? – and if that is our conclusion, what are the structural and/or stylistic elements in his text (in this case, the *Roman de Brut*) that contribute to that impression? What are the features that make his text so recognizable, if not actually familiar? In comparing the anonymous verse texts to Wace's *Brut*, however, I would like to steer clear of consistently invoking a normative-derivative model, except for purposes of highlighting textual differences: where we get into trouble is making

---

8 Foucault, "Qu'est-ce qu'un auteur?" *Bulletin de la Société française de philosophie* 6.3 (1969): 74–103, repr. in *Dits et Écrits 1954–88*, 4 vols., ed. Daniel Defert, François Ewald, and Jacques Lagrange (Paris: Gallimard, 1994), 1:789–821. On the distinctiveness of Wace's authorial presence in relation to the relatively "pale" authorial figures of anonymous texts, in the context of religious works, but also with reference to Wace's work more broadly – and by extension, the anonymous verse *Bruts* – see esp. J. Blacker, "Authorial Voice in Wace's *Assomption* and Anonymous Versions," in *Court and Cloister: Studies in the Short Narrative in Honor of Glyn S. Burgess*, ed. Jean Blacker and Jane H. M. Taylor, Medieval and Renaissance Texts and Studies 517 (Tempe, AZ: Arizona Center for Medieval & Renaissance Studies, 2018), 231–55, esp. 236–41 and nn. 13–24; eadem "Le rôle de la *persona* – ou la voix auctoriale – dans la *Conception Nostre Dame*, le *Roman de Brut* et le *Roman de Rou*"; David Hult, "Author/Narrator/Speaker"; and Sarah Kay whose article on Chrétien de Troyes is very helpful in gaining perspective on how we tend to approach anonymous authors in our passion for identification ("Who was Chrétien de Troyes?" *Arthurian Literature* 15, ed. James P. Carley and Felicity Riddy, Cambridge: D. S. Brewer, 1997, 1–35). Kay notes that the "process [of identification] is conditioned by the way we read the texts, and by the assumptions we bring to them" (2). She adds that among the criteria we use to identify authors – when that is what we seek to do, which is not always the case with anonymous texts – "the principles summarized by Foucault in his account of the development of the 'author function' in modern thought play a major part, namely consistency with respect to quality, subject matter, expression and outlook" (3). We discuss this further in the conclusion of this chapter.

388   CHAPTER 6

judgments of a text based on what is "missing from" or has been "added to" the text that is considered the normative model.

3   Overview: Anonymous Verse *Brut*s

Although all now fragmentary, the anonymous corpus demonstrates that there were probably multiple anonymous Old French *Brut* poems in verse, most of which may have been eclipsed by Wace's *Brut* in the sense that the latter was copied in its entirety frequently[9] whereas none of the anonymous *Brut*s are extant in their entirety – and as far as we know, in only one copy each – though BL Harley 1605 is extant in 5 distinct parts, including an alexandrine version of the Prophecies of Merlin (see Appendix 11).[10] None of these anonymous texts which may have been whole at some point were as completely eclipsed however by Wace's *Brut* as Gaimar's no-longer-extant *Estoire des Bretuns* since they have managed to survive and the latter hasn't; the four copies of Gaimar's

---

9   See Appendix 1 below, which illustrates how the *Brut* copies were bound on either side of the Channel. There is no way to solve the dilemma posed by the popularity of Wace's poem: was Wace's text more popular because it was more readily available to be copied or was it more available and widely copied because it was more well liked, which has resulted in its being considered the normative version and the only complete French verse *Brut* extant? This popularity could be attributed in part to two of Wace's "innovations" – his recording of the Round Table and the Invention of the True Cross (*Inventio Crucis*) being the most well known, the latter narrative part of a legend serving to associate Constantine's mother Helena with the discovery of this Christian relic (5720–24; Houck, *Sources*, 246–47) – or the encyclopedic nature of his vision of Arthur. For Wace's Arthur has something for everyone – military campaigns, maritime adventures, battles with giants, negotiations with and domination of pagan tribes and the Romans, as well as the monarch's presiding over the Round Table, and a bit of knights, ladies, and love casuistry. Wace's text is also known for his lively use of dialogue which makes the "action" come alive to a greater extent than in a number of the anonymous texts, particularly the Royal *Brut*, which often has the distant and detached tenor of an annal. On Wace's use of dialogue, see especially Le Saux, *Companion*, 88 n. 9, 100, 106, 113, 134–37, 140, 217, 225, 239, and 244.

10   On Harley 1605, see Peter Damian-Grint who presents fragments 1–4, "Vernacular History in the Making: Anglo-Norman Verse Historiography in the Twelfth Century," unpub. Ph. D. thesis, University of London (Birkbeck), 1994, Appendix 11, 368–473, and Brian Blakey on fragment 5, "The Harley *Brut*: An Early French Translation of Geoffrey's *Historia Regum Britannie*," *Romania* 82.325 (1961): 44–70. Technically speaking, this is the first of three volumes of MS. Harley 1605 (1605/1, though scholars do not always use this designation). See the British Library Digitised Manuscripts at http://www.bl.uk/manuscripts/FullDisplay.aspx?ref=Harley_MS_1605/1.

THE ANONYMOUS VERSE BRUT TRADITION 389

Estoire des Engleis are found following Wace's text in each manuscript, rather than following the *Estoire des Bretuns*.[11]

In terms of possible relationships among these fragmentary witnesses, on the one hand, Takamiya may have been a copy of Harley 4733 which it resembles closely, but it also could have been part of a larger poem, yet another presentation of Galfridian material to French-speaking audiences. With respect to Harley 4733, given resonances found by Peter Damian-Grint with the Royal *Brut*,[12] it is not impossible that either Takamiya or Harley were originally part of the Royal *Brut*, which itself – when it was a whole poem, if it ever were, and not just created for the purpose of "rectifying" a large portion of Wace's *Brut* – may have predated Wace, as early as the 1140s (rather than dating from the first third of the thirteenth century, which was Alexander Bell's surmise when working on his edition);[13] as we have it now, though,

---

11   On the MSS of Gaimar's remaining work the *Estoire des Engleis*, see Short, ed., xvii–xxii. On the *Estoire des Bretuns*, Ian Short observes that "the existence of this now lost *Estoire des Bretuns* is further corroborated by Gaimar's epilogue [in the *Estoire des Engleis*] where he records that his history of the English had begun with Jason and the Argonauts, and that he was bringing it to a close during the early years of the 12th century [ll. 6528–6531]. None of the other six [now eight incl. College of Arms roll 12/45A and Takamiya 115] extant vernacular versions of the *Historia Regum Britanniae*, mostly fragmentary, can, however, be identified with Gaimar's missing text. Almost everything about it remains, therefore, unknown" ("What was Gaimar's *Estoire des Bretuns*?" 144).

12   "A 12th-century Anglo-Norman *Brut* Fragment (MS BL Harley 4733, f. 128)," in *Anglo-Norman Anniversary Essays*, ed. Ian Short, Anglo-Norman Text Society Occasional Publications Series 2 (London: Anglo-Norman Text Society, 1993), 87–104, cited at 95. Damian-Grint observes, however, that "despite certain echoes of the Royal *Brut*, our text [Harley 4733] gives every appearance of representing a quite independent 12th-century *Brut* tradition" (95), lending further credence to the notion that each of these texts tells its own story, with its own perspectives on the legendary history of Britain, though depending on the text, each provides the "vital core" which makes the story recognizable to its audiences. On Geoffrey of Vinsauf's notion of a narrative's "vital core," that is, the nucleus or central details without which the story would be unrecognizable, see Douglas Kelly, "Brevity as Emphasis in the Narrative Lay: The Long and the Short of It," in *Court and Cloister: Studies in the Short Narrative in Honor of Glyn S. Burgess*, 1–16, esp. 4–6. Given the resemblances found recently between Takamiya and Harley 4733, it is quite possible that those two fragments may be based on the same – as yet unknown/unidentified – poem. For an edition and study of the Takamiya fragment, see Jean Blacker and Peter Damian-Grint, "More about Arthur: the anonymous verse *Brut* fragment in Yale University Beinecke Library MS Takamiya 115," *Medium Ævum* 92.1 (2023): 67–103.

13   *Anglo-Norman Brut*, ed. Bell, xxxiv. The philological evidence Damian-Grint provides is compelling, both for a twelfth-century dating, and for early in the century as well. Furthermore, he adds that, "there is, then, nothing to invalidate Bell's own hypothesis that the Royal *Brut* and the *Description of England*, both twelfth-century works, may have

390   CHAPTER 6

Royal is fragmentary and substitutes for a large portion of Wace's text in the Royal MS.[14]

The relationships among the verse fragments, their manuscript witnesses, and how many versions of the Galfridian material are represented therein – telling their own stories – have yet to be fully explored. As far as we know definitively at this point, only the five fragments in British Library Harley 1605 appear to have been parts of a single whole *Brut*; any remaining parts of any of the other anonymous *Brut* fragments have yet to be found or identified as such.[15]

---

come from the same pen," which leads Damian-Grint to raise the intriguing possibility that the *Description of England* and the Royal *Brut* may also have been fragments of the same text ("Redating the Royal *Brut* Fragment," 285), and not just two works by the same author; see Alexander Bell, "The Anglo-Norman *Description of England*: An Edition." In addition, Damian-Grint observes ("Redating," 283–84 n. 4) that following John Gillingham, Lesley Johnson argues for the "certainty" of a twelfth-century dating of the *Description* based on manuscript and internal evidence (Gillingham, "The Context and Purposes of Geoffrey of Monmouth's *History of the Kings of Britain*," 33 and nn. 80–81; Johnson, "The Anglo-Norman *Description of England*: An Introduction," cited at 11 n. 1). The earliest witness of the *Description* is found in late twelfth-century Durham Cathedral Library, MS. C.iv.27, which also contains a copy of Gaimar's *Estoire des Engleis*, Wace's *Roman de Brut* (with an interpolation of Merlin's Prophecies containing a 172-line preamble which Bell speculated might have been part of another "lost" translation of the *Historia*; *L'Estoire des Engleis by Geffrei Gaimar*, ed. Alexander Bell, xvii), and Jordan Fantosme's *Chronicle* (ed. and trans. R. C. Johnston, Oxford: Clarendon Press, 1981).

14   The anonymous verse *Brut* in the early 14th c. Anglo-Norman MS, British Library, Royal 13.A.xxi, known as the Royal *Brut* or the Anglo-Norman *Brut*, is the longest fragment, containing 6,237 octosyllabic lines. In its current codicological situation, the Royal *Brut*, quite possibly originally part of a complete *Brut*, is preceded by the first 52 lines of Wace's *Brut*, and followed by the remainder of Wace's 14,866-line poem (the 6,237 lines are thought to have "substituted" for Wace's lines 53–8728, hence the label of interpolation, though the poem's editor, Alexander Bell, suggests that Wace's poem may have been used to fill out the missing parts of the Anglo-Norman poem, and not vice versa (*An Anglo-Norman Brut* (*Royal 13.A.xxi*), ed. Alexander Bell, Anglo-Norman Text Society 21–22 (Oxford: Basil Blackwell, 1969), x. See also Alexander Bell, "The Royal *Brut* Interpolation," *Medium Aevum* 32.3 (1963): 190–202; based on a number of omissions in comparison with Wace, Bell concluded that the Royal *Brut* was not a reworking of Wace, nor did he find that there were enough similarities between Royal and the Munich *Brut* to warrant considering a relationship between those two texts either). The Royal *Brut* narrative extends from the foundation story of the Trojan ancestors up to King Uther's arrival at Tintagel. Thus, the Royal *Brut* never treats Arthur's reign and conquests, or any events following.

15   See n. 12 above regarding Takamiya and Harley 4533 as possibly copied from the same original, though too overlapping to be "missing" parts of the same manuscript (as Harley 1605 fragments are parts of the same manuscript with no overlap).

THE ANONYMOUS VERSE BRUT TRADITION   391

That the majority of the anonymous fragmentary texts are preserved in Anglo-Norman manuscripts is not surprising, though, since the history of Britain might have been more compelling for audiences in England than in France.[16] However, while it may be odd that not one complete anonymous *Brut* remains, another pattern of preservation is perhaps even more odd – none of the anonymous texts contain material on the Saxons following the reign of King Arthur – and in fact, only Egerton, and Harley 1605 have any coverage of Arthur at all. In other words, in the majority of the anonymous verse *Brut*s there is nothing on Gormund's Donation, St. Augustine's conversion of the English, King Athelstan's uniting of the realm under a single leadership or other events in the passage of dominion from the Britons to the English (Germanic settlers/invaders and their descendants). Unless this lack of post-Arthurian material is an accident of preservation, we should consider at least one other possibility: that French-speaking English audiences were apparently more interested in the early history of the Britons when they sought out "translations" (or treatments) of Geoffrey's vulgate *Historia* – and some on Arthur's reign – or at least not too interested in the tumultuous successions or in the establishing of continuities between the Britons, Saxons, and Normans. With the latter portion of the Otho-Laȝamon lost to fire in the eighteenth century, in terms of the early verse traditions, it is only Wace's *Brut* and the Caligula Laȝamon whose post-Arthurian sections on the fall of the Britons and the rise of the English that have come down to us.[17]

---

16   See Appendix 1 below containing an up-to-date chart of the *Brut* in Anglo-Norman and Continental codices and Appendix 2 updating the anonymous verse *Brut*s.

17   On Laȝamon manuscripts, see *Layamon's Brut*, ed. G. L. Brook, R. F. Leslie, EETS, 2 vols. (Oxford: Early English Text Society, 1963), and esp. Jonathan Watson, "Affective Poetics and Scribal Reperformance in Lawman's *Brut*: A Comparison of the Caligula and Otho Versions," *Arthuriana* 8.3 (1998): 62–75; Elizabeth Bryan, *Collaborative Meaning in Medieval Scribal Culture: The Otho Laȝamon*, Editorial Theory and Literary Criticism Series (Ann Arbor: University of Michigan Press, 1999); Françoise H. M. Le Saux, *Laȝamon's Brut: The Poem and its Sources*, 1–13; Erik Kooper, "Laȝamon's Prosody: Caligula and Otho – Metres Apart," in *Reading Laȝamon's Brut*, 419–41; and Stephen M. Yeager, "Diplomatic Antiquarianism and the Manuscripts of Laȝamon's *Brut*," *Arthuriana* 26. 1 (2016): 124–40.

392   CHAPTER 6

4   **Common Content of the Anonymous Verse *Brut*s Relative to the**
        Historia and Wace[18]

EARLY AND EARLY-TO-MID SECTIONS OF THE _HISTORIA_

Munich, Bayerische Staatsbibliothek C. Gall. 29 early 13th (Continental) octosyllabic	4180 lines (§§5–32, descr. of Britain, arrival of Brutus, to Cunedagius's victory over Marganus [two of Leir's grandsons])* *(lines 3693–4180 extend past *Historia* §32, on founding of Rome) -- overlaps with Wace, Coll. of Arms, Royal
London, BL Royal 13.A.XXI 1st half 14th octosyllabic	6237 lines (§§6–137, Aeneas's marriage to Uther's arrival at Tintagel ; prophecies omitted) -- "Royal *Brut*" interpolated into Wace's *Brut*, replacing ll. 53–8728; overlaps with Wace, Egerton, Harley 1605, Bekker, Coll. of Arms, Munich
London, College of Arms 12/45A (roll) late 13th octosyllabic (with prose)	approx. 2500 lines (§§23–133; Humber's attack to Merlin's prediction of Uther's reign; corresp. to Wace ll. 1293–8338, many many lacunae; Prophecies omitted) -- overlaps with Wace, Egerton, Royal, Bekker, Harley 1605, Munich [there is also an incomplete copy of Wace's *Brut* on the reverse side of the roll]

---

18   For the contents of the very short prophecies fragment in London, BL Add. 48212.O (mid 14th c.) and the six complete Prophecies MSS (not including Harley 1605 listed above), see Appendix 2. The table here is not intended to be as complete as Appendix 2 which lists all the anonymous verse *Brut*s currently known, including the MSS which contain the Prophecies: the texts are listed here according to their contents, that is, on the basis of the first section of the *Historia* they treat and neither on their dates of composition nor on the dates of their manuscripts. Thus: 1) Munich; 2) Royal; 3) London College of Arms 12/45A; 4) Harley 1605; and 5) Egerton. See also n. 3 above.

THE ANONYMOUS VERSE BRUT TRADITION 393

Mid sections of the *Historia*

London, BL Harley 1605
mid-13th
alexandrine monorhymed
laisses

3361 lines:
1) 1280 lines (§§73–94, death of King
Lucius to arrival of Hengist)
2) 1279 lines (§§113–36, **Prophecies**
[missing lines 1–73], to
beginning of Uther's reign)
3) 80 lines (§§152–54, reinstatement of
Loth)
4) 81 lines (§§155–56, Bedevere, Kay
enfoeffed, feast at City of
Legions)
5) 641 lines (§§165–69, Mt.-St.-Michel
giant, first encounter of
Arthur and Emperor Lucius)
-- **overlaps with Coll. of Arms, Bekker,
Wace, Royal (excepting Prophecies)**

Krakow, Jagiellonian
Univ. Lib. Gall. fol. 176
[Bekker frag.]
late 12th (Continental)
alexandrine monorhymed laisses

136 lines (§§127–30, assembling
Stonehenge)
-- **overlaps with Wace, Egerton, Royal,
Harley 1605, Coll. of Arms**

New Haven (Conn.), Yale U,
Beinecke Lib.
Takamiya 115
mid-13th
octosyllabic

161 lines, with gaps (end of §142-§143,
Arthur's initial coronation,
battle against Colgrinus)
-- **overlaps with Wace, Egerton,
Harley 4733**

London, BL Harley 4733
late 12th
octosyllabic

256 lines, with gaps (§§143–47, Arthur's
coronation, pursuit of
Saxons to Somerset)
-- **overlaps with Wace, Egerton,
Takamiya**

394   CHAPTER 6

MID-TO-LATE SECTIONS OF THE *HISTORIA*

London, BL Egerton 3028 **mid-14th** **octosyllabic**	2914 lines (not including 354-line continuation of English history to 1338–40) (§§65–205, sons of Cymbeline to near end ; corresp. to Wace ll. 4883–14842, many lacunae ; Prophecies omitted) **-- overlaps with Wace, Takamiya, Harley 4733, Royal, Harley 1605, Coll. of Arms**

5   Anonymous Verse *Brut*s

5.1   *Munich* Brut (*Munich, Bayerische Staatsbibliothek C. Gall. 29*)

5.1.1   Background

The second-longest anonymous verse *Brut*, the Munich *Brut* (hereafter *MB*), is the only Continental fragment[19] other than the very short Bekker fragment.[20]

---

19   In her edition, Patricia Grout has lengthy discussions of the language of the manuscript, including a chapter on the language of the author (118–34) as well as one on the language of the scribe (135–40), concluding that both the author's and the scribe's language shows Northern or North-Eastern influence, concurring with Bell on his assessment of Picard-Walloon (Alexander Bell, "The Munich *Brut* and the *Estoire des Bretuns*," *Modern Language Review* 34.3 (1939): 321–54, 327); all citations from *MB* come from Grout (P. B. Grout, "An Edition of the Munich *Brut*," unpublished Ph.D. thesis, University of London, 1980). She also provides copious references to Hofmann and Vollmöller's edition and their discussion of language as well (*Der Münchener Brut. Gottfried von Monmouth in französischen Versen des XII. Jahrhunderts*, ed. Konrad Albrich Hofmann and Karl Gustav Vollmöller, Halle: Max Niemeyer, 1877); see also eadem "The Author of the Munich *Brut*, His Latin Sources and Wace," *Medium Ævum* 54.2 (1985): 274–82, 274–75; Karl Jenrich, *Die Mundart des Münchener Brut* (Halle: E. Karrss, 1881), and Bell, "The Munich *Brut* and the *Estoire des Bretuns*." On the nuances of the language in the manuscript and distinctions between author and scribe of the *MB*, François Zufferey provides numerous examples which "plaident en faveur d'une origine normande de l'auteur, plus particulièrement de Haute-Normandie" (138), and for the scribe "quant à la langue de la copie, elle peut être rattachée à l'aire d'interférence picardo-wallonne" (139). In addition to the author's Norman language and the copyist's Picard-Walloon features, Zufferey provides substantial evidence of the manuscript having made a detour through England, which left "light traces" of Anglo-Norman influence ("l'exemplaire doit avoir fait un détour par l'Angleterre, qui a laissé des traces légères d'une composante anglo-normande," 140), though continental features dominate (*Le Roi Leïr: Versions des XIIᵉ et XIIIᵉ siècles*, ed. François Zufferey, trans. [modern French] Gilbert Nussbaumer, with an introduction by Alain Corbellari and an extract of Laȝamon by Valérie Cangemi, Champion Classiques 41, Paris: Honoré Champion, 2015, 133–93 [Munich *Brut*]).

20   For a thorough study of the Bekker fragment (Krakow, Jagiellonian Univ. Lib. Gall. fol. 176), so-called because it was first transcribed (partially) by Immanuel Bekker (*Der roman*

THE ANONYMOUS VERSE BRUT TRADITION   395

As noted by P. B. Grout, the Munich *Brut* is a "substantial" fragment, 4180 lines
corresponding to Geoffrey's chapters 5–32, from the description of Britain to
the point where Romulus and Remus have just founded Rome (though the last
nearly 500 lines, 3693–4180, extend beyond *Historia* §32, and expand upon the
founding of Rome); up to this point in the narrative, Wace's version has 2110
lines, and thus *MB* has nearly doubled Wace in the early Trojan-foundation
part of the text. Grout writes that "this disparity is occasioned partly by the
fact that the author of *MB* is much more prolix than Wace, but also by the fact
that his text contains two major additions to the material to be found in the
Historia: lines 91–342, and lines 3693–4180."[21] Grout adds that in her reading,
MB is closer to the vulgate than Wace whose text is closer to the First Variant,
though as we have seen above in Chapter 5, any assessment of Wace's reliance
on the FV depends on which section of Wace's narrative one is referring to.[22]
Grout found on the whole that in the places where *MB*'s text is based on the
Historia, his translation is a "faithful" one; however, beyond the very minor
changes, there remain major and significant additions.[23]

5.1.2   Roman Material/Universal History
Typical of the Continental Wace *Brut* manuscripts which are most often bound
with Trojan-related romances – unlike Anglo-Norman manuscripts which
for the most part "package" Wace's poem with other insular histories[24] – the
Munich author evinces a fascination for early Trojan/Roman history, adding
material from the *Aeneid*, Landulphus Sagax's expanded version of Paul the
Deacon's *Historia Romana*, St. Jerome's translation of Eusebius, and Ovid's
Fasti.[25] The first addition in lines 91–342 contains amplifications on Geoffrey
and FV's briefer versions of the war between Aeneas and Turnus, the marriage of Aeneas and Lavinia, the death of Aeneas followed by the succession of
Ascanius, the founding of Alba and the birth of Silvius: *MB* amplifies the war

---

  von Fierabras, provenzalisch, ed. I. Bekker, Berlin: G. Reimer, 1829, pp. 182–83, in n. to
  l. 3311 of the *Fierabras*), deemed unfindable right after the second world war (by Tatlock),
  and rediscovered by Sylvie Lefèvre in the 1980s in the Biblioteka Jagiellónska in Krakow,
  see Lefèvre, "Le fragment Bekker et les anciennes versions françaises de l'*Historia regum
  Britanniae*," *Romania* 109 (1988): 225–46. See also Tatlock, *Legendary History*, 458, and
  Damian-Grint, *The New Historians*, 64.

21 Grout, "The Author of the Munich *Brut*, His Latin Sources and Wace," cited here at 275. See
  also 276–77 on the contents and sources of the second expansion on Roman history.

22 See Chapter 4, n. 2 and Chapter 5, n. 7.

23 Grout, "The Author of the Munich *Brut*," 275.

24 Including the incomplete copy of Wace's *Brut* in the genealogical roll, CA 12/45 A (the only
  known copy of any kind of Wace's *Brut* in a roll). See Appendix 1 below on the binding of
  Wace's *Brut* in Anglo-Norman and Continental manuscripts.

25 *MB*'s major sources, in addition to the vulgate *Historia* and in places (particularly in
  Brutus's parentage), the FV; see Grout, "The Author of the Munich *Brut*," 277, on the
  non-Galfridian sources.

396   CHAPTER 6

between Aeneas and Turnus, between Ascanius and Turnus's ally Mezentius, the building of Alba (which became a colony of Lavinium) by Ascanius, and his choice of Silvius Postumus, his half-brother, as his heir, in preference to his own son. The great majority of the extra details are from the *Aeneid*, or Servius's commentary; two details are from St. Jerome's translation of Eusebius – that Silvius (Postumus) succeeded his half-brother Ascanius, and the fifteen kings in Silvius's line.[26]

In addition to the Munich author's passion for Roman history, it would appear that the incorporation of this material in his (or her) *Brut* can be associated with an impulse to create a universal history, as is often seen in later interpolations in medieval histories such as that of a Life of Edward the Confessor into MS. BnF fr. 1416 of Wace's *Brut* (in the place of 12 lines on Edward the Elder, 14763–74).[27] In fact, before launching into the roughly 500-line addition of the material in 3693–4180, where the poem ends – whose contents include (but are not confined to) a list of the kings of Latium before Latinus, kings from Aeneas to Procas, the birth and early days of Romulus and Remus, the restoration of their grandfather and the founding of Rome – the author says that he would list all the kings of Rome up to the birth of Christ before returning to his British material (3699–704).

This editorial comment on the part of the author is both a strong suggestion of the universalizing efforts and also perhaps an unwitting admission of

---

26   Grout, "The Author of the Munich *Brut*," 276. Contrary to the vulgate, but found in some of the FV MSS – see Chapter 3, n. 52 – the MB author has confused Silvius Postumus son of Aeneas with Silvius son of Ascanius, which is apparently chronologically impossible: Silvius Postumus was supposed to have succeeded Ascanius (l. 268), and himself reign for 29 (ll. 341, 3770) or 39 years (l. 332), making it impossible for him to have been the father of Brutus, the latter who was conceived during Ascanius's lifetime, and was destined to kill his father around 16 years later (Grout, "The Author of the Munich *Brut*," 281, n. 13, and ed., 43–45). Grout also observes that "further confusion is to be seen later in the Munich *Brut* (2073–6) here, following the Vulgate Version of the *Historia* (ed. Faral, XXII 22–3), that same Silvius, son of Aeneas, earlier given by the Munich *Brut* (though not by the Vulgate Version of the *Historia*) as Brutus' father, is described as his uncle and 'tierz rois latin' (2075). The preceding two were, of course, Aeneas and Ascanius. The author of the Munich *Brut* motivates [sic] Ascanius' choice of his half-brother Silvius as his heir, by explaining that his own son Iulus (Julis, 320) was too young to take on the duties of kingship" (44–45). She adds that there is no mention of this in the *Historia*, nor was she able to find it in Servius's commentary, although it does appear in Jerome's translation of Eusebius, Paul the Deacon's *Historia Romana*, and Landulfus Sagax's version of the latter (45). See also Wright, ed., vol. II, c–ci.

27   Not only does this interpolation reflect a universalizing impulse, it also denotes a confusion between Edward the Elder who reigned from 899 until his death in 924 and Edward the Confessor who reigned 1042–1066. On BnF fr. 1416, Arnold's MS. J, see Bliss and Weiss, "The 'J' Manuscript of Wace's *Brut*."

THE ANONYMOUS VERSE BRUT TRADITION   397

the peripheral nature of the Roman material with respect to the history of the
founding of Britain, as he reminds his audience that he will get back to the
matter at hand eventually: even though the author's stated plan was to resume
the British material, he did not hesitate to take major excursions away from
his primary model – presumably Geoffrey – before proceeding back to what
may have been for him (or her) of secondary importance – i.e., the history of
the Britons – if we can judge from the extant "sample" we have with its use of
Geoffrey's narrative on Romulus and Remus as a springboard for an excursus
on Roman history before Latinus, though of course we cannot confirm this
since the remainder of the poem, which might indeed have returned to the
narrative on the Britons, has never been found.

5.1.3   Description of Britain
As seen in the table above of the overlapping contents, the Munich MS. is the
only vernacular verse text containing a description of Britain, that is, a version of *Historia* §5; Wace's *Brut* (which of course was not anonymous) also
does not contain that section. Grout mentions a number of minor changes to
the description in the vulgate, including that the island had thirty-one important cities (ll. 53–54), each with a bishop where the vulgate has twenty-eight
(§5.38–39), while changing the order of some of the details such as that the
three big rivers are mentioned before the easy access to France from the south
rather than afterwards as in the vulgate.[28] However, Grout neglects to mention
an important detail, that *MB* lists five peoples in Britain: the Britons as the
first, then the Normans, the Saxons – whom people called "the English" (l. 70
"Sainnes, que l'un apele Englois") – and the Scots and the Picts. The vulgate
gives the Normans (primacy of place, though not chronology), the Britons, the
Saxons, the Picts and the Scots (§5.43–44), followed by the authorial commentary that the Britons lost the island "when their pride brought divine retribution," giving way to the Picts and the Saxons (§5.44–45); as noted, *MB* does not
eschew authorial commentary, but in general, he avoids commentary on the
failings of the Britons. It was quite possibly *MB*'s interest in the Romans which
led Hofmann and Vollmöller to list "Normans" as a rejected reading in favor of
"Romans," while Geoffrey and other historians writing in Latin curiously do not
list the Romans by name as occupiers of the island.[29]

---

28   Grout ed., 55.
29   Hofmann and Vollmöller, ed., 109 (under the category "Anmerkungen" and marked
      with an H. to indicate Hofmann). As noted above in Chapter 3, the group of occupiers
      who are surprisingly not mentioned as such by those writers who give lists of inhabit-
      ants of Britain – that is, Bede, Geoffrey, or the First Variant redactor (or by William of
      Malmesbury or Henry of Huntingdon for that matter) – is the Romans. This is a surprising

398 CHAPTER 6

5.1.4   More Roman History/War against Pandrasus/ Founding of
          New Troy

Grout focuses much of her critical attention on the two sections where the MB author has expanded on early Roman history, as well as on the lengthy expansion of the Leir episode. The first Roman passage is contained in lines 90–342, where MB devotes more time and energy to Aeneas than either Wace or Royal (or the Galfridian material). For events surrounding Aeneas – including information on the Trojan heroes Helenus and Antenor (99–104), Aeneas's arrival in Italy and his reception by Latinus, the death of Aeneas and the war against Mezentius (145–266), on the birth of Silvius Postumus and the founding of the line of Alban kings (272–342) – MB supplements Geoffrey and the FV with details from either the *Aeneid* itself or Servius on the *Aeneid*.[30]

While the section on the war against Pandrasus (533–922) does not contain a wealth of information gathered from non-Galfridian sources, MB seems to relish the description of the varied stages of Brutus's victory against the Greek king, presenting a passage roughly 33% longer than Wace's and 50% longer than Royal's, paralleling Geoffrey's eight sections (§8–16), while emphasizing Brutus's craftiness in defeating the Greek monarch.[31]

Following the elaborated war against Pandrasus, come the narrative events involved in the relationship between Brutus and Corineus after whom Cornwall is eventually named, where MB devotes double the space as Wace (MB 1293–2327; Wace 779–1201), including the Trojans' defeat of the Franks (Poitevins) (MB 1325–1828; Wace 853–930) before heading to the island, and the eventual founding of New Troy (MB 2013–56; Wace 1169–1201). In terms of MB's presentation of the Britons, relative to the giants the Trojans found upon their arrival in Britain, MB would appear to try to compromise between Wace and Geoffrey (§21). Where Wace goes much further than Geoffrey by saying that the land was "cleansed" of the giants as well as of their progeny (*R de B*, 1169–70),[32] MB says the giants were chased out "eschaciez" (2015) – though not using the vulgate's "driving off to mountain caves any giants they came upon" ("repertos gigantes ad cauernas montium fugant" §21.456–57) – but then adds the carnage (though no mention is made of succeeding generations as

---

silence in this context since as Peter Turner comments with respect to Gildas's *De Excidio*, the Romans "are not bit players; we receive more information about them than about any other foreign group," a situation which is even more pronounced in the vulgate *Historia*, given the relative length of that work. See Chapter 3, n. 46.

30   Grout ed., 42–43. On Silvius Postumus, see also n. 87 below.
31   See Grout ed., 56–65 on the amplified war against Pandrasus (MB 533–922; Wace 253–492; Royal 115–464).
32   See Chapter 5, n. 15.

THE ANONYMOUS VERSE BRUT TRADITION 399

in Wace) "que morz les out et detrenciez" (2016; "they [the Britons] killed and slaughtered them"). Brutus's control was total: "le païs tint entierement; / tot i fist sun commandement" (2017–18; "He held the country entirely; all obeyed his command").

MB follows very closely the vulgate's §22 on the founding of New Troy. The passage recounting how Kaerlud was named after Lud, and the tension between Lud and his brother Nennius since the former wanted to suppress the name of Troy in the realm is not found in the FV, though it is in *MB*, including the authorial aside that since Gildas treated that conflict, the *MB* author would not, though *MB* does not state that Gildas was an historian (vulgate §22.498–503; *MB* 2049–56). Wace, like the FV, omits the reference to the tension between the brothers, but elaborates at length on the etymology of London's names (1223–50), certainly more than FV, and more than *MB*.

While a line-by-line analysis of the Munich *Brut* could well turn up other parallels with Wace in particular, one parallel is worthy of mention at this juncture, and that is the naming of the children of King Ebraucus, who, with twenty wives, had twenty sons and thirty daughters. As mentioned below, Royal does not name the progeny, though Wace does, following the vulgate and First Variant (§26). While the majority of Wace MSS read "Luor" as one of the sons (1547), MS. K (the Guiot MS.) reads "Ivor" as does Munich. Although the Guiot MS. – which also has the interesting feature of having suppressed Wace's authorship – dates from the thirteenth century, it is possible that Munich used an earlier prototype of Wace similar to Guiot. However, since Munich lacks so many of the passages which make Wace's poem unique – for example, the Round Table, Arthur's plenary court, and foreign conquests – we will never know for certain regarding Munich's possible Wace prototype, or if he/she even used one, having likely been completely independent.[33]

---

33 As noted above, although I am making comparisons between Wace and the anonymous verse *Brut*s in order to highlight narrative content and techniques, it is very likely only Egerton which had a copy of Wace and referred to it; Royal was inserted into a Wace MS but was quite likely initially written independently of Wace. With respect to Wace's poem and descriptions and the Munich *Brut* – since it is so difficult to avoid these sorts of comparisons as Wace's poem dominates "the field" – Grout, in principle, would like to come to a conclusion about "literary talent," a type of assessment which I avoid at all costs: "Unfortunately no important piece of description – except for some battle description in the war against Pandrasus (275–302; 317–36; 467–83) and the account of Corineüs' wrestling bout with Goëmagog (1107–68) – occurs in the part of Wace's *Brut* which runs parallel to the Munich *Brut*. In consequence one is tempted to see the author of the Munich *Brut* has having more literary talent than Wace, but to claim this on so little evidence would be unjustifiable" (ed., 78).

400   CHAPTER 6

5.1.5   Leir

Almost immediately preceding the second expansion on early Roman history which closes the extant part of the Munich *Brut* (3693–4180 [end]) – not Galfridian in origin though Grout states that the 500-line narrative may have been prompted by Geoffrey's chronologizing note to Romulus and Remus[34] – comes the lengthy passage on Leir (2734–3620) intended to parallel Geoffrey's §31 (which is an unusually long section in the *Historia*). Here we see *MB*'s use of direct speech and characters' emotions as the core of his *amplificatio*,[35] especially in comparison with the two texts where there is important overlap, Wace and Royal, the latter seeming to evince little concern for the pathos (similarly to CA as well). Beginning with Royal who uses pathos sparingly, toward the end of the passage, the Royal poet gives Leir two short speeches. In the first, Leir addresses Cordelia in her absence, openly acknowledging his guilt in her banishment:

---

34   In the vulgate *Historia* §32, Geoffrey relates that after Cordelia's peaceful 5-year reign, two of her sister's sons Marganus and Cunedagius, rebelled against her. Following her imprisonment and suicide, Marganus and Cunedagius fight among themselves; Cunedagius, victorious, "took control of the whole island and for thirty-three years ruled it in splendour. At that time lived the prophets Isaiah and Hosea and Rome was founded on April 21st by the twins Romulus and Remus" (§32.282–85). It is this dating gesture which Grout finds to be the incentive for the *MB* author's inclusion of the second "original" excursus on Roman history, original because it is not part of the Galfridian narrative. For a detailed account of the contents and probable sources of lines 3693–4180, see Grout, "The Author of the Munich *Brut*, His Latin Sources and Wace," 276–77.

35   *MB* 888 lines (2734–3620), Wace 413 lines (1655–2066) and Royal 265 lines (1466–1203). On *MB*'s addition of speeches relative to the vulgate and Wace, Grout observes "that both Old French authors have extended this use of direct speech: Wace gives us in addition a very nasty avaricious speech of Gonorille to her husband (1863–82), and Leïr's comment when driven from pillar to post: 'Caitif mei, dist il, mar i vinc!/ Si vil fui la, plus vil sui ça' (1900–1; 'Miserable me, he says, cursed be the day I came! Were I wretched there, I am more wretched here'). The author of the Munich *Brut* has added much more. He attributes a brief remark to Gonorille (3137–60), doubles Leïr's monologue (3197–248; 3251–94), and retails [sic] in considerable detail Cordeïlle's speech to the messenger in France, emphasising her loyalty to her father, and giving instructions on how he is to be restored to kingly status and dignity (3334–6; 3349–88)" (ed., 74–75); one can add to this the description of Leïr's feelings on 3153–72. For excerpted passages with commentaries (and modern French translations) on Leir from the vulgate *Historia* (39–57), Wace (61–93), Laȝamon (97–129), *MB* (133–93), Royal (197–223), and the *Chastoiement d'un père à son fils* (228–57), see Zufferey et al, *Le Roi Leïr*. On Leir in Wace, see also Laurence Mathey-Maille, "Le roi Leir chez Geoffroy de Monmouth et Wace: la naissance d'une figure mythique," in *Pour une mythologie du Moyen Âge*, ed. Bominique Boutet and Laurence Harf-Lancner (Paris: Presses de l'École Normale Supérieure, 1988), 99–115.

THE ANONYMOUS VERSE BRUT TRADITION   401

"Ohi!" fet il, "Cordoille,   "O, Cordelia," he said,
Tu le me diseis, belle fille: "You told me, fair daughter,
Tant cum les grant aveirs aveie,   That as long as I had great wealth,
Tant m'amouent, tant valeie;   They would love me so much, I would
                                              be valued so much;
Cum aveie les riches citez,   As I had rich cities,
Les chastels, les fermetez,   Castles, fortresses,
Entr'eles estoie sire apelez.   Among them, I would be called sire.
Ore sui povre e dechacez."   Now I am poor and chased away."[36]
      (Royal, 1327–34)

Then, through indirect discourse, the poet relates how Leir cursed Lady
Fortune (1335–38). What would ordinarily be considered the body of Leir's
lament is compressed into four lines:

"Ahi!" feit, il "que devendrei?   "Alas!" he said, "what will become
                                              of me?
En quele terre m'en irrei?   To what land will I go?
Jo ne sai quel part turner,   I do not know which way to turn,
Isci ne puis pur hunte ester."   I cannot stay here in shame."
      (Royal, 1339–42)

The Royal poet tells us several lines later that the king was crying; Queen
Cordelia is said to have often shed tears in private over the fate of her father
(1403–4); and her death from sorrow and suicide in prison are also reported.
    As can be seen in a close reading of both passages in Royal, the Anglo-Norman
poem conveys many of the same emotions as Wace's but not nearly to the same
degree. At the end of a lengthy speech, Wace intensifies the sense of shame
and self-pity, by adding "no one loves me" to the declarations of "woe is me"
and "I have wronged (blamed, reproached) Cordelia":

"E des que jo, las! apovri,   "And no sooner was I, alas!
                                              impoverished,
Amis, parenz, serganz perdi.   I lost friends, family, retainers.
Jo n'ai un sul apartenant   I do not have a single kinsman
Ki d'amur me face semblant."   Who shows any sign of love for me."
      (WACE, Brut, 1933–46)

---

36   As in Chapter 5, I am using Arnold's text of Wace's Brut, referring to notes, emendations,
      and translations in Weiss where needed. All translations from the Old French in this
      chapter are my own (including of Wace). All citations from Royal are from Bell's edition.

Wace plays on the irony of the false testimony recognized too late, painting, with a short list, a portrait of complete loss and utter despair. Throughout the speech in Wace (1913–72), the extensive use of the pronoun "jo" – 12 instances in the space of 60 lines – contributes to the vortex effect of the king's situation: what tends to be stressed in the Royal *Brut* is the eventual reconciliation between Cordelia and her father rather than the father's profound sense of dejection which he had to reach before deciding to act. The lighter tone and the use of the terms "corteis" and "sage" to describe the abject king lends the Royal text – while "historically accurate" in the sense that it retains the Galfridian parameters – a more dispassionate air whereas Wace's poem is more theatrical, aimed at evoking much stronger emotions in the audience.

However, in comparison with the Munich version, Wace's is the dispassionate one. At the beginning of Wace's central speech (60 lines, 1913–72), Leir refers to himself as a wretch and speaks of Cordelia twice in passionate terms:

"Las mei, dist il, trop ai vescu

Quant jo cest mal tens ai veü."
   (WACE, *Brut*, 1913–14)

"Wretched me," he said, "I have lived too long

When I have seen this evil time."

The king later refers to Cordelia in the third person:

"Bien me dist veir ma mendre fille,
Que je blasmoe, Cordeïlle,
Ki dist que tan cum jo avreie
Tant preisiez, tant amez sereie.
N'entendi mie sa parole
Ainz la blasmai e tinc pur fole ..."

   (WACE, *Brut*, 1938–43)

"Cordelia, my youngest daughter,
Whom I blamed, told me the truth,
That I would be esteemed and loved,
According to what I possessed.
But I did not listen to her at all
Thus I blamed her and thought her mad ..."

"Bien me dist Cordeïlle veir,
Mais ne m'en soi aparceveir";
   (WACE, *Brut*, 1949–50)

"Cordelia surely told me the truth,
But I did not perceive it in my heart";

While it is much easier to feel the king's sorrow and regret in Wace than in Royal, Munich increases the pathos further – not to mention increasing the number of lines by one third – by having Leir call out to God – in addition to referring to Fortune alone as Wace does – and to Cordelia twice, in direct address, albeit in her absence:

"Oi Deus! Verrai ge mais lo jor que de nul bien aie retor. (MB, 3251–52)	"O God, will I ever see the day When I ever return to prosperity.
A! Cordeïlle! Cordeïlle! Cum voir respondis, bele file! (MB, 3257–58)	Ah Cordelia, Cordelia! How truly you answered, beautiful daughter!
Ah! Cordeïlle! Cordeïlle! A toi cum vendrai, bele fille, u prendrai ge cel hardement que sueffre tun regardement? Ne sai s'avrai ja la cunsence que venir puisse en ta presence." (MB, 3277–82)	Ah! Cordelia, Cordelia! How will I come to you, beautiful daughter, Where will I get the courage To suffer your gaze? I know not if I will even have permission To be able to come into your presence."

The Munich author also has the king repeat what Cordelia said to him, thus adding to the keen sense of regret, loss, and anguish communicated in the rest of the speech (and in the passage as a whole of nearly one hundred lines, 3197–3294).

Despite the fact that Leir was a king of the Britons, in the Munich *Brut* the amount of text devoted to the king's emotions and those of his daughters, tends to drown out any political import of this section, emphasizing what has happened to Leir as a man and father, and less what has happened to Britain as a result of his tragic story: for example, after Cordelia's marriage to the French king Aganippus, Geoffrey states that "much later, when Leir began to grow weary with age, the dukes to whom he had given Britain and his daughters rose up against him. They deprived him of the kingdom and his royal authority which up to then he had exercised well and with glory" (§31.186–89; "Post multum uero temporis, ut Leir torpor coepit senio, insurrexerunt in illum praedicti ducis quibus Britanniam cum filiabus diuiserat; abstulerunt autem ei regnum regiamque potestatem, quam usque ad illud tempus uiriliter et gloriose tenuerat").[37] *MB* instead emphasizes the cruelty of the sons-in-law, without

---

37   Wright declines to translate "uiriliter" directly – he gives "well and with glory" for "uiriliter et gloriose"; the *MB* author certainly makes no reference to Leir's masterful reign over his dominion during the "glory days," though he tries to keep up with Geoffrey's structural

404 CHAPTER 6

mentioning Britain as a political entity or how Leir had exercised power in the past before having arranged the inheritance with his two sons-in-law ("Trop li furent crueil si gendre, / il ne li voldrent s'onor rendre," 3030–31; "His sons-in-law were very cruel to him, they did not want to pay him his due honor"),[38] contributing to a scene of great pathos, resembling more how the king is remembered in romance and other literature in centuries to follow.

Following Cordelia's suicide in line 3620, *MB* returns briefly to the history of the Britons, with the strife between Marganus and Cunedagius and the latter's victory (*Historia* §32). It would appear that *MB* takes the last line of §32 which Geoffrey uses to "date" the material about Marganus and Cunedagius, "at that time lived the prophets Isaiah and Hosea; and Rome was founded on April 21st by the twins Romulus and Remus" as what Grout aptly surmises was a "springboard" for an excursus into Roman history yet again.[39]

As mentioned above, *MB* does provide an authorial commentary explaining how he will return to the history of the Britons after focusing more on the founding of Rome:

Briément vos vuel dire la summe	Briefly, I want to give you a summary
de toz les rois d'Albe et de Rome	Of all the kings of Alba[40] and Rome
ki lo regnë en ordre tindrent,	Who held the kingdoms in order
des icel tens que Troien vindrent	From the time that the Trojans came

---

details, naming the two dukes, etc. Wace focuses on the avariciousness of the sons-in-law, Maglaurus (in Geoffrey; FV Maglaunus; Manglanus in Wace), king of Scotland (Geoffrey has "duke" of Scotland §31.190) and Henuinus (unnamed in Wace), duke of Cornwall who couldn't wait to get their hands on their inheritance, which Leir had divided between the two of them: "They ... so battled and pursued him, that they took his kingdom from him by force. Their father-in-law had left it all to them, but they arranged that one of them would lodge him and provide for him" (1835–41, Wace), which in fact, did not turn out well for Leir, since the sons-in-law do not keep their word, harassed by the daughters, Gonorille and Ragau, to essentially forsake Leir. Leir eventually sees the error of his ways, crosses to France, makes peace with Cordelia, and Aganippus helps him return to Britain to regain his former lands (2029–2040). Grout finds Wace more "detached" and more "judgmental" than sympathetic (ed., 76), concluding that "the account in the Munich *Brut*, despite its repetitiveness, [can be found] more appealing and more moving" (ed., 76). Value judgments of literary quality aside, *MB* can be seen to underplay the administrative aspects found in the *Historia*, and Wace's *Brut*.

38   "S'onor rendre" can also be translated "to give him back his domains" or his "dignity, authority."

39   "The Author of the Munich *Brut*," 276.

40   Alba Longa, an ancient city in Central Italy, destroyed by Rome around the seventh century BCE. According to legend, Romulus and Remus, the founders of Rome, came from the royal dynasty of Alba Longa. In Virgil's *Aeneid*, that was Aeneas's bloodline as well.

THE ANONYMOUS VERSE BRUT TRADITION

jusqu'al tens que Jesus fu neiz,	Until the time Jesus was born,
par cui li mundes fu salveiz.	Through whom the world was saved.
Altres premiers i voldrai metre,	I would like to put the others first,[41]
tant cum j'en puis savoir par letre,	As I have learned through writing,
ki roi furent de Lumbardie,	Those who were kings of Lombardy,
ainz que Eneas l'eüst saisie.	When Aeneas took it over.
Quant vos arai d'icels parlei,	When I have told you of all those,
quanque g'en sai de veritei,	Such as I know it for truth,
a ma matiere revendrai	I will come back to my topic
et des Bretuns racunterai.	And I will tell you about the Britons.

(*MB*, 3699–3712)

However, the promised narrative on the Britons never materializes since the poem breaks off after line 4180, with no signs of returning to the author's stated mission of telling of the history of the kings of Britain.

5.1.6 Conclusion: Comparative Look Back at Membritius; *MB*'s Political Agenda

Before turning to the Royal *Brut* section, a comparison of the Membritius passage among Wace, Royal, and Munich is illustrative of how each of these texts tells its own story and points suggestively to the "political programs" of their authors: Royal, to distill the material to its essence (the passage is half the length of that in either *MB* or Wace, 22 lines, 467–88) while adding some new interpretations; Munich, to highlight the early section of the text within the context of Roman history; and Wace wishing to see both sides. Wace devotes 44 lines (518–58) to Menbritius's speech where the latter persuades the Trojans to ask permission to leave Greece, reasoning that the Greeks will never forget the damage the Trojans have done:

"Jamais as Greus nen avrom pais,	"We will never be at peace with the Greeks,
Kar il n'ublierunt jamais	For they will never forget
Lur parenz, lur uncles, lur peres,	Their relatives, their uncles, their fathers,
Lur cosins, lur nevus, lur freres	Their cousins, their nephews, their brothers

---

41   Precisely to whom "the others" refers is not clear, but it probably refers either to all the leaders (and peoples) who preceded Aeneas in Rome, or the kings of Lombardy, all of whom the author wishes to write about before returning to his main topic, the Britons.

Ne lur altres amis precains	Nor their other close friends
Que nus avum morz a noz mains."	Who died at our hands."

(WACE, *Brut*, 529–34)

Munich also devotes more than 40 lines to the speech (943–88), but the passage notably takes place 400 lines later in the text due to the inserted passage on early Latin history and does not emphasize the anticipated future hardships for the Greeks caused by the Trojans' brutality.[42]

While each text has Menbritius state that the Trojans would never have peace if they stayed, perspectives differ, and it would appear that neither Royal nor Munich sought to recast Wace, but rather to put their own "spin" on the history of the Britons. First, Royal's passage is significantly shorter than those of Wace and Munich, in keeping with the text's efforts to provide a spare narrative; second, Royal is more aggressive, the only one of the three texts declaring that if the Greeks don't do what the Trojans ask (lit., if Pendrasus doesn't do what the Trojans ask) – that is, provision them with gold silver, ships, etc. for their voyage, plus Pandrasus's daughter Imogen as Brutus's wife – they should kill them [him] (485–86; "E si il ço ne volt furnir/ De mal[e] mort le facez murir")! Third, Munich adds a note about Inogen's beauty – "Clere est, et bele cumme gemme" (979; "She is fair, and beautiful as a gem") whereas Royal does not even name her ("E sa fille doinst a uxour/A dan Bruz nostre seignur," 481–82; "And that he should give his daughter as a wife to lord Brutus, our feudal lord"); and fourth, Wace is the only one who sees both sides, putting in the mouth of Membritius blame on the Trojans for their atrocities against the Greeks.

In fact, this passage in Wace contains a number of aspects typical of that poet's style and attitude: the repetition of the verb "duinst" in the same position in four lines, three consecutively (519–21; 523); repetition of similar sounding verbs "descrestrums" and "descharrums" (549, 550); the use of the pronoun "jo" three times, toward the end and at the end, of Menbritius's speech, to make the advice seem more immediate and heartfelt on Menbritius's part (542, 556–58), and perhaps more importantly, Wace's unfailing desire to see both sides – in this case, the Trojans' as well as the Greeks' – a tendency which one finds in even fuller evidence in his second history, the *Roman de Rou* (and which could have been a source of irritation for audience and patrons of that text).[43]

---

42   The *MB* author remains steadfastly on the side of the Romans, and by extension, the Trojans.

43 | | |
|---|---|
| "Duinst nus li reis or e argent, | "The king should give us gold and silver, |
| Duinst nus nés e duinst nus furment, | He should give us ships and provisions, |
| E doinst nus quanquë ad mestier | And give us whatever we need |
| As nés e conduire e a mangier; | To guide the ships, and to eat; |

THE ANONYMOUS VERSE BRUT TRADITION   407

Again, Royal gets the job done quickly, almost like an annal, Wace – who is often seen as dispassionate when compared with other contemporary vernacular writers including Laȝamon[44] – adds a personal touch through the use of the pronoun "jo" and an attempt at impartiality, and Munich makes sure we know who all the players are and how beautiful the woman is. If one were compelled to assess the courtly nature of these three texts, one might be tempted to rank Munich first, but in terms of a political agenda – though courtly description can be seen as a political agenda in many contexts – it is difficult to say more than underscore Munich's efforts to weave in as many details about ancient Roman history as he could without submerging his Galfridian source, though his major digression toward the end of the fragment listing all the Roman leaders before the birth of Christ constitutes a considerable derailing of Geoffrey's aim. While the Munich author may well have wanted to tap into the popularity of universal histories, most likely it was the growing popularity of the *romans d'antiquité* and their contribution to views of the classical world which led him to shape his *Brut* in the ways he did.

E doinst al duc, nostre seinnor,	And that he give to the duke, our lord,
Innogen, sa fille a oisur; ...	Innogen, his daughter, as a wife; ...
(519–24)	
Nus descrestrums e il crestrunt,	We will weaken and they will prosper,
Nus descharrums e il sordrunt; ...	We will decline and they will rise up; ...
(549–50)	
Jo ne quid que nul en i ait	I don't believe that there is a one [among them]
Ki n'ait par nus damage eü ...	Who hasn't suffered harm at our hands ...
(542–43)	
Pur si fait mal cum jo vus di	On account of this evil situation as I describe to you
Vus lo jo mettrë a la veie,	I advise you to set forth on the way,
Se Brutus, nostre dux, l'otreie."	If Brutus, our leader, agrees."
(Wace, 556–58)	

On Wace's seeing both sides of an issue as a potential irritant for patrons, see Chapter 5, nn. 180 and 255.

44 On Wace as less passionate in his portrayals of major characters and situations, see n. 37 above, for Grout's assessment. For a very useful comparison in Laȝamon and Wace of the emotions involved in friendship and in Leir's family situation, see Erin Mullally, "Registers of Friendship in Layamon's *Brut*," *Modern Philology* 108.4 (2011): 469–87.

408   CHAPTER 6

5.2   The Royal Brut (*London, British Library Royal 13.A.XXI*)

5.2.1   Overview

The anonymous verse *Brut* in the early 14th c. Anglo-Norman MS, British Library, Royal 13.A.xxi, known as the Royal *Brut* or the Anglo-Norman *Brut*,[45] is the longest fragment, containing 6,237 octosyllabic lines. In its current codicological situation, the Royal *Brut*, quite possibly originally part of a complete *Brut*, is preceded by the first 52 lines of Wace's *Brut*, and followed by the remainder of Wace's 14,866-line poem: the 6,237 lines are thought to have "substituted" for Wace's lines 53–8728, hence the label of interpolation, though the poem's editor, Alexander Bell, suggests that Wace's poem may have been used to fill out the missing parts of the Anglo-Norman poem, and not vice versa.[46] The Royal *Brut* narrative extends from the foundation story of the Trojan ancestors up to King Uther's arrival at Tintagel. Thus, the Royal *Brut* never treats Arthur's reign and conquests, or any events following.

Based on a number of omissions in comparison with Wace, Bell concluded that the Royal *Brut* was not a reworking of Wace, nor did he find that there were enough similarities between Royal and the Munich *Brut* to warrant considering a relationship between those two texts either;[47] if Peter Damian-Grint is right (and it would appear he is) about the early nature of the Royal text, as early as the 1140s (rather than the first third of the thirteenth century which was Bell's surmise),[48] then the Royal author – who appears to have been from the north of England – would not have had Wace's *Brut* available to him anyway, nor even the First Variant, and in that case, most likely relied on an early copy of Geoffrey's *Historia*, the text which he appears to have followed the most closely of the three possible sources being considered here.

In broad outline, the Royal *Brut* author – or redactor, depending on one's perspective on the question of whether Royal was constructing a version of the Galfridan material independent of Wace's *Brut* (i.e., an author) or whether he as trying to "improve" upon Wace's poem in a variety of ways (i.e., a redactor of Wace's *Brut*) – preserves Geoffrey of Vinsauf's notion of a narrative's "vital core," that is, the nucleus or central details without which the story would be unrecognizable.[49] For example, for one of the early British rulers, King Ebraucus, who had twenty wives and ruled for sixty years, Royal provides

---

45   *An Anglo-Norman Brut (Royal 13.A.xxi)*, ed. Alexander Bell. On the dating of the MS and its text, see also Appendix 2, n. 1.

46   *Anglo-Norman Brut*, ed. Bell, x. See also Alexander Bell, "The Royal *Brut* Interpolation."

47   *Anglo-Norman Brut*, ed. Bell, xix.

48   See n. 13 above.

49   See Douglas Kelly, "Brevity as Emphasis in the Narrative Lay: The Long and the Short of It," esp. 1–9.

THE ANONYMOUS VERSE BRUT TRADITION 409

nearly all the characters in Wace's section, both major and minor, and details including the size of his navy, his founding of the city of Kaerbrauc north of the Humber (York) and Alclud in Albany (Dumbarton),[50] all with less detail than Wace, though: Royal mentions that Ebraucus had fifty children, twenty sons and thirty daughters, but Wace names them all, as do Geoffrey and the First Variant author, whereas Royal does not include the names of the sons and daughters, nor the name of the Maidens' Castle. In addition to all the names of the offspring, Wace tells the audience that Ebraucus built a castle called "Les Puceles" on Mount Agned,[51] and then devotes nine more lines to explaining that he doesn't know how it got its name, with his use of the now well known *"jo ne sai" topos*, that is, a stance which expresses his preference to claim ignorance rather than providing information that might turn out to be false:

E el mont Agned chastel fist	And [he] had a castle built on Mt. Agned
Qui des Pulceles ad surnun;	Which is named "Castle of the Maidens";
Mais jo ne sai par quel raisun	But I don't know for what reason
Li chastels out nun des Pulceles	The castle is called "Castle of the Maidens"
Plus que de dames ne d'anceles;	Rather than "of the Ladies" or "of the Handmaidens";
Ne me fu dit ne jo nel di	It [the reason] wasn't told to me, nor am I making it up
Ne jo n'a mie tut oï	Nor have I heard all about it
Ne jo n'ai mie tut veü	Nor have I seen everything about it
Ne jo n'ai pas tut entendu,	Nor have I understood it all,
E mult estovreit home entendre	And he who would like to give a complete account
Ki de tut vuldreit raison rendre.	Must understand it all very well.

(WACE, *Brut*, 1526–36)

---

50 See notes to lines 1333 and 1335, pp. 416–17, in Lawman, *Brut*, trans. Rosamund Allen.

51 Allen notes that Maidens' Castle "is not the place in Dorset, but probably Edinburgh" and that in Geoffrey, it appears as the Castellarum Puellarum (Lawman, *Brut*, trans., n. to l. 1340, p. 417, citing Thorpe, trans., p. 79). See Wright trans., "Ebraucus also built the city of Dumbarton towards Scotland, the town of Mount Agned, now called Edinburgh, and Mons Dolorosus" (*HRB*, §27.92–94; "Condidit etiam Ebraucus urbem Aldclud versus Albaniam et oppidum Montis Agned, quod nunc Castellum Puellarum dicitur, et Montem Dolorosum").

410 CHAPTER 6

Not that the Royal author fabricates, but he certainly does not call attention to the act of writing or to the possibility of his own ignorance.

As Alexandre Micha observes in his brief discussion of six fragmentary translations of Geoffrey's *Historia*,[52] the Royal *Brut* is essentially a work of *abbreviatio*; the relevant section in Wace's *Brut* – lines 53 to 8729 – is reduced by 2439 lines, or roughly by 28%. In terms of how he (or she) accomplishes the task of *abbreviatio*, what the Royal narrator has done most substantially is eliminate Wace's *discours interprétatif*, including cleansing the text of all of Wace's commentaries on his own ignorance – the *"jo ne sai" topos* – at least fifty of them, as in the case of Ebrauc's castle Les Puceles. The Royal *Brut* author has also eliminated Wace's numerous passages on etymology, one of Wace's passions, though it is important to add that through Wace's frequent explanations of etymology and toponymics, we can also see his attitudes toward migration, changes in leadership, and other more substantive themes, rather than simply picturesque details or a fascination with the evolution of languages; while some of Wace's etymological passages are borrowed from the Latin, many are original. Royal also cuts a number of speeches, though he adds a few new ones; he also cuts kings numbers 14–20 (and possibly a few others) from the early part of Geoffrey's *Historia*.

Like Egerton – in this case, following Wace – Royal omits the book of Merlin's Prophecies, though he does not include any hint of Wace's justification for that omission, since he assiduously avoids any sort of commentary whatsoever on the act of writing. Royal has the red and white dragons in two hollow stones under Vortigern's tower, but the pools are not drained, nor are the dragons fighting. Wace mentions the fighting dragons but not Merlin's politically charged interpretation (7523–35), but he does have Merlin predict the coming of Aurelius, Uther, and Arthur (in the guise of the boar of Cornwall) (7571), whereas in Royal, Merlin remains silent on the fates of Aurelius and Uther and the coming of Arthur, which in the *Historia*, is contained in a separate prophecy Merlin utters just following the book of Prophecies (*HRB*, §118. 7–21). Wace includes these latter points despite his cutting of the book of Prophecies itself, as they are important aspects of both the vulgate and First Variant versions of the history of the Britons. For Royal thus this is a very notable omission,

---

52 The Munich *Brut* (Staatsbibliothek Cod. Gall. 29), the Bekker fragment (Krakow, Jagiellonian Univ. Lib. Gall. fol. 176), Arundel 220 (London, BL), Harley 4733 (London, BL), Harley 1605 (London, BL), the decasyllabic preamble to the interpolated prophecies in Durham, Cathedral Lib. C.iv.27 and in Cologny-Geneva, Fond. Bodmer 67 (which Micha refers to by its former designation, the D'Arcy Hutton MS.), and the Royal *Brut* (*Étude sur le "Merlin" de Robert de Boron, Roman du XIIIe siècle*, Publications Romanes et Françaises 151, Geneva: Droz, 1980, 32–34).

THE ANONYMOUS VERSE BRUT TRADITION 411

even in the interests of *abbreviatio*, an omission which suggests that Royal may have found any of Merlin's prophecies, let alone the entire book of Prophecies, a more politically hot potato than Wace did.[53]

5.2.2 Trojan Foundation Myth

A number of medieval texts, including the *Historia Brittonum*,[54] one of Geoffrey's main sources, provide evidence of a Trojan foundation myth for Britain, but it is Geoffrey's version that is probably the best known and which certainly provides the most details, revealing Geoffrey's attempt to create what might be construed as an entire universe for the Britons, a shared ethnicity over generations, a link to the Romans and yet also a distinction from them, and certainly a distinction from the Saxons, whom he generally demonizes in the *Historia*.

The central kernel of this particular version of the Trojan foundation myth in the vulgate §6 is the Brutus story: Aeneas's grandson, Silvius, has a secret passion for Lavinia's niece, marries her, and from their union Brutus is born. Fate has decreed that he should bring about the death of both his mother and his father. As a result, Brutus is banished from Italy by his relatives, and after much wandering with a band of Trojan followers he had liberated from bondage in Greece, he arrives in Britain, where he gives his name to the island, dubbing the Trojans Britons. Brutus rules for twenty-four years, creates many laws, and upon his death, his kingdom is divided among his three sons: Locrinus who rules England, Albanactus who rules Scotland, and Kamber who rules Wales.[55]

---

53   See Blacker, "'Ne vuil sun livre translater': Wace's Omission of Merlin's Prophecies from the *Roman de Brut*."

54   Ed. and trans. John Morris. Most scholars today have been convinced by David Dumville's extensive and painstaking work that the attribution to Nennius is erroneous; see esp. David N. Dumville, "Nennius and the *Historia Brittonum*," and idem, "*Historia Brittonum*: An Insular History from the Carolingian Age."

55   Although the earliest version of this story (in connection with Britain) dates to the early ninth century, the archeologist John Creighton believes "it may have been of Roman origin, partly in view of the overwhelming evidence for the appropriation of Graeco-Roman myth by British rulers in the era before the Claudian conquest" in 43 AD. (Creighton, *Coins and Power in Late Iron Age Britain*, Cambridge: Cambridge University Press, 2000, esp. 137–45; Creighton summarized by Nico Roymans, "Hercules and the Construction of a Batavian Identity in the Context of the Roman Empire," in *Ethnic Constructs in Antiquity: The Role of Power and Tradition*, ed. Ton Derks and Nico Roymans, Amsterdam Archaeological Studies 13 (Amsterdam: Amsterdam University Press, 2009), 219–38, at 237). For examples of a number of "creative appropriations" of the dominant Trojan foundation myth particularly in late antique Gaul and Britain and a discussion of how "deeply rooted was the Trojan descent myth in the northern provinces" (221) and on the "need of communities conquered by Rome to forge a link to Graeco-Roman mythology in the context of their political relationship with Rome" (220), see Roymans, 219–23. See also

412   CHAPTER 6

In Royal, the broad outline of Brutus's liberation of the enslaved Trojans under the Greek king Pandrasus, the prophecy of Brutus's founding of Britain delivered to Brutus at the temple of Diana – either by the goddess herself or in a dream – on the deserted isle of Loegetia ("Leogence") follows the vulgate and First Variant – and Wace, up to a point (though in Royal, Brutus's uncertainty about the delivery of the message is gone – it is the goddess herself who makes the prophecy). Royal also diverges from Wace by following more closely the vulgate and the First Variant on the arrival of the Trojans in Britain. Wace diverges in important details – to which I will return shortly – but for the order of the narrative he follows the First Variant: that is, in Wace, the short description of the land (this is not the "description of Britain" passage found very early in the vulgate and FV, but a later description) follows the passage about the giants and Gogmagog, whereas in the vulgate and Royal, the description of the land precedes the narrative about the giants and Gogmagog.

5.2.3   Giants; Group Identities

In the vulgate, Geoffrey writes that the island had no inhabitants except for a few giants; after exploring this very "pleasant" land and "driving off to mountain caves any giants they came upon," Brutus's followers portion out the land and begin cultivating crops, "so that, in a short time, the country appeared to have been occupied for many years" (*HRB*, §21.452–59) – by human beings, that is. At this juncture, Brutus calls the island Britain and his followers "Britons." He also renames the Trojan language – which had been called "crooked Greek" – into British; this term of Geoffrey's, "crooked Greek," "curuum Graecum," (*HRB*, §21.462) is not found elsewhere, either in Wace or the First Variant. In fact, in Royal doesn't mention the change in language at all, apparently not considering language an important marker of identity as Wace frequently does.

In the vulgate, one day when Brutus is holding a feast at the port where the Britons had landed, twenty Cornish giants fall upon them and wreak great slaughter. The Britons are ultimately victorious, killing them but sparing their leader, Gogmagog, so that the Cornish leader Corineus can fight with him in hand-to-hand combat, since he was "always most eager to fight giants" (§21.476–77); Corineus is victorious and throws the giant into the sea. Nothing more is heard of the other giants who had been said originally to have been

---

Jonathan Barlow, who argues that "the association of Franks with the Troy myth [and the association for a number of other peoples] had a long history stretching back into the Roman empire," and thus its association with the Franks in particular did not originate with Fredegar in the seventh century ("Gregory of Tours and the Myth of the Trojan Origins of the Franks," *Frühmittelalterliche Studien* 29 (1995): 86–95, cited at 86).

THE ANONYMOUS VERSE BRUT TRADITION   413

chased into the mountains, and the Britons settle happily, eventually dividing
the land among Brutus's three sons after his death. The Royal *Brut* follows this
narrative very closely, including in the order in which it is presented.

As discussed in Chapter 5, but which bears repeating in this context of
Royal's treatment of the material on the giants, Wace however adds details to
the Galfridian narrative that have significant implications. Mindful of Michelle
Warren's characterization of Geoffrey's *Historia* as a portrayal of "the forgotten
empire of a marginalized people in reaction to an urgently present colonial
dynamic,"[56] we may be surprised to see references to what amounts to genocide and ethnic separatism perpetrated by the Britons early in the narrative,
that is, before the time when they themselves are either exterminated, driven
into Wales or off the island.

In Wace's *Brut*, the opening couplet of the passage on Brutus's naming of the
land might easily be missed:

Quant la terre fud neïee	When the land was cleansed
Des gaianz e de lur lignee,	Of the giants and their line,
Li Troïen s'aseürerent,	The Trojans felt secure.
Maisuns firent, terres arerent,	They built houses, cultivated the lands,
Viles e burcs edifierent,	Built cities and towns,
Blez semerent, blez guaainerent.	Sowed corn, and reaped it.
La terre aveit nun Albion,	The land was called Albion,
Mais Brutus li chanja sun nun.	But Brutus changed its name.

(WACE, *Brut*, 1169–76)

Wace goes further regarding the demise of the native population: the *Roman
de Brut* is the only one of these texts – or any Galfridian text, as far as I know –
to mention the complete removal of the giants,[57] implying that there were
more than just a few, i.e., a whole population, including offspring. He uses
the past participle "neïee" which means "washed away, wiped out, drowned"
or "cleansed." In addition, Wace with his customary thoroughness, says the
Trojans – soon to become Britons – make sure to rid the land of the giants' line
or chance of progeny, "lur lignee" as well, presumably so that there would be
no question later as to whom the land belonged once the Trojans had firmly

---

56   *History on the Edge*, 116.
57   Sylvia Huot comments that "Geoffrey of Monmouth, though couching his narrative in an
     overall framework that promotes the eradication of giants, does not shy from acknowledg-
     ing the element of enjoyment that the Trojans found in their interactions with Britain's
     indigenous inhabitants," nor on the other hand does he explicitly describe the eradication
     as Wace does (*Outsiders*, 65).

414   CHAPTER 6

established themselves, and brought civilization to Britain, taking no chances
that members of an anterior group would remain to make claims or compete
for natural resources.[58]

If the Royal *Brut* author set about to "correct" or "sanitize" Wace's version,
one can see why he eliminated Wace's passage on the complete removal and
cleansing of any trace of the native group of giants, since this is not a particularly attractive activity perpetrated by any newly arrived group upon another
pre-existing population, even if the latter were characterized as sub-human,
or perhaps especially so. Or, rather than relying on a copy of Wace, if Royal
had been working with a copy of the vulgate *Historia* – which he seems to
follow more closely than the First Variant – if the FV had even been available
at the time Royal author was writing (of which there were probably far fewer
copies at the time – there are certainly far fewer extant today), then Royal's
non-genocidal version is to be expected, though it is not without bloodshed
(and Geoffrey's etymology):

Aval la faleise le geta,	Over the cliff he [Cornieus] threw him,
La faleise en est ensanglanté,	The cliff was bloody,
Li geianz en est tut depescé.	The giant was all in pieces.
Li Troien en sunt mult lé,	The Trojans were very happy,
A la faleise un sun nun duné	They gave the cliff his name
Car si cum dient li paisant,	As the peasants called it,
De Geomagog est ço le salt.	That is, Gogmagog's Leap.
Brutus veit par le pais	Brutus traveled through the land
Cum cil kin est poestifs.	As one who was in charge of it.
Un liu trovat mult avenant	He found a very suitable place
U fist une cité vaillant, ...	Where he made a distinguished city, ...

(Royal, 1016–26)

---

58   Huot: "As the indigenous inhabitants of an island that is nonetheless uninhabited and
      ready for settlement, giants illustrate Samira Kawash's characterization of the native as
      'non-existent' in the eyes of the colonizer, for whom the indigene fades into the back-
      ground as merely part of the landscape awaiting management and rule: the "thing that has
      been excluded as the condition for the colonizer's view of the 'empty landscape'" (Huot,
      Outsiders, 42–43, citing Kawash, "Terrorists and Vampires: Fanon's Spectral Violence
      of Decolonization," in *Franz Fanon: Critical Perspectives*, ed. Anthony C. Alessandrini,
      London and New York: Routledge, 1999, 237–57, cited at 253). See also in Chapter 1 in the
      context of Geoffrey's vulgate, Jeffrey Cohen on the biblical subtext of the "first Trojan
      encounter with the aboriginal giants" and the inherent ironies of that encounter for the
      portrayal of the Britons (*Of Giants: Sex, Monsters, and the Middle Ages*, 34–35), and also
      on giants as aboriginals in both the narratives of early Britain and elsewhere in medieval
      French literature, see Sylvia Huot, *Outsiders*, esp. 9–11, 37, 42–43, 55–56, and 65–68.

THE ANONYMOUS VERSE BRUT TRADITION   415

Further on in the narrative, however, on the theme of group identities, somewhat less easy to explain is Royal's elimination of the origin story of the Picts, more specifically, how they got their wives. According to Geoffrey, during the reign of Marius, the 77th king of the Britons,[59] the Picts arrive from Scythia, bent on ravaging the land – in Royal, "la terre prist a deguaster" (3258). Marius defeats the Picts and beheads Rodric, king of the Picts, and erects a memorial to that event; Marius then gives the Picts a large part of Caithness. Wace, Geoffrey, and First Variant all relate that the land gifted was a wasteland, and also that the Picts asked the Britons for wives but they refused (Geoffrey adds, that "they refused to marry their daughters and other female relatives to such people," §70.386). The Picts then cross over to Ireland and bring back wives from there. Geoffrey adds further "but enough of the Picts, since it is not my intention to write either their history or that of the Scots, who are descended from them and the Irish" (§70.386–88). Neither Wace, nor Royal, nor the First Variant indulges in Geoffrey's bit of ethnic disparagement, that the Picts were not worthy to marry British women (Geoffrey is not particularly positive about the Irish either).

Alexander Bell notes that while Geoffrey mentions Caithness in four contexts – the Rodric episode, plus Cordelia's nephew's inheritance, Brennius's inheritance, and the northernmost point of Belinus's road stretching from the tip of Cornwall to the tip of Caithness – Royal keeps only the Rodric reference.[60] In two other instances Royal uses the name Caithness – the northernmost tip of modern-day Scotland – where Geoffrey simply names Scotland or a region near Scotland (once for the donation by the usurper Carensius[61] to the Picts (3441), and the other by Aurelius to the Saxons Octa and Eosa (5586)). According to Bell, the Royal author seems to have regarded Caithness as "a dumping-ground for undesirable aliens."[62] Also significant is

---

59   In Reeve's Index, Marius is listed as the 86th king of the Britons; see Chapter 1, n . 4.

60   *Anglo-Norman Brut*, ed. Bell, xiii.

61   In the Royal *Brut*, Bell, presumably following the manuscript, gives the following spellings for the same king: "Carense" (3422), "Carenses" (3389, 3422, 3454), "Carensius" (3457), "Carisius" (3365); the Latin "Carausius" (used by Geoffrey and the First Variant) is given as the modern equivalent in the Index (p. 196). Weiss has "Carais" in both her text of Wace and her translation.

62   *Royal Brut*, ed., Bell, xiii. Regarding Carausius's donation to the Picts, Geoffrey has "a home in Scotland" ("where they have remained ever since, mixed with the British," §75.60–2) – Wace has "He [Carais] sent the Picts into Scotland; he gave them towns and lands; from that time on, the Picts have been completely intermingled with the Scots" (5471–74; "Les Pics en Escoce enveia; / Viles e terres lur duna; / Des cel tens unt li Pic esté / Tuit as Escoz entremellé"); and for Aurelius's donation to Octa, Geoffrey has "the region adjacent to Scotland" (§126.189) as does Wace (7957–60). As far as Royal's suggested propensity to see

416 CHAPTER 6

Royal's elimination of Geoffrey's comments that when Carausius gave the Picts "a home in Scotland" (§75. 60–62) – or Wace's comment that the Picts remained in "a land near [next to] Scotland" ("[une] terre ... / ... / Dejuste Escoce," 7957, 7959) – the Picts remained "ever since, mixed with the British" (§75. 62). It is possible that Royal was uncomfortable with the whole subject of overlapping identities – Picts, Britons, and Saxons – that is, any form of ethnic mixing, or perhaps he feared that members of his audience might be wary of such a concept.

5.2.4 Coming of Christianity to Britain

Discrepancies also exist in the texts' reporting of the conversion of the Britons which is said to have taken place during the reign of Lucius, the 79th king[63] directly following Marius's son Coillus (of course, not all of Geoffrey's 107 named kings and queens from early British history can be verified, though a few can). Munich, Royal, Harley 1605, and College of Arms 12/45A report that Lucius sends to Pope Elutherius a message requesting someone to baptize him and teach Christianity to his people. Dunian and his companion, Fagan, arrive and accomplish the task, preaching to the people and setting up bishoprics and archbishoprics; Wace omits the locations of the administrative establishments, and their subdivisions, as well as Geoffrey's comment that he won't include more details "in his inferior style" since Gildas has already written about it "in so distinguished a work" (*HRB*, §72.431–33). The First Variant provides the locations, subdivisions and a very perfunctory remark at the end that the acts of Elutherius's servants "are clearly set forth in the book that Gildas the historian composed" (FV, §72.8), adding language and a few phrases of a more religious or conventionally devout nature over the course of the section, particularly about the eradication of idolatry (FV, §72).

Royal reverses the order in which the *Historia* names the three archbishoprics; according to Bell, by including the originally British kingdom of Bernicia

---

Caithness as "a dumping-ground for undesirable aliens," could this possibly be related to attitudes toward the Scandinavian invaders who made incursions in the north including Caithness (largely initially from Norway, but later from Denmark) (both historical, as far as Royal's sources were concerned, but also contemporary in terms of his own background or audience)? As Sally M. Foster writes, their "first recorded attack on Britain and Ireland [by the Vikings] took place in 793 on Lindisfarne in Bernicia"; according to contemporary annals, attacks increased, "'amounting to devastation of all the island of Britain by the gentiles [pagans]'... by the later 9th century Norse settlement was firmly established in the Northern Isles and Caithness. Ultimately, it was the presence of the Vikings and their continuing expansionist tendencies that were instrumental in the final unification of the Dál Riata and Picts" (*Picts, Gaels and Scots: Early Historic Scotland*, 5–6).

63 In Reeve's Index, Lucius is listed as the 88th king; see Chapter 1, n. 4.

THE ANONYMOUS VERSE BRUT TRADITION 417

along with Scotland and the British kingdom of Deira under the jurisdiction of York, Royal is in agreement with the Welsh *Brut* in Oxford, Jesus College MS. 61, and not with Wace, Geoffrey, or the First Variant (in the edited versions currently available to us), thereby expanding the number of formerly British kingdoms under York's jurisdiction, possibly emphasizing British origins or British input in the formation of Northumbria.[64] Bell notes other reminiscences of the Welsh translation, but merely suggests that the Royal and Welsh translators may have used the same copy of Geoffrey (without commenting on any implications).[65]

5.2.5 The *Adventus Saxonum*

The coming of the Saxons, or the *adventus Saxonum*, basically divides early historians into those who represented the Anglocentric perspective of Vortigern's having invited the immigrants who later achieved great things, and those who represent the British or Celtic perspective that the Saxons came as an invading army, uninvited, though depending on the author, with Vortigern's blessing, thereby significantly contributing to his – and ultimately their – demise or diminution. The *adventus* thus is potentially revealing of one aspect of Royal's attitudes toward the history he is translating – and adapting. First, to remind us of the major features of this section from major sources: 1) in sixth-century British historian Gildas's *De Excidio Britanniae*, Vortigern invites the Saxons – or rather, they were not exactly invited, but "admitted" by the "ill-fated tyrant" (ch. 23, 5 and 4, p. 26);[66] 2) in Bede's Anglocentric eighth-century *Historia Ecclesiastica gentis Anglorum*, Vortigern invites the Saxons;[67] 3) in the ninth-century *Historia Brittonum*, often ascribed to Nennius, the Saxons come as

---

64 Printed by Griscom in English translation beneath the Latin text in his edition of the vulgate; *Anglo-Norman Brut*, ed. Bell, note for lines 3313–22, p. 179. See Barbara Yorke, *Kings and Kingdoms of Early Anglo-Saxon England*, 74.

65 *Anglo-Norman Brut*, ed. Bell, xv–xvi. On the twelfth-century copies of the vulgate and FV *Historia* (and other copies), see Chapter 3, nn. 9, 10, and 21, and also Michael D. Reeve "The Transmission of the *Historia Regum Britanniae*."

66 "Igitur intromissi in insulam barbari" and "infausto tyranno" (ch. 23, 5 and 4, p. 97; Gildas, *The Ruin of Britain and other works*, ed. and trans. Michael Winterbottom). However, "intromissi" can also mean "introduced," which carries more the implication of invitation.

67 "Tunc Anglorum siue Saxonum gens, inuitata a rege praefato" (*HE*, I.15, ed. and trans. Colgrave and Mynors). Among the extensive sources on Bede's Anglocentric perspectives and his construction of Englishness, see especially Christopher Highley, *Catholics Writing the Nation in Early Modern Britain and Ireland* (Oxford: Oxford University Press, 2008), 84–91; T. M. Charles Edwards, "Bede, the Irish and the Britons"; Patrick Wormald, "Bede, the *Bretwaldas* and the Origins of the *Gens Anglorum*"; and Barbara Yorke, *The Conversion of Britain: Religion, Politics and Society in Britain, 600–800* (New York: Pearson, 2006; repr. London and New York: Routledge, 2014), 21.

418 CHAPTER 6

exiles, uninvited, arriving purely by chance (ch. 31); but later, sin is ascribed to Vortigern for having "received the English people";[68] 4) in Geoffrey's *Historia* and the First Variant, the Saxons come as exiles (having cast lots, due to over-population), uninvited, and arrive purely by chance (§98); 5) in Henry of Huntingdon's *Historia Anglorum*, "The race of Saxons, or English, invited by the above-mentioned king [Vortigern], came to Britain in three long ships, in the year of grace 449";[69] in the remainder of the section, Henry lists their regions and genealogies; 6) in Henry's *Epistola ad Warinum*, ostensibly a summary of the high points of Geoffrey's *Historia* (with important discrepancies) composed not long after Robert de Torigni showed Henry a copy of the *Historia* at Le Bec in 1139, Vortigern invites the Saxons "only to be betrayed by them" (*EW*, ch. 8, p. 111);[70] 7) in Wace, the Saxons come, uninvited, arrive purely by chance, explaining that their land was overpopulated – Wace makes a point of their foreign speech and physical beauty (6703–66); and lastly, 8) in the Royal *Brut*: Saxons come, uninvited, with three lines about their physical appearance and prowess; they explain about the overpopulation, but not at such great length as in Wace (4589–4622). Thus, Royal takes the ostensibly pro-British Galfridian position, though remaining as neutral as possible, certainly not demonizing the Saxons as Geoffrey most often does in the *Historia*.

5.2.6 Revival of Christianity among the Britons

In the vulgate, Royal, First Variant, and Wace, the narrative order and emphases differ in the accounts of the revival of Christianity among the Britons. Following the eradication of the Pelagian heresy by St. Germain (bishop of Auxerre) and St. Lupus (bishop of Troyes), the vulgate proceeds to present

---

68   *HB* (ed. and trans. John Morris): The Saxons were "driven into exile from Germany" (but the text doesn't say why) (ch. 31, p. 26); in ch. 48 regarding Vortigern, "When he was hated for his sin, because he received the English people ["†propter susceptionem populi Saxonici†," phrase brought in from Mommsen's edition, ch. 48, p. 73], by all men of his own nation ...," recounting how Vortigern "wandered from place to place until at last his heart broke, and he died without honour" (ch. 48, p. 33); – but "received" in the context of "propter susceptionem" does not automatically imply "invited."

69   That is, "during the reign of Marcian and Valentinian, whose imperial rule lasted seven years, and in the twentyfourth [*sic*] year after the kingdom of the Franks had begun, whose first king was Faramund" (11.1) (*HA*, ed. and trans. Diana Greenway, 79).

70   Neil Wright, "The Place of Henry of Huntingdon's *Epistola ad Warinum*." One of the more interesting discrepancies is a reference in ch. 9 to the Breton hope of Arthur's return (following the mention that the king as well as Mordred "too fell"), the "hope" not mentioned explicitly in Geoffrey's *Historia* (Wright, 79); without mentioning the "hope," Geoffrey nonetheless leaves Arthur's ultimate fate ambiguously open to interpretation, where the king is said to have been mortally wounded but also taken to Avalon "to have his wounds tended" (§178.81–84).

THE ANONYMOUS VERSE BRUT TRADITION 419

how Vortigern's son Vortimer manages to defeat the Saxons and send them back to their own land. Vortimer's victory comes about since the Britons feared that they would be thoroughly overrun by Saxons. They appeal to Vortigern who does nothing since he is married to Hengist's daughter, Ronwen, but also because the Saxons have helped him defeat his other enemies, the Picts; the Britons ultimately overthrow Vortigern, replacing him with his son, Vortimer:

> Quod cum uidissent Britones, timentes proditionem eorum dixerunt regi ut ipsos ex finibus regni sui expelleret. Non enim debebant pagani Christianis communicare nec intromitti, quia Christiana lex prohibebat; insuper tanta multitudo aduenerat ita ut ciuibus terrori essent; iam nesciebatur quis paganus esset, quis Christianus, quia pagani filias et consanguineas eorum sibi associauerant. (*HRB*, §101.389–95)

> When the Britons saw this [i.e., that Hengist kept inviting more and more ships of settlers], they feared that they would be betrayed and told the king to expel the Saxons from the kingdom. Pagans ought not to communicate or mix with Christians, as it was forbidden by Christian law; moreover so many of them had arrived that his subjects feared them; no one knew who was pagan and who Christian, since the pagans had married their daughters and relatives. (§101, p. 130)

Royal follows in broad outline, but as very often, abridges the source(s):

"Sire reis, nus vus prium	"Lord king, we beg you
E cum seignur vus requerum,	And as [our] sovereign we entreat you,
Ceste gent mais ne maintenez,	Don't protect these people,
Mais fors del pais les getez	But throw them out of the land
Kar il trestut sunt paien	For they are all pagans
E nus sumes crestien,	And we are Christians,
Ensemble ne devem ester	We must not be together
Ne od els bevre ne manger."	Nor drink or eat with them."
(Royal *Brut*, 4851–58)	

The kernel of not mixing with the pagans is retained – interestingly, in the social setting of dining, emphasizing the conduct aspect of religion, rather than the spiritual: the focus is on the sociopolitical, as an element of group identity. However, the Royal translator has eliminated Geoffrey's specific references to the negative aspects of intermarriage. Could this be to avoid casting

420   CHAPTER 6

aspersions on his Anglo-Norman patrons who may have been rapidly assimilating with the English including through intermarriage?

Wace also cuts Geoffrey's comment about intermarriage (as does the First
Variant) but on the other hand expands on what is found in both of the Latin
texts as if to compromise between the two:

Emprés vindrent altres suvent	Afterwards others often came
De jur en jur menuement	Little by little, day after day
Od quatre nés, od cinc, od sies,	With four ships, with five, with six,
Od set, od uit, od nof, od dies.	With seven, with eight, with nine, with ten.
Tost furent si paien munté	Soon the number of pagans had gone up so much
As crestïens entremeslé,	Intermingling with the Christians,
Avisunques conuisseit l'un	That no one hardly knew
Ki ert crestïen e ki nun.	Who was a Christian and who wasn't.
As Bretuns ad mult ennuied	This really annoyed the Britons
Si unt al reit dist e preied	Who said to the king, and beseeched [him]
Que cele estrange gent ne creie	That he not trust this foreign people
Kar a vcüc se desleie;	For they had been seen to be disloyal;
Trop ad de cels paiens atrait,	He had attracted too many of these pagans,
Vilanie est, grant hunte fait,	Which was base and caused great disgrace,
Departe les, cument que seit,	He should make them leave, no matter how,
Ou tut u le plus en enveit.	Send them away, either all or most.

(WACE, *Brut*, 7059–74)

In Geoffrey, following Vortigern's refusal to yield to this request, he is overthrown, his son Vortimer is enthroned, and subsequently defeats the Saxons,
who leave for their homeland, leaving behind their sons and wives. At this
point in Wace, after chasing out the Saxons, Vortimer restores "to everyone
what they had each lost through them [the Saxons]" (7133–34; "E Vortimer a tuz
rendi / Ço que chescuns par els perdi"), rebuilds churches and paves the way
for the arrival of St. Germain and St. Lupus. Whereas in Geoffrey and Royal, the
two saints come to reverse the decline of religion due to the pagans' presence
as well as the Pelagian heresy, Wace changes the narrative order and explains
that Christianity was poorly observed because Hengist "had corrupted it" (7138;

THE ANONYMOUS VERSE BRUT TRADITION   421

"Pur Henguist ki l'out corumpue"), without mentioning the Pelagian heresy; the First Variant uses the same narrative order as Wace, but retains Geoffrey's explanation about the Pelagian heresy (FV, §102), and praise for Gildas which Geoffrey has earlier in §101. Royal restores the narrative order in the Galfridian Latin source, specifically cites the Pelagian heresy, and retains the Latin references to Gildas (which Wace had also passed over). A very different perspective is provided by Bede who writes that the two prelates came to England expressly to squelch the Pelagian heresy, which he claims was introduced by Agricola, the son of the Pelagian bishop Severianus, a detail not found in Royal, Geoffrey, or the First Variant. In a fairly rare moment, Bede credits the Britons with reaching out to Germanus and Lupus "wisely" to rid them of that scourge; he certainly doesn't blame Hengist or the Saxons (HE, I.17).[71]

---

71 Often, though not categorically, Bede tends to be critical of the Britons with respect to ecclesiastical matters. On the many aspects of Bede's portrayal of the Britons, see especially W. Trent Foley and Nicholas Higham, "Bede on the Britons"; Ian Wood, "Who are the Philistines? Bede's Readings of Old Testament Peoples," in *The Resources of the Past in Early Medieval Europe*, ed. Clemens Gantner, Rosamond McKitterick, and Sven Meeder (Cambridge: Cambridge University Press, 2015), 172–87; Alexander Murray, "Bede and the Unchosen Race," in *Power and Identity in the Middle Ages: Essays in Memory of Rees Davies*, ed. Huw Pryce and John Watts (Oxford: Oxford University Press, 2007), 52–67; and Stephan J. Shustereder, *Strategies of Identity Construction: The Writings of Gildas, Aneirin and Bede* (Göttingen: V & R unipress, 2015), 264–66. Murray cautions that "in any indictment of Bede, [his] public must be brought into the reckoning. Bede's *History* was dedicated to an English king, Ceolwulf, and envisaged a public of similar cast of mind" (66), and draws a parallel with the Bayeux Tapestry which was made necessary by the Normans' need to justify the Conquest, suggesting that Bede's *History* was "the Bayeux Tapestry of the Anglo-Saxon Conquest" (67). In a lecture where she examines Bede's largely negative presentation of the Britons in the *Ecclesiastical History*, Clare Stancliffe writes that given Bede's dating of the coming of the Saxons to 449, "the three hundred years [after which time from the British perspective via Gildas "the bloody Saxon warfare and occupation would end"] would be up in less than twenty years from the time he completed his *Ecclesiastical History* in 731" and thus "it is small wonder, then, that Bede felt apprehensive about the future of Northumbria ... that one of the imponderable threats appeared to him to be that represented by the Britons" (*Bede and the Britons*, cited at 39–40). Stancliffe finds that Bede does shower accolades on certain Britons, such as St. Ninian (who converted the southern Picts) and St. Alban (first recorded Briton Christian martyr), but they are "isolated figures" and that "when Bede generalises from individual to people in his history, it is Cadwallon [king of Gwynedd 625–34/5 and Northumbria 633–34/5, the last Brythonic-speaker who ruled over much of eastern Britain], not Ninian, who typifies the Britons" (41). For additional information and perspectives, see Chapter 1, n. 75 and Chapter 2, n. 120.

5.2.7 Conclusion

In conclusion, descriptions of situations are sometimes shorter in Royal than in Wace's *Brut*; for example Royal uses twenty verses to relate how, after the death of Lucius and the conversion of the Britons, the latter were leaderless, how Severus was sent by the Romans and how he built a wall between Scotland and Deira (3336–56). Wace devotes eighty lines to Severus's (Sever's) activities.[72] In contrast to descriptions of events, descriptions of people are often longer in Royal than in Wace, particularly of women, such as Inogen, Brutus's wife, or King Cole's daughter, Helen – a princess educated in the liberal arts (3591–96) – neither of whom Wace describes. Most of the character descriptions are stock though, where the individual rises above the group only through his or her function as a member of the group. Most evident are Royal's disdain for *discours interprétatif* – and Wace's uniqueness in that regard – as well as Royal's discomfort with – or disinterest in – multiple or overlapping cultural and ethnic identities. Although he often follows Geoffrey's events and pro-Briton perspectives (though not slavishly), he eschews Geoffrey's disdain for the Saxons and disparaging comments on other groups, with no interest in narrating genocide either (like Wace). Royal's story is neat and tidy.

I have only scratched the surface of what the Royal *Brut* can reveal about early vernacular views of the legendary history of Britain in Anglo-Norman England. Much remains to be explored in that text and the other verse *Brut*s in relation to the Galfridian material (and the First Variant), to Wace, and presentation of the Trojan ancestors in the *romans d'aniquité*. Looking at Wace and the Royal *Brut*, we have an excellent example of Barbara Herrnstein Smith's views on versions versus stories, which bear repeating here: once the variables, from major events to the smallest of semantic markers, are rearranged in response to political, social, linguistic, and even metrical functions and expectations, we no longer have different versions of the same story, but actually different stories.[73]

---

72 Narrative events including his building of a dike ("un fossé" 5309) across the land – which could refer to Septimius Severus's building of a defensive Wall which has been linked to either the reinforcing of the Antonine Wall (c. 208), but most frequently to the rebuilding of Hadrian's Wall (*c.*208–11) – chasing of the Britons and their leader, the baron Fulgene(s) (*HRB* and FV, §74 Fulgenius (II – that is, the rebel against Severus, not the 48th king [not 57th] of the Britons, Fulgenius (I), §52)) into Scotland, their deaths in battle, and Severus's burial with honor at York (5273–5352). See Weiss, trans., 135, nn. 1–3, and Simon Elliott, *Septimius Severus in Scotland: The Northern Campaigns of the First Hammer of the Scots* (London: Greenhill Books, 2018).

73 "Narrative Versions, Narrative Theories."

THE ANONYMOUS VERSE BRUT TRADITION   423

5.3   *London, College of Arms 12/45A*

5.3.1   Overview of the Narrative(s); Prologues

This roll (hereafter CA), the fifth-longest of the anonymous verse *Bruts* at approximately 2500 lines, appears to have been copied in England between 1284 and 1290[74] – though the text itself may well predate 1200. It contains a fragment of an anonymous *Brut* which follows roughly verses 1293–8338 of Wace's *Brut* (with many lacunae), that is, corresponding roughly to Geoffrey's sections §§23–133.[75] Except for the lacunae relative to the vulgate (which the

---

74   Short, "Un *Roman de Brut* anglo-normand inédit," 277. A note of "housekeeping" for read-
       ers: Olivier de Laborderie apparently did not number the verses in his transcription; I am
       grateful to Dr. Di Lella for having supplied to me his copy of Laborderie's transcription
       from the latter's thesis. Short uses his own numbering for the two extracts he publishes –
       the passages are not consecutive on the roll (though he numbers them 1–255 and 256–674
       and indicates with a symbol that the passages are not consecutive; 104 lines separate
       the two passages); the first, on Merlin's background, the opening of the Prophecies and
       foretelling of Vortigern's death, corresponds roughly to the vulgate §§105–108, 111–112.1
       and 118, and the second to Aurelius's commanding the moving of the giants' stones from
       Ireland to Stonehenge and the king's poisoning and death, to vulgate §§127–133; Di Lella's
       edition of this anonymous *Brut* text is in progress. Thus, in my references here, the lines
       of College of Arms 12/45 A currently remain unnumbered, since, in addition, it is not clear
       how the redactor(s) intended the prose extracts to be interpreted, particularly the shorter
       extracts interspersed among the verse lines. For example, some of the short prose pas-
       sages could conceivably be divided into octosyllabic lines (accounting for the irregularity
       of Anglo-Norman verse, there would be longer lines as well), yielding at times 5–8 lines,
       for example; the longer prose passages, such as the 900-word narrative of Cassibellanus,
       appear intended as prose, though again, how they too should be tallied with respect
       to line numbers, remains an editorial decision I am not prepared to make at this time,
       deciding that it would be best to leave the numbering and similar structural questions to
       the text's eventual editor (Short also does not number the lines of the prose prologue he
       reproduces before the opening of his first extract, p. 278). See also n. 89 below regarding
       Short's tally of 2500 lines for the anonymous verse text (not the selections from Wace's
       Brut), and also 119 below on my decision to number the prose passages (but not the lines
       within them) in the continuation of English history at the end of the roll; I have elected to
       refer to the prose passages in the genealogical continuation as "paragraphs."

75   According to Laborderie, in the great majority of cases, the genealogies in roll form do
       not take up the history of the Britons from the age of Brutus, but rather begin with the
       period of the early English Heptarchy (AD 500–85) (*Histoire, mémoire et pouvoir*, 200).
       Many are made up of prose passages, but at least one other contains verse: College of
       Arms roll 20/2. Since I have not seen this roll, and thus it is not clear to me how much
       verse it contains – though it apparently contains the standard prologue of the *Livere de
       Reis de Brittanie*, excerpts from Nicholas Trevet's *Cronicles*, lines from Wace's *Brut*, and
       a fragment of the Royal *Brut* – it will not be discussed in this study; see Di Lella, "Il *Roll
       Brut* (prima parte)," 40. John Spence reports that 20/2 "contains a full account of British
       history in Anglo-Norman prose from a separate textual tradition"; as of the publication of

424   CHAPTER 6

author was using) and to Wace (which the author may have been using)[76] – the lacunae are too numerous to list here since they often consist of 2–5 lines – the anonymous *Brut*'s narrative runs from Locrinus's and Kamber's vengeance of Albanacus, who had been defeated by Humber, king of the Huns, and the latter's death in the river which bears his name, to Merlin's prediction to Uther that he would have a son who would be victorious over France and beyond. Thus, this text, like the seven other anonymous verse *Brut*s (not counting those which only have Merlin's Prophecies) contains no post-Arthurian material and in this case, in fact, no Arthurian material whatever.[77]

Structurally, the narrative of the anonymous *Brut* on the CA roll contains unusual features (with respect to other anonymous verse texts, that is, though not necessarily with respect to genealogical rolls), such as its beginning with a diagram of the Heptarchy, the sparse summation of vulgate §§5–22, the interspersal of prose among the octosyllabic verses, such as the passage on King Leir

---

    his study, Spence had also not seen MS (roll) 20/2 (*Reimagining History in Anglo-Norman Prose Chronicles*, York: York Medieval Press, 2013, 14 and n. 68).

76   The anonymous verse *Brut* redactor may indeed have had a version of Wace to hand, as the fragment of Wace's *Brut* on the roll's dorse suggests, but also the fact that the anonymous text contains some Wace lines included following the narrative of Ebraucus and his progeny: Wace's lines 1597–1670 – though missing lines 1615–16, 1621–26, 1632, 1635–36, 1639–42, and 1663–66 – which recount the reigns of Leil, Ruhundibraz, Bladud, and the start of Leir's reign, preceding the condensed prose section on Leir and his daughters. See Ian Short, "Un *Roman de Brut* anglo-normand inédit," 274 and n. 5, and also Di Lella, "Il *Roll Brut* (prima parte)," 43. Short also observes that a significant number of the Wace variants in the copy on the roll resemble elements in *Roman de Brut* MS. P (BL Additional 45103) (274, n. 4).

77   While it might appear that a genealogy and its commentary continue on the reverse side, beginning with a barely legible rondel of Arthur, the material is actually extracts from Wace's *Brut*, beginning with the lines 9059–65 (ed. Arnold), that is, Uther's death, up through 13675–80 – how the English had no crowned king after Gormund's departure (Laborderie, "Ligne de Reis," 1080–121). The Wace text is followed by prose sections, beginning with Gormund's death, the Pentarchy, up through a mention of the reign of Henry III's first son, Edward I (see Appendix 1 below); Gormund's death is not narrated either in the Galfridian tradition or by Wace (perhaps the CA redactor confused this Gormund with Harthacanute's son of the same name in Rauf de Boun's *Petit Bruit*?; on Harthacanute's [Hardknout's] son, see John Spence, *Reimagining History in Anglo-Norman Prose Chronicles*, 89). Interestingly, anonymous verse fragments Harley 4733 and Takamiya 115 begin roughly where the Wace section on the verso of College of Arms 12/45A does: that is, with the end of §142, the death of Uther, and §143, the (non-ceremonial) coronation of Arthur. An examination of Harley 4733 and Takamiya 115 which correspond roughly (at times very roughly) to Wace ll. 9005–9274 (the former more extensively than the latter) suggests that neither fragment was based on Wace, though their similarities to each other suggest that they could have been based on the same – as yet unknown/unidentified – poem.

THE ANONYMOUS VERSE BRUT TRADITION 425

and his daughters or that of Cassibellanus, making it an atypical text, if only for its mixture of media, as it were.[78] A selection of the more important of these narrative features will be analyzed here, in addition to the narrative of the *adventus Saxonum*, and CA's inclusion of the opening of Merlin's Prophecies toward the end of the fragment, to give a sense of the movement of the text, and suggest some of the redactor's possible motivations in presenting such a diverse production. In addition, the way in which CA's anonymous *Brut* ends around line 8338 of Wace and then the reverse of the roll picks up very soon after with Wace's line 9059, concluding with prose continuations, a genealogical text up to the reign of Henry III's first son, Edward I, suggests the possibility that the entire roll was meant not as a collection of "random" texts but as a unified history of England in French, from Brutus – very sketchily – through Edward I, including Arthur's reign supplied by the Wace *Brut* text – though with many lacunae.[79] Some of the more outstanding of the Wace lacunae will also be discussed briefly at the end of this section.

The narrative of the roll opens with a pictorial representation of the Heptarchy (roundels), accompanied by short commentaries explaining the locations of the different regions, followed by a longer prose commentary:

[P]ar ceste figure desus, l'en poet savoyr les divers regnes ke furent jadis en Engleterre. E si fait a savoyr[80] ke Engletere est bellonge. E si poet l'en savoyr par ceste figure [coment] les regnes furent assis, c'est a savoyr[81] li queus devers le este e li queus devers le vest, et li queus devers le north, et li queus devers le suth. Car ele est asise entre le north e le vest, des queus ele receit tote sa temperance, c'est a savoyr du vest chalur e du north freidure. E por ceo Engleterre, kie jadis fu apele Bretaigne la Majour[82] por

---

78   On the more typical and less typical structural components of this roll with respect to other genealogical rolls, see below n. 86, in addition to n. 77 above.

79   Short confirms that it is the same redactor, or at the least, that the roll was copied by the same scribe: "Le tout, décoré de diagrammes et de médaillons rouges, bleus et dorés qui parsèment les deux textes, et copié à longues lignes, est écrit de la même main" (274). I must leave to future researchers the fascinating questions which will inevitably be raised by the prospect of this roll as a unified effort to trace English/British history, rather than a collection of "random" texts.

80   John Spence notes that "Anglo-Norman prose chronicles announce key facts by prefacing them with "Fait assavoir" (*Reimagining History*, 6), which I have translated as "let it be known," but it can also read "we know."

81   "That is to say" (Spence, *Reimagining History*, 6).

82   On this unusual usage, see Stefan Jurasinski, "Andrew Horn, Alfredian Apocrypha, and the Anglo-Saxon Names of the *Mirror of Justices*," *The Journal of English and Germanic Philology* 105.4 (2006): 540–63, pp. 549 and 559.

426 CHAPTER 6

le nun du primer habitur, ke avoit a nun Bruto, quant les gyans furent vencuz, de totes ylles c'est la plus benoite. Ore fait a dire de Bruto e de son poer ke conquistrent Engleterre sur les gyanz e coment il urent primerement seignurie en Engleterre.

Through the drawing above, one can learn about the different regions that made up England at that time. And let it be known that England was oblong/oval. And one can know by means of this drawing how the different regions were placed, that is to say, which were on the east and which on the west, and which on the north, and which on the south. For she [England] is situated toward the north and the west, from which she gets all her moderate temperatures, warmth from the west, and cold from the north. And for this reason, England, which was called "Britannia Major" from the name of its first inhabitant, who was named Brutus, when the giants were conquered; of all the isles, it is the most blessed. Now we will talk about Brutus who conquered England against the giants and how they [the Britons] first had dominion over England.[83]

This commentary is followed by a rubric – *Icestui Brutus conquist Engleterre sur les VII gyants* – which is puzzling and may be a unique reference to specifically seven giants who had inhabited the island before the arrival of the Trojans (Britons).[84]

Immediately following this short prose commentary is the prologue proper:

[Q]uatre mil e trentedous anz après ke Deu avoit le mund crié e Adam e Eve, e mil e dous cens anz avant ke Jesu Crist nasqui en Bethleem de gloriouse virgine seynte Marie, le avant dit Brut, le filz Silve, vint de la bataille de Troye, a ky Pandrasie, le roy de Grece, avoit sa fille, Ynnogen a nun, doné a femme, si ariva en Deveneshyre, a Totenesse, od CCC e XXIII nefs.[85] En tote Engleteerre ne en Escoce ne en Wales ne esteit homme ne femme for VII gyanz, e lur mestre fu apelé Gogmagog, ke Corne, uncle Brut, ocist, e les autres tuz s'en fuirent. Brut de sun nun l'ylle apela Bretaigne e ses compagnuns Bretuns. Sur Tamise fist la ville des Lundres, si l'apela Novele Troie. En ceu tens fu Hely le prestre juges des Jeus en la Terre Seynte. Brut engendra de Innogen, a femme, la fille Pandrasii, rei

---

83 The translations are my own.

84 This specific reference in the italicized line (a rubricated line within in a roundel or hollow circle? See n. 86 below) and in the text to seven giants remains elusive.

85 324 ships, vulgate §16. 267, Totnes as the arrival spot §21.452.

THE ANONYMOUS VERSE BRUT TRADITION 427

de Grece treis filz. Le nun du premer : Locryn ; li autre : Albanac ; li tierz : Kamber. E regna Brutus en Engleterre, en Escoce e en Wales xxiiii anz e morut e fu enterré a Londres.[86]

[F]our thousand and thirty two years after God created the world and Adam and Eve, and one thousand two hundred years before the birth of Jesus Christ in Bethlehem from the glorious Virgin Holy Mary, the aforesaid Brutus, the son of Silvius,[87] came from the battle of Troy where Pandrasus, king of Greece, had given his daughter named Immogen to

---

86   In Laborderie's transcription, following the two italicized lines (one made up of three phrases separated by slashes and the other independent) – "*Icestui Locryn fu son primer filz. / Albanak fu son autre filz. / Kamber fu son tierz fils*" and "*Locrin regna après son pere Brutus*" – are two lines also in prose which Short includes at the end of the prologue: "Aprés les treis filz Brut les reaumes entre eus partirent: Locryn aveit tut Engleterre, Albanac, Escoce, Kamber, Wales. [Q]uant le regne urent partiz, mult prant piece regn-erent e bien s'entreamerent" (ed., 278; "After the three sons of Brutus divided the kingdom among themselves: Locrin had all of England, Albanacus, Scotland, Kamber, and Wales. [W]hen they had divided the realm, they reigned for a long time and loved each other well"). Without the last two lines, the prologue covers vulgate §§16–22; the dividing of Brutus's kingdom among his sons occurs in §23. I am grateful to John Spence for hav-ing shared with me (in a private communication) the possibility that the italicized lines in Laborderie's transcription of ca, either separated by slashes in clusters or standing independently, may represent phrases associated with roundels as seen in Laborderie's article on the Schøyen roll (among others), or as seen in the Chaworth roll (Olivier de Laborderie, "Les généalogies des rois d'Angleterre sur rouleaux manuscrits (milieu xiiie siècle–début xve siècle). Conception, diffusion et fonctions," in *La généalogie entre sci-ence et passion*, ed. Tiphaine Barthelemy and Marie-Claude Pingaud, Paris, Éditions du Comité des Travaux Historiques et Scientifiques, 1997, 181–99; Alixe Bovey, *The Chaworth Roll: A Fourteenth-Century Genealogy of the Kings of England*, London: Sam Fogg, 2005; the latter source contains beautifully reproduced photos of that roll (functioning as both a study and an exhibition catalogue of the Chaworth Roll, 3–24 March 2005), providing an excellent idea of the appearance of highly illuminated genealogical rolls). However, ca 12/45 A may well be atypical with respect to its manner of illustration; that is, at times, instead of always filling roundels in its genealogical trees with colored or gilded figures or faces, with writing around the borders of individual roundels, the "circles" are filled with rubricated phrases, with colors around the borders (but not words), as seen in the black-and-white reproduction of membrane 3 recto of 12/45 A, on p. 66 of Di Lella's "Il *Roll Brut* (prima parte)." Since I have been unable to see the roll myself (as noted above), Dr. Di Lella has kindly reiterated for me (in a private communication) the nature of the italicized lines in Laborderie's transcription (at least with reference to the first text): "les lignes en italique ... représentent les textes (rubriqués) qui se trouvent à l'intérieur des cercles rouges et verts qui composent l'arbre généalogique. Le texte de la généalogie est copié tout autour de cet arbre."

87   There is no indication whether this is Silvius, son of Ascanius, or Silvius Postumus, half-brother of Ascanius.

428   CHAPTER 6

wife, arrived in Devonshire, at Totnes, with 324 ships. In all of England, nor in Scotland, nor in Wales was there a man or a woman except for seven giants, whose leader was called Gogmagog, whom Corineus, Brutus's uncle, killed and all the others fled. Brutus called the island Britain after his own name, and his companions he called Britons. On the Thames he founded the city of London, which was called New Troy. At that time, Helius was high priest of the Jews in the Holy Land. Brutus had with Innogen, his wife, the daughter of Pandrasus, king of Greece three sons. The name of the first one: Locrin; the other: Albanac; the third: Kamber. And Brutus reigned in England, in Scotland and in Wales 24 years and died and was buried in London.

It is as if the "pre-prologue" substitutes for the description of Britain in Galfridian §5 – with no explanation of how the English Heptarchy came to stand in for either the Bedan or Galfridian version in this sort of a text on the Britons, as if the Heptarchy had become standard in thirteenth century genealogies and was thus expected, even as an introduction to material on the Britons, which apparently, in some cases it had. In fact, John Spence notes that "Anglo-Norman prose chronicles can appear uncertain how to handle Anglo-Saxon history with its multiple, warring kingdoms rather than a unified England. The earliest Anglo-Norman prose chronicle of English kings does not begin until after the unification of these kingdoms. ..." He continues that "in almost all the complete surviving manuscripts of [the] roll-chronicles, the approach taken is to preface the narrative with a circular diagram representing the Heptarchy."[88] Although CA 12/45A is not strictly a prose chronicle in its entirety, it does appear to be following this model of opening with a pictorial representation of the Heptarchy.

The prologue proper is also striking in its tremendous haste, that is, covering Galfridian sections 5–22 in one paragraph. It is worth noting that Aeneas is never mentioned, although Pandrasus is; the foundation myth is breezed through in record fashion, ending with the foundation of New Troy, the division of the island among Brutus's sons, and the king's death and burial in London.

In the roughly 90 verses which follow (with a few lines of prose interspersed), the author races through the reign of Locrinus, his choice of his wife Estrild and the anger of his intended father-in-law Corineus, whose daughter he scorned, and he reigns of Maddan and Mallyn. Ebrauc (Ebraucus) follows; the narrative of names of his progeny is in prose, with 20 sons named but only 21 daughters, rather than naming 20 sons and 30 daughters. Leil succeeds Brutus

88   *Reimagining History in Anglo-Norman Prose Chronicles*, 76.

THE ANONYMOUS VERSE BRUT TRADITION 429

Greenshield, Ruhundibraz after Bladud, with Leir after Bladud. The narrative of Leir and his daughters is very condensed into one long prose paragraph (approximately 400 words),[89] with a return to verse for Leir's interactions with Cordelia (around 40 lines), and three lines of prose for his speech to Cordelia. CA give the essential "facts" of the Leir narrative, without drama, but also without implications for Britain or the Britons.

5.3.2   Comparative Study of Cassibellanus (Geoffrey, Wace, Royal, and CA)

Following the king lists after the mention of Cordelia's reign, the most substantial section is on Cassibellanus (the reigning king of the Britons at the time of Julius Caesar's arrival), a prose passage of approximately 900 words. CA's choice of details is most unusual, especially in comparison with Geoffrey (§§53.381–64.268, Cassibellaunus), Wace (3791–4840, Cassibellan), and Royal (2167–2946, multiple spellings), the latter which is distinguished by its tendency to condense (but here the section is only 300 lines shorter than in Wace).

In Geoffrey, some of the most outstanding features are:

1.   After Julius Caesar conquers Gaul, he arrives in Flanders, and covets Britain, rationalizing that the Romans and Britons share a common ancestry (§54);

2.   Caesar sends a letter to Cassibellanus, demanding tribute (§54) and Cassibelanus replies, refusing (§55);

3.   Caesar arrives, and Cassibellanus and the Britons triumph after much bloodshed (§56);

4.   Cassibellanus rejoices, Caesar retreats, but two years later, tries again (§§57–60);

5.   Cassibellanus rejoices this second time, holds celebratory festivities, during which his nephew, Hirelglas, is beheaded by Androgeus's son following an insult match (§61);

6.   Androgeus (one of Lud's sons and thus another of Cassibellanus's nephews) goes to Caesar, begging to be defended against Cassibelanus who is raging (§61);

7.   In another battle, Caesar corners Cassibellanus trying to starve him and his troops out and Cassibellanus now begs Androgeus to reconcile him to Caesar, "lest his capture should dishonour the race to which they both

---

89   It is not completely clear whether Short has included the passages which appear in prose form (then possibly converted them to poetic lines) in his approximate count of 2500 lines.

430   CHAPTER 6

belonged" (§62.232–33; "ne dignitas gentis ex qua natus fuerat capto ipso deleretur");

8. Androgeus tells Caesar that his revenge is complete, and begs for leniency for Cassibelanus; Caesar agrees, accepting a yearly tribute of three thousand pounds of silver (§63); Cassibellanus reigns seven more years and is buried at York.

Wace follows Geoffrey closely, with some notable changes:

1. When Caesar is first introduced, Weiss notes, "Wace extends the panegyric of Julius Caesar, whom he sees as an ideal ruler, though he mistakenly thinks he became emperor";[90] earlier, I had called this type of description "reflex praise," or "automatic praise for a famous figure," which in my view differs from panegyric since it has no function – i.e., no hope of gain – outside the text;[91]

2. In the passage where Caesar remarks that the Romans and the Britons come from the same stock, Wace inserts a pro-Briton point about Belinus and Brennius, having Caesar state that they grew so powerful that they took the city of Rome and destroyed the Senate (3877–80), rather than as in Geoffrey where Caesar states that the Britons have degenerated and are no longer the Romans' equals ("degenerate sunt a nobis"), having forgotten how to be soldiers (§54.9–10); thus in the vulgate, Caesar is seen to reassert Rome's dominion without showing any recognition of any historical weakness whatever;

3. Wace gets a dig in against the French, about whom he says that when hearing that the Britons had routed the Romans the first time, they "mult haeient leur seinurie / E cremeient lur felonie" (4157–58; "hated very much their domination and feared their cruelty") but when they spoke with Caesar, their "arrogance" ended since Caesar "was good at taming evil-doers and restraining the arrogant" (4163–66; "Mais l'orguil as

---

90 Weiss, trans., p. 99, n. 1.

91 "For Geoffrey, Julius Caesar is first an enemy of the British people and second the famed Roman general. Caesar receives no praise from Geoffrey, yet he does from Wace. This praise does not carry the same weight as praise found in panegyric since it serves no purpose outside the text; rather, it simply acts as a point of information" and "This description [3833–42] filled with superlatives is not intended to make Caesar a sympathetic figure, thereby drawing the reader's sympathy away from the Britons whom Caesar was striving to enslave. Rather it represents an automatic response on the author's part to clothe a famous figure in terms which were becoming characteristic of descriptions of heroes in twelfth-century Old French narrative poetry: *vaillanz* (worthy), *pruz* (noble), *savies* (usually *sage*, wise), and *de grant chevalerie* (having a great army or possessed of chivalric qualities or both). These terms serve here as a means of identification, not as a means of persuasion" (*Faces of Time*, 97–98, 1994).

THE ANONYMOUS VERSE BRUT TRADITION   431

Franceis fina / Des que Cesar od els parla. / Cesar sout bien felun danter / E orguillus amesurer");

4. Caesar builds the tower of Ordre (not found in the *Historia*), though later in §60, Caesar retreats to a tower at Odnea;[92]

5. During the last battle, Wace adds a reference to the wheel of Fortune which this time had turned against the Britons, and thus, Cassibellanus was forced to beg Androgeus to reconcile him with Caesar;

6. Before Caesar leaves Britain, he founds Exeter (4826); not in Geoffrey.

In Royal:

1. The flattering description of Caesar from Wace is absent, however his conquests are listed, though he is not an emperor here;

2. Cassibellanus has a "conestable" ("chief officer of the household/ governor") named Belinus, but this is not a nod to Caesar's reference to Belinus and Brennius in Wace;

3. The festivities after Cassibellanus's first victory are expanded, with a great number of cattle and sheep sacrificed (2584–2604);

4. More "courtly" language is used to describe the Britons' suffering at the third battle;[93]

5. Caesar leaves Britain, without founding Exeter.

In CA:

1. The circumstances which explain why Caesar is coming to Britain are absent, that is, virtually all of points 1–4 above in Geoffrey are missing; the third sentence simply states "[C]assibellian enjeta Julius Cesar, empereur de Rome, fors de Engleterre dous fiez" ("Cassibellanus threw Julius Caesar, emperor of Rome, out of England twice");

2. The bulk of the passage is devoted to the murder of Cassibellanus's nephew by Androgeus's son and how that family feud is ultimately resolved through Caesar's intervention; and the third battle which ensues between Caesar – sought by Androgeus – and Cassibellanus ends in Caesar's favor;

3. The letter from Androgeus to Caesar is the longest "speech" thus far in the CA text;

4. On the third day of the battle, Cassibellanus is being starved out, and Androgeus goes to plead to Caesar – this time, Androgeus makes a speech

---

92 See Arnold II, 800, Houck, *Sources*, 216, and Weiss, 102 n. 2 on the tower of Ordre (lighthouse, tour d'Ordre at Boulogne-sur-Mer) created by Caligula and restored by Charlemagne.

93 The Royal narrator exclaims, "Ahi! Quel dol de chevaler, / De gentil rei, de bon guerrer ... E or trestut en fuiant / Est tant pruz e tant vaillant ... Li plus hardiz en out pour" (2823–24, 2827–28, 2834; "Ai! what knightly sorrow about the noble king, good warriors ... And now all are fleeing so worthy, and so valiant ... [even] the most bold are afraid").

432   CHAPTER 6

> in person rather than sending a message; he addresses Caesar as "Sire
> empereur"; when Caesar doesn't respond, Androgeus makes another
> speech, offering tribute if Caesar lets Cassibellanus and his troops live;
> Caesar accepts the covenant.

This passage contains the most direct address of any in CA, and perhaps is
meant to act as an example of "courtly" interaction, and resolution of family
disputes, though at quite a cost – the Britons' subjugation – though they are
not forced into serfdom. Nonetheless, what may be most important here is that
CA leaves out the Romans' rationale for subjugating the Britons, and details of
the Britons' victories before the final capitulation, leaving Caesar as ultimate
victor without any demonstration of the Romans' greed and lust for power, as
in Geoffrey's *Historia*.

5.3.3   Hengist and Horsa

Annalistic as it is, CA does contain a passage (in verse) on the arrival of Hengist
and Horsa in three longboats. They are characterized as "bels bacheliers," echoing Wace's comment on their handsome appearance, though not nearly as fulsomely: "With their well-built bodies, and shining faces; they were taller and
more handsome than all the other youths" (Wace, 6724–26; "As cors bien faiz,
as faces cleres, / Ki plus grant erent e plus bel / Que tuit li altre juvencel").[94]
They say they come offering their service, though the story of how, when the
population grows too big at home, the fittest are sent away to seek their fame
and fortune elsewhere (§98.259–70) as told in in Geoffrey and Wace (6740–66),
does not appear in CA. As in the *Historia*, Vortigern expresses sorrow that they
are not Christians, but enlists their aid in helping him deal with the Picts
nonetheless.

CA does slip in the comment that when Hengist heard that which he desired
("[Q]uant Henges oi ceo qu'il desire") – as if that had been the brothers' plan all
along – he flatters Vortigern, agreeing to offer help:

"Beals sire rois, vous le verrez	"Fair lord, king, you will see
Si tost cum mester averez	As soon as you will have need [of us]
Cum voz enemis veincerum[95]	How we will defeat your enemies
E cum por vous combaterum."	And how we will fight for you."

---

94   See also Chapter 5, n. 50.

95   Laborderie has "veincerunt (?)" indicating doubt as to the third person plural "veince-
       runt." "Veincerum" would appear more logical, not only because the first person plural
       form corresponds to "combaterum" as couplets in CA are either rhymed or assonanced,
       but also because the meaning corresponds to the Galfridian material, although in
       Geoffrey, Hengist does not openly promise to conquer Vortigern's enemies, but that is in

THE ANONYMOUS VERSE BRUT TRADITION   433

The Saxons defeat the Picts in short order. Vortigern gives them the castle they asked for – Swangcastre[96] – and encourages them to send for reinforcements from Germany. Eighteen ships arrive, including Hengist's daughter Rowen (Ronwen). The "Wasshail/Drinkhail" passage is reproduced faithfully, with Vortigern giving Hengist Kent as a wedding gift for his permission to marry Ronwen. As in other texts, the Britons grow to mistrust the Saxons since so many arrive; in the vulgate and Wace, "soon the number of pagans went up so much, intermingling with the Christians, that one hardly knew who was a Christian and who wasn't" (7063–66); the vulgate goes further to state that the intermingling was against Christian law.[97] In CA, there are no references to undesirable – or unlawful – intermingling; the Britons ask Vortimer to throw the Saxons out, because they are getting no results from Vortigern, since the

---

    effect what happens early on in the relationship between the Briton king and the Saxons (§98.295–98).

96   *HRB*: "dictum nameque fuit postmodum Britannice Kaercarrei, Saxonice uero Thancastre, quod Latino sermone Castrum Coirrigiae appellamus" (§99.335–37; "for it was later called in British Kaercarrei, and in English Thancastre, or Castrum Corrigiae in Latin"). Wace elaborates, never wishing to miss an etymological description, even if, as he admits, he doesn't know all the reasons:

Cest nun Thwancastre li ad mis	He [Hengist] gave it the name Thwancastre
En language de sun païs.	In the language of his land
Thwancastre* sun nun del quir prent	Thongcaster takes its name from the [bull's] hide
Sil puet l'um numer altrement	One can call it otherwise
Chastel de cureie en rumanz,	Castle of the "cureie" in French
Kaër Carreï en bretanz,	"Kaër Carreï" in British,
Pur ço que li fu mesurez	Because it was measured
Od la curreie e compassez. (6917–24)	And marked out with the thong. (6917–24)
Premierement ot nun Thwancastre	It was first called Thwangcaster;
Or l'apelent plusurs Lancastre	Now many call it Lancaster.
Si ne sevent pas l'achaisun	They don't know the reason
Dunt Thwancastre ot primes cest nun.	That it first had the name Thwancaster.

    *Arnold prints in the variants that both of his base manuscripts P and D have "Wancastre" everywhere the name of the castle appears (I, p. 367: l. 6917 "*PD* Wancastre partout"). The lines in italics are noted by Weiss (174, n. 6), to the effect that MSS PHKRN have four more lines omitted by Arnold as an interpolation, though they appear with his text as variants, with slight differences from what appears here (ed., I, 367 and see also I, xliv; the most significant variant among these four lines which themselves are variants is in N which has "De Wancastre ot pris cest nun" for the fourth line). According to Arnold, *Thwangcestre* was the medieval name for Caistor, near Grimsby (ed., II, 804–5, n. to l. 6917) (Weiss, trans., 175, n. 1). See also Chapter 5, n. 43 above.

97   See Chapter 3, nn. 63–64.

434   CHAPTER 6

latter does not want to alienate the Saxons on account of his wife. Vortimer defeats the Saxons and gives Gorangone "his earldom/county" ("sa conté") back, and to others their lands as well.[98]

The remainder of the narrative involving Hengist and Horsa follows the general outline of the vulgate, without omission of major points: Vortigern reigns again after Ronwen has Vortimer poisoned; Vortigern and the Saxons plan for a May Day assembly to arrange a peace. The events which ensue – Hengist's plot for his men to come armed to the meeting while the Britons are unarmed, leads to the episode that is commonly called the "Night of the long knives" where the Saxons hide knives in their boots and draw them at the secret cry, "Nimez ut oure saxas"! According to CA, the Saxons kill three thousand and sixty Britons – Geoffrey has around ("circiter") four hundred and sixty (§104.470), FV the same as the vulgate (§104.3), and Wace four hundred and sixty as well (7256–57); Vortigern flees into Wales.

CA gives no mention of the Saxons having threatened Vortigern until he gave them what they wanted, and that then they proceeded to take York, Lincoln, and Winchester, laying waste to all regions as in *HRB* (§105.494–95); this does not mean however, that CA is a pro-Saxon text, while it is true that it certainly does not convey Geoffrey's animosity to the Saxons, even when the narrative is "fairly faithful." Wace provides a fuller account than CA, which is not surprising, given the latter's tendency to annalistic narration: that Vortigern gives the Saxons London, Winchester, Lincoln, York, and Chichester, and in order to have himself released from the ransom and prison, he gives them in fee Sussex, Essex, and Middlesex, because, Wace says, those lands adjoined Kent which Vortigern had given to Hengist previously.[99]

---

98   Gorangonus in the vulgate, count of Kent (§100.364). Wace omits this reference.
99   Typical of Wace, he opens a parentheses here to explain the etymology of the suffix "sex" as it was the English word for knives (7297–7309). He goes on to explain that in order to forget the ignominy of this treachery, the English changed their words for "knives" so that the names of the regions would not serve as a reminder (7303–08). According to Weiss, it is MS. P which adds Vortigern's gift of Sussex, Essex, and Middlesex, and the false etymological link, MSS J and H omitting the gift as well as the false etymology, and F the false etymology (185, n. 1); however, Arnold's variants would indicate that a significant number of MSS (DLCSFAGT) are missing rather the gift of the cities (7289–90), and not the gift of Sussex, Essex, and Middlesex (Arnold, I, 386). Even if the gift of the regions and the false etymology are a minority reading with respect to the MSS of the *Brut*, the story of this ransom is also found in the *Historia Brittonum*, Essex and Sussex in an earlier version, with Middlesex added later (Morris, ed., §46, p. 73), and may have also been circulating in Welsh lore (Williams, I., "GWRTHEYRN (VORTIGERN)," *Dictionary of Welsh Biography*.

THE ANONYMOUS VERSE BRUT TRADITION

5.3.4 Vortigern's Search for Merlin, Opening of the Prophecies

The last unusual feature of CA to be discussed here is the fairly complete narrative of how Vortigern finds Merlin in order to learn how to repair his tower and make it stand, and the subsequent inclusion of the opening section of Merlin's Prophecies, in octosyllabic couplets (vulgate §112.34–39):[100]

"Way al chaitif ruge dragun,	"Woe to the wretched red dragon,
Car pres est sa confusion.	For its destruction is nigh.
Li blans draguns sa fosse averad	The white will take over its lair
E fors del estanc le mettrad.	And put the red out of the pond.
Li blans les Saisnes signifie,	The white signifies the Saxons,
Que preistes en compaignie,	Whom you brought into [our] midst,
E li chaitif ruge draguns	And the wretched red dragon
Cil signifie les Bretuns."[101]	Signifies the Britons."

8 lines of 20

Retrieved 28 Mar 2020, from https://biography.wales/article/s-GWRT-HEY-0400). See also Chapter 5, nn. 47–48.

100   Except for the aspect of impersonal expression mentioned below in n. 101 which CA has in common with the alexandrine version of the Anglo-Norman verse prophecies as represented in the Lincoln manuscript, the fragment of the Prophecies in CA does not resemble the decasyllabic or alexandrine versions closely enough either lexicographically or morphologically to suggest that it was copied from any of those witnesses; in addition to the edited texts themselves, see also the critical apparatus in *Anglo-Norman Verse Prophecies*, ed. and trans. Blacker, 73–96. The previously only known extant octosyllabic witness to the Prophecies, London, BL Additional 48212.O, only contains §116.33–42, that is, the narrative from the awakening of the Daneian forest to the heron's three eggs, and thus does not provide any direct evidence from the opening of the text that CA's version could have been derived from that witness (which was not edited with the decasyllabic and alexandrine versions). However, that there are now two known witnesses to an octosyllabic vernacular verse Prophecies text – BL Additional 48212.O and CA – suggests that there may have been a complete octosyllabic version at one time.

101   Although I have translated "compagnie" in CA as "into [our] midst" (assuming an understood pronoun), in the aspect of their impersonal expression, these few verses in CA resemble more closely the alexandrine version of the Anglo-Norman verse Prophecies as represented by the Lincoln manuscript, rather than the decasyllabic version as represented by the Durham manuscript (*Anglo-Norman Verse Prophecies*). Durham refers to "we" and "us," as if the narrator identifies with the Britons, though no such identification is made openly for Merlin by Geoffrey (§112.34–37):

"Guaiment e dolur al ruge dragun,	"Woe and sorrow to the Red Dragon,
Car mult haste sa destructiun.	For its destruction is nigh.
E ses cavernes purprendrat li blancs,	The White will take over its caves,
Ki signifie Engleis e Alemans	Which means the Angles and the Alemans

436   CHAPTER 6

In CA, when Merlin has finished this short explanation of the red and white
dragons, Vortigern asks to have his death foretold. Merlin obliges, explaining to
Vortigern that the sons of Constantine will exact their revenge, leaving Brittany
("la Bretayne Petite") seeking to regain Britain ("Bretaine le Grant"); Aurelius
and Uther will come, and in the end both will die of poison. Although CA adds:
"Mais li senglers de Cornwaille / Les devorad par sa bataille" ("But the boar of
Cornwall will devour them through its battle"), it neglects to say that it is the
traitors that the Boar of Cornwall will devour. One only learns that from Wace:

"Ses fiz, ki iert de Cornoaille,   "His son, who will come from
                                              Cornwall,

Cum senglers fiers en bataille,   As a boar fierce in battle,
Les traïturs devurera   Will devour the traitors
E tuz tes parens destruira;   And will destroy all of your relatives;
Cil sera mult vailllanz e pruz,   He will be very brave and noble,
Ses enemis conquerra tuz."   He will conquer all his enemies."

    (WACE, *Brut*, 7577–82)

E les Sednes ki sunt attrait par vus.   And the Saxons, who have been brought
                                              here by you.
Li ruges draguns signifie *nus*   The Red Dragon signifies *us*
Ki de Bretaine major sumes né   Who were born in Great Britain;
Li blancs destreindrat *nostre* parenté ..." The White will destroy *our* lineage ..."
       (Durham, 1–8) (emphasis added)

However, in the vulgate, Merlin does say to Vortigern, addressing him directly, "the Saxons
whom *you* have summoned" (§112.35), and that is repeated in CA, but not in Lincoln
which has the third person, less personal, "the king" ("Li blancs, ceo sunt la Seisne que *li
reis* mandad"):

"Guai al ruge dragun, quar sa destructiuns   "Woe to the red dragon, for its destruction
Est tute apparailliee, e preste la saison.   Is all prepared, and near is its time,
Les fosses des vermail, li blancs les   The pits of the red, the white will besiege
purprendrad: them:
Li blancs, ceo sunt la Seine que li reis   The white are the Saxons whom the king
mandad,   summoned,
Li ruges, li Bretun, que li blancs   The red, the Britons, whom the white will
prendrad ..."   take ..."
         (Lincoln, 1–5)

See *ANP*, p. 33 for Durham (with translation), and p. 59 for Lincoln (here the translation is
mine, but the edition does not contain a translation of Lincoln, only of Durham). In light
of research done for the present book, it would also be possible to translate Durham's
ll. 4–5 as "Which means the English and the Germans / And the Saxons ..." In this introductory prophecy of the red and white dragons under Vortigern's castle, Geoffrey only has
"Saxons" (§112.35) as does the FV.

THE ANONYMOUS VERSE BRUT TRADITION 437

In addition, CA neglects to mention however, that the boar is Uther's son; Wace does mention this fact, but he does not use the name Arthur, who was traditionally associated with the savior Boar of Cornwall.[102] Following Merlin's prophecy of Vortigern's end, roughly 500 lines cover the reign of Aurelius, the burning of Vortigern in his tower, Aurelius's battle against Hengist and the latter's defeat and death,[103] the moving of the stones to Stonehenge, Paschent's plot against Aurelius (in, Wace, 8241–84), Aurelius's death and Uther's ascent to the throne. Merlin comforts Uther at the loss of his brother, that he must fight his enemies.

5.3.5 Ending of CA's Anonymous Verse *Brut*

CA is not clear at the end as parts of lines are missing, particularly in its reference to France, where Merlin explains the appearance of a comet to Uther:

"Ne vous signifie ceste esteile	"This star means you[104]
Que devant vous ne seile (?).	Which before you does not hide itself.
E li draguns k'ist de desuz	And the dragon which comes out on top
Cil vous fait reis sur nous tuz.	He will make you king over us all.
Li draguns qui si est ardans	The dragon which is so keen
Mustre que vous serrez [...]	Shows that you will be [...]
Lais que s'en turne vers France	There where it turns toward France
A Deu sei signefiance	God will know the meaning
[...]" [105]	[...]"

---

102 Vulgate §118.20–21, the Boar will devour Vortigern's progeny who "will have a share in this treason," i.e., the murders of both Uther and Aurelius.

103 Octa's beseeching Aurelius for mercy upon his father's death would appear to be omitted.

104 Rather than remove the negative particle "Ne" as an emendation, I have chosen not to translate it, since in terms of the meaning of the passage, I find it unlikely that the author/scribe thought the star did *not* refer to Uther.

105 Laborderie has "lais" rather than "Lais." Here, CA may have been trying to echo the vulgate: in Geoffrey, regarding the comet, "the ray that extends over France foretells that you will have a most powerful son, whose might shall possess all the kingdoms beneath it; the other ray indicates a daughter, whose sons and grandsons will rule Britain in turn" (§133.369–72; "Radius autem qui uersus Gallicanam plagam porrigitur portendit tibi filium futurum et potentissimum, cuius potestas omnia regna quae protegit habebit; alter uero radius significat filiam, cuius filii et nepotes regnum Britanniae succedenter habebunt"). CA however does not have many of the pertinent details including those of the sons and daughter.

438 CHAPTER 6

However, if one looks to Wace again for clarification, he takes up the relay, as it were, and expands upon this passage, particularly with respect to Uther's son's conquests:

"Li uns des rais, ço est uns fiz	"One of the rays [of the star], that's a son
Que tu avras, de grant puissance,	You will have, of great strength,
Ki conquerra jesq'ultre France;	Who will conquer up to and beyond France;
Par l'altre rai, ki ça turna,	By the other ray, as it turned,
E en set rais se devisa,	And split into seven rays,
T'est une fille demustree,	Is meant that you will have a daughter,
Ki vers Escoce ert mariee.	Who will marry in Scotland.
Plusurs bon eir de li naistrunt	Many good heirs will be born from her
Qui mers e terres conquerunt."	Who will conquer seas and lands."
(WACE, *Brut*, 8336–44)	

Wace's version implies foreign conquests for the progeny of Uther's future daughter, certainly more so than Geoffrey's whose version prophesies dominion over Britain, but not necessarily beyond.

5.3.6   Introduction to Incomplete Copy of Wace's *Brut*, and Summary of
          Remainder of Dorse

Here, CA's anonymous *Brut* leaves off; one turns to the dorse of the roll, the redactor/scribe adding a rondel of Arthur and what is now a barely legible accompanying text.[106] What follows is a condensed fragmentary copy of Wace's *Brut*, beginning with lines 9059–65 and ending with 13675–680 (vulgate §§143–188) – from Arthur's battle against Colgrim, the first following coming to the throne, up until Pope Gregory sends Augustine to convert the English – with significant lacunae, totaling roughly 1400 lines (down from 4600 lines in Wace or one-third of the *Brut* in complete manuscripts). As if meant to complete the history of Britain/England which runs, on the recto up to the end of the anonymous verse *Brut*, through – on the verso – the excerpted end of Wace's *Brut*, we find at the end of the verso what is in effect a Continuation of English history (resembling histories of the English, including Anglo-Norman, Anglo-Angevin kings, but not the British, except in versions

---

106   See n. 79 above on the roll having been either originally compiled by the same person
        from texts sought out to make an assemblage, or even written by the same person, translated from Geoffrey or copied from Wace, plus others.

THE ANONYMOUS VERSE BRUT TRADITION 439

with a "prequel" on the Britons):[107] this final text contains prose paragraphs with headings, beginning in earnest (after rubrics and two summative headings)

---

107   At this stage of research (including my own), I would like to reserve judgment on the identity of this text, but this "continuation" could possibly be a version of the *Livere de Reis de Brittanie*, which is found in many permutations, including with a "prequel" to borrow John Spence's term on the history of the Britons "based ultimately" on Geoffrey, and which often run from the Pentarchy (sometimes the Heptarchy) to Edward I's reign, but occasionally to John's reign or those of Edward II or Henry III; Spence dates the text – or textual tradition – found thus far in 28 manuscripts "almost all from the thirteenth or early fourteenth centuries," to the reign of King John or Henry III, but also suggests that the text in CA in particular may belong rather to another tradition of genealogies, though sharing a textual ancestor with *LRB* (Spence, *Reimagining History*, esp. 12–14 (cited above at 12–13), 46–50, 76–77, 91, and 110, and on the other tradition of genealogies, see the resources he provides in n. 67, pp. 13–14; I am grateful to Dr. Spence for clarification on these traditions, expressed in a private communication). On this very complex text which has not yet been extensively studied (*LRB*), see also Ruth Dean (with Maureen Bolton), *Anglo-Norman Literature*, item 13 (pp. 12–15); Cecily Clark, "Appendix: The Anglo-Norman Chronicle" in *The Peterborough Chronicle: The Bodleian Manuscript Laud Misc. 636*, ed. Dorothy Whitelock, Early English Manuscripts in Facsimile 4 (Copenhagen: Rosenkilde and Bagger, 1954), 39–43; and the editions/translations, *Le Livere de Reis de Brittanie e Le Livere de Reis de Engleterre*, ed. and trans. J. Glover, Rolls Series, London, 1865, and *Kritische Ausgabe der Anglonormannischen Chroniken: Brutus, Li Rei de Engleterre, Le Livere de Reis de Engleterre*, ed. C. Foltys, Berlin, 1962, pp. 45–114 (inaugural-dissertation) (Foltys refers to the prologue of the *LRB* as "Brutus" and the body of the text as "Li Rei de Engleterre"; see Dean and Boulton, item 23, p. 20, for the *Livere de Reis de Engleterre* [*LRE*]). Cf. The database Jonas of the IRHT which identifies CA 12/45 A as a witness to a "généalogie des rois d'Angleterre," not the *LRB* (Section romane, notice de "Généalogie des rois d'Angleterre, Anonyme" dans la base Jonas-IRHT/CNRS, permalink: http://jonas.irht.cnrs.fr/oeuvre /9709), and also Di Lella who identifies the historical text at the end of the dorse of CA 12/45 A as a copy of the "standard" version of the *LRB* (i.e., without the "prequel" on the Britons) ("Il *Roll Brut* [prima parte]," 43). Thus far, it is known that two manuscripts associated with Wace, one containing the complete *Brut*, MS. T (Cambridge Corpus Christi College 50) and one fragmentary Wace MS. Cologny-Geneva, Bibliotheca Bodmeriana 67 each contain the *LRB* (as identified as witnesses in Dean and Boulton, *Anglo-Norman Literature*, item 13, p. 13); see also nn. 166 and 171 below on the anonymous Egerton *Brut*'s verse "continuation," Appendix 1, nn. 5 and 6 (on Wace MSS with "continuations"), and Appendix 2, n. 6 (on the Egerton "continuation"); see also Maud Becker, "Une édition de la Continuation du *Roman de Brut* de Wace, contenue dans le manuscript British Library Cotton Vitellius A.X," unpublished doctoral thesis, University of Aberystwyth, 2019; work remains to be done comparing the "continuations," where applicable. However, it should be added that along with resonances shared with the *LRB*, the genealogical text in College of Arms 12/45 A bears an even more striking resemblance (at times almost verbatim) to the prose "Manual I" edited by Thomas Wright (*Feudal Manuals of English History, A Series of Popular Sketches of our National History, Compiled at Different Periods, From the Thirteenth Century to the Fifteenth, for the Use of the Feudal Gentry and Nobility*, London, 1872, 1–37). On the latter "Manual I" once in the possession of Joseph Mayer (Liverpool), but now missing, see Olivier de Laborderie, "The First Manuals of English History: Two Late Thirteenth-Century Genealogical Rolls of the Kings of England

440   CHAPTER 6

with a short exposition of how the seven kingdoms of the Heptarchy seemed like five,[108] the importance of Egbert's reign[109] (771/775–839, king of Wessex),[110]

---

in the Royal Collection," *Electronic British Library Journal*, article 4, 2014: 1–25, esp. 1–4 (https://www.bl.uk/eblj/2014articles/article4.html).

108 "<E> puis ke les regnes furent partiz, les rois de adunc regnerent si comencere(n)t a estriver entre els, e furent les uns vencuz et les VII regiuns resemblés en cinc" (paragraph 1; "<And> then the kingdoms were divided; the kings who ruled there began to fight among themselves, and some were vanquished and the 7 regions resembled five").

109 Like the *Livere de Reis de Brittanie* which provides descriptions of each kingdom of the Heptarchy but not accounts of each of their separate histories, CA also begins the narrative with the moment of unification under Egbert, who is called Aethelbrith here as in *LRB*; see Spence, *Reimagining History*, 76.

110 Laborderie writes that the anonymous authors of the late thirteenth-century genealogical rolls, first written in Latin and then translated into Anglo-Norman French, broke with Matthew Paris whose other "prototypes" they ordinarily followed, and followed instead William of Malmesbury and Ailred of Rievaulx among others in placing Egbert as their choice of first king of a united England and head of the royal line, rather than his grandson Alfred: "At the end of the thirteenth century, the fierce competition (obviously posthumous and by proxy) between Egbert and his grandson Alfred as to who should be regarded as the first king of England seems to have turned out to Egbert's advantage, in spite of Matthew Paris' intellectual authority and prestige. Henceforward, although some people still stand for Alfred and consider him the first effective king of England, no leading historian ever contemplated, as far as I know, choosing him to be the head of a genealogy of the kings of England, as Matthew Paris had done in the mid-thirteenth century. Conversely, more and more 14th century chroniclers considered the reign of Egbert, because he was seen as responsible for the unification of England, as a watershed in English history"; on the subtleties of this debate, see O. de Laborderie, "The First King of England? Egbert and the Foundations of Royal Legitimacy in Thirteenth-Century Historiography," in *Image and Perception of Monarchy in Medieval and Early Modern Europe*, ed. Sean McGlynn and Elena Woodacre (Newcastle upon Tyne: Cambridge Scholars Publisher, 2014), 70–83, cited at 81. Chris Given-Wilson states that "William divided his history of pre-conquest England (449–1066) into two books separated by the reign of Ecgberht, King of Wessex (802–839). Ecbgerht had been the first English king who 'made himself sole ruler of almost the whole island,' thereby bringing to completion the progression from regnal multiplicity to unity ... in William's view, therefore, it was the unification of England under the West Saxon dynasty which marked out the ninth century as a watershed in English history" (*Chronicles: The Writing of History in Medieval England*, Hambledon, London, and New York: 2004, 118–19). Wace on the other hand, follows Geoffrey of Monmouth in naming tenth-century Athelstan as the first king of a united England, rather than either Alfred or Egbert who appear in neither the *HRB* or Wace's poem (since naming those 8th–9th century kings would have undermined Geoffrey's political agenda of shared dominion between the Britons and the Saxons for approximately three hundred years following Arthur whom they appear to place in the late fifth to early sixth centuries). See also Chapter 5, n. 198, on Wace's efforts to finesse Geoffrey's (and the FV's) chronology at the end of his narrative.

THE ANONYMOUS VERSE BRUT TRADITION   441

and running up through the list of the fourteen children of Edward I, first son
of Henry III.[111]

5.3.7   Lacunae in CA's Copy of Wace's *Brut*
The more notable lacunae[112] in CA's copy of Wace's *Brut* are:

1)   9193–9206: how the Britons guarded Celidon wood where the Saxons had
     fled, and how hungry the Saxons were after 3 days without provisions;
2)   9243–52: how the Saxons were spared but returned to ravage Devonshire,
     Somerset and much of Dorset, but the people of Bath held out against
     them;
3)   9759–88: how the knights at the Round Table came from many lands;
4)   10175–96: rejoicing, celebrating Arthur's return from the continent: how
     women kissed their husbands, aunts their nephews, etc.;
5)   10211–37: the richness of the land;
6)   10249–10302: at the festivities, missing the names of the second group of
     barons[113] and some of the foreign guests as well (10305–12);
7)   10333–358: missing servants, food, furs;
8)   10449–59: the Trojan custom of how people were seated at feast tables;
9)   10490–10588: the queen, her servants, the games;
10) 10591–620: Arthur's gift giving;
11) 10741–50: the ills of idleness;
12) 10763–76: Gawain: peace is good after war and so is love;

---

111   See also Short: "La fin de la généalogie nous permet d'en attribuer l'écriture à la période
      allant de 1284 (date de naissance du dernier des quatorze enfants d'Édouard Ier réperto-
      riés) jusqu'à environ 1290 (aucune mention de la mort de sa première femme) ou 1300
      (premier enfant du second lit, non répertorié). La provenance insulaire du rouleau va de
      soi, la *scripta* et les rimes du *Brut* inédit, nous le verrons, la confirment" ("Un *Roman de
      Brut* anglo-normand inédit," 274).
112   There may be well over 100 of the very short lacunae of 2–5 lines mentioned above, and
      thus it is impractical to report on them here. See Di Lella's thesis where he has a fuller list,
      108–9.
113   The vulgate gives a second list of 14 barons, 12 of whose Welsh family names begin with
      "map" (or "mab," that is, "son" or "son of") (§156.340–44), followed by the phrase "and
      many others too numerous to name" ("plures quoque alii, quorum nomina longum est
      enumerare" §156.343–44); the First Variant eliminates the names of those Welsh attend-
      ees, keeping only the comment that there were too many to name "multi quos longum est
      enumerare uel nominare" (§156.6); Wace uses "fiz" for nine of these lesser barons, and for
      four others, he only uses their given names (10271–82), also commenting that "D'altres de
      menur teneüre / I avait tant, n'en sai mesure" (10287–88; "of others of lesser rank, there
      were so many, I don't know how to count them").

442   CHAPTER 6

13) 10803–18: in Arthur's speech to the Britons following the letter from the Roman ambassadors: they've insulted us enough!; 10821–24: they ask tribute of other islands and France as well;

14) 10831–40: Arthur: What is taken by force is not justly held;

15) 11013–40: second half of Angusel's speech is missing;

16) 11063–72: praise for Arthur from the Roman ambassadors on their return to Lucius;

17) 11093–11124: 31 lines: the emperor Lucius did not delay, summoning many kings and dukes from the far reaches of the empire;

18) 11133–63: 30 lines, the thousands who came to join Arthur's army;

19) 11143–80: Arthur's dream of the bear and the dragon;

20) 11293–11318: no one had the courage to fight the giant of Mont-Saint-Michel;

21) 11561–98: Arthur's single combat against the giant;

22) 11940–12262: 321 lines missing: much of the battle of the Britons against the Romans;

23) 12309–92: 82 lines: Arthur arranges his troops;

24) 12447–554: 107 lines missing: praise for Lucius; Lucius's speech to the Romans; opening of the final battle;

25) 12591–626: 33 lines: Bedevere's death;

26) 12749–786: 37 lines: more important deaths;

27) 13385–400: a positive portrayal of Gormund[114]

28) 13415–514: 100 lines: the Saxons fight the Britons; they hear of Gormund, make a truce with the Britons, but then send for Gormund who invades Britain;

29) 13519–538: missing Ysembard altogether;

30) 13623–36: following how the city of Cirencester was lost due to the stratagem of the flame-carrying sparrows, Gormund destroys many cities, castles of ancient times, bishoprics, and abbeys which have never since been restored; [115]

31) 13639–652: how the land came to be called England. [116]

---

114   See n. 91 above on Wace's awarding of "reflex praise" for important characters who are not necessarily heroes, such as Julius Caesar, or as in the case of Gormund, completely villainous.

115   On the stratagem of the sparrows, see Chapter 4, n. 39, and Weiss, 342, n. 2.

116   The 10-line passage on the changing of the name at the time of Gormund was added by Wace, including the comments that the Saxons had no wish to use any other language or to adapt their customs to those of any other group (see Chapter 5 for the passage and an English translation, p. 370); the FV at the beginning of §186 does mention the change of name ("Hinc Angli Saxones uocati sunt") but nothing about the Saxons' "deliberately maintained separateness" as Elizabeth Tyler has put it in reference to their wish to not associate themselves with other groups' identity connections with the Trojans (Chapter 5,

THE ANONYMOUS VERSE BRUT TRADITION 443

In addition to the fact that the CA anonymous *Brut* is a relatively annalistic text and that this tendency to cut description and speeches may well have carried over into the roll's copy of Wace's *Brut* as a matter of course, a pattern does emerge from these more substantial lacunae. While some of the lacunae concern descriptions of battle scenes, the majority fall into the category of "local color." However, although the CA redactor may have thought them expendable, descriptions of Arthur's retinue, court festivities, and other cultural events have a deeper meaning and are not simply "decorative." As can be seen in Wace's text – particularly in the lengthy descriptions surrounding the Round Table – original to Wace, at least textually – and Arthur's plenary court – drawn from Geoffrey of Monmouth, with embellishments – the Norman poet appears to have tried to convey as detailed a picture as possible (without being overly wordy), to provide his audience with a collection of gestures, for example, which signal cultural meaning, explain behaviors, and characterize social patterns, descriptions which contemporary anthropologists (and cultural sociologists) then rely on to understand those cultures.[117]

Regardless of whether Wace was trying to reflect contemporary social "reality" for his audience through these descriptions or whether they were meant to serve as a model for future behaviors, these descriptions were evidently of no interest to the CA redactor, for reasons that remain unclear. Although he may have thought they were less important than the "facts," most scholars today would agree that cultural descriptions are themselves "facts," and certainly for Wace they were very essential ones, whether they signaled matters of pride for the descendants of the Britons, and by extension, the Anglo-Norman elites who were ruling during Wace's time, or whether they were "advice for princes" or any combination of meanings, symbolism, or cultural capital along a broad continuum.[118]

5.3.8   Continuation of the Anonymous *Brut* and Wace Text; Conclusion
The continuation of the anonymous *Brut* and Wace text in prose paragraph form[119] contains standard, though as well perhaps some anomalous, opinions,

---

n. 243). On these and other manifestations of insularity of the Saxons, according to Wace, see also Chapter 5, nn. 199–200.

117   See Clifford Geertz in particular, "Thick Description: Toward an Interpretive Theory of Culture," in idem, *The Interpretation of Cultures* (New York: Basic Books, 1973; rev. ed. 2000), 3–32.

118   See esp. Laurie A. Finke and Martin B. Shichtman, "Profiting from the Past: History as Symbolic Capital," and "The Romance of Empire: Vernacular and the Structuration of Power," in *King Arthur and the Myth of History*, 35–70 and 71–102.

119   See n. 107 regarding the possibility that the "continuation" is a version of the *Livere de Reis de Brittanie*. As mentioned above in n. 74, since I am not editing these texts, I have not numbered the lines of the anonymous *Brut*, nor the lines of the paragraphs of the

444   CHAPTER 6

which may be useful to note for literary scholars of prose chronicles as well
as historians:

1)   that "Willame Bastard, conqueror de Engleterre" conquered the realm
      in a battle against Harold who held the land wrongly "que le tint a tort"
      (paragraph 24), a perspective which certainly is not pro-English;

2)   the paragraph (25) on William Rufus is standard in its condemnation,
      though without mention of homosexuality per se ("Totes les choses ke
      pleseient a Deu, si lui despleisent"; "Everything that was pleasing to God,
      displeased him");

3)   that Stephen of Blois reigned, like Harold, "a tort": "[I] cestui Estevene,
      ke fut filz Ele la duchesce, regna aprés a tort et en guerre e en travail tut
      son tens qu'il vesqui" (paragraph 28; "This Stephen, who was the son of
      Ele the duchess reigned after her wrongly and in war and in turmoil the
      whole time he lived");[120]

4)   the section on Henry II, announced by a rubric like all the other sections,
      was apparently left out (though this may have been an accident);

5)   section 30 on "Le roi Ricar le pruz" is uniformly glowing, as one might
      expect, though the following (31) on King John (without epithet) is not:
      "Entre trestuz les reis crestiens morteus il fud le plus franc e par son
      eyndegré il se fist meimes serf e mist le glorius reaume de Engleterre en
      truage" ("Among all the Christian kings who have lived, he was the most
      open[121] and by his own free will, he made himself a slave and placed the
      most glorious kingdom of England in tributary").[122]

Even more surprising, about John, the redactor goes on to exclaim: "Alas! tant
cum il vesqui il out assez de tribulations e travaus e perdi assez de ses terres

---

       continuation (as is the norm done by editors of prose texts ordinarily, such as *The Oldest
       Anglo-Norman Prose Brut Chronicle*, ed. and trans. Julia Marvin [Woodbridge: Boydell
       and Brewer, 2006]), though those texts are ordinarily of a less "mixed media" nature than
       either the anonymous *Brut* or the continuation (genealogical text) in CA 12/45 A; I am just
       citing the continuation with "paragraph" numbers. I am grateful for the readers' under-
       standing of these decisions regarding these texts as yet unedited (or not edited in full). On
       the other hand, lines of the Wace text from this roll are numbered in my citations, with
       reference to both Weiss, trans., and Arnold, ed.

120   Among the chroniclers, opinion on Stephen was mixed; for a survey, see R. H. C. Davis,
       King Stephen 1135–1154 (New York: Longman, 1967; rev. ed 1977), Appendix III, "The
       Chronicle Sources," 146–52. "Ele" must be Adele (Adela) countess of Blois, daughter of
       William the Conqueror.

121   *Franc* can also mean "generous, noble, worthy, gracious," but it is difficult to see how the
       redactor might have wished to convey any of those more positive meanings in this context.

122   On John's loss of Plantagenet lands, see Gillingham, *The Angevin Empire*, and *King John:
       New Interpretations*, ed. S. D. Church (Woodbridge, Suffolk: Boydell, 1999).

THE ANONYMOUS VERSE BRUT TRADITION 445

k'il out outre mer" ("Alas! as long as he lived he had rather a lot of trials and tribulations and lost rather a lot of his lands overseas"), surprising because, as in the case of the narrative on Stephen, the redactor expresses what could be construed as personal dismay at the difficulties endured by those two kings, striking almost a personal tone, a far remove from the very neutral tone of the anonymous *Brut*. In CA we have then a range of seemingly personal interjections from our single redactor – though it is also possible that he may not have been the original author of the texts (and may have even been working with Wace at second or third remove), but rather the assembler which does of course involve vision and planning and is not completely mechanical:[123] in the anonymous (largely) verse text, the redactor eschews all narratorial *discours interprétatif*; he does though include a few of Wace's editorial remarks in his copy of the *Roman de Brut*; and finally he closes with 34 prose paragraphs, some of which contain editorial exclamations as seen in the paragraphs about kings Stephen and John.[124]

5.4 *The Harley* Brut (*London, British Library Harley 1605*)

5.4.1 Overview of the Five Fragments

Harley 1605, while containing fewer lines than Royal, is the only fragment – actually, set of fragments – which gives a clear impression that they come from a completed original, due to the variety of passages covered by the fragments, lack of overlap, as well as stylistic considerations. In terms of Harley 1605 (the fourth-longest text) resembling other manuscripts, in Appendix II of his 1994 doctoral thesis, Peter Damian-Grint, who provides a transcription of the first four fragments,[125] observes that from among all the anonymous *Brut* fragments, Harley 1605 bears the closest resemblance to the Bekker fragment,

---

123 See the discussion below in the context of the Egerton *Brut*, on reassessing – and thus often redeeming – the role of scribes in medieval literature.

124 We need to keep in mind however, David Hult's cautionary remarks, that often in medieval texts, expressions that may sound personal, may be trying to evoke reactions in the audience or make general cultural comments, for example, rather than expressing an authentic personal opinion. See Chapter 5, n. 20.

125 "Vernacular History in the Making: Anglo-Norman Verse Historiography in the 12th Century," Appendix II: "The Harley *Brut*: MS BL Harley 1605, Art. 1," 368–473. For an edition and discussion of the fifth fragment, see Brian Blakey, "The Harley *Brut*: An Early French Translation of Geoffrey of Monmouth's *Historia Regum Britanniae*." See also Beatrice Barbieri, "Una traduzione anglo-normanna dell'*Historia Regum Britannie*: la *Geste des Bretuns in alessandrini* (*Harley Brut*)," *Studi Mediolatini e volgari* 57 (2011):163–76, and eadem, "La *Geste des Bretuns en alexandrins* (*Harley Brut*): Une traduction de l'*Historia* aux teintes épiques," in *L'Historia regum Britannie et les "Bruts" en Europe*, I, 141–55.

446   CHAPTER 6

Krakow Jagiellonian 176.[126] While it is true that Bekker which is Continental and Harley which is Anglo-Norman are the only two extant in alexandrine monorhymed laisses, they exhibit many more similarities than the octosyllabic versions do to one another.[127] The quantity of "close verbal echoes" has prompted Damian-Grint to propose that the Bekker fragment could in fact have been based on an earlier version of the Harley manuscript.[128] Brian Blakey speculates that the original upon which the Harley manuscript is based could possibly predate Wace, and like Gaimar's *Estoire des Bretuns*, have been superseded by Wace's more popular version, though this is impossible to prove.[129]

In another context, I also agree with Damian-Grint when he finds similarities between Harley and Royal – the fragment with which Harley has the greatest overlap in terms of content – to be minimal, no greater than those one would expect from two efforts to present a source – or multiple sources on the same "topic" – translating from Latin into the French vernacular within roughly the same time frame.[130]

For the purposes of comparison, the following is a summary of the contents of the five fragments of Harley 1605, totaling 3361 lines:

1)   Fragment 1: 1280 lines, §§73–94, from the death of King Lucius (legendary second century king credited with bringing Christianity to the Britons)[131] to the arrival of Hengist and Horsa; Severus fights Fulgenius (though the former is not given credit for building Hadrian's wall);[132]

---

126   "Vernacular History in the Making," 369–71.

127   Except for possibly Harley 4733 and Takamiya 115. See nn. 12 below and 77 above.

128   Damian-Grint provides a comparison of the lines in common between Bekker and Harley 1605 (fragment 2), showing that the narrative is about 10% longer in Harley than in Bekker, and that about 25% of the lines are very similar, with some being almost identical (370–71).

129   "The Harley *Brut*," 46.

130   "Vernacular History in the Making," 370. We need to remember though that "to translate" did not necessarily mean, at this time, a strict language-to-language transfer; Wace's "translation" admits of multiple sources. On the issue of translation and its various meanings in this period, see Damian-Grint, especially *The New Historians*, 20–32 passim, 117–20, and 228–33 passim.

131   *HB* has the Lucius story as does William of Malmesbury (in the *De Antiquitate*), but as Alan Smith notes, "the Lucius story reaches its highest development in Geoffrey of Monmouth" ("Lucius of Britain and alleged Church Founder," *Folklore* 90.1 (1979): 29–36, cited at 30). See also Felicity Heal, "What Can King Lucius do for You? The Reformation and the Early English Church," who quips at the start of her excellent study, "many uncomplimentary things have been said about Geoffrey of Monmouth over the last 900 years, but he has rarely been accused of failing to tell a good story" among which "one of his best" is that of King Lucius (593).

132   The narrative in Harley is much more skeletal than in Wace, who narrates how Severus built the "dike" across the north to shut out Fulgenius, as well as many Britons, Scots and

THE ANONYMOUS VERSE BRUT TRADITION 447

2)   Fragment 2: 1279 lines, §§113–136; contains an alexandrine version of Merlin's Prophecies, missing lines 1–72 (514-line Prophecies text); the fragment then runs up to the Britons' capture of Octa and Eosa at the beginning of Uther's reign;

3)   Fragment 3: 79 lines: §§152–54, Arthur restores "Angulose" (Wace Angusel, Latin Auguselus) to royal power over Scotland, makes his brother Urianus king of Moray, and restores to Loth the earldom of Lothian and "its associated provinces" ("ceterarumque comprouinciarum quae ei pertinebant" §152.207–8); Arthur marries Guinevere, and enjoying great renown in Britain, prepares to conquer foreign lands, heading first to Norway to ensure that Loth would inherit from Sichelmus (§154); Norway and Denmark are conquered and Lot gains his inheritance as king of Norway; Arthur's meeting with and defeat of Frollo (the Roman tribune of Gaul) in single combat are omitted or, most likely, are missing at the end of this fragment (§155);

4)   Fragment 4: 80 lines: §156, Bedevere and Kay are enfeoffed, feast at the City of Legions; among the guest names omitted are all the Welsh (*map/mab* "son") comprising the second set of guests, as well as many aspects of the festivities;[133]

5)   Fragment 5: 641 lines, §§165–69: Mont-Saint-Michel giant, first encounter between Arthur and the Roman emperor Lucius.

In his comparative analysis of Wace's *Brut* and the Harley fragments, Blakey finds that the Harley poet's approach to the *Historia* "differs considerably from that of Wace," claiming that "the Harley poet shows throughout a more manifest respect for his source" (though Blakey does not offer examples). The extant portions of the Harley *Brut* do not contain any "innovations equal in stature to Wace's Round Table or Invention of the True Cross," divergences from the *Historia* – of which Blakey states he has found around 300, though more than half of these he states "do not fall into any recognizable category."[134] Unlike CA

Picts, so that Deira would be "so well sealed off that Fulgenius dare not enter" ("Quant Deïre fu si bien close / que Fulgenes entrer n'i ose" 5319); along with some of the Britons, Severus fights against Fulgenius, the remainder of the Britons, the Scots and the Picts; both are mortally wounded. On various sources including the vulgate, Bede, Gildas, and Wace regarding Hadrian's wall, see Weiss, 135, n. 3, and also n. 72 above.

133   CA also eliminates the Welsh guests at the court festivities; see n. 113 above. Brian Blakey sees a pattern here, in that the translator apparently omitted Welsh place names in two passages (although Blakey does not state which passages), along with a "considerable condensation of Geoffrey's eulogy of Caerleon," probably referring to Geoffrey's praise of the City of Legions as site of Arthur's plenary court (§156. 310–26) which Blakey found to be "all indicative of a lack of interest in Welsh matters" (47).

134   "The Harley *Brut*," 46.

448   CHAPTER 6

which has practiced a fair bit of *abbreviatio*, omitting numerous small clusters of verses, Harley has apparently indulged in *amplificatio* – Blakey has found that "expansions of the Latin text are far more numerous than contractions" – including the "much more extensive use in the [Harley] *Brut* of direct speech, both where Geoffrey reports and where no speech of any sort exists in the *Historia*."[135]

Interestingly, while Harley may have amplified Geoffrey's narrative, relative to Wace, he has also cut a fair bit: Harley contains less dialogue and demonstrates less interest in the universality of representation at Arthur's court, a more bookish interest in classical tales, and in general less interest in aggrandizing Arthur. Arithmetically, while Harley has longer lines than Wace (4 more syllables per line on average), each roughly equivalent passage in Harley is shorter than in Wace: fragment 1 by 250 lines (Wace lines approx. 5260–6792), fragment 2 by 370 lines (Wace approx. 7542–8917, excepting the prophecies which are not found in Wace), fragment 3 is less than half the length of the equivalent in Wace (approx. 9617–9814), fragment 4 one-sixth the length (Wace approx. 10153–329), and fragment 5, three-fourths the length of the corresponding section in Wace (approx. 11288–12180, which does not include the description of Biblical images in Arthur's tent (ship?), absent in Wace). In terms of specific omissions in Harley, in addition to the lack of Welsh names among the second group of plenary court attendees and omission of Welsh place names, and the omission of praise for Caerleon, the Harley redactor also omits or curtails ecclesiastical references.[136]

In Blakey's analysis, it is fragment 5 that contains the greatest degree of *amplificatio*, of which one major example will suffice. This fragment begins in the middle of a long descriptive passage which Otto Wendeburg and J. S. P. Tatlock see as a description of Arthur's tent at the high feast in Glamorgan (§§156–57); H. L. D. Ward and Robert Fletcher interpret the description as being of Arthur's ship (in which he was sailing to Barfleur, and where he has the dream of the bear and the dragon), although there is no parallel for a description of a ship in Geoffrey (end of §165.104–7), nor does this description of the tent panels appear in Wace.[137]

---

135   "The Harley *Brut*," 47.
136   "The Harley *Brut*," 47.
137   Blakey, "The Harley *Brut*," 48–49. Otto Wendeburg, *Über di Bearbeitung von Gottfried von Monmouths Historia Regum Britanniae in der HS. Brit. Mus. Harl. 1605*, dissertation Universität Erlangen. Braunschweig: Albert Limbach, 1881, esp. 7–8 and 16; Tatlock, *Legendary History*, 458; H. L. D. Ward, *Catalogue of Romances in the Manuscript Department of the British Museum*, 3 vols. (vols. 1 and 2, Ward, vol. 3 J. A. Herbert)(London: Trustees of the British Museum, 1883–1910), I, 272–4; R. H. Fletcher, *Arthurian Material in the Chronicles*,

THE ANONYMOUS VERSE BRUT TRADITION   449

Blakey posits a third alternative, based on the context of what follows
the description: that the description of the paintings in the first 120 lines of
fragment 5 (2720–2840) is an invention of the poet, an amplification on the
phrase "tentoria sua figentes" ("they immediately pitched their tents," §164.30)
inserted into the mention of Arthur's tent at Barfleur, since the description is
immediately followed by the news of the Mont-Saint-Michel giant reaching
Arthur, as in the vulgate (opening of §165). While this third alternative appears
the most plausible, to claim that "the passage is not then a complete innovation, but an interesting amplification of Arthur's pavilion in Barfleur" since "its
presence does not imply the omission of any *Historia* narrative, nor is it in any
way contrary to the translator's usual technique," seems specious – except for
the opinion that it is not contrary to the translator's methods; Blakey also speculates that if this were a description of the pavilion at Caerleon, then it would
have meant that the translator had omitted eight chapters of Geoffrey's narrative (counting via Griscom's edition IX, xiv-x, iii), which does seem unlikely.[138]
However, his claim that the description "is not a complete innovation" is very
difficult to accept, certainly with respect to Geoffrey's text, since the description is of a panel showing Moses's parting of the Red Sea, and his appearance
with horns; the second panel of David anointed by Saul, and defeat of Goliath;
the third panel on Ulysses encounter with Circe; the fourth panel, the apocryphal story of Judith and Holofernes;[139] and lastly the guards at the door of
the tent. Perhaps the passage is not "a complete innovation" since it has precedents in biblical and classical literature.[140] Regardless of one's perceptions
of the origins of this passage, nonetheless, it most certainly provides us with
another example in the anonymous *Brut*s of the impulse to create a universalizing narrative.

5.4.2   Fragment 1: the *Adventus Saxonum*

With respect to the major topics of this book that intersect with issues of identity, cultural positioning and conflicts – the Trojan foundation myth, the *adventus Saxonum*, Arthur's reign, and the passage of dominion – fragments 1, 3 and
4 are the most germane, with fragment 2 of interest due to the Prophecies and
how they are embedded in the text, and fragment 5 of importance more for

---

  especially those of Great Britain and France, orig. published in *Harvard Studies and Notes in
  Philology and Literature* 10 (Boston, 1906; repr. New York: Burt Franklin, 1958), 143.

138 "The Harley *Brut*," 49–50.

139 A version of this apocryphal story is found in at least one other Old French text, the
  Roman en vers de Girart de Rossillon (Blakey, "The Harley *Brut*," 53 n. to lines 81–105).

140 See Blakey, "The Harley *Brut*," p. 50, notes to lines 1–120, 2–28, and 13; pp. 51, numerous
  references to 1 Samuel; and p. 53, notes to lines 81–105.

450 CHAPTER 6

stylistic reasons, though with some cultural overtones. Fragment 1 contains the *adventus Saxonum*, and has very few original moments, quite possibly because the passage is so short, ll. 1200–80 (§98.250–85), narrating just the arrival of the two brothers with three keels of knights from Germany. Since Hengest was older and wiser, it is he who explains that they had drawn lots and were chosen to go into exile, due to overpopulation at home. Hengist explains as well that they followed the guidance of Mercury; he adds that they worship Saturn, Jupiter, and Freya as well. Vortigern proceeds to say he regrets their belief system but that their arrival is good timing since "Mi enemi me funt mult granz oppressïons"[141] (1280; "My enemies are oppressing me greatly"). The fragment breaks off there.

A notable difference between Harley fragment 1 and Wace is the narrative of the shipwreck and drowning of Ursula and the 11,000 virgins. In Harley, 26 lines are devoted to the tragedy whose narrative is interrupted by a story about Wanis, Melga, and Maximien. Wace devotes 60 lines to the passage, including an elaborate description of what happened to the ships when the storm arose suddenly; as seen elsewhere, maritime vocabulary is one of Wace's signature traits.[142] Wace's narrative on Wanis, Melga, and Maximien follows the central narrative on the virgins and is more closely tied in thematically than the interrupting story in Harley because Wace uses the material to demonstrate how those young women who did survive the storm were then cruelly killed since they would not consent to have sex with these heathens who found some of them still alive lost at sea.[143] The Harley interruption further lessens the pathos of the tragedy through its opening lines where the author states, "Un aventure avint que or voil reconter / de un[s] rei[s] escumengé, que jo sai bien nomer" (694–95; "An adventure happened which I now want to tell you about a detested king, whose name I know well"). Ironically, the Harley author uses a variation on one of Wace's frequently used phrases seen most often in the *Roman de Rou* "jo ne sai nomer" – I don't know how to name (whose names I don't know) – which the latter uses not to interrupt pathos but to create (or maintain) an image of honesty through admission of incomplete knowledge.[144]

---

141 Citations from fragments 1, 3–4 are from Peter Damian-Grint's thesis (Appendix 11), and for fragment 5, Blakey's "The Harley *Brut*." References to fragment 2 containing the Prophecies are to *ANP*, Blacker, ed. and trans. All translations are my own.

142 See Chapter 5, n. 99.

143 "Des meschines firent ocirre / Plusurs qu'il voldrent purgesir / Ki nel vuleient consentir; / Nes ocieient pas pur el, / Paen esteient cil cruel" (6082–86; "They had the maidens killed, many that they wanted to have sex with, because they did not want to consent; they didn't kill them for any other reason, they were cruel pagans").

144 See Chapter 5, n. 13.

THE ANONYMOUS VERSE BRUT TRADITION   451

5.4.3   Fragments 3 and 4: Arthur's Reign
The two shortest fragments 3 and 4 (80 and 81 lines respectively) concern Arthur's reign, and are somewhat more suggestive of possible socio-political agendas. In fragment 3, Guinevere is described in 4 lines as "pleine de corteisie," Roman-born and raised in the home of Cador. Wace devotes 14 lines to the new queen "une cuinte e noble meschine" (9646) who was "bele ... e curteise e gent" (9647), including the same "information" as Harley but using many more adverbs and adjectives from the courtly lexicon, increasing Guineviere's stature and status.[145] Arthur conquers the same realms in the two passages – Ireland, Iceland, Orkney, and Gotland (though Wace adds the mysterious Wenelande, not in Geoffrey or FV)[146] – though more swiftly in Harley, and without Wenelande. In Harley, after Arthur's conquests, Arthur returns to Normandy (2609) (*Historia* §153.223, "in Britanniam"), whereas in Wace he returns "en Engleterre" (9729). There is no mention of the Round Table in Harley, and thus no mention of knights from around the western world seated enjoying equal status, though the latter text mentions the breadth of Arthur's realm and its "curteisie" (2616). The twelve-years' peace is mentioned as having been apparently enjoyed in Normandy (2611), after which time Arthur is eager to dominate all of Europe "Quand Artur le oï dire por icel achaison, / en ad jurei li reis sun chés e sun menton / que il avrat Europe en sa subjectïon" (2627–29; "When Arthur had heard that [foreign leaders were making defensive preparations][147] for this reason, he swore on his head and his beard that he would have all Europe in his sway"), a capsule of what we read in Geoffrey: "When Arthur learned of this, he exulted at being universally feared and decided to conquer all Europe" (§154.234–36). For Harley, Guinevere is less

---

145   See Chapter 5, n. 109 for Wace's passage on Guinevere.
146   Weiss, 245 n. 1. See also Ernest C. York, "Wace's Wenelande: Identification and Speculation."
147   Harley gives the short version of what he probably found in Geoffrey, that Arthur is eager to dominate all of Europe, especially when he hears that foreign leaders of neighboring countries were making defensive preparations against his potential attack: "kings of nations overseas became very frightened that he would attack and deprive them of their subjects. Overcome by nagging doubts, they began to put their cities and fortifications in order and built castles in appropriate spots as places of last resort should Arthur attack them. When Arthur learned of this, he exulted at being universally feared and decided to conquer all Europe" (§154.230–36; "... reges transmarinorum regnorum nimius inuadebat timor ne inquietatione eius oppressi nationes sibi subditas amitterent. Mordacibus ergo curis anxiati, urbes atque urbium turres renouabant, oppida in congruis locis aedificabant, ut si impetus Arturum in illos duceret refugium si opus esset haberent. Cumque id Arturo notificatum esset, extollens se quia cunctis timori erat, totam Europam sibi subdere affectat").

452   CHAPTER 6

important than she is for Wace, but Arthur is just as land-hungry as in Geoffrey (and Wace).

Harley fragment 4 is devoted to the festivities at King Arthur's court at Pentecost. Judging from the arrangement of details, while the passage is incomplete, it is also significantly abridged relative to the 450 lines Wace devotes to the scene (10171–10621) (Harley frag. 4, 80 lines, 2640–2719). Harley chooses to omit the joyful kissing and crying upon Arthur's return from war, as well as a large number of the guest list. Most notably excluded are the kings of North and South Wales, and nearly everyone's sons. Some of the attendees are named such as "Bos li quens de Oxeneford" (2680), "Heldins li quens de Flandres" (2688), "Horeals, le quens del Mans" (2693), "Höels, cil d'Amorice" (2698), Bedevere and Kay, and the twelve peers of France (2691, 2694, and 2696). At the end of the fragment, regions are named but not individual attendees, and certainly not the next generation.[148] Wace's genealogical guest list is far more complete than Harley's, and in fact, MS. J adds 14 more lines of names of regional groups of those summoned, which suggests that some redactors of Wace's poem found even his fulsome list lacking.[149]

More importantly, in Harley, the church service (the coronation itself), the costumes, games and much of the gift-giving are omitted, as are the references to the knights' prowess in hopes of winning the love of the ladies. It is possible that Harley rearranged the parts of the passage, and that those parts we think were omitted are simply lost since they were part of a non-existent fragment, but this is unlikely. Harley trims with respect to Wace – who was not his model, admittedly – but the guest list in particular is much shorter than that of the vulgate (§156.326–55), as well as Geoffrey's version of the festivities in §157. Wendenburg suggests that the general guest list by region stems from Geoffrey's "non remansit princeps alicuius precii citra Hispaniam quin ad istud edictum ueniret" (§156.353–5; "there was no prince worth his salt this side of Spain who did not answer such a call"); Wace's passage corresponds "N'out remés barun des Espaine / Dessi al Rim vers Alemainne, / Ki a la feste ne

---

148   Weiss writes that Wace "seems closer to the names of people and cities in the *vv* here [Variant Version]" than to the vulgate (259, n. 2); the First Variant excludes the sons with the Welsh prefix *map*. However, Wace does include some of those sons, using the term *fiz*, but not as a prefix to the name itself as in the vulgate, e.g. "Li fiz Apo i fu, Donaud,/ E Regeïm, le fiz Elaud; / Fiz Coïl i fu, Cheneüs ..." (10271–73; "Donaud, the son of Apo, was there, and Regeïm, the son of Elaud; Cheneüs, son of Coïl, was there") (vulgate §156.340–41: "Donaut Mappapo, Cheneus Mapcoil, ... Regin Mapclaut ..."). See also Chapter 5, nn. 131–32, and also n. 113 above.

149   Weiss, 258, n. 1, and for the contents of the variant in MS. J, see Arnold, note for line 10246, II, pp. 537–38.

THE ANONYMOUS VERSE BRUT TRADITION

venist / Pur ço ke la sumunse oïst" (10327–9: "No baron remained from Spain to the Rhine toward Germany, who did not come to the feast, provided he heard the summons"). Wendenburg suggests, then, that Harley's generalized guest list is followed by a list of gifts Arthur made, inspired by Geoffrey's "largitas namque Arturi" (§156.354–5) (where Wace instead has a lyric explanation of why the guests came, as provided below in the note):[150]

De si que en Espaigne, ço dit en la lecçon,	As the text says, no knight,
n'ad remis chevalier, conte ne baron ne seit tot venu a cel asembleison,	count or baron remained up to Spain [who] did not come to this assembly
kar tot i sunt venu: e Provençal e e Guascon,	for they all came: Provençalers and Gascons
li Alvernaz i furent e tuit li Borginon,	Those from Auvergne and all the Bourgignons,
Mansel e Peitevin e Norman e Breton	Those from Le Mans and Poitou, Normans and Bretons
e Flemeng e Norreis e Tieis e Frison,	and Flemish and Norse and German and Frisian,
e li Franceis i vindrent trestot a entençon	and the French came as soon as they heard
de cel jor que il murent çascun de sa maison:	that from that day everyone grew better with respect to his home:
en aprés a çascun donat li reis livreison.	after that the king paid each one tribute.

---

150 Wendenburg, *Über di Bearbeitung*, 12. See Chapter 5, n. 140, on Wace's enumeration of Arthur's gifts (ll. 10599–10620), which occurs just before the arrival of the Roman ambassadors brings an abrupt end to the court festivities. Earlier, after the comment about "no baron from Spain, etc." (10327–29), we hear Wace's lyric explanation of why the guests came:

Tant pur Artur, tant pur ses duns,	As much for Arthur as for his gifts,
Tant pur cunustre ses baruns,	As much to meet and know his barons,
Tant pur veeir ses mananties,	As much to see his riches,
Tant pur oïr ses curteisies,	As much to hear his noble sentiments,
Tant pur amur, tant pur banie,	As much out of love for him, and for his decrees,
Tant pur enur, tant pur baillie.	As much for honor, as much for power.
(10331–336)	

454   CHAPTER 6

La pëusez veeir tan[t] urs e tant lion,	There you could have seen so many bears and lions,
la pëusez veir tant valtre e tant bruon,	there you could have seen so many hunting dogs and hounds,
e tant bons esperviers, tant ostors e falcon,	and so many good sparrow-hawks, so many goshawks and falcons,
e tant riches mantels e tant bon peliçon,	and so many fine cloaks and fine furs,
e tant bliald de pailes, tant riche ciclaton.	and so many brocades, rich silk tunics.
Se il i sunt venuz, il unt dreit acaison,	If they came, they had good reason,
kar cil ne set li rei ne n'ait gueredon;	for they knew the king had rewards;
sun or e sun argent lur done a grant foison,	He gave his gold and his silver in great abundance,
chevals e palefreis lor livre il a bandon.	horses and palfreys he gave them freely.

(HARLEY 2701–19 [end of fragment 4])

Although quite compressed, at the end of the fragment, Harley would appear to be trying to make up for lost time as it were, trying to cover as many of the bases as possible in a short space, as if he realized he had left something out, for example where Wace (10301–326) and Geoffrey (§156) give specific names of individuals and their regions, Harley only gives regions, as well as some regions not in Wace or Geoffrey (such as Provence and Gascony) – even the contents of the two lines "Tant i out chevals, palefrez e destriers,/ des tant i out falcons e ostors e esperviers" (2699–2700; "There were so many horses, palfreys, and war horses, so many falcons and goshawks, and sparrow-hawks") appear in some-what different form in 2701, as if in a reprise, as seen in the passage above. A close analysis of fragment 4 in comparison with other fragmentary anony-mous *Bruts* (and not necessarily alexandrine) – if and when any further ones are discovered – might indeed prove interesting and valuable, but for the moment, especially the last 16 lines of fragment 4 (Damian-Grint's CLXII, ll. 2704–19) appear at times unique and not completely logical in their narra-tive ordering, not resembling Geoffrey or Wace.

5.4.4   Fragment 5: the Last of Arthur's Battles

As noted above in the discussion of *amplificatio*, fragment 5 is made up of 641 lines: the description of the panels of Arthur's tent at Barfleur (1–120

THE ANONYMOUS VERSE BRUT TRADITION   455

[2720–2840]);[151] Bedevere and Helen's nurse's sorrow (126–305 [2846–3025]);
Arthur's single combat with the giant (209–305) – perhaps this was an extra
motivation for the narrative about David and Goliath in the tent; and the
remainder on the battles with Lucius and the Romans (306–641 [3026–3361]).
Although no major events appear to be added with respect to Arthur's reign
per se, the Harley redactor does indulge in material description of Gawain,
Bos, and Gerin's gear, including short lances inlaid with the finest gold (342;
"Cascun porte un espiéd neeléd a or fin"); also, emperor Lucius's tent was made
of rich oriental purple cloth, one flap was white and the other purple, the third
was a brocade of Alexandrine silk (346–48; "Le tref l'emperëor fud fait de un
osterlin;/ Li un geron fud blanc e li altre porprin,/ Le tierz esteit fait de un paile
alisandrin"). Some of these details about the emperor's tent are repeated in the
next stanza, as if mimicking the technique of *laisses similaires* in widespread
use in the epic tradition, intended to slow down the action and emphasize
the scene,[152] while at the same time echoing the growing romance tradition in
which one finds descriptions of opulence as a matter of course, to both identify with classical and biblical models, and also to evoke the cultural superiority of the ruling elites.[153] These additions are odd however, when viewed in the
context of the descriptions absent from the scenes at Arthur's plenary court;
granted Geoffrey's descriptions of the latter are shorter than in Wace, but it still
seems mysterious that Harley left so much out even relative to Geoffrey, his
model (and given the organization of Harley, these would appear to be omissions rather than accidents of preservation).

5.4.5   Fragment 2: Merlin's Prophecies and Merlin's Prediction of
         Vortigern's Death Up through Uther's Capture of Octo and Eosa
As noted above, Harley's ANP in fragment 2 contains prophecies 7 to the end,
beginning with the line equivalent to l. 73 in the Lincoln MS. and l. 74 in BL,
Addition 45103; the latter two manuscripts have the ANP interpolated into

---

151   The first line numbers refer to the fragment itself; the second line numbers refer to the
       fragments collectively (based on Blakey, with fragment 5 picking up where fragment 4
       leaves off, l. 2719 as in Damian-Grint, thesis, Appendix II, p. 472).
152   See Emmanuèle Baumgartner on *laisses similaires*, "introduisant dans le récit les 'grandes
       haltes lyriques'" (https://www.universalis.fr/encyclopedie/la-chanson-de-roland/1-la-lai
       sse-une-cellule-narrative/ and Jean Rychner, *La Chanson de geste: essai sur l'art epique des
       jongleurs* (Geneva: Droz, 1955).
153   These sorts of descriptions of feudal opulence may also be evocative of the East, which
       was common at the time of the crusades. See Geraldine Heng, *Empire of Magic*, 328.

456   CHAPTER 6

copies of Wace's *Brut*, but in Harley the copy is the only one independent of Wace.[154] There is no internal indication of why the Prophecies in Harley begin with prophecy 7; this may simply be an accident of preservation, admitting the possibility that Harley originally contained a complete text of the ANP. Blakey asserts that "the Merlin prophecies of the Lincoln and Additional MSS were not as Tatlock assumed, mere ad hoc concoctions, designed to remedy Wace's omissions but were extracted from the work of which the Harley fragments alone survive."[155]

Although it is possible that Additional and Lincoln were not created simply in order to "complete" Wace's text, we can't assume either than they were derived from Harley. As mentioned in my edition, "just as the *PM* [*Prophetiae Merlini*] circulated apart from the *Historia*, the ANP could have also circulated separately, being taken up by the *H* poet and incorporated into a larger whole of which only five fragments now remain."[156] Following their versions of the Prophecies, the Harley Prophecies fragment is also unique in another way: Lincoln contains a 10-line transitional passage almost identical to a passage in H, and not found in Additional or the decasyllabic versions. Lincoln's transitional passage contains some of the same details found in Wace, ll. 7543–54 – that is, the lines which immediately follow Wace's disclaimer where he states that he will not translate the Prophecies, 7535–42, and which tell of Vortigern's attention to Merlin and his questions about his death. In Lincoln, the Wace text resumes at 7543, with a lengthy passage on Vortigern's death (to l. 7582, not all of which will be reproduced here). Harley on the other hand continues on with its own version of Merlin's narrative to Vortigern on his death (rather than switching to Wace's *Brut*, as the Lincoln MS does):

Lincoln	*Harley*
Quand li rei Vortiger ot escuté Merlin,	Quant li reis Vortiger out escolté Merlin,
Jurad qu'unques mes ne vit sis mestre devin.	Jurat que unkes mais n'oid si maistre devin.
"Di moi si tu sez de ma mort le train."	"Di mei, se tul sez, de ma mort la train."
"Sire, vols tu saveier e cunustre ta fin?	"Sire, volz tu saveir e conoistre ta fin?"

---

154   *ANP*, ed. and trans., Blacker, 9.

155   "The Harley *Brut*," 45.

156   Blacker, ed. and trans., 9. For evidence that the decasyllabic and alexandrine ANP had separate origins, see 9–10.

THE ANONYMOUS VERSE BRUT TRADITION 457

Bien te garde del feu as dous fiz Constentin,
Cil sunt en Armoriche e sunt mult bel meschin.
E sunt od els Bretun, Mansel e Peitevin.
Li sire d'Amoriche icil sunt si cusin,
E tresqu'a poi tens serrunt nostre veisin;
En Toteneis serrunt anuit u le matin." [1–10]

Li reis ad mult loé Merlin (7543)

E mult le tint a buen devin;

Demanda li quant il murreit

E par quel mort il finereit,

Kar de sa fin ert en effrai.

"Garde, dist il [Merlin], guarde tei[157]
Del feu aux enfanz Constentin,

Kar par lur feu vendras a fin.

D'Armoriche sunt ja meü

Par mer siglent a grant vertu.

De ço te puis faire certein

Qu'a Toteneis vendrunt demain.

Mal lur as fait, mal te ferunt,

De tei griefment se vengerunt.

Bien te guarde del feu as dous filz Co[n]stentin
Cil sont en Armorice e sunt mul bel meschin,
e sunt od els Breton, Mansel e Peitevin,
li sire de Amorice, kar il sunt si cosin.
En tresque a poi d'ore serront voster veisin;
A Toteneis serrunt u seir u a matin."

"Par tei fud mort lur piere par [ta] grant traïson.
par tei vindrent li Seigne en iceste regïon,
par tei de iceste terre sun occis li baron.
Li dui filz Co[n]stentin te en ren-dront guerredon,
En une tor te arderunt, la n'avras guarison:
e së il mal te funt, il unt juste açaison,
kar par ta malveisté sunt honi li Breton.
Quant tu seras occis par tele confusïon
dunc contre les Seines esmoverunt la tençon.
Quant Hengistes iert mort e tut si compaignon,
Aurelies serrat reis par dreit eslectïon.
Icil ferat grant pais par dreit ententïon
e referat iglises par en coste e en viron.
Cil morrat par venim, ço ferunt li felon.

---

157   Weiss restores P's "Merlin" in this line, replacing the "dist il" with "dist Merlin."

458   CHAPTER 6

A tun mal lur frere traïs	Pois ert ses freres reis, danz Uther Pendragon,
E a tun mal rei te feïs	tote la terre averat en sa possessïon:
E a tun mal en cest païs	cil morrat par venim." – Ço dit en la lesçon.
Paens e Saisnes atraïs ...	Tot si come Merlin l'out dit e aconté ...
(Lincoln 1–10 and Wace 7543–60)[158]	(Harley, frag. 2, 1796–1823)

When King Vortigern had listened to Merlin	When King Vortigern had listened to Merlin
He swore he had never seen such an excellent diviner	He swore he had never heard such an excellent diviner
"Tell me if you know the manner of my death."	"Tell me, if you know, the manner of my death."
"Sire, do you want to know your end?"	"Sire, do you want to know your end?"
Protect yourself from the fire of the two sons of Constantine,	Protect yourself from the fire of the two sons of Constantine,
They are in Armorica and are very handsome boys.	They are in Armorica and are very handsome boys.
And with them are Bretons, and those from Maine and Poitou.	and with them are Bretons, and those from Maine and Poitou.
The lords of Armorica, for they are his cousins	the lords of Armorica, for they are his cousins,
And very soon will be our neighbors;	In a short while they will be your neighbors;
Either tonight or tomorrow they will be in Totnes." (Lincoln 1–10)	They will be in Totnes either tonight or tomorrow."
The king praised Merlin greatly	"Their father died at your hands through your great treason
And considered him a very great diviner;	through you the Saxons came to this region
He asked him when he would die	through you great barons of this land died

---

158   The passage from Wace in italics of Merlin's predictions of Vortigern's end, etc. (of which 7543–60 are cited here), continues another 22 lines to 7582. My translations of Lincoln, Wace (7543–60) and Harley follow.

THE ANONYMOUS VERSE BRUT TRADITION 459

*And by what death he would meet his
end,
For he was very frightened about this
death.
"Beware, he said [Merlin], protect
yourself
From the fire of the children of
Constantine,
For through their fire you will meet
your end.
They are already leaving Armorica
They are sailing over the sea with
great strength.
About this I can tell you with certainty
that
They will come tomorrow to Totnes.*

*You harmed them, and they will harm
you,
They will avenge themselves on you
harshly.
Through your wickedness you betrayed
their brother
Your wickedness which made you king*

*And your wickedness which attracted
the
Pagans and Saxons to this land ..."*

(WACE, 7543–60)

The two sons of Constantine will pay
you back,
They will burn you in a tower, you
will have no escape:
and if they do harm to you, it will be
justified,
for through your wickedness you
have shamed the Britons.
When you will be killed in such
shameful circumstances,
war will break out against the Saxons.
When Hengist is dead and all his
companions,
Aurelius will be king by rightful
election.
He will make great peace through
great judgement
and he will rebuild the churches
nearby and in the vicinity.
He will die by poison, inflicted by the
traitors.
Then his brother will be king, lord
Uther Pendragron,
he will have the whole land in his
possession
he will also die of poison." – That is
what the book says.
All as Merlin said it and told it ...

(HARLEY, frag. 2, 1796–1823)

In Harley, this passage is not followed by Wace's ll. 7534–54, or by any sections
of Wace (including the disclaimer), since Harley is an independent text. Harley
continues on with its own version of the *Historia*, §118.7–21 (Merlin foretell-
ing Vortigern's death), with the mention of Hengist's death, and the omission
of the Boar of Cornwall "who will conquer all his enemies" (Wace, 7582) being
the major differences from Wace's version (as well as from Geoffrey's, where
the element of the Saxons' faces being "red with blood" is also omitted by both
Wace and Harley).

As noted above, Blakey remarked that the Harley redactor did not seem too
interested in ecclesiastical matters, though he does not list specific passages

460   CHAPTER 6

omitted. One such passage would have come in fragment 2, where Aurelius
has convened his people for Pentecost to celebrate the victory over the Saxons
(2281–92). In the *Historia*, at this juncture, Geoffrey describes how with the
"assent of the people," Aurelius bestowed York on Samson, and Caerleon on
Dubricius (§130.290–94), details which are lacking in Harley. One variant
toward the end of the fragment suggests either a different source or a misunderstanding or both: in Merlin's interpretation of the comet for Uther, Geoffrey
writes "attached to the tail was a fiery mass stretching out like a dragon from
whose mouth issued two rays, one of which seemed to extend beyond the
skies of France, the other toward the Irish sea and to end in seven smaller rays"
(§132.350–54). Merlin interprets the dragon as Uther, and the ray over France
as a presage of Uther's powerful son "whose might shall possess all the kingdoms beneath it; the other ray indicates a daughter, whose sons and grandsons
will rule Britain in turn" (§133.369–72); in Geoffrey, Ireland or the Irish sea are
not mentioned in the interpretation proper, nor are they in Wace, where the
daughter will be "married to Scotland" (8342, "Ki vers Escoce ert mariee") and
give birth to sons and daughters who will conquer seas and lands (8341–44).[159]
The Irish are mentioned slightly later in Wace in connection with their ensuing
battle with the Britons (8350–56), though not by name in Geoffrey, probably
represented by Gillomanius, the Irish king.

    In Harley, the ray over France still signifies the son, but there's a ray which
ends below Ireland:

"Li rai ki en Iberne est ça aval terminez,	"The ray which extends below Ireland,
signifie une fille que vos engenderez;	signifies a daughter you will have;
e nieces e nevoz de celle fille avrez,	and you will have from this daughter nieces and nephews,
dunt li uns aprés l'aultre tendrat voz eritiez."	Who will hold your heritage one after the other."
(HARLEY, frag. 2, 2442–45)	

While Geoffrey devotes §§118–136 to this part of the narrative following
Merlin's prediction of Vortigern's death through Uther's capture of Octo and
Eosa, and Wace nearly 1000 lines (7583–8540), Harley devotes approximately
775 lines (1825–2599) to roughly the same material.[160] Early on in the passage,

---

159   The daughter is not mentioned in CA's version; see n. 105 above.
160   On the one hand, it should be noted that there are a large quantity of short speeches in
      the passage following the Prophecies, making the dialogue livelier than in Wace, though

THE ANONYMOUS VERSE BRUT TRADITION   461

Harley appears to follow Wace's lead by cutting short Aurelius's speech, just as
it was done in the First Variant; in the vulgate, Aurelius reminds duke Eldol of
Vortigern's betrayal of Aurelius's father, Constantinus, "who had saved him and
our country from the invading Picts" (§119.40–41); then he reminds him of his
betrayal of Aurelius's brother Constans. Aurelius feels that the Saxons deserve
"to be applauded" for having driven Vortigern out of the kingdom, and yet the
land must be freed of them since they "laid waste our fertile land, destroyed
our holy churches and wiped out the Christian faith almost from shore to
shore" (§119.47–50).

Where Geoffrey never passes up an opportunity to castigate the Picts
as well as the Saxons for their perpetual offenses against individual Britons
and all Britons, Wace's 12-line speech simply retains the element of betrayal
of Constantine and Constans, and evokes revenge on Vortigern (7629–40).
Here Harley goes a bit farther in its 15-line speech (1849–63) to mention the
destruction of churches and Christianity, being more critical of the Saxons
than the First Variant tends to be as a general rule, evoking vengeance not just
on Vortigern but on the Saxons and their families and progeny: "Que vengez
en seium, baron, ore en pensez, / e puis aprés des Seisnes e de lor parentez"
(1862–63; "Let us be avenged, barons, now and think of it [of Vortigern] and
then afterwards, of the Saxons and their kin"). A bit like Wace's use of "reflex
praise," Harley's narrator tells his audience – "Seinors" echoing epic style –
that those from Germany were strong and well armed, that they would fight
"splendidly"[161] but lose their lives (1995–96; "Seinors, mult sun hardi la gent
de Germanie, / e furent trés bien armé e des armes guarnie; / richement se
combat come por perdre sa vie"); the use of monorhymed laisses in the battle
scenes adds to the epic tenor of the passage.[162]

The epic tenor of fragment 2 continues through the scenes where the king
of Ireland, Gillomanies, is appalled that the Britons want to come to Ireland
to fight the Irish for the giants' stones – don't they have their own stones?!:
"Baron, ore tieng Bretons por fols e esbaïz!" (2247; "Barons, I consider now the

---

  again thereby reducing the tension of many a moment, and not building up the Britons
  or the future arrival of Arthur.

161 "Richement" can be translated as "magnificently," "strenuously," "powerfully," or even
  "splendidly," the latter which conveys an even more noble connotation than "powerfully."

162 In fact, monorhymed laisses are used throughout the poem, but in the battle scenes, they
  are more reminiscent of epic which may have been the author's intention from the outset. Two more *laisses similaires* are found in [CXLVII] and [CXLVIII] on Paschent's death
  (Pascenties, Pascencies), and even a very rare instance of narratorial *discours interprétatif*
  in epic style: "Quant Aurelies fud morz – ço fud duel e pecchez!" (2483; "When Aurelius
  was dead – it was a sorrow and a sin!").

462   CHAPTER 6

Britons to be fools and stupefied!"). In the central part of the passage, 4–5 line speeches are numerous, more than descriptions of the battle.[163] The last longish speech relating to the battle (and not to Merlin's predictions) is put in the mouth of Gorlois of Cornwall, who advises the Britons to attack the Saxons by stealth, which they do, and are ultimately victorious (2528–37). In Wace, Gorlois's speech contains more religious imagery than in Harley – which in fact contains none – including advice to the Britons to pray to God for support (8473–8504), to give up their "wickedness" ("felonies") which they had committed all their lives (8495–96), again resembling the more pious tone of the FV, and as Weiss notes, "considerably more pious than in *HRB*"; the latter (vulgate) focuses exclusively on strategy (§136.420–28).[164]

5.4.6   Tentative Conclusions

Further research is needed on Harley and its potential sources to determine if there is any pattern to a political agenda that could be suggested by changes made in the text, or if it is anything other than an accident of preservation – available hides? – that the first two fragments are virtually identical in length, as are the third and fourth. For the moment, it is impossible to say if the patrons, whoever they may have been, wanted anything more than a copy in French of Arthurian/British history that they could refer to, learn from, and not spend too much time reading or listening to or worrying over the details, including any more than the bare minimum of authorial/narratorial *discours interprétatif* or other bits beyond the "vital core."

5.5   *The Egerton* Brut (*London, British Library Egerton 3028*)
5.5.1   Overview of the Manuscript, the Poem, Authorial Voice, and Egerton's Goals

In the late 1330s to early 1340s, an English scribe, possibly trained at St. Albans, created for a family of the lesser nobility of the southwest Marches a form of abridgment of Wace's *Brut* in Anglo-Norman.[165] The manuscript contains a

---

163   The longest speech is Merlin's 19 lines interpreting the comet (2427–45), discussed above.
164   Weiss, 215 n. 1. Wace does not add however, FV's comment on the Saxons' paganism: "to free us from our threatening adversaries, who themselves are enemies of the living God, and worshippers of idols" (Burchmore, §136.4; "ut liberet nos ab imminentibus aduersariis qui et ipsi inimici sunt Dei uiui, ydolorum cultores" Wright, ed. II, §136, p. 130). This comment is not surprising, given that one of the only criticisms FV levels against the Saxons was their perceived offense against God and Christianity.
165   "An Anglo-Norman Metrical 'Brut' of the 14th Century," ed. Vivien Underwood, 41; citations from the Egerton *Brut* are from this edition; as above, citations from Wace's *Roman de Brut* (here "Wace") are from Ivor Arnold's edition, unless otherwise noted. All translations are

THE ANONYMOUS VERSE BRUT TRADITION   463

narrative in octosyllabic rhymed couplets which reduces nearly 10,000 lines of Wace's *Brut* (4883–14842) to 2,914 lines; 12% of the poem or 337 lines have been added to the 88% made up of Wace's lines.[166] On every recto, there is a miniature, sixty-three in all, preceded by two to three lines which situate each miniature within the narrative; these verses preceding each miniature are all original, non-Wace verses. In addition to the original lines preceding the miniatures, the Egerton scribe also used short passages to summarize material cut or to provide transitions between the Wace sections; these summative passages make up most of the remainder of the 12% of original lines. The Egerton *Brut* is the only extant illustrated metrical French *Brut*, from among the nearly fifty metrical *Brut* manuscripts: nineteen complete or nearly complete manuscripts of Wace's *Brut*; fifteen manuscripts containing incomplete copies (either extracts or fragments) of Wace's poem; nine fragmentary anonymous *Bruts*; plus eight anonymous copies of all or part of the Prophecies (some bound with Wace manuscripts).[167]

At least three areas of inquiry present themselves vis-a-vis this poem: 1) the interactive creation of meaning between illustration and text (a very rich area which cannot be fully explored within the context of this study); 2) the relationship between scribe and author, and the role of authorial voice or author-function in defining texts; and 3) the Egerton poet's possible political, social as well as aesthetic motives for using Wace in the ways he did – including his treatment of the *adventus Saxonum*, Arthur's reign, and the passage of

---

      my own, unless otherwise indicated. See also my "Courtly Revision of Wace's *Roman de Brut* in British Library Egerton MS 3028," and Appendix 2 below.

166   The British Library catalogue of digitized manuscripts reads: "ff. 1r–56v: An abridged version of Wace's *Roman de Brut*, beginning at line 4883 of the longer version (Weiss ed. (2002), p. 124); the first quire is misbound so the correct order of the text is ff. 2, 8, 3, 4, 5, 6, 7, 1 (most illegible), 9. The text is imperfect at the beginning: the lost leaves (probably five gatherings of 8 leaves, or about 2080 lines) corresponded to ll. 1–4999 of Wace's *Brut* and the last 10301 lines of Wace are represented here by about 2800 lines, to the death of Cadwalader (f. 56r). ff. 56v–63r: Continuation from Egbert to Edward III (1338–39)." For more details on the 354-line octosyllabic chronicle continuation from Egbert to Edward III, including an account of historical inaccuracies, see the catalogue of digitized manuscripts at http://www.bl.uk/manuscripts/FullDisplay.aspx?ref=Egerton_MS_3028.

167   See Appendix 1, and also Weiss, xxviii–xxix. This tally does not include Pierre of Langtoft or other later adaptations of Galfridian material in French verse (*Édition critique et commentée de Pierre de Langtoft, Le Regne d'Édouard 1er*, ed. Jean-Claude Thiolier, Créteil: C.E.L.I.M.A., 1989–). For a more diverse range of French translations and adaptations of Galfridian material, see Blacker, "The Anglo-Norman and Continental French Reception of Geoffrey of Monmouth's Corpus from the 12th to the 15th Centuries."

464 CHAPTER 6

dominion[168] – rather than simply writing his own poem without Wace's words, or copying another anonymous *Brut*, or making a complete copy of Wace, with illustrations, since they seem so key to the pleasure of the text. Subjects 2) and 3) will form the basis of this study, though the role of the miniatures will be touched on briefly.

By referring to the Egerton *Brut* as a form of abridgment of Wace's *Brut*, I may have already gone too far in identifying this poem with Wace's. A safer label for the poem might be the one chosen by Vivien Underwood who edited the poem in his 1937 University of London doctoral thesis, "An Anglo-Norman Metrical 'Brut' of the 14th Century." Yet this label, too, is less than satisfactory because the metrical chronicle in Egerton 3028 is not a completely independent treatment of the Brutus legend, as Underwood amply demonstrates.[169] It is difficult to *not* identify this text with Wace since 88% of the poem's verses appear to come from several Anglo-Norman manuscripts of the *Roman de Brut* (1155).[170] However, the kind of cutting and pasting done by the Egerton writer who may also have been the illustrator of this text, reveals a set of authorial intentions not always consonant with Wace's. A close reading of the poem reveals that in addition to providing visual aids and greatly reducing the number of lines, the Egerton author made changes which significantly violate Wace's intent, including the trimming of battle scenes, elimination of etymological passages (one of Wace's passions), reduction of the use of direct speech, as well as shortening lists of names and descriptions of social gatherings, such as the festivities at King Arthur's plenary court, not to mention suppression of Wace's claim to authorship by elimination of the epilogue where Wace's name appears (*Brut*, 14859–66), and inclusion of only half of his disclaimer as to why he didn't want to translate and include the Prophecies.[171]

---

168   Since the beginning of the Egerton *Brut* is missing, it does not contain a version of material on the foundation story of Britain (and Wace himself did not include a Description of the island, so we wouldn't expect that unless the Egerton poet contributed one independently, which he did not).

169   See esp. "An Anglo-Norman Metrical 'Brut'," 42–64.

170   Although it is not possible to confirm this exhaustively but given the similarities with some of the Anglo-Norman manuscripts as seen in Arnold's copious variants, it is logical to think that Egerton's Wace model was one of the Anglo-Norman exemplars.

171   Egerton ends (the *Brut* section, not including the continuation) at roughly line 14702 of Wace's text, adding an original six lines to wrap up the reign of Cadwallader, omitting lines 14711–866, and proceeding directly to the 354-line (octosyllabic) genealogical continuation on English history from Egbert to the reign of Edward III (this text remains to be identified more definitively). In terms of Wace's disclaimer regarding the Prophecies, Egerton includes the first four of eight lines, but not the four lines where Wace explains why he does not want to provide and translate the Prophecies:

THE ANONYMOUS VERSE BRUT TRADITION   465

By simultaneously preserving Wace's voice yet modulating it freely, the Egerton *Brut* sits squarely at the center of one of the liveliest debates in medieval textual criticism: where does the author's text leave off, and that of the scribe begin? Like Bernadette Masters in her article, "Anglo-Norman in Context: The Case for the Scribes," I would like to argue for a reassessment of the scribal role in medieval literary creation, especially in the field of Anglo-Norman texts where scribes have often been dismissed as merely corrupters of Continental texts.[172] However, unlike Masters, I do not find "the forms of creativity represented by author-centered models and scribal-centered models" mutually exclusive, but rather complementary, as two intertwined aspects of medieval literary production.[173] However, even if we accept the complementarity of scribe and author as a model, the model is difficult to apply here because the Egerton writer goes beyond the normal boundaries of scribal redaction, which we associate more often than not with a spectrum of copying strategies, though the spectrum is broad.[174] In Egerton, we appear to have in fact two

Dunc, dit Merlin, les prophecies	Then, Merlin said, the prophecies
Ke vous avez, ceo crei, oiez,	Which you have, I believe, heard,
Des Reis qe a venir esteieint,	About the kings who were to come,
Ke la terre tenir deveient.	Who were to hold the land.
(Eg., 1331–34; corresponding to Wace, 7535–38)	
Ne vuil sun livre translater	I do not wish to translate his book
Quant jo nel sai interpreter;	since I do not know how to interpret it;
Nule rien dire ne vuldreie	I would not like to say anything
Que si ne fust cum jo dirreie.	In case what I say does not happen
(Wace 7539–42)	[lit. "In case it might not happen as I might say [it]"].

See also Chapter 5, n. 178.

172 *Exemplaria* 6.1 (1994): 167–203.

173 Masters, "Anglo-Norman in Context: The Case for the Scribes," 169.

174 Cf. Francesco Di Lella who argues that my qualifying Egerton (in my 2006 article) as an autonomous anonymous *Brut* rather than as a Wace fragment is "un ipotesi poco giustificabile," ("a hardly justifiable hypothesis"; thesis, 111, n. 30), yet ironically on the pages following he supports my point by demonstrating that there are so many thematic divergences that Egerton 3028 – in my view – cannot in all likelihood be considered a Wace fragment (thesis, 113–115), Wace fragments often being simpler, more "random" collections of passages (if they are not continuous). The extent and nature of scribal "tampering" – not simply lacunae as for example in the Wace fragment in CA – may signal distinctions between fragments and independent texts. Thus, this difference of opinion may have much to do with perceptions of scribal activity and intent, and probably cannot be solved in absolute terms. On the range of scribal activity in primarily thirteenth- and fourteenth-century Old French manuscripts, see Keith Busby, *Codex and Context: Reading Old French Verse Narrative in Manuscript*, 2 vols. (Amsterdam and New York: Rodopi, 2002), esp. vol. 1, ch. 2, "Scribal Behaviour," 59–126.

466   CHAPTER 6

authors – Wace through many of his words and our constructed projection of his voice – and the Egerton poet, the scale of whose literary modifications characterizes him more as an author than as a scribe, especially if we perceive an author (or the author category) as a constructed entity, both belonging to, and transcending, individual texts, as Foucault suggests: as an informing principle beyond the simple identification of a specific creator, an informing principle made up of a complex patterns of signs and operations in the texts which distinguish his (or her) work from that of another and which invariably enter into – often subconsciously – our idea of who a particular author is as a separate entity from the texts themselves.[175]

The Egerton manuscript has 118 folios, written on vellum, of small format (19.5 cm × 12 cm), reduced from its original size by trimming, probably done in the nineteenth century to fit a new binding.[176] It contains three texts: first on ff. 1–63, the *Brut* with a continuation from Egbert to the reign of Edward III; followed by a version of the *Destruction de Rome* on ff. 64–83; and lastly the *Roman de Fierabras*, ff. 84–118. The events at the close of the continuation – subsequent to Edward's landing at Antwerp but preceding the victory at Sluys – as well as the script and other material factors, suggest a date of 1338–40, according to Underwood.[177] The style of writing, lining, and illustrating indicate a single scribe, or possibly multiple scribes – the author as head

---

175   Michel Foucault, "Qu'est-ce qu'un auteur?"; see also n. 8 above and n. 209 below.
176   Underwood, "An Anglo-Norman Metrical 'Brut'," 1–2. Alison Stones observes that Egerton 3028, "with a total of no fewer than 118 miniatures, it belongs to a special category of densely illustrated secular manuscripts made between c. 1250 and 1350 in England for patrons, mostly anonymous, who were particularly interested in historical, hagiographical and literary works in Latin and French" ("The Egerton *Brut* and its Illustrations," 167; the colors in the illustrations reproduced in this article are very close to those of the manuscript itself). Additionally, regarding the miniatures, Philippa Hardman and Marianne Ailes note that "if the arms used throughout the whole manuscript are considered more closely, an even greater political engagement with the English claim to the French throne may be discerned. In the *Brut* section, the early rulers of England, Hengist, Arthur and Edward I bear the *gules three lions passant guardant or*, which was by then [c.1138–40] the established royal arms of England [folios 18r, 27r, 41r, 53r, and 63r]... [and in the *Brut*] moreover, Arthur not only defeats (and kills) Frolle [the Roman ruler of France, bearing a coat of arms associated with France, *azure three fleurs de lis or*]: he then wins the whole of France which he claims as his own" (*The Legend of Charlemagne in Medieval England: The Matter of France in Middle English and Anglo-Norman Literature*, Cambridge: D. S. Brewer, 2017, esp. pp. 138–46, cited here at 141–42, 144). On the early history of the royal arms of England, see Adrian Ailes, *Royal Arms of England* (Reading: University of Reading, 1982). On the depictions of Arthur typically bearing a coat of arms *azure three crowns or*, see Michel Pastoureau, *Les Chevaliers de la Table Ronde: Anthropologie d'une société imaginaire* (Lathuile: Éditions de Gui, 2006), 29–35.
177   Underwood, "An Anglo-Norman Metrical 'Brut'," 5–6.

THE ANONYMOUS VERSE BRUT TRADITION   467

of a team? – trained in the same school. Orthographic and historical evidence suggest that the manuscript was produced by a resident (or residents) of the southwestern Marches, possibly near Gloucester.[178] While it is possible that Egerton 3028 is a copy of an abridgment, my instinct is that it is the original, a single work commissioned to serve specific purposes – as many of the anonymous *Brut*s may have been.[179]

As noted above, the Egerton *Brut* is imperfect at the beginning, having lost probably five gatherings of 8 leaves or about 2080 lines[180] – but even if the beginning were extant, the number of lines in Egerton would only equal approximately one third of those in the *Roman de Brut*. In addition to the narrative of Egerton beginning *in medias res*, we also can be reasonably sure that the *Brut* is missing at least some initial folios since both the *Destruction* and the *Fierabras* are preceded by full-page miniatures with decorated borders on the verso facing their opening folios (63v and 83v respectively). Both of those texts have their second miniatures – each taking up a half-page – two folios later, on the recto side (66r and 86r), with miniatures occurring on each subsequent recto. The *Brut* begins with its first half-page miniature on 1r, with the rest following consecutively. The versos contain an average of thirty-eight lines in a single column, the rectos on average eighteen lines, with the miniatures filling approximately half the column; the sixty-three illustrations in the *Brut* are most often found halfway down a folio, but sometimes toward the top of the column, or toward the bottom.[181]

Since I have only seen the manuscript on microfilm, I cannot personally vouch for the colors of the miniatures. The Museum Catalogue states, "the style is curious with dull, ugly colours (hair and beards nearly always purple) and very little gold (for crowns, etc.). There is a profusion of imaginary heraldry."[182] In their study on the artistic representation of the Roland legend in medieval literature, Rita Lejeune and Jacques Stiennon note that the hair and beards in the *Fierabras* miniatures in Egerton are almost always in red, with a bit of

---

178   Underwood, "An Anglo-Norman Metrical 'Brut'," 41.

179   I agree with Underwood that this may be an autograph; Hardman and Ailes however find this suggestion "no more than speculation" (*Legend of Charlemagne*, 138, n. 62).

180   Underwood, "An Anglo-Norman Metrical 'Brut'," 4. See also n. 5 above, and the British Library Catalogue of Illuminated Manuscripts which reports that "the first quire [is] misbound; the right order being ff. 2, 8, 3–7, 1, 9." https://www.bl.uk/catalogues/illuminated manuscripts/record.asp?MSID=6654.

181   *The British Museum Catalogue of Additions to the Manuscripts 1916–1920* (London, 1933, 338–42) provides a list of the illustrations in the codex (340–42).

182   *Catalogue 1916–20*, 340.

gold ornamentation.[183] In the miniatures from the *Fierabras* in the Lejeune and Stiennon volume, shades of reddish orange and brown dominate, though the shoes, stockings and lining of the king's cloak appear to be a dark green.[184] Lejeune and Stiennon note that the style of writing and illustration in Egerton is very similar to that of the Hanover *Fierabras*, also a mid-fourteenth-century manuscript with Anglo-Norman characteristics.[185]

David J. A. Ross has also pointed out the stylistic similarities between Hanover MS. Niedersächsische Landesbibliothek IV 578 and Egerton 3028, in his study of mid-thirteenth-century manuscripts containing pen and ink drawings reminiscent of Matthew Paris's and executed quite possibly at St. Albans Abbey.[186] Ross calls for further study on manuscripts illustrated in this style of color-washed line drawings, suggesting that we have "evidence of the existence of a lay establishment specializing in the copying and illustration of secular Anglo-Norman literature in the second quarter of the thirteenth century," which would be early for the existence of this type of enterprise.[187] Ross cites the Hanover and Egerton MSS as evidence of the production of secular manuscripts containing this distinctive type of illustration well into the fourteenth century.[188]

Thus, the Egerton manuscript may be one of a group of manuscripts produced in a scriptorium in southwest or south-central England in the mid-fourteenth century, not a de luxe edition, but one in which illustrations played an important part in the presentation. The patron or original owner of the manuscript was likely literate, though it is not inconceivable that the copy was presented following oral performances or readings of the poem, as a souvenir, with the pictorial images intended to stimulate the owner's memory of the narrative, since the images on the whole reiterate the narrative line but do not advance it, that is, they don't tell anything new.

---

183   Rita Lejeune and Jacques Stiennon, *La Légende de Roland dans l'art du Moyen Âge*, 2 vols. (Brussels: Arcade, 1966), I, 218.

184   In the ICLS Madison Congress session (2004) where I originally presented the paper which was revised for the *Courtly Arts* volume, Keith Busby observed that the reproductions in Lejeune and Stiennon are more orange-colored than the miniatures actually appear in the manuscript.

185   Lejeune and Stiennon, *La Légende de Roland dans l'art du Moyen Âge*, vol. 1, 218.

186   "A Thirteenth Century Anglo-Norman Workshop," in *Mélanges offerts à Rita Lejeune, professeur à l'Université de Liège*, 2 vols. (Gembloux: J. Duculot, 1969), vol. 1, 689–94.

187   Ross, "A Thirteenth Century Anglo-Norman Workshop," 694.

188   Ross, "A Thirteenth Century Anglo-Norman Workshop," 694.

THE ANONYMOUS VERSE BRUT TRADITION 469

The following are but three of the many examples of this repetitive/reiterative tendency in the use of the miniatures, where the narrative is illustrated but not moved forward to the next stage:

1) the miniature of three barons who beseech seated King Constantine to remove Maxenz, the Roman emperor, and declare himself emperor (f. 6r): this miniature is preceded by the lines, "Les barons ni volent a Rome meindre, / A Costantin alerent pleindre" (Eg., 277–78; "The barons didn't want to stay in Rome, they went to Constantine to complain"), and followed by "D'aler a Rome cil aprismast, / Archiers et chivalers amenast" (Eg., 279–80: "He was on the point of going to Rome, he took archers and horsemen with him"), declaring that Constantine has resolved to go to Rome (omitting the six lines in which Wace relates that the barons were so insistent, and flattering, that this decision was virtually assured, *Brut*, 5704–9);

2) the miniature of two ships and seven maidens on high seas, depicting the imminent shipwreck of Ursula and the 11,000 virgins (f. 10r), preceded by the lines, "Ki dunc oist crier meschines, / Et enhaucier voices femines" (Eg., 503–4; "Who thus heard the maidens crying out and lift their women's voices") and followed by "Mult par io out Nefs [*sic*] perilez / Et meschines a doel neiez" (Eg., 505–6; "Many ships perished there and the maidens drowned in pain"). While the Egerton poet uses fifty-two lines where Wace has seventy-seven – a fairly large proportion of lines relative to Wace in this case – the illustration nonetheless does not supplant or in any way furnish what has been omitted, that is, primarily Wace's descriptions of the weather, the sea and the pathos of the tragedy where the great majority of the maidens were drowned. Rather, it reinforces what has been included already in the Egerton narrative; and

3) the miniature of the coronation of King Arthur surrounded by two bishops and two barons (f. 37r) preceded by the lines "Arthur Ie fiz Uther maunderent, / A Circestre le coronerent" (Eg., 1933–34; "They sent for Arthur son of Uther, they crowned him in Cirencester") and followed by "Qant Arthur fu Reis novelement / De sun gré fist un sereement" (Eg., 1936–37; "When Arthur was newly king, he swore an oath of his own accord"), referring to how Arthur swears the Saxons will have no peace as long as they remain in the kingdom (Wace, 9034–35). In neither Egerton nor Wace's *Brut* do we see the names of the bishops and barons pictured in the Egerton miniature; in addition, Egerton omits twenty lines of Wace's narrative 9013–32, a passage which relates Arthur's attributes and his generosity which were evident as early as the age of 15 when he

470   CHAPTER 6

was crowned, Egerton skipping from Wace l. 9012 ("A Cilcestre le coru-
nerent"), picking up again at l. 9033 with the mention of the oath Arthur
makes to his men before embarking on campaigns against the Saxons.[189]
That the Egerton *Brut* was originally bound with two poems associated with
the legendary history of France, and that it contains a continuation of English
history up through the midway point of Edward III's reign, suggests that the
Egerton *Brut* was considered an historical text, as Wace's *Brut* appears to have
been in most of the Anglo-Norman manuscripts, and which was likely consonant with Wace's intention when originally writing. If we consider the Egerton
Brut to be a Wace manuscript – multiple fragments sewn together to make a
new whole, sewn together from the cloth of Wace – the Egerton manuscript
is the only Anglo-Norman Wace manuscript to bind the *Brut* with either a
roman d'antiquité or with a poem associated with the Charlemagne cycle of
epics, that is, with legendary French history. Appendix 1 reveals that the latter
presentation, or binding, is typical of Continental Wace manuscripts, whereas
Anglo-Norman manuscripts in general group the *Brut* with English histories or
liturgical texts. Thus, the Egerton *Brut* is again unusual, this time in its contextualization of the poem as part of a combined insular and Continental corpus
of vernacular historico-legendary works.

However, if we consider the Egerton *Brut* a "non-Wace" *Brut*, it is one of
eight vernacular verse *Bruts* (not containing the Prophecies) all of which are
fragmentary, though of course, they may not have been at the time they were
produced.[190] Of all the anonymous vernacular verse *Bruts*, the Egerton *Brut*
contains the largest proportion of sections of Geoffrey of Monmouth's vulgate *Historia Regum Britanniae* and the First Variant because it covers nearly
the "whole story" albeit in greatly reduced format. It is also the text that most
closely resembles Wace's *Brut*, given the use of Wace's lines, as well as its omission of Merlin's Prophecies (though neither the Royal *Brut*, London, BL Royal
l3.A.xxi, nor College of Arms roll 12/45 A contain the Prophecies either).
The Egerton text is the most Wace-like of the non-Wace texts since 88% of
Egerton is made up of Wace lines taken virtually verbatim from Anglo-Norman

---

189   The miniature of Arthur's coronation is reproduced in color in Valentine Fallan, "King
       Harold's chanson: An English Reading of the *Roman de Rou*," an essay occasioned by
       the publication of Glyn S. Burgess's translation, *Wace: The Roman de Rou* (see the *Times
       Literary Supplement*, 5277 [21 May 2004], 12–13). On both stylistic details and larger pat-
       terns of organization among the miniatures, see Alison Stones, "The Egerton *Brut* and its
       Illustrations."
190   See Appendix 2. In a way, in terms of the count, Harley 1605 does "double-duty" as it is an
       anonymous verse *Brut*, but it also contains a nearly complete version of the Prophecies.

THE ANONYMOUS VERSE BRUT TRADITION   471

manuscripts D, L, C, S and possibly F.[191] Continental manuscripts G and R
are the next two most likely source manuscripts, according to the variants
listed by Ivor Arnold. Perhaps the Egerton poet was working from a Wace
manuscript no longer extant since it is unlikely that he had access to so many
manuscripts. Nonetheless, his goal was not to reproduce Wace *qua* Wace but
a much shorter text with its own political and social agendas, among the most
outstanding are: 1) to de-emphasize the evolution of the island and its peoples
particularly the Britons, presenting the amalgamated England as more of
fait accompli than a tumultuous work-in-progress; 2) to tone down the military aspects of the narrative; and 3) to incorporate a no-fuss attitude toward
peacetime finery and love.

5.5.2   Egerton's Cutting of Passages to Achieve Its Goals
5.5.2.1   *Trimming of Maritime and Martial Scenes*
It has been well demonstrated by William Sayers, Matthew Bennett, and
Elisabeth van Houts among others, that Wace in both the *Brut* and the *Rou*
displays a passion for maritime and martial scenes.[192] In Egerton, many of the
battle narratives are greatly curtailed or cut altogether. The most conspicuous "revisions" among them include: the omission of 300 lines on Severus's
campaigns in Scotland and how the Picts, sent into Scotland by the rogue king
Carais, became indistinguishable from the Scots (Wace, 5285–568); 100 lines of
Uther's war against Octa (Wace, 8434–531) are replaced by a five-line summation (Eg., 1772–76); a twelve-line paraphrase (Eg., 1941–52) replaces 300 lines
cut from Arthur's war with Colgrin and Cheldric, followed by the omission of
Arthur's conquest of Scotland and Ireland and tales of the marvelous lakes
told to Hoel (Wace, 9039–639); and the narrative of the conquest of Gaul is
curtailed (Wace, 9930–60, 10015–40, 10151–70 are provided), with eleven lines
given of Wace's seventy-seven for the conquest of Scandinavia, plus a five-line
paraphrase (Wace, 9799–876; Eg., 2017–32). The cutting of over 700 lines
(Wace, 11617–12371) from Arthur's campaign against the Emperor Lucius in
Gaul, replaced by a nine-line paraphrase, has the effect not only of minimizing the weight of the lead-up to the passage where Arthur is victorious over
Rome, but also of eliminating the role of Gawain as warrior; his earlier speech
defending peace is cut as well (Wace, 10765–72). In fact, in Egerton, Gawain is
only mentioned in two lines of the text, where he is named as Arthur's nephew
(Eg., 2733 and 2745). This is puzzling, since by the time the Egerton *Brut* was

---

191   This is suggested by Underwood (47), and tentatively confirmed by a survey of Arnold's
      variants.
192   See Chapter 5, n. 99.

472   CHAPTER 6

produced, Gawain was a character already well established in the romance tradition both in France and England.

5.5.2.2   *Trimming of Speeches*

With regard to trimming speeches in Wace's text, Underwood remarks: "Besides the battle pieces, the long-winded eloquence of Wace's characters very properly suffers condensation."[193] Properly or not, the Egerton scribe cuts many speeches by as much as 90%, while eliminating others. For example, much of the description of Uther's passion for Igerne is cut and of the eleven lines asking Ulfin for advice, all that remain are:

"Ulfin," dist il, "cunseille mei,	"Ulfin," he said, "advise me,
Mis conseilz est trestut en tei.	I am relying on you entirely for advice.
L'amour Ygerne m'ad suspris,	Love for Ygerne has surprised me,
Tut m'ad vencu, tut m'ad conquis."	Conquered me, vanquished me completely."

(WACE, 8657–60; Eg., 1819–22, with minor changes)

Egerton was not interested in the seven lines recounting how the king thought he would die if his love were not consummated posthaste (Wace, 8661–67). Similarly, the thirteen lines of chitchat in Ulfin's reply are reduced to two lines of advice to ask Merlin, "Ne vus en sai conseil duner; / Mais faites Merlin demander" (Wace, 8675–76; Eg., 1823–24, with minor changes) ("I don't know how to advise you; / Go ask Merlin"). Thus, not only are many of the "pre-battle harangues," to use Underwood's less-than-flattering term, omitted, with the exception of Arthur's reading of the threatening letter from Lucius brought by the Roman ambassadors, but also the brief moments of love dialogue, albeit between sovereign and advisor.

The fact that Egerton retains 60% of the letter Arthur reads from the Roman ambassadors preceding his battle with Lucius supports Underwood's suggestion that the Egerton *Brut* was meant to serve at least in part as war propaganda for Edward III. The emperor's claim that Arthur held France and Flanders wrongly (Wace, 10686) and that he would take Britain and France from him (Wace, 10700) might have been one pre-battle harangue Edward's entourage would have wanted to hear, since Edward, who apparently claimed the French throne whenever expedient,[194] wished to emulate Arthur by

---

193   Underwood, "An Anglo-Norman Metrical 'Brut'," 50.

194   Anne Curry, "The Hundred Years War, 1337–1453," in *The Practice of Strategy: From Alexander the Great to the Present*, ed. John Andreas Olsen and Colin S. Gray (Oxford: Oxford University

THE ANONYMOUS VERSE BRUT TRADITION 473

successfully proving the emperor – in the fourteenth-century context, the King of France – wrong. Propaganda to enhance Henry Plantagenet's hold on the throne – the *Brut* was supposedly completed in 1155, one year after Henry's ascent to the throne of England – was likely among Wace's intentions, since he wrote for Henry whose land holdings in France were ultimately the most vast of any English monarch, far greater than those of the King of France until fifteen years after Henry's death in 1189.[195] By 1360, although he had temporarily set aside his claim to the French throne, Edward held the largest proportion of French territory of any English monarch since Henry Plantagenet.[196]

5.5.2.3 *Trimming of Naming Passages, and Other Cultural Markers Such as Court Festivities*

Wace's numerous etymological and toponymic passages – one of his passions, where he even expands on Geoffrey of Monmouth, his main source – are almost all removed by the Egerton poet who appears distinctly uninterested in how names changed as territories changed hands. Admittedly, the great majority of the etymological and toponymic passages in Wace's *Brut* precede the beginning of the Egerton text as we have it, yet the Egerton poet avoids the few chances he did have to include them. If the Egerton poet was possibly from the area around Gloucester or had ties there, as Underwood suggests, it is curious that he eliminates Wace's fourteen-line description of how Gloucester got its name (Wace, 5075–88) since he would not have gained that much space by omitting it. Gone, too, are Hengist's description of how Wednesday and Friday were named after Saxon gods (Wace, 6775–92), and at the end of the text, the passage on how the Welsh got their name is gone, since that passage appears in Wace's concluding account of Yvor's and Yni's return to Britain (Wace, 14843–66), which is missing from Egerton.

The Egerton poet also does not appear to have been too interested in the aesthetic aspects of festivities at Arthur's court, though by extension, the aesthetic is bound up with the ceremonial and is thus integrally connected to issues of power and cultural dominance. Even though the proportion of his text devoted to Arthur is virtually identical to that of Wace – 27% to 28% – and thus, by mathematical proportion greater than in Wace, Arthur still does not appear as important a ceremonial figure in Egerton as in Wace. Of the

---

Press, 2011), chapter 5, Oxford Scholarship Online 2012 https://www.oxfordscholarship .com/view/10.1093/acprof:oso/9780199608638.001.0001/acprof-9780199608638.

195 On John's loss of Plantagenet lands, see n. 122 above.
196 C. Warren Hollister, *The Making of England, 55 B.C. to 1399*, 4th ed. (Lexington, MA: Heath, 1983), 259.

424 verses Wace devotes to the festivities at Arthur's court following his conquest of Gaul, Egerton retains 171. One hundred and fourteen lines have been cut from the guest list – where Wace uses much of Geoffrey's material, enhancing the section on whose sons were present (though not the Welsh sons, which he largely retains but does not expand upon) – and are replaced by a seven-line paraphrase which hits the high points but names no one individual. Perhaps Egerton's patron was not interested in hearing if his or her ancestors were members of the Round Table or present at Arthur's plenary court. The closing note in the seven-line paraphrase that many came on horseback in handsome groups could be construed as participation in a courtly lexicon and ethic, but this element is significantly understated in comparison with Wace.

Egerton also cuts 139 verses from the account of the festivities themselves following the guest list, including passages of gift-giving, the luxurious aspects of the queen's entourage, even the celebrated passage on how the knights seeking to impress the ladies were braver in jousting, and thus the ladies more restrained in responding to their admirers (Wace, 10511–20). Wace's fourteen lines on Guinevere at the wedding, mentioning her beauty, lineage and Arthur's love for her (as well as their inability to have children) is replaced by a four-line paraphrase as a wedding scene:

Devant la Reine Gonovre alerent	Before Queen Guinevere went
Qatre dames qui portoient	Four ladies carrying
Qatre columbes blauncs plumez:	Four doves with white feathers:
Mult furent beles et afaitez.	They were very beautiful and well attired.

(Eg. 2214–17)

While on the one hand Wace's less-than-courtly comment that the royal couple was childless is omitted, so are the details of Guinevere's Roman heritage, in other words, her genealogy, as well as the king's love for her. As a consequence of these editorial decisions by the Egerton author, the focus on the ceremonial aspects of Arthur's peacetime activities is substantially diminished, as is the love element, and genealogy, which in Guinevere's case is significant, since in the following scenes Arthur goes on to defeat the Romans, demonstrating his equality to them through marriage plus his superiority to them through military prowess.

In the context of the cutting of names of guests, description of food, music, and jousting, it is somewhat surprising to find that toward the end of the festivities section, the Egerton poet retains a handful of verses stating that Kay the seneschal and Bedevere the cup-bearer served Arthur at table (Eg., 2332–37;

THE ANONYMOUS VERSE BRUT TRADITION   475

Wace, 10463–66, 10471–72). The roles of these two figures are substantially enhanced relative to their importance in Wace's text, if only through cutting of other passages and characters, including Gawain. The Egerton poet's increased emphasis on Kay, and particularly on Bedevere, suggests that he may have been related to the close assistants of Edward III, or at least that he valued the service provided by close assistants more than he valued gift-giving, jousting, and general merriment.

5.5.3   Egerton and the Church
Egerton's "general tidying up" includes significant changes in the story of St. Augustine's conversion of the English. Egerton omits the narrative of how the mischievous residents of Dorchester hung rays' tails on the back of Augustine's vestments, and as a result of God's vengeance, how all their descendants thenceforth had tails (Wace, 13715–44), a passage of ethnic critique found in writing only in Wace; gone as well, however, are the much more positive accounts of the miraculous spring discovered by Augustine and the founding of Cerne Abbey (Wace, 13745–812).[197] Egerton also omits Augustine's conflicts with the British Church and the massacre of the Bangor monks at Chester (Wace, 13825–926). Thus, in the Egerton *Brut*, all one learns about Augustine is contained in a few lines about his arrival and successful conversion of the Saxons without mention of the protest from the British clergy that they did not need to be converted and their refusal to owe allegiance to Augustine but to their own prelate (Wace, 13880–84). The Egerton scribe adds a few original lines about a trip Augustine was supposed to have taken to Rome to confirm to the pope the success of his mission (Eg., 2859–62). By eliminating the ethnic slurs about tailed Englishmen and material on divisions in the Church, and by adding the original lines about Augustine's trip to see the pope, Egerton presents a more unified and palatable picture of Augustine's mission than Wace does. One could go so far as to say that his presentation of Augustine's mission suggests a more pro-English approach to this material, but at the least, this is another example of Egerton's lack of interest in evoking sympathy for the Britons.

5.5.4   The *Adventus Saxonum*
A further example of Egerton's relative lack of interest in the fate of the Britons is his account of the *adventus Saxonum*. Hengist and Horsa show up on schedule and assist Vortigen against the Picts; they ask for castles and the king grants them "Suongcastre" (Eg., 984). The Egerton poet devotes much less narrative

---

197   See J. Blacker, "Why Such a Fishy Tale?"

476   CHAPTER 6

space than either Geoffrey or Wace on the thought of so many Saxons arriving that one couldn't tell the pagans from the Christians (Eg. 1072–1075).[198] He
omits the arrival of St. Germanus to help bring Christianity back to Britain
(Wace 7131–54);[199] he does, though, include the Night of the Long Knives (Eg.,
1125–60), but not the four lines describing the quantity of the carnage inflicted
on the unsuspecting Britons, 460 Britons slaughtered through the Saxon
treachery (Wace, 7255–58).

5.5.5   Future of the Britons

As mentioned above, although Egerton maintains nearly the same percentage of his text devoted to Arthur as Wace – 27% to Wace's 28% – he portrays a
less prepossessing monarch and shows less interest in the future of the Britons
than Wace. Like Wace, Egerton leaves out Merlin's Prophecies which form
chapters 112–17 of both the vulgate and First Variant versions of Geoffrey of
Monmouth's *Historia Regum Britanniae*.[200] But Egerton goes further than Wace
in leaving out as well Merlin's prophecy of Arthur's possible return (Wace,
13285–98), of all but the barest mention of the arrival of Gormund and the
defeat of the Britons represented by his "Donation" (Wace's over two hundred
lines 13382–610 are replaced by an eleven-line summation), and of the eventual
return of the Britons to power only after they would be able to return the relics
of their saints from Rome to Britain.[201] Egerton also reduces the narrative of

---

198   See the discussion of the Britons' fear of being overrun by Saxons and the ills of too much
      mingling of pagan Saxons and Christian Britons as portrayed in the vulgate, FV, Wace and
      Royal above under Royal, section 2f ("Revival of Christianity among the Britons").

199   Wace does not mention as do Bede (1.17) and Geoffrey (§101; and FV §102) the particular
      detail that St. Germanus comes to fight the Pelagian heresy in addition to reestablishing
      the Christian faith (which according to Geoffrey and the FV was necessary due to both the
      influx of pagan Saxons and the heresy). As mentioned above in Chapter 5, Wace in effect
      blames the results of the Pelagian heresy on the Saxons without mentioning the heresy
      itself (Wace, 7136–7138), which is understandably not Bede's perspective, though the lat-
      ter does show sympathy here for the Britons whom he says could not combat Pelagius on
      their own, even though they did not want to accept the heresy.

200   As noted above in Chapter 1, Reeve does not number the book of Prophecies but they
      retain the section numbers 112–117. For the First Variant see Geoffrey of Monmouth, *The
      Historia Regum Britannie of Geoffrey of Monmouth II*, ed. Neil Wright (1988), §§112–17.

201   The vulgate *Historia Regum Britanniae* reads, "Dicebat etiam populum Britonum per
      meritum suae fidei insulam in futuro adepturum postquam fatale tempus superu-
      eniret; nec id tamen prius futurum quam Britones, reliquiis eius potiti, illas ex Roma in
      Britanniam asportarent; tunc demum, reuelatis etiam ceterorum sanctorum reliquiis
      quae propter paganorum inuasionem absconditae fuerant, amissum regnum recuperar-
      ent" (§205.568–73; "It is said that through his blessing the British people would one day
      recover the island, when the prescribed time came, but that this would not happen before
      the British removed Caualadrus' body from Rome and brought it to Britain; only then

THE ANONYMOUS VERSE BRUT TRADITION 477

Cadwallader's reign from roughly 200 lines (Wace, 14657–842) to twenty-three (Eg., 2891–914): there is no mention of Cadwallader's sending his nephews, Yvor and Yni, back to the island to rule over those Britons who stayed behind during the famine (Wace, 14818–24), nor of the king's death during his pilgrimage to Rome, and his burial there (Wace, 14827–40). In the Egerton *Brut*, Cadwallader dies after only one month in Brittany (Eg., 2908–14), and the modified abridgement of Wace's narrative ends there, without mention of Athelstan's reigning over a united England (except for Wales and Cornwall) (Wace, 14757–60). In the overall organization of the Egerton *Brut*, Arthur remains a center of interest as an historic figure and symbol, albeit toned down, but the destiny of the Britons does not, the passage of dominion barely notable, and certainly not a source of sorrow or shame for the Britons.[202]

would they recover their lost kingdom, after the discovery of the bodies of the other saints which had been hidden from the invading pagans.") Wace gives a rough translation of the first sentence, but apparently not of the second, not defining exactly whose remains are referred to here – but it would appear just Cadwallader's, and not those of other figures – and not referring specifically to saints' relics (though the mention of "relics" evokes saints in and of itself): "Ne ja ço estre ne purreit / Desi la que li tens vendreit / Que les reliques de *sun cors*, [my emphasis] / De sepulture traites fors, / Serreient de Rome aportees / E en Bretaine presentees (Wace, 14795–800) ("That it would never come to pass until the time came when his body's relics, taken from his tomb, would be brought from Rome and presented [laid forth] in Britain"). Egerton avoids this prophecy altogether. See Chapter 2, n. 37 on Geoffrey's possibly confusing the story of Cadwallader's pilgrimage to Rome with Bede's account of Cædualla of Wessex's pilgrimage to Rome, and also how in the tenth-century Welsh prophetic poem, the *Armes Prydein*, Cadwallader (Cadwaladr; king of Gwynedd, d. late 7th c.; son of Cadwallon) appears along with a prince named Cynan (Conan Meriadoc), as one of two messianic leaders expected to restore the Britons to the sovereignty of Britain following the expulsion of the Saxons. A full exploration of these legends and their appearance in Welsh prophetic poetry is beyond the scope of this study.

202   Not only is Wace's authorship suppressed by omission of the last eight lines, but also the reminder for the audience that this was a history of the Britons, and of the lineage of the barons descended from Brutus, even though Wace underscores that the Britons held the island for a long time, but *in the past*:

Ci falt la geste des Bretuns	Here ends the history of the Britons
E la lignee des baruns	And the line of the barons
Ki del lignage Bruti vindrent,	And they who came from the Brutus's lineage,
Ki Engleterre lunges tindrent.	Who held England for a long time. One thousand one hundred and fifty-five years,
Puis que Deus incarnatiun	Since the Incarnation of our Lord
Prist pur nostre redemptiun	[Who was] taken [into Heaven] for our salvation

5.5.6 Scotland

Underwood points out that Egerton was not interested in Scotland or the north.[203] I would like to go further to suggest that the poet purposefully minimizes any possible allusions to claims of even limited authority or domination on Scotland's part, likely in light of Edward's numerous "brutal and inconclusive campaigns" in Scotland, prior to his victory over the Scots at the battle of Neville's Cross in 1346, when he took King David II captive and devastated the Scottish countryside.[204] In addition to cutting 300 lines on Severus's campaigns in Scotland, thereby eliminating altogether Arthur's conquest and division of Scotland, Egerton demotes the king of Scotland in his account of Arthur's battalions (Eg., 2602–17) on the eve of the battle with the Emperor Lucius.

The Egerton poet's first step in this plan is to increase the number of battalions from eight to twelve (though the heads of the second and eighth battalions are not named). He then moves the king of Scotland from his position as head of the first battalion to head of the twelfth, promoting Kay and Bedevere from the fifth battalion to the first. The count of Flanders and Guichard of Poitou also receive a promotion in Egerton – from the sixth battalion to the third – replacing the kings of Denmark and Norway who disappear. Further shuffling results in a promotion for Jugein of Leicester (seventh to fourth) and Jonathan of Dorchester (seventh to fifth), Corsalen of Chester (eighth to sixth) and Urgen of Bath (eighth to seventh), and a demotion for Boso of Oxford (second to ninth). Hoel – whom we should remember was the king of Brittany, second home of the Britons, and Arthur's nephew – and Gawain, another of Arthur's nephews, fall from the third battalion and disappear, and the tenth, eleventh, and twelfth battalions are created for the counts of Lincoln, Warwick, and the king of Scotland respectively. This reorganization seems far from arbitrary, especially since Egerton's habit is often to eliminate nonessential material; he evidently thought the disposition of Arthur's army was absolutely essential, and was not going to dignify the king of Scotland with a place at the head of the first battalion. His continued favoritism for Kay the seneschal and near

---

> Mil e cent cinquante e cinc anz,
> Fist mestre Wace cest romanz.   Master Wace wrote this work in French.
>   (Wace, 14859–866)

203 Underwood, "An Anglo-Norman Metrical 'Brut'," 74.

204 Hollister, *The Making of England*, 4th ed., 255. This probably also means that the Egerton author would not have been interested in either Geoffrey's positioning of Arthur as ostensible lord of Scotland, or any broader connections Arthur may have had as king of the Britons with the "men of the North." On this vastly complex subject, see esp. Tim Clarkson, *The Men of the North*, 9–33.

THE ANONYMOUS VERSE BRUT TRADITION 479

obsession with Bedevere the butler are puzzling but inescapable. Gawain had to be eliminated here for internal narrative consistency, since he is mentioned only twice in passing and thus relegated to the rank of a very minor character in the text, for reasons that remain unclear.

5.5.7 Continuation of the Egerton *Brut* on English History

In brief, the 354-line continuation of the Egerton *Brut* on English history does not distinguish itself by bringing new information to light or perhaps by attempting to sort out the involved juggling of the Heptarchy, which it does not include.[205] Egerton's continuation text is notable for 1) its historical inaccuracies, such as the statement that Henry I was the son of Stephen of Blois; 2) its confusion, including skipping the reign of Alfred altogether by going straight from Aethelwolf to Athelstan, having begun with Egbert (Egbrid in this text); 3) providing the Norman perspective on the Conquest through presentation of the Norman version as Wace did in the *Roman de Rou* (c.1160–74); and 4) its gingerly treatment of William Rufus, whose disputes with the Church and alleged homosexuality go unmentioned.[206] Henry II's disputes with the Church – specifically with Becket – are emphasized in Egerton's continuation, however, in the capsule summary of his reign. Further details of how Egerton's continuation on English history compares with those found in Wace manuscripts C and J, and the newly discovered history (quite possibly a version of the *Livere de reis de Britannie*) following the Wace fragment in College of Arms 12/45 A remain to be taken up in future studies.

---

205 See also n. 107 above on CA's prose continuation, also beginning with Egbert, but with the Heptarchy (which it explains was actually a Pentarchy). As noted above, the differences between the Egerton octosyllabic history and CA's remain to be investigated.

206 As noted above in Chapter 4, R. R. Davies comments on Gaimar's "remarkable portrait of William Rufus as a world-conquering, Arthur-imitating figure" (n. 5). Among contemporary historians, to the best of my knowledge, Gaimar is the only twelfth-century writer to have been an apologist for William Rufus, while at the other end of the scale, as Frank Barlow notes, Orderic Vitalis was one of the monarch's harshest critics (*The Ecclesiastical History*, ed. and trans. Marjorie Chibnall, 6 vols., Oxford Medieval Texts, Oxford: Clarendon Press, 1969–80, esp. vol. 4, bk. 8); see Barlow, *William Rufus* (Berkeley and Los Angeles: University of California Press, 1983), 435, and also Emma Mason, *William II Rufus the Red King* (Stroud: Tempus, 2005), 7–8, 18–19, 204–6, who proposes that Wace (in the *Rou*) also wrote a largely favorable portrait of that king (19), though in my view, not nearly as positive as Gaimar's. It is possible that Egerton's brief yet largely positive treatment of the monarch was standard for the middle of the fourteenth century, but this, too, remains to be investigated elsewhere.

480   CHAPTER 6

5.5.8   Egerton: Conclusions

The Egerton *Brut* prompts us to ask "Who is Wace or what is a Wace text?" because it replaces many of Wace's intended meanings while retaining so many of Wace's words. To use Peter Shillingsburg's distinction, the Egerton scribe was more conservative in his treatment of Wace's "intention to do" – that is, the intention to record specific words in a specific order – and much more liberal with Wace's "intention to mean" – his intention to convey a particular meaning or set of meanings through the specific arrangement of words.[207] The Egerton poet has made more radical changes to Wace's *Brut* than a hypothetical scribe who may have "Anglo-Normannized" a French original by applying notoriously fluid Anglo-Norman metrical standards to Continental French verse lines. The Egerton poet has retained the largely Anglo-Norman lines[208] but has recalibrated the content, foregrounding some elements through the elimination of others, plus making additional changes.

It is very difficult to read the Egerton *Brut* without having in mind a concept of Wace's voice which goes beyond this manuscript, and beyond either the insular or Continental manuscripts of his *Roman de Brut*, following the lead of Michel Foucault here – "le résultat d'une opération complexe qui construit un certain être de raison qu'on appelle l'auteur ... la projection dans des termes plus ou moins psychologisants ... du traitement qu'on fait subir aux textes ... des traits qu'on établit comme pertinents, des continuités qu'on admet" – not only because we cannot divorce ourselves from an author-centered notion of editorial practice, but also because Wace is still so present together with the Egerton author.[209] Perhaps the Egerton poet used Wace in order to associate his poem with that of the famous poet or with his audience's idea of what Wace would sound like. But why he did that so extensively yet making many significant changes remains a mystery. If the Welsh and British historical aspects of Wace's poem were less important, as were ceremony, love, and certainly Scotland, why not simply write a version in his own words, like the authors of the other anonymous *Brut*s, most notably Munich, Harley 1605, and

---

207   *Scholarly Editing in the Computer Age: Theory and Practice*, 3rd ed. (Ann Arbor: University of Michigan Press, 1996), 4–35.

208   See n. 191 above.

209   M. Foucault, "Qu'est-ce qu'un auteur?" in *Dits et ecrits* 1954–88, I, cited at 800–01 ("Nevertheless these aspects of an individual, which we designate as making him an author are only a projection, in more or less psychologizing terms, of the operations that we force texts to undergo, the connections that we make, the traits that we establish as pertinent, the continuities that we recognize, or the exclusions that we practice," trans. Josué V. Haran, in *Contemporary Literary Criticism: Literary and Cultural Studies*, 4th ed., ed. Robert Con Davis and Ronald Schliefer (New York: Longman, 1998. 364–76, here 370).

THE ANONYMOUS VERSE BRUT TRADITION   481

Royal? Whether the Egerton patron specifically commissioned an illustrated
Wace abridgment tailored to suit mid-fourteenth-century tastes we cannot
know with certainty.

The Egerton *Brut* begs us to simultaneously forget and remember Wace,
by presenting a very different text through a patchwork of the original (or
originals, depending on one's critical orientation); in addition, formulating
a consistent political or courtly agenda for the poem based on the disparate
elements discovered in this patchwork is even more problematic than block-
ing out our preconceived ideas of Wace and his text. While it is easier to see
that this is not a nearly complete Wace manuscript, it is less easy to answer
the question: What distinguishes this patchwork from a simple assemblage
of fragments, or from an interpolated manuscript, such as D, B, C, P, H, J, and
L? Perhaps the coherent quality of the fragments, including the goals behind
the assemblage? Or the quantity, that is, the numerous and often consecutive nature of the fragments? Or the inclusion of miniatures bolstering the
text where paraphrases sometimes replace long passages? If the Egerton *Brut*
is merely an assemblage of fragments, then it should be considered a fragmentary Wace manuscript which this study suggests it is not, nor is it a pure
abridgement in the modern sense of the term, abridgements themselves raising the question of their status in relation to the original in a medieval context of often extreme textual fluidity.

Although possibly even more unique than has been suggested within the
limits of this study and thus less representative of widespread patterns of
textual production than we might have originally assumed, the Egerton *Brut*
nonetheless urges us to define more precisely what we mean by an author, a
fragment, or even scribal redaction, or at the least it should make us more aware
of the definitions which already inform our reading and editorial practices.

6   Chapter Conclusion

It has been difficult to do complete justice to these anonymous texts in the limited context of this chapter, but I hope to have demonstrated at the least that
each merits analysis as a separate text, with stylistic and thematic attributes
of its own, and not necessarily as derivative of Wace, or in other ways lacking.
However, medieval audiences – or at least the makers of books – did apparently
see Wace's *Brut* as a superior text, and, in closing this chapter, I would like to
examine the possible criteria upon which this judgment may have been based.

As mentioned above in n. 9, first, we have a classic chicken-or-the-egg
dilemma: was Wace's text more popular because it was more readily available

482   CHAPTER 6

to be copied or was it more available and widely copied because it was more well liked, which for us, has ultimately resulted in its being the only complete French verse *Brut* text extant? While this dilemma cannot be solved, my instinct is that Wace's *Brut* had something that kept audiences coming back, and this something is closely connected with what Michel Foucault termed the "author-function" of a text. In his essay, "What is an author?" Foucault suggests that the four functions outlined by St. Jerome still affect the ways in which modern critics view authors: first, that the author is defined as a "constant level of value" – that is, that each of his works are of equal quality and inferior works must be struck from his canon; second, that the author is "defined as a field of conceptual or theoretical coherence" (371), that his doctrine cannot contain any major internal contradictions; third, that the author is "conceived as a stylistic unity"; and fourth, that the author is seen as an "historical figure at the crossroads of a certain number of events" (371). The author-function is not simply the assigning of a name to a text but "the result of a complex operation which constituted a rational being that we call 'author'" ultimately "a projection of the operations that we force texts to undergo, the connections that we make, the traits that we establish as pertinent, the continuities that we recognize, or the exclusions that we practice" (370). Those connections we make are based on signs in the text which often unconsciously contribute to our idea of what constitutes a work of the particular author in question. Thus, we come to anonymous *Brut*s with our idea of Wace, which in turn has been formed by a variety of factors – vocabulary, self-reference, use of direct and indirect discourse, etc.

The four modalities outlined by Jerome and reformulated by Foucault in his discussion of how readers create authors can be applied to Wace and affect our reading of his *Brut*: first, with respect to the "constant level of value," material is seen as Wace or non-Wace and often non-Wace is deemed inferior (among the French texts, not Laȝamon or others) – Ivor Arnold made those kinds of decisions when assembling his edition, and these decisions affect editors constantly. Second, regarding consistency of doctrine, scholars have often pointed out that in the *Rou* (more so than in the *Brut*) there are inconsistencies of viewpoint that have made them question the "authenticity" of various passages, reveling an expectation that the historian must always be consistent; scholars also seem to expect that because Wace wrote in French his *Brut* would demonstrate a decidedly pro-French bias, which it does not: Françoise Le Saux, along with Emily Albu among others, have shown that if Wace demonstrates any bias in favor of a political group – and I still hold to my earlier view that in general, Wace has largely "depoliticized" the material he found in the vulgate *Historia* and the First Variant, in that he has tried to be more neutral

THE ANONYMOUS VERSE BRUT TRADITION 483

(rather than removing political content per se), for example by praising the "villains" – for example, the Casesars, Hengist and Horsa, and Gormund – in keeping with their stature and not demeaning them purely because they were enemies of the Britons as Geoffrey did – if he evinces bias, it is a Norman bias, not pro-French.[210]

Third, with respect to Laȝamon for example, some past generations of scholars of the English verse *Brut* have tended to impose a perceived stylistic unity upon Wace – a courtly vision – that while present, does not dominate and, in fact, competes with his interests in etymology, military affairs, geography, and meteorology to name only a few.[211] Lastly, Wace's innovations – the Round Table and the Invention of the True Cross being the most well known – have tended to make him an "historical figure at the crossroads of a certain number of events," and thus have tended to restrict the ways in which his work has been read, and at least until recently, had often relegated him to the status of the author of the Round Table, becoming a literary landmark with ironically relatively few stopping by to do more than take a snapshot.[212] However, if we can judge by the number of extant manuscripts in relation to other vernacular chronicles of the twelfth century, medieval audiences and manuscript owners did not share this minimizing, modern "touristic" perspective toward Wace's *Brut*.

Le Saux has taken note of some of the most important features that make Wace's *Brut* so Wace-like: the nostalgic, in fact at times sorrowful, tone in which he recounts the passing of time, the changing of place names and other historical shifts; the use of a courtly lexicon – though I want to underscore the fact that the anonymous authors do so as well, some to a larger degree

---

210 Le Saux, *Companion*, esp. 160–208, and Albu, *The Normans in their Histories: Propaganda, Myth and Subversion* (Woodbridge: Boydell, 2001), 215–20, 222–37.

211 In Chapter 4, "The French Connection," of her groundbreaking study on Laȝamon (*Laȝamon's Brut: The Poem and its Sources*, 59–93), Françoise Le Saux examines scholarship on Wace's "courtliness" and although Donald Hoffman writes in his review that Le Saux is "hampered by a somewhat simplistic notion of the 'courtly'," she ably demonstrates how the concept of Wace's "courtliness" had dominated at least one substantial branch of Laȝamon scholarship, concluding both that the Norman poet's vision was much more complex than previously thought, but also that, given the possible breadth of Laȝamon's exposure to French literature, "the French influence on the *Brut* cannot be said to be restricted to Wace, and it is more pervasive than was once thought" (93) (Hoffman, *Quondam et Futurus* 1.1 [1990]: 91–94, cited at 92).

212 As noted in Chapter 4, n. 1, while doing the literature search for my annotated bibliography on Wace, I was repeatedly struck by the large proportion of scholarship which mentioned Wace in passing as the first to record the story of the Round Table, but then said nothing more about him or the *Brut*. Those essays of course were not included in the bibliography.

than others; the use of military and maritime vocabulary, two interlocking vocabulary groups which also need to be emphasized, for Wace's *Brut* is probably more a military manual than a courtly one; his use of pathos which in comparison with the Caligula Laʒamon, for example, may seem less significant than it really is.

The combination of all these elements – plus that Wace is simply a very good storyteller, to paraphrase Felicity Heal, "no one could accuse Wace of failing to tell a good story"[213] – contributed in the 12th–14th centuries to make his *Brut* the normative French version. Even in manuscripts, such as the famous BnF fr. 794, the "Guiot" manuscript, where Wace is not named – and thus his authorship is literally suppressed – his authorial voice is heard and the stories – Belinus and Brennius, Arthur's conquests, Augustine's conversion of the English, the Britons' flight from the island to Brittany and back – remain largely intact. Wace's vision including his presentation of Arthur is more encyclopedic than often assumed: there's something for everyone – military campaigns, maritime adventures, battles with giants, negotiations with and domination of pagan tribes and the Romans (and the French!), the Round Table, and a bit of knights and ladies and love. Wace's Arthur is less courtly, more military, while at the same time more detached than assumed by some – but never as distant or detached as Royal's Arthur, for example, which seems to have the goal of simply depersonalizing rather than elevating the monarch. The sense of detachment Wace creates for Arthur on the other hand contributes to the monarch's universality, lending an aura of impersonal, transcendent grandeur that was inevitably fated to pass – though we shouldn't forget that Wace was the only French writer to include the "Breton hope" of Arthur's eventual return to lead his people once again – just as the triumphs of the Caesars or other famous leaders were fated to be replaced by adversity as Fortune turned her wheel.

In conclusion, we find many elements while comparing all these *Brut*s, elements we might not have noticed without points of comparison, but nevertheless sometimes we do these texts an injustice as well, by minimizing their authors to the role of scribe or redactor, a habit of reading which likewise tends to inhibit our capacity to see the relationship between authorial voice and political or social program. On the one hand, by perceiving of Wace and Caligula Laʒamon (since that is the more complete of the two manuscripts) as authors – i.e., in the modern view, more important than scribes or redactors – we create them in our own image of what these authors were, and thus limit our possibilities of discovery. On the other hand, we have invested them with an authority that ideally ought not to interfere with our perceptions of those

---

213   See n. 131 above.

texts somehow considered inferior. The less popular texts need to come out of the shadow of the popular ones, despite our occasional temptation to see the former as perfunctory products by second-rate writers in response to patrons' requests: we need a French translation of the history of the kings of Britain, and can't afford (or find) a copy, so please sit down and produce one! Our evaluation of the more popular or more influential ones – Wace and Laȝamon[214] – should continually be redefined in light of new discoveries, both intra- and extra-textual. With those expansive goals in mind, unlike the early anonymous French verse *Brut*s which never seemed to manage to write much about the Saxons, we as a community of scholars, will never run out of angles.

---

214 Although extant in only two manuscripts today, Laȝamon's *Brut* remains without question very influential. See the extensive bibliographical references in Jonathan Davis-Secord, "Revising Race in Laȝamon's *Brut*," *Journal of English and Germanic Philology* 116.2 (2017): 156–81, and in *Reading Laȝamon's Brut: Approaches and Explorations*, ed. Allen, Roberts, and Weinberg (2013).

Conclusion

From Geoffrey of Monmouth's counter-history which effectively launched a tradition of exploration of early history, underscoring its role in the recognition of a more comprehensive, inclusive history, to the five Old French fragmentary verse *Brut*s discussed in Chapter 6 – which in a way, represent the last stop in the journey to the Anglo-Norman prose *Brut* of the thirteenth century (and beyond), one of the most popular historical texts of the Middle Ages – we have seen a tremendous range of treatments of, and attitudes towards, the foundational history of the Britons, and of course, of Arthur, Geoffrey's lasting legacy to both historiography and literature.

Perhaps it shouldn't surprise us how each author discussed in this book has put a different "spin" on his (or her) story of the Britons within English history, from Bede, William of Malmesbury, and Henry of Huntingdon's essentially Anglocentric visions of the Saxon "achievement" – though their views are certainly not monolithic – and Geoffrey's responses to those visions, drawing inspiration from, and greatly expanding on, Gildas and the *Historia Brittonum*, to the First Variant's rejection of some of Geoffrey's favoritism for and emphasis on the Britons, to Wace's numerous attempts at reconciliation of the various presentations and often conflicting visions he found in his sources, to the anonymous verse *Brut*s whose authors/scribes each have had their own political preoccupations (or seeming lack thereof).

In large part, Wace's synthetic approach toward multiple sources, including oral sources, provides new perspectives on the development of the history of Britain, and on the development of historical writing as well, as he tried to understand and present how marginalized groups could – and should – contribute to the evolution of multiple societies over time. In particular, I would like to focus here first on his passion for etymology and toponymics as a tool of historical interpretation, further expanding on Joanna Bellis's very useful analysis of Wace's use of etymologies. As noted above,[1] Bellis argues that for Geoffrey, Wace, and Laȝamon, "etymologizing the landscape was a means of giving Britain a glorious and self-authenticating history, independently from their problematic sources" (321), finding that "Laȝamon in particular relates to the national myth very differently from Wace, his source, identifying with the conquered rather than the conquerors, history's losers rather than its victors"; according to Bellis, unlike Wace, who used etymologies as "certifiers of the veracity of his account" Laȝamon's "etymological truth-claims function more

---

1 Chapter 5, n. 6.

CONCLUSION   487

as elegies for the erosion of the glory of the national myth, and as prophecies
for its ultimate reinstatement" (322); Bellis also suggests that in Wace "etymology is not static but fluid, an unfinished and developing story rather than a
closed master narrative" (336).[2] It is this idea that etymological discourse can
manifest fluidity rather than fixity, illustrating the evolution of peoples paralleling the evolution of languages, names of peoples, and place names, rather
than the codification of the national narrative that is new in Wace studies, and
illuminating.

Although it is still possible to read Wace's etymological discourses in the
Brut as I did over twenty-five years ago – as often redolent of nostalgia and a
sense of loss as territories perpetually changed hands and nothing, from rulers to names of cities, ever stayed the same[3] – it appears now necessary in
light of the contextualization of the *Brut* within the broader frameworks of
the foundation myth of the Britons, the *adventus Saxonum*, the conversion of
the English, and the passage of dominion, in light of the developing traditions
of the authors treated in this study, to see these same etymological impulses
in a more positive light, as illustrative of a more fluid vision of social integration, seeing the interconnectedness for Wace between his views of the evolution of language and of metamorphoses and assimilation of peoples. While
on the one hand it would appear that Wace viewed Gormund's Donation as
a cataclysmic event wherein the Britons were exiled to the outskirts of their
own lands, in other contexts, he would appear to subscribe to a more contemporary anthropologists' view of gradual infusions of the Saxon groups into the
Britons' social fabric, in a more peaceable light. Wace neither proposes the
adventus as an "achievement," nor does he vilify the Saxons as Geoffrey does;
he also rarely mentions the speakers of Anglo-Norman except to say that they
used "Londres" as their word for "Lundene" since they couldn't pronounce the
latter, due to a lack of linguistic talent rather than through any inflexibility

---

2   "Mapping the National Narrative: Place-Name Etymology in Laȝamon's *Brut* and its Sources."
    For further perspectives on the blending of languages and cultures in Laȝamon's *Brut*, see
    also these inevitably interwoven complexities of conquerors and conquered which are also
    summed up by Julia Marvin at the end of her review of Kenneth Tiller's post-colonial study
    of Laȝamon's perspectives on Anglo-Norman rule and vision of history (*Laȝamon's Brut and
    the Anglo-Norman Vision of History*, Cardiff: University of Wales Press, 2007): "His analysis
    re-illuminates the essential strangeness and complexity of the position of Laȝamon's *Brut*
    as a post-Conquest English verse account of mostly British history: the conquered, drawing
    on the languages and texts of the conquerors, telling in the language of the conquered the
    largely heroic story of the previously conquered, with the English language itself a token of
    victory, defeat, and resistance all at once" (*Arthuriana* 20.4, 2010: 108–9, cited at 109).
3   In the original of *Faces of Time* (1994).

or prejudice or refusal to take on new customs, as he implies for the Saxons, a criticism, granted, yet not completely a vilification.

Interestingly, Jacqueline M. Burek argues that for Laȝamon, it was the Britons who were inflexible in their approach to other cultures and thus were unable to conquer or adapt, and the Saxons who were flexible, the opposite perception from that we have found in Wace, though perhaps not surprising since Laȝamon was writing from a more English perspective than his French model (and roughly forty years later, for different audiences).[4] In terms of the blending of cultures, Scott Kleinman comments that for Laȝamon, "the story of the passage of dominion between the Britons and the Saxons turns out to be the story of the historical process by which multiple cultures contributed to the making of the cultural melting pot of his own day."[5] Burek adds to Kleinman's assessment "that Laȝamon specifically presents the English, and not the Britons, as the creators and beneficiaries of such a cultural melting pot."[6] Continuing with the "melting pot" image for a moment, we also see in Wace (7059–74) less of a resistance to assimilation (or simply intermingling) between the Britons and the Saxons than in Geoffrey (§101), perhaps due to his Norman origins, the Normans, by reputation at least, apparently rapidly trying to blend in with those they conquered.[7] By the same token, Wace appears to have felt on one level a sense of identification with the Britons as a marginalized people in their own land,[8] a sentiment which is clearly in evidence looking back at his reporting of Gormund's Donation and how Wace says that the latter and his "army" thoroughly destroyed the land – having been shown the way by the Saxons, it must be added – before handing over what remained of it to the Saxons, who then proceeded to exile the Britons (1193–1200, 13463–87, and 13625–37).

However, Wace is such an eclectic, synthetic writer that the only way to propose a consistent, unified historical vision for him in my view is through the metaphor of Arthur and the Round Table. Unlike with Geoffrey – although scholars don't always agree on interpretations – one can follow or develop an interpretation through the narrative in a fairly consistent way; in Geoffrey, there are not nearly as many twists and turns as in Wace, since his approach is less synthetic and he is arguing certain points to the exclusion of others – not

---

4 "'Ure Bruttisce speche': Language, Culture, and Conquest in Laȝamon's *Brut*.
5 "*The Æðelen of Engle*: Constructing Ethnic and Regional Identities in Laȝamon's *Brut*," *Exemplaria* 16.1 (2004): 95–130, cited at 128.
6 "'Ure Bruttisce speche'," 123, n. 16.
7 Chapter 2, n. 150.
8 On Wace's origins on the isle of Jersey and the various ways they may have his informed his historical writing, see Chapter 5, n. 20.

CONCLUSION   489

admitting to other "evidence" because it will undermine his "agenda," whereas
Wace will provide a variety of perspectives – as in the *Rou* for example where
he provides multiple views on the events leading up to the Conquest (English,
Norman, and Edward's deathbed recantation),[9] ostensibly leaving it up to his
audience to decide which version seems the most plausible.

As I've observed elsewhere,[10] Wace's providing multiple perspectives reveals
an apparent lack of confidence in any historian's ability to access the "absolute
truth" which exists beyond the "facts" narrated in texts – because those narra-
tions are perforce dependent on the imperfect tool of language – and is a very
modern position, in fact a postmodern one; an outstanding characteristic of
the postmodern condition, according to Jean-François Lyotard, is the disbelief in *métarécits*, great heroes, great dangers, great goals.[11] Gabrielle Spiegel
reminds us that

> if, as [Jean-François] Lyotard argues, there are no longer any master nar-
> ratives, still less are there any certainties about the nature and status
> of history itself, whether as an object of study or a subject of practice.
> Our confidence in the totality and ultimate unity of the greater histori-
> cal enterprise is gone. Like so much else, history has been subject to the
> fracturing and fragmentation that has beset all aspects of postmodern
> thought. Not only are there no master narratives, there is no consensus
> of even the possibility of historical knowledge uncontaminated by the
> hermeneutic circle.[12]

That is not to say that Lyotard denies the existence of History with a capital
"H" – as some for example deny the existence of the Holocaust – but that in
his view, postmodern society no longer believes in the great ideas of the past
which were often seen to link the "facts" through historical themes. Spiegel herself tries to find a middle ground between, on the one hand, the postmodern
disbelief in History and the lack of confidence in the referentiality of language,

---

9   *Faces*, new Introduction, 31–32 and n. 76, on Wace's multiple versions leading up to
    the Conquest.
10 "Le rôle de la *persona* – ou la voix auctoriale – dans la *Conception Nostre Dame*, le *Roman
    de Brut* et le *Roman de Rou* de Wace."
11 "En simplifiant à l'extrême, on tient pour "postmoderne" l'incrédulité à l'égard des
    métarécits ... La fonction narrative perd ses foncteurs, le grand héros, les grands perils,
    les grands périples et le grand but" (*La Condition postmoderne. Rapport sur le savoir*, Paris:
    Éditions de Minuit, 1979, cited here at 7–8).
12 Gabrielle M. Spiegel, *The Past as Text: The Theory and Practice of Medieval Historiography*
    (Baltimore and London: Johns Hopkins University Press, 1997), xxi–xxii.

490   CONCLUSION

and on the other hand, the necessity of historians' efforts to discover and present "facts" as evidence in order to advance our knowledge of the past.[13]

Despite his resistance to providing a unified vision – if it means choosing some facts while repressing others that might not fit a certain "agenda" – Wace continues to believe in the importance of the historical enterprise, and also in the value of heroic actions, heroic leaders and honorable groups, as seen particularly in his portrayal of Arthur. Wace follows the general structure Geoffrey provides in terms of Arthur's domestic and foreign campaigns, but he makes significant changes as well. The first is the addition of the Round Table, the second the contrast between Arthur and Gormund as leaders and conquerors, and the third is the personal relationship which Arthur has with Mary – whom he sees in battle *on the inside* of his shield. Each of those additions is essential to who Arthur becomes in the *Roman de Brut*, and to Wace's historical vision, via the metaphor of King Arthur.

In terms of Arthur's "otherness," each of these various elements bears repeating here, especially as they pertain to his status as both insider and outsider, and how that impacts him as a leader and model, as Wace both adapted and expanded – "improved upon" – Geoffrey's essential core. The following elements, each of which points to Arthur's status as insider or outsider, and sometimes as both simultaneously, each of these statuses contribute to his plasticity as a literary/historical figure across eras and genres of historiographical or romance narrative:

1)   illegitimate son – outsider (Merlin's use of herbs and other forms of deception to disguise Uther);
2)   son of a king and future queen – insider;
3)   inherits the throne thus, by extension, through magical means – outsider;[14]
4)   earns the right to be king through his own seemingly transcendental prowess, tolerance of many other cultures (though not of the Saxons or the Romans, each of whom want to subjugate him), and generosity – characterized as the "greatest king" (and other superlatives) – insider;
5)   belongs to a "barbarian group" when seen from the perspective of the soon-to-be-dominant group, the Saxons (Angles/English, in the eleventh hour) – outsider;

---

13   *The Past as Text*, esp. Chapter 3, "Towards a Theory of the Middle Ground," 44–56.

14   Absent from the Galfridian material – including from Wace – the motif of the test of Arthur pulling the sword from the stone in order to prove his descendance from the regal line apparently enters the written tradition in Robert de Boron's late twelfth-early thirteenth century *Roman de Merlin*; see Rosemary Morris, *The Character of King Arthur*, 36–49.

CONCLUSION 491

6) functions as a civilizer through his founding of the Round Table which carries socio-linguistic as well as socio-political connotations – insider;
7) member of a colonizing group and a colonized group, conqueror and conquered – insider and outsider;
8) dies but doesn't – human and messianic figure, "Breton hope" – both within the human realm and outside it – the consummate insider/outsider.

While admittedly Arthur swears to his men as soon as he is crowned that the Saxons will never have peace as long as they inhabit the island with the Britons, Arthur's form of annexing other territories – while certainly a form of colonialism – can be seen as more tolerant of other cultures, leaving the original cultures intact, as for example in Gaul when he fights the Roman legate Frollo in single combat so as not to wreak havoc on Paris and its inhabitants (in the vulgate, Frollo requests the single combat since his army is outnumbered, but in the *Brut*, Frollo asks in order to save Paris, demonstrating Wace's recognition of the importance of "not destroying the village in order to save it"); as if to balance out his fierceness in battle, Wace makes sure that Arthur magnanimously demonstrates mercy for the Scots, while they retain the lands of their ancestors (or at least, their homelands), but under the direction of the leaders Arthur whom installs: Angusel, Loth and Urien. When Arthur leaves Denmark and Norway, the former's King Aschil becomes Arthur's liegeman, and Arthur installs Loth as king of Norway (according to his inheritance), but life goes on in those two countries as it had before, without occupation by colonizing armies or new governments and the cultural and social upheaval that would have brought; no one is forced to assimilate, or make any changes to their culture or way of life. In contrast, as we have seen, Gormund is a different kind of conqueror than Arthur; after he conquers Ireland and has himself proclaimed king – since he wanted to rule somewhere he didn't inherit (though he does not ultimately rule Ireland in the narratives), Gormund moves on to the land of the Britons, destroying everything in his path, without even permitting "forced assimilation" (not that that is an ideal or recommended situation) with the help of the Saxons, and then hands the island over to the Saxons as he had promised, sending the Britons into exile.

While this could seem too anachronistically modern for some scholars, in my view, Wace's introduction of the Round Table suggests an understanding that societies can be valued by the degree of diversity they allow and encourage, and the degree of unity they maintain while being diverse; societies don't want to be so diverse that they fall apart, but they also don't want to maintain themselves through authoritarianism. The genius of Wace is that through the Round Table, Arthur is seen to allow the diversity and equality of others without letting any groups try to be the first among equals; thus the Round Table

492   CONCLUSION

promotes diversity while at the same time maintaining unity. Without the Round Table, Arthur might have been an ordinary ruler of a kingdom where the "other" gains power then feels threatened by the "other others" and subsequently clamps down and destroys diversity in order to maintain unity. With the Round Table, Arthur is the perfect example of the outsider who becomes insider without squelching diversity and other groups, making his "state" more flexible and thus more durable.

Wace's vision of unity through diversity – which, as an ideal, would continue to function throughout historical time into the future – is bolstered by his almost instinctual faith in Mary which he also transfers to Arthur. While Mary focuses both Arthur's and Wace's personal piety, Arthur allows Wace to focus on a national vision, a potential way out of perpetual wars, political domination, and cultural imperialism. In the *Brut*, it is as if Mary gives both Arthur and Wace the strength to focus and unify their personal piety, so that they can then have the courage and imagination to identify and promote a national, flexible, diverse unity, where no one would be second class citizens in their own land.

Another important image of piety and departure of Wace from Geoffrey of Monmouth and the First Variant is his addition of Helena's voyage to Jerusalem where she finds the True Cross (5720–24), "ki lunges out esté celee" (5724; "which had long been hidden").[15] Although Fiona Tolhurst ultimately seeks to emphasize that in Wace "this traditional female role displaces her potential reign," I agree with her in signaling the historical importance of Wace's portrayal: "By presenting Eleine as traveling to the Holy Land, working with Jewish wise men, and making possible the recovery of the greatest of Christian treasures, Wace gives her a place in Christian history that she does not possess in either of his main sources [the vulgate and FV]."[16] Although this earlier Constantine is not shown in the Galfridian texts to be directly related to Arthur, the broader associations are compelling.

In the last analysis, although reasons differ among members of the general public and scholars, what the continued growth of the "Arthurian industry" demonstrates is the fascination for, and the need of, Arthur and all he represents. From those who want to know if he really existed, to those intrigued by his continuous appeal despite the lack of provable historicity, Arthur maintains his position as one of the most enduring figures and metaphors of Western literature. Richard Trachsler reminds us that in the *Prophetiae Merlini* from Geoffrey's *Historia*, referring to the Boar of Cornwall who is often identified

---

15   Helena (in Wace, Eleine), daughter of King Coel, wife of King Constantius, and mother of Constantine I.

16   *Geoffrey of Monmouth and the Translation of Female Kingship*, 185–86.

CONCLUSION 493

as Arthur (though not directly in the texts examined in this book), "Merlin annonce, comme on sait que la gloire du roi sera immense et immortelle: *In ore populorum celebrabitur et actus eius cibus erit narrantibus*" ("Merlin announces that as we all know the king's glory will be immense and immortal"; *HRB*, §112. 42–43, "He will be celebrated in the mouth of nations and his deeds will feed those who tell them").[17] As Geraldine Heng remarks, citing in fact the same passage as Trachsler, "In Arthurian literary history, the interventions of Merlin conjure so efficacious a magical aura that the magus is eventually imported into the constellation of Arthurian romance, with which he is not, in fact, initially associated ... And Arthur himself would become a marvel."[18] Andrew Galloway goes as far as to say that Laȝamon, referring to a passage which hearkens back this same passage from the Prophecies, "makes Arthur emphatically eucharistic in this expansion, as he does his own poem in the prologue. For those storytellers drinking and eating from his tongue and breast, Arthur is both a sacred and a festive endless gift, a fragile island of pure gift ...".[19]

Neither Geoffrey nor the First Variant mention the "Breton hope," though Henry of Huntingdon does in passing at the very end of his *Epistola ad Warinum*, and William of Malmesbury is quite skeptical; it is Wace who tries to set the "hope" in context, refusing to declare Arthur's death one way or the other. While this equivocation can be seen merely as typical of Wace's desire to present what he knows – and that can sometimes be conflicting information – but not declare what he cannot prove, it has a deeper meaning, since for Wace, it is what Arthur represents – diversity, unity, generosity, tolerance, and perhaps more importantly, hope for those who have been displaced, misjudged, or written off – and not necessarily the king as a messianic figure above all else.

---

17 "Le visage et la voix. L'auteur, le narrateur et l'enlumineur dans la littérature narrative médiévale," *Bibliographical Bulletin of the International Arthurian Society* 57 (2005): 349–71; my translation of the French, Latin translation from Reeve/Wright.

18 *Empire of Magic*, 50.

19 "swa him sæide Merlin . þe witiȝe wes mære. / þat a king sculde cume . of Vðere Pendragune. / þat gleomen sculden wurchen burd . of þas kings breosten. / and þer-to sitten . scopes swiðe sele. / and eten heore wullen . ær heo þenne fusden. / and winscenches ut teon . of þeos kinges tungen. / and drinken & dreomen . daies & nihtes. / þis gomen heom sculde i-lasten . to þere weorlde longe." (11,492–99; "Thus Merlin, who was a famous wise man, said about him / that a king would come from Uther Pendragon / such that minstrels would make a table of food from the king's breast / and many splendid poets would sit down to it / and eat their fill, before they journeyed thence, / and draw out wine drafts from the king's tongue, / and drink and make merry day and night: / this game would last for them as long as the world will," Galloway's translation of Laȝamon's *Brut*, 11492–99, ed. Brook and Leslie; "Laȝamon's Gift," *PMLA* 121.3 (2006): 717–34, at 726. See also Lawman, *Brut*, trans. Rosamund Allen, note to l. 11494, p. 450, and Le Saux, *Sources*, 117.

494   CONCLUSION

Although it may seem odd to give Laȝamon the last word in conclusion, but the phrasing pointed out by Michael Faletra says volumes about Arthur's importance and enduring appeal:

> Here, perhaps for the first time, one is treated to an overt statement of the prophecy of Arthur's return, spoken from the king's own lips [14273–82]. If Arthur's authority alone is not enough Lawman reminds us of Merlin's predictions a few lines later: *Bute while wes an witeye, Mærlin ihate, / he boden mid worde his quithes weoren sothe, / that an Arthur sculde yete cum Anglen to fulste* [But once there was a seer called Merlin who prophesied – his sayings were true – that an Arthur should come again to aid the people in England] (ll. 14295–14297).[20] The first historian to include the legend of Arthur's return,[21] Lawman does of course hedge his bets by having Merlin claim that '*an* Arthur' and not '*the* Arthur' shall return, a tactic that further underscores Arthur's status as a *symbol* of the hope and resurgence of the Britons.[22]

It is important to note that in Laȝamon, it is Arthur who first utters the prediction that he will come again, but as noted above, it is Merlin who backs him up, in a more neutral way:

> And I shall voyage to Avalon, to the fairest of all maidens,
> To the Queen Argante, a very radiant elf,
> And she will make quite sound every one of my wounds,
> Will make me completely whole with her health-giving potions.

---

20   In the Otho Laȝamon, the reading is "Bruttes: 'aid to the British'" whereas in Caligula, it is "Anglen, 'to aid the English'" (Allen, trans., note to l. 14297). Allen also comments that Eric G. Stanley "doubts that the English had the same hopes of that Arthur as the Bretons" ("The Date of Laȝamon's *Brut*," *Notes and Queries* 213, 1968: 85–88). Stanley, however, was in fact rejecting Tatlock's theory that Laȝamon was paying "a compliment to Prince Arthur of Brittany, who in his infancy was proclaimed heir by Richard I" (*Legendary History*, 504–5), concluding that "the authorities cited by Tatlock hardly allow us to see Arthur of Brittany as the hope of the English" (87). Nonetheless, this particular discrepancy between the two manuscripts' renditions of the "Breton hope" for "an" Arthur to save the English rather than the Britons is certainly suggestive of a variety of interpretations.

21   Actually, Wace, not Laȝamon, was the first to develop this theme, though as noted above, Henry of Huntingdon does mention it in passing, and William of Malmesbury refers to it as "old wives' tales." See Chapter 2, n. 59.

22   Faletra, "Once and Future Britons: The Welsh in Lawman's *Brut*," *Medievalia et Humanistica* 28 (2001): 1–23, cited at 15.

CONCLUSION   495

And then I shall come back to my own kingdom
And dwell among the Britons with surpassing delight. (14277–82)[23]

Rosamund Allen reminds us that Geoffrey does not mention Arthur's return, "but speaks of him as mortally wounded and taken to Avalon so that his wounds could be tended to, which Wace echoes (*Fud el cors nafrez mortel-ment*), but adds that he, Wace, will say no more than Merlin did: that his death would be doubtful."[24] However, it should be added that Wace, as usual, takes the middle ground: he does say that Arthur is still in Avalon, awaited by the Britons, "as they say and understand," but not committing himself completely, using the third person "ne volt plus dire de sa fin" (13283; "[he] does not want to tell any more about his end"), emphasizing that Merlin is right about the doubtful nature of Arthur's end:

Encore i est, Bretun l'atendent,	He is still there, the Britons await him,
Si cum il dient e entendent;	As they say and give one to understand;
De la vendra, encore puet vivre.	From there he will come, he can still go on living.
Maistre Wace, ki fist cest livre,	Master Wace, who composed this book,
Ne volt plus dire de sa fin	Does not want to say any more about his end
Qu'en dist li prophetes Merlin;	Than the prophet Merlin said about it;
Merlin dist d'Arthur, si ot dreit,	Merlin said about Arthur, and he is right,
Que sa mort dutuse serreit.	That his death would be in doubt.
Li prophetes dist verité;	The prophet spoke the truth;
Tut tens en ad l'um puis duté,	Ever since then one has doubted,
E dutuera, ço crei, tut dis,	And will doubt, I believe, for all time,
Se il est morz u il est vis.	Whether he is dead or he is alive.

(13279–90)

Suffice it to say that since I am not a Laȝamon scholar, I won't presume to discuss his political and cultural goals in his version of the *Brut* story. As we have seen, Geoffrey of Monmouth has written a highly political history – though it

---

23   Allen, trans., 364–65.
24   Allen, trans., note to ll. 14281–82, 14290–7, pp. 461–62.

depends on one's perspectives as to what form Geoffrey's politics took beyond bringing the Britons into history by legitimizing their role in historical narrative, by demonstrating their longstanding claims and the legitimacy of their rivalry as equals with the Saxons, though ultimately relegated to the geographical fringes of the island. For Wace, Arthur becomes more of a symbol of an outsider who through strength, wisdom and ambition, rises to help his people without transforming the "other others" into marginalized groups – though for the Saxons, the wish to do so on his part is hard to deny. While Arthur may have wanted to triumph over the Saxons, he is not shown to decimate or subjugate others, and through the Round Table, Wace's Arthur is shown to establish a seat of government where all are equal, and none are first among equals. Arthur refuses to capitulate to the Romans, setting an example of tolerant behavior, though not without feistiness, and determination to prevail over those who chose to dominate him or the Britons.

But it is Laȝamon who takes all of Wace's symbolism a step further, in a way, out of time and space. By saying that the Britons await *"an* Arthur" rather than *"the* Arthur," the king becomes a symbol for all the downtrodden, for all those waiting to be saved from marginalization, to be brought back to their rightful place in history, to be brought to the table as equals among equals, natives among newcomers, regardless of how "other" they may seem to some who judge them by their differences, and not by their common humanity. This universal symbolism of Arthur both contributes to his place in history and historical writing, and takes him beyond history, and undoubtedly contributes to the monarch's lasting appeal both to scholars and in popular culture, an illustration of how necessary myth – that is, uplifting myth – is to the global imagination. Although it may be true, as Nicholas Higham concludes that "we can now agree to discount King Arthur as a 'real' figure of the past, leaving him and his deeds to the 'smoke' and 'highland mist' of make-believe and wishful thinking ...[that] it is there that he properly belongs,"[25] the "highland mist of make-believe" is nonetheless crucial to the global imagination because it has the capacity to pull all of us out of separatism, colonial oppression, and cultural imperialism toward dreams of building a more equal, just, and hopeful world.

---

25   Nicholas J. Higham, *King Arthur: The Making of the Legend*, 279.

APPENDIX 1

Wace's *Roman de Brut* in Its Manuscript Contexts

Complete or nearly complete copies in MSS containing only Wace's Brut[1]

ANGLO-NORMAN (1 of 9)

S 1) Paris, BnF nouv. acq. fr. 1415 (14th)

CONTINENTAL (6 of 10)

E 1) London, BL Harley 6508 (14th)

R 2) Paris, Bibl. de l'Arsenal 2981 (14th)
   (missing ll. 13994–14013 and 14064–866 [end],
   fol. 100 having ll. 14014–14063)

N *3) Paris, BnF fr. 1454 (15th)

O *4) Paris, BnF fr. 12556 (15th)

V *5) Vienna, Österr. Nat. Bibl. 2603 (15th)

   6) Paris, Bibl. de l'Arsenal 2982 (18th-c.
      copy of Bibl. Ste.-Gen. 2447, but without "Dits
      et proverbes des philosophes")[2]

---

1   This is an updated version of the list recently published in J. Blacker, "'But That's Another Story': Wace, Laȝamon, and the Early Anonymous Old French Verse *Bruts*," *Arthuriana* 31.4 (2021): 47–102, Appendix I, 83–92. The notes below contain select references in article form primarily of less well known manuscripts or fragments, and not library catalogues which are often on-line now due to the digitalization of manuscripts; see also the invaluable Ruth J. Dean, *Anglo-Norman Literature: A Guide to Texts and Manuscripts*, with the collaboration of Maureen B. M. Boulton, for further bibliographical references (for Anglo-Norman manuscripts), and "Jonas: Répertoire des textes et des manuscrits médiévaux d'oc et d'oïl," l'Institut de recherche et d'histoire des textes (IRHT) and Le Centre national de la recherche scientifique (CNRS), https://jonas.irht.cnrs.fr/. In this chart, which aims to demonstrate patterns of codicological assemblage for Wace's *Roman de Brut* in insular and continental manuscripts, I have reported the foliation from my sources, including Dean and Boulton and Jonas, as well as articles, editions, and collection catalogues; readers should keep in mind that not all sources are internally consistent in the formats they use in their own reporting (e.g., the last three items in the Guiot MS reported as on fols. 361ra–394vc, 349v–430, and 430v–433v, the latter two without column designations, though it is of course possible that those later folios were not written in multiple columns), and I have chosen to not sacrifice elements in their reporting for the sake of consistency. Nonetheless, I have sought to be consistent wherever possible, while providing as much information as possible (on foliation, that is, though refraining from reporting information on quires, script, provenance, etc.).

2   Reported by Antoine Le Roux de Lincy, ed., *Le Roman de Brut de Wace*, 2 vols. (Rouen: É. Frère, 1836–38), vol. I, lxx–lxxi, but not by Arnold (ed., *Le Roman de Brut de Wace*, 2 vols., SATF, Paris, 1938–40). Since this is a copy of a complete 14th-c. manuscript, rather than, for example, a 19th-c. anthology containing excerpts as does Albi, Bibl. mun. Rochegude 8, I am including Arsenal 2982 here.

© KONINKLIJKE BRILL NV, LEIDEN, 2024 | DOI:10.1163/9789004691889_010

498   APPENDIX 1

Complete or nearly complete copies in MSS *containing other texts as well as Wace's Brut:*

ANGLO-NORMAN (8 of 9)

A 2) London, Coll. of Arms Arundel XIV (14th)

  a) *Brut*, fols. 1r–92v

  b) Gaimar, *Estoire des Engleis*, fols.
    93r–124v

  c) *Lai d 'Haveloc*, fols. 125v–132r

  d) Langtoft, *Regne d'Edouard le Ier*, fols.
    133r–147v

  e) *Lignee des Bretuns et des Engleis*, fols.
    148r–149r

  f) Chrétien, *Perceval* (only A-N copy),
    fols. 150r–221v

  g) Walter de Henley, *Hosebonderie*, fols.
    222r–229v

  h) an allegorical love poem (A-N), fols.
    230r–238r

D 3) Durham, Cathed. Lib. C.IV.27 (late 12th–
early 13th)

  a) *Brut* (+ ANP),[4] fols.1r–94r

  b) Gaimar, *Estoire des Engleis*,
    fols. 94r–137r

  c) *Description of England* (A-N),
    fols. 137r–138v

CONTINENTAL (4 of 10)

G 7) Paris, Bibl. Ste.-Geneviève 2447 (14th)

  a) *Brut*, fols. 1r–90r

  b) "Dits et proverbes des philosophes"
    (4 ff.) (OF),
    fols. 91r–94r

J 8) Paris, BnF fr. 1416 (13th)[3]

  a) *Eneas*, fols. 1r–63r

  b) *Brut*, fols. 63v–156v, 181r–182r
    (incl. 4414-line *Vie d'Edouard le
    Confesseur*, replacing ll. 14763–74),
    fols. 157r–181r

  c) 405-line chron. of England, cont. of
    Brut, from William the Conqueror to
    the Siege of La Rochelle 1224 (OF),[5] fols.
    182r–184v

---

3 Jane Bliss and Judith Weiss, "The 'J' Manuscript of Wace's *Brut*," *Medium Ævum* 81 (2012):
    222–48.

4 See Appendix II below. For the decasyllabic and alexandrine Prophecies, see *Anglo-Norman
    Verse Prophecies of Merlin*, ed. and trans. Blacker.

5 Le Roux de Lincy, ed., *Le Roman de Brut de Wace*, vol. I, pp. cxv–cxxvii. More work remains
    to be done in order to determine the relationships between the "continuations" and gene-
    alogies in MSS C, J, College of Arms 12/45 A (roll), and the LRB (*Le Livere de Reis de Brittanie
    e Le Livere de Reis de Engleterre*, ed. and trans. John Glover, Rolls Series 42, London, 1865
    and *Kritische Ausgabe der anglonormannischen Chroniken: Brutus, Li rei de Engleterre, Le
    livere de reis de Engleterre*, ed. Christian Foltys, inaugural-dissertation, Berlin, 1961, Berlin:

WACE'S ROMAN DE BRUT IN ITS MANUSCRIPT CONTEXTS   499

d) Short epilogue to Gaimar, fol. 138v
e) Jordan Fantosme, Chronicle, fols.
   139r–167v

L 4) Lincoln, Cathed. Lib. 104 (13th)
a) *Brut* (+ ANP), fols. 1r–108r

b) Gaimar, *Estoire des Engleis*, fols.
   108v–157v
c) *Description of England* (Λ-N), fol. 157v
d) Jordan Fantosme, *Chronicle*, fols.
   158r–189v

H 9) Paris, BnF fr. 1450 (13th)
a) Benoît de Ste.-Maure, *Roman de Troie*,
   fols. 1ra–83rb
b) *Eneas*, fols. 83rb–112vb

c) *Brut* (ll. 1–9798), fols. 112vb–139v
d) Chrétien, *Erec et Enide*, fols. 140–158

e) Chrétien, *Perceval*, fols. 158r–184v
f) *First Continuation*, fols. 184v–188v
g) Chrétien, *Cligès*, fols. 188r–207r
h) Chrétien, *Yvain*, fols. 207–221
i) Chrétien, *Lancelot* (frag., from l. 5642),
   fols. 221–225
Brut (ll. 9799–14866 [end]), fols. 225–238
j) *Roman de Dolopathos* (end missing),
   fols. 238–264

C 5) London, BL Cotton Vitellius A.X (13th)
a) annal to 1325 (Canterbury) (bound
   with B) in 16th–17th c.) (L), fols. 1–18
b) *Brut*, fols. 19–115v
c) 3227-line chron. of Anglo-Saxon and
   Norman kings to Henry III (A-N),
   fols. 115v–137v[6]
d) Wace, *Conception* (frag., ll. 1129–1203)
   (at bottom of fols. 123v–127r)

K 10) Paris, BnF fr. 794 (13th) [Guiot MS]
a) Chrétien, *Erec et Enide*, fols. 1ra–27ra

b) Chrétien, *Lancelot*, fols. 27–54
c) Chrétien, *Cligès*, fols. 54rb–79rc
d) Chrétien, *Yvain*, 79va–105rc

e) *Athis et Prophilias*, 106r–182v

Druck E. Reuter-Gesellschaft 1962, 45–114; Foltys refers to the prologue of the *LRB* as "Brutus"
and the main text as "Li Rei de Engleterre"). The chronicle "continuation" in MS J would not
appear to be closely related to the others. On the genealogical text in the College of Arms roll,
see Chapter 6 above, and on the "continuation" in the anonymous Egerton *Brut*, and other
"continuations," see Appendix 2, below, n. 6.

6   See Maud Becker, "Une édition de la Continuation du *Roman de Brut* de Wace, contenue
    dans le manuscript British Library Cotton Vitellius A.x," unpub. Ph.D. thesis, University
    of Aberystwyth, 2019. Work remains to compare this "continuation" with others where
    applicable.

500 APPENDIX 1

e) 2nd book of Langtoft's *Chronicle*,
   fols. 139r–157v

f) account of the abbots of Malmesbury
   Abbey (L), fols. 158–160

g) Consistory statutes of Henry
   Burghersh (L) (1334) (15th c.),
   fols. 161–162

h) Statutes of Litchfield Cathedral (late
   15th) (L; ME), fols. 163r–205

f) Benoît de Ste.-Maure, *Roman de Troie*,
   fols. 184ra–286ra

g) *Brut*, fols. 286rb–342rb

h) Calendre, *Les Empereurs de Rome*,
   fols. 342va–360vc

i) Chrétien, *Perceval*, fols. 361ra–394vc

j) *First Continuation*, fols. 394v–430

k) *Second Continuation*, fols. 430v–433v

F 6) London, BL Additional 32125 (13th)

a) *Brut* (missing ll. 10527–12772),
   fols. 1r–57v

b) *Description of England* (A-N, frag.),
   fol. 58r–58v

c) *Roman del Saint Graal*, fols. 59r–205v

d) Robert de Boron, *Merlin*,
   fols. 206r–245v

P 7) London, BL Additional 45103 (13th)

a) *Hystoria Troianorum et Grecorum*, fols.
   1r–10r, incl. account of origin of the
   Franks (L), fols. 8rb–9rb

b) *Brut*, fols. 13r–166r (+ ANP,
   fols. 86r–97r)

c) first statute of Westminster (1275)
   (A–N), fols. 167r–183r

d) *La Petite Philosophie*, fols. 185r–212r

e) poem on the Four Daughters of God
   (A–N), fols. 212r–214v

f) poem on the Apocalypse (A–N),
   fols. 214v–215r

g) *La Seinte Resurreccion* (play),
   fols. 215r–220r

T 8) Cambridge, Corpus Christi Coll. 50 (13th)

a) genealogy of the kings of Britain (L),
   fols. 1r–7r

WACE'S ROMAN DE BRUT IN ITS MANUSCRIPT CONTEXTS   501

b) *Brut*, fols. 7v–89v

c) *Livere de Reis de Brittanie* (kings
from Egbert to Henry III) (A–N),
fols. 90r–91r[7]

d) "Romanz de un chivaler e de sa
dame e de un clerk" (fabliau; A–N),
fols. 91r–94v

e) *Amis et Amilun*, fols. 94v–102r

f) poem on the Four Daughters of God
(A-N), fol. 102r–102v

g) *Gui de Warwic*, fols. 103r–181r

9) Vatican City, Bibl. Apos. Vat. Ottoboniani
lat. 1869 (13th)
[a) list of bishops (L); b) *Généalogie
d'Adam*;

c) *Vita sancti Thome martyris*; d)
Speculum peccatoris;

e) William of Waddington, *Le Manuel des
Pechiez*;

f) treatise of confessions and orations
(A-N)][8]

---

7   Identified as a witness of the *Livere de Reis de Brittanie* by Dean and Boulton, item 13, p. 13; see
also n. 5 above, n. 13 below, and https://parker.stanford.edu/parker/catalog/sp968bx9690.

8   Edith Brayer, "Deux manuscrits du *Roman de Brut* de Wace, Vatican, Ottoboni lat. 1869; La
Haye, Bibl. Royale 73.J.53," in *Studi in onore di Angelo Monteverdi*, ed. Augusto Guidi, 2 vols.,
Modena: Società Tipografica Modenese, 1959, vol. I, 100–08 (101). Brayer reported that the
first six texts of this MS are not extant and that the table of contents records their former
existence in the MS. However, since she wrote, Maria Careri has confirmed that the end of the
fourth item, a Latin text which would probably be identified as the *Speculum peccatoris* (on
"f. 1rA, la fine un testo latino che va probabilmente identificato con lo 'Speculum peccatoris'"),
the fifth item fols. 1r–61r which has the first five books of the *Manuel de pechiez*, and the sixth
item, fols. 62r–92r which has books 6–9 of the *Manuel* are to be found in Vatican MS Pal. Lat.
1970 (late 13th–early 14th c.) ("Per la storia di un testimone poco utilizzato del *Brut* di Wace
(*membra disiecta*)," in *Studi di filologia romanza offerti a Valeria Bertolucci Pizzorusso*, ed.
Pietro G. Beltrami, Maria Grazia Capusso, Fabrizio Cigni, and Sergio Vatteroni (Pisa: Pacini,
2006), 421 [419–24]); on items 1–3 and 4 (except for 4's *explicit* which is found in Pal. lat. 1970),
see also Careri, "Per la storia," 424. Although Careri writes that the *Manuel* ends on fol. 95r,
according to the digitized version of the MS in Heidelberg, the text ends on 92r, and the last few
folios through 95v are blank (https://digi.ub.uni-heidelberg.de/diglit/bav_pal_lat_1970/0192).
As to the "treatise of confessions and orations" in the table of contents of the Ottoboni MS
as reported by Brayer, perhaps that was meant to be a description of the last books of the

502   APPENDIX 1

g) *Brut*, fols. 96r–183r

h) "Britannia insularum nobilissima,"
   fols. 183r–187vb

i) Honorius of Autun, *Imago mundi*,
   188r–193r

j) "Gesta salvatoris cum aliis,"194r–210r

MSS containing fragmentary texts of Wace's Brut

ANGLO-NORMAN (10)

B 1) London, BL Royal 13.A.xxi
   (late 13th–early 14th)

a) Herman de Valenciennes, Bible (frag.)
   2r–11v

b) Honorius of Autun, *Imago mundi*,
   12v–39v

c) *Brut* (ll. 1–52), fols. 40v–41r (following
   Heptarchy platte, 40v)
   A-N or Royal *Brut* (6237 lines),
   fols. 41r–77r
   Brut (ll. 8729–14866 [end]), fols. 77v–113r

d) Gaimar, *Estoire des Engleis*,
   fols. 113r–150r

e) misc. theological tracts (L),
   fols. 151r–192v

f) subject Index to Statues of England to
   Henry VI, fols. 193–194, trimmed and
   used as flyleaves

CONTINENTAL (5)

M 1) Montpellier, Bib. Interuniv. Sect. Médecine
   251 (13th)

a) Benoît de Ste.-Maure, *Roman de Troie*,
   fols. 1r–147v

b) *Eneas*, 148ra–207va

c) *Brut* (ll. 1–5664), fols. 207vb–242[9]

Manuel, as there would not appear to be any text remaining after the *Manuel*, at least not in Pal. lat. 1970 (though it could possibly be elsewhere). According to Dean and Boulton, the often "hesitantly accepted" identification of William of Waddington as author of the *Manuel* has been "validated from documentary evidence" presented by Matthew Sullivan, "The Original and Subsequent Audiences of the *Manuel des Péchés*," unpub. D. Phil. thesis, Oxford University, 1990 (*Anglo-Norman Literature*, item 635, 349).

9 See the site "Medieval Francophone Literary Culture outside France" on MS Montpellier, Bib. Interuniv. Sect. Médecine 251 at http://www.medievalfrancophone.ac.uk/browse/mss /356/manuscript.html.

WACE'S ROMAN DE BRUT IN ITS MANUSCRIPT CONTEXTS

X 2–3) Oxford, Bodl. Lib. Rawlinson D 913
(late 12th–early 13th, 14th): medieval mis-
cellany Containing numerous OF and A-N
frags. from 2 MSS, including:
fols. 83–84 *Brut,* 2 frags. (ll. 7029–148;
7391–510) (late 12th–early 13th) (A-N)[10]
fol. 85 sermon (A-N verse)
fol. 85 *Voyage de saint Brendan*
fols. 86–89v *Gui de Warewic*
fol. 90 *Protheselaus*
fol. 91 Hugh de Roteland, *Ipomedon*
fol. 92r–92v *Brut,* 2 frags. (ll. 4346–64;
4453–71) (14th) (OF)

fol. 93 A-N satirical poem

fols. 94–97 *Roman de la Rose* (8 frags.)
fols. 103–105 *Roman d'Alexandre*

Y 2) Paris, BnF fr. 12603 (late 13th–early 14th)

a) *Chevalier aux deux epees,* fols. 1r–71r

b) Chrétien, *Yvain,* fols. 72ra–111rb
c) *Eneas* (frag.), fols. 111rb–144vb
d) *Brut* (ll. 67–1950), fols. 144vb–155ra
e) *Enfances Oger le Danois,* fols. 156ra–202va
f) *Fierabras,* fols. 203ra–238ra
g) 18 fabliaux, fols. 239ra–279rb
h) Marie de France, *Fables* (103 fables),
fols. 279rb– 301rb
i) fabliau ("La dame qui conquist son
baron") (frag.), fol. 301va–vb

Z 4) New Haven, Yale Beinecke Lib. 395
(late 13th–early 14th); *olim* Phillipps 4156
a) Herman de Valenciennes, Bible (frag.),
fols. 1r–68r
b) H. de v., *Assomption de Notre Dame,*
fols. 68r–75r
c) P. Alphonsus, *Disciplina clericalis* (A-N),
fols. 75r–97v
d) A-N poem on Genesis, fols. 98r–110r
e) Robert de Ho, *Les Enseignements,* fols.
111r–129v

**3) The Hague, Konink. Bibl. 73.1.53 (13th)[11]

Brut frag. only (scattered 7348 lines out of
14866)

---

10   Hans-Erich Keller, "Les Fragments oxoniens du *Roman de Brut* de Wace," in *Mélanges de langues et littératures romanes offerts à Carl Théodore Gossen,* ed. Germán Colón and Robert Kopp (Bern: Francke; Liège: Marche Romane, 1976), 453–67. According to Keller, fols. 83–84 contain the oldest witness to Wace's *Brut* (456), as confirmed by Maria Careri, Christine Ruby, and Ian Short, *Livres et écritures en français et en occitan au XIIe siècle: Catalogue illustré,* with the collaboration of Terry Nixon and Patricia Stirnemann, Scritture e libri del medioevo 8 (Rome: Viella, 2011), 146.

11   Maartje Draak, "The Hague Manuscript of Wace's *Brut,*" in *Amor Librorum: Bibliographic and Other Essays, a Tribute to Abraham Horodisch on his Sixtieth Birthday,* ed. not listed (Amsterdam: Erasmus Antiquariaat; Zurich: Safaho Foundation, 1958), 23–27.

504　　　　　　　　　　　　　　　　　　　　　　　　　　APPENDIX 1

f) *Partonopeu de Blois* (frag.),
   fols. 129v–130v
g) *Vie de saint Eustache*, fols. 131r–145r
h) letter of Prester John to Emperor
   Manuel Conmenus (A-N verse trans. by
   Raoul d'Arundel), fols. 145r–152v
i) Guillaume Ie Clerc, *Bestiaire*,
   fols. 153r–179r
j) "Liber sompniorum et lunarum" (A-N),
   fols. 180r–183v
k) *Le voyage du Chevalier Owen au*
   Purgatoire
   de saint Patrice, fols. 184r–188v
l) *Brut* (ll. 1–7141), fols. 189r–224v

5) Vatican City, Bibl. Apos. Vat. Pal. lat. 1971
   (13th)
a) *Partenopeu de Blois,* fols. 1r–59v
b) *Amadas et Idoine* (frag.), fols. 61r–68v
c) *Brut* (ll. 1219–2421, 3613–4752), fols.
   69v–84v
d) *Floire et Blanchefleur* (frag.), fols.
   85r–90v
e) *Chanson d'Aspremont* (frag.), fols.
   91r–98v

**4) Zadar (Croatia), Gradska Bib. (13th)[12]

a) octosyll. love song (OF, Ital.)
b) *Brut* (ll. 13485–629, with lacunae;
   14287–443, with lacunae)

6) Cologny-Geneva, Bibl. Bodmeriana 67
   (13th)
a) *Gui de Warewic* (end missing), fols.
   1ra–44vc
b) *Brut* (ll. 13642–14866 [end]), fols.
   45ra–49vb

** 5) Berkeley, UCB Bancroft Lib. 165 (late 13th)

   2 frags. (ll. 387–580, 1769–954)

   (unpub. discov. by John F. Levy, Univ. of
   California, Berkeley, 1996)[13]

---

12   Muhamed Nezirović, "Les Fragments de Zadar du *Roman de Brut* de Wace," *Romania* 98.391
       (1977): 379–89. Although exact foliation is not stated, the article (written while the MS was
       held by the Archdiocese of Zadar) provides details of the columns involved in the *Brut*
       fragments and is followed by a transcription of the fragments.
13   Nancy Vine-Durling, "The UC Berkeley *Brut* Fragment: A New Transcription and Assess-
       ment," in *L'Historia regum Bitannie et les "Bruts" en Europe, II: Production, circulation et
       réception (XIIe–XVIe siècle)*, ed. Hélène Tétrel and Géraldine Veysseyre, Rencontres 349,
       Civilisation médiévale 32 (Paris: Classiques Garnier, 2018), 103–24.

WACE'S ROMAN DE BRUT IN ITS MANUSCRIPT CONTEXTS 505

c) ANP (follows *Brut,* not interpol.),
  fols. 49vc–52vc
d) *Florence de Rome,* fols. 53ra–81rc
e) *Livere de Reis de Brittanie* (beg. with
  Pentarchy, with account of kings from
  Egbert to John in 1216) (A-N), fols.
  81vc–82vd[14]
f) genealogical table of Norman dukes
  and kings of Eng. to John in 1216 (L),
  fol. 83

**7) London, Univ. Lib. 574 (14th, 15th)
MS contains numerous short texts and
fragments, the majority of which are Latin
and French liturgical and scientific texts;
frag. of one leaf contains parts of the
Brut (ll. 6680–710, 6782–812)

**8) London, Westminster Abbey,
  Muniments Rm.
  C.5.22 (early 13th) (discov. by Judith
  Weiss)[15]
2 frags. (ll. 9065–74, 9077–98, 9101–08,
9212–16, 9219–32, 9235–40, 9245–48,
9253–62, 10329–30, 10359–80, 10385–400,
10523–32, 10589–98, 10621–30, 10633–42,
with lacunae; 11407–12, 11447–52, 11487–92,
11529–34, with lacunae)

---

14 Identified as a witness of the *Livere de Reis de Brittanie* by Dean and Boulton, *Anglo-Norman Literature,* item 13, p. 13. See also Françoise Vielliard, "Cologny, Fondation Martin Bodmer, Cod. Bodmer 67," in eadem, *Bibliotheca Bodmeriana Catalogue II: Manuscrits français du Moyen Âge* (Cologny-Geneva: Fondation Martin Bodmer, 1975), 23–31 and http://e-codices.unifr.ch/en/description/fmb/cb-0067/.

15 Judith Weiss, "Two Fragments from a Newly Discovered Manuscript of Wace's *Brut,*" *Medium Ævum* 68.2 (1999): 268–77.

506 APPENDIX 1

**9) London, College of Arms 12/45A (roll) (late 13th–early 14th)
(discov. by Olivier de Laborderie)[16]
a) anonymous verse *Brut*, membranes 1–7, recto
b) fragment of Wace's *Brut* (ll. 9059–13680,
with numerous lacunae), membranes
1–4 dorse[17]
c) genealogy of the kings of England (beg. with Pentarchy,
with account of kings from Egbert to Edward I) (A-N),
membranes 4–7 dorse[18]

**10) Durham, Univ. Lib. Additional 1950.A.8 (early–mid-13th)[19]
surviving lines: 1287–88, 1324–26, 1364–67, 1405–7;
2453–55, 2493–95, 2533–35, and 2575–77

Note: Line numbers of the *Brut* correspond to Arnold (ed., *Le Roman de Brut de Wace*,
2 vols., SATF, Paris, 1938–40)

Legend: A   Arnold's sigla
         A-N   Anglo-Norman
         ANP   texts edited in *Anglo-Norman Verse Prophecies of Merlin*
                (J. Blacker, ed. and trans.)
         L   Latin
         ME   Middle English
         OF   Old French (may include texts not yet identified as
                Anglo-Norman)
         *   according to Arnold, ed., vol. I, xi, xiii, these MSS appear to be
                identical
         **   MSS unknown to Arnold

---

16   See Appendix 2 below, n. 5.
17   Ian Short demonstrates that the anonymous *Brut* runs the full extent of the seven mem-
     branes on the recto ("Un *Roman de Brut* anglo-normand inédit," 274). On the makeup
     of the remainder of the roll, see also Francesco Di Lella, "Il *Roll Brut* nel rotolo London,
     College of Arms, 12/45 A (prima parte)," *Critica del testo* 22.1 (2019): 37–66, esp. 41–43,
     and also idem, "Il *Roll Brut* nel rotolo London, College of Arms, 12/45 A (seconda parte),"
     Critica del testo 22.2 (2019): 61–83.
18   On other "continuations" and genealogies, see Appendix 2 below, n. 6.
19   From the digitized Durham University Library Archives and Special Collections Cata-
     logue: "Fragment from Wace, *Roman de Brut* written in England early/mid 13th century
     reused as a hinge strip in an early 15th century binding"; for more details, see the digitized
     Catalogue at https://n2t.durham.ac.uk/ark:/32150/t1mpz50gw15j.html.

APPENDIX 2

Anonymous Verse *Brut*s

Legend: §§= sections of *HRB* (Reeve, ed., Wright, tr. 2007)

NB: All MSS are Anglo-Norman except Munich and Bekker

[W] = interpolated into, or bound with Wace's *Roman de Brut* (1155)

overlaps = approximate overlapping of narratives

OCTOSYLLABIC[1]

1) London, BL Harley 4733[2]
late 12th
fol. 128

256 lines, with gaps (§§143–47, Arthur's coronation, pursuit of Saxons to Somerset)
-- overlaps with Wace, Egerton, Takamiya

2) Munich, Bayerische
Staatsbibliothek C. Gall. 29[3]
early 13th (Continental)
(the only text in this MS; 1r–23v)

4180 lines (§§5–32, descr. of Britain, arrival of Brutus to battle at Tours, Leir, and reign of Cunedagius)
-- overlaps with Wace, Royal, Coll. of Arms

3) New Haven (Conn.), Yale
Univ. Beinecke Lib.

161 lines, with gaps (end of §142-§143, Uther's death, Arthur's coronation, battle against Colgrinus)

---

1   This is an updated version of the list published in J. Blacker, "'But That's Another Story': Wace, Laȝamon, and the Early Anonymous Old French Verse *Brut*s," *Arthuriana* 31.4 (2021): 47–102, Appendix II, 92–97. Most if not all of these texts (except for Egerton which was likely composed around the time the manuscript was assembled with its illuminations) date from the twelfth century, though nearly all the MSS are later; approximate dates of the MSS are given here. On dating of the texts, see Ian Short, "Un *Roman de Brut* anglo-normand inédit," 275.

2   Peter Damian-Grint, ed., "A 12th-century Anglo-Norman *Brut* Fragment (MS BL Harley 4733, f. 128)," in *Anglo-Norman Anniversary Essays*. In the 1993 edition, a couplet was missed after v. 90: "[Encunte Baldolf l'e]nvead, / Sis cent chevaliers li baillat" [Damian-Grint, private communication]. See also Maria Careri, Christine Ruby, and Ian Short, *Livres et écritures en français et en occitan au XIIᵉ siècle: Cataloque illustré*, with the collaboration of Terry Nixon and Patricia Stirnemann, Scritture e libri del medioevo 8 (Rome: Viella, 2011), item 41, 92–93, and the Catalogue of Illuminated Manuscripts at the British Library which describes the foliation as follows: "A late-12th century fragment of the 'Brut' in Anglo-Norman, is bound as a flyleaf with the reverse as a recto (f. 128). Wormholes indicate f. 128 has been bound with Harley 4733 for a long while" (https://www.bl.uk/catalogues/illuminatedmanuscripts/record.asp?MSID =4627&CollID=8&NStart=4733).

3   P. B. Grout, "The Manuscript of the Munich *Brut* (Codex Gallicus 29 of the Bayerische Staatsbibliothek, Munich)"; see also Zufferey, ed., et al, *Le Roi Leïr*, 133–41.

© KONINKLIJKE BRILL NV, LEIDEN, 2024 | DOI:10.1163/9789004691889_011

508   APPENDIX 2

Takamiya 115[4]   — overlaps with Wace, Egerton, Harley 4733
mid 13th
fragment of 1 folio

4) [W][5] London, Coll. of Arms   approx. 2500 lines (§§23–133; Humber's attack to Merlin's
12/45A (roll)   prediction of Uther's reign; rough correspondance to Wace lines
late 13th   1293–8338, many lacunae; Prophecies omitted)
recto   — overlaps with Wace, Egerton, Royal, Bekker,
                                   Harley 1605, Munich
                                   [W = a fragmentary copy of Wace's *Brut* on the dorse
                                       of the roll ; lines 9059–13680, many lacunae]

---

4 I and my colleague Peter Damian-Grint owe a debt of gratitude to Ian Short, Diana Tyson,
   and Alice Ford-Smith of Bernard Quaritch Antiquarian Booksellers for the help they
   afforded me along the circuitous path to determining the current location of this manuscript (no longer in the Martin Schøyen Collection MS. 650, its last known location before it
   was rediscovered in 2018 in the Toshiyuki Takamiya Collection of the Beinecke Library, Yale
   University, where it had been since 2013). The first printed notice is found in the Bernard
   Quartich Catalogue (London, 1991); the second more broadly available notice is as item
   16 (without location) – "*Brut* Fragment" – in Dean and Boulton, *Anglo-Norman Literature*,
   p. 16. A digital file of this MS leaf is available through the Yale University Beinecke Library at
   https://brbl-dl.library.yale.edu/vufind/Record/4428130.

5 This copy of Wace's *Brut*, on the dorse of the same roll as the anonymous *Brut* discovered
   by Olivier de Laborderie ("'Ligne de reis,'" 380–85; rev. ed. in *Histoire, mémoire et pouvoir: les
   généalogies en rouleaux des rois d'Angleterre 1250–1422*) brings the current total to 19 complete or nearly complete copies of Wace's *Brut*, plus 15 incomplete copies that survive either
   as extracts or as manuscript fragments (the number of fragments and extracts increases if
   different extracts within the same manuscript are counted separately); see Ian Short's edition of part of the anonymous *Brut* in this roll, and also Francesco Di Lella, "Il *Roll Brut* nel
   rotolo London, College of Arms, 12/45 A (prima parte)," *Critica del testo* 22.1 (2019), 37–66
   and idem, "Il *Roll Brut* nel rotolo London, College of Arms, 12/45 A (seconda parte)," *Critica
   del testo* 22.2 (2019), 61–83. For sources on the identification of the anonymous verse *Bruts*
   (non-Prophecies texts), see Short, "Un *Roman de Brut* anglo-normand inédit," 273–74 n. 2, and
   Ruth J. Dean, *Anglo-Norman Literature: A Guide to Texts and Manuscripts*, with the collaboration of Maureen B. M. Boulton, items 3, 15–17 (16, "*Brut* fragment," p. 16, is now Yale, Beinecke
   Takamiya 115), 19–22, and 50 (including verse Prophecies MSS). Short demonstrates that the
   anonymous *Brut* runs the full extent of the seven membranes on the recto ("Un *Roman de Brut*
   anglo-normand inédit," 274), and that the correspondence to Wace lines 1293–8338 is very
   approximate due to the high number of lacunae (p. 275). On the makeup of the remainder of
   the roll (dorse) (Wace extracts, membranes 1–4 and the genealogy of the kings of England,
   beginning with a division into a pentarchy, with an account of kings from Egbert to Edward I,
   membranes 4–7), see Francesco Di Lella, "Il *Roll Brut* nel rotolo London, College of Arms,
   12/45 A (prima parte)," 43, and also on the genealogy (but not Wace), see Diana B. Tyson, "The
   Old French *Brut* rolls in the London College of Arms," in *Guerres, voyages et quêtes au Moyen
   Âge: Mélanges offerts à Jean-Claude Faucon*, ed. Alain Labbé, Daniel W. Lacroix et Danielle
   Quéruel (Paris: Honoré Champion, 2000), 421–7, 423.

ANONYMOUS VERSE BRUTS

5) London, BL Arundel 220
early 14th
fols. 4–5

258 lines (§§106–8, Vortigern's tower, discovery of Merlin)
— **overlaps with Wace, Egerton, Royal**

6) London, BL Egerton 3028
mid 14th
fols. 1–56

2914 lines (not including 354-line "continuation" of English history, Egbert to Edward III 1338–40, on fols. 56–63)[6] (§§65–205, sons of Cymbeline to near end; corresponds roughly to Wace lines 4883–14842,[7] many lacunae; Prophecies omitted)
— **overlaps with Wace, Royal, Harley 1605, Harley 4733, Takamiya, Coll. of Arms**

7) London, BL Add. 48212.O
mid 14th
fols. 103v–104r

117 lines (§116 :33–42, **Prophecies** frag., from awakening of Daneian forest to heron's three eggs)
— **overlaps with Prophecies MSS only**

8) [W] London, BL Royal
13.A.XXI
1st half 14th

6237 lines (§§6–137, Aeneas's marriage to Uther's arrival at Tintagel; Prophecies omitted)
— **interpolated** ("replacing" *Brut* lines 53–8728); Wace fols.

---

6   More work remains to be done to determine whether this "continuation" is possibly a version of the *Livere de Reis de Brittanie* or another genealogical chronicle termed a "feudal manual" by its editor, Thomas Wright, and the interrelationships between these chronicles and those found in College of Arms 12/45 A (also a Wace MS [roll]) and Wace MSS J, Paris, BnF fr. 1416 and C, London, BL Cotton Vitellius A.x (*Le Livere de Reis de Brittanie e Le Livere de Reis de Engleterre*, ed. and trans. J. Glover, Rolls Series, London, 1865 and *Kritische Ausgabe der Anglonormannischen Chroniken: Brutus, Li Rei de Engleterre, Le Livere de Reis de Engleterre*, ed. C. Foltys, Berlin, 1962, 45–114, inaugural-dissertation); Thomas Wright, ed., *Feudal Manuals of English History* (London, 1872); see also Dean, *LRB*, items 13 (pp. 13–15) and "Genealogical Chronicles," item 6 (pp. 7–10), and John Spence, *Reimagining History in Anglo-Norman Prose Chronicles* (York: York Medieval Press, 2013), 12–14 and nn. 65–68. The chronicles in Wace MSS T, Cambridge, Corpus Christi College 50 and Cologny-Geneva, Bibl. Bodmeriana 67 (containing a fragment of Wace), with accounts of kings from Egbert to Henry III and John respectively, have been identified by Dean as versions of the *LRB* (item 13); Di Lella considers the genealogy on the dorse of CA 12/45 A to be a "standard text" of the *LRB* ("Il Roll *Brut*," prima parte, 43); see also Appendix 1 above on the dorse of CA 12/45 A and Appendix 1 in J. Blacker, "'But That's Another Story': Wace, Laȝamon, and the Early Anonymous Old French Verse *Bruts*," 83–92. On MS J, see esp. Jane Bliss and Judith Weiss, 'The "J" Manuscript of Wace's *Brut*', *Medium Ævum* 81.2 (2012): 222–48. On MS C, see Maud Becker, 'Une édition de la Continuation du *Roman de Brut* de Wace, contenue dans le manuscript British Library Cotton Vitellius A.x', unpublished doctoral thesis, University of Aberystwyth, 2019.

7   On Cadwallader's reign, for example, reduced from roughly 200 lines to 23, see J. Blacker, "Courtly Revision of Wace's *Roman de Brut* in British Library Egerton MS 3028," in *Courtly Arts and the Art of Courtliness*, 247.

510   APPENDIX 2

41r–77v[8]   40–113, interp.

                                        overlaps with Wace, Egerton, Harley 1605, Bekker,
                                        Coll. of Arms, Munich

DECASYLLABIC[9]

1) [W] Durham, Cathedral   **Wace** *Brut* + interpolated **Prophecies** ("replacing" lines 7333–
Library, C.IV.27   7582): 668 lines (§§112–17), preceded by 172-line preamble[10] and
late 12th–early 13th   with 6-line epilogue attributing the translation of the Prophecies to
fols. 42v–48r   "Helias"

2) Cambridge, Fitzwilliam   **Prophecies:** 665 lines (§§112–17), preceded by 166-line preamble
Museum 302   (2-line epilogue, attributed to "Helys")
2nd half 13th
fols. 90v–99r

3) [W] Cologny-Geneva,   **Wace** *Brut* **frag.** (end of poem 13642–14866)[11]
Bibl. Bodmeriana 67   + **Prophecies:** 668 lines (§§112–17), preceded by lines 63–172 of
2nd half 13th   preamble (no epilogue)
fols. 49r–52r

4) Oxford, Bodleian Lib.   **Prophecies:** 669 lines (§§112–17), preceded by 169-line preamble
Hatton 67   (no epilogue)
2nd half 13th
fols. 18r–25v

ALEXANDRINE

1) Krakow, Jagiellonian   136 lines (§§127–30, assembling Stonehenge)
Univ. Lib. Gall. fol. 176   — **overlaps with Wace, Egerton, Royal, Harley 1605,**

---

8   Bell, ed., *An Anglo-Norman Brut*, p. xi; see also British Library Catalogue of Illuminated
     Manuscripts, http://www.bl.uk/catalogues/illuminatedmanuscripts/record.asp?MSID=5
     535&CollID=16&NStart=130121.

9   For the decasyllabic and alexandrine Prophecies, see *Anglo-Norman Verse Prophecies
     of Merlin*, ed. and trans. J. Blacker. The very short octosyllabic prophecy fragment in
     BL Additional MS 48212.O was not edited along with the decasyllabic and alexandrine
     Prophecies.

10   On the full preamble (as edited in decasyllabic base MS Durham, Cathedral Lib. C.IV.27),
     see *Anglo-Norman Verse Prophecies of Merlin*, 6–9.

11   Although the last line number given is 14864, the printed transcription of the last folio
     (49b) indicates 14866 lines: see *Bibliotheca Bodmeriana Catalogue II: Manuscrits fran-
     çais du Moyen Age*, établi par Françoise Vielliard, Cologny-Geneva, 1975, 23–31 (27);
     http://e-codices.unifr.ch/en/description/fmb/cb-0067/. It is possible that there are two
     lines missing earlier in the text.

ANONYMOUS VERSE BRUTS   511

[Bekker frag.][12] late 12th (Continental)	Coll. of Arms
2) London, BL Harley 1605[13] mid 13th	3361 lines: 1) 1280 lines (§§73–94, death of King Lucius to arrival of Hengist) 2) 1279 lines (§§113–36, **Prophecies** [missing lines 1–72 and 4 others ; 515 lines, no prologue, 10-line transitional passage similar to that in Lincoln], to beginning of Uther's reign) 3) 80 lines (§§152–54, reinstatement of Loth) 4) 81 lines (§§155–56, Bedevere, Kay enfoeffed, feast at City of Legions) 5) 641 lines (§§165–69, Mt-St-Michel giant, first encounter of Arthur and Emperor Lucius) — **overlaps with Coll. of Arms, Bekker, Wace, Royal (but none of those have Prophecies)**
3) [W] Lincoln, Cathedral Library 104 2nd half 13th fols. 48r–57v	Wace *Brut* + interpolated **Prophecies** (between *Brut* lines 7542 and 7543): 587 lines (§§ 112–17), with 28-line prologue by "Willeme," followed by 10-line transitional passage (unattributed)
4) [W] London, BL Add. 45103 late 13th fols. 86r–97r	Wace *Brut* + interpolated **Prophecies** (between *Brut* lines 7584 and 7585): 584 lines (§§112–17) (no prologue, no transitional passage)

---

12   For a thorough study of the Bekker fragment (Krakow, Jagiellonian Univ. Lib. Gall. fol. 176), so-called because it was first transcribed (partially) by Immanuel Bekker, (*Fiérabras*, ed. I. Bekker, Berlin, 1829, pp. 182–83, in n. to l. 3311), deemed unfindable right after the second world war (by J. S. P. Tatlock, *The Legendary History of Britain*, 458), and rediscovered by Sylvie Lefèvre in the 1980s in the Biblioteka Jagiellónska in Krakow, see Lefèvre, "Le fragment Bekker et les anciennes versions françaises de l'*Historia regum Britanniae*," *Romania* 109 (1988): 225–46. See also Peter Damian-Grint, *The New Historians of the Twelfth-Century Renaissance*, 64.

13   On printed sources, see Chapter 6, n. 10 above. Technically speaking, this is the first of three volumes of MS Harley 1605 (1605/1, though scholars do not always use this designation). See the British Library Digitised Manuscripts at http://www.bl.uk/manuscripts/FullDisplay.aspx?ref=Harley_MS_1605/1. The folios are as follows: 1) 1r–16v; 2) Prophecies 17r–23r; remainder of fragment 23r–32v; 3) 33r–v; 4) 34r–v; 5) 35r–42v.

APPENDIX 3

Arthur's "Twelve Battles": Comparative Chart

Historia Brittonum (9th c.)	*HRB* (mid-12th c.)	First Variant (mid-12th)	H. Huntingdon (*HA*, mid-12th)	Wace's *Brut* (mid-12th)
1) river Glein	—	—	river Glein	—
2) river Duglas*	river Duglas, York	river Duglas, York	—	river Duglas, defeat of Colgrim
3) river Duglas	—	—	river Duglas	—
4) river Duglas	—	—	river Duglas	—
5) river Duglas, in the region of Lindsey	Lincoln	Lincoln	river Duglas, in the district of Lindsey	Lincoln
6) river Bassas	—-	—	Bassas	—
7) Celyddon forest, battle of Celyddon Coed (Colidon Wood)	forest of Colidon	Colidon Wood	Celyddon forest, Celyddon Coed	Celidon Wood

---

* Morris translates as "Douglas" in *HB* rather than "Duglas" as in *HRB* (Reeve ed., Wright trans.), FV (Wright ed., Burchmore trans.) and Wace in the original (Arnold ed.); Weiss (trans.) has "Douglas" as does Greenway (*HA*, ed. and trans.). I am choosing "Duglas" here in Appendix 3 and elsewhere to disambiguate from the River Douglas, in the north-west, and not the same (possibly unlocatable) river referred to in *HB*, allegedly in Lindsey. In terms of its location, among other sources cited in Chapter 1, n. 76, see Andrew Breeze who argues for Douglas Water, Scotland ("The Historical Arthur and Sixth-Century Scotland," *Northern History* 52.2, 2015: 158–81, 174).

8)	Guinnion fort – Arthur carries image of Mary "on his shoulders"	*pagum Badonis* – Arthur carries Mary on his shield (Bath? Badon?)	*pagum Badonis* (Mary on the shield)	castle of *Guinnion* – Arthur carries Mary "on his shoulders"	Battle of Bath – Arthur carries Mary *inside* his shield
9)	City of the Legion	Thanet (two sentences)	—	City of Legions (Caerleon)	—
10)	Bank of the river Tryfrwyd	Loch Lomond	Lake Lumonoy	river Tryfrwyd	Loch Lomond
11)	hill called Agned	*Castellum Puellarum* [Edinburgh]; much earlier; no battle; before Arthur's time	Mt. Agned (Castle of the Maidens; much earlier in text; no battle; no Arthur)	hill called Brevoin "Catbregion" (Arthur's 11th battle)	Mt. Agned (Castle of the Maidens; much earlier in text; no battle; no Arthur)
12)	Badon Hill	—	—	*HA, monte Badonis*; [*EW* (mid-12th), *Bade*; only named battle]	—

BATTLES FOLLOWING ARTHUR'S INTERNATIONAL CONQUESTS**

—	Camblan – Arthur's final battle, against Modredus	River Camlan – Arthur's final battle, against Modredus	*EW* (loc. unnamed) final battle against Modredus	"Camble" – Arthur's last battle, against Modred
De Excidio (Gildas early 6th c.) Britons' victory at *Mons Badonicus* (no Arthur)	Bede (*HE*, 8th c.) Britons' victory at *Mons Badonicus* (no Arthur)	*Annales Cambriae* (mid-10th c. orig.) Battle of Badon, Arthur carries the Cross of Jesus	W. of Malmesbury (*GRA*, early 12th) Mount Badon, Arthur carries image of Mary "on his arms"	
—	—		—	

** Battle of Camlann in which Arthur and Modred (Mordred) fell

Bibliography

Primary Sources

Alfred of Beverley, *Annales, sive Historia de gestis regum Britanniae*, ed. Thomas Hearne (Oxford, 1716).

The Anglo-Norman Prose Chronicle of Early British Kings or the Abbreviated Prose Brut, Text and Translation, ed. and trans. Heather Pagan and Geert de Wilde. The Medieval Chronicle X (2015). 225–319.

"An Anglo-Norman Metrical 'Brut' of the 14th Century (British Museum Ms Egerton 3028)," ed. Vivien Underwood, unpublished Ph.D. thesis. University of London, 1937.

An Anglo-Norman Brut (Royal 13.A.xxi), ed. Alexander Bell, Anglo-Norman Text Society 21–22 (Oxford: Basil Blackwell, 1969).

Anglo-Norman Verse Prophecies of Merlin, ed. and trans. Jean Blacker (Dallas, TX: Scriptorium, 2005; rev. ed. of "The Anglo-Norman Verse Prophecies of Merlin," *Arthuriana* 15.1 [2005]: 1–125).

The Anglo-Saxon Chronicle: A Collaborative Edition. Volume 8, MS F, ed. Peter Baker (Cambridge: D. S. Brewer, 2000).

The Anglo-Saxon Chronicles, ed. and trans. Michael Swanton (London: J. M. Dent & Sons, 1996; rev. ed., London: Phoenix, 2000).

"The *Annales Cambriae* and the Old-Welsh Genealogies from *Harleian MS*. 3859," ed. Egerton Phillimore, *Y Commrodor* 9 (1888): 141–83 (repr. in John Morris, *Genealogies and Texts*, ed. and trans. Morris, Arthurian Period Sources 5, Chichester: Phillimore, 1995, 13–55).

Annales Vedastini in *The Annals of Fulda: Ninth Century Histories, volume II*, trans. Timothy Reuter, Manchester Medieval Sources (Manchester: Manchester University Press, 1992); Manchester Medieval Sources Online (Manchester, 1992), online Dec. 2012, http://manchester.metapress.com/.

Armes Prydein: The Prophecy of Britain from the Book of Taliesin, ed. Ifor Williams, trans. Rachel Bromwich, Mediaeval and Modern Welsh Series 6. Dublin: School of Celtic Studies Dublin Institute for Advanced Studies, 1972; repr. 1982, 2006 [orig. published in Welsh in 1955].

Asser, *Asserius de rebus gestis Alfredi* in *Asser's Life of King Alfred together with the Annals of St Neots*, ed. William Henry Stevenson (Oxford: Clarendon Press, 1904; repr. with introductory article by Dorothy Whitelock, 1959).

Asser, *Alfred the Great: Asser's Life of King Alfred and Other Contemporary Sources*, trans. Simon Keynes and Michael Lapidge (London: Penguin, 1983, 2004).

Becker, Maud, "Une édition de la Continuation du *Roman de Brut* de Wace, contenue dans le manuscrit British Library Cotton Vitellius A.X," unpublished doctoral thesis, University of Aberystwyth, 2019. http://hdl.handle.net/2160/a630fa13-ca0b-42e5-922b-ed82def554db.

Bede, *Chronica Maiora ad a. DCCXXV*, ed. Theodor Mommsen, Monumenta Germaniae Historica Auctores Antiquissimi XIII (Berlin: Weidmann, 1898), 223–327.

Bede, *Chronica Maiora = De Temporum Ratione Liber cap. LVI–LXXI seu Chronica Maiora*, ed. Charles W. Jones, Corpus Christianorum, Series Latina 123 B (Turhout: Brepols, 1977), 461–544.

"Bekker fragment," in *Der roman von Fierabras, provenzalisch*, ed. Immanuel Bekker (Berlin: G. Reimer, 1829, pp. 182–83, in n. to l. 3311 of the *Fierabras*).

"The Anglo-Norman *Description of England*: An Edition," ed. Alexander Bell, in *Anglo-Norman Anniversary Essays*, ed. Ian Short, Anglo-Norman Text Society Occasional Publications Series 2 (London: Anglo-Norman Text Society, 1993), 31–47.

Geffrei Gaimar, *Estoire des Engleis: History of the English*, ed. and trans., Ian Short (Oxford: Oxford University Press, 2009).

Geffrei Gaimar, *L'Estoire des Engleis by Geffrei Gaimar*, ed. Alexander Bell. Anglo-Norman Text Society 14–16 (Oxford: Basil Blackwell, 1960; repr. New York: Johnson Reprint Corp., 1971).

Geoffrey of Monmouth, *Geoffrey of Monmouth: Historia Regum Britanniae. A Variant Version edited from manuscripts*, ed. Jacob Hammer (Cambridge, MA: Medieval Academy of America, 1951).

Geoffrey of Monmouth, *The Historia Regum Britanniae of Geoffrey of Monmouth, with Contributions to the study of its place in Early British History ... Together with a literal translation of the Welsh Manuscript No. LXI of Jesus College, Oxford, by Robert Ellis Jones*, ed. Acton Griscom (New York: Longmans, Green, 1929).

Geoffrey of Monmouth, *The Historia Regum Britannie of Geoffrey of Monmouth, I: Bern Burgerbibliothek, MS. 568*, ed. Neil Wright (Cambridge: D. S. Brewer, 1984).

Geoffrey of Monmouth, *The Historia Regum Britannie of Geoffrey of Monmouth, II: The First Variant Version: a critical edition*, ed. Neil Wright (Cambridge: D. S. Brewer, 1988).

Geoffrey of Monmouth, *The History of the Kings of Britain: An Edition and Translation of the De gestis Britonum [Historia Regum Britanniae]*, ed. Michael D. Reeve, trans. Neil Wright, Arthurian Studies 69 (Woodbridge: Boydell, 2007).

[Anonymous] *The History of the Kings of Britain: The First Variant Version*, ed. and trans. David W. Burchmore, Dumbarton Oaks Medieval Library 57 (Cambridge, MA: Harvard University Press, 2019).

Gerald of Wales, *Geraldi Cambrensis opera*, ed. J. S. Brewer et al, 8 vols., 6: *Itinerarium Kambriae et Descriptio Kambriae*, ed. James F. Dimock [1868], Rolls Series (London, 1861–91).

Gerald of Wales, *The Journey Through Wales / The Description of Wales*, trans. Lewis Thorpe (Harmondsworth, Middlesex: Penguin Books, 1978).

BIBLIOGRAPHY 517

Gerald of Wales, *Instructione Principis* (*On the Instruction of a Prince*), trans. Scott McLetchie, 1994, Internet Medieval Sourcebook (no line numbers). https://source books.fordham.edu/source/1223gerald-arthurtomb.asp.

Gervase of Canterbury, *Historical Writing in England. The Historical Works of Gervase of Canterbury*, ed. W. Stubbs, 2 vols., Rolls Series (London, 1879–80).

Gildas, *The Ruin of Britain and other works*, ed. and trans. Michael Winterbottom. Arthurian Period Sources, 7 (London: Phillimore, 1978). [*De Excidio Britanniae*]

The Gododdin of Aneirin: Text and Context from Dark-Age North Britain, ed. and trans. John T. Koch (Cardiff: University of Wales Press, 1997).

Gormont et Isembard. Fragment de chanson de geste du XIIe siècle, ed. Alphonse Bayot, CFMA (Paris: Honoré Champion, 1921).

Goscelin, *Vita S. Augustini, majus opusculum* (*Vita major*), *Acta Sanctorum* 19:6 (Paris: Victor Palme, 1866). 26 May, 370–92.

Hariulf, *Chronique de l'abbaye de Saint-Riquier* (*Ve siècle – 1104*), ed. Ferdinand Lot (Paris: Picard, 1894).

Henry, Archdeacon of Huntingdon, *Historia Anglorum: The History of the English People*, ed. and trans. Diana Greenway, Oxford Medieval Texts (Oxford: Clarendon Press, 1996).

Henry, Archdeacon of Huntingdon, *Henry of Huntingdon: The History of the English People 1000–1154*, ed. and trans. Diana Greenway, Oxford World's Classics (Oxford: Oxford University Press, 1996, 2002).

Henry, Archdeacon of Huntingdon, "The place of Henry of Huntingdon's *Epistola ad Warinum* in the text-history of Geoffrey of Monmouth's *Historia regum Britannie*: a preliminary investigation," ed. and trans. Neil Wright. In *France and the British Isles in the Middle Ages and Renaissance: Essays by Members of Girton College, Cambridge, in Memory of Ruth Morgan*, ed. Gillian Jondorf and David N. Dumville (Woodbridge, Suffolk: Boydell and Brewer, 1991), 71–113.

Historia Brittonum, ed. Theodore Mommsen (*Chronica Minora*, Berlin, 1892).

Historia Brittonum, ed. Edmond Faral. In *La Légende arthurienne: études et documents*, 3 vols. (Paris: Champion, 1929), vol. 3, 2–62 [facing-page edition of the Chartres MS (the manuscript was since destroyed during WWII) and the Harley MS (Faral also includes the *Annales Cambriae* where they are found in Harley between the main part of ch. 66 and the list of cities in ch. 66a)].

The Historia Brittonum, 3: The "Vatican" Recension, ed. David N. Dumville (Cambridge: D. S. Brewer, 1985).

John of Salisbury, *Letters of John of Salisbury, vol. 1: The Early Letters* (*1153–61*), ed. and trans. W. J. Millor, H. E. Butler, and Christopher N. L. Brooke, Oxford Medieval Texts (Oxford: Clarendon Press, 1986).

Jordan Fantosme, *Jordan Fantosme's Chronicle*, ed. and trans. Ronald Carlyle Johnston (Oxford: Clarendon Press, 1980).

518 BIBLIOGRAPHY

Kritische Ausgabe der Anglonormannischen Chroniken: Brutus, Li Rei de Engleterre, Le Livere de Reis de Engleterre, ed. Christian Foltys, Berlin, 1962, pp. 45–114 (inaugural-dissertation).

Le Lai d'Haveloc and Gaimar's Haveloc Episode, ed. Alexander Bell (Manchester: The University of Manchester Press, 1925).

Lawman, *Brut*, trans. Rosamund Allen (New York: St. Martin's, 1992).

Layamon, *Layamon's Arthur. The Arthurian Section of Layamon's Brut (lines 9299–14297)*, ed. and trans. William Raymond Johnston Barron and Carole Weinberg (Harlow: Longman, 1989; rev. ed. Exeter: Exeter University Press, Exeter Medieval English Texts and Studies, 2001).

Layamon, *Layamon's Brut*, ed. George Leslie Brook, Robert Frank Leslie, EETS, 2 vols. (Oxford: Early English Text Society, 1963), vol. 1, lines 1–8020; 1978, vol. 2, lines 8021–end.

Le Livere de Reis de Brittanie e Le Livere de Reis de Engleterre, ed. and trans. John Glover, Rolls Series (London, 1865).

"Manual I" (genealogical text), ed. Thomas Wright. In *Feudal Manuals of English History, A Series of Popular Sketches of our National History, Compiled at Different Periods, From the Thirteenth Century to the Fifteenth, for the Use of the Feudal Gentry and Nobility* (London, 1872), 1–37.

Marie de France, *Lais*, ed. Alfred Ewert (Oxford: Basil Blackwell, 1944; reissued with new Introduction and Bibliography, Glyn S. Burgess, London: Bristol Classical Texts, 1995).

Der Münchener Brut. Gottfried von Monmouth in französischen Versen des XII. Jahrhunderts, ed. Konrad Albrich Hofmann and Karl Gustav Vollmöller (Halle: Max Niemeyer, 1877).

"An Edition of the Munich *Brut*," ed. Patricia B. Grout, unpublished Ph.D. thesis, University of London, 1980.

Nennius: British History and the Welsh Annals, ed. and trans. John Morris, Arthurian Period Sources 8 (London: Phillimore, 1980) [contains the *Annales Cambriae*, the earliest extant version, inserted in the Harley MS between ch. 66 and ch. 66a (the list of cities of Britain) of the *Historia Brittonum*, pp. 85–91, with a prefatory note and English translation on pp. 44–49].

The Oldest Anglo-Norman Prose Brut: An Edition and Translation, ed. and trans. Julia Marvin (Woodbridge: Boydell, 2006).

Orderic Vitalis, *The Ecclesiastical History*, ed. and trans. Marjorie Chibnall, 6 vols., Oxford Medieval Texts (Oxford: Clarendon Press, 1969–80).

Pierre of Langtoft, *Édition critique et commentée de Pierre de Langtoft, Le Regne d'Édouard I er*, ed. Jean-Claude Thiolier (Créteil: C.E.L.I.M.A., 1989–).

The "Prophetia Merlini" of Geoffrey of Monmouth: A Fifteenth-Century English Commentary, ed. and trans. Caroline D. Eckhardt, Speculum Anniversary Monographs 8 (Cambridge, MA: Medieval Academy of America, 1982).

BIBLIOGRAPHY 519

Prose Brut to 1332, ed. Heather Pagan, Anglo-Norman Texts 69 (Manchester: Anglo-Norman Text Society, 2011).

Le Roi Leïr: Versions des XIIᵉ et XIIIᵉ siècles, ed. François Zufferey, trans. [modern French] Gilbert Nussbaumer, with an introduction by Alain Corbellari and an extract of Laʒamon by Valérie Cangemi, Champion Classiques 41 (Paris: Honoré Champion, 2015, 133–93 [Munich *Brut*]).

Robert of Torigni, *Chronique de Robert de Torigni*, 2 vols., ed. Léopold Delisle, Société de l'histoire de Normandie (Rouen: A. Le Brument, 1872–73).

Sigebert of Gembloux, *Chronographia*, ed. L. C. Bethmann, Monumenta Germaniae Historica: Scriptores 6 (1844; repr. Leipzig, 1925), 268–374.

Trioedd Ynys Prydein: The Triads of the Island of Britain, ed. and trans. Rachel Bromwich (Cardiff: University of Wales Press, 1961, 4th ed. 2014).

Wace, *The Hagiographical Works: The Conception Nostre Dame and the Lives of St Margaret and St Nicholas*, trans. with introduction and notes, Jean Blacker, Glyn S. Burgess (trans.) and Amy V. Ogden, Studies in Medieval and Reformation Traditions 169, Texts and Sources 3 (Leiden: Brill, 2013).

Wace, *La Partie arthurienne du Roman de Brut de Wace*, ed. Ivor D. O. Arnold and Margaret M. Pelan (Paris: Klincksieck, 1962).

Wace, *Le Roman de Brut de Wace*, ed. Ivor D. O. Arnold, 3 vols. (Paris: Société des Anciens Textes Français, 1938–40).

Wace, *Le Roman de Brut de Wace*, ed., Antoine Le Roux de Lincy, 2 vols. (Rouen: É. Frère, 1836–38).

Wace, *Le Roman de Rou de Wace*, ed. Anthony J. Holden, 3 vols. Société des Anciens Textes Français (Paris: Picard, 1970–73; repr. with translation in Wace, *The Roman de Rou*, trans. Glyn S. Burgess, St. Helier: Société Jersiaise, 2002; *The History of the Norman People*, Wace's *Roman de Rou*, trans. Glyn S. Burgess, Woodbridge: Boydell, 2004 [original not included]).

Wace, *Wace's Roman de Brut: A History of the British: Text and Translation*, trans. Judith Weiss (Exeter: Exeter University Press, 1999; 2nd ed. 2002).

William of Malmesbury, *Gesta Regum Anglorum*, 2 vols., vol. 1, ed. and trans. Roger Aubrey Baskerville Mynors, Rodney M. Thomson, and Michael Winterbottom, Oxford Medieval Texts (Oxford: Clarendon Press, 1998) and vol. 2: *General Introduction and Commentary*, Rodney M. Thomson in collaboration with Michael Winterbottom (Clarendon Press, 1999).

William of Malmesbury, *Willelmi Malmesbiriensis Monachi Gesta Pontificum Anglorum, Libri quinque*, ed. Nicholas Esterhazy Stephen Armytage Hamilton, Rolls Series 52 (London: Longman, 1870).

William of Newburgh, *Historia rerum Anglicarum*, ed. Richard Howlett, Rolls Series 82 (1884–85).

William of Newburgh, [*Historia rerum Anglicarum*] *William of Newburgh: The History of English Affairs*, trans. Peter G. Walsh and Michael J. Kennedy, Aris and Phillips Classical Texts (Oxford: Oxbow Books, 1988).

William of Rennes, *Gesta Regum Britannie* of William of Rennes: *Historia Regum Britannie of Geoffrey of Monmouth, v. Gesta Regum Britannie*, ed. and trans. Neil Wright (Woodbridge: D. S. Brewer, 1991).

Secondary Sources

Ailes, Adrian. *Royal Arms of England*. Reading: University of Reading, 1982.

Aird, William M. *Robert Curthose, Duke of Normandy c. 1050–1134*. Woodbridge: Boydell, 2008.

Allen, Rosamund, Jane Roberts, and Carole Weinberg, eds. *Reading Laʒamon's Brut: Approaches and Explorations*. Amsterdam – New York: Rodopi, 2013; *DQR Studies in Literature* 52.1.

Albu, Emily. *The Normans in their Histories: Propaganda, Myth and Subversion*. Woodbridge: Boydell, 2001.

Anderson, Benedict. *Imagined Communities: Reflections on the Origin and Spread of Nationalism*. London and New York: Verso, 1983; rev. ed. 2006.

Anderson, Marjorie O. "Dalraida and the Creation of the Kingdom of the Scots." In *Ireland in Early Mediaeval Europe: Studies in Memory of Kathleen Hughes*, ed. Dorothy Whitelock, Rosamond McKitterick, and David Dumville. Cambridge: Cambridge University Press, 1982. 106–32.

Archibald, Elizabeth and Ad Putter, eds. *The Cambridge Companion to the Arthurian Legend*. Cambridge: Cambridge University Press, 2009.

Arnold, Ivor D. O. and Harry Lucas. "Le Personnage de Gormont dans la *Chanson de Gormont et Isembard*." In *Mélanges de philologie romane et de littérature médiévale offerts à Ernest Hoepffner par ses élèves et ses amis*. Publications de la Faculté des Lettres de l'Université de Strasbourg, 113. Paris: Les Belles Lettres, 1949. 215–26.

Aronstein, Susan. *Introduction to British Arthurian Narrative*. Gainesville: University Press of Florida, 2012.

Aurell, Martin. "Le discrédit de l'incroyable histoire de Geffroi de Monmouth au XIIe siècle." In *La verité et crédibilité: construire la verité dans le système de communication de l'Occident XIIIe–XVIIe siècle*), ed. Jean-Philippe Genêt. Paris-Rome: Publications de la Sorbonne, 2015. 499–520.

Aurell, Martin. "Geoffrey of Monmouth's *History of the Kings of Britain* and the Twelfth-Century Renaissance," *Haskins Society Journal* 18 (2006): 1–18.

Baczko, Bronislaw. *Les imaginaires sociaux: Mémoires et espoirs collectifs*. Paris: Payot, 1984.

BIBLIOGRAPHY

Balsom, Denis. "The Three-Wales Model." In *The National Question Again: Welsh Political Identity in the 1980s*, ed. J. Osmond. Llandysul: Gomer Press, 1985. 1–17.

Bammesberger, Alfred and Alfred Wolmann, eds. *Britain 400–600: Language and History*. Anglistische Forschungen 205. Heidelberg: Carl Winter, 1990.

Bancourt, Paul. *Les Musulmans dans les chansons de geste du cycle du roi*, 2 vols. Aix-en-Provence: Université de Provence, 1982.

Barber, Richard, ed. *Arthurian Literature II*. Cambridge: D. S. Brewer, 1982; Totowa, N.J.: Rowman and Littlefield.

Barber, Richard, ed. *Arthurian Literature IV*. Cambridge: D. S. Brewer, 1984.

Barber, Richard, ed. *Arthurian Literature VI*. Cambridge: D. S. Brewer, 1986.

Barber, Richard, ed. *King Arthur: Hero and Legend*. New York: St. Martins, 1961; repr. 1986.

Barbieri, Beatrice. "Una traduzione anglo-normanna dell'*Historia Regum Britannie*: la *Geste des Bretuns in alessandrini (Harley Brut)*." *Studi Mediolatini e volgari* 57 (2011):163–76.

Barbieri, Beatrice. "La *Geste des Bretuns en alexandrins (Harley Brut)*: Une traduction de l'*Historia* aux teintes épiques." In *L'Historia regum Britannie et les "Bruts" en Europe*, ed. Hélène Tétrel and Géraldine Veysseyre, I, 141–55.

Barlow, Frank. *William Rufus*. Berkeley and Los Angeles: University of California Press, 1983.

Barlow, Jonathan. "Gregory of Tours and the Myth of the Trojan Origins of the Franks." *Frühmittelalterliche Studien* 29 (1995): 86–95.

Barrow, Geoffrey. "Anglo-French Influences." In *Who are the Scots? and The Scottish Nation*, ed. Gordon Menzies. Edinburgh: Edinburgh University Press, 2002; orig. pub. in *Who are the Scots?* London: BBC, 1971 (51–65). 85–97.

Barrow, Geoffrey. *The Anglo-Norman Era in Scottish History*. Oxford: Clarendon Press, 1980.

Barrow, Geoffrey. *David I of Scotland (1124–1153): The Balance of New and Old*, The Stenton Lecture 1984. Reading: University of Reading, 1985.

Barrow, Geoffrey. "King David, Earl Henry and Cumbria," CWAAS (Cumberland and Westmoreland Antiquarian and Archeological Society) 99 (1999): 117–27.

Barrow, Geoffrey. "Wales and Scotland in the Middle Ages." *Welsh History Review* 10.3 (1981): 302–19.

Bartlett, Robert. *England under the Norman and Angevin Kings 1075–1225*. The New Oxford History of England. Oxford: Clarendon Press, 2000.

Bartrum, Peter C. "Was There a British 'Book of Conquests'?" BBCS 23 (1968–70): 1–6.

Bassett, Steven. "How the west was won: the Anglo-Saxon takeover of the west midlands." *Anglo-Saxon Studies in Archaeology and History* 11 (2000): 107–118.

Bates, David. *William the Conqueror*. New Haven, CT: Yale University Press, 2016.

Bates, David. *The Normans and Empire*. Oxford: Oxford University Press, 2013.

Baumgartner, Emmanuèle. "*Laisses similaires.*" In https://www.universalis.fr/encyclo pedie/la-chanson-de-roland/1-la-laisse-une-cellule-narrative/.

Baxter, Stephen. "Lordship and Labour." In *A Social History of England, 900–1200*, ed. Julia C. Crick and Elisabeth Van Houts. Cambridge: Cambridge University Press, 2011. 98–114.

Bell, Alexander. "Gaimar's Early 'Danish' Kings." *PMLA* 65 (1950): 601–40.

Bell, Alexander. "The Munich *Brut* and the *Estoire des Bretuns*," *Modern Language Review* 34.3 (1939): 321–54.

Bell, Alexander. "The 'Prologue' to Gaimar." *Modern Language Review* 15.2 (1920): 170–75.

Bell, Alexander. "The Royal *Brut* Interpolation." *Medium Ævum* 32.3 (1963): 190–202.

Bellis, Joanna. "Mapping the National Narrative: Place-Name Etymology in Laȝamon's *Brut* and its Sources." In *Reading Laȝamon's Brut*, ed. Rosamund Allen, Jane Roberts, and Carole Weinberg. 321–42.

Bennett, Matthew. "The Uses and Abuses of Wace's *Roman de Rou*." In *Maistre Wace*, ed. Glyn S. Burgess and Judith Weiss. 31–40.

Bennett, Matthew. "Wace and Warfare." In *Anglo-Norman Studies XI: Proceedings of the Battle Conference, 1988*, ed. R. Allen Brown. Woodbridge: Boydell Press, 1989. 37–57.

Bennett, Matthew. "Poetry as History? The 'Roman de Rou' of Wace as a Source for the Norman Conquest." In *Anglo-Norman Studies V: Proceedings of the Battle Conference 1982*, ed. R. Allen Brown. Woodbridge: Boydell Press, 1983. 21–39.

Benton, John. "The Evidence for Andreas Capellanus Re-Examined Again." *Studies in Philology* 59 (1962):471–78.

Berard, Christopher M. "King Arthur and the Canons of Laon." *Arthuriana* 26.3, 2016: 91–119.

Berard, Christopher M. *Arthurianism in Early Plantagenet England: From Henry II to Edward I*. Woodbridge: Boydell, 2019.

Bédier, Joseph. *Légendes épiques. Recherches sur la formation des chansons de geste.* 4 vols., 3rd ed. Paris: Honoré Champion, 1926–29.

Bérat, Emma. "The Patron and her Clerk: Multilingualism and Cultural Transition." *New Medieval Literatures* 12 (2010): 23–45.

Berberich, Christine. "'I Was Meditating about England': The Importance of Rural England for the Construction of 'Englishness'." In *History, Nationhood and the Question of Britain*, ed. Brocklehurst and Phillips. 375–85.

Bernau, Anke. "Beginning with Albina: Remembering the Nation." *Exemplaria* 21.3 (2009): 247–73.

Bernau, Anke. "Myths of Origin and the Struggle Over Nationhood in Medieval and Early Modern England." In *Reading the Medieval in Early Modern England*, ed. Gordon McMullan and David Matthews, Cambridge: Cambridge University Press, 2007. 106–18, 249–53 (notes).

BIBLIOGRAPHY

Beyers, Rita. "La Conception Nostre Dame de Wace: premier poème narrative sur la Vierge en ancien français." In *Serta devota in memoriam Guillelmi Lourdaux. Pars posteriora: Cultura medievalis*, ed. Werner Verbeke, Marcel Haverals, Raphaël De Keyser and Jean Goossens. 2 vols. Medievalia Lovaniensia, series 1, 21. Leuven: Leuven University Press, 1992–95. II, 359–400.

Biddle, Martin. "Seasonal Festivals and Residence: Winchester, Westminster and Gloucester in the Tenth to Twelfth Centuries." In *Anglo-Norman Studies VIII: Proceedings of the Battle Conference 1985*, ed. R. Allen Brown. Woodbridge: Boydell, 1986. 51–63.

Birns, Nicholas. "The Trojan Myth: Postmodern Reverberations." *Exemplaria* 5 (1993): 45–78.

Blacker, Jean. "The Anglo-Norman and Continental French Reception of Geoffrey of Monmouth's Corpus from the 12th to the 15th Centuries." In *A Companion to Geoffrey of Monmouth*, ed. Georgia Henley and Joshua Byron Smith. Brill's Companions to European History 22. Leiden: Brill, 2020. 454–66. https://brill.com/view/title/39588.

Blacker, Jean. "Arthur and Gormund: Conquest, Domination and Assimilation in Wace's *Roman de Brut*." In *"Si sai encore moult bon estoire, chançon moult bone et anciene": Studies in the Text and Context of Old French Narrative in Honour of Joseph J. Duggan*, ed. Sophie Marnette, John F. Levy, and Leslie Zarker Morgan. Medium Ævum Monographs. Oxford: The Society for the Study of Medieval Languages and Literature, 2015. 261–82.

Blacker, Jean. "Authorial Voice in Wace's *Assomption* and Anonymous Versions." In *Court and Cloister*, ed. Jean Blacker and Jane H. M. Taylor. 231–55.

Blacker, Jean. "Courtly Revision of Wace's *Roman de Brut* in British Library Egerton MS 3028." In *Courtly Arts and the Art of Courtliness: Selected Papers from the Eleventh Triennial Congress of the International Courtly Literature Society, University of Wisconsin-Madison, 29 July–4 August 2004*, ed. Keith Busby and Christopher Kleinhenz. Cambridge: D. S. Brewer, 2006. 237–58.

Blacker, Jean. "'Dame Custance la gentil': Gaimar's Portrait of a Lady and her Books." In *The Court and Cultural Diversity: Selected Papers from the Eighth Triennial Congress of the International Courtly Literature Society, The Queen's University of Belfast 26 July–1 August 1995*, ed. Evelyn Mullally and John Thompson. Cambridge: D. S. Brewer, 1997. 109–19.

Blacker, Jean. *The Faces of Time: Latin and Old French Historical Narrative of the Anglo-Norman Regnum*. Austin: University of Texas Press, 1994; rev. electronic ed., 2019, Amazon Kindle; new Introduction, 1–50.

Blacker, Jean. "Narrative Decisions and Revisions in the *Roman de Rou*." In *Maistre Wace: A Celebration*, ed. Glyn S. Burgess and Judith Weiss. 55–71.

Blacker, Jean. "'Ne vuil sun livre translater': Wace's Omission of Merlin's Prophecies from the *Roman de Brut*." In *Anglo-Norman Anniversary Essays*, ed. Short. 49–59.

Blacker, Jean. "Le rôle de la *persona* – ou la voix auctoriale – dans la *Conception Nostre Dame*, le *Roman de Brut* et le *Roman de Rou* de Wace." In *Le Style de Wace: Actes du colloque de la* SERAM, *Jersey juillet 2019*, ed. Denis Hüe, Françoise Laurent, Michel Vital Le Bossé and Laurence Mathey-Maille. Orleans: Éditions Paradigme, 2020. 51–71.

Blacker, Jean. "Transformations of a Theme: The Depoliticization of the Arthurian World in the *Roman de Brut*." In *The Arthurian Tradition: Essays in Convergence*, ed. Mary Flowers Braswell and John Bugge. Tuscaloosa: University of Alabama Press, 1988. 54–74, notes pp. 204–9 [published under the name Blacker-Knight].

Blacker, Jean. *Wace: A Critical Bibliography*, with the collaboration of Glyn S. Burgess (St. Helier: Société Jersiaise, 2008).

Blacker, Jean. "Where Wace Feared to Tread: Latin Commentaries on Merlin's Prophecies in the Reign of Henry II," *Arthuriana* 6.1 (1996): 36–52.

Blacker, Jean. "Why Such a Fishy Tale? St. Augustine's Conversion of the English in Wace's *Roman de Brut*." *Romance Quarterly* 52.1 (2005): 45–53.

Blacker, Jean. "Will the Real *Brut* Please Stand Up? Wace's *Roman de Brut* in Anglo-Norman and Continental Manuscripts." In *Text: An Interdisciplinary Annual of Textual Studies* 9, ed. David C. Greetham and William Speed Hill. Ann Arbor: The University of Michigan Press, 1996. 175–86.

Blacker, Jean and Peter Damian-Grint, "More about Arthur: the anonymous verse *Brut* fragment in Yale University Beinecke Library MS Takamiya 115," *Medium Ævum* 92.1 (2023): 67–103.

Blacker, Jean and Jane H. M. Taylor, eds. *Court and Cloister: Studies in the Short Narrative in Honor of Glyn S. Burgess*. Medieval and Renaissance Texts and Studies 517. Tempe, AZ: Arizona Center for Medieval & Renaissance Studies, 2018.

Blakey, Brian. "The Harley *Brut*: An Early French Translation of Geoffrey's *Historia Regum Britannie*," *Romania* 82.325 (1961): 44–70 (fragment 5 of Harley 1605/1).

Bliss, Jane and Judith Weiss. "The 'J' Manuscript of Wace's *Brut*." *Medium Ævum* 81 (2012): 222–48.

Bloch, R. Howard. *Etymologies and Genealogies: Literary Anthropology of the French Middle Ages*. Chicago: University of Chicago Press, 1983.

Bond, C. J. "Monastic Fisheries." In *Medieval Fish, Fisheries and Fishponds in England*. 2 vols., ed. Michael Aston, BAR British Series 182 (i), Oxford: BAR, 1988. I, 69–112.

Boutet, Dominique. "De la *translatio imperii* à la *finis saeculi*: progrès et decadence dans la pensée de l'histoire au Moyen Age." In *Progrès, reaction, decadence dans l'occident médiéval*, ed. Emmanuèle Baumgartner and Laurence Harf-Lancner. Geneva: Droz, 2003. 37–48.

Bovey, Alixe. *The Chaworth Roll: A Fourteenth-Century Genealogy of the Kings of England*. London: Sam Fogg, 2005.

BIBLIOGRAPHY

Brady, Lindy. *Writing the Welsh Borderlands in Anglo-Saxon England*. Manchester: Manchester University Press, 2017.

Brault, Gerard Joseph. *Early Blazon: Heraldic Terminology in the Twelfth and Thirteenth Centuries with Special Reference to Arthurian Literature*. Woodbridge: Boydell, 1997, 2nd ed.

Brayer, Edith. "Deux manuscrits du *Roman de Brut* de Wace, Vatican, Ottoboni lat. 1869; La Haye, Bibl. Royale 73.J.53." In *Studi in onore di Angelo Monteverdi*, ed. Augusto Guidi, 2 vols. Modena: Società Tipografica Modenese, 1959. I, 100–08.

Breen, Colin. "Maritime Connections: Landscape and Lordship among the Gaelic Atlantic Seaboard of Scotland and the North of Ireland during the Middle Ages." *Journal of the North Atlantic* 12.1 (2019): 3–15. https://doi.org/10.3721/037.012.sp202.

Breeze, Andrew. "The Historical Arthur and Sixth-Century Scotland." *Northern History* 52.2, 2015: 158–81. http://dx.doi.org/10.1179/0078172X15Z.00000000085.

Breeze, Andrew. "The Arthurian Battle of Badon and Braydon Forest, Wiltshire." *Journal of Literary Onomastics* 4.1 (2015): 20–30.

Brett, Caroline. "Soldiers, Saints, and States? The Breton Migrations Revisited." *Cambrian Medieval Celtic Studies* 61 (2011): 1–56.

Brewer, Derek. "Englishmen With Tails: Laȝamon, 'Muggles' and a Transhistorical Ethnic Joke in English." In *Medieval Heritage: Essays in Honour of Tadahiro Ikegami*. Tokyo: Yushodo, 1997. 3–15.

Broadhurst, Karen. "Henry II of England and Eleanor of Aquitaine: patrons of Literature in England?" *Viator* 27 (1996): 53–84.

Brocklehurst, Helen and Robert Phillips, eds. *History, Nationhood and the Question of Britain*. Houndmills and New York: Palgrave Macmillan, 2004.

Brooke, Christopher N. L. "Geoffrey of Monmouth as an Historian." In *Church and Government in the Middle Ages: Essays Presented to C. R. Cheney on his Seventieth Birthday*, ed. C. N. L. Brooke, David Edward Luscombe, G. H. Martin and Dorothy Owen. Cambridge: Cambridge University Press, 1976, rev. 1978. 77–91.

Brooks, Nicholas. "Canterbury, Rome and the Construction of English Identity." In *Early Medieval Rome and the Christian West: Essays in Honor of Donald A. Bullough*, ed. Julia M. H. Smith. Leiden: Brill, 2000. 221–46.

Brooks, Nicholas. "The Creation and Early Structure of the Kingdom of Kent." In *The Origins of Anglo-Saxon Kingdoms*, ed. Steven Bassett. London and New York: Leicester University Press, 1989. 55–74.

Brooks, Nicholas. "The English Origin Myth." In Nicholas Brooks, *Anglo-Saxon Myths: State and Church 400–1066*. London: Hambledon Press, 2000. 79–90.

Brooks, Nicholas. "From British to English Christianity: Deconstructing Bede's Interpretation of the Conversion." In *Conversion and Colonization in Anglo-Saxon England*, ed. Catherine E. Karkov and Nicholas Howe. Medieval and Renaissance Texts and Studies 318, Essays in Anglo-Saxon Studies 2. Tempe, AZ: Arizona Center for Medieval and Renaissance Studies, 2006. 1–30.

Broun, Dauvit. "Alba: Pictish Homeland or Irish Offshoot?" In *Exile and Homecoming: Papers from the Fifth Australian Conference of Celtic Studies, University of Sydney, July, 2004*, ed. Pamela O'Neill. Sydney: Sydney Celtic Studies Foundation, University of Sydney, 2005. 234–75.

Broun, Dauvit. *The Irish Identity of the Kingdom of the Scots: From the Picts to Alexander III*. Woodbridge: Boydell, 1999.

Broun, Dauvit. *Scottish Independence and the Idea of Britain: From the Picts to Alexander III*. Edinburgh: Edinburgh University Press, 2007, 2013/2014.

Broun, Dauvit. "When did Scotland become Scotland?" *History Today* 46.10 (1996): 16–21.

Bromwich, Rachel, Alfred Owen Gughes Jarman, and Brynley F. Roberts, eds. *The Arthur of the Welsh: The Arthurian Legend in Medieval Welsh Literature*. Cardiff University of Wales Press, 1991.

Bromwich, Rachel. "Brittany and the Arthurian Legend." In *The Arthur of the Welsh*, ed. Rachel Bromwich, A. O. H. Jarman, and Brynley F. Roberts. 249–72.

Bromwich, Rachel. "Concepts of Arthur." *Studia Celtica* 10/11 (1975–76): 163–81.

Brown, Arthur C. L. "The Round Table Before Wace." *Studies and Notes in Philology and Literature* 7 (1900): 183–205 (repr. Boston: Atheneum, 1900).

Brown, Arthur C. L. "Camlann and the Death of Arthur." *Folklore* 72.4 (1961): 612–21.

Brown, Reginald Allen. *The Normans and the Norman Conquest*. Woodbridge: Boydell, 1985.

Bryan, Elizabeth. *Collaborative Meaning in Medieval Scribal Culture: The Otho Laȝamon*. Editorial Theory and Literary Criticism Series. Ann Arbor: University of Michigan Press, 1999.

Bullock-Davies, Constance. "'*Exspectare Arturum*': Arthur and the Messianic Hope." *Bulletin of the Board of Celtic Studies* 29 (1980–81): 432–40.

Burek, Jacqueline. "'Ure Bruttisce speche': Language, Culture and Conquest in Laȝamon's *Brut*." *Arthuriana* 26.1 (2016): 108–23.

Burgess, Glyn S. "Women in the Works of Wace." In *Maistre Wace: A Celebration*, ed. Glyn S. Burgess and Judith Weiss. 91–106.

Burgess, Glyn S. and Karen Pratt, eds. *The Arthur of the French*. Cardiff: University of Wales Press, 2006.

Burgess, Glyn S. and Judith Weiss, eds. *Maistre Wace: A Celebration, Proceedings of the International Colloquium held in Jersey 10–12 September 2004*. St. Helier: Société Jersiaise, 2006.

Busby, Keith. "Scribal Behaviour." In Keith Busby, *Codex and Context: Reading Old French Verse Narrative in Manuscript*, 2 vols. Amsterdam and New York: Rodopi, 2002. 59–126.

Caldwell, Robert A. "Geoffrey of Monmouth, Prince of Liars." *North Dakota Quarterly* 39 (1963): 46–51.

BIBLIOGRAPHY

Caldwell, Robert A. "Wace's *Roman de Brut* and the *Variant Version* of Geoffrey of Monmouth's *Historia Regum Britanniae.*" *Speculum* 31 (1956): 675–82.

Caldwell, Robert A. "The use of sources in the *Variant* and vulgate versions of the *Historia Regum Britanniae* and the question of the order of the versions." *Bibliographical Bulletin of the International Arthurian Society* 9 (1957): 123–4.

Calin, William C. *The Old French Epic of Revolt: Raoul de Cambrai, Renaud de Montauban, Gormond et Isembard.* Geneva: E. Droz, 1962.

Cam, Helen M. "The Legend of the Incendiary Birds." *English Historical Review* 31.121 (1916): 98–101.

Campbell, Ewan. "Were the Scots Irish?" *Antiquity* 75 (2001): 285–92.

Campbell, James. "Some Twelfth-Century Views of the Anglo-Saxon Past." *Peritia* 3 (1984): 131–50 (repr. in Campbell, *Essays in Anglo-Saxon History*, London: Hambledon Press, 1986, 209–28).

Careri, Maria. "Per la storia di un testimone poco utilizzato del *Brut* di Wace (*membra disiecta*)." In *Studi di filologia romanza offerti a Valeria Bertolucci Pizzorusso*, ed. Pietro G. Beltrami, Maria Grazia Capusso, Fabrizio Cigni, and Sergio Vatteroni. Pisa: Pacini, 2006. 419–24.

Careri, Maria, Christine Ruby, and Ian Short, *Livres et écritures en français et en occitan au XIIᵉ siècle: Catalogue illustré*, with the collaboration of Terry Nixon and Patricia Stirnemann. Scritture e libri del medioevo 8. Rome: Viella, 2011.

Carver, Martin. "Lost, found, repossessed or argued away – the case of the Picts." *Antiquity* 85.330 (2011): 1479–83.

Carver, Martin. "What were they thinking? Intellectual Territories in Anglo-Saxon England." In *The Oxford Handbook of Anglo-Saxon Archaeology*, ed. Helena Hamerow, David A. Hinton, and Sally Crawford. Oxford: Oxford University Press, 2011. 914–47.

Cassard, Jean-Christophe. "La Tradition royale en Bretagne armorique." *Revue Historique* 281.1 (569) (1989): 15–45.

Chadwick, Hector Munro. "Vortigern." *Studies in Early British History*, ed. Nora K. Chadwick et al. Cambridge: Cambridge University Press, 1954. 26–27.

Chadwick, Nora K. "The Colonization of Brittany from Celtic Britain." *Proceedings of the British Academy* 51 (1965): 235–99.

Charles-Edwards, Thomas M. "The Arthur of History." In *The Arthur of the Welsh*, ed. Bromwich, Jarman, and Roberts. 15–32.

Charles-Edwards, Thomas M. "The Authenticity of the Gododdin: An Historian's View." In *Astudiaethau ar yr Hengerdd: Studies in Old Welsh Poetry*, ed. Rachel Bromwich and R. Brinley Jones. Cardiff: University of Wales Press, 1978. 44–71.

Charles-Edwards, Thomas M. "The Origins of Brittany." In Thomas Charles-Edwards, *Wales and the Britons 350–1064*. Oxford: Oxford University Press, 2013. 56–74.

Charles-Edwards, Thomas M. *Wales and the Britons, 350–1064.* Oxford: Oxford University Press, 2013.

Chibnall, Marjorie. *Anglo-Norman England 1066–1166.* Oxford: Basil Blackwell, 1986.

Church, Jordan. "'The Play of Elves': Supernatural Peripheries and Disrupted Kingship in Layamon's *Brut.*" *Philament* 24.1 (2018): 15–32. http://www.philamentjournal.com.

Church, Stephen D., ed. *King John: New Interpretations.* Woodbridge: Boydell, 1999.

Church, Stephen D. "Paganism in Conversion-Age Anglo-Saxon England: The Evidence of Bede's *Ecclesiastical History* Reconsidered." *History* 93.2 (310) (2008): 162–80.

Clark, Cecily. "Appendix: The Anglo-Norman Chronicle." In *The Peterborough Chronicle: The Bodleian Manuscript Laud Misc. 636,* ed. Dorothy Whitelock, Early English Manuscripts in Facsimile 4. Copenhagen: Rosenkilde and Bagger, 1954. 39–43.

Clark, John. "Trinovantum – the evolution of a legend." *Journal of Medieval History* 7.2 (1981): 135–51.

Clarkson, Tim. *The Men of the North: The Britons of Southern Scotland.* Edinburgh: John Donald, 2010.

Clarkson, Tim. *Strathclyde and the Anglo-Saxons in the Viking Age.* Edinburgh: John Donald, 2016.

Clayton, Mary. *The Cult of the Virgin Mary in Anglo-Saxon England.* Cambridge Studies in Anglo-Saxon England 2. Cambridge: Cambridge University Press, 1990.

Cohen, Jeffrey Jerome. *Of Giants: Sex, Monsters, and the Middle Ages.* Medieval Cultures 17. Minneapolis: University of Minnesota Press, 1999.

Cohen, Jeffrey Jerome. "Green Children from Another World or the Archipelago in England." In *Cultural Diversity in the British Middle Ages,* ed. Cohen, New Middle Ages Series. New York: Palgrave MacMillan, 2008. 75–94.

Cowan, Edward J. "Myth and Identity in Early Medieval Scotland." *Scottish Historical Review* 63:176, pt. 2 (1984): 111–32.

Crane, Susan. "Anglo-Norman Cultures in England, 1066–1460." In *The Cambridge History of Medieval English Literature,* ed. David Wallace. Cambridge: Cambridge University Press, 1999. 35–60.

Creighton, John. *Coins and Power in Late Iron Age Britain.* Cambridge: Cambridge University Press, 2000.

Crick, Julia. "The British Past and the Welsh Future: Gerald of Wales, Geoffrey of Monmouth and Arthur of Britain." *Celtica* 23 (1999): 60–75.

Crick, Julia. "Geoffrey of Monmouth, Prophecy and History." *Journal of Medieval History* 18.4 (1992): 357–71.

Crick, Julia. *The Historia Regum Britannie of Geoffrey of Monmouth, III: A Summary Catalogue of the Manuscripts.* Cambridge: D. S. Brewer, 1989.

Crick, Julia. *The Historia Regum Britannie of Geoffrey of Monmouth, IV. Dissemination and Reception in the Later Middle Ages.* Cambridge: D. S. Brewer, 1991.

Croizy-Naquet, Catherine. "César et le *romanz* au XIIe siècle." *Cahiers de Recherches Médiévales* (special issue: *La Figure de Jules César au Moyen Âge et à la Renaissance*), 13 (2006): 39–49.

Croizy-Naquet, Catherine. "L'*Estoire des Engleis* de Geiffrei Gaimar, ou comment faire mémoire du passé." In *Le Passé à l'épreuve du présent: appropriations et usages du passé au Moyen Âge à la Renaissance*, ed. Pierre Chastang, Mythes, Critique et Histoire. Paris: Presses de l'Université Paris-Sorbonne, 2008. 61–74.

Crouch, David. *The Chivalric Turn: Conduct and Hegemony in Europe before 1300*. Oxford: Oxford University Press, 2019.

Crouch, David. *The Normans: The History of a Dynasty*. London and New York: Hambledon Continuum, 2002.

Cunliffe, Barry. *Britain Begins*. Oxford: Oxford University Press, 2012.

Curley, Michael J. Geoffrey *of Monmouth*. Twayne's English Authors Series 509. New York: Twayne, 1994.

Curry, Anne. "The Hundred Years War, 1337–1453." In *The Practice of Strategy: From Alexander the Great to the Present*, ed. John Andreas Olsen and Colin S. Gray. Oxford: Oxford University Press, 2011, Chapter 5, Oxford Scholarship Online 2012 https://www.oxfordscholarship.com/view/10.1093/acprof:oso/9780199608638 .001.0001/acprof-9780199608638.

Dalton, Paul. "The Date of Geoffrey Gaimar's *Estoire des Engleis*, the Connections of his Patrons, and the Politics of Stephen's Reign." *Chaucer Review* 42 (2007): 23–47.

Dalton, Paul. "Geoffrei Gaimar's *Estoire des Engleis*, Peacemaking, and the 'Twelfth-Century Revival of the English Nation'." *Studies in Philology* 104 (2007): 427–53.

Dalton, Paul. "Topical Concerns of Geoffrey of Monmouth's *Historia Regum Britannie*: History, Prophecy, Peacemaking, and English Identity in the Twelfth Century." *Journal of British Studies* 44.4 (2005): 688–712.

Damian-Grint, Peter. *The New Historians of the Twelfth Century Renaissance: Inventing Vernacular Authority*. Woodbridge: Boydell, 1999.

Damian-Grint, Peter. "Propaganda and *essample* in Benoît de Sainte-Maure's *Chronique des ducs de Normandie*." In *Medieval Chronicle IV*, ed. Erik Simon Kooper. Amsterdam and Atlanta, GA: Rodopi, 2006. 39–52.

Damian-Grint, Peter. "Redating the Royal *Brut* Fragment." *Medium Ævum* 65.2 (1996): 280–85.

Damian-Grint, Peter. "Truth, Trust and Evidence in the Anglo-Norman *Estoire*." In *Anglo-Norman Studies XVIII. Proceedings of the Battle Conference 1995*, ed. Christopher Harper-Bill. Woodbridge: Boydell, 1996. 63–78.

Damian-Grint, Peter. "Vernacular History in the Making: Anglo-Norman Verse Historiography in the Twelfth Century," unpub. Ph. D. thesis, University of London (Birkbeck), 1994, Appendix II, 368–473 (fragments 1–4 of Harley 1605/1).

Damian-Grint, Peter. "A 12th-century Anglo-Norman *Brut* Fragment (MS BL Harley 4733, f. 128)." In *Anglo-Norman Anniversary Essays*, ed. Ian Short. 87–104.

Damian-Grint, Peter and Françoise Le Saux, "The Arthur of the Chronicles." In *The Arthur of the French*, ed. Glyn S. Burgess and Karen Pratt. 93–111.

Daniel, Norman A. *Heroes and Saracens: An Interpretation of the Chansons de Geste*. Edinburgh: Edinburgh University Press, 1984.

Davies, R. Rees. *Domination and Conquest: The experience of Ireland, Scotland and Wales 1100–1300*. Cambridge: Cambridge University Press, 1990.

Davies, R. Rees. *The First English Empire: Power and Identities in the British Isles 1093–1343* (*The Ford Lectures Delivered in the University of Oxford in Hilary Term 1998*). Oxford: Oxford University Press, 2000.

Davies, R. Rees. "Lordship or Colony?" In *The English in Medieval Ireland: proceedings of the first joint meeting of the Royal Irish Academy and the British Academy, Dublin, 1982*, ed. James Lydon. Dublin: Royal Irish Academy, 1984. 142–60.

Davies, R. Rees. *The Matter of Britain and Matter of England: An Inaugural lecture delivered before the University of Oxford on 29 February 1996*. Oxford: Clarendon Press, 1996.

Davies, R. Rees. "Nations and National Identities in the Medieval World: An Apologia." *Journal of Belgian History* 34 (2004): 567–79.

Davies, R. Rees. "The Peoples of Britain and Ireland, 1100–1400: IV. Language and Historical Mythology." *Transactions of the Royal Historical Society*, Sixth Series, vol. 7 (1997): 1–24.

Davies, R. Rees. "Presidential Address: The Peoples of Britain and Ireland, 1100–1400. II. Names, Boundaries and Regnal Solidarities." *Transactions of the Royal Historical Society*, Sixth Series, vol. 5 (1995): 1–20.

Davies, R. Rees. "Race Relations in Post-Conquest Wales: Confrontation and Compromise." The Cecil-Williams Lecture for 1973, *Transactions of the Honourable Society of Cymmrodorion* (1974–75): 32–56.

Davies, Wendy. *Wales in the Early Middle Ages*. Leicester: Leicester University Press, 1982.

Davis, R. H. C. "The Chronicle Sources." In *Davis, King Stephen 1135–1154*. New York: Longman, 1967; rev. ed 1977. Appendix III, 146–52.

Davis-Secord, Jonathan. "Revising Race in Laȝamon's *Brut*." *Journal of English and Germanic Philology* 116.2 (2017): 156–81.

Delbouille, Maurice. "Le Témoignage de Wace sur la légende arthurienne." *Romania* 74 (1953): 172–99.

Delusier, Alex. "L'Illusion stylisque du réalisme dans le *Roman de Brut* de Wace." Academia, 2020. https://www.academia.edu/43191879/Lillusion_stylistique_du_r%C3%A9alisme_dans_le_Roman_de_Brut_de_Wace.

BIBLIOGRAPHY

Denzin, Norma K., Yvonna S. Lincoln, and Linda Tuhiwai Smith, eds. *Handbook of Critical and Indigenous Methodologies*. Los Angeles: Sage Publications, 2008.

De Vries, Jan. "La Chanson de *Gormont et Isembart*." *Romania* 80.317 (1959): 34–62.

Di Lella, Francesco. "Il *Roll Brut* nel rotolo London, College of Arms, 12/45 A (prima parte)." *Critica del Testo* 22.1 (2019): 37–66.

Di Lella, Francesco. "Il *Roll Brut* nel rotolo London, College of Arms, 12/45 A (seconda parte)." *Critica del Testo* 22.2 (2019): 61–83.

Di Lella, Francesco. "Il *Roman de Brut* in Inghilterra: Tradizione manoscritta e tradizioni letterarie," unpublished PhD thesis, Università di Roma "La Sapienza" and Université de la Sorbonne, Rome and Paris, 2018.

Downham, Clare. Review of James Fraser *From Caledonia to Pictland and Alex Woolfe, From Pictland to Alba 789–1070*. *Journal of Scottish Historical Studies* 29.2 (2009): 141–43.

Draak, Maartje. "The Hague Manuscript of Wace's *Brut*." In *Amor Librorum: Bibliographic and Other Essays, a Tribute to Abraham Horodisch on his Sixtieth Birthday*, ed. [not listed]. Amsterdam: Erasmus Antiquariaat; Zurich: Safaho Foundation, 1958. 23–27.

Duggan, Joseph John. "Medieval Epic as Popular Historiography." In *Grundriss der Romanischen Literaturen des Mittelalters*, XI.1, *Littérature historiographique des origines à 1500*, ed. Hans Ulrich Gumbrecht, Ursula Link-Heer, and Peter-Michael Spangenberg. Heidelberg: Carl Winter, 1986–87. 285–311.

Dumville, David N. "The Anglian Collection of Royal Genealogies and Regnal Lines." *Anglo-Saxon England* 5 (1976): 23–50.

Dumville, David N. "Brittany and 'Armes Prydein Vawr'." *Études Celtiques* 20.1 (1983): 145–59.

Dumville, David N. "The Chronology of *De Excidio Britanniae*, Book I." In *Gildas: New Approaches*, ed. Michael Lapidge and David Dumville. 61–84.

Dumville, David N. "The Corpus-Christi 'Nennius'." *Bulletin of the Board of Celtic Studies*, 25 (1972–74): 369–80 (repr. in Dumville, *Histories and Pseudo-histories of the Latin Middle Ages*).

Dumville, David N. "Gildas and Maelgwn: problems of dating." In *Gildas: New Approaches*, ed. Michael Lapidge and David Dumville. 51–60.

Dumville, David N. "*Historia Brittonum*: An Insular History from the Carolingian Age." In *Historiographie im frühen Mittelalter*, ed. Anton Scharer and Georg Scheibelreiter, Veröffentlichungen des Instituts für Österreichische Geschichtsforschung 32. Munich and Vienna: Oldenbourg, 1994. 406–34.

Dumville, David N. "The Historical Value of the *Historia Brittonum*." *Arthurian Literature* VI, ed. Richard Barber. Cambridge: D. S. Brewer, 1986. 1–26.

Dumville, David N. *Histories and Pseudo-histories of the Insular Middle Ages*. Aldershot: Variorum, 1990.

Dumville, David N. "'Nennius' and the *Historia Brittonum*." *Studia Celtica* 10/11 (1975/6): 78–95 (repr. in Dumville, *Histories and Pseudo-histories of the Insular Middle Ages*).

Dumville, David N. "On the north British section of the *Historia Brittonum*." *Welsh History Review* 8 (1976/7): 345–54 (repr. in Dumville, *Histories and Pseudo-histories of the Insular Middle Ages*).

Dumville, David N. "Some aspects of the chronology of the *Historia Brittonum*." *Bulletin of the Board of Celtic Studies*, 25 (1972–74): 439–45 (repr. in Dumville, *Histories and Pseudo-histories of the Insular Middle Ages*).

Dumville, David N. "Sub-Roman Britain: history and legend." *History N. S.* 62 (1977): 173–92 (repr. in Dumville, *Histories and Pseudo-histories of the Insular Middle Ages*).

Duncan, A. A. M. *The Kingship of the Scots, 842–1292*. Edinburgh: Edinburgh University Press, 2002.

Duncan, A. A. M. *Scotland: The Making of the Kingdom*. Edinburgh: Oliver & Boyd, 1975, 254–55).

Dunbar-Ortiz, Roxanne. *An Indigenous People's History of the United States*. ReVisioning American History 3. Boston: Beacon Press, 2014.

Eastwood, David. Review of *Celtic Identity and the British Image*, by Murray G. H. Pittock, Manchester: Manchester University Press, 1999. *English Historical Review* 116.465 (2001): 249–50.

Echard, Sián. *The Arthur of Medieval Latin Literature: The Development and Dissemination of the Arthurian Legend in Medieval Latin*. Cardiff: University of Wales Press, 2011.

Echard, Sián. *Arthurian Narrative in the Latin Tradition*. Cambridge: Cambridge University Press, 1998.

Echard, Sián. "'Hic est Artur': Reading Latin and Rereading Arthur." In *New Directions in Arthurian Studies*, ed. Alan Lupack. Cambridge: D. S. Brewer, 2002. 49–67.

Echard, Sián. "*Historia Brittonum*." In *The Encyclopedia of Medieval Literature in Britain*. Chichester, West Sussex and Hoboken, NJ: John Wiley & Sons, 2017. 1019–20.

Eckhardt, Caroline D. "The *Prophetia Merlini* of Geoffrey of Monmouth: Latin Manuscript Copies." *Manuscripta* 26.3 (1982): 167–76.

Eisenstadt, Shmuel N. *The Political Systems of Empires*. New York: The Free Press, 1969.

Ekwall, Eilert. *The Concise Oxford Dictionary of Place Names*. 4th ed. Clarendon: Oxford University Press, 1966.

Eley, Penny and Philip E. Bennett. "The Battle of Hastings according to Gaimar, Wace and Benoît: Rhetoric and Politics." *Nottingham Medieval Studies* 43 (1999): 47–78.

Elliott, Simon. *Septimius Severus in Scotland: The Northern Campaigns of the First Hammer of the Scots*. London: Greenhill Books, 2018.

Emanuel, Hywel D. "Geoffrey of Monmouth's *Historia Regum Britanniae*: a Second Variant Version." *Medium Ævum* 35 (1966): 103–11.

BIBLIOGRAPHY

Evans, Andrew J., John Nettleship, and Stephen Perry. "*Linn Liuan/Llynn Lliw*: The Wondrous Lake of the *Historia Brittonum's de Mirabilibus Britanniae* and *Culhwch ac Olwen*." *Folklore* 119 (2008): 295–318.

Evans, Daniel John. "Welshness in 'British Wales': negotiating national identity at the margins." *Nations and Nationalism: Journal of the Association for the Study of Ethnicity and Nationalism* 25.1 (2019): 167–190.

Evans, Nicholas. "Royal Succession and Kingship among the Picts." *The Innes Review* 59.1 (2008): 1–48. https://doi.org/10.3366/E0020157X000140.

Evison, Vera. "Distribution maps and England in the first two phases." In *Angles, Saxons, and Jutes. Essays presented to J. N. L. Myres*, ed. V. I. Evison. Oxford: Clarendon Press, 1981. 126–67.

Fahy, Dermot. "When did Britons become Bretons?: A Note on the Foundation of Brittany." *The Welsh History Review* 2 (1964–65): 111–24.

Faletra, Michael A. "The Conquest of the Past in the History of the Kings of Britain." *Literature Compass* 4.1 (2007): 121–33.

Faletra, Michael. "Narrating the Matter of Britain: Geoffrey of Monmouth and the Norman Colonization of Wales." *The Chaucer Review* 35.1 (2000): 60–85.

Faletra, Michael. "Once and Future Britons: The Welsh in Lawman's *Brut*." *Medievalia et Humanistica* 28 (2001): 1–23.

Faletra, Michael. *Wales and the Medieval Colonial Imagination: The Matters of Britain in the Twelfth Century*. New York: Palgrave MacMillan, 2014.

Farrel, Jennifer. "History, Prophecy and the Arthur of the Normans: The Question of Audience and Motivation behind Geoffrey of Monmouth's *Historia Regum Britanniae*." In *Anglo-Norman Studies 37: Proceedings of the Battle Conference 2014*, ed. Elisabeth van Houts. Woodbridge: Boydell, 2015. 99–114.

Faull, Margaret Lindsay. "Semantic Development of Old-English *Wealh*." *Leeds Studies in English* 8 (1975): 20–44.

Fenton, Kristen. *Gender, Nation and Conquest in the Works of William of Malmesbury*. Woodbridge, Suffolk: Boydell, 2008.

Feurherd, Paul. *Geoffrey von Monmouth und das alte Testament mit Berücksichtigung der Historia Britonum des Nennius*, Inaugural-Dissertation, Friedrichs-Universität Halle-Wittenberg. Halle, 1915.

Field, Peter J. C. "Arthur's Battles." *Arthuriana* 18.4 (2008): 3–32.

Field, Peter J. C. "Nennius and his History." *Studia Celtica* 30 (1996): 159–65.

Field, Peter J. C. "Gildas and the City of the Legions." *Heroic Age* 1 (1999): http://www.heroicage.org/issues/1/hagcl.htm (accessed 2019).

Finley, Moses I. "Colonies – An Attempt at a Typology." *Transactions of the Royal Historical Society* 26 (1976): 167–88.

Finke, Laurie A. and Martin B. Shichtman. "Exegetical History: Nazis at the Round Table." *Postmedieval: A Journal of Medieval Cultural Studies* 5 (2014): 278–94.

Finke, Laurie A. and Martin B. Shichtman. *King Arthur and the Myth of History.* Gainesville: University Press of Florida, 2014.

Finke, Laurie A. and Martin B. Shichtman. "The Mont St. Michel Giant: Sexual Violence and Imperialism in the Chronicles of Wace and Laȝamon." In *Violence against Women in Medieval Texts*, ed. Anna Roberts. Gainesville: University Press of Florida, 1998. 56–74.

Fitzpatrick-Williams, Keith. "The xxuiii ciuitates brittaniȩ of the *Historia Brittonum*: Antiquarian Speculation in Medieval Wales." *Journal of Literary Onomastics* 4.1 (2015): 1–19.

Flack, Christopher H. "Writing Conquest: Traditions of Anglo-Saxon Invasion and Resistance in the Twelfth Century," unpublished doctoral thesis, University of Minnesota, Sept. 2013. http://hdl.handle.net/11299/159710.

Fletcher, Robert Huntington. *Arthurian Material in the Chronicles, especially those of Great Britain and France*, orig. published in *Harvard Studies and Notes in Philology and Literature* 10. Boston, 1906; repr. New York: Burt Franklin, 1958.

Fleuriot, Léon. *Les origines de la Bretagne: l'émigration.* Paris: Payot, 1980.

Fleuriot, Léon. "Le patriotisme brittonique et l'histoire légendaire." In *Histoire littéraire et culturelle de la Bretagne*, ed. Jean Balclou and Yves Le Gallo. Paris: Champion, 1987. 105–19.

Flint, Valerie. "The *Historia Regum Britanniae* of Geoffrey of Monmouth: Parody and its Purpose." *Speculum* 54 (1979): 447–68.

Flood, Victoria. "Arthur's Return from Avalon: Geoffrey of Monmouth and the Development of the Legend." *Arthuriana* 25.2 (2015): 84–110.

Flood, Victoria. *Prophecy, Politics and Place in Medieval England: From Geoffrey of Monmouth to Thomas of Erceldoune.* Cambridge: D. S. Brewer, 2016.

Foley, W. Trent and Nicholas J. Higham. "Bede on the Britons." *Early Medieval Europe* 17.2 (2009): 154–85.

Foot, Sarah. "The Making of *Angelcynn*: English Identity Before the Norman Conquest." *Transactions of the Royal Historical Society*, ser. 6. Cambridge: Cambridge University Press, 1996. 25–50.

Forsyth, Katherine. *Language in Pictland: The Case Against "Non-Indo-European Pictish."* Studia Hameliana 2. Utrecht: Stichting Uitgeverij de Keltische Draak, 1997.

Forsyth, Katherine. "Origins: Scotland to 1100." In *Scotland: A History*, ed. Jenny Wormald. Oxford: Oxford University Press, 2005. 1–38.

Forsyth, Katherine. "Picts." In *Celtic Culture: An Historical Encyclopedia*, ed. John T. Koch. IV, 1446–48.

Foster, Sally M. *Picts, Gaels and Scots: Early Historic Scotland.* London: Batsford, 1996; 2nd ed. 2004; rev. ed. London: Birlinn, 2014.

BIBLIOGRAPHY

Foucault, Michel. "Qu'est-ce qu'un auteur?" *Bulletin de la Société française de philosophie* 6.3 (1969): 74–103 (repr. in *Dits et Écrits 1954–88*, 4 vols., ed. Daniel Defert, François Ewald, and Jacques Lagrange. Paris: Gallimard, 1994. 1:789–821).

Foucault, Michel. "What is an author?" trans. Josué V. Haran. In *Contemporary Literary Criticism: Literary and Cultural Studies*, 4th ed., ed. Robert Con Davis and Ronald Schliefer. New York: Longman, 1998. 364–76.

Fox, Robin. "In the Company of Men: Tribal Bonds in Warrior Epics." In Fox, *The Tribal Imagination: Civilization and the Savage Mind*. Cambridge, MA: Harvard University Press, 2011. 196–225.

Fraser, James. "From Ancient Scythia to *The Problem of the Picts*: Thoughts on the Quest for Pictish Origins." In *Pictish Progress: New Studies in Northern Britain in the Middle Ages*, ed. Stephen T. Driscoll, Jane Geddes, and Mark A. Hall. Leiden: Brill, 2010. 16–43.

Fraser, James. *From Caledonia to Pictland: Scotland to 795*. New Edinburgh History of Scotland 1. Edinburgh: Edinburgh University Press, 2009.

Frazer, William O. "Introduction," in *Social Identity in Early Medieval Britain*, ed. Frazer and Andrew Tyrell. London and New York: Leicester University Press, 2000. 1–22.

Freeman, Elizabeth. "Geffrei Gaimar, Vernacular Historiography, and the Assertion of Authority." *Studies in Philology* 93.2 (1996): 188–206.

Freeman, Edward A. *Four Oxford Lectures: Teutonic Conquest in Gaul and Britain*. London, 1888.

Fulton, Helen, ed. *A Companion to Arthurian Literature*. Blackwell Companions to Literature and Culture 58. Oxford: Blackwell, 2009; Chichester: John Wiley & Sons, 2012.

Fulton, Helen. "History and Myth: Geoffrey of Monmouth's *Historia Regum Britanniae*." In *A Companion to Arthurian Literature*, ed. Fulton. 44–57.

Fulton, Helen. "Originating Britain: Welsh Literature and the Arthurian Tradition." In *A Companion to British Literature: Volume 1: Medieval Literature 700–1450*, ed. Robert DeMaria, Jr., Heesok Chang, and Samantha Zacher. Hoboken, NJ: John Wiley & Sons, 2014. 308–22.

Galbraith, Vivian Hunter. "Good Kings and Bad Kings in English History." *History* n.s. 30 (1945): 119–32.

Gallais, Pierre. "La *Variant Version* de l'*Historia Regum Britanniae* et le *Brut* de Wace." *Romania* 87 (1966): 1–32.

Galloway, Andrew. "Laȝamon's Gift." *PMLA* 121.3 (2006): 717–34.

Geertz, Clifford. "Thick Description: Toward an Interpretive Theory of Culture." In Geertz, *The Interpretation of Cultures*. New York: Basic Books, 1973; rev. ed. 2000. 3–32.

Gelling, Margaret. "Why Aren't We Speaking Welsh?" *Anglo-Saxon Studies in Archaeology and History* 6 (1993): 51–56.

George, Karen. *Gildas's "De excidio Britonum" and the Early British Church.* Studies in Celtic History 26. Woodbridge: Boydell and Brewer, 2009.

Gerould, Gordon H. "King Arthur and Politics." *Speculum* 2 (1927): 33–51.

Giandrea, Mary Frances. *Episcopal Culture in Late Anglo-Saxon England.* Woodbridge: Boydell, 2007.

Gillingham, John. *The Angevin Empire.* London: Arnold, 2nd ed. 2001.

Gillingham, John. "Conquering the Barbarians: War and Chivalry in Twelfth-Century Britain," *Haskins Society Journal* 2 (1992): 67–84 (repr. in Gillinhgham, *The English in the Twelfth Century.* 41–58).

Gillingham, John. "The Context and Purposes of Geoffrey of Monmouth's *History of the Kings of Britain.*" In *Anglo-Norman Studies XIII. Proceedings of the Battle Conference, 1990,* ed. Marjorie Chibnall. Woodbridge: Boydell, 1991, 99–118 (repr. in Gillinhgham, *The English in the Twelfth Century.* 19–39).

Gillingham, John. *The English in the Twelfth Century: Imperialism, National Identity and Political Values.* Woodbridge: Boydell, 2000.

Gillingham, John. "The Foundations of a Disunited Kingdom." In *Uniting the Kingdom? The Making of British History,* ed. A. Grant and K. Stringer. London: Routledge, 1995, 48–64 (repr. in Gillinhgham, *The English in the Twelfth Century.* 93–109).

Gillingham, John. "Gaimar, the Prose *Brut* and the Making of English History." In *L'Histoire et les nouveaux publics dans l'Europe médiévale,* ed. Jean-Philippe Genet. Paris: Publications de la Sorbonne, 1997, 165–76 (repr. in Gillingham, *The English in the Twelfth Century.* 113–22).

Gillingham, John. "Kingship, Chivalry and Love. Political and Cultural values in the Earliest History Written in French: Geoffrey Gaimar's *Estoire des Engleis.*" In *Anglo-Norman Political Culture and the Twelfth Century Renaissance,* ed. C. Warren Hollister. Woodbridge: Boydell, 1997, 33–58 (repr. in Gillingham, *The English in the Twelfth Century.* 233–58).

Gillingham, John. "Richard of Devizes and 'a rising tide of nonsense': How Cerdic met King Arthur." In *The Long Twelfth-Century View of the Anglo-Saxon Past,* ed. Martin Brett, David A. Woodman. London: Routledge, 2015. 141–56.

Gillingham, John. "A Second Tidal Wave? The Historiography of English Colonization of Ireland, Scotland and Wales in the Twelfth and Thirteenth Centuries." In *Historiographical Approaches to Medieval Colonization of East Central Europe,* ed. J. Piskorski. Boulder, CO: University of Colorado Press, 2003. 303–27.

Giot, Pierre Roland, Philippe Guignon, and Bernard Merdrignac. *Les premiers Bretons d'Armorique.* Rennes: Presses Universitaires de Rennes, 2003; published simultaneously in English as *The British Settlement of Brittany: The First Bretons in Armorica,* Stroud: Tempus, 2003.

Given-Wilson, Chris. *Chronicles: The Writing of History in Medieval England.* Hambledon, London, and New York: 2004.

BIBLIOGRAPHY

Gransden, Antonia. "Bede's reputation as an historian in medieval England." *Journal of Ecclesiastical History* 32 (1981): 397–425 (repr. in Gransden, *Legends, Traditions and History in Medieval England*, London and Rio Grande, OH: Hambledon Press, 1992, 1–29).

Gransden, Antonia. *Historical Writing in England, c. 550–c. 1307*. Ithaca, NY: Cornell University Press, 1974.

Green, Thomas. *Concepts of Arthur*. Stroud, Glos.: Tempus Publishing, 2007.

Green, Thomas. "The British Kingdom of Lindsey." *Cambrian Medieval Celtic Studies*, 56 (2008): 1–43.

Greene, Virginie. "Qui croit au retour d'Arthur?" *Cahiers de Civilisation Médiévale* 45.180 (2002): 321–40.

Greenway, Diana. "Authority, convention and observation in Henry of Huntingdon's *Historia Anglorum*." In *Anglo-Norman Studies XVIII, Proceedings of the Battle Conference 1995*, ed. Christopher Harper-Bill. Woodbridge: Boydell, 1996. 105–21.

Greenway, Diana. Review of Wright's edition of the First Variant and Alexander Nequam's *Speculum Speculationum*, ed. Rodney M. Thompson. *Albion* 22.1 [1990]: 102–4.

Grimmer, Martin. "Invasion, settlement or political conquest: changing representations of the arrival of the Anglo-Saxons in Britain." *Journal of the Australian Early Medieval Association* 3 (2007): 169–186.

Grisward, Joël H. "Uter Pendragon, Arthur, et l'idéologie royale des Indo-européens." In *Le Moyen Âge aujourd'hui, Europe*, 654, 1983, 111–120 (repr. in D. Hüe, *Fils sans père, études sur le Merlin de Robert de Boron*, Medievalia 35, Orleans: Paradigme, 2000. 103–13).

Grout, Patricia B. "The Author of the Munich *Brut*, His Latin Sources and Wace." *Medium Ævum* 54.2 (1985): 274–82.

Guenée, Bernard. "L'historien et la compilation au XIIᵉ siècle." *Journal des savants* (1985): 119–35.

Guenée, Bernard. "L'historien par les mots." In Guenée, *Politique et histoire au Moyen Age, Recueil d'articles sur l'histoire politique et l'historiographie médiévale, 1956–1981*. Paris: Publications de la Sorbonne, 1981. 221–37.

Guy, Ben. "Constantine, Helena, Maximus: on the appropriation of Roman history in medieval Wales, c. 800–1250." *Journal of Medieval History* 44.4 (2018): 381–405.

Guy, Ben. "Geoffrey of Monmouth's Welsh Sources." In *A Companion to Geoffrey of Monmouth*, ed. Georgia Henley and Joshua Byron Smith. 32–66.

Guy, Ben. *Medieval Welsh Genealogy: An Introduction and Textual Study*, Studies in Celtic History 42. Woodbridge: Boydell Press, 2020.

Guy, Ben. Review of *History of the Kings of Britain. The First Variant Version*, ed. and trans. David W. Burchmore, Dumbarton Oaks Medieval Library 57. Cambridge, MA: Harvard University Press, 2019. *The Journal of Medieval Latin* 32 (2022): 300–7.

Hamerow, Helena. "Migration Theory and the Anglo-Saxon 'Identity Crisis'." In *Migrations and Invasions in Archaeological Explanation*, ed. John Chapman and H. Hamerow. *British Archaeological Reports* Series 664 (1997): 33–44.

Hammer, Jacob. "A Commentary on the *Prophetiae Merlini*." *Speculum* 10 (1935): 3–30.

Hammer, Jacob. "A Commentary on the *Prophetia Merlini* (Geoffrey of Monmouth's *Historia Regum Britanniae*, Book VII) (Continuation)." *Speculum* 15 (1940): 409–31.

Hammer, Jacob. "Remarks on the Sources and Textual History of Geoffrey of Monmouth's 'Historia Regum Britanniae' with an Excursus on the 'Chronica Polonorum' of Wincenty Kadlubek (Magister Vincentius)." *Bulletin of the Polish Institute of Arts and Sciences in America* 2.2 (1944): 500–64.

Hammond, Matthew H. "Ethnicity and the Writing of Medieval Scottish History." *The Scottish Historical Review* 85.1 (2006): 1–27.

Hanning, Robert W. *The Vision of History in Early Britain: From Gildas to Geoffrey of Monmouth*. New York: Columbia University Press, 1966.

Hardman, Philippa and Marianne Ailes. *The Legend of Charlemagne in Medieval England: The Matter of France in Middle English and Anglo-Norman Literature*. Cambridge: D. S. Brewer, 2017.

Hardt, Michael and Antonio Negri. *Empire*. Cambridge, MA and London: Harvard University Press, 2000.

Harris, Joseph and Karl Reichl. "Performance and Performers." In *Medieval Oral Literature*, ed. Karl Reichl, De Gruyter Lexikon. Berlin and Boston: De Gruyter, 2012. 141–202.

Harris, Sara. *The Linguistic Past in Twelfth-Century Britain*. Cambridge Studies in Medieval Literature 100. Cambridge: Cambridge University Press, 2017.

Harris, Stephen J. *Race and Ethnicity in Anglo Saxon Literature*. London and New York: Routledge, 2003.

Harvey, David C. and Rhys Jones. "Custom and Habit(us): The Meaning of Traditions and Legends in Early Medieval Western Britain." *Geografiska Annaler, Series B, Human Geography* 81.4 (1999): 223–33.

Hay, Denys. "The Use of the Term 'Great Britain' in the Middle Ages." *Proceedings of the Society of Antiquaries of Scotland* 89 (1955–56): 55–66; repr. in *Hay, Europe: The Emergence of an Idea*, Edinburgh: Edinburgh University Press, 1957, rev. ed. 1968. 128–44.

Heal, Felicity. "What Can King Lucius do for You? The Reformation and the Early English Church." *The English Historical Review* 120.487 (2005): 593–614.

Hechter, Michael. Internal *Colonialism: The Celtic Fringe in British National Development, 1536–1966*. Berkeley and Los Angeles: University of California Press, 1975; 2nd ed., New Brunswick, NJ: Transaction Publishers, 1999.

Helbert, Daniel. "'an Arður sculde ȝete cum': The Prophetic Hope in Twelfth-Century Britain." *Arthuriana* 26.1 (2016): 77–107.

BIBLIOGRAPHY   539

Henderson, Isabel. "The Problem of the Picts." In *Who are the Scots?*, ed. Gordon Menzies. London: BBC, 1971. 51–65.

Heng, Geraldine. *The Invention of Race in the European Middle Ages*. Cambridge: Cambridge University Press, 2018.

Henley, Georgia. "Transnational book traffic in the Irish Sea zone. A new witness to the First Variant version of Geoffrey of Monmouth's *De gestis Britonum*." *North American Journal of Celtic Studies* 4.2 (2020): 131–162.

Henley, Georgia and Joshua Byron Smith, eds. *A Companion to Geoffrey of Monmouth*. Brill's Companions to European History 22. Leiden: Brill, 2020. https://brill.com /view/title/39588.

Herrn, Michael. "Gildas and Early British Monasticism." In *Britain 400–600: Language and History*, ed. Alfred Bammesberger and Alfred Wollmann. 65–78.

Hicks, D. Emily. *Border Writing: The Multidimensional Text*. Minneapolis: University of Minnesota Press, 1991.

Higham, Nicholas John. "Introduction." In *Britons in Anglo-Saxon England*, ed. N. J. Higham. Publications of the Manchester Centre for Anglo-Saxon Studies 7. Woodbridge: Boydell, 2007. 1–15.

Higham, Nicholas J. "Early Latin Sources: Fragments of a Pseudo-Historical Arthur." In *A Companion to Arthurian Literature*, ed. Helen Fulton. 30–43.

Higham, Nicholas J. *The English Conquest: Gildas and Britain in the Fifth Century*. Manchester University Press, 1994.

Higham, Nicholas J. *King Arthur: Myth-making and History*. London: Routledge, 2002.

Higham, Nicholas J. *Kingdom of Northumbria: AD 350–1100*. Stroud, Gloucestershire: Sutton, 1993.

Higham, Nicholas J. "Old Light on the Dark Age Landscape: the Description of Britain in the *De Excidio Britanniae* of Gildas." *Journal of Historical Geography* 17.4 (1991): 361–72.

Higham, Nicholas J. *Rome, Britain and the Anglo-Saxons*. London: Seaby, 1992.

Higham, Nicholas J. "From Tribal Chieftains to Christian Kings." In *The Anglo-Saxon World*, ed. Nicholas J. Higham and Martin J. Ryan. New Haven, CT and London: Yale University Press, 2013. 126–78.

Hill, Christopher. *Intellectual Origins of the English Revolution – Revisited*. Oxford: Oxford University Press, rev. ed. 2001.

Hines, John. "Philology, Archaeology and the *Adventus Saxonum vel Anglorum*." In *Britain 400–600: Language and History*, ed. Alfred Bammesberger and Alfred Wollmann. 17–36.

Hodges, R. *The Anglo-Saxon Achievement*. London: Duckworth, 1989.

Hoffman, Donald. Review of Françoise Le Saux, *Laȝamon's Brut: The Poem and its Sources. Quondam et Futurus* 1.1 [1990]: 91–94.

Hollister, C. Warren. *The Making of England, 55 B. C. to 1399*, 4th ed., Lexington, MA: D. C. Heath, 1983; 5th ed., 1988.

Holsinger, Bruce W. "Medieval Studies, Postcolonial Studies, and the Genealogies of Critique." *Speculum* 77.4 (2002): 1195–1227.

Horne, Gerald. *The Counter Revolution of 1776: Slave Resistance and the Origins of the United States of America*. New York: New York University Press, 2016.

Horne, Gerald. *The Apocalypse of Settler Colonialism: The Roots of Slavery, White Supremacy, and Capitalism in Seventeenth-Century North America and the Caribbean*. New York: Monthly Review Press, 2018.

Houck, Margaret. *Sources of the Roman de Brut of Wace*. University of California Publications in English, 5. Berkeley and Los Angeles: University of California Press, 1941. 161–356.

Howe, Nicholas. *Migration and Mythmaking in Anglo-Saxon England*. New Haven, Yale University Press, 1989; 2nd ed. South Bend, IN, University of Notre Dame Press, 2001.

Hoxie, Frederick E. "The Presence of Native American History." In *The Organization of American Historians and the Writing and Teaching of American History*, ed. Richard S. Kirkendall. Oxford: Oxford University Press, 2011. 198–206.

Hüe, Denis. "Les Variantes de la séduction: autour de la naissance d'Arthur." In *Le Roman de Brut entre mythe et histoire: actes du colloque, Bagnoles de l'Orne, septembre 2001*, ed. Claude Letellier and Denis Hüe. Medievalia 47. Orleans: Paradigme, 2003. 67–88.

Hulme, Obadiah. *An Historical Essay on the English Constitution*. London: Edward and Charles Dilly, 1771.

Hult, David. "Author/Narrator/Speaker: The Voice of Authority in Chrétien's *Charrete*." In *Discourses of Authority in Medieval and Renaissance Literature*, ed. Kevin Brownlee and Walter Stephens. Hanover, NH and London: University Press of New England, 1989. 76–96 (notes, 267–69).

Huot, Sylvia. *Outsiders: The Humanity and Inhumanity of Giants in Medieval French Prose Romance*. Notre Dame, IN: University of Notre Dame Press, 2016.

Hurlock, Kathryn and Paul Oldfield, eds. *Crusading and Pilgrimage in the Norman World*. Woodbridge: Boydell, 2015.

Hutton, Robert. "The Early Arthur: History and Myth." In *The Cambridge Companion to the Arthurian Legend*, ed. Archibald and Putter. 11–35.

Ingledew, Francis. "The Book of Troy and the Genealogical Construction of History: The Case of Geoffrey of Monmouth's *Historia regum Britanniae*." *Speculum* 69.3 (1994): 665–704.

Jackson, Kenneth H. "On the northern British Section in Nennius." In *Celt and Saxon: Studies in the Early British Border*, ed. N. K. Chadwick. Cambridge: Cambridge University Press, 1963. 21–62.

BIBLIOGRAPHY

Jackson, Kenneth H. "The Site of Mount Badon." *Journal of Celtic Studies* 2 (1953): 152–55.

James-Raoul, Danièle. *La Parole empêchée dans la littérature arthurienne*. Paris: Honoré Champion, 1997.

Janulak, Karen. *Geoffrey of Monmouth*. Cardiff: University of Wales Press, 2010.

Jaski, Bart. "'We are all of the Greeks in our Origin': New Perspectives on the Irish Origin Legend." *Cambrian Medieval Celtic Studies* 46 (2003): 1–53.

Jirmounsky, M. Malkiel. "Essai des analyses des procédés littéraires de Wace." *Revue des Langues Romanes* 63 (1925–26): 261–96.

Johns, Susan M. *Noblewomen, Aristocracy and Power in the Twelfth-Century Anglo-Norman Realm*. Manchester: Manchester University Press, 2003.

Johnson, Lesley. "The Anglo-Norman *Description of England*: An Introduction." In *Anglo-Norman Anniversary Essays*, ed. Short. 11–30.

Johnson, Lesley. "Etymologies, Genealogies, and Nationalities (again)." In *Concepts of National Identity in the Middle Ages*, ed. Simon Forde, Lesley Johnson, and Alan V. Murray. Leeds Texts and Monographs, new series 14. Leeds: School of English, University of Leeds, 1995. 125–36.

Johnson, Lesley. "Returning to Albion." In *Arthurian Literature XIII*, ed. James P. Carley and Felicity Riddy. Cambridge: D. S. Brewer, 1995. 19–40.

Jones, Bedwyr L. Review of *Armes Prydein: The Prophecy of Britain from the Book of Taliesin*." *Medium Ævum* 43 (1974): 181–85.

Jones, Mari C. "Identity Planning in an Obsolescent Variety: The Case of Jersey Norman French." *Anthropological Linguistics* 50.3–4 (2008): 249–65.

Jones, Michael E., and John Casey. "The Gallic Chronicle Restored: A Chronology for the Anglo-Saxon Invasions and the End of Roman Britain." *Britannia* 19 (1988): 367–98.

Jones, Nerys Ann. "Arthurian References in Early Welsh Poetry." In *Arthur in the Celtic Languages: The Arthurian Legend in Celtic Literatures and Traditions*, ed. Ceridwen Lloyd-Morgan and Erich Poppe. Arthurian Literature in the Middle Ages IX. Cardiff: University of Wales Press, 2019, repr. 2020. 15–34.

Jones, William Richard. "England Against the Celtic Fringe: A Study in Cultural Stereotypes." *Cahiers d'Histoire Mondiale* 13.1 (1971): 155–71.

Jones, William Richard. "Medieval State-Building and the Churches of the Celtic Fringe." *Journal of Church and State* 16.3 (1974): 407–19.

Jurasinski, Stefan. "Andrew Horn, Alfredian Apocrypha, and the Anglo-Saxon Names of the *Mirror of Justices*." *The Journal of English and Germanic Philology* 105.4 (2006): 540–63.

Kabir, Ananya Jahanara. "Analogy in Translation: Rome, England, India." In *Postcolonial Approaches to the European Middle Ages: Translating Cultures*, ed. A. J. Kabir and Deanne Williams, Cambridge Studies in Medieval Literature. Cambridge: Cambridge University Press, 2006. 183–204.

Kawash, Samira. "Terrorists and Vampires: Fanon's Spectral Violence of Decolonization." In *Franz Fanon: Critical Perspectives*, ed. Anthony C. Alessandrini. London and New York: Routledge, 1999. 237–57.

Kay, Sarah. "Who was Chrétien de Troyes?" *Arthurian Literature* 15, ed. James P. Carley and Felicity Riddy. Cambridge: D. S. Brewer, 1997. 1–35.

Kearns, Carol Bubon. "The Influence of the Trojan Myth on National Identity as Shaped in the Frankish and British Trojan-origin myths and the *Roman de Brut* and the *Roman de Troie*," upub. Ph.D. dissertation, University of Florida, 2002.

Kearny, Hugh. *The British Isles: A History of Four Nations*. 2nd ed. Cambridge: Cambridge University Press, 2006.

Keen, Maurice. Review of Malcom Vale, *The Princely Court: Medieval Courts and Culture in North West Europe, 1270–1380*. *English Historical Review* 117.473 (2002): 903–5.

Keller, Hans-Erich. *Étude descriptive sur le vocabulaire de Wace*. Deutsche Akademie der Wissenschaften zu Berlin, Veröffentlichungen des Instituts für Romanische Sprachwissenschaft 7. Berlin: Akademie-Verlag, 1953.

Keller, Hans-Erich. "Les Conquêtes du roi Arthur en Thulé." *Cahiers de Civilisation Médiévale* 23 (1980): 29–35.

Keller, Hans-Erich. "Les Fragments oxoniens du *Roman de Brut* de Wace." In *Mélanges de langues et littératures romanes offerts à Carl Théodore Gossen*, ed. Germán Colón and Robert Kopp. Bern: Francke; Liège: Marche Romane, 1976. 453–67.

Keller, Hans-Erich. "Wace et Geoffrey de Monmouth: problème de la chronologie des sources." *Romania* 98 (1977): 379–89.

Kelly, Douglas. "Brevity as Emphasis in the Narrative Lay: The Long and the Short of It." In *Court and Cloister*, ed. Jean Blacker and Jane H. M. Taylor. 1–16.

Kelly, Douglas. "The Trojans in the Writings of Wace and Benoît de Sainte-Maure." In *People and Texts: Relationships in Medieval Literature: Studies Presented to Erik Kooper*, ed. Thea Summerfield and Keith Busby. Costerus New Series 166. Amsterdam and New York: Rodopi, 2007. 123–41.

Kerlouégan, François. "Le Latin du *De Excidio Britanniae* de Gildas." In *Christianity in Britain, 300–700, Papers presented to the Conference on Christianity in Roman and Sub-Roman Britain held at the University of Nottingham 17–20 April 1967*, ed. M. W. Barley and R. P. C. Hanson. Leicester: Leicester University Press, 1968. 151–76.

Kerlouégan, François. *Le De Excidio Britanniae de Gildas. Les destinées de la culture latine dans l'île de Bretagne au VIe siècle*. Paris: Presses de La Sorbonne, 1987.

King, Edmund. *King Stephen*. New Haven, CT: Yale University Press, 2010.

Kinoshita, Sharon. *Medieval Boundaries: Rethinking Difference in Old French Literature*. Philadelphia: University of Pennsylvania Press, 2006.

Kleinman, Scott. "*The Æðelen of Engle*: Constructing Ethnic and Regional Identities in Laʒamon's *Brut*." *Exemplaria* 16.1 (2004): 95–130.

BIBLIOGRAPHY 543

Knight, Stephen T. *Arthurian Literature and Society*. London and New York: Macmillan, 1983.

Koch, John T., ed. *Celtic Culture: An Historical Encyclopedia*. 5 vols. Santa Barbara, CA: ABC-CLIO, 2006.

Koch, John T. "The Celtic Land." In *Medieval Arthurian Literature: A Guide to Recent Research*, ed. Norris J. Lacy, Routledge Library Editions: Arthurian Literature 7. New York and London: Garland, 1996. 239–322.

Kooper, Erik. "Laȝamon's Prosody: Caligula and Otho – Metres Apart." In *Reading Laȝamon's Brut*, ed. Rosamund Allen, Jane Roberts, and Carole Weinberg. 419–41.

Krappe, Alexander Haggerty. "The Sparrows of Cirencester." *Modern Philology* 23 (1925–26): 7–16.

Labordelie, Olivier de. "The First King of England? Egbert and the Foundations of Royal Legitimacy in Thirteenth-Century Historiography." In *Image and Perception of Monarchy in Medieval and Early Modern Europe*, ed. Sean McGlynn and Elena Woodacre. Newcastle upon Tyne: Cambridge Scholars Publisher, 2014. 70–83.

Labordelie, Olivier de. "The First Manuals of English History: Two Late Thirteenth-Century Genealogical Rolls of the Kings of England in the Royal Collection." *Electronic British Library Journal*, article 4, 2014: 1–25. https://www.bl.uk/eblj/2014 articles/article4.html.

Labordelie, Olivier de. "Les généalogies des rois d'Angleterre sur rouleaux manuscrits (milieu XIIIᵉ siècle–début XVᵉ siècle). Conception, diffusion et fonctions." In *La généalogie entre science et passion*, ed. Tiphaine Barthelemy and Marie-Claude Pingaud. Paris: Éditions du Comité des Travaux Historiques et Scientifiques, 1997. 181–99.

Labordelie, Olivier de. "L'incorporation de l'*Histoire des rois de Bretagne* de Geoffrey de Monmouth dans les généalogies des rois d'Angleterre (XIIᵉ–XIVᵉ siècles)." In *L'Historia regum Britannie et les "Bruts" en Europe, II*, ed. Hélène Tétrel and Géraldine Veysseyre. 255–80.

Labordelie, Olivier de. "'Ligne de reis': Culture historique, représentation du pouvoir royal et construction de la mémoire nationale en Angleterre à travers les généalogies royales en rouleau du milieu du 13e siècle au milieu du 15e siècle," unpublished PhD thesis, École des Hautes Études en Sciences Sociales, Paris, 2002 (revised version in *Histoire, mémoire et pouvoir: Les généalogies en rouleau des rois d'Angleterre (1250–1422)*. Bibliothèque d'histoire médiévale, 7. Paris: Classiques Garnier, 2013).

Labordelie, Olivier de. "A New Pattern for English History: The First Genealogical Rolls of the Kings of England." In *Broken Lines: Genealogical Literature of Medieval England and France*, ed. Raluca L. Radulescu and Edward Donald Kennedy. Turnhout: Brepols, 2008. 45–61.

Lacy, Norris. "Arthurian Research in a New Century: Prospects and Projects." In *New Directions in Arthurian Studies*, ed. Alan Lupack, Arthurian Studies 51. Cambridge: D. S. Brewer, 2002. 1–20.

Lacy, Norris, ed. *A History of Arthurian Scholarship*. Cambridge: D. S. Brewer, 2006.

Lamont, Margaret. "Becoming English: Ronwenne's Wassail, Language, and National Identity in the Middle English Prose *Brut*." *Studies in Philology* 107.3 (2010): 283–309.

Lamont, Margaret. "When are Saxons 'Ænglisc'? Language and Readerly Identity in Laȝamon's *Brut*." In *Reading Laȝamon's Brut*, ed. Rosamund Allen, Jane Roberts, and Carole Weinberg. 295–319.

Lamy, Marielle. *L'Immaculée Conception. Étapes et enjeux d'une controverse au Moyen Âge (XIIᵉ–XVᵉ siècles)*. Collection des Études Augustiniennes: Moyen Âge et Temps Modernes 35. Turnhout: Brepols, 2000.

Lane, Alan, "The End of Roman Britain and the Coming of the Saxons: An Archaeological Context for Arthur?" in *A Companion to Arthurian Literature*, ed. Fulton. 15–29.

Lapidge, Michael and David N. Dumville, eds. *Gildas: New Approaches*. Studies in Celtic History 5. Woodbridge: Boydell, 1984.

Latham, Ronald Edward. *Revised Medieval Latin Word-List from British and Irish Sources*. London: Oxford University Press for the British Academy, 1965; orig. *Medieval Latin Word-List*, ed. J. H. Baxter and Charles Johnson, 1934.

Leckie Jr., R. William. *The Passage of Dominion: Geoffrey of Monmouth and the Periodization of Insular History in the Twelfth Century*. Toronto: University of Toronto Press, 1981.

Lefèvre, Sylvie. "Le fragment Bekker et les anciennes versions françaises de l'*Historia regum Britanniae*." *Romania* 109 (1988): 225–46.

Legge, M. Dominica. *Anglo-Norman Literature and its Background*. Oxford: Oxford University Press, 1963.

Lejeune, Rita and Jacques Stiennon, *La Légende de Roland dans l'art du Moyen Âge*, 2 vols. Brussels: Arcade, 1966.

Le Saux, Françoise Hazel Marie. "'La geste des trois fils Guillaume': Henry I in Wace's *Roman de Rou*." *Reading Medieval Studies* 12 (2008): 191–207.

Le Saux, Françoise H. M. "On Capitalization in Some Early Manuscripts of Wace's *Roman de Brut*." In *Arthurian Studies in Honour of P. J. C. Field*, ed. Bonnie Wheeler, Arthurian Studies 57. Woodbridge: Boydell. 29–47.

Le Saux, Françoise H. M. "Layamon's Ambivalence Reconsidered." In *The Text and Tradition of Layamon's Brut*, ed. Le Saux. Cambridge: D. S. Brewer, 1994. 171–82.

Le Saux, Françoise H. M. *Layamon's Brut: The Poem and its Sources*. Arthurian Studies 19. Cambridge: D. S. Brewer, 1989.

Lloyd, John Edward. "The Death of Arthur." *Bulletin of the Board of Celtic Studies* 11 (1941–4): 158–60.

Lloyd, John Edward. *A History of Wales.* 2 vols. London, 1939.

Lloyd, James William. "The West Country Adventures of Saint Augustine of Canterbury." *Folklore* 31 (2020): 413–34.

Loomba, Ania. *Colonialism/Postcolonialism.* Abingdon, Oxon: Routledge, 3rd ed. 2015.

Loomis, Roger Sherman. "The Legend of Arthur's Survival." In *Arthurian Literature in the Middle Ages: A Collaborative History,* ed. Loomis. Oxford: Clarendon Press, 1959. 64–71.

Lot, Ferdinand. "*Gormond et Isembard.* Recherches sur les fondements historiques de cette épopée." *Romania,* 27 (1898): 1–54.

Lowenthal, David. "The Island Garden: English Landscape and British Identity." In *History, Nationhood and the Question of Britain,* ed. Brocklehurst and Phillips. 137–48.

Lowman, Emma Battell. "*An Indigenous Peoples' History of the United States*: A Review." *Decolonization: Indigeneity, Education & Society* 4.1 (2015): 118–28.

Loyn, Henry Royston. *Anglo-Saxon England and the Norman Conquest.* New York: St. Martin's Press, 1962, 2nd ed. 1991.

Lyotard, Jean-François. *La Condition postmoderne. Rapport sur le savoir.* Paris: Éditions de Minuit, 1979.

MacColl, Alan. "The Meaning of 'Britain' in Medieval and Early Modern England." *Journal of British Studies* 45 (2006): 248–69.

MacDougall, Hugh A. *Racial Myth in English History: Trojans, Teutons, and Anglo-Saxons.* Montreal: Harvest House, 1982.

Martin, Kevin M. "The 'aduentus Saxonum'." *Latomus* 33 (1974): 608–39.

Marvin, Julia. Review of Kenneth J. Tiller, *Laȝamon's Brut and the Anglo-Norman Vision of History,* Cardiff: University of Wales Press, 2007. *Arthuriana* 20.4 (2010): 108–9.

Masters, Bernadette A. "Anglo-Norman in Context: The Case for the Scribes." *Exemplaria* 6.1 (1994): 167–203.

Matheson, Lister M. *The Prose Brut: The Development of a Middle English Chronicle.* Medieval and Renaissance Texts and Studies, 180. Tempe, AZ: Medieval and Renaissance Texts and Studies, 1998.

Mathey-Maille, Laurence. "L'Étymologie dans le *Roman de Rou* de Wace." In *"De sens rassis": Essays in Honor of Rupert T. Pickens,* ed. Keith Busby, Bernard Guidot, and Logan Whalen. Faux Titre 259. Amsterdam and New York: Rodopi, 2005. 403–14.

Mathey-Maille, Laurence. "Figures de femmes dans le *Roman de Brut* de Wace." In *Désir n'a repos: hommage à Danielle Bohler,* ed. Florence Bouchet and Danièle James-Raoul. Pessac: Presses Universitaires de Bordeaux, 2015. 415–26.

Mathey-Maille, Laurence. "La géographie anglo-normande dans le *Roman de Brut* et le *Roman de Rou* de Wace." In *Troisième journée d'études anglo-normandes. Adaptation, parodie et autres emplois,* ed. Michel Zink. Paris: Académie des inscriptions et belles-lettres, 2014. 45–54.

Mathey-Maille, Laurence. "De l'*Historia Regum Britanniae* de Geoffroy de Monmouth au *Roman de Brut* de Wace: la naissance du roman." In *Le Travail sur le modèle*, ed. Danielle Buschinger. Médiévales 16. Amiens: Presses du Centre d'Études Médiévales, 2002. 5–10.

Mathey-Maille, Laurence. "Mythe troyen et histoire romaine: de Geoffrey de Monmouth au *Brut* de Wace." In *Entre fiction et histoire: Troie et Rome au Moyen Age*, ed. Emmanuèle Baumgartner and Laurence Harf-Lancner. Paris: Presses de la Sorbonne Nouvelle, 1997. 113–25.

Mathey-Maille, Laurence. "La pratique de l'étymologie dans le *Roman de Brut* de Wace." In *"Plaist vos oïr bone cançon vallant": mélanges de langue et de littérature médiévales offerts à François Suard*, ed. Dominique Boutet, Marie-Madeleine Castellani, François Ferrand and Aimé Petit. Université Charles de Gaulle – Lille 3, Collection Travaux et Recherches, 2 vols. Lille: SEGES, 1999. II, 579–86.

Mathey-Maille, Laurence. "Le roi Leir chez Geoffroy de Monmouth et Wace: la naissance d'une figure mythique." In *Pour une mythologie du Moyen Âge*, ed. Bominique Boutet and Laurence Harf-Lancner. Paris: Presses de l'École Normale Supérieure, 1988. 99–115.

Mathey-Maille, Laurence. "Le *Roman de Brut* de Wace: une œuvre inclassable?" In *L'Œuvre inclassable: Actes édités par Marianne Bouchardon and Michèle Guéret-Laferté*. Actes du colloque 18. Rouen: University of Rouen, CÉRÉdI, 2016. 1–6. http://ceredi.labos.univ-rouen.fr/public/?l-oeuvre-inclassable.html.

Mathey-Maille, Laurence. "De la Vulgate à la Variant Version de l'*Historia regum Britannie: Le Roman de Brut* de Wace à l'épreuve du texte source." In *L'Historia regum Britannie et les "Bruts" en Europe, I*, ed. Hélène Tétrel and Géraldine Veysseyre. 129–39.

Meecham-Jones, Simon. "Early Reactions to Geoffrey's Work," in *A Companion to Geoffrey of Monmouth*, ed. Georgia Henley and Joshua Byron Smith. 181–208.

Meecham-Jones, Simon. "Where was Wales? The Erasure of Wales in Medieval English Culture." In *Authority and Subjugation in Writing of Medieval Wales*, ed. Meecham-Jones and Ruth Kennedy. London: Palgrave Macmillan, 2008. 27–55.

Merdrignac, Bernard. "Conan Meriadoc." In *Celtic Culture: An Historical Encyclopedia*, ed. John T. Koch. II, 473–75.

Meyer, Paul. "Ballade contre les Anglais." *Romania* 21 (1892): 50–52.

Micha, Alexandre. *Étude sur le "Merlin" de Robert de Boron, Roman du XIIIe siècle*. Publications Romanes et Françaises 151. Geneva: Droz, 1980.

Miller, Molly. "Geoffrey's Early Royal Synchronisms." *Bulletin of the Board of Celtic Studies* 28 (1978–80): 373–89.

Miller, Molly. "Matriliny by Treaty: The Pictish Foundation-Legend." In *Ireland in Early Mediaeval Europe: Studies in Memory of Kathleen Hughes*, ed. Dorothy Whitelock, Rosamond McKitterick, and David Dumville. Cambridge: Cambridge University Press, 1982. 133–61.

BIBLIOGRAPHY

Miller, Sarah Allison. *Medieval Monstrosity and the Female Body*. Routledge Studies in Medieval Religion and Culture 8. New York and Abingdon: Routledge, 2010.

Molyneaux, George. "Did the English Really Think they were God's Elect in the Anglo-Saxon Period?" *Journal of Ecclesiastical History* 65.4 (2014): 721–37.

Morris, Rosemary. *The Character of King Arthur in Medieval Literature*. Arthurian Studies 4. Cambridge: D. S. Brewer, 1982; repr. 1985.

Morris, Rosemary. "The *Gesta Regum Britanniae* of William of Rennes: An Arthurian Epic?" In *Arthurian Literature VI*, ed. Barber. 60–125.

Muhlberger, Stephen. "The Gallic Chronicle of 452 and its Authority for British Events." *Britannia* 14 (1983): 23–33.

Mullally, Erin. "Registers of Friendship in Layamon's *Brut*." *Modern Philology* 108.4 (2011): 469–87.

Murray, Alexander. "Bede and the Unchosen Race." In *Power and Identity in the Middle Ages: Essays in Memory of Rees Davies*, ed. Huw Pryce and John Watts. Oxford: Oxford University Press, 2007. 52–67.

Myres, John Nowell Linton. *Anglo-Saxon Pottery and the Settlement of England*. Oxford: Oxford University Press, 1969.

Myres, John Nowell Lynton. *English Settlements*. Oxford History of England. Oxford: Oxford University Press, 1989.

Myres, John Nowell Lynton. "Pelagius and the end of Roman Rule in Britain." *JRS* 50 (1960): 21–36.

Naismith, Rory and Francesca Tinti. "The Origins of Peter's Pence." *English Historical Review* 134.568 (2019): 521–52.

Nezirović, Muhamed. "Les Fragments de Zadar du *Roman de Brut* de Wace." *Romania* 98.391 (1977): 379–89.

O'Brien, Conor. "Chosen Peoples and New Israels in the Early Medieval West." *Speculum* 95.4 (2020): 987–1009.

O'Brien, Jean M. *Firsting and Lasting: Writing Indians out of Existence in New England*. Minneapolis: University of Minnesota Press, 2010.

Oram, Richard. *David I: The King who Made Scotland*. Stroud: Tempus, 2004.

O'Sullivan, Thomas. *The De Excidio of Gildas: Its Authenticity and Date*. Columbia Studies in the Classical Tradition 7. Leiden: E. J. Brill, 1978.

Otter, Monica. "Functions of Fiction in Historical Writing." In *Writing Medieval History*, ed. Nancy Partner. London: Hodder Arnold, 2005. 109–30.

Otter, Monica. *Inventiones: Fiction and Referentiality in Twelfth-Century English Historical Writing*. Chapel Hill: University of North Carolina Press, 1996.

Over, Kristin Lee. *Kingship, Conquest, and Patria: Literary and Cultural Identities in Medieval French and Welsh Arthurian Romance*. New York: Routledge, 2005.

Pace, Edwin. "Athelstan, 'Twist-Beard,' and Arthur's Tenth-Century Breton Origins for the *Historia Regum Britanniae*." *Arthuriana* 26.4 (2016): 60–88.

Padel, Oliver James. "Geoffrey of Monmouth and Cornwall." *Cambridge Medieval Celtic Studies* 8 (1984): 1–28.

Pähler, Heinrich. *Strukturuntersuchungen zur Historia Regum Britanniae des Geoffrey of Monmouth*. Bonn: Universität Bonn, 1958.

Paradisi, Gioia. *Le passioni della storia: Scrittura e memoria nell'opera di Wace*. Dipartimento di Studi Romanzi Università de Roma "La Sapienza." Testi, Studi e manuali 16. Rome: Bagatto Libri, 2002.

Park, Hwanhee. "Arthur and the Mont St. Michel Giant in Laȝamon's *Brut*: Exposing the Fragility of Kingship." *Arthuriana* 26.1 (2016): 5–21.

Partner, Nancy F. *Serious Entertainments: The Writing of History in Twelfth-Century England*. Chicago and London: University of Chicago Press, 1977.

Pastoureau, Michel. *Les Chevaliers de la Table Ronde: Anthropologie d'une société imaginaire*. Lathuile: Éditions de Gui, 2006.

Pattison, John E. "Integration versus apartheid in post-Roman Britain: A response to Thomas et al (2008)." *Human Biology* 83 (2011): 715–33.

Pickens, Rupert T. "Implications of Being 'French' in Twelfth-Century England." In *"Chançon legiere a chanter": Essays in Old French Literature in Honor of Samuel N. Rosenberg*, ed. Karen Fresco and Wendy Pfeffer. Birmingham, AL: Summa Publications, 2007. 373–86.

Piggott, Stuart. "The Sources of Geoffrey of Monmouth: I. The pre-Roman king-list." *Antiquity* 15 (1941): 269–86.

Piquemal, Catherine. "Culwch and Olwen: A Structured Portrayal of Arthur?" *Arthuriana* 10.3 (2000): 7–26.

Pohl, Walter. "Ethnic Names and Identities in the British Isles: A Comparative Perspective." In *The Anglo-Saxons from the Migration Period to the Eight Century: An Ethnographic Perspective*, ed. John Hines. Woodbridge: Boydell, 1997. 7–32.

Press, Alan R. "The Precocious Courtesy of Geoffrey Gaimar." In *Court and Poet. Selected Proceedings of the Third Congress of the International Courtly Literature Society 1980*, ed. Glyn S. Burgess. Liverpool: Francis Cairns, 1981. 267–76.

Pryce, Huw. "British or Welsh? National Identity in Twelfth-Century Wales." *English Historical Review* 116.468 (2001): 775–801.

Purdie, Rhiannon. "Dice-games and the Blasphemy of Prediction." In *Medieval Futures: Attitudes to the Future in the Middle Ages*, ed. J. A. Burrow and Ian P. Wei. Woodbridge: Boydell, 2000. 167–84.

Rambaran-Olm, Mary and Erik Wade. "The Many Myths of the Term 'Anglo-Saxon'." *Smithsonian Magazine* July 14, 2021: https://www.smithsonianmag.com/history/many-myths-term-anglo-saxon-180978169/.

Reeve, Michael D. "The Transmission of the *Historia Regum Britanniae*." *Journal of Medieval Latin* 1 (1991): 73–117.

BIBLIOGRAPHY

Reuter, Timothy. "Assembly Politics in Western Europe from the eighth century to the twelfth." In *The Medieval World*, ed. Peter Linehan, Janet L. Nelson, and Marios Costambeys. London: Routledge, 2001. 432–50.

Reynolds, Susan. "Medieval 'Origines Gentium' and the Community of the Realm." *History* 68 (1983): 375–90.

Reynolds, Susan. "What Do We Mean by 'Anglo-Saxon' and 'Anglo-Saxons'?" *Journal of British Studies* 24 (1985): 395–414.

Richter, Michael. "Bede's *Angli*: Angles or English?" *Peritia* 3, 1984: 99–114.

Rickard, Peter. *Britain in Medieval French Literature*. Cambridge: Cambridge University Press, 1956.

Rickard, Peter. "*Anglois coué* et *L'Anglois qui couve*." *French Studies* 7 (1953): 48–55.

Riddy, Felicity. "Contextualizing *Le Morte Darthur*: Empire and Civil War." In *A Companion to Malory*, ed. Elizabeth Archibald and A. S. G. Edwards. Cambridge: D. S. Brewer, 1996. 55–73.

Roberts, Brynley Frances. "Geoffrey of Monmouth and the Welsh Historical Tradition." *Nottingham Mediaeval Studies* 2 (1976): 29–40.

Robertson, Kelli. "Geoffrey of Monmouth and the Translation of Insular Historiography." *Arthuriana* 8.4 (1998): 42–57.

Rollo, David. *Historical Fabrication, Ethnic Fable and French Romance in Twelfth-Century England*. Edward C. Armstrong Monographs on Medieval Literature 9. Lexington, KY: French Forum Publishers, 1998.

Ross, David John Athole. "A Thirteenth Century Anglo-Norman Workshop." In *Mélanges offerts à Rita Lejeune, professeur à l'Université de Liège*, 2 vols. Gembloux: J. Duculot, 1969. I, 689–94.

Rothwell, William. "Language and Governance in Medieval England." *Zeitschrift für französische Sprache und Literatur* 93 (1983): 258–70.

Rouse, Richard, and Cory Rushton. "Arthurian Geography." In *The Cambridge Companion to the Arthurian Legend*, ed. Archibald and Putter. 218–34.

Roymans, Nico. "Hercules and the Construction of a Batavian Identity in the Context of the Roman Empire." In *Ethnic Constructs in Antiquity: The Role of Power and Tradition*, ed. Ton Derks and Nico Roymans. Amsterdam Archaeological Studies 13. Amsterdam: Amsterdam University Press, 2009. 219–38.

Russell, Paul. Review of *History of the Kings of Britain. The First Variant Version*, ed. and trans. David W. Burchmore, Dumbarton Oaks Medieval Library 57. Cambridge, MA: Harvard University Press, 2019. *North American Journal of Celtic Studies* 4.2 (2020): 237–41.

Russell, Trevor. "National Identity, Propaganda, and the Ethics of War in English Historical Literature, 1327–77," unpub. PhD thesis, University of Leeds, 2017.

Sargent-Baur, Barbara Nelson. "*Dux Bellorum/Rex Militarum*/roi fainéant: La Transformation d'Arthur au XIIᵉ siècle." *Le Moyen Age: Revue d'Histoire et de Philologie* 90.3–4 (1984): 357–73 (repr. as "*Dux Bellorum/Rex Militarum/roi fainéant*: The

Transformations of Arthur in the Twelfth Century." In *King Arthur: A Casebook*, ed. Edward D. Kennedy. New York: Garland, 1996. 29–43).

Sargent-Baur, Barbara Nelson. "From Heroic King to *Roi fainéant*: Arthur of Romance." In *The Encyclopedia of Medieval Literature in Britain*, ed. Siân Echard, Richard Rouse, and Jacqueline A. Fay. Hoboken, NJ: John Wiley, 2017. 178–82.

Sayers, William J. S. "Arthur's Embarkation for Gaul in a Fresh Translation of Wace's *Roman de Brut*." *Romance Notes* 46.2 (2006): 143–56.

Sayers, William. *The Beginnings and Early Development of Old French Historiography (1100–1274)*. Berkeley: University of California Press, 1967.

Sayers, William. "A Norse Etymology for Luff, 'Weather Edge of a Sail'." *American Neptune* 66.1 (2001): 25–38.

Sayers, William. "Rummaret de Wenelande: A Geographical Note to Wace's *Brut*." *Romance Philology* 18 (1964): 46–53.

Schirmer, Walter F. *Die frühen Darstellungen des Arthurstoffes*. Arbeitsgemeinschaft für Forschung des Landes Nordrhein-Westfallen, Geisteswissenschaften 73. Cologne and Opladen: Westdeutscher Verlag, 1958.

Schirmer, Walter F. and Ulrich Broich. *Studien zum literarischen Patron am England des 12. Jahrhunderts*. Wissenschaftliche Abhandlungen der Arbeitsgemeinschaft für Forschung des Landes Nordrhein-Westfalen 23. Cologne: Springer Fachmedien Wiesbaden, 1962.

Schmolke-Hasselmann, Beate. "The Round Table: Ideal, Fiction, Reality." In *Arthurian Literature II*, ed. Richard Barber. 41–75.

Schwartz, Susan M. "The Founding and self-betrayal of Britain: An Augustinian approach to Geoffrey of Monmouth's *Historia Regum Britanniae*." *Medievalia et Humanistica* n. s. 10 (1981): 33–53.

Shichtman, Martin B. and Laurie A. Finke. "Profiting from the Past: History as Symbolic Capital in the *Historia Regum Britanniae*." In *Arthurian Literature XII*, ed. James P. Carley and Felicity Riddy. Cambridge: D. S. Brewer, 1993, 1–35; repr. as ch 2 in *King Arthur and the Myth of History*, ed. Finke and Shichtman. 32–70.

Short, Ian, ed. *Anglo-Norman Anniversary Essays*. Anglo-Norman Text Society Occasional Publications Series 2. London: Anglo-Norman Text Society, 1993.

Short, Ian. "Gaimar's Epilogue and Geoffrey of Monmouth's *Liber vetustissimus*." *Speculum* 69.2 (1994): 323–43.

Short, Ian. "Language and Literature." In *A Companion to the Anglo-Norman World*, ed. Christopher Harper-Bill and Elisabeth van Houts. Woodbridge: Boydell, 2002. 191–213.

Short, Ian. "Un *Roman de Brut* anglo-normand inédit." *Romania* 126 (2008): 273–95.

Short, Ian. "What was Gaimar's *Estoire des Bretuns*?" *Cultura Neolatina* 71 (2011): 147–49.

Shustereder, Stephan J. *Strategies of Identity Construction: The Writings of Gildas, Aneirin and Bede*. Göttingen: V & R unipress, 2015.

Sims-Williams, Patrick. "Celtic Civilization: Continuity or Coincidence?" *Cambrian Medieval Celtic Studies* 64 (2012): 1–45.

Sims-Williams, Patrick. "The Early Welsh Arthurian Poems." In *The Arthur of the Welsh*, ed. Bromwich, Jarman, and Roberts. Cardiff University of Wales Press, 1991. 33–72.

Sims-Williams, Patrick. "Gildas and the Anglo-Saxons." *Cambridge Medieval Celtic Studies* 6 (1983): 1–30.

Sims-Williams, Patrick. "The Settlement of England in Bede and the *Chronicle*." *Anglo-Saxon England* 12, ed. Peter Clemoes. Cambridge: Cambridge University Press, 1983. 1–41.

Sims-Williams, Patrick. "Some functions of origin stories in early medieval Wales." In *History and Heroic Tale: A Symposium*, ed. Tore Nyberg, Iørn Piø, Preben Meulengracht Sørensen, and Aage Trommer. Odense: Odense University Press, 1985. 97–131.

Sims-Williams, Patrick. "The Visionary Celt: the Construction of an Ethnic Perception." *Cambridge Medieval Celtic Studies* 11 (1986): 77–96.

Sims-Williams, Patrick. "The Welsh Versions of Geoffrey of Monmouth's 'History of the Kings of Britain'." In *Adapting Texts and Styles in a Celtic Context: Interdisciplinary Perspectives on Processes of Literary Transfer in the Middle Ages: Studies in Honour of Erich Poppe*, Studien und Texte zur Keltologie 13, ed. Axel Harlos and Neele Harlos. Munster: Nodus Publikationen. 2016. 53–76.

Smith, Alan. "Lucius of Britain and alleged Church Founder." *Folklore* 90.1 (1979): 29–36.

Smith, Barbara Herrnstein. "Narrative Versions, Narrative Theories." *Critical Inquiry* 7.1 (1980): 213–36.

Smith, Linda Tuhiwai. *Decolonizing Methodologies: Research and Indigenous Peoples*, 2nd ed. London: Zed Books, 2012.

Southern, Sir Richard W. "Aspects of the European Tradition of Historical Writing: 1. The Classical Tradition from Einhard to Geoffrey of Monmouth." *Transactions of the Royal Historical Society*, 5th ser. 20 (1970): 173–96.

Southern, Sir Richard W. "Aspects of the European Tradition of Historical Writing: 3. History as Prophecy." *Transactions of the Royal Historical Society*, 5th ser., 22 (1972): 159–80.

Southern, Sir Richard W. "The English Origins of the 'Miracles of the Virgin." *Medieval and Renaissance Studies* 4 (1958): 176–216.

Southern, Sir Richard W. *Western Views of Islam in the Middle Ages*. Cambridge, MA: Harvard University Press, 1962.

Southward, E. C. "Gormont roi d'Afrique." *Romania* 69 (1946–47): 103–12.

Snyder, Christopher A. "Arthur and Kingship in the *Historia Brittonum*." In *The Fortunes of King Arthur*, ed. Norris J. Lacy. Cambridge: D. S. Brewer, 2005. 1–12.

Sønnesyn, Sigbjørn. "The Rise of the Normans as *Ethnopoiesis*." In *Norman Tradition and Transcultural Heritage: Exchange of Cultures in the "Norman" Peripheries of*

Medieval Europe, ed. Stefan Burkhardt and Thomas Foerster. London: Routledge, 2016. 203–18.

Sowerby, Richard. "Hengest and Horsa: the manipulation of history and myth from the *adventus Saxonum* to *Historia Brittonum*." *Nottingham Medieval Studies*, 51 (2007): 1–19.

Spence, John. *Reimagining History in Anglo-Norman Prose Chronicles*. York: York Medieval Press, 2013.

Spiegel, Gabrielle M. "Towards a Theory of the Middle Ground," chapter 3 in Spiegel, *The Past as Text: The Theory and Practice of Medieval Historiography*. Baltimore and London: Johns Hopkins University Press, 1997. 44–56.

Trachsler, Richard. "Le visage et la voix. L'auteur, le narrateur et l'enlumineur dans la littérature narrative médiévale." *Bibliographical Bulletin of the International Arthurian Society* 57 (2005): 349–71.

Spivak, Gayatri Chakravorty. "Can the subaltern speak?" In *Marxism and the Interpretation of Culture*, ed. Cary Nelson and Lawrence Grossberg. Urbana and Chicago: University of Illinois Press, 1988. 271–313.

Stafford, Pauline. "Aelfryth." In *The Wiley Blackwell Encyclopedia of Anglo-Saxon England*, ed. Michael Lapidge, John Blair, Simon Keynes, and Donald Scragg. Chichester and New York: John Wiley and Sons, 2nd ed., 2014.

Stafford, Pauline. "The Anglo-Saxon Chronicles, Identity and the Making of England." *The Haskins Society Journal* 19 (2008): 28–50.

Stanley, Eric G. "The Date of Laȝamon's *Brut*." *Notes and Queries* 213 (1968): 85–88.

Stenton, Frank Merry. *Anglo-Saxon England*. Oxford: Oxford University Press, 1943, 1947; 3rd ed. 1971. 16–17.

Stephen, Leslie and Sidney Lee. "St. Augustine of Canterbury." In *Dictionary of National Biography*, ed. Stephen and Lee, 22 vols., 8 suppl. London: Oxford University Press, 1937–39. I, 727–29.

Stones, Alison. "The Egerton *Brut* and its Illustrations." In *Maistre Wace: A Celebration*, ed. Glyn S. Burgess and Judith Weiss. 167–76.

Stringer, Keith John. *The Reign of Stephen: Kingship, Warfare and Government in Twelfth-Century England*. London: Routledge, 1993.

Stroh, Silke. "Colonial Beginnings? Celticity, Gaeldom and Scotland until the end of the Middle Ages." *Scottish Cultural Review of Language and Literature, suppl. Uneasy Subjects: Postcolonialism in Scottish Gaelic Poetry* 17 (2011): 43–68.

Sullivan, Matthew. "The Original and Subsequent Audiences of the *Manuel des Péchés*," unpub. D. Phil. thesis, Oxford University, 1990.

Summerfield, Thea. "Filling the Gap: Brutus in the *Historia Brittonum, Anglo-Saxon Chronicle* MS F, and Geoffrey of Monmouth." In *The Medieval Chronicle VII*, ed. Juliana Dresvina, Nicholas Sparks, Erik Kooper. Amsterdam: Rodopi, 2011. 85–102.

BIBLIOGRAPHY 553

Szerwiniack, Olivier. "L'*Epistola ad Warinum* d'Henri de Huntingdon, première adaptation latine de l'*Historia regum Britannie*." In *L'Historia regum Britannie et les "Bruts" en Europe, 1*, ed. Hélène Tétrel and Géraldine Veysseyre. 41–52.

Tahkokallio, Jakko. *The Anglo-Norman Historical Canon: Publishing and Manuscript Culture*. Cambridge: Cambridge University Press, 2019.

Tahkokallio, Jakko. "Publishing the *History of the Kings of Britain*." In *L'Historia regum Britannie et les "Bruts" en Europe, II*, ed. Hélène Tétrel and Géraldine Veysseyre. 45–57.

Tahkokallio, Jakko. "Update to the List of Manuscripts of Geoffrey of Monmouth's *Historia regum Britanniae*." In *Arthurian Literature XXXII*, ed. Elizabeth Archibald and David F. Johnson. Woodbridge: Boydell, 2015. 187–203.

Tatlock, John Strong Perry. "The Dates of the Arthurian Saints' Legends." *Speculum* 14.3 (1939): 345–65.

Tatlock, John Strong Perry. *The Legendary History of Britain: Geoffrey of Monmouth's Historia Regum Britanniae and its Early Vernacular Versions*. Berkeley: University of California Press, 1950; repr. New York: Gordian Press, 1974.

Taylor, Charles. *Modern Social Imaginaries*. Durham, NC: Duke University Press, 2004.

Tétrel, Hélène. "Trojan Origins and the Use of the *Aeneid* and Related Sources in the Old Icelandic *Brut*." *The Journal of English and Germanic Philology* 109.4 (2010): 490–514.

Tétrel, Hélène and Géraldine Veysseyre, eds. *L'Historia regum Britannie et les "Bruts" en Europe, I: Traductions, adaptations, réappropriations* (*XIIe–XVIe siècle*). Rencontres 106, Civilisation médiévale 12. Paris: Classiques Garnier, 2015.

Tétrel, Hélène and Géraldine Veysseyre, eds. *L'Historia regum Britannie et les "Bruts" en Europe, II: Production, circulation, reception* (*XIIe–XVIe siècle*). Rencontres 349, Civilisation médiévale 32. Paris: Classiques Garnier, 2018.

Thomas, Hugh M. *The English and the Normans: Ethnic Hostility, Assimilation, and Identity, 1066–c. 1220*. Oxford: Oxford University Press, 2003.

Thomas, Rebecca. "Geoffrey of Monmouth and the English Past." In *A Companion to Geoffrey of Monmouth*, ed. Henley and Smith. 105–28.

Tilliette, Jean-Yves. "Invention du récit: La 'Brutiade' de Geoffroy de Monmouth (*Historia regum Britanniae*, § 6–22)." *Cahiers de civilisation médiévale* 39 (1996): 217–233.

Tolan, John. *Saracens: Islam in the Medieval European Imagination*. New York: Columbia University Press, 2002.

Tolhurst, Fiona. "Geoffrey of Monmouth's *Historia regum Britannie* and the Critics." *Arthuriana* 8.4 (1998): 3–11.

Tolhurst, Fiona. *Geoffrey of Monmouth and the Feminist Origins of the Arthurian Legend*. Arthurian and Courtly Cultures. New York: Palgrave MacMillan, 2012.

Tolhurst, Fiona. *Geoffrey of Monmouth and the Translation of Female Kingship.* Arthurian and Courtly Cultures. New York: Palgrave MacMillan, 2013.

Tolhurst, Fiona. "What ever Happened to Eleanor? Reflections of Eleanor of Aquitaine in Wace's *Roman de Brut* and Lawman's *Brut.*" In *Eleanor of Aquitaine: Lord and Lady*, ed. Bonnie Wheeler and John Carmi Parsons. New Middle Ages. New York: Palgrave Macmillan, 2003. 319–36.

Traschler, Richard, ed. *Moult obscures paroles: Études sur la prophétie médiévale*, with Julien Abed and David Expert. Paris: Presses de l'Université Paris-Sorbonne, 2007.

Traschler, Richard. "Le visage et la voix. L'auteur, le narrateur et l'enlumineur dans la littérature narrative médiévale." *Bibliographical Bulletin of the International Arthurian Society* 57 (2005): 349–71.

Trevelyan, George Macaulay. *History of England.* London, 1926.

Turner, Peter. "Identity in Gildas's *De Excidio et Conquestu Britanniae.*" *Cambrian Medieval Celtic Studies* 58 (2009): 29–48.

Turville-Petre, Joan Elizabeth. "Hengest and Horsa." *Saga Book of the Viking Society for Northern Research* 14 (1953–57): 273–90.

Tyler, Elizabeth M. "England between Empire and Nation in the 'Battle of Brunanburh'." In *Whose Middle Ages? Teachable Moments for an Ill-Used Past*, ed. Andrew Albin, Mary C. Erler, Thomas O'Donnell, Nicholas L. Paul, Nina Rowe, and David Perr. New York: Fordham University Press, 2019. 166–80.

Tyson, Diana. "The Old French *Brut* rolls in the London College of Arms." In *Guerres, voyages et quêtes au Moyen Âge: Mélanges offerts à Jean-Claude Faucon*, ed. Alain Labbé, Daniel W. Lacroix, and Danielle Quéruel. Paris: Honoré Champion, 2000. 421–7.

Tyson, Diana. "A Study of Medieval French *Brut* Manuscripts in London Collections." In *L'Historia regum Britannie et les "Bruts" en Europe, II*, ed. Hélène Tétrel and Géraldine Veysseyre. 125–45.

Urbanski, Charity. *Writing History for the King: Henry II and the Politics of Vernacular Historiography.* Ithaca, NY and London: Cornell University Press, 2013.

Vine-Durling, Nancy. "The UC Berkeley *Brut* Fragment: A New Transcription and Assessment." In *L'Historia regum Britannie et les "Bruts" en Europe, II*, ed. Hélène Tétrel and Géraldine Veysseyre. 103–24.

Vielliard, Françoise. "Cologny, Fondation Martin Bodmer, Cod. Bodmer 67." In Françoise Vielliard, *Bibliotheca Bodmeriana Catalogue II: Manuscrits français du Moyen Âge.* Cologny-Geneva: Fondation Martin Bodmer, 1975. 23–31. http://e-codices .unifr.ch/en/description/fmb/cb-0067/.

Walters, Lori. "Wace and the Genesis of Vernacular Authority." In *"Li premerains vers": Essays in Honor of Keith Busby*, ed. Catherine M. Jones and Logan E. Whalen. Amsterdam and New York: Rodopi, 2011. 507–16.

BIBLIOGRAPHY 555

Ward, Henry Leigh Douglas. *Catalogue of Romances in the Manuscript Department of the British Museum*. 3 vols. (vols. 1 and 2, Ward, vol. 3 J. A. Herbert). London: Trustees of the British Museum, 1883–1901.

Ward, John H. "Vortigern and the End of Roman Britain." *Britannia* 3 (1972): 277–89.

Ward-Perkins, Bryan. "Why Did the Anglo-Saxons Not Become More British?" *The English Historical Review* 115. 462 (2000): 513–33.

Warner, Lawrence. "Geoffrey of Monmouth and the De-Judaized Crusade." *Parergon* 21.1 (2004): 19–37.

Warren, Michelle R. *History on the Edge: Excalibur and the Borders of Britain, 1100–1300*. Minneapolis: University of Minnesota Press, 2000.

Warren, Michelle R. "Making Contact: Postcolonial Perspectives through Geoffrey of Monmouth's *Historia regum Britannie*." *Arthuriana* 8.4 (1998): 115–34.

Warren, Michelle R. "Memory out of Line: Hebrew Etymology in the *Roman de Brut* and *Merlin*." *Modern Language Notes* 118.4 (2003): 989–1014.

Watson, Jonathan. "Affective Poetics and Scribal Reperformance in Lawman's *Brut*: A Comparison of the Caligula and Otho Versions." *Arthuriana* 8.3 (1998): 62–75.

Weiss, Judith. "Arthur, Emperors, and Antichrists: The Formation of the Arthurian Biography." In *Writers of the Reign of Henry II: Twelve Essays*, ed. Ruth Kennedy and Simon Meecham-Jones. The New Middle Ages. New York: Palgrave Macmillan, 2006. 239–48.

Weiss, Judith. "The Text of Wace's *Brut* and How it is Treated by its Earliest Manuscripts." In *L'Historia regum Britannie et les "Bruts" en Europe, II: Production, circulation, réception*, ed. Hélène Tétrel and Géraldine Veysseyre. 83–101.

Weiss, Judith. "Two Fragments from a Newly Discovered Manuscript of Wace's *Brut*." *Medium Ævum* 68.2 (1999): 268–77.

Weissig, Lisa Lampert. *Medieval Literature and Postcolonial Studies*. Postcolonial Literary Studies. Edinburgh: Edinburgh University Press, 2010.

Wendeburg, Otto. *Über di Bearbeitung von Gottfried von Monmouths Historia Regum Britanniae in der HS. Brit. Mus. Harl. 1605*. Dissertation Universität Erlangen. Braunschweig: Albert Limbach, 1881.

Wheeler, Gemma. "Rewriting the Past: Women in Wace's *Roman de Brut*." *Reading Medieval Studies* 37 (2011): 59–77.

Whitaker, Cord J. *Black Metaphor: How Modern Racism Emerged from Medieval Race-Thinking*. Philadelphia: University of Pennsylvania Press, 2019.

White, Donald A. "Changing Views of the *Adventus Saxonum* in Nineteenth and Twentieth Century English Scholarship." *Journal of the History of Ideas* 32 (1971): 585–94.

Williams, I. "GWRTHEYRN (VORTIGERN)." *Dictionary of Welsh Biography*. Retrieved 28 Mar 2020, from https://biography.wales/article/s-GWRT-HEY-0400.

Williams, Mary. "King Arthur in History and Legend." *Folklore* 73 (1962): 73–88 (Presidential Address to the Folklore Society).

Wilton, David. "What Do We Mean by *Anglo-Saxon*? Pre-Conquest to the Present." *Journal of English and Germanic Philology* 119.4 (2020): 425–56.

Winkler, Emily. *Royal Responsibility in Anglo-Norman Historical Writing*. Oxford: Oxford University Press, 2017.

Winkler, Emily. "William of Malmesbury and the Britons." In *Discovering William of Malmesbury*, ed. Rodney M. Thomson, Emily Dolmans, and Emily A. Winkler. Woodbridge: Boydell, 2017. 189–201.

Winterbottom, Michael. "The Preface of Gildas' *De Excidio*." Transactions of the Honourable Society of Cymmorodorion (1974–5): 277–87.

Woledge, Brian. "Notes on Wace's Vocabulary." *Modern Language Review* 46.1 (1951): 16–30.

Wood, Ian. 'The End of Roman Britain: Continental Evidence and Parallels." In *Gildas: New Approaches*, ed. Michael Lapidge and David Dumville. 1–25.

Wood, Ian. "Before and After the Migration to Britain." In *The Anglo-Saxons from the Migration Period to the Eighth Century: An Ethnographic Perspective*, ed. John Hines, Studies in Historical Archaeoethnology 2. Woodbridge: Boydell, 1997. 41–54.

Wood, Ian. "The Mission of Augustine of Canterbury to the English." *Speculum* 69.1 (1994): 1–17.

Wood, Ian. "Who are the Philistines? Bede's Readings of Old Testament Peoples." In *The Resources of the Past in Early Medieval Europe*, ed. Clemens Gantner, Rosamond McKitterick, and Sven Meeder. Cambridge: Cambridge University Press, 2015. 172–87.

Woolfe, Alex. "Apartheid and Economics in Anglo-Saxon England." In *Britons in Anglo-Saxon England*, ed. Higham. 115–29.

Woolfe, Alex. "Community, Identity and Kingship in Early England." In *Social Identity in Early Medieval Britain*, ed. Tyrrell and Frazer. 91–110.

Woolfe, Alex. *From Pictland to Alba 789–1070*. New Edinburgh History of Scotland 11. Edinburgh: Edinburgh University Press, 2007.

Woolfe, Alex. "Geoffrey of Monmouth and the Picts." In *Bile ós Chrannaibh: A Festschrift for William Gillies*, ed. William McLeod, et al. Ceann Drochaid, Perthshire: Clann Tuirc, 2010. 439–50.

Wormald, Patrick. "Bede, the *Bretwaldas* and the Origins of the *Gens Anglorum*." In *Ideal and Reality in Frankish and Anglo-Saxon Society*, ed. Wormald. Oxford: Oxford University Press, 1983. 99–129.

Wright, Neil. "Did Gildas read Orosius?" *Cambridge Medieval Celtic Studies* 9 (1985): 31–42.

Wright, Neil. "Geoffrey of Monmouth and Bede." *Arthurian Literature VI*, ed. Richard Barber. 27–59.

Wright, Neil. "Geoffrey of Monmouth and Gildas." *Arthurian Literature II*, ed. Richard Barber. 1–40.

Wright, Neil, "Geoffrey of Monmouth and Gildas Revisited." *Arthurian Literature IV*, ed. Richard Barber. 155–63.

Wulf, Charlotte A. T. "A Comparative Study of Wace's Guenevere in the Twelfth Century." In *Arthurian Romance and Gender; masculin/féminin dans le roman arthurien medieval; Geschlechterrolen in mittelalterlichen Artusroman*, ed. Friedrich Wolfzettel. Amsterdam and Atlanta, GA: Rodopi, 1995. 66–78.

Wulf, Charlotte A. T. "The Coronation of Arthur and Guenevere in Geoffrey of Monmouth's *Historia regum Britanniae*, Wace's *Roman de Brut*, and Lawman's *Brut*." In *Reading Laȝamon's Brut*, ed. Rosamund Allen, Jane Roberts, and Carole Weinberg. 229–51.

Yeager, Stephen M. "Diplomatic Antiquarianism and the Manuscripts of Laȝamon's *Brut*." *Arthuriana* 26.1 (2016): 124–40.

York, Ernest C. "Wace's 'Wenelande': Identification and Speculation." *Romance Notes* 22.1 (1981): 112–18.

Yorke, Barbara. "Anglo-Saxon Origin Legends." In *Myth, Rulership, Church and Charters: Essays in Honour of Nicholas Brooks*, ed. Julia Barrow and Andrew Wareham. Aldershot: Ashgate, 2008. 15–29.

Yorke, Barbara. "The Bretwaldas and the origins of overlordship in Anglo-Saxon England." In *Early Medieval Studies in Memory of Patrick Wormald*, ed. Steven Baxter, Catherine Karkov, Janet L. Nelson, and David Pelteret, Studies in Early Medieval Britain. Aldershot: Ashgate 2009; repr. London: Routledge, 2017. 81–96.

Yorke, Barbara. *The Conversion of Britain: Religion, Politics and Society in Britain, 600–800.* New York: Pearson, 2006; repr. London and New York: Routledge, 2014.

Yorke, Barbara. "Northumbria". In Yorke, *Kings and Kingdoms of Early Anglo-Saxon England.* Milton Park, Abingdon: Taylor & Francis, 1990. Chapter 8, 72–99.

Yorke, Barbara. "Political and Ethnic Identity: A Case Study of Anglo-Saxon Practice." In *Social Identity in Early Medieval Britain*, ed. Tyrrell and Frazer. 69–89.

Young, Frank. "Reactive Subsystems." *American Sociological Review* 35.2 (1970): 297–307.

Zara, Véronique. "The Historical Figure of Arthur in Wace's *Roman de Brut*." *Arthuriana* 18.2 (2008): 17–30 (Lagniappe Festschrift in Honor of Norris J. Lacy).

Zatta, Jane. "Translating the *Historia*: The Ideological Transformation of the *Historia Regum Britannie* in the Twelfth Century Vernacular Chronicles." *Arthuriana* 8.4 (1998): 148–61.

Index of Persons

Nota Bene   1: Some names have been standardized to follow more widely recognized traditions (for example, Walwein to Gawain, Artur to Arthur, Ganhumara to Guinevere, Eneas to Aeneas) and others include the more well known Latin equivalents (either historical personages or legendary ones, the latter often, but not always, created by Geoffrey of Monmouth) in addition to the forms Wace used, such as Cassibellan (Cassibellanus) and Ebrauc (Ebraucus) or English equivalents Adelstan (Athelstan). If there is an alternative French spelling as well as a Latin one, they will be in parentheses.

Nota Bene   2: Since Geoffrey of Monmouth (and the vulgate *Historia Regum Britanniae*) appear on nearly every page and the First Variant (FV) appears nearly as often, they have not been indexed here, nor has Arthur who has over 1300 references. *Not all legendary figures have been indicated as such in this Index.*

Aaron   87

Aeneas (Eneas)   21, 50, 61, 84, 116, 158, 180, 261–62, 264, 392, 395–96, 398, 405, 411, 428, 509

Aethelred, king   978–1013, 1014–16, Edward the Martyr's half-brother, c. 963–78, k. 975–78   252

Africans   131–32, 208, 210, 234, 347, 349

Aganippus, king of France, Cordelia's husband   403–4

Anglo-Saxon Chronicle(s)   12, 19, 54, 62, 67–68, 76–77, 79, 81, 91, 99, 110, 126, 141, 163, 240, 250, 254, 256, 325, 344, 381

Alain, king of Brittany   136

Alban(s)   50, 139, 187, 398 (line of Alban kings) St Alban   421

Albanactus (Albanac), Brutus's third son   343, 411, Albanacus   424, 427–8

Aldroenus, king of Brittany   116, 183–4, 332

Alvret, English king Alfred (Alfred the Great)   92, 96, 255, 344, 346, 377, 440, 479

Alfred, sacrist of Beverley, author of a history of Britain/England from Brutus to Henry I, c. 1148–51   34, 36, 254

Amphibalus   187

Androgeus, son of Lud, nephew of Cassibellan   429–32

Angles   5, 12, 23, 29, 50 (East Angles), 68–9, 71, 75–6, 78, 89, 117, 139–40, 175, 208–9, 211, 227, 250, 254, 273, 281, 290, 303, 348, 351–54, 435, 490

Anna, Arthur's sister   207

Antenor, Trojan lord   60–61, 264, 398

Apo, Donaud's father   452

Ascanius (Aschanius), son of Aeneas   50, 180, 395–96, 427

Aschil (also Aschillus), king of Denmark   202, 310, 357, 491

Asclepiodotus, duke of Cornwall   187

Athelstan, king of the Anglo-Saxons   924–27 and king of the English   927–39, except for Wales and Cornwall   19, 21, 23, 31, 85–86, 92, 94, 96, 100, 107, 116–17, 137, 148, 168, 178, 205, 208, 211, 222–24, 227–28, 230, 233, 251, 256, 261, 343, 371–74, 381, 391, 440, 477, 479 (also Adelstan   256, 372)

Auguselus, in Geoffrey of Monmouth, king of Scotland   126, 147, 199–200, 236, 333, 378, 447 (also Angusel   198, 305, 318, 327–28, 333, 336, 338, 447, 491)

Augustine (Augustin), saint, sent by Pope Gregory to convert the English   24, 52, 69, 86, 94, 103–4, 126, 131, 133–34, 168, 190, 204–5, 208–11, 213–19, 235, 237, 256–59, 261, 359–67, 380, 382, 391, 438, 475, 484

Augustus Caesar, Roman emperor   212

Aurelius Ambrosius, king of Britain, brother of Uther and Constant   20, 71, 82, 97, 99, 101, 109, 187, 213, 234

Bassianus, king of the Britons   145

Bede, English monk, author, scholar, 672/3–735   5, 13–14, 24, 34, 37–38, 40, 43–44, 46, 51–52, 54, 56, 58–59, 62, 65, 67–72, 75–82, 86, 96, 98, 101, 103–5, 110, 113, 121, 126, 135, 138–39, 145, 154, 159,

INDEX OF PERSONS

Bede, English monk (*cont.*)
163, 165, 170–71, 174–79, 184, 189, 205,
208, 211–12, 217–18, 221, 225, 228, 232,
234, 240, 242, 244, 246, 254, 257, 260,
265, 281, 303, 353, 360–62, 366, 377, 381,
397, 421, 447, 476, 486, 514
Belinus (1), legendary king of the Britons,
brother of Brennius   84, 92, 96, 142, 199,
205–6, 261, 331–32
Belinus (2), Cassibellan's seneschal   431
Bladud, king of Britain   424, 429
Bledric, lord of Cornwall   216, 372
Bedevere, Arthur's cupbearer   98, 114, 127,
177, 202, 311, 315–16, 318, 320, 334, 336,
352, 355, 358, 393, 442, 447, 474–75,
478–79, 511
Borel, count of Le Mans   312, 334
Bos(o), count of Oxford 1202   478
Brennius, brother of Belinus, legendary duke
of Burgundy, ruler of Rome   92, 142, 205,
261, 331, 333, 336, 415, 430–31, 484
Bretons   7–9, 27, 37–38 113, 116–17, 152, 229,
237, 255, 270, 279, 307–8, 334, 339, 341,
453, 458, 461, 494
Brien, nephew of Chadwalein   380
Britons   5, 7–9, 12–16, 18–21, 23–26, 29,
31–32, 35, 37–38, 40, 42–54, 57–63,
65–75, 77–107, 109–11, 115–18, 122–24,
127–28, 130–40, 142, 144–47, 151–55, 162,
164, 168, 170–90, 192–94, 188–89, 201–2,
204, 207–19, 221–32, 234–37, 240–46,
248–70, 273–74, 276–80, 283–84, 286,
290, 293, 296, 299, 303–5, 307–9, 319,
324–33, 335–36, 339–41, 343, 347–50,
352–55, 359–62, 368–80, 383, 384, 391,
397–99, 403–6, 410–23, 426, 428–36,
439–62, 472, 475–78, 484–84, 486–88,
492, 49496, 514
Brutus, grandson of Ascanius, legendary
founder of Britain   5, 7–8, 21, 24, 29, 44,
48–50, 54–61, 82, 84–85, 92, 116, 121, 136,
158, 173, 180–81, 261, 264–66, 268–69,
272, 275–77, 343, 353, 392, 395–96,
398–99, 406–7, 411–14, 422–28, 439,
464, 477, 498–99, 507
Burgundians   50

Cador, duke of Cornwall   22, 102, 115, 125–26,
130, 292, 293, 299, 306, 327, 329, 334,
339, 341–42, 351

Cadwallader, king of Gwynedd in Wales
c. 655–682 and last king of Britain (in
Galfridian legend)   21, 24, 29, 84, 91–92,
94, 106–7, 115–16, 131, 135–37, 148,
204–5, 219, 221–25, 227–29, 234–36, 261,
286, 295, 314, 368–69, 371, 373–74, 464,
477, 509
Caliburnus (Excalibur), Arthur's sword
124–25, 193–94, 298
Caradoc of Llancarfan, "colleague" of
Geoffrey of Monmouth   35, 39, 230–31,
374
Carais (Carausius), pirate ruler of Britain
21, 145, 415–16, 471
Cariz, legendary king of Britain   211, 342;
also Keredic   94, 211, 255
Cassibellanus, king of Britain   84, 423, 425,
429–32
Catellus (Lucius Catellus), Roman senator
who became a war leader with emperor
Lucius   202
Chadwalein (also Caduallo, Cadwallo), king
of Britain south of the Humber   261, 368
Cadwan, king of South Wales   261, 372, 382
Cerdic, king of Wessex   514–39 246–47,
249–50, 254–57, 262, 281, 337
Cheldric, Saxon warlord   96, 248–49, 337,
355, 471
Cheneus, Arthurian lord   452
Coel, of Gloucester, king of England   80,
332, 492
Claudius, Roman emperor   92, 332
Coillus, son of Marius, king of Britain   416,
452
Colgrim, Colgrimus (also Colgrin, Colgrinus),
Saxon leader   96, 112, 123, 19–92, 293–94,
393, 438, 471, 507, 512
Constant, monk and brother of Aurelius
and Uther, crowned by Vortigern then
betrayed   22, 101, 205, 261, 461
Constantius, Roman senator, legate to
Britain, then crowned king of Britain,
marries Helen (daughter of Coel), father
of Constantine I   332, 492
Constantine (Costentin): son of Constantius
and Helen (daughter of Coel) and Roman
emperor (Constantine I [*HRB* Thorpe
trans.])   199, 332, 492
Constantine (Constentin), Breton
king of Britain, brother of Aldroen

560   INDEX OF PERSONS

Constantine (Constentin) (*cont.*)
(Constantine II [*HRB* Thorpe trans.]),
founder of the House of Constantine   22,
93, 101, 116, 122, 261, 332
Constantine (Costentin), king of Britain,
son of Cador, succeeds Arthur in
Geoffrey (Constantine III [*HRB* Thorpe
trans.])   246, 332, 341
Cordelia, third (youngest) daughter of
King Leir   400–4, 415, 429
Corineus, legendary Trojan lord and warrior
after whom Cornwall was named   55–56,
60, 92, 181, 265, 267–69, 272, 398–400,
412, 428
Cornish   7–9, 18, 55, 78, 88, 181, 372, 412
Creusa, Aeneas's first wife, mother of
Ascanius   180
Cunan (also Conan), king of Brittany,
nephew of Octavius   261, 278–80, 342;
Aurelius Conanus   477
Cunedagius, legendary king of the Britons
392, 400, 404, 507

Danes   58, 68, 129–30, 176–77, 206, 242,
244–45, 248, 250–51, 253, 303, 337–38,
344, 378–79
Dardanus, ancestor of the Trojans   48–50
David, king of Israel, author of many of
the Psalms   41
David I, king of Scotland (1124–53)   144, 148,
181, 264, 269, 283–84, 332
David II, king of Scotland (1329–71)   478
Diana, goddess and prophetess   412
Diocletian, Roman emperor (284–305, reign
noted for the last great persecution of the
Christians)   93, 187–88, 212
Dionot, temporary ruler of Britain in Cunan's
absence   279–80
Doldani, king of Gotland   307
Donaud, Arthurian lord, son of Apo   452
Dubricius, 6th c. British ecclesiastic and
bishop of Caerleon, later archbishop and
Roman legate   123, 193, 315–19, 323, 460
Dumwallo, king of Britain   380
Dunian, bishop, baptizes King Lucius   416

Ebissa, cousin of Octa. *See also* Eosa   72,
100–2, 165, 186

Ebraucus, legendary king of the Britons,
founder of York, fathered twenty sons and
thirty daughters with twenty wives   124,
165, 250, 399, 408–9, 424, 428
Edward the Elder, king of the Anglo-Saxons
899–924, father of Athelstan   96,
251–52, 396; and Peter's Pence   371
Edward the Confessor, last king of the House
of Wessex 1042–1066   382, 396, 466, 489
Edward the Martyr, king of the
English 975–978   252
Edward I, king of England 1272–1307; son of
Henry III (king of England 1216–1272)
236, 424–25, 439, 441, 506, 508
Edward II, king of England 1307–1327   26,
385
Edward III, king of England 1327–1377
463–64, 466, 470, 472–73, 475, 478, 509
Edwin, king of Northumbria 616–632/633
94, 96, 104, 134, 136, 261, 380–2
Elaud, father of Regeim   452
Eldadus, bishop, brother of Edulf   101, 189
Eldol, legendary king of Britain   461
Eldulf, count of Gloucester   284
Eleine (1) (St Helena), daughter of Coel
(Geoffrey of Monmouth, Henry of
Huntingdon), mother of Constantine (1),
first Christian empress, thought to
have discovered the "True Cross" (in
Jerusalem)   492
Eleine (2), niece of Hoel, raped and killed by
giant of Mont-St-Michel   334
Elenus, son of Priam   151
Eleutherius (Pope Eleutherius,
2nd c. AD)   213
Elfrid (Ethelfrid, Edelfridus), king of
Northumbria, relative of Adelbert, king
of Kent: Elfrid   261, Ethelfrid   361–62,
Edelfridus   86, 94, 104, 134, 214, 217
Eosa, Octa's kinsman. *See also* Ebissa
96–97, 101–2, 192, 261, 290, 415, 447,
455, 460
Equitius, appointed consul by emperor
Valentinianus   72. *See also* Gratian
Estrild, wife of Locrinus   428

Faganus, bishop sent with Dunian to baptize
King Lucius and the Britons   212–13, 416
Freya, Saxon goddess   450

INDEX OF PERSONS   561

French (people, not language)   39, 41, 60,
    64, 119–20, 129, 140, 148–49, 153, 160,
    183–84, 241–42, 255, 266–67, 271,
    273–74, 277, 279–80, 294, 309, 312,
    318–19, 325–26, 344–45, 365–68, 376,
    382–83, 389, 391, 403, 430, 453, 466,
    470, 472–73, 482–84
Frollo, Roman governor of France   97, 114,
    127, 311, 315, 358, 447, 491
Fulgenius I, king of Britain   422
Fulgenius II, leader of northern Britons, rebel
    against Severus   422, 446–47

Gaimar, Geoffrei Gaimar, Anglo-Norman
    poet and historian, fl. 1130s   13, 24–25, 29,
    34, 56, 89, 120, 160–64, 241–59, 262, 265,
    267, 281, 337, 346, 350, 374–75, 388–90,
    446, 479, 498–99, 502
Galaes, Welsh queen   106–7, 150, 225–26,
    230–31
Gauls   55, 60, 71, 140, 145, 181, 266, 278, 309,
    447
Gawain, Loth's eldest son, Arthur's cousin
    (though sometimes referred to as his
    nephew)   113, 125–26, 202, 441, 455,
    471–72, 475, 478–79 (Walwein   296,
    329, 334–38)
Gerinus, count of Chartres   128, 202, 455
Germain, saint and bishop of Auxerre
    (378–c. 440s), sent to Britain with
    St Lupus by Pope Romain to re-establish
    Christianity   418, 420
Germans   199–200, 327–28, 333, 418
Gildas, 6th-c. British monk and historian
    14, 20, 24, 37, 43–44, 46, 48, 53, 53,
    56–59, 62, 64–68, 70–72, 76–78, 98,
    101, 108–9, 113, 117, 121, 123, 131, 138–39,
    154, 169, 170–71, 174–75, 177–78, 181, 184,
    187, 189, 206–7, 213, 221, 232, 249, 260,
    281, 303, 332, 352, 398–99, 416–17, 421,
    447, 486
Gillomanius, king of Ireland at the time
    Merlin moves the "Giants' Dance,   460,
    Gillomanies   461
Gillomar (Gillomarus, Gillamurius [HRB]),
    king of Ireland in Arthur's time   307
Goemagog, leader of the giants in Britain
    before the arrival of Brutus   399;
    Goemagog's Leap   268
Goffar the Pict, king of Poitiers   55;
    Goffarius Pictus, Aquitanian king   60

Gonorille, eldest of King Leir's daughters
    400, 404
Gonvais, king of Orkney   307
Gorbonian, king of Britain   318
Gorlois, count of Cornwall   236, 288–89, 462
Gormund (in Geoffrey African king)   24–25,
    85–86, 89, 92, 94, 97, 103, 116, 131–32,
    191, 198, 204–5, 207–9, 211, 234, 239,
    250, 255–57, 259, 261, 272–74, 278, 301,
    307, 343–51, 353, 355, 357–60, 371, 382,
    391, 424, 442, 476, 483, 487–88, 490–91;
    Gormund's "Donation"   24–25, 85–86,
    89, 92, 97, 99–100, 132, 209, 244–45,
    255–59, 261, 272–74
Gotlanders   102, 131, 307, 317, 329, 343, 451;
    Gotland   356; king Doldanius of
    Gotland   127
Gratian. See also Equitius, who was appointed
    consul by emperor Valentinian I, eldest
    son of Valentinian I, emperor of Western
    Roman Empire 367–383   72
Greeks   50, 60, 171, 262, 264, 405–6
Gregory, saint and pope (590–604), sent
    St Augustine (later first archbishop
    of Canterbury 597) to convert the
    English   68, 133, 213, 215, 218, 361, 438
Gualon (Guales), Welsh duke   107
Guinevere, Arthur's queen   22, 93, 112, 115,
    126, 306, 314, 327–28, 338, 447, 451, 474
Guithelinus, king of Britain, husband of
    Marcia   96 (of Marcian law)
Guithelinus, archbishop of London   182–84

Helenus (and Antenor), Trojan heroes   398
Hengist, Saxon leader   64, 68, 70, 72–74, 82,
    91, 93, 98, 100–2, 164, 185–86, 189, 198,
    236, 244, 248–50, 256–57, 261, 281–84,
    285, 293, 337, 393, 419–21, 432–34, 437,
    446, 450, 457, 459, 466, 473, 475, 483,
    511; also Hengest, 76–77, 85, 96, 99,
    122, 246, 254; also Henguist   283–84,
    337, 421
Henry of Huntingdon, English historian,
    c. 1088–1157   13, 23, 33–35, 39, 54,
    56–59, 64, 77, 79, 83, 88–89, 103, 111, 120,
    146, 156–57, 7, 162–63, 170, 177, 184, 189,
    230–31, 242, 246, 260, 281, 293, 339–40,
    344, 353, 361, 371, 374, 379, 397, 418,
    486, 493–94, 514; Epistola ad Warinum,
    33, 59, 81, 83, 89, 98, 112, 339–40, 418,
    493, 514

562   INDEX OF PERSONS

Hirelglas, nephew of Cassibellan   429
Hoel, Arthur's nephew, king of Brittany   115,
        198–99, 202–3, 295, 318, 323–24,
        327–29, 332–34, 378, 451, 471, 478; also
        Hoelus   116, 125, 128
Holdin, count of Flanders   312, 358
Homer, Greek poet   266
Horsa, brother of Hengist   5, 64, 68, 70,
        72–74, 76, 82, 91, 93, 96–98, 164, 185,
        244, 248–50, 254, 256–57, 261, 281, 286,
        293, 432, 434, 446, 475, 483
Huns   68, 93, 280, 424

Innogen, Brutus's wife, daughter of
        Pendrasus   181, 407, 426, 428
Irish (noun and adjective)   37, 45–46,
        49–50, 52, 57–59, 72, 74, 77, 79, 82,
        95–97, 102, 114, 118–19, 125, 131, 138–39,
        145, 147, 149, 165, 171–72, 175–76, 178,
        204, 219, 241, 300–1, 304, 307, 338,
        345–56, 369, 378, 415, 418, 460–61
Isaiah, prophet of Israel   400, 404
Isembard, (legendary) nephew of King
        Louis   131, 255, 345–46, 348; also
        Ysembard   442

Jesus Christ (figure and dating)   52, 110, 215,
        218, 257, 295, 298, 332, 405, 417, 427, 514
Jews   10, 38, 340, 428
Jugein, count of Leicester   478
Julius Caesar   25, 46, 56, 59, 61, 82, 84, 92,
        177, 180, 187–88, 287, 295, 330–31, 335,
        349, 354, 429–31, 442
Jupiter   50, 450

Kamber, son of Brutus, king of Kambria
        (Cambria)   341, 411, 424, 427–28
Katigern, son of Vortigern   186
Kay, Arthur's seneschal   114, 127, 311, 315–17,
        320, 336, 358, 393, 447, 452, 474–75, 478, 511
Kentish   70, 73–74, 104, 256
Kinlint, Arthurian lord   318

Latinus, king of Latium (in Italy)   50,
        396–98
Lavinia, second wife of Aeneas   50, 180,
        395, 411
Leil, legendary king of the Britons   424, 428

Leir, legendary king of the Britons   84, 92,
        392, 398, 400–4, 407, 424, 429, 507
Ligier, count of Boulogne   312
Locrinus, first son of Brutus   143, 343, 411,
        424, 428
Loth, of Loeneis, Arthur's brother-in-law,
        king of Norway   97, 102, 125–27, 305, 310,
        356–57, 393, 447, 491, 511
Louis III, king of France [West Francia],
        879–882 (and legendary/unnamed
        figures)   344–46, 348
Lucius Hiberius, Roman emperor (first
        appearing in Geoffrey of Monmouth, and
        killed by Arthur)   93, 115, 128, 190,
        197–99, 202, 277, 305, 314, 327–30,
        344–36, 442, 447, 455, 471–72, 478, 511
Lucius, supposed 2nd c. king of the Britons,
        traditionally credited with bringing
        Christianity to the Britons   84, 187, 205,
        212–13, 393, 416, 422, 446
Lud, king of Britain   56, 84, 181, 272–73,
        276–77, 399
Luor, one of Ebrauc's sons   399
Lupus, St, an early bishop of Troyes   188,
        283, 418, 420–21

Maglaurus (in Geoffrey, duke of Scotland; FV
        Maglaunus, king of Scotland and Wace
        Manglanus, king)   404
Malgo, king of Britain   44, 102, 131, 143, 233,
        261, 341–43
Marcia, legendary queen and regent of
        Britain, also lawmaker   96 (Marcian law
        281, 430, HRB §47.256–61)
Margadud, (Geoffrey refers to this king of the
        Demetae, late Iron Age tribe of Southwest
        Wales)   135, 214, 216, 372
Marganus, nephew of Cordelia   392, 400,
        404
Margoid, Arthurian lord   318
Maxenz, Roman emperor   469
Maximianus, king of Britain   54, 93, 142, 199;
        also Maximien   278–80, 331, 450
Maximianus Herculius, inquisitor and
        persecutor of Christians   187–88
Melga, king of Scythia   280, 450
Menbritius, wise Trojan   405–6
Mercury, Greco-Roman, Saxon god   450

INDEX OF PERSONS

563

Merlin, prophet and magician 60, 93,
101–2, 106, 115, 137, 205–6, 222–23, 225,
288, 290, 340–41, 347, 373, 392, 410,
423–24, 435–37, 455–60, 462, 465,
472, 476, 490, 493–95, 508–9; Merlin's
Prophecies: 25–26, 39, 42, 60, 93–95,
115, 167–69, 261–62, 332, 347, 383–84,
388, 390, 410–11, 423–25, 435, 447,
455–56, 470, 476, 492
Mezentius, in Roman mythology Etruscan
king 396, 398
Minerva 283
Mordred (Modred , Modret), Arthur's
"son/nephew" 22, 93–94, 102, 110, 113, 115,
124–26, 130–31, 198, 204, 246–47, 251,
261, 288, 292, 327–28, 330, 336, 338, 342,
418, 514; Mordred's "Donation" 244,
248–49, 254–55, 337
Mustensar, African king 347

Nennius, monk and possibly author, fl. c. 800
24, 40, 44, 46–48, 51, 56–57, 59, 61–62,
109–10, 124, 181, 213, 352, 411, 417
Nennius, of Canterbury, younger brother of
Cassibellan, son of Heli 181, 272, 399
Neton, father of Run 318
Normans 12, 19, 21, 42, 58–60, 80, 97–98,
117–18, 120–21, 140, 143, 146–47, 149–53,
162, 168, 170, 172, 175–77, 229, 242, 245,
253, 270, 273–74, 314, 353–54, 359, 391,
397, 421, 488
Norwegians 338, 378–79

Octa, son of Hengist 96–97, 100–2, 165, 186,
192, 261, 290, 437
Octavius, count of Wales (HRB, duke of the
Gewissei) and then (legendary) king of
Britain 278
Orderic Vitalis, English/Norman monk and
historian of Normandy, 1075–c. 1142
58–59, 149, 479
Oswald, Christian king of Northumbria 86,
96, 134
Oswi, brother of Oswald 105, 134–35

Pandrasus, king of Greece 55, 181, 398–99,
406, 412, 426–28

Paris, Trojan (son of Priam) who kidnapped
Helen of Greece 130, 262
Paschent, son of Vortigern 186, 437, 461
Penda, Anglo-Saxon king of Mercia
c. 632–655 86, 94, 96, 105, 134, 136, 368,
381–82; also Peanda 105, 117, 135–36,
225, 147
Peter of Langtoft, English chronicler
d. c. 1307 3, 299, 463
Peter (Pierre), saint; "St Peter's pence" 371
Philistines 61
Picts 5, 7, 9, 44–46, 51–52, 54, 57–58, 66,
72, 77, 80, 82, 93, 96–98, 114, 124–25,
136, 139–40, 144–46, 149, 171–73,
175–76, 178–79, 184–85, 191–92, 204,
218, 220–22, 234, 242, 246, 248, 251–52,
254, 261, 280, 282, 300–1, 303–4, 369,
378–79, 397, 415–16, 419, 421, 432–33,
447, 461, 471, 475
Poitevins 55, 266, 398
Pridwen, Arthur's shield 110–11, 114, 124, 193,
295, 297–98

Ragau, the second daughter of King Leir
404
Regeim, of Puntif 452
Remus, brother of Romulus (founders of
Rome) 48, 395–97, 400, 404
Richier, Arthurian lord 312, 334
Riculf, Norwegian baron 310
Rodric, of Scythia, king of the Picts 145, 415
Romans 9, 14, 20, 44–46, 48, 50–51,
58–59, 60–61, 64–66, 71–72, 80–81,
85, 90, 92–93, 96, 100, 109, 112, 115,
117, 121, 128–30, 132, 136, 139, 140, 145,
155, 177–80, 182–84, 190, 198–203,
205, 220–22, 246, 249, 261, 278,
288, 303–4, 314, 326–33, 335–36,
354, 369, 388, 397–98, 406, 411, 422,
429–30, 432, 442, 455, 474, 484, 490,
496; "Annals of the Romans" 50;
Roman occupation 44, 59, 71, 73,
155; Roman Senate 93, 145, 197;
Post-Roman Britain 14, 152, 376;
Roman Britain 54, 65–66, 69, 376;
Sub-Roman Britain 44, 218, 332
Romulus, brother of Remus (founders of
Rome) 48, 395–97, 400, 404

564   INDEX OF PERSONS

Ronwen, daughter of Hengist, wife of
    Vortigern   73, 93, 99–100, 185–86, 188–89,
    283–84, 419, 433–34
Rummaret, king of Wenelande (both
    unknown)   307

Samson, saint, bishop of York   460;
    Archbishop Samson of Dol   323
Saturn, Greco-Roman, Saxon god   450
Saul, king of Judah   449
Saxons   5, 7, 12, 14, 19–23, 25, 29, 32, 42, 44,
    50–54, 57–58, 62, 64, 69, 71–75, 97–104,
    106–7, 114, 116–17, 122–26, 128, 130–38,
    140–44, 146, 150–52, 153–54, 163, 170,
    172, 175–79, 182, 184–94, 200, 204,
    207–11, 214–25, 227, 230, 232–35, 237,
    240–45, 247–50, 252–58, 261, 272–73,
    278, 281–86, 290–93, 299, 302–5, 314,
    333, 337–38, 342–43, 345–55, 357,
    369–71, 373–80, 382, 391, 393, 397, 411,
    415–22, 433–36, 440–443, 458–62,
    469–70, 475–77, 486, 487–88, 490–91,
    496, 507
Scots   5, 7, 20, 37, 45–46, 48, 54, 58, 66, 72,
    77, 80, 82, 96–97, 114, 118–21, 124–26,
    136, 140, 144–49, 168, 170–73, 175–76,
    178–79, 184, 191–92, 204, 220–22, 229,
    234, 241, 246, 248, 251–52, 254, 282, 294,
    299–305, 343, 355, 357, 378–80, 397,
    415, 446–47, 471, 478, 491
Sergius, saint and pope   222–23, 225
Septimius Severus, Roman senator and
    emperor (193–211), builder of the wall
    "between Deira and Albany"   422
Sibyl   223, 332
Silvius, son of Ascanius and father of Brutus
    (according to some texts)   49–50, 56,
    120, 395–96, 411, 427
Silvius Postumus, son of Aeneas (according
    to some texts)   61, 180, 396, 398, 427
Simeon of Durham, English chronicler,
    d. after 1129   34, 371
Sodomites (referring to biblical group)   131

Trojans   5, 19, 55, 59–60, 87, 115, 138, 153, 176,
    178–82, 235, 239, 254, 262, 264–70, 276,
    326, 332, 382, 398, 404–6, 411–14, 426,
    442
Turks   345

Turnus (1), duke of Tuscany   50, 395–96
    (ally of Mezentius)
Turnus (2), nephew of Brutus   55, 235, 179,
    265–66

Ulfin, confidant of Uther   472
Urgen, count of Bath   478
Urien, father of Yvain, king of Moray, brother
    of Loth   305, 318, 491
Ursula, daughter of Dionot (both legendary),
    sent to Brittany with thousands of
    companions, shipwrecked, raped,
    drowned   279–80, 450, 469
Uther Pendragon, brother of Aurelius, father
    of Arthur, king of the Britons   22, 41,
    93, 101–2, 116, 122–23, 192–93, 205–6,
    261, 288–91, 314–15, 378, 390, 392–93,
    408, 410, 424, 436–38, 447, 455, 458–60,
    469, 471–72

Valentinian(us) I, Roman emperor   364–75
    281, 418
Vespasien, Roman general and emperor
    69–79, 92
Virgin Mary   52, 76, 110, 114, 283, 294–96, 334
Vortigern, king of Britain (fl. 425–450, two
    separate reigns)   22, 29, 54, 65–66, 72–74,
    76–78, 82, 85, 93, 97–101, 122, 184–86,
    189–90, 234, 261, 281–85, 293, 303, 337,
    351, 417–19, 432–37, 450, 456, 458, 461
Vortimer, son of Vortigern, deposes father
    and reigns briefly, but poisoned by
    stepmother Ronwen   29, 53, 72–74, 79,
    100, 186, 188–89, 205, 283–84, 293,
    419–20, 433–34
Vortipor, mid-6th c. ruler of Dyfed in Wales
    44, 342 (also Vortiporius   102)

Wace, Norman poet and historian,
    c. 1110–c. 1174   17, 21, 25–27, 53, 56, 61, 64,
    69, 85–86, 89, 92–93, 99, 110, 116,
    122–23, 131–33, 151–54, 157, 159, 160,
    166, 179–81, 188, 196, 208, 211, 217, 235,
    239–44, 255, 260–92, 294–314, 316–20,
    322, 324–46, 348–63, 365–87, 389–90,
    392–95, 398–402, 404–18, 420–22,
    424–25, 429–34, 436–48, 450–60,
    462–66, 469–97, 499, 507–12
Wanis, king of Hungary   280, 450

INDEX OF PERSONS

565

Welsh (people) 7–9, 18–19, 21, 26, 20, 35, 37, 39–43, 46–47, 49–50, 59, 65, 78–79, 86, 94–95, 104, 106–7, 118–19, 121, 131, 137, 141, 144, 146–48, 150–52, 154, 160–62, 164–65, 182, 194, 222–23, 226, 228–31, 236–37, 244, 252, 261, 304–5, 315, 317–18, 325, 332, 338, 346, 360, 371, 374, 377, 384, 441, 447–48, 452, 473–74, 480

William of Malmesbury, half-Norman English historian, c. 1095–c. 1143 8, 13, 17, 24, 26, 35, 39–40, 53–59, 64, 68, 75, 77, 79, 88, 98–100, 110–11, 113, 118–19, 121, 141, 148, 152, 154, 156, 163, 170, 177, 230–31, 242, 287, 293, 296, 324–25, 340, 353, 360, 363–64, 367, 371–72, 374, 377, 397, 440, 486, 493, 494, 514

Woden, Saxon god (Mercury) 70, 76, 83, 257

Ygerne, Uther's queen, Arthur's mother 22, 93, 288–89, 472; also Igerne 206

Yne, ancestor of Edward and Athelstan 371

Yni, son/nephew of Cadwallader 90, 106, 137, 222–23, 226, 229–31, 261, 374, 477

Yvain, son of Urien 246–47

Yvor, son of Cadwallader 261, 374, 473, 477; also Ivor 90, 106, 137, 222–23, 225–26, 228–31, 235